"The name 'Jungmann' is synonymous with the history of the Mass. Have a question about the origins of some part of the Sunday Eucharist? 'Look it up in Jungmann,' people will say. These volumes are both historical and historic. This new edition will make this timeless research more available to the eager reader."

Rev. Paul Turner
Author of *Glory in the Cross*

"What a delight to have this classic work in print again! It still remains the most reliable and detailed guide to the evolution of the Roman mass, to which every student of liturgical history should turn."

Paul Bradshaw
Professor of Liturgy
University of Notre Dame

Joseph A. Jungmann, S.J. (1889–1975), an Austrian Roman Catholic priest and scholar, was ordained to the priesthood in 1913 and entered the Society of Jesus (the Jesuits) four years later. He spent most of his career as professor of pastoral theology at the University of Innsbruck, where he taught both catechetics and liturgy. With the exception of the years during which Hitler closed down the theological faculty (1939–45), Jungmann's entire teaching career was spent at Innsbruck, where for a time he also served as rector of the community of Jesuits.

Jungmann is best known for his contributions to Catholic catechetics and liturgical studies. In particular, he is associated with the renewal of the Eucharistic liturgy and served on the Second Vatican Council's commission that produced *Sacrosanctum Concilium*, a document on liturgy and worship, in 1964. He authored many books, including *Liturgical Worship, Christian Prayer through the Centuries*, and *The Mass of the Roman Rite*.

The Mass of the Roman Rite:

ITS ORIGINS AND DEVELOPMENT

(Missarum Sollemnia)

By
Rev. JOSEPH A. JUNGMANN, S.J.
Professor of Theology,
University of Innsbruck

Translated by
Rev. FRANCIS A. BRUNNER, C. SS. R.
Professor of Theology,
St. Joseph's College, Kirkwood, Mo.

VOLUME ONE

Christian Classics *Notre Dame, Indiana*

First published in English in 1951. Translated from the German revised edition of *Missarum Solemnia*, 1949.

"The Commingling," published here as an appendix to volume 2, was part of the revised and abridged edition of *The Mass of the Roman Rite*, Burns and Oates, London, 1959.

Imprimi Potest: Francis J. Fagen, C.Ss.R.
Provincial, St. Louis Province of Redemptorist Fathers
March 10, 1950

Nihil Obstat: Cardinal Francis Spellman
Archbishop of New York
Given at New York, September 22, 1950

The Nihil Obstat and *Imprimatur* are official declarations that a book or pamphlet is free of doctrinal or moral error. No implication is contained therein that those who have granted the *Nihil Obstat* or *Imprimatur* agree with its contents, opinions, or statements expressed.

Christian Classics™, Ave Maria Press®, Inc., P.O. Box 428, Notre Dame, IN 46556.

Founded in 1865, Ave Maria Press is a ministry of the United States Province of Holy Cross.

www.christian-classics.com

	Hardcover Edition	Paperback Edition
Complete Set	ISBN-10 0-87061-271-9	ISBN-10 0-87061-274-3
	ISBN-13 978-0-87061-271-8	ISBN-13 978-0-87061-274-9
Volume 1	ISBN-10 0-87061-272-7	ISBN-10 0-87061-275-1
	ISBN-13 978-0-87061-272-5	ISBN-13 978-0-87061-275-6
Volume 2	ISBN-10 0-87061-273-5	ISBN-10 0-87061-276-X
	ISBN-13 978-0-87061-273-2	ISBN-13 978-0-87061-276-3

Cover image © The Image Bank / Walter Bibikow.

Cover and text design by John R. Carson.

Printed and bound in the United States of America, 2012.

Author's Foreword

THIS I AM SURE NO ONE WILL DOUBT: IF A STUDY OF OUR TRANSMITTED culture is worth the trouble not only of securing a surface knowledge, but of delving with all available care and love to gain an insight into its essence and its course of development, and to grasp the meaning of every last detail, certainly it is no less true—even aside from higher considerations—with regard to the liturgy of Holy Mass, which is daily celebrated on a hundred thousand altars, and to which, Sunday after Sunday, the whole Catholic population streams.

Of course there is no dearth of penetrating studies. Year after year they make their appearance for the widest possible circles of readers. Nor is there a want of scientific research. In the last few decades investigations of every sort have happily been on the increase. But a work of greater magnitude, which would assemble and evaluate the results of so many separate inquiries—that was hardly to be looked for!

That the present writer undertook such a task is to be laid, in a sense, to the evil times through which we have passed. When the theological faculty at Innsbruck was abolished a few months after the invasion of the Nazi forces into Austria, the business of teaching could at first be carried on, at least in essentials and with scarcely a diminution of students, outside the confines of the University. But then came the second blow. On October 12, 1939 the Collegium Maximum was closed and given up, along with the Canisianum which had already been seized. But only a few days later, even before my departure from Innsbruck, I made up my mind to dedicate the time thus left free to me to an exposition of the Mass-liturgy. For that seemed to me to be the theme most useful to handle in a time of stress like this. Besides it was this subject that my previous studies and writings, and the great amount of notes and my moderately large collection of books would have best fitted me for. The dissolution of the college had of course involved not only the loss of the extensive college library, but likewise all access to the stacks of the liturgical seminar which had been built up through the years with much trouble and pain.

But I began the work anyway. To be sure, the notion that I could get along with just a few books soon proved to be a big mistake, for I wanted to build a solid structure that did not rest on conjecture and on the unexamined acceptance of the data of earlier authors. But in my new residence in Vienna I found that the friendliness of the authorities concerned opened up many libraries for my convenience—the house libraries of my own order, of course, and the collections open to all in the public libraries; also several important church libraries, especially the seminary library and the library of the Schotten Institute, all of which favored me by granting the continued and prolonged loan of fundamental books—for which I am deeply grateful.

Little by little, too, my own small stock began to grow, thanks especially to the energetic exertions of Father Joseph Miller, at that time our Provincial, who managed to rescue some of my own books by buying what he could from bookstores and antique-shops; thanks, too, to confreres who were serving in the war in France and elsewhere, who acquired for me many a precious volume from foreign publishers. Finally, because of the cooperation of the officials in charge, I was also able to secure the loan of some important items from the collection of the Innsbruck liturgical seminar.

Thus I could get on with the work with some assurance. But it did not begin really to take shape till in 1942 I was able to exchange my residence in Vienna for one in the country—an ideal place, considering the conditions of war. This was the home of the School Sisters of St. Pölten, in Hainstetten, in the little wedge of land formed by the confluence of the lower Ybbs with the Danube, peacefully nestled in fertile hill country. Here, along with the moderate duties in a little church attached to the convent, I was granted not only the undisturbed quiet of a peaceful countryside, but—under the watchful care of the good Sisters—all the material conditions conducive to successful labor. The distant rumble of the war—which, it is true, often increased to the whistle of bombs and the shaking of the whole house— served only as an incentive to gather up all my resources in order to prepare, at least in one point, for the spiritual reconstruction which was sure to come.

By degrees my method became clearer and more secure. The medieval development, I found, would have to be worked out anew from the sources. For, although by and large the phenomena were all connected by a common tie, still a more precise insight into origins and motive forces could be gained only by carefully determining the place of provenance and the stage of development of the texts that have come down to us, texts which in some particulars were still further disparate and divided. From what the sources had to offer—and I mean not only modern editions of the text but older collections as well, especially Martène, two hundred and more years old and still valuable—excerpts had to be made systematically. The rows of paragraphs and chapters began to grow, in parallel columns that stretched out yard after yard, and with dozens and even hundreds of smaller strips; and, to make it easier to establish relationships and basic forms, all shimmering in every color of the rainbow! By thus collating the texts I could at last arrive at a thorough understanding of the evolution of a given piece. Yet this work is presented to the reader most of the time in just a few sentences, with a dozen or so selected source references in the footnotes, offering the critical student the sought-for assurance and the basis for further work, and in no way disturbing the ingenuously unconcerned reader. It was no easy thing to arrange the results of hundreds of detailed investigations, discoveries, hints and controversies in such a way that the exposition would be readable, and the little stones would be fashioned into a mosaic in which would appear a picture of the Roman Mass which, in spite of many a retouching and adaptation, still peers down at us today in pacific brightness.

By the beginning of May, 1945, when the waves of war, already subsiding, settled down, so to say, before our walls from East and West, the last sheets of manuscript were being readied in clean copy. My return at last to Innsbruck and to the library of the liturgical seminar gave me an opportunity not only to fill in many unhappy lacunæ, but also to finish a job which I had already started at Vienna. Long ago, while in Franz Josef Dölger's classes, I had had drummed into me, as a sort of scientific conscience, the exacting demand: *Check every citation!* This took another six months and more of strenuous work.

It is due to the persistence of the Herder publishing firm in Vienna that, despite innumerable obstacles, the setting and printing of the German book was pushed through with such dispatch and with all the careful attention I could have wished for.

Do not think I am deluding myself with the belief that, for all this diligence, the work does not suffer certain weaknesses. It is a child of war; children of war have a claim to a milder judgment. It was difficult, and in some instances—even after the war—impossible, to procure the pertinent new literature from the foreign press. And manuscripts and incunabulæ for the whole period under consideration were for all practical purposes unavailable. But that was not too bad, since nearly all the worthwhile sources for the period up to the late Middle Ages, and for the period following till 1570, at least the most typical samples of a tremendous flood of liturgical books were at hand in modern editions. Some student to come will probably find much to supplement and, I am sure, much to straighten out, especially if later on the liturgical manuscripts in various countries (including, in part, Germany) are published, and critical editions of such important sources as the Roman *Ordines* are prepared. Much, too, is to be looked for in materials that only border on the liturgical, like the *Consuetudines* of medieval monasteries and convents. And anyone who will become conversant with the various liturgies of the Orient and the partially existent monastic variants of the Roman rite, not only through source books, but, where possible, in actual performance, will, I think, be able to shed more light on many details of our Roman Mass. Finally, there is work to be done regarding the participation of the faithful, which is also a part of divine service and therefore belongs to liturgy; a study of the customs of each country—hardly to be found in books—ought to prove valuable. Among the important historical questions of a more particular kind, there is room for research in that aggregation of written witnesses to the reform of the Roman Mass around the year 1000, the aggregation previously grouped together as the Séez-group; the sudden blossoming of ecclesiastical life in Normandy during the tenth and eleventh centuries serves as a background. The history of liturgy has in every case many problems to solve, even in the narrower sphere of the Mass-liturgy.

So what I am able to offer, I beg the reader to accept. And may I make a last remark: this book is not meant to serve only for knowledge—even the knowledge of the most precious object in the Church's accumulated treasure—but it is intended for life, for a fuller grasp of that mystery of which Pope Pius XII says in his encyclical *Mediator Dei* (§ 201): "The Mass is the chief act of divine worship; it should also be the source and center of Christian piety."

Jos. A. Jungmann, S.J.

Innsbruck,
Easter 1948.

TRANSLATOR'S NOTE

Father Jungmann needs no introduction. This learned Jesuit and eminent liturgical scholar, at present editor of one of the foremost German theological magazines, is well-known throughout the Catholic world. His genetic study of the Roman Mass, entitled *Missarum Sollemnia*, first published at Vienna in 1948, has already reached a second German edition. It is a "must" for anyone desiring an over-all view of the history of the western Mass, its theology and its ceremonial. The translation represents in substance the second (revised) edition of the German. In the notes, however, the translator has sometimes substituted or added English references where they were advisable. If by his English version of this tremendous work the translator has contributed to a wider and deeper knowledge of the holy sacrifice, he is humbly grateful.

The translator has to thank several of his students and confreres for their ready aid while he was preparing this work, particularly the Very Rev. A. T. Zeller, C.Ss.R., and the Rev. M.S. Bringazi, C.Ss.R., who read proofs and manuscript respectively and generously offered helpful suggestions, contributing no little thereby to make this rendering fit to stand by the side of the original.

Grateful acknowledgment is also made to Sheed and Ward, publishers of Monsignor Knox's translation of the New Testament for gracious permission to use quotations from that work.

Francis A. Brunner, C.Ss.R.

St. Joseph's College,
Kirkwood, Mo.

ABBREVIATIONS

BIBLIOGRAPHY
Books and Articles Cited in Brief

D'ACHERY, J. L., O.S.B. *Spicilegium sive Collectio veterum aliquot scriptorum*. 2nd. ed. in 3 vols. Paris, 1723.

AIGRAIN. See *Liturgia*.

ARNOLD, A. *Der Ursprung des christlichen Abendmahls im Lichte der neuesten liturgiegeschichtlichen Forschung*. 2nd ed. (Freiburger Theologische Studien, 44). Freiburg, 1939.

ALBERS, BR. *Consuetudines monasticæ*. 5 vols. Monte Cassino, 1905-1912.

ANDRIEU, M. *Les Ordines Romani du haut Moyen-Age. I. Les Manuscrits*. (Spicilegium Sacrum Lovaniense, 11). Louvain, 1931.

——*Le Pontifical Romain au Moyen-Age*. 4 vols.: I. *Le Pontifical Romain du XIIe siecle;* II. *Le Pontifical de la Curie Romaine au XIIIe siecle;* III. *Le Pontifical de Guillaume Durand;* IV. *Tables*. (Studi e Testi, 86, 87, 88, 99). Vatican City, 1938-1941.

ATCHLEY, E. G. CUTHB. F. *A History of the Use of Incense in Divine Worship*. (Alcuin Club Collections, 13). London, 1909.

BATIFFOL, P. *Leçons sur la Messe*. 7th ed. Paris, 1920.

BAUMSTARK, A. *Liturgie comparée. Conférences faites au Prieuré d'Amay*. Edition refondue. Chevetogne o. J., 1940.

——*Missale Romanum. Seine Entwicklung, ihre wichtigsten Urkunden und Probleme*. Eindhoven-Nimwegen o. J., 1929.

——*Die Messe im Morgenland*. (Sammlung Kösel). Kempten, 1906.

——*Vom geschichtlichen Werden der Liturgie*. (Ecclesia Orans, 10). Freiburg, 1923.

BECK, A. *Kirchliche Studien und Quellen*. Amberg, 1903.

BEISSEL, S., S.J. *Bilder aus der Geschichte der altchristlichen Kunst und Liturgie in Italien*. Freiburg, 1899.

——*Entstehung der Perikopen des Römischen Messbuches*. Freiburg, 1907.

BENEDICT XIV. *De sacrosancto sacrificio Missæ libri tres*. Denuo ed. J. Schneider. Mainz, 1879.

BERLIÈRE, U., O.S.B. *L'ascèse bénédictine des origines à la fin du XIIe Siècle*. Maredsous, 1927.

BERTHOLD VON REGENSBURG. *Vollständige Ausgabe seiner deutschen Predigten*, with introduction and notes by Fr. Pfeiffer and J. Strobl. 2 vols. Vienna, 1862-1880.

BIEHL, L. *Das liturgische Gebet für Kaiser und Reich*. (Görresgesellschaft, Veröffentlichungen der Sektion für Rechts- und Staatsgeschichte, 75). Paderborn, 1937.

BINTERIM, A. J. *Die vorzüglichsten Denkwürdigkeiten der christkatholischen Kirche*. 7 vols. Mainz, 1825-1841.

BISHOP, E. *Liturgica historica*. Oxford, 1918.

BLUDAU, A. *Die Pilgerreise der Ätheria*. (Studien zur Geschichte und Kultur des Altertums, XV, 1-2). Paderborn, 1927.

BLUME, CL., S.J. *Tropen des Missale im Mittelalter. II. Tropen zum Proprium Missarum*. (Analecta hymnica, 49). Leipzig, 1906.

BLUME CL. and BANNISTER, H. M. *Tropen des Missale im Mittelalter. I. Tropen zum Ordinarium Missæ*. (Analecta hymnica, 47). Leipzig, 1905.

BONA, J. *Rerum liturgicarum libri duo.* Cologne, 1674.

BOTTE, B., O.S.B. *Le Canon de la Messe Romaine.* Critical edition, with introduction and notes. Mont César, 1935.

BRAUN, J., S.J. *Der christliche Altar in seiner geschichtlichen Entwicklung.* 2 vols. Munich, 1924.

——*Das christliche Altargerät in seinem Sein und in seiner Entwicklung.* Munich, 1932.

——*Die liturgische Gewandung im Occident und Orient nach Ursprung und Entwicklung, Verwendung und Symbolik.* Freiburg, 1907.

——*Die liturgischen Paramente in Gegenwart und Vergangenheit. Ein Handbuch der Paramentik.* 2nd ed. Freiburg, 1924.

BREMOND, H. *Histoire littéraire du Sentiment religieux en France.* Paris, 1916.

BRIDGETT, T. E., C.SS.R. *A History of the Holy Eucharist in Great Britain,* with notes by H. Thurston, S.J. London and St. Louis, 1908.

BRIGHTMAN, F. E. *Liturgies eastern and western.* I. *Eastern liturgies.* Oxford, 1896.

BRINKTRINE, J. *Die heilige Messe.* 2nd ed. Paderborn, 1934.

——*Die feierliche Papstmesse und die Zeremonien bei Selig- und Heiligsprechungen.* "Ordo et Canon missæ (Cod. Vet. Ottobon. lat. 356)," *Eph. liturg.,* 51 (1937), 198-209.

BROWE, PETER, S.J. *Die häufige Kommunion im Mittelalter.* Münster, 1938.

——*Die Pflichtkommunion im Mittelalter.* Münster, 1940.

——*Die Verehrung der Eucharistie im Mittelalter.* Münster, 1933.

BRUININGK, H. v. *Messe and kanonisches Stundentgebet nach dem Brauche der Rigaschen Kirche im späteren Mittelalter.* Riga, 1904.

BUENNER, D. *L'ancienne Liturgie Romaine. Le Rite Lyonnais.* Lyons o. J., 1934.

CABROL, FERNAND. *Origines liturgiques.* Paris, 1906.

CAGIN, P., O.S.B. *L'Eucharistia canon primitif de la Messe. (Scriptorium Solesmense,* 2). Paris, 1912.

CALLEWAERT, C. *Sacris erudiri. Fragmenta liturgica collecta a monachis S. Petri de Aldenburgo in Steenbrugge, ne pereant.* Steenbrugge, 1940.

CODRINGTON, H. W. *The Liturgy of Saint Peter.* (LQF, 30). Münster, 1936.

Concilium Tridentinum. Diariorum, actorum, epistolarum, tractatuum nova collectio Edidit Societas Görresiana. Freiburg. 1901 ff.

CONNOLLY, R. H. *The liturgical Homilies of Narsai.* (Texts and Studies, VIII, 1). Cambridge, 1909.

CORBLET, J. *Histoire dogmatique, liturgique et archéologique du sacrement de l'Eucharistie.* 2 vols. Paris, 1885-86.

DE CORSWAREM, P. *De liturgische boeken der kollegiale O. L. Vr.-Kerk van Tongeren voor het Concilie van Trente.* Ghent, 1923.

Cours et Conférences des Semaines liturgiques. III. Louvain, 1925, ff.

Decreta authentica Congregationis Sacrorum Rituum. 5 vols. Rome, 1898-1901. Appendix I (1912), Appendix II (1927).

DEKKERS, E. O.S.B. *Tertullianus en de geschiedenis der liturgie.* (Catholica, VI, 2). Brussels-Amsterdam, 1947.

DENZIGER, H. and UMBERG, J. B. *Enchiridion Symbolorum.* 15th ed. Freiburg, 1922.

DESTEFANI, GASPARE. *La Santa Messa nella Liturgia Romana.* Turin, 1935.

VAN DIJK, A., O.S.B. "De fontibus 'Opusculi super missam' Fr. Gulielmi de Melitona O.M. (mit Textausgabe)." *Ephemerides liturgicæ,* LIII (1939), 291-349.

DIX, GREGORY. *The Treatise on the Apostolic Tradition of St. Hippolytus of Rome.* London, 1937.

——*The shape of the Liturgy.* 2nd ed. Westminster, 1945.

DOELGER, F. J. *Sol salutis. Gebet und Gesang im christlichen Altertum. Mit besonderer Rücksicht auf die Ostung in Gebet und Liturgie.* 2nd ed. (LF 4-5). Münster, 1925.

DUCANGE-FAVRE. *Glossarium mediæ et infimæ Latinitatis.* 10 vols. Niort, 1883-87.

DUCHESNE, L. *Le Liber pontificalis.* 2 vols. Paris, 1886-92.
——*Christian Worship: Its Origin and Evolution.* 5th ed. trans. from the 3rd French ed. by M. T. McClure, London, 1927.

DUMOUTET, E. *Le desir de voir l'Hostie et les origines de la devotion au Saint-Sacrement.* Paris, 1926.

DURANDUS, G. *Rationale divinorum officiorum.* Lyons, 1574. (In our citations we quote the chapters and numbers, since these recur in all modern editions.)

EBNER, A. *Quellen und Forschungen zur Geschichte und Kunstgeschichte des Missale Romanum im Mittelalter. Iter. Italicum.* Freiburg, 1896.

EICHMANN, E. *Die Kaiserkrönung im Abendland. Ein Beitrag zur Geistesgeschichte des Mittelalters.* 2 vols. Würzburg, 1942.

EISENHOFER, L. *Handbuch der katholischen Liturgik.* 2 vols. Freiburg, 1932-33.

ELBOGEN, I. *Der jüdische Gottesdienst in seiner geschichtlichen Entwicklung.* 2nd ed. Frankfurt, 1924.

ELFERS, H. *Die Kirchenordnung Hippolyts von Rom.* Paderborn, 1938.

ELLARD, G., S.J. *The Mass of the future.* Milwaukee, 1948.

FELTOE, CH. L. *Sacramentarium Leonianum.* Cambridge, 1896.

FÉROTIN, M., O.S.B. *Le Liber ordinum en usage dans l'église wisigothique et mozarabe d'Espagne du Ve au XIe siècle.* Paris, 1904.
——*Le Liber mozarabicus sacramentorum et les manuscrits mozarabes.* Paris, 1912.

FERRERES, J. B., S.J. *Historia del Misal Romano.* Barcelona, 1929. (Contains descriptions of the liturgical MSS of the ecclesiastical provinces of Valencia and Taragona.)

FIALA, V., O.S.B. *Der Ordo missæ im Vollmissale des Cod. Vat. lat. 6082 aus dem Ende des 11. Jh.: Zeugnis des Geistes.* Gabe zum Benedictus-Jubiläum, dargeboten von der Erzabtei Beuron (Beiheft z. 23. Jahrg. d. *Benediktinischen Monatschrift*). Beuron, 1947.

FINSTERWALDER, P. W. *Die Canones Theodori Cantuariensis und ihre Uberlieferungsformen.* Weimar, 1929.

FISCHER, L. *Bernhardi Cardinalis et Lateranensis Ecclesiæ Prioris Ordo officiorum Ecclesiæ Lateransis.* Munich, 1916.

FORTESCUE, A. *The Mass. A Study of the Roman Liturgy.* London, 1912.

FRANZ, A. *Die Messe im deutschen Mittelalter. Beiträge zur Geschichte der Liturgie und des religiösen Volkslebens.* Freiburg, 1902.

FRERE, W. H. *The use of Sarum.* 2 vols. Cambridge, 1898-1901.

FRIEDBERG, E. *Corpus Iuris Canonici.* 2 vols. Leipzig, 1879-1881.

FUNK, FR. X. *Didascalia et Constitutiones Apostolorum.* 2 vols. Paderborn, 1905.

GARDELLINI, A. *Decreta authentica Congregationis S. Rituum.* 3rd ed. in 2 vols. Rome, 1856-1858.

GASQUET, AIDAN. *Parish Life in Medieval England.* New York, 1906.

GASSNER, JEROME, O.S.B. *The Canon of the Mass. Its History, Theology and Art.* St. Louis, 1949.

GATTERER, M., S.J. *Praxis celebrandi functiones ordinarias sacerdotales.* 3rd ed. Innsbruck, 1940.

GAVANTI, B. and MERATI, C. M. *Thesaurus sacrorum rituum.* 5 vols. Venice, 1723.

GEISELMANN, J. R. *Die Abendmahlslehre an der Wende der christlichen Spätantike zum Frühmittelalter.* Munich, 1933.

GERBERT, M. *Monumenta veteris Liturgiæ Alemannicæ.* 2 vols. St.-Blaise, 1777-1779.
——*Vetus Liturgia Alemannica.* 2 vols. St.-Blaise, 1776.

GIHR, NICHOLAS. *The Holy Sacrifice of the Mass.* Rev. trans. St. Louis, 1949.

GOOSSENS, W. *Les origines de l'Eucharistie.* Paris, 1931.

GÖTZ, J. B. *Das Pfarrbuch des Stephan May in Hipoltstein vom Jahre 1511.* (Reformationsgeschichtliche Studien und Texte, 47-48). Münster, 1926,

GREVING, J. *Johann Ecks Pfarrbuch für U. L. Frau in Ingolstadt.* (Reformationsgeschichtliche Studien and Texte, 4-5). Münster, 1908.

GUERRINI, F. M., O.P. *Ordinarium iuxta ritum sacri Ordinis Fratrum Prædicatorum.* Rome, 1921.

HABERSTROH, L., S.V.D. *Der Ritus der Brechung und Mischung nach dem Missale Romanum.* (St. Gabrieler Studien, 5). Mödling, 1937.

HAMM, F. *Die liturgischen Einsetzungsberichte im Sinne vergleichender Liturgieforschung untersucht.* (LQF, 23). Münster, 1928.

HANSSENS, J. M., S.J. *Institutiones Liturgicæ de ritibus orientalibus.* Tome II-III: *De Missa rituum orientalium.* Rome, 1930-1932.

HARDOUIN, J., S.J. *Acta Conciliorum et Epistolæ decretales.* 11 vols. Paris, 1715.

HARTZHEIM, J., S.J. *Concilia Germaniæ.* 5 vols. Cologne, 1759-1763.

HAULER, E. *Didascaliæ Apostolorum fragmenta Veronensia.* Leipzig, 1900.

HEILER, FR. *Das Gebet. Eine religionsgeschichtliche und religionspsychologische Untersuchung.* 4th ed. Munich, 1921.

HENNECKE, E. *Neutestamentliche Apokryphen.* 2nd ed. Tübingen, 1924.

HERRGOTT, M. *Vetus disciplina monastica.* Paris, 1726.

HESBERT, R. J., O.S.B. *Antiphonale Missarum sextuplex.* Brussels, 1935.

HIERZEGGER, R. "Collecta und Station. Die römischen Stationsprozessionen im Frühen Mittelalter," *ZkTh,* LX (1936), 511-554.

HITTORP, M. *De divinis catholicæ Ecclesiæ officiis ac ministeriis.* Cologne, 1568.

HOEYNCK, F. A. *Geschichte der kirchlichen Liturgie des Bisthums Augsburg.* Augsburg, 1889.

JAVOR, E., O.S.B. *Hét kéziratos Pozsony Missale a Nemzeti Múzeumban.* Budapest, 1942.

JEDIN, H. "Das Konzil von Trient und die Reform des Römischen Messbuches," *Liturgisches Leben,* VI (1939), 30-66.

——"Das Konzil von Trient und die Reform der Liturgischen Bücher," *Ephemerides Liturgicæ,* LIX (1945), 6-38, with fullest bibliographical references.

JUNGMANN, J. A., S.J. *Die Stellung Christi im liturgischen Gebet.* (LF, 7-8). Münster, 1925.

——*Die lateinischen Bussriten in ihrer geschichtlichen Entwicklung.* Innsbruck, 1932.

——*Gewordene Liturgie. Studien und Durchblicke.* Innsbruck, 1941.

——*Liturgical Worship. An Inquiry into its Fundamental Principles.* New York, 1941.

KENNEDY, V. L., C.S.B. *The Saints of the Canon of the Mass.* (Studi d'Antichita Cristiana, 14). Vatican City, 1938.

KING, ARCHDALE A. *Notes on the Catholic Liturgies.* London, 1930.

KLAUSER, TH. *Das römische Capitulare evangeliorum. Texte und Untersuchungen zu seiner ältesten Geschichte.* I. Typen. (LQF, 28). Münster, 1935.

——"Die liturgischen Austauschbeziehungen zwischen der römischen und der fränkisch-deutschen Kirche vom 8. bis zum 11. Jh," *Historisches Jahrbuch der Görresgesellschaft,* LIII (1933), 169-189.

KÖCK, J. *Handschriftliche Missalien in Steiermark.* Graz, 1916.

KÖSSING, J. *Liturgische Vorlesungen über die heilige Messe.* 2nd ed. Regensburg, 1856.

KRAMP, J., S.J. "Messgebräuche der Gläubigen in der Neuzeit," *StZ,* CXI (1926, II), 206-223.

——"Messgebräuche der Gläubigen in den ausserdeutschen Ländern," *StZ,* 113 (1927, II), 352-367.

KRAZER, AUG. *De apostolicis necnon antiquis ecclesiæ occidentalis liturgiis . . . liber singularis.* Augsburg, 1786.

KÜNSTLE, K. *Ikonographie der christlichen Kunst.* 2 vols. Freiburg, 1926-28.

KUNZE, G. *Die gottesdienstliche Schriftlesung. I. Stand und Aufgaben der Perikopenforschung.* (Veröffentlichungen der evang. Gesellschaft f. Liturgieforschung, 1). Göttingen, 1947.

LE BRUN, P. *Explication litterale, historique et dogmatique des prières et des cérémonies de la Messe.* 4 vols. Lyons, 1860.

LEFÈVRE, P. F., O. PRÆM. *L'Ordinaire de Prémontré d'après des mss. du 12. et du 13. siècle.* Louvain, 1941.

LEGG, J. WICKHAM. *Tracts on the Mass.* (HBS, 27). London, 1904.

——*Missale ad usum Ecclesiæ Westmonasteriensis.* 3 Pts. (HBS, 1, 5, 12). London, 1891-1897.

LEITNER, F. *Der gottesdienstliche Volksgesang im jüdischen und christlichen Altertum.* Freiburg, 1906.

LEITZMANN, A. *Kleinere geistliche Gedichte des 12. Jh.* 2nd ed. (Kleine Texte, 54). Berlin, 1929.

LEPIN, M. *L'idée du sacrifice de la Messe d'après les Théologiens depuis l'origine à nos jours.* Paris, 1926.

LEROQUAIS, V. *Les Sacramentaires et les Missels manuscrits des bibliothèques publiques de France.* 4 vols. Paris, 1924. (Citations of the author's name alone refer to this work.)

——*Les Pontificaux des bibliothèques publiques de France.* 4 vols. Paris, 1937.

——"L'Ordo Missæ du Sacramentaire d'Amiens," *Eph. liturg.,* XLI (1927), 435-445.

LIETZMANN, H. *Das Sacramentarium Gregorianum nach dem Aachener Urexemplar.* (LQ, 3). Münster, 1921.

——*Messe und Herrenmahl.* (Arbeiten zur Kirchengeschichte, 8). Bonn, 1926.

LINSENMAYER, G. *Geschichte der Predigt in Deutschland von Karl d. Gr. bis zum Ausgang des 14. Jh.* Munich, 1886.

LIPPE, R. *Missale Romanum Mediolani 1474.* 2 vols. (HBS, 17, 33). London, 1899-1907.

Liturgia. Encyclopédie populaire des connaissances liturgiques. Published under the direction of R. Aigrain. Paris, 1935.

DE LUBAC, H., S.J. *Corpus mysticum. L'Eucharistie et l'Eglise au moyen-age.* (Theologie, 3). Paris, 1944.

MANSI, J. D. *Sacrorum Conciliorum nova et amplissima collectio.* 31 vols. Florence, 1759-1798.

MARTÈNE, E., O.S.B. *De antiquis Ecclesiæ ritibus.* 2nd ed., 4 vols. Antwerp, 1736-1738. (In order to facilitate reference to other editions, the citations are made according to Martène's own divisions, but the volume and page numbering of the second Antwerp edition are appended in parentheses.)

MARTINUCCI, P. *Manuale decretorum S. Rituum Congregationis.* 4th ed. Regensburg, 1873.

MASKELL, W. *The ancient liturgy of the church of England according to the uses of Sarum, York, Hereford and Bangor.* 3rd ed. Oxford, 1882.

MERK, K. J. *Abriss einer liturgiegeschichtlichen Darstellung des Mess-Stipendiums.* Stuttgart, 1928.

METZGER, F. M. *Zwei karolingische Pontifikalien vom Oberrhein.* (Freiburger Theologische Studien, 17). Freiburg, 1914.

Miscellanea Liturgica in honorem L. Cuniberti Mohlberg, Vol. I. (Bibliotheca "Ephemerides Liturgicæ," 22). Rome, 1948.

MOHLBERG, K. O.S.B. *Das fränkische Sacramentarium Gelasianum in alamanischer Uberlieferung.* 2nd ed. (LQ, 1-2).Münster, 1939. (This second edition contains on pp. 293-339 a table of concordance compiled by G. Manz.)

——*Radulph de Rivo, der letzte Vertreter der altrömischen Liturgie.* Vol. I. *Studien.* Louvain, 1911; Vol. II. *Texte.* Münster, 1911-1915.

MOHLBERG, K. and BAUMSTARK, A. *Die älteste erreichbare Gestalt des Liber Sacramentorum anni circuli der römischen Kirche.* (LQ, 11-12). Münster, 1927.

DE MOLÉON, JEAN G. *Voyages liturgiques de France.* Paris, 1718.

MONACHINO, V. *La cura pastorale a Milano, Cartagine e Roma nel secolo IV.* (Analecta Gregoriana, 41). Rome, 1947.

MURATORI, L. A. *Liturgia Romana Vetus*. 2 vols. Venice, 1748.

NETZER, H. *L'introduction de la Messe romaine en France*. Paris, 1910.

NICKL, G. *Der Anteil des Volkes an der Messliturgie im Frankenreiche von Chlodwig bis auf Karl den Grossen*. Innsbruck, 1930.

NIELEN, JOSEPH M. *The Earliest Christian Liturgy*. Trans. P. Cummins. St. Louis, 1941.

OESTERLEY, W. O. E. *Jewish Background of the Christian Liturgy*. Oxford, 1925.

Ordinarium Cartusiense pro divinis officiis in Ordine Cartusiensi uniformiter celebrandis. Grande Chartreuse, 1932.

PARSCH, PIUS. *Volksliturgie. Ihr Sinn und Umfang*. Klosterneuburg, 1940.

DE PUNIET, P., O.S.B. *Das römische Pontifikale. Geschichte und Kommentar*. Trans. from the French. Klosterneuburg, 1935.

QUASTEN, JOHANNES. *Monumenta eucharistica et liturgica vetustissima*. Bonn, 1935-1937.

——*Expositio antiquæ liturgiæ Gallicanæ Germano Parisiensi ascripta*. (Opuscula et Textus, ser. liturg., 3). Münster, 1934.

RADÓ, P., O.S.B. *Libri liturgici manu scripti bibliothecarum Hungariæ*. I. *Libri liturgici ms. ad Missam pertinentes*. (Editiones Bibliothecæ Szechenyanæ Musæi Nationalis Hungariæ, 26). Budapest, 1947.

RAES, A., S.J. *Introductio in liturgiam orientalem*. Rome, 1947.

RAHMANI, IGNATIUS E. *Testamentum Domini Nostri Jesu Christi*. Mainz, 1899.

RENAUDOT, E. *Liturgiarum orientalium collectio*. 2nd ed. in 2 vols. Frankfurt, 1847.

RICHTER, G. and SCHOENFELDER, A. *Sacramentarium Fuldense sæc. X*. Fulda, 1912.

RIEDEL, W. *Die Kirchenrechtsquellen des Patriarchats Alexandrien*. Leipzig, 1900.

RIGHETTI, M. *Manuale di storia liturgica*. Vol. III: *L'Eucaristia sacrificio e sacramento*. Milan, 1949.

ROCK, DANIEL. *The Church of Our Fathers*. Newly ed. by Hart and Frere. London, 1903.

ROETZER, W., O.S.B. *Des hl. Augustinus Schriften als liturgie-geschichtliche Quelle*. Munich, 1930.

RÜCKER, A. *Die syrische Jakobusanaphora. Mit dem griechischen Paralleltext*. (LQ, 4). Münster, 1923.

——*Ritus Baptismi et Missæ, quem descripsit Theodorus ep. Mopsuestenus in sermonibus catecheticis*. (Opuscula et Textus, ser. liturg., 2). Münster, 1933.

RUETTEN, F. "Philologisches zum Canon Missæ," StZ, CXXXIII (1938, I), 43-50.

SAWICKI, P., O.S.P.I.ER. *De missa conventuali in Capitulis et apud Religiosos. Historice, canonice, liturgice. Cui accedit appendix De Missa* conventuali in Ordine *S. Pauli I. Er.* Cracow, 1938.

SCHABES, L. *Alte liturgische Gebräuche und Zeremonien an der Stiftskirche zu Klosterneuburg*. Klosterneuburg, 1930.

SCHMITZ, H. J. *Die Bussbücher und das kanonische Bussverfahren*. Düsseldorf, 1898.

SCHNEIDER, F., O.CIST. "Vom alten Messritus des Cistercienser Ordens," *Cistercienser-Chronik*, XXXVII (1925), 145-152, with continuations till XL (1928), 77-90.

SCHREIBER, G. *Untersuchungen zum Sprachgebrauch des mittelterlichen Oblationswesens*. Wörishofen, 1913.

——*Gemeinschaften des Mittelalters. Recht und Verfassung, Kult und Frömmigkeit*. (Gesammelte Abhandlungen, Vol. 1). Münster, 1948.

SCHROEDER, H. J. *Canons and Decrees of the Council of Trent*. St. Louis, 1941.

SCHUEMMER, J. *Die altchristliche Fastenpraxis mit besonderer Berücksichtigung der Schriften Tertullians*. (LQF, 27). Münster, 1933.

SCHUSTER, ILDEFONSO. *The Sacramentary. Historical and Liturgical Notes on the Roman Missa*. 5 vols. Trans. from Italian by A. Levelis-Marke. New York, 1924-1930.

SILVA-TAROUCA, C., S.J. *Giovanni "Archicantor" di S. Pietro a Roma e L'Ordo Romanus da lui composto.* (Atti della pont. Accademia Romana di Archeologia, Memorie, I, 1). Rome, 1923.

SIMMONS, THOS. F. (ed.) *The Lay Folks Mass Book.* (Early English Text Society, original series, 71). London, 1879.

SMITS VAN WAESBERGE, M., S.J. "Die misverklaring van Meester Simon van Venlo," *Ons geestelijk Erf,* XV (1941), 228-261; 285-327; XVI (1942), 85-129; 177-185.

SÖLCH, G. G., O.P. *Hugo von St. Cher, O.P. und die Anfänge der Dominikanerliturgie. Eine liturgiegeschichtliche Untersuchung zum "Speculum Ecclesiæ."* Cologne, 1938.

SRAWLEY, J. H. *The Early History of the Liturgy.* Rev. ed. Cambridge, 1947.

STAPPER, R. *Ordo Romanus primus de Missa papali.* (Opuscula et Textus, ser. liturg., 1). Münster, 1933.

STRACK, H. L. and BILLERBECK, P. *Kommentar zum Neuen Testament aus Talmud und Midrasch.* Vol. IV. Munich, 1928.

THIEL, A. *Epistolæ, Romanorum Pontificum.* Braunsberg, 1868.

TOMMASI, J. M. *Opera.* Ed. Vezzosi. 7 vols. Rome, 1747-1754.

TRAPP, W. *Vorgeschichte und Ursprung der liturgischen Bewegung vorwiegend in Hinsicht auf das deutsche Sprachgebiet.* Regensburg, 1940.

URSPRUNG, O. *Die katholische Kirchenmusik.* Potsdam, 1931.

VIERBACH, A. *Die liturgischen Anschauungen des Vitus Anton Winter. Ein Beitrag zur Geschichte der Aufklärung.* (Münchener Studien zur historischen Theologie, 9). Munich, 1929.

VOLK, P., O.S.B. *Der Liber ordinarius des Lütticher St. Jakobs-Klosters.* (Beiträge zur Geschichte des alten Mönchtums und des Benediktinerordens, 10). Münster, 1923.

VAN WAEFELGHEM, M., O.PRÆM. *Le Liber ordinarius d'après un ms. du 13.-14. siècle.* Louvain, 1913.

WAGNER, PETER. *Einführung in die gregorianischen Melodien.* I. *Ursprung und Entwicklung der liturgischen Gesangsformen bis zum Ausgang des Mittelalters.* 3rd ed. Leipzig, 1911. II. *Neumenkunde.* 2nd ed. Leipsig, 1912.

WARNER, G. F. *The Stowe Missal.* 2 vols. (HBS, 31-32). London, 1906, 1915.

WARREN, F. E. *The Liturgy and Ritual of the Celtic Church.* Oxford, 1881.

WILMART, A., O.S.B. *Auteurs spirituels et Textes dévots du moyen-âge latin. Etudes d'histoire littéraire.* Paris, 1932.

WILSON, H. A. *The Gelasian Sacramentary.* Oxford, 1894.

——*The Gregorian Sacramentary under Charles the Great.* (HBS, 49). London, 1915.

YELVERTON, E. E. *The Mass in Sweden.* (HBS, 57). London, 1920.

ZIMMERMANN, B., O.CARM. *Ordinaire de l'ordre de Notre Dame du Mont-Carmel par Sibert de Beka.* (Bibliothèque Liturgique, 13). Paris, 1910.

TABLE OF CONTENTS

Introduction

EVER SINCE THE GOD-MAN WALKED THIS EARTH OF OURS AND CLOSED His career with the redemptive sacrifice of the Cross, there has been in the midst of men that mystery-filled renewal of His world-saving offering which has continued from age to age and from land to land, and which will so continue till He comes again. Sometimes with pomp and splendor in the midst of thousands, sometimes in the quiet of a lonely chapel, in the poverty of a tiny village church, in some out-of-the-way spot from which men consecrated to God go out to their works of love, everywhere the same mystery is daily consummated in endless repetition. Hardly separated by even a thin wall from the market-place of everyday life, it is found in the very midst of men who throng forward toward the heavenly grace which here rises resplendent, who stretch out their hands seeking help to prevent their sinking into nothingness, into a life estranged from God.

From the very beginning Jesus designed this institution precisely for this purpose, to rise in the midst of the people. Here is the wood of the cross standing firm and erect; here our Lord's words find their fulfillment: "And I, if I be lifted up from the earth, will draw all things to myself" (John 12:32). A mighty process of assimilation, tending ever farther and farther, is centered in this glowing hearth—a process of conformation or at least of approximation of the earthly to the heavenly, of the sinful life of man to the offering of the Son of God to His Father's will.

But the very fact that Christ's power is continually hedged in by men and surrounded by surging life made it imperative from the very beginning that there be some protecting form, some firm dwelling in which the Holies would be guarded against rough hands and the dust of the streets, safe from desecration and dishonor. It would have to be a form in which what is going on beneath is enveloped without being hidden from men's senses, so that its inmost riches and its uplifting power might be made manifest. This form is the *liturgy of Holy Mass.*

Christ Himself gave us only the essential core of the liturgical celebration; the externals had to be furnished by men. These the Church has worked out in a slow development, year by year. And as in a structure which has been building for centuries, the Mass-liturgy is not always constructed along the same uniform lines, either in whole or in its single parts. Of course, the basic outline, the form of the Eucharist, once it was chosen, remained untouched. And we are bound to admire the piety that held fast to what was established and seldom allowed new ideas to tamper with what was long existing and familiar. But in other matters, what changes! In stressing certain aspects, in responding to the religious temper of the times,

1

and in veering with the general atmosphere through which the Church has had to pass, some things were brought to the fore, others, on the contrary, allowed to disappear.

The liturgy of the Mass has become quite a complicated structure, wherein some details do not seem to fit very well, like some venerable, thousand-year-old castle whose crooked corridors and narrow stairways, high towers and large halls appear at first sight strange and queer. How much more comfortable a modern villa! But in the old building there is really something noble. It treasures the heirloom of bygone years; the architectures of many successive generations have been built into its walls. Now these must be recovered by the latest generation. So, too, in the Mass-liturgy, only a historical consideration of the evolutionary work of the centuries can make possible a proper appreciation. Of course it would not be unthinkable—rather it would be the ideal toward which all further development should tend—that the Mass-liturgy should be so constructed that, while remaining true to the past, it should be understandable, both in general plan and in single details, without reference to history. Many an old cathedral—as I myself noticed especially on a visit to Trier's revered *Dom*—displays such a solution perfectly. If this were the case, explanations could be reduced to a minimum. A consideration of the growth would then really be of only historical interest, something about which people would not ordinarily have to bother.

But this is not the case with the Roman Mass. To gain a thorough understanding of it, whether as a complete unit or in detail, one is forced to rely on historical investigation. Such historical investigation, serving as it does to explain what is actually at hand, has since the sixteenth century been zealously turned to the analysis of the liturgy of Holy Mass. The last few centuries have been at it with special diligence and considerable success. To summarize the results of these inquiries and to round them out as much as possible is the task the following pages propose to do.

To determine just how broad the field must be which this historical analysis will cover, it is important to discover the precise meaning of the word "liturgy." Is it concerned only with the activity of the priest who celebrates, so that the participation of the people and the forms under which he celebrates are only accidental concomitants, to be considered perhaps in pastoral theology and canon law but not in a liturgical disquisition? Or are the Christian people joined to the priest in the compass of the term? A cursory glance at the older periods of Christian worship forces the latter solution, for in early times the Mass-liturgy was definitely cast in the form of a communal exercise. The Council of Trent, too, declares that Christ left the Mass to his *Church*. The Church, however, is something more than just the clergy; it is the whole Christian people under the leadership of proper authority.

If nowadays we appear to be stressing more and more the participation of the laity in the liturgical function, this is only a result of a return to that larger concept of the Church which the circumstances of the time and the demands of the cure of souls have forced upon us.[1] If this enlarged concept is clearly kept in mind, new light will be shed on many questions regarding the Mass-liturgy.

From what has been said, one can formulate the plan of this book. The main portion of the book is concerned with a genetic explanation of the various rites and prayers of the Roman Mass. This is preceded by two introductory and preparatory parts. The first is a quick glance at the history of the Mass from the first Maundy Thursday till today. Non-Roman liturgies must must also be considered, for the comparative study of these will help us to derive the lines of development. This historical prospectus will bring to our notice more plainly the various forces that have in the course of centuries contributed to building the structure of the Mass, and thus can be outlined the larger phases of the development which the complete picture unfolds and which will be repeated more specifically at numerous points. Of this development the earlier period has indeed been presented often. Batiffol, in his *Leçons sur la Messe* has given us a fine picture of the developments of the early Middle Ages. Of the later period, a more precise view is offered for the first time in the following pages.

The second preparatory section deals with those changes in the liturgy of the Mass which arise from the diversity of the ways of the Church's particpaton. On the one hand there are the various modes of celebration necessitated by the variety of celebrants—from pontifical functions right down to private Masses. On the other hand there are various modes of congregational participation, limited by considerations of ritual as well as of time and place. Here in particular the function of the people in relationship to the liturgy must be carefully worked out. To test the conclusions regarding the part the people play in the celebration of Holy Mass, a chapter is-prefixed on the essence of the sacrifice of the Mass, to illustrate the essential meaning of the sacrifice of the Mass as worship, in contrast to the sacrifice of the Cross. We can see at the same time in this offering of worship that the role of the Church—and therefore of the people—is not that of passive by-standers; that, rather, all active resources must be drawn upon in taking part in the sacerdotal work of the High-Priest Eternal who—in regard to the material offering—sanctifies and transfigures even the sensible world of unreasoning creation.

The Mass has been called the central artistic achievement of Christian culture. The dramatist Hugo Ball (d. 1927) held the opinion: "For the Catholic there can really be no theater. The play which dominates his life and enthralls his every morning is holy Mass."[2] Paul Claudel, after the initial impressions which culminated in his conversion, was thrilled by the sacred drama unfolded at Notre Dame in Paris. "It was the most profound

---

[1] See J. A. Jungmann, "Was ist Liturgie?" ZkTh, LV (1931), 83-102; reprinted in the volume *Gewordene Liturgie*, 1-27.

[2] E. Hennings-Ball, *Hugo Balls Weg zu Gott* (Munich, 1931), 42.

and grandiose poetry, enhanced by the most august gestures ever confided
to human beings. I could not sufficiently satiate myself with the spectacle
of the Mass. . . ."[3]

These are the words of seers, words that compel our attention. When an
inspired faith has grasped the invisible mystery hidden beneath these
forms, then these modest forms themselves begin to shine under the reveal-
ing light of the mystery.

We must not, of course, be deceived into thinking that the words "artistic
work" as usually understood, tell more than a half-truth. There is wanting
a disciplined conservativeness in incident—and this is true not only of the
Roman liturgy; there is wanting, even up to the final outgrowths, any
consciously determined and accomplished plan. Men of many centuries
and speaking many languages have all contributed to the work, perhaps
with some common ideal that was itself subjected to a diversity of shades
and accents—as we learn from the history of dogma and even more from
the still unwritten history of Christian preaching. Still these men were all
members of one Church, men, in fact, so identified with that Church that
we but seldom know their names; and the common ideal was a pattern of
such force that their work did not fall apart but preserved its unity and
so gained a special beauty. However, it is not properly the beauty of an
art-product which is manifested here, but rather the beauty of a living
thing such as we admire in a blossoming tree which, no matter how irregu-
lar and haphazard the branches and twigs and leaves and flowers might
be, yet maintains a dominant symmetry, because a life-principle, a soul,
guides its growth. It is in this sense that Sigismund von Radecki speaks
of the accomplishment of the prophetic and operative words of Holy Mass:
"This is not art but rather the pattern and source towards which all art
is striving."[4] In Holy Mass the world beyond reaches down into our earthly
world. In the power of this invasion, in the fire of this meeting of man with
God, the irridescent form of earthly artistry is lost and entangled in the
balanced rhythm of resonant human words.

On the other hand the greatness of the thing, the reverent enthusiasm
for the sublime work which is given us men to do, lures us on to dare the
very heights. In a thousand different attempts the Church in the course
of her long history has endeavored to reform and improve her liturgy by
means of the most diverse agencies, which time and again were called in
to retouch the work in orderly and accomplished fashion. Nor will she
in future desist from this pressing and eternally unfinished task. We may
hope that this care for the holy of holies which she guards will prove to be
all the more fruitful as the ideal patterns which for centuries have guided
this care become clearer.

---

[3] From "In the Grip of God," in S. and
Lamping, *Through Hundred Gates* (Milwaukee, 1939), 202.
[4] S. v. Radecki, *Wort und Wunder* (2nd

S. ed.; Vienna, 1942), p. 51, in the essay, "Das
Verborgene Wort." Also in *Liturgisches
Leben*, VI (1939), 73.

It is the task of the history of the liturgy to bring to light these ideal patterns of past phases of development which have been hidden in darkness and whose shapes are all awry. After the tiresome preparation of studying and transcribing manuscripts, publishing, dating and localizing them properly, and assembling and interpreting facts, history must gather these all together to reproduce and focus the ideal patterns. In many points this review of pictures of older forms will serve to make us understand—and so to cherish—what we have received as our inheritance. It is not the fact of antiquity that makes liturgical customs valuable, but their fulness of content and their expressive value. Even newer ceremonies, like the priest's blessing at the end of Mass, can possess a great beauty.

In not a few places this objective review will bring to notice many rites gained and many rites lost which ought not to have been. With reference to the position taken by the deacon while singing the Gospel at a solemn Mass, the saintly Cardinal Bona (d. 1674) makes the rather cogent remark:

> *Hinc apparet, quam verum sit . . . multa hodie pro lege haberi in his quæ pertinent ad ecclesiasticas observationes, quæ sensim ex abusu irrepserunt; quorum originem cum recentiores ignorent, varias conantur congruentias et mysticas rationes invenire, ut ea sapienter instituta vulgo persuadeant.*[5]

Of course it stands to reason that not any and everyone can start these reforms on his own initiative. The great Mabillon (d. 1707), when publishing his edition of the Roman *Ordines*, prefaced it with a pertinent warning, while at the same time he expressed the wish that those whose concern it was to see to the proper conduct of divine worship might keep these older patterns in mind.

> *Hæc autem non eo animo referimus, quasi veterum huiusmodi rituum usus privata auctoritate revocari velimus, aut recentiorum (quod absit) induci contemptum, sed ut eos qui eiusmodi officiis præpositi sunt invitemus ad consulendam antiquitatem, quæ quanto fonti propior, tanto venerabilior est.*[6]

---

[5] Bona, *Rerum liturg.* 1. II, 7, 3 (670). The rubricist, Cardinal Merati (d. 1744), uses almost the same words: Gavanti-Merati, *Thesaurus* I, 11, 6 (I, 111).

[6] J. Mabillon, *In ord. Rom. Commentarius prævius*, c. 21 (PL LXXVIII, 934 D).

Part I

THE FORM OF THE MASS THROUGH THE CENTURIES

1. Mass in the Primitive Church

THE FIRST HOLY MASS WAS SAID ON "THE SAME NIGHT IN WHICH HE was betrayed" (1 Cor. 11:23). Judas' resolution had been taken, the next few steps would bring our Lord to the Mount of Olives where an agony would overtake Him and His enemies seize Him. In this very hour He gives His disciples the Holy Sacrament which for all time would be the offering of the Church. The setting was significant—the paschal meal. Since the withdrawal of the people out of Egypt the paschal lamb had served year after year to prefigure the great expectation. The fulfillment, too, would serve to recall the exodus not only from Egypt but from the land of sin, and the arrival not into a promised land but into God's kingdom. From this hour on it was to continue as a fond reminiscence from generation to generation.[1] But the records of the Last Supper contain few details concerning the ceremonial of the meal, probably because this ceremonial was not meant to be the lasting setting of the celebration.[2]

And still we should like to know more about that first Mass. Attempts have been made, through research into the form of the paschal meal in Christ's time and a thorough study of the New Testament accounts, to reconstruct the events of the Last Supper.[3] Attention must be called to the apparent differences in these accounts—differences even in detailing the

---

[1] The thought of Christ as the true Easter Lamb is emphasized in John 19: 36. For this same reason, to show clear proof that Christ was *pascha nostrum*, St. John appears to lay stress on the fact that Jesus died on the very day when the Sanhedrists were eating the paschal lamb, on the παρασκευὴ τοῦ πάσχα (John 19:14). On the other hand, almost all exegetes are at one in considering our Lord's Last Supper on Thursday night a paschal meal. For the problem this creates, and the various solutions suggested, see: W. Goossens, *Les origines de l'Eucharistie* (Paris, 1931), 110-127; A. Merk, "Abendmahl," LThK,

I, 17-19; A. Arnold, *Der Ursprung des christlichen Abendmahles im Lichte der neuesten liturgiegeschichtlichen Forschung* (2nd ed.; Freiburg, 1939), 57-73.

[2] The hypothesis, that the primitive form of the ecclesiastical celebration of the Eucharist is to be explained from the paschal supper, is defended by G. Bickell, *Messe und Pascha* (Mainz, 1872) and recently by J. B. Thibault, *La liturgie Romaine* (Paris, 1924), 11-37 (Ch. I, "La liturgie primitive et le grand Hallel"). The hypothesis is generally discarded.

[3] Matt. 26:26-29; Mark 14:22-25; Luke 22:15-20; 1 Cor. 11:23-25.

7

form of the words of institution; these differences must arise from the differences in the liturgical practice from which the accounts sprang.[4] In Matthew and Mark the words spoken over the bread are followed by those over the chalice, while in Luke and Paul a more or less large interval elapses: μετὰ τὸ δειπνῆσαι—as the Roman rite itself announces: *simili modo postquam cœnatum est.* Seemingly at the Last Supper the presentation of the eucharistic Chalice was separated from the presentation of the sacramental Body. It was the liturgical practice of the primitive Church which first brought them together. The older exegesis, indeed, apparently attempted a justification of the time elements of the text without sundering the two consecrations.[5] But the modern interpretation, even of Catholics, is almost unanimous in taking the words at their face value.[6] Besides the natural meaning of the words, another argument is to be found in the ease with which we can thus dovetail the narrative into the paschal rite current in our Lord's time, as research has revealed it.[7]

In Christ's day the paschal meal was surrounded with a very complicated ceremonial. Before the meal proper, at which the Easter lamb was eaten, there was a little preliminary—a serving of bitter herbs and unleavened bread that recalled the want felt during the journey out of Egypt. Both before and after this preludial meal the cup was filled. Then the son of the family or the youngest of those present had to place the question: what did these unusual customs signify? With a prayer of thanks to God, the father of the house then told the story of the ancient days in Egypt and of the liberation from darkness into light, from bondage into freedom *(Haggada).* This closed with the singing of the first part of the *Hallel* (Vulgate, Psalms 112; 113:1-8), in which all those at table joined by answering "Alleluia" after each half verse.

Only after this did the meal proper begin. The father of the house took one of the loaves of unleavened bread, broke it, pronounced over it a little blessing and passed it around. This ceremony of brotherly communion in one bread was the signal for starting the meal. Then the paschal lamb was

---

[4] F. Hamm, *Die liturgischen Einsetzungsberichte im Sinne vergleichender Liturgieforschung untersucht,* LQF, XXIII, (Münster, 1928), 2; J. Gewiess, *Die urapostolische Heilsverkündigung nach der Apostelgeschichte* (Breslau, 1939),158f., 164f., 167; Brinktrine, *Die Hl. Messe,* 18f.
[5] Cf. R. Cornely, *Commentarius in I. Cor.* (Paris, 1890), 342f.; W. Berning, *Die Einsetzung der hl. Eucharistie in ihrer ursprünglichen Form nach den Berichten des. N. T.,* kritisch untersucht (Münster, 1901), 243f. Both place the double consecration at the end of the meal.
[6] J. M. Hanssens, S.J., *Institutiones liturgicæ de ritibus orientalibus* (Rome, 1930),

II, 407-413 (cf. 410, in reference to the same author's studies for clarifying the theological difficulties); Goossens, *Les origines,* 151; J. Sickenberger, *Die Briefe des hl. Paulus an die Korinther und Römer* (4th ed.; Rom. 1932), 54; Arnold, 75-79.
[7] H. L. Strack - P. Billerbeck, *Kommentar zum Neuen Testament aus Talmud und Midrasch* (Munich, 1928), IV, 41-76. H. L. Strack, *Pesachim. Der Mischnatraktat "Paschafest" mit Berücksichtigung des N.T. und der jetzigen Paschafeier der Juden nach Hss und alten Drucken, herausgegeben, übersetzt und erläutert* (Leipzig, 1911).

eaten, with no ritual to hem in the eating and drinking. But after the meal was over the father of the house took the cup, newly filled with wine, and sitting upright he lifted it slightly while he spoke the grace after meal, the real table prayer. Then all drank of it. This was the third cup, called "the cup of the blessing," or "chalice of benediction."[8] All then sang the second and larger part of the Hallel (Vulgate, Psalms 113:9—117:29 and 135) and, after a last blessing, drank the fourth ceremonial cup.

Into this arrangement our Lord's Last Supper fits very easily. The consecration of the bread is connected with the blessing before the eating of the lamb, grafted on to the rite of breaking the bread. For this blessing Matthew and Mark employ not the word εὐχαριστήσας, but another word which better describes such a prayer, εὐλογήσας.[9] The bread which the father of the house passed around in the preliminary Haggada was to be accompanied (according to an old Aramaic formulary) with the words: "See the bread of misery which was eaten by our fathers who passed out of Egypt." Our Lord hands it to His disciples with the weighty words, "This is my body which is to be given for you."[10] The consecration of the chalice is connected with the grace after meal and with the third cup,[11] the cup of the blessing (chalice of benediction), of which all could partake in common, whereas during the rest of the meal each of those at table drank from his own individual cup.[12] For the table prayer a special formula was prescribed; Jesus devised one of His own.[13]

Our Lord concluded the institution with the command, "Do this for a commemoration of me." How did the Apostles and the primitive Church carry out this order? As the New Testament accounts intimate by their omission of nearly all details of the paschal feast, the setting of the paschal rite was not considered. Its repetition was not only impracticable, because of the surrounding ceremonial, but it was impossible from the standpoint of law, for in the Old Testament law, to which the Apostles still clung, the eating of the paschal lamb was set for only one time of the year. Promi-

---

[8] For the meaning of this "chalice of benediction" also at other meals, cf. H. Lietzmann, Messe und Herrenmahl (Bonn, 1926), 208f.

[9] The fact that Paul, and after him Luke, employ the word εὐχαρτισήσας is explained as a Græcism. For a discussion of this, see Gewiess, 164.

[10] Hanssens, 412; J. Jeremias, Die Abendmahlsworte Jesu (Göttingen, 1935), 23.

[11] This is clear from the reference to a "hymn" following immediately (Matt. 26:30; Mark 14:26). The exegetes who have the two consecrations follow each other immediately place them therefore in this spot at the end of the meal. The fourth cup was apparently not used at our Lord's paschal supper.

[12] Goossens, 151 f., referring to G. Dalmann, Jesus-Jeschua (Leipzig, 1922), 140f. Strack - Billerbeck, IV, 58 f., 76, consider the common cup an exception. For the designation of "cup of the blessing," cf. τὸ ποτήριον τῆς εὐλογίας in St. Paul (1 Cor. 10:16: "a cup that we bless").

[13] The disciples at Emmaus recognized our Lord in the "breaking of the bread" (Luke 24:31); what is meant perhaps is His manner of saying the table-prayer attached to the action—His address to the heavenly Father or His gaze uplifted heavenward; cf. Goossens, 170-172.

The formulæ we will have occasion to refer to later, infra Notes 24 and 25.

nent in the narrative of St. Luke and St. Paul is the placing of the consecration of the chalice after the meal; Matthew and Mark do not take any
special notice of this peculiar circumstance. When Matthew and Mark
wrote, it must have already been customary in their locality to put the
two consecrations together. Does that mean that Paul and his disciple Luke
still suppose an actual separation? At least in this case there would be some
basis for the related opinion that in the early community the Eucharist
was, as a rule, bound up with a meal. But unfortunately we cannot clear
up this or any similiar question, nor can we recreate the form of the Mass-
liturgy up to the middle of the second century except through little vestiges and hints and by deductions from later facts.

The Acts of the Apostles mentions three times the "breaking of bread"
in the Christian congregation[14]—mentions it in such a way that it designates not some introductory ceremony at a meal but a complete and self-
contained action. In this term "breaking of bread" we have an entirely
new, Christian mode of expression, a term alien to both Jewish[15] and classical literature. The term evidently corresponds to a new thing, the holy
Bread of the Christian community.[16] The neo-converts of Whitsunday lived
in holy happiness; "and continuing daily with one accord in the temple
. . . , and breaking bread in their houses" (Acts 2:46). Besides the liturgy
of the Old Law in which everyone regularly took part,[17] there was also this
new celebration, which was referred to only by suggestion, and to which
the Christians had to come in smaller groups and in their own dwellings.
"And they continued steadfastly in the teaching of the Apostles and in the
communion of the breaking of the bread and in the prayers" (Acts 2:42).
Reference is made to prayer conjoined to the breaking of bread.[18] We can
discover nothing further.

In a later chapter we read that there was an assembly one Sunday night
at Troas "for the breaking of bread" (Acts 20:7). A long sermon by
St. Paul precedes this "breaking of bread" and partaking of the Eucharist
(Acts 20:11).[19] From the words "breaking of bread" we cannot infer any-

---

[14] Acts 2:42, 46; 20:7.

[15] Only Jer. 16:7 employs it poetically in
the particular meaning of "to hold a funeral
feast" or "to hold a wake."

[16] The latest investigators rather generally
agree that in all these instances there is
reference to the Eucharist. Goossens, 170-
174; Arnold, 43-47; Gewiess, 152-157.
This explanation is given for at least Acts
2:42, 46 in a fundamental study by Th.
Schermann, "Das Brotbrechen im Urchris-
tentum," *Bibl. Zeitschrift* VIII (1910), 33-
52; 162-183; esp. 169f. But some writers
are explicitly opposed to the opinion that
the Eucharist is meant: A. Steinmann, *Die*

Apostelgeschichte (4th ed.; Bonn, 1934),
40-42; J. M. Nielen, *The Earliest Christian Liturgy* (St. Louis, 1931), 29ff.; A.
Wikenhauser, *Die Apostelgeschichte*
(Regensburg, 1938), 35f.

[17] Cf. Acts 3:1.

[18] O. Bauernfeind, *Die Apostelgeschichte*
(Theol. Handkommentar zum N.T., 5,
Leipzig [1939]), 54, is inclined to interpret
the whole passage, 2:42, in a liturgical
sense: listening to the teaching of the Apostles, making one's offering, breaking the
bread and praying. "What Luke is really
saying is: Their fellowship was essentially
a fellowship in the evening meal."

[19] Cf. Goossens, 136.

thing more. Since the words were not used simply for "to have a meal," we cannot conclude from them alone that the essential sacramental rite, which our Lord had instituted with the breaking of bread, and which was thereafter so spoken of, was always bound up with a real meal.

But several other arguments do lead to this conclusion. When we see the Apostles gathered together after our Saviour's resurrection, it seems to be the common table that brings them together. That could also have been the case after Pentecost. This was then the opportunity at set times to combine with it the memorial meal of the Lord, just as He Himself had combined it with a meal.[20] Every meal was already impressed with a reverential character, since it was always begun and ended with prayer.[21] Especially the Sabbath meal—the meal on Friday night which initiated the Sabbath—possessed a highly religious stamp. An expansion of the table company beyond the family circle was a well-loved practice on this day just as at the Easter meal.[22] Like these Sabbath meals in character were the community banquets which were held on certain occasions for one's circle of friends (Chaburah).[23]

One of the ceremonies which appears to have been part and parcel of the practice at such meals was for the master of the house to bless the bread, break it and distribute it.[24] Thus the entire company was drawn together by the blessing and the eating in common. Of course the blessing of the wine would naturally be added. The "cup of the blessing" itself was filled at the end of the meal, right before the saying of grace which concluded the meal. As an invitation to drink of this cup, a prescribed formula was used. At a later period the prayer was composed of four doxologies of which the first two can be traced back to the time before the destruction of Jerusalem, namely, the "Praise of the Meal" and the "Praise of the Land."[25]

Certain it is that this custom (with the proper changes) was continued within the Christian communities. We have striking proof of this in the prayer of the Didache near the end of the first century:

[20] Goossens, 133. Perhaps we must regard our risen Saviour's companionship at meals with His disciples as a link between the Last Supper and the eucharistic meal of the primitive church. In fact, if we dare stress the symbolical meaning attached to the meal, we will be able to trace a very significant line from the accounts of the evangelists regarding these meals and the great messianic meal of eternity, and thereby gain a new light into the eucharistic mysteries. See Y. de Montcheuil, "Signification eschatalogique du Repas eucharistique," Recherches de Science religieuse, XXXIII (1946), 10-43.

[21] E. Kalt, Biblisches Reallexikon, (2nd ed.; Paderborn, 1939), II, 868f.

[22] Cf. Luke 14:1.

[23] Lietzmann, Messe und Herrenmahl, 206-210.

[24] Strack - Billerbeck, IV, 621; Lietzmann, 206. According to Berachah 6, 1, the blessing reads: "Praised be Yahweh, our God, the king of the world, who makes the bread to come from the earth."

[25] Strack - Billerbeck, IV, 627-634. The praise of the land begins: "We thank Thee, Yahweh, our God, for having given our forefathers as their inheritance this lovable, good and wide land, for having led us, O Yahweh, our God, out of the land of Egypt and for having freed us from the house of bondage. We thank Thee for Thy covenant, which Thou hast sealed on our flesh, for Thy Torah which Thou hast taught us. . . ."; ibid., 631.

(9.) Regarding the Eucharist. Give thanks as follows:
First concerning the cup:
"We give Thee thanks, our Father, for the Holy Vine of David Thy servant, which Thou hast made known to us through Jesus, Thy Servant."
"To Thee be the glory forevermore."
Next, concerning the broken bread:
"We give Thee thanks, our Father, for the life and knowledge which Thou hast made known to us through Jesus, Thy Servant."
"To Thee be the glory forevermore."
"As this broken bread was scattered over the hills and then, when gathered, became one mass, so may Thy Church be gathered from the ends of the earth into Thy Kingdom."
"For Thine is the glory and the power through Jesus Christ forevermore."
Let no one eat and drink of your Eucharist but those baptized in the name of the Lord; to this, too, the saying of the Lord is applicable: *Do not give to dogs what is sacred.*
(10.) After you have taken your fill of food, give thanks as follows:
"We give Thee thanks, O Holy Father, for Thy holy name which Thou hast enshrined in our hearts, and for the knowledge and faith and immortality which Thou hast made known to us through Jesus, Thy Servant."
"To Thee be the glory forevermore."
"Thou, Lord Almighty, hast created all things for the sake of Thy name and hast given food and drink for men to enjoy, that they may give thanks to Thee; but to us Thou hast vouchsafed spiritual food and drink and eternal life through [Jesus,] Thy Servant."
"Above all, we give Thee thanks because Thou art mighty."
"To Thee be the glory forevermore."
"Remember, O Lord, Thy Church: deliver her from all evil, perfect her in Thy love, and from the four winds assemble her, the sanctified, in Thy kingdom which Thou hast prepared for her."
"For Thine is the power and the glory forevermore."
"May grace come, and this world pass away!"
"Hosanna to the God of David!"
"If anyone is holy, let him advance; if anyone is not, let him be converted. *Maranatha!* " "Amen."
But permit the prophets to give thanks as much as they desire.[26]

Much as these prayers have been discussed, little has been achieved in the way of clarifying their precise meaning and import. In every case we have table prayers in the setting of a Christian meal: Blessing of wine and bread, and grace at the end. That the meal included the sacramental Eucharist is hardly likely.[27] The call at the end of the final grace may per-

[26] Tr. J. A. Kleist, S.J., *The Didache* (Ancient Christian Writers, VI; Newman Press, Westminster, Md., 1948), 20-21. Quoted with permission of the publisher.
[27] However the opinion has again been advocated lately in a thorough discussion of the two *Didache* passages by C. Ruch, "La messe d'après les Pères," DThC, X (1928), 865-882. In his reconstruction the prayers of the congregation are said in common, but no one joins in the prayers of the officiant. The opinion comes up against one objection particularly, in the expression: μετὰ δὲ τὸ ἐμπλησθῆναι; this does not appear in a solemn prayer (like the *Satiati* of the Roman post-communions), but in a rubric. On the other hand, εὐχαριστία and εὐχαριστεῖν do not refer unequivocally to the Blessed

haps relate to the Eucharist. But again it is not clear how it is connected here.[28] At a much later time, after the close of the second century, we learn more about the agapes which the Christian community conducted for the benefit of the poor and to foster the spirit of Christian concord.[29] But these agapes are absolutely separate from the Eucharist. We cannot therefore directly derive anything more from them than the picture of a religion-sponsored meal.[30]

From what has already been said, this only can be deduced with certainty, that the various forms of table customs taken over by the young

Sacrament, for the terms are used even in the following centuries in a wider sense. Cf. *inter alia* Arnold, 23-29; Baumstark, *Liturgie comparée*, 50f.; P. Cagin, *L'Eucharistia* (Paris, 1912), 252-288.

[28] Th. Schermann, *Die allgemeine Kirchenordnung, frühchristliche Liturgien und kirchliche Uberlieferung*, (Paderborn, 1915), II, 282f., holds the opinion that what is here in question was the consecrated bread preserved from the previous Sunday's celebration. We would then have a first form of the *Missa præsanctificatorum*. We could also, with A. Baumstark, *Vom geschichtlichen Werden der Liturgie*, 7f., think of a house-Mass in the proper sense, with a real consecration of the bread and wine. This opinion about a domestic Mass was already advanced in P. Drews, "Untersuchungen zur Didache IV," *Zeitschrift f. d. neut. Wissenschaft*, V (1904), 74-79. Such a domestic Mass could be considered only if there was present someone possessing the power to consecrate—which was seldom the case; cf. *Did.* 15, 1. The booklet itself, which was intended not for bishops but for the congregation and its catechists (cf. possibly the διδάσκαλοι in Hermas, *Pastor*, Mand. 4, 3, 1), did not have to contain the consecratory texts. Cf. in the same sense, Arnold, 26-29. Against the opinion that the thanksgiving prayer in c. 10 is to be considered a consecratory eucharistic prayer, cf. ZkTh, LXIII (1939), 236 f.

A new explanation, based on reasons of sound worth, is developed by E. Peterson, "Didache cap. 9, 10," *Eph., liturg.* LVIII (1944), 3-13. According to this, the prayers which are used in the *Didache* as table prayers have the form of a christological hymn, such as was early used at the celebration of the Eucharist, at the *fractio panis*.

[29] Tertullian, *Apol.*, c. 39. Hippolytus, *Trad. Ap.* The textual material in Dix. 45-53. The fullest text is the Ethiopian, but it too is mixed up; cf. the text as set forth by E. Hennecke, *Neutestamentl. Apokryphen*, p. 581; complemented in ZkTh, LXIII (1939), 238.

These are the proceedings as described by Hippolytus: In the evening all gather for the agape. The deacon brings a light into the room; the light is blessed with a prayer to which are prefaced "The Lord be with you" and "Let us give thanks to the Lord" (but not "Up with your hearts," which is reserved for the celebration of the Eucharist), and the respective replies. Then the deacon takes the cup and intones an alleluia-psalm; the presbyter and bishop do the same. The gathering responds with an alleluia. Then the meal begins. Before he starts eating, each one accepts a piece of blessed bread from the bishop; "this is 'eulogy', but not 'eucharist' like the Body of the Lord." Each one also takes his cup, says a blessing over it, and then drinks and eats. The catechumens receives exorcized bread, but may not take part in the meal. Everyone may eat his fill, and also take home what is left over (the ἀποφορητόν), but so that there is enough for the host to send to others. Talk at table is led by the bishop, or by the priest or deacon in his place; no one talks unless he is called upon or questioned. Proper conduct is continually inculcated. In the case of a meal for the widows, care should be taken that they get home before dark.

[30] It is significant that various features clearly indicate the connection with the Jewish meal ceremonial: the responsorial psalmody at the beginning, the initial breaking of the bread, the cup-blessing spoken by the individuals.

Church from Judaism[31] easily led to employing for Christ's institution the setting of a meal even outside the paschal meal. The grace after meals was the given occasion for the consecration of the chalice, no matter whether the consecration of the bread had occurred earlier, at the very start of the meal, or took place here.[32]

To prove that in this early period of the Church the Eucharist was actually bound up with a meal, we have only one corroborating fact in the example of Corinth, as described by St. Paul.[33] The first undoubted fact is that the Corinthians really connected the holy celebration with a great banquet, but certain abuses had crept in which were in glaring contradiction to the spirit of Christ's institution. As might have been expected,[34] the meal was supplied not from a common stock but from the provisions brought by the well-to-do. But instead of spreading out all in common and awaiting the start of the supper, the people divided into little groups and consumed their own supplies with a selfishness that was often climaxed by drunkenness. Under such circumstances the words and the ceremonies of the holy action became a secondary matter, a formality which the officiant could perform at his own table and scarcely be noticed. Add to the scandal the painful situation of those guests who had brought nothing. Denouncing such conduct, St. Paul speaks with solemn seriousness of the content and worth of Christ's institution. It might surprise us that he introduces the phrases about the chalice with the words already noticed, μετὰ τὸ δειπνῆσαι, and thus has the intervening meal of the community precede. That would hardly make it appear as if he wanted to suppress the meal itself.[35] Rather we have an indication of how Paul wanted it set in order—and it was to be enclosed by the two consecrations! And so he could very correctly speak of the whole thing as a unit under the term "a supper of the Lord."[36]

[31] E. von der Goltz, *Tischgebete und Abendmahlsgebete in der altchristlichen und in der griechischen Kirche,* TU, XXIX, 2b. (Leipzig, 1905).

[32] For the consecration of the bread at this latter spot a favorable starting point was thought to have been the Jewish practice of keeping a piece of the bread broken at the beginning till the end of the meal and then producing it; cf. von der Goltz, *Tischgebete,* 6f. But the observance seems to be of a later date, and not Palestinian but Babylonian in origin; cf. A. Marmorstein, "Miszellen I. Das letzte Abendmahl und der Seder-Abend," *Zeitschrift f. d. neutest. Wissenschaft,* XXV (1926), 249-253; Arnold, 55f.

[33] 1 Cor. 11:17-34. Cf. especially E. B. Allo, *Première épître aux Corinthiens* (Paris, 1934), 269-316.

[34] Reference is made to the statement regarding the *cultores Dianæ et Antinoi* of Lanuvium (*Corpus Inscriptionum Latinarum,* XIV, n. 2112 [II, Z. 14-16]), according to which the four members whose turn it was that year were to bring to the six annual *cœnæ*: each an amphora of good wine, for each guest a loaf of bread, four sardines, a cushion to lie on, and service.

[35] This is to be stressed, in opposition to the concept of Goossens, 136-141, and some other interpreters, that Paul condemned the meal itself as an abuse, and that by the emphatic τοῦτο ποιεῖτε he meant to declare that nothing was to be done except what he called attention to in his account.

[36] That the words κυριακὸν δεῖπνον (1 Cor. 11:20) refer to the whole proceeding is defended by Arnold, 101-105, following E. B. Allo, *op. cit.* In Hippolytus, *Trad.*

That we are not making a mistake in this deduction is indicated by another remnant which we meet about the beginning of the third century. In the church regulations of Hippolytus of Rome, a special provision is made for the Easter Mass at which the newly baptized are to receive their first Holy Communion. After the Body of the Lord is given them, they are to receive, besides the consecrated chalice, also two others, one filled with milk and honey and the other with water, and these, it would seem, before the consecrated chalice, which comes at the very end.[37] As new-born children of God they get the children's meal, milk and honey, to strengthen them and to recall to their minds God's promises; they receive, too, the water that suggests that cleansing of soul which they have just experienced.[38] Although the consecration had already for a long time been bound together by a single eucharist, this solemn Communion at Eastertide harks back to a time when the meal was interposed before the consecration of the chalice.

The drawing together of the doubled thanksgiving prayer into one was naturally the concomitant of the drawing together of the two consecrations. And this must have occurred even in apostolic times, when the meal was still connected with the celebration of the Eucharist. If the latter followed the meal, the next step was to take up and enlarge the closing thanksgiving prayer—a solution which the appearance of later liturgies clearly points to. But the eucharistic celebration, along with the prayer of thanksgiving, could also be set first, and there are traces of such a solution too.[39]

On the basis of all these facts we can now attempt to outline the probable development of the eucharistic celebration in the first century of its existence. The Apostles fulfilled the command of our Lord given them at the Last Supper by celebrating regularly in the setting of a meal which was conducted with the ritual forms of a Jewish community meal. The most important point of contact was the grace after meals and the "cup of blessing" (chalice of benediction) connected with it. The grace or prayer of thanks was introduced by an invitation from the host to the guests.[40] This

Ap. (Dix, 46) the independent agape still bears the name "Lord's Supper."

Perhaps these and other details in Hippolytus' arrangement of the agape can be taken to indicate that at an earlier period the agape was actually connected with the Eucharist; see H. Elfers, *Die Kirchenordnung Hippolyts von Rom* (Paderborn, 1938), 169.

[37] Hippolytus, *Trad. Ap.* (Dix, 40-42). The later version of the baptismal rite in *Canones Hippolyti*, c. 19, 15 (Riedel, 213) has the milk and honey follow the consecrated chalice, obviously out of regard for the law of fasting.

[38] Elfers, 166-175. The confusion in later

versions of the Church Order shows that there was no longer any knowledge of the old rite; *ibid.*, 174. See below, p. 22.

[39] In the *Epistola apostolorum*, a work of the middle of the second century, preserved in two translations, a Coptic and an Ethiopian, the Coptic for the celebration of Easter night calls for the Remembrance of the Lord first, and then the agape, the Ethiopian in reverse, agape first and then the Remembrance of the Lord. C. Schmidt, *Gespräche Jesu* (TU, XLIII; Leipzig [1919]), 54 f.

[40] *Berachoth*, VII, 3: "How does one word the invitation? If there are three persons

invitation must have fused already in this early period into the double exclamation, *Sursum corda* and *Gratias agamus*, which we find, along with their corresponding answers, practically unaltered in all the succeeding liturgical traditions. The grace or thanksgiving prayer itself, which even in its pre-Christian original had led from gratitude for food and drink into gratitude for the benefits of the grace-filled guidance of God's people,[41] could and did take on Christian features.

This new Christian concept is revealed in the prayers of the *Didache*, which are ever so much more meaningful if they are considered simply as table prayers. Besides, the *Didache* also stresses (10, 7) the improvisation of this prayer of thanks by the "prophets." Certainly if anything in the story of Redemption was to be the occasion for happy remembrance and thanksgiving, it would be this moment of fulfillment in Christ. To build up these thoughts expressly, the example of the Jewish Easter and feast-day Haggada would provide a model, although this was scarcely necessary since the apostolic preaching itself supplied ample material for such memories. Many of the heavenly songs which in St. John's Apocalypse are sung to God and the Lamb can very well be placed in the mouth of an earthly congregation which is gathered with its officiant for the celebration of the Eucharist.[42]

The consecration of the bread which stands at the beginning of the service must have been drawn over to the consecration of the cup of blessing, and this very soon, perhaps even in the first generation, at least in the sense that bringing them together was considered admissible. Our Lord's words of institution used on these two occasions were thus merged into a single two-part account, and the εὐλογία—εὐχαριστία spoken over the bread became then a thanksgiving prayer which introduced or even enclosed the account and the double consecration therein contained. For the words, "For as often as you shall eat this bread and drink the cup, you proclaim the death of the Lord," with which St. Paul continues his narrative of the institution, and even the sense of Jesus' own command, would early have given rise to the practice of expressing these thoughts right after the account itself, as we again actually find it in all the liturgies, namely in the anamnesis.[43]

Since, on the one hand, the prayer of thanks was thus enriched and rounded out and settled in form, and on the other, the growing communi-

present, he says, 'Let us praise (him whose food it is we have eaten)!'" At larger gatherings the invitation was more solemn. Strack - Billerbeck, IV, 629. An invitation of this sort presupposes chiefly a situation where the transition to prayer is not from a previous silence but from conversation. Hence, to keep the practice even after conversation and meal were dropped could be significant of the special holiness of the action that followed.

[41] *Vide supra,* Note 25.

[42] Apoc. 4:11; 5:9-14; 17f.; 15:3f. Cf. C. Ruch, "La Messe d'après la S. Ecriture," DThC, X, 858, 860.

[43] Cf. amongst others Gewiess, *Die urapostolische Heilsverkündigung,* 165, who takes the καταγγέλλετε of 1 Cor. 11:26 as an imperative, so that a "heralding" or proclamation in words is demanded.

ties became too large for these domestic table-gatherings, the supper-character of the Christian assembly could and did fall out, and the eucharistic celebration stood out as the proper form of divine worship. The tables disappeared from the room, except for the one at which the presiding official pronounced the eucharist over the bread and wine. The room was broadened into a large hall capable of holding the whole congregation. Only in isolated instances was the connection with a meal continued into the following centuries.[44] And the ideal toward which all energetically strove was to hold in each congregation only one single Eucharist.[45]

It was both the Jewish and hellenistic practice to hold the meal, as a δεῖπνον, at an evening hour, but once the meal disappeared there was nothing to hinder the choice of another time of the day for the celebration. Since Sunday, as the day of the Resurrection, was very early promoted as the day for the celebration,[46] and attention was thus focused on the remembrance of the story of Redemption and especially of its glorious outcome, the next step was easy, namely, to transfer all to the morning hours, since it was in the morning before sunrise that Christ had risen from the dead.[47] The earliest Easter celebration known to us was an evening celebration but it followed the time-schedule mentioned and its climax was not reached till early in the morning at cockcrow.[48] Sunday service, too, would fit nicely into this scheme, for if one began to see in the sunrise a picture of Christ rising from the dead,[49] one would lay considerable store in the notion of greeting Christ himself with the rising of the sun.[50] And besides, as long as Christianity was not publicly acknowledged, the circumstances of the laborer's life would have urged the choosing of an hour outside the usual time of work.

[44] For Maundy Thursday, St. Augustine, *Ep.* LIV, 7, 9 (CSEL XXXIV, 168) tells of the practice of imitating the Last Supper by having a meal just before the evening Mass. Last vestiges of this custom were still to be found in the fourteenth century; Eisenhofer, II, 304.

In Egypt, according to Socrates, *Hist. eccl.*, V, 22 (PG LXVII, 636), it was still customary in the fifth century to celebrate the Eucharist on Saturday as the conclusion of a meal.

Besides, we must remark that in the domestic celebrations of Mass, which were continued alongside the congregational celebrations for several centuries (see *infra*, Part II, ch. 5), the connection with a meal was maintained considerably longer, since here there were not the difficulties that confronted the congregational celebrations.

[45] Ignatius of Antioch, *Ad Philad.*, c. 5, Σπουδάσατε οὖν μιᾷ εὐχαριστίᾳ χρῆσθαι.

[46] Acts 20:7; *Didache* 14.

[47] Lietzmann, *Messe und Herrenmahl*, 258, thinks that the connection with the service of reading and prayer held in the synagogue on the Sabbath morning was what drew the eucharistic celebration from the evening to the morning. But then the reading and prayer service would have to be considered the main thing. Lietzmann also mentions (*ibid.*, Note 2) the idea of H. Usener, that the transfer was in some way conjoined to the Greek custom of "sacrificing to the gods of heaven at sunrise," but very properly puts no stock in the influence of this observance.

[48] O. Casel, "Art und Sinn der ältesten christlichen Osterfeier," JL XIV (1938), 1-78, esp. 5, 23 f., 29.

[49] Dölger, *Sol salutis*, 364-379; cf. 123 f.

[50] *Ibid.*, 119 f., with reference to the passage in Wis. 16:27 f., which concerns the manna but was early given a Christian turn: δεῖ φθάνειν τὸν ἥλιον ἐπ' εὐχαριστίαν σου.

When about 111-113 A.D., Pliny the Younger, Legate of Bithynia, had arrested and examined a number of Christians, he established the fact that they were in the habit of meeting on a certain fixed day before dawn (stato die ante lucem) and of singing in alternate verses a song to Christ their God; they bound themselves by solemn oath not to do any wrong; they then dispersed but assembled again at a later hour for a harmless meal.[51] Quite probably we have in the first-named gathering the celebration of the Eucharist, and in the hymn sung alternately the prayer of thanks which opened with alternate prayer and closed with the Amen of the people and which might even have included the Sanctus said in common.[52] The second assembly, which was considered less important and which was discontinued after Pliny intervened, would then be the evening agape as we see it continuing even later on.[53] If these conjectures are right, then we have further in the act of moral obligation bound in with the morning celebration, a distant parallel to the Sunday confession of sins, of which the Didache speaks.[54] Although we are completely in the dark as to the form and performance of this act, the general sense of it is doubtless the securing of that state of mind which Paul had already demanded for the Eucharistic celebration[55] and which in one case is looked upon as a contrite confession, in the other as a resolve and sacred promise of amendment. We see later on, time and again, new forms arising from the same root.[56] Besides we can acknowledge that the kiss of peace which we soon

For the early morning divine service cf. also Dölger, 118 ff.; Schümmer, Die altchristliche Fastenpraxis, 109 ff.

Later Cyprian, Ep. 63, 15 f. (CSEL III, 713 f.) expressly witnesses to it: We celebrate the Eucharist as a morning sacrifice, in sacrificiis matutinis, even though it was instituted in the evening, because we commemorate therewith the Resurrection of the Lord.

The injunction to remember the Resurrection during home morning prayers is frequently met with in the pertinent writings, e.g. Cyprian, De or. dom., c. 35 (CSEL III, 292).

[51] Pliny, Ep. ad Trajanum, X, 96. For the text of the letter see Kirch, Enchiridion fontium hist. eccl. (5th ed.; Freiburg, 1941), 22 ff.; also Dölger, Sol salutis, 105 f., who discusses some of the contents more thoroughly, 106-136.

[52] See Volume II, Chapter 2, 4. The Ter-Sanctus is probably an acquisition from the Jewish schema, and even then was to be said before sun-up; Berachoth I, 2; Dölger, 121.

[53] A Eucharistic celebration in the morning and an agape at night is also the sur-

mise of C. Mohlberg, La Scuola cattolica, LXIV (1936), 211-213; idem., "Carmen Christo quasi Deo," Revista d'Archeologia Cristiana, XIV (1937), 93-123. Dölger, Sol salutis, 127 f., considers the hymns to be of the type of those in the Apocalypse, which, of course, are exactly the materials for eucharistic prayer; see Note 22 above. Other interpretations are reviewed in A. Kurfess, "Plinius und der urchristliche Gottesdienst," Zeitschrift f. d. neutest. Wissenchaft, XXXV (1936), 295-298.

[54] Didache 14, 1 (Quasten, Mon., 12 f.) : Κὰτα κυριακὴν δὲ κυρίου συναχθέντες κλάσατε ἄρτον καὶ εὐχαριστήσατε προεξομολογησαμένοι τὰ παραπτώματα ὑμῶν, ὅπως καθαρὰ ἡ θυσία ὑμῶν ᾖ.

[55] 1 Cor. 11 : 28 f.

[56] Here belong the various formulas of self-accusation which especially since the early Middle Ages appeared as apologias in the priest's prayers both East and West. In our Roman Mass we have the Confiteor at the beginning and just before the distribution of Communion. To the latter corresponds the "prayer of penance" in every Mass of the Ethiopian rite, after which the priest turns to the people and pronounces

will meet up with and which we have already supposed as the opening of the holy celebration even in this early period[57] had a similar function.[58] If we thus see forming in this early period the large outlines of the later Mass-liturgy, there still remains the task of pointing out a great many details of a later and even present-day practice, in which, within the Mass celebration, a primitive and apostolic liturgy survives, a liturgy adapted by the Apostles from the usage of the synagogue.[59] Here belongs the common way of starting and ending the prayer: At the beginning came the greeting with *Dominus vobiscum* or a similar formula, the answer to which was the genuinely Hebraic *Et cum spiritu tuo*. The close of the prayer referred in some way to God's boundless dominion, which lasts *in sæcula sæculorum*. The stipulated answer of the people remained, in fact, untranslated: Amen. Thus with particular reference to the prayer of thanks, the general scheme remained unaltered, no matter how the contents changed. This holds true in every instance for the conclusion just mentioned and likewise for the introductory dialogue of which we spoke earlier. For the opening formula of the prayer of thanks itself, the formula of the customary Jewish *berachah*[60] did not persist; but even the opening with *Vere dignum et justum est* must have been adapted by the primitive congregation from some older tradition. For the further conduct of the prayer of thanks and for the transition into the triple *Sanctus* various hints from the Sabbath service of the synagogue must have been at work for this contained a very expansive praise of God for His creation and His provident care of Israel.[61] It could even be that the first phrase of the *Sanctus* stems from this source.

an absolution. Cf. Brightman, 235-237.

A rite for the purification of the souls of the assembled congregation at the beginning of the Mass proper appeared after the tenth century in the form of a *culpa* or "public confession" to which was added a formal absolution. See *infra*, p. 492. We may take the exhomologesis in *Didache* 14, 1 in much the same sense; cf. B. Poschmann, *Pænitentia secunda* (Bonn, 1940), 88-92, who considers it parallel to the *Confiteor* and designed to forgive venial sins, but he excludes sacramental penance. But in opposition see K. Adam, "Buszdisziplin," LThK, II (1931), 657, who in reference to the testimonies for the absolution prayers of the Church, alludes to the *Did.* 14, 1, as follows: "This 'confession' (ἐξομολογεῖσθαι, Jas. 5 : 16) in church, made effectual by the prayer of the liturgical congregation, is, for sins not mortal, the ordinary form of apostolic church-penance."

[57] It is remarkable how often the letters of the Apostles close with an invitation to greet one another with this kiss of fellowship: Rom. 16:16; 1 Cor. 16:20; 2 Cor. 13:12; 1 Thess. 5:26; 1 Pet. 5:14. Perhaps the reading of the letter was annexed to the celebration of the Eucharist.

[58] An indication of this is the fact that we encounter the kiss of peace as well as the prayer of penance at the start of the Mass proper and at the preparation for Communion.

[59] For further discussions, see the authors cited for the individual texts and formulas.

[60] The name "Berachah" comes from the opening word of the grace at table, "Praised." The type beginning in this fashion survives, e.g., in the formula of our table prayer, *Benedictus Deus in donis suis* . . . The beginning of the table prayer in the *Didache*, εὐχαριστοῦμέν σοι — also stemming, no doubt, from pre-Christian tradition—we will find again as the start of the eucharistic prayer in Hippolytus.

[61] Baumstark, *Liturgie comparée*, 54f. This element is clearly evident in the

A second stream of adaptation from the primitive judæo-Christian community emerges in the service of readings of the fore-Mass, as we shall meet it in Justin. The tie with the Temple, which (according to the Acts of the Apostles 2:46) the emergent Christian church still maintained along with its own eucharistic gatherings, entailed above all, here as elsewhere, attendance at the synagogue for the Sabbath service, which was primarily a reading of the Scriptures. Only after the break with the synagogue, consequent upon the persecution of the year 44, did the hour of worship devoted to reading take on a specially Christian shape, and gradually combine with the eucharistic celebration as the fore-Mass. This old legacy is also definitely retained in the imitation of the two-fold division of the Law and the Prophets (which is at the basis of several Christian pericope lists) and in the arrangement of the singing in between.

In all these instances we are concerned only with the materials and the ground-plan which were taken over in the new structure of Christian worship. But there was also a new soul by which it was transformed. And what is of greater consequence in this formation and growth is not the age of the materials used in the building, but the building itself, the new architecture of the Mass itself which arose from within, the body which the new soul had shaped for itself from the old material and which even in the earliest phases of development—and precisely in these—had undergone a considerable change of appearance.

From the very start the basic motif was to observe the memorial of our Lord, the remembrance of His redemptive Passion, in the form of a meal. Therefore at first, the framework of a supper remained in the foreground. The faithful sat at table; under cover of simple nourishment they feasted upon the Body and Blood of Him who had laid down His life for us all and who should some day come again to gather His own into His Kingdom. The spoken word would slip easily from the recital of the words of institution and the command therein contained into such thoughts of memory and expectation. Union with our Lord in His glory came as strongly into the consciousness as union amongst themselves came visibly to the eye by means of the meal. But this framework of a meal could not even in the very beginning delimit and define the type of eucharistic service. The meal was not an ordinary meal but a sacred banquet, not only hallowed and inspired by the memory which gave it value and which in its course was sacramentalized, but also borne Godwards by the word of the prayer that was added to it. For if, in primitive Christian culture, every meal imported not only various blessings but the prayer of thanks as well, it was truer still of this meal.

The mind of a man not blinded by pride will be turned toward God even by a natural meal. Nowhere is it more plainly and visibly seen that man

eucharistic prayer of the *Apostolic Constitutions* (*infra,* Chapter 4), and also,   e.g., in certain prefaces of the Spanish *Missale mixtum* (PL LXXXV, 271f., 286f.).

is a receiver, than when he takes nourishment to keep his life powers together. Therefore a meal has always been the incentive to acknowledge one's own creation by means of a prayer of thanks which is bound up with the meal. In Christianity man is a double receiver. Not only is he fitted out with goods of the natural order, but he is gifted beyond measure and beyond his capacity; because it is God who imparts Himself to man. That prayer of thanks is the right echo responding to God's wondrous benefits to man.

Nothing is therefore more natural than that thanksgiving to God should be the very basis of Christian conduct, that thanksgiving in the prayer of the nascent Church should become a mighty sound growing ever stronger, that as the εὐχαριστία it should be combined with that holy meal in the sacramental core of which the highest of God's gifts is continually renewed.

Hallowing the meal by means of the Eucharist soon accomplished a result which affected its liturgical appearance very much, namely a gradual ousting of the meal itself. This result corresponds to that spiritualization in matters of worship which is for incipient Christianity—in contrast to the synagogue—very significant.[62] For the conduct or guidance of those who participated, the movement of prayer became—if it had not already been so from the very start—settled and determined. The Eucharist became the basic form and shape of the Mass-liturgy.[63]

The prayer of thanks in the adopted table customs of the judæo-Christian communities was thus combined with our Lord's εὐχαριστήσας to form

[62] Cf. H. Wenschkewitz, *Die Spiritualisierung der Kultusbegriffe Tempel, Priester und Opfer im Neuen Testament* (Leipzig, 1932) ; see O. Casel, JL, XII (1934), 301-303.

[63] A certain *visible* residue of the ancient fundamental meal form is still to be noted in the Mass today: the table, on which bread and wine are set, and the partaking of the transubstantiated gifts in Communion. The sacrificial or offering element is also indicated to the eye in the gestures of presentation at the offertory, in the course of the canon, and especially in the little elevation at the closing doxology at the end of the canon. Such a lifting on high belonged to the ritual of table prayer in the olden Jewish banquet: at the start of the meal the person presiding took the bread lying before him in his hands and spoke the blessing. He likewise picked up the cup while saying the blessing over the wine. But especially with regard to the "cup of the blessing"—the one reciting the grace was to grasp it with both hands, and then hold it with his right hand a few inches off

the table as he spoke the blessing. Strack-Billerbeck, IV, 621-628. Psalm 115:4 (13) : *Calicem salutaris accipiam,* is explained as referring to this ceremony ; see the passages from Talmud bab., Pesach f. 119b, in Lietzmann, *Messe und Herrenmahl,* 209. For the elevation or lifting of the bread, cf. E.v.d. Goltz, *Tischgebete,* TU XXIX, 2 b, 7, 57 ff.

On the other hand, stress on the prayer posture at the Eucharist outweighed the previous table posture, so that for a long time all stood up, the presiding officiant and the *circumstantes.*

The problem of the basic form of the Eucharist has been discussed by R. Guardini, *Besinnung vor der Feier der heiligen Messe,* II (Mainz, 1939), 73 ff. I was able to argue out the matter in a number of conversations with the author, and thus arrive at the distinctions already pointed out. Cf. also G. Söhngen, *Das sakramentale Wesen des Messopfers* (Essen, 1946), 57-61. J. Pascher, *Eucharistia* (Münster, 1947. J. A. Jungmann, "Um die Grundgestalt des messfeier," StZ, CXLIII, p. 310.

the starting point of a development which seemed to demand externaliza-
tion. In the hellenistic surroundings this development found just the soil
it needed to grow.[64]

The *Didache* already uses a double phrase, and in reference to Sunday
worship combines with the old term "breaking of bread" the newer term
"offering thanks."[65] Ignatius of Antioch simply employs εὐχαριστία as the
name of the Sacrament of the "Eucharist."[66]

2. From Justin to Hippolytus of Rome

Justin, the philosopher and martyr, who wrote his *First Apology* in
Rome about 150, preserved to us the first full account of a Christian Mass
celebration. The picture is valid in the first instance only for Rome, but
surely the features included hold true for the whole Christian world through
which Justin had travelled from East to West.[1] After speaking about Christian Baptism, Justin continues . . .

> (c. 65) After we have baptized him who professes our belief and associates
> with us, we lead him into the assembly of those called the Brethren, and we
> there say prayers in common for ourselves, for the newly-baptized, and for
> all others all over the world. . . . After finishing the prayers, we greet each
> other with a kiss. Then bread and a cup of water and wine mixed are
> brought to the one presiding over the brethren. He takes it, gives praise
> and glory to the Father of all in the name of the Son and of the Holy Ghost,
> and gives thanks at length for the gifts that we were worthy to receive
> from Him. When he has finished the prayers and thanksgiving, the whole
> crowd standing by cries out in agreement: "Amen." "Amen" is a Hebrew
> word and means, "So may it be." After the presiding official has said thanks
> and the people have joined in, the deacons, as they are styled by us, distrib-
> ute as food for all those present, the bread and the wine-and-water mixed,
> over which the thanks had been offered, and also set some apart for those
> not present.

---

[64] A strong tendency in the philosophic and
popular-philosophic thinking at the time
of Christianity's inception, a tendency
molded by Plato and the Stoics, liked to
emphasize how little the deity required our
gifts, since the deity was ἀνενδεής. The
only offering worthy of the deity was silence or at most a prayer clothed in the
pure garment of words, the εὐλογία. According to Plato, the activity most conformable to God's nature is doing good,
the activity most conformable to that of
creation, thanking God (εὐχαριστεῖν), since
creation can present no adequate counter-
performance. The beauty and order of the
cosmos, which at that time had been newly
disclosed by maturing natural sciences,
formed the foremost theme of such medi-

tations. O. Casel, *Das Gedächtnis des
Herrn in der altchristlichen Liturgie* (Ecclesia Orans 2; Freiburg [1918]).

[65] *Didache* 14, 1 (Quasten, *Mon.*, 12f):
κλάσατε ἄρτον καὶ εὐχαριστήσατε.

[66] Ignatius of Antioch, *Ad Eph.* 13; *Ad
Philad.* 4; *Ad Smyrn.* 7, 1; *ibid.* 8, 1
(Quasten, *Mon.*, 335 f.).

[1] The local diversity of the earliest liturgies, which is emphasized by A. Baumstark,
*Vom geschichtlichen Werden der Litur-
gie*, 29 ff., must be understood only in the
sense that, for want of precise legislation,
certain minutiæ might change from place
to place; Justin, to cite an instance, did not
know of any fixed text for the thanksgiving prayer.

(c. 66) And this food itself is known amongst us as the Eucharist. No one may partake of it unless he is convinced of the truth of our teaching and is cleansed in the bath of Baptism. . . .

(c. 67) . . . And on that day which is called after the sun, all who are in the towns and in the country gather together for a communal celebration. And then the memoirs of the Apostles or the writings of the Prophets are read, as long as time permits. After the reader has finished his task, the one presiding gives an address, urgently admonishing his hearers to practice these beautiful teachings in their lives. Then all stand up together and recite prayers. After the end of the prayers, as has already been remarked above, the bread and wine mixed with water are brought, and the president offers up prayers and thanksgivings, as much as in him lies. The people chime in with an Amen. Then takes place the distribution, to all attending, of the things over which the thanksgiving had been spoken, and the deacons bring a portion to the absent. Besides, those who are well-to-do give whatever they will. What is gathered is deposited with the one presiding, who therewith helps orphans and widows. . . ." [2]

The double picture shows precisely that the liturgical appearance of the Mass at this time was essentially defined by the εὐχαριστία. Notice, too, the sharp emphasis which Justin puts on the seemingly unimportant matter of the congregation's Amen. The thanksgiving spoken by the one presiding comes from the heart of the whole assembly and is confirmed by all. Justin, who was himself a layman, bears witness by this detail how much value the faithful set on their pronouncing this word. This community spirit, this feeling of oneness which was so immediately expressed when the celebration had the character of a meal, continues thus to put its stamp on the worship. And it was even more strongly impressed in the Communion which by its nature united the entire community.

What was received in Communion was designated the "Thank-you gift" (τὰ εὐχαριστηθέντα, ὁ εὐχαριστηθεὶς ἄρτος), and the Amen was intoned as a *thanksgiving*. In Justin's description of the Mass, the expression of thanks, the very notion of thanks, stand out as the second significant and characteristic feature.

That we really have here an idea which was currently operative in the Christian community can be gathered not only from the fact that εὐχαριστία is now generally used as the technical term for the Mass,[3] but even more from the explanation which is given this word. Justin himself says elsewhere[4] that Christ gave us "the bread of the Eucharist" as a memorial of His Passion, and "that through it we might thank God, both for establishing the world and all that is in it for man's sake, and for freeing us from the evil in which we were born and, through Him who had willingly undertaken to suffer, entirely destroying the Powers and Forces." Irenæus also sets it down as a basis for the institution: the disciples of Christ should

[2] Greek text of Chapters 61 and 65-67, with explanatory notes, in Quasten, *Mon.*, 13-21. Cf. Schuster, *The Sacramentary*, I, 59-61.
[3] The expression is also in the semi-Gnostic apocryphal Acts of the Apostles. Cf. Th. Schermann, "εὐχαριστία und εὐχαριστεῖν in ihrem Bedeutungswandel bis 200 n. Chr.," *Philologus*, LXIX (1910), 375-410.
[4] Justin, *Dial. c. Tryphone*, 41, 1 (Quasten, *Mon.*, 337).

"not be sterile and ungrateful."[5] Origen maintains: "We are not men with thankless hearts. True, we do not make any offerings, we do not sacrifice in worship things which, far from being of benefit to us, are really our enemies. But toward God, who has showered us with benefits . . . we are ashamed not to be grateful. The token of our gratitude to God is the Bread which we call Eucharist."[6]

One cannot help but notice with what enthusiasm the ecclesiastical writers of this period describe God's benefactions; first of all, those in the order of creation, but more especially those with which the children of the Church have been favored. And with what energy they urge that deep feeling of self-sacrifice and of subservient obedience, from which gratitude proceeds. According to Clement of Alexandria, the Christian owes God a life-long gratitude; this is the expression of true reverence.[7] "The offering of the Church," thus Clement continues, "consists in a prayer in which all our thoughts, given over to God, are wrapped up along with the offering."[8]

The subjectiveness and spirituality of worship and the offering of the heart to God are so emphasized in the Christian sources of this period[9] that one might have supposed that there was an absence of outward offering; before Irenæus (so runs the opinion), no offering was recognized in the Church except that which consisted in thanksgiving.[10] Actually, many pronouncements during this period lend a semblance of verity to this supposition and appear to our ears very exaggerated. God "does not demand an offering of victim or drink nor of any visible things."[11] He requires "not blood-oblations and drink, not the odor of flowers or of incense, since He is the perfect perfume, without want or blemish." The highest sacrifice one can offer Him is to acknowledge Him and tender Him our spiritual service.[12] The only honor worthy of Him is to put His gifts to use for ourselves and for the poor, and to "be thankful and by our spirit send heavenward

[5] Irenæus, *Adversus hær.*, IV, 17, 5 (Quasten, *Mon.*, 346).

[6] Origen, *Contra Celsum*, VIII, 57 (PG XI, 1601 f.).

[7] Clement of Alexandria, *Stromata*, 7, 7 (PG IX, 449 C).

[8] *Ibid.*, (PG IX, 444 C). Cf. the exposition of the devotional ideas which form the background for the eucharistic teaching of the second century, in Elfers, *Die Kirchenordnung Hippolyts*, 263-275. From a later period, cf. for thanksgiving as a basic Christian notion, Cyril of Jerusalem, *Catech. myst.*, V, 5 (Quasten, *Mon.*, 100), Chrysostom, *In Matth. hom.*, 25, 3 (PG LVII, 331); *In I Cor. hom.*, 24, 1 (PG LXI, 199).

[9] Cf. the chapter "Das Opfer im Geiste" in O. Casel, *Die Liturgie als Mysterienfeier* (5th ed.; Ecclesia Orans 9; Freiburg

[1923]), 105-134, and the other works of the same author there referred to, 105.

[10] Fr. Wieland, *Der vorirenäische Opferbegriff* (Munich, 1909). Wieland had expressed the same ideas in two earlier writings (since 1906), which led to a controversy with E. Dorsch; see esp. E. Dorsch, *Der Opfercharakter der Eucharistie einst und jetzt* (2nd ed.; Innsbruck, 1911). See the summary of the results of the dispute in G. Rauschen, *Eucharistie und Busssakrament in den ersten Jahrhunderten der Kirche* (2nd ed.; Freiburg, 1910), 71-95; Goossens, *Les origines de l'Eucharistie*, 58-71; 367-369.

[11] Aristides, *Apology*, par. 1, in *The Ante-Nicene Fathers*, Vol. IX. (New York, 1912.)

[12] Athenagoras, *Legatio*, c. 13 (TU IV, 2, p. 14).

songs of praise and hymns of glory for our creation and for every means of prosperity, for the qualities of the different kinds of things, and for the changes of season."[13] For this reason, the apologists explained, the Christians had no altar and no temple.[14]

But if one were to decide from such expressions that in the minds of the Christians of the time there was a Eucharist but no eucharistic sacrifice properly so called, one would be jumping to conclusions. Along with phrases of this sort, meant to emphasize the differences between Christianity and paganism, there are found from the very beginning other phrases which not only declare that the eucharist was pronounced over the bread and wine, but which speak plainly enough of gifts which are sacrificed to God in the Eucharist,[15] or which simply designate the Eucharist as an oblation or presuppose its *sacrificial* character.[16] There are expressions which can be interpreted, without violence, in a broader sense, like the repeated reference to the prophecy of Malachy which is fulfilled in the celebration of the Christian Eucharist.[17]

We are therefore certain from the very start that in the Eucharist not only do prayers of thanksgiving rise from the congregation to God, but that at the same time a gift is offered up to God.[18] It is another question, however, how the offering of a gift is evaluated in the rite of that period. But remember, it is not necessary that the details of eucharistic theology appear in the rite. Even in the developed Mass-liturgy of today many pertinent points of dogma are entirely omitted. So it is quite understandable that in a primordial form of the celebration, evolving chiefly either from the memorial of our Lord,[19] or from the prayer of thanks, little would be

---

[13] Justin, *Apolog.* I, 13 (PG VI, 345) ; cf. also Clement of Alexandria, *Stromata,* 7, 3, 6 and elsewhere.

[14] Minucius Felix, *Octavius,* c. 32, 1, CSEL II, 45; cf. c. 10, 2, *ibid.,* 14; Tertullian, *De spect.,* c. 13 CSEL XX, 15.

[15] Clement of Rome, *Ad Cor.* 36, 1: Clement calls Christ τὸν ἀρχιερέα τῶν προςφορῶν ἡμῶν. Cf. *ibid.,* 40-44.

Justin, *Dial. c. Tryphone,* c. 41, (PG VI, 564) ; cf. for this Elfers, pp. 257-259.

[16] *Didache,* 14: The Sunday Eucharist is twice called θυσία. In Ignatius of Antioch, it is true, θυσιαστήριον is not yet the material altar of sacrifice. But at least in *Ad Philad.,* 4, the expression is used in connection with the Eucharist: The Flesh of Jesus Christ and the chalice of His Blood form a θυσιαστήριον to which the Christians gather ; cf. Elfers, 287 f.

For Heb. 13:10, cf. the exegetic discussion in Goossens, *op. cit.,* pp. 212-222. He is inclined to understand by the

θυσιαστήριον, which is contrasted to the Old Testament expiatory sacrifice, not only the sacrifice of the Cross, but the eucharistic altar too. In any case, here as in 1 Cor. 10:21 the existence of a sacrificial meal is taken for granted. Further bibliography on the Eucharist as a sacrifice, in Arnold, *op. cit.,* pp. 97 ff.

[17] *Didache,* 14, 3 ; Justin, *Dial. c. Tryphone,* 41 ; cf. *ibid.,* 28, 117.

[18] How much this thought coincides with the notion of εὐχαριστία is manifest from the fact that already in Philo εὐχαριστία does not mean only thanksgiving but a sacrifice for the purpose of rendering thanks. Schermann, *op. cit.,* 385 f. ; cf. p. 379.

[19] Such a form, for instance, as is found in the spurious *Acts of St. Thomas,* a second/third century work of Gnostic origin, c. 158 (Hennecke, *Neutestamentl. Apokryphen,* 287 f. ; Quasten, *Mon.,* 345). Another conjecture suggests that the prayer that comprised the Eucharist might have been

said about oblation and sacrifice. Such, in fact, is our conduct whenever we present a gift that is due; we do not talk much about the gift we are tendering, preferring instead to concentrate on the labors and merits that occasioned the gift.

But actually we do find in the oldest text of the Eucharist, in Hippolytus of Rome, an expression of sacrifice, immediately connected with the anamnesis, right where all later Catholic liturgies employ a similar word: *memores igitur mortis et resurrectionis eius offerimus tibi panem et calicem . . .*[20] It is possible that these words of oblation, or words like them, were included in the prayer of thanks at an earlier stage, perhaps even from the very first.[21]

On the other hand, many obstacles had to be overcome before the oblation to God—and with it, the sacrificial character of the Eucharist—would be expressed not only in words but in the external appearance of the celebration, and thus stretch out beyond the framework of a prayer of thanks connected with a meal. We have already heard the apologists of the second century who set the heathen sacrifice with its intoxication of the senses and its external pageantry over against the simple and spiritual worship of the Church, a worship that strives only to prove the grateful offering of those hearts assembled before God in Christ. The only outward symbol of this offering added to the words of the prayer, was something exalted high above the offerings of heathen and of Jew—the body of our Lord, which had been obediently sacrificed, and the blood that He shed, manifested to the eye as a piece of bread and a chalice of wine. The New Law does not have an oblation that is a "man-made one."[22] Thus was excluded the notion that a true and genuine oblation to God could be discerned in the gifts of bread and wine which were placed on the table for the Eucharist, or in those things presented by the faithful for the agape or for alms. This view Justin holds quite firmly.[23] Tertullian has watered it down.[24] But Irenæus plainly takes a new stand. In explaining the Eucharist,

drawn from the thoughts contained in Christ's farewell address and his high-priestly prayer; see Ruch, "La Messe," DThC, X, 855 f.

[20] Hauler, 107; Dix, 8 f.

[21] In reference to the whole passage see also Lietzmann, *Messe und Herrenmahl*, 181: "What stands there could . . . have been spoken in Corinth or Ephesus in the time of the Apostle Paul. Lietzmann would like to make Paul the creator not only of the liturgical type to be found in Hippolytus, but also of the eucharistic doctrine and the eucharistic practice therein contained regarding bread and chalice. As a further application of his biblio-critical method, he contrasts with the Pauline basic type another basic type in the primitive congrega-

tion at Jerusalem, a chaliceless type which continued for a short while in Egypt. This second type did not endure. Regarding Lietzmann's theories, cf. Arnold, 11-53; Goossens, 86-96; 353-359.

[22] *Epistle of Barnabas*, c. 2, 6: μὴ ἀνθρωποποίητον ἔχῃ τὴν προσφοράν: "its (the New Law's) oblation should not be a man-made one."

[23] Justin, *Dial. c. Tryphone*, c. 117.—*Apol. I*, 67, 1. 6, the collect is cited; it follows the celebration of the Eucharist and is not marked by any words as a sacrifice or offering to God. Ruch, "La messe d'après les Pères," DThC, X, 905 ff. Cf. Elfers, *Die Kirchenordnung Hippolyts*, 236 ff.

[24] Tertullian, *De or.*, c. 28 (CSEL, XX, 198 f.); *De exhort. cast.*, c. 11 (CSEL

he emphasized the fact that we offer the firstlings of creation.[25] At the Last Supper our Lord took "bread growing out of creation" and a "chalice coming from our creation," spoke the words over them, and thus taught His disciples the new oblation of the New Testament. He had therefore commanded the disciples "to offer up to God the firstlings of creatures, not because He needed them, but that they themselves might not be sterile and ungrateful."[26] These words show that for Irenæus no less than for his predecessors, it was the inner intention, the offering of the heart that was decisive before God,[27] and that only the Eucharist of the body and blood of Christ presented the clean oblation of which Malachias had spoken.[28] For only in Christ is all creation gathered together and sacrificed to God, as Irenæus does not tire of repeating.[29]

But in taking a position against the exaggerated spiritualism of the Gnostics, Irenæus appears to be compelled to defend the worth of earthly creation. With clear vision he sees the symbolic meaning of what occurred at our Lord's institution of the Blessed Sacrament, when things of this earth of ours were so exalted that by the word of God they became Christ's flesh and blood and were thus empowered to enter into the clean oblation of the New Covenant.

Once the natural gifts of bread and wine were recognized as symbols of the internal oblation of the heart, nothing stood in the way of developing the ceremony of their presentation into an oblation to God, and so giving a stronger expression to the sacrificial element which was at the center of the Eucharist—not only in words but in the external rite. Since the beginning of the third century there appear accounts of an offering by the faithful preceding the eucharistic prayer. From then on this is liturgically revised in various ways and gradually shaped into a genuine offertory procession.[30] But even so, it is only the broader notion of oblation that receives a liturgical stamp, not the narrow idea of a sacrifice in the sense of the changing or destruction of a gift.[31] We get the first

<hr>

LXX, 146 f.). See the explanation of both these passages in Elfers, 294 f.

[25] Irenæus, *Adversus hær.* IV, 18, 1 (PG VII, 1024 f.; *al.* IV, 31, 1, Harvey, II, 201).

[26] *Ibid.*, IV, 17, 5 (PG VII, 1023; *al.* IV, 29, 5, Harvey, II, 197 ff.). Cf. Tertullian, *Adv. Marcionem*, I, 14 (CSEL XLVII, 308).

[27] *Ibid.*, IV, 18, 3: "The sacrifice does not hallow the man, for God does not require sacrifice, but the conscience of the offerer, if it is pure, hallows the sacrifice and effects God's accepting it as from a friend." Cf. *ibid.*, IV, 18, 4 (PG VII, 1026 f.; *al.* IV, 31, 2 f., Harvey, II, 203 f.). On the devotional doctrine behind St. Irenæus' eucharistic teaching, cf. Elfers, 263-274.

[28] *Ibid.*, IV, 17, 5; cf. V, 2, 3.

[29] *Ibid.*, III, 18, 1; 19, 3; 21, 10, and *passim*.

[30] A more complete discussion in Vol. II, Chapter 1, 1.

[31] In the Orient an expressive and interpretative oblation in the narrower sense is worked out in the prelude to the sacrifice, within the proskomide, namely the rite of "Slaughtering the Lamb," that is, dividing the species of bread with the "holy lance"; see Brightman, 356 f. The ceremony is already extant in the oldest form of the explanation of the liturgy by Ps.-Germanus, assigned to the ninth century; Hanssens, III, 22. The Latin Middle Ages often explained the breaking of the host after the *Pater noster* in much the same sense.

inklings of the liturgical development of the rite in question in the church regulations or church order of Hippolytus of Rome. Over this document which brings the history of the Mass-liturgy out of the twilight of scattered accounts into the light of day, we must delay awhile. For in it we find for the first time the complete text of the eucharistic prayer.

3. From Hippolytus to the Separation of Liturgies

The work we are here dealing with was known for a long time under the title *The Egyptian Church Order*. But it was not till recently that its authorship was ascribed to the Roman presbyter, Hippolytus, the skilful controversialist writer of the third century.[1] He had come into sharp conflict with two popes, Zephyrinus (d. 217) and Callistus (d. 222), had in fact set himself up as anti-pope in opposition to the latter, but at last he was reconciled with the Church and died as a martyr (235), as his cultus in Rome bears witness even up to this very hour. He is commemorated on August 13. The name of the work, composed in Greek, is Ἀποστολικὴ παράδοσις. As representative of the conservative wing, Hippolytus had in mind compiling what were esteemed as the "apostolic traditions" in the regulation of ecclesiastical life. The work was probably completed about 215, before the schism which broke out when Callistus was chosen pope. The division that followed, together with the fact that the work was done in Greek, explains why the *Apostolic Tradition*, like so many of the writings of Hippolytus, was almost entirely forgotten in Rome and in the West, while in the Orient, in Egypt as well as in Syria, precisely because it claimed to present the apostolic tradition and because it came from Rome, it had a tremendous success. And that explains why, except for a few tiny fragments, it has survived not in the original text, but in translation—in Coptic, Arabic, Ethiopian and partly in Syrian. Some important fragments of a Latin version have also come down, contained in a collection of oriental legal papers.[2] For our knowledge of ecclesiastical life in Rome in the third century, this document is the most important source.[3]

[1] E. Schwartz, *Uber die pseudoapostolischen Kirchenordnungen* (Strassburg, 1910); R. H. Connolly, *The So-called Egyptian Church Order* (Cambridge, 1916). In opposition to the opinions previously expressed, the authorship of Hippolytus is convincingly vindicated by H. Elfers, *Die Kirchenordnung Hippolyts von Rom* (Paderborn, 1938).

[2] E. Hauler, *Didascaliæ apostolorum fragmenta Veronensia* (Leipzig, 1900), 101-121.

[3] No absolutely critical text has so far been published. The most important investigation is G. Dix, *The treatise on the Apostolic Tradition of St. Hippolytus of Rome* (London, 1937). Other studies and editions are cited in Quasten, *Monumenta*, 27. The text has been made available to wider circles through the anonymous (H. Edmayr) volume, *Die Apostolische Uberlieferung des hl. Hippolytus* (Klosterneuburg, 1932).

The text begins with directions for the consecration of a bishop. The newly-consecrated prelate is acclaimed with the cry: ἄξιος. Then the deacons bring up the gifts (προσφορά). Accompanied by all the presbyters, the bishops lay their hands over the gifts and begin the prayer of thanks:

> Dominus vobiscum. Et cum spiritu tuo. Sursum corda. Habemus ad Dominum. Gratias agamus Domino. Dignum et iustum est. Et sic iam prosequatur.
> Gratias tibi referimus, Deus per dilectum puerum tuum Jesum Christum, quem in ultimis temporibus misisti nobis salvatorem et redemptorem et angelum voluntatis tuæ. Qui est Verbum tuum inseparabile, per quem omnia fecisti et bene placitum tibi fuit. Misisti de cœlo in matricem Virginis, quique in utero habitus incarnatus est et Filius tibi ostensus est ex Spiritu Sancto et Virgine natus. Qui voluntatem tuam complens et populum sanctum tibi adquirens extendit manus cum pateretur, ut a passione liberaret eos qui in te crediderunt. Qui cumque traderetur voluntariæ passioni ut mortem solvat et vincula diaboli dirumpat et infernum calcet et iustos inluminet et terminum figat et resurrectionem manifestet, accipiens panem gratias tibi agens dixit: Accipite, manducate: hoc est corpus meum, quod pro vobis confringetur. Similiter et calicem dicens: Hic est sanguis meus qui pro vobis effunditur. Quando hoc facitis, meam commemorationem facitis. Memores igitur mortis et resurrectionis eius offerimus tibi panem et calicem gratias tibi agentes quia nos dignos habuisti adstare coram te et tibi ministrare. Et petimus ut mittas Spiritum tuum Sanctum in oblationem sanctæ Ecclesiæ. In unum congregans des omnibus qui percipiunt sanctis in repletionem Spiritus Sancti ad confirmationem fidei in veritate, ut te laudemus et glorificemus per puerum tuum Jesum Christum, per quem tibi gloria et honor Patri et Filio cum Sancto Spiritu in sancta Ecclesia tua et nunc et in sæcula sæculorum. Amen.[4]

At the conclusion the remark is added: If anyone offers oil, or cheese or olives, a similar prayer of thanks may be said over it—and, as an example, a short blessing is appended.[5] After some regulations about the other degrees of orders, and about church offices, there follow precepts for the catechumenate and Baptism. At the conclusion of this last we find—as in Justin— further mention of the Mass. But here there is only the note that the participation of the newly-baptized in the service of the congregation begins with the common prayer and the kiss of peace before the offering of the gifts.[6] There are also regulations for the peculiar usage—already touched upon—of offering at this Mass of the newly-baptized, besides the sacramental Eucharist, also a chalice filled with milk and honey and a third one with water.[7]

It would be a mistake to envision in this text which Hippolytus proposes, the Roman Mass of the third century, pure and simple. That would hardly coincide with the stage of liturgical development reached at that

[4] Hauler, 106 f.; Dix, 7-9.

[5] A portion of this came by a very roundabout way into the Roman Pontifical, and here survives within the ceremony for the consecration of the oils on Maundy Thursday, at the close of the canon, as in Hippolytus; cf. J. A. Jungmann, "Beobacht-

ungen zum Fortleben von Hippolyts 'Apostolischer Uberlieferung'," ZkTh, LIII (1929), 579-585. The additional prayers for communion found in the Egyptian text-transmission are not Hippolytus'.

[6] Dix, 39 f.; Hauler, 111 f.

[7] Supra, Chapter 1, p. 15.

period. At this time there is still no fixed formulary for the Mass-liturgy, but only a fixed framework which the celebrant fills out with his own words, as older accounts clearly indicate.[8] Hippolytus presents his text only as a suggestion, and expressly stresses the right freely to extemporize a text[9] as a right which remained long in force.[10] This right Hippolytus himself here laid claim to. Favorite thoughts, favorite turns of expression from his other writings recur time and again.[11]

The Eucharist of Hippolytus does on the whole exhibit a type of the contemporary liturgy, but not the only type then in use.[12] For it is rather

[8] Didache, 10, 6; Justin, Apol. I, 67; see supra, Chapter 2, p. 22.

[9] As an appendix to the prayers for ordination (Dix, 19) : "It is absolutely not necessary for the bishop to use the exact wording which we gave above, as if he were learning them by heart for his thanksgiving to God. Rather each one should pray according to his capability. If he is ready to pronounce a grand and solemn prayer, that is well; if on the contrary he should say a prayer according to a set form, no one may hinder him. But the prayer must be correct and orthodox." Cf. also J. Lebreton in Fliche-Martin, Histoire de l'église, II (1935), 70, note 3.

There is a significant commentary on the development of the liturgical practice in the fact that the Arabic and Ethiopian texts leave out the "not" in the quotation cited; they read: "It is absolutely necessary . . ."

[10] The free creation of a text—which need not mean improvising in the strict sense, but like a good sermon could be a work carefully drawn-up and well-memorized— was still in practice at Rome when in the year 538 (or perhaps 558) a preface of the Leonine Sacramentary mirrored the one single case of the anniversary of a Pope's ordination coinciding with Maundy Thursday; see Baumstark, Missale Romanum, 32 f. In Spain fixed texts were the rule, but the right to compose Mass formulas freely is still demonstrable in the seventh century; P. Sejourné, S. Isidore de Séville (Paris, 1929), 175.

In general fixed texts were the rule since the fourth century.

For the beginning of liturgical books, see Fortescue, The Mass, 113 ff.; also Abbot Cabrol, The Books of the Latin Liturgy (London and St. Louis, 1932), 13-19.

Even when liturgical books were in existence, the texts were not necessarily read off; rather—as Hippolytus seems to provide for (cf. previous note)—they had to be learnt by heart and recited, a thing not too difficult in the case of the uniform formulas of oriental liturgies. In the West there is testimony to the reading of the texts in Gregory of Tours (d. 594), Hist. Franc., II, 22 (PL LXXI, 217 f.). Sidonius [d. about 489] was able to dispatch everything correctly even when the wonted libellus was taken away; Vitæ patrum, c. 6 (PL LXXI, 1075). Cf. Eisenhofer, I, 59 f.

[11] Elfers, 50-54, adduces six such instances in the eucharistic prayer alone. The expression Verbum inseparabile is intended to counter the suspicion raised against Hippolytus of teaching a separation between God and His Logos. For the striking phrase extendit manus there is a commentary in Hippolytus, De Antichristo, c. 61: "Nothing is left for the Church in persecution except the wings of the great Eagle, that is, of belief in Jesus Christ, who stretched out His hands on the holy wood . . . and [who] calls to Himself all who believe in Him and guards them as a bird guards its young." Even the meaning of the puzzling expression ut terminum figat is cleared up somewhat by a fragment of Hippolytus: Christ wanted to teach the just about the moment of the general resurrection. (Elfers, 54). The final doxology too, at least in regard to the interpolated naming of the three divine Persons, could well be Hippolytus' own work. Cf. also R. H. Connolly, "The Eucharistic Prayer of Hippolytus," Journal of theol. Studies, XXXIX (1938), 350-369, where other parallels are cited.

[12] The distinction here borne in mind has nothing in common with the distinction made by Lietzmann, who contrasts with the

surprising that ideas derived from the Old Testament, which play such a major role in most of the later texts, and which one rightly deduces from synagogue traditions, are here entirely absent. No reference is made to the work of creation, nor to God's salvific plan in the pre-Christian era—a point which remained the rule in later Greek liturgies. The *Sanctus*, too, is missing, along with the corresponding introduction. Only the work of Redemption is gratefully delineated, and in such an ingenious way that the account of the Institution is organically conjoined. The prayer therefore gives the impression of a well-rounded completeness. Hippolytus appears to have striven consciously for this completeness in his model formulary, sharply distinguishing it from the forms at hand in which the connection seems somewhat loose. Perhaps this other type developed from the circumstance that, when the Eucharist was disjoined from the evening agape, it was linked with an already existent Sunday morning church service, in which the Sabbath morning service of the synagogue—already mentioned[13]—lived on, with its readings on the one hand and on the other its praise of God for the creation and for His gracious guidance of His people, with its mention of the angelic choirs and its cry of the threefold *Sanctus* from the vision of Isaias.[14]

But besides the strictly christological type of Hippolytus and the type derived from the synagogue, a third type must also have developed quite early, a type of thanksgiving, or rather of praise, in which the thoughts of the Christian acknowledgment of God were clothed in the phrases of hellenist philosophy. The infinite greatness of God was presented by the repetition of negative attributes, as a rule formed with the privative *a*: "God non-inchoate, unsearchable, inexpressible, incomprehensible to everything made."[15] Or creation is reviewed, with that feeling for nature that is reawakened in those centuries, and from this is shaped a glorification of God's power and wisdom.[16]

It stands to reason that these types did not ever have independent forms

type in Hippolytus a second primitive type which was originally chaliceless; see *supra*, Chapter 2, note 21.

[13] *Supra*, p. 19.

[14] Thus Baumstark, *Liturgie comparée*, 54-56, in reference to the *Epistle of St. Clement*, ch. 24 (*lege* 34).

The passage in Clement is sometimes regarded as the earliest indication of the use of the *Sanctus* in the liturgy of primitive Christianity; cf. H. Engberding, "Trishagion," L ThK, X (1938), 295.

For an appreciation of the eucharistic prayer of Hippolytus, cf. Arnold, *Der Ursprung des christlichen Abendmahls*, 164-166.

[15] This is the form of address in Serapion's anaphora (Quasten, *Mon.*, 59 f.).

Cf. Th. Schermann, *Die allgemeine Kirchenordnung, frühchristliche Liturgien und kirchliche Überlieferung* (Paderborn, 1915), II, 462-465.

[16] Justin already mentions thankfulness for creation in the eucharistic prayer; cf. *supra* p. 25.

An early example of a religious contemplation of the wondrous work of nature is found in St. Clement of Rome's *Epistle to the Corinthians*, ch. 20. Cf. O. Casel, *Das Gedächtnis des Herrn in der altchristlichen Liturgie* (Ecclesia Orans 2, Freiburg [1918]), 15 ff., 31 ff. Also G. Bardy, "Expressions stoiciennes dans la Prima Clementis," *Rech. des sciences rel.*, XII (1922), 73-85.

or exist by themselves in a pure state, for the basic Christian and christo-logical motif of the prayer of thanks could indeed wane but never entirely vanish.[17] But they comprise components which formed parts of the eucha-ristic prayer, or directions toward which it tended—until the word of authority and the official text put a stop to the development. In the sources of the Mass-liturgy surviving from the fourth century, we meet, besides the organic growth of liturgical forms and usages, also concrete examples of the types noticed.

From what has been said we are forced to conclude that the liturgical prayer texts were, in the third century, still elastic and continually subject to new influences. But at the same time there is a good deal to show that, for the general course of the liturgy in the Church as a whole, there was a unified order, a network of still flexible regulations stamped with the authority of custom. These statutes regulated the building of the house of God, the time and manner of service, the division of functions, the way prayers were to begin and end, and so forth. The fundamental design of the prayer of thanks—the Eucharist—is everywhere the same: it begins invariably with a short dialogue and closes with the Amen of the people. When in 154 Bishop Polycarp of Smyrna visited Pope Anicetus at Rome, the latter invited him to celebrate the Eucharist in church,[18] an honor for the episcopal guest which the Syrian Didascalia of the third century makes compulsory in analogous instances.[19] There was no fear, therefore, of any disturbing deviation because of the strange liturgies. The same thing is indicated by the transfer of the liturgical formulary of Hippolytus from Rome to distant Egypt and as far away as Ethiopia where it remains even till today, the usual Mass formulary under the title "Anaphora of the Apostles." What was here set down fitted without trouble into the indi-genous order of the strange country. We can therefore, in this wider sense, speak of a unified liturgy of the first centuries.[20]

[17] Schermann, op. cit., 469 f., enumerates, in addition to the judaistic, christological and hellenistic types, a fourth type, the trinitarian, but he does not have the Mass-liturgy precisely in mind.

In this connection, however, one could just as well speak about a christological-trinitarian type instead of a christological one, since the work of salvation, lauded in the Great Prayer, is extended to include its completion through the operation of the Holy Spirit. Even Hippolytus pre-sumes this extension in the prayer for the fullness of the Holy Ghost. The laudatory mention of the Holy Ghost, and the con-joined naming, one after the other, of the three divine Persons in the manifestation of their work for our sanctification is reg-ularly found since the fourth century in the Mass-liturgy of the Orient, where the Holy Ghost epiklesis is an established law.

In this sort of anaphora, constructed much like the symbol, W. H. Frere, The Anaphora or Great Eucharistic Prayer. An eirenical study in liturgical history (London, 1938), perceives the ideal of the eucharistic prayer.

[18] Eusebius, Hist. eccl., V, 24.

[19] Didascalia, II, 58, 3 (Funk, I, 168). When the guest, through modesty, excuses himself from this honor, he should at least speak the words over the chalice. The later revision, in Const. Ap., II, 58, 3 (ibid., 169) substitutes for the last remark: he should at least pronounce a blessing over the people.

[20] Fortescue, 51-57. The idea of an una, sancta, catholica et apostolica liturgia has

4. The Mass In the Orient after the Fourth Century

With the coming of the fourth century an important differentiation makes its appearance. In the organization of the Church, especially within Greek territory, there grew up, bit by bit, over and above the individual communities with their episcopal overseers, certain preponderant centers, above all Alexandria and Antioch. From these centers and their provincial synods there radiated special legislation that in time gave a particular stamp to the church life of those affected. Thus, too, divergent liturgies gradually acquired their fixed form. This was a necessary development. The speedy spread of congregations, for whom, since Constantine, numberless buildings of often vast proportions had been erected, required a more rigid control of common worship, and demanded a greater carefulness about the text of the prayers than was needed in the smaller groups where the officiant might perhaps on occasion extemporize.

So it became more and more the rule that the text should be set down in writing. And so, too, it became necessary to borrow texts from other churches. The possibility of a strict control was also heightened. In North Africa they were satisfied to issue a warning that this borrowing should not be haphazard, but that the texts should be carefully passed upon by capable brethren (in episcopal office).[1] The result was the gradual standardization of formulas to be used unvaryingly throughout a province.

From the turn of the fourth century, however, there survive two collections of liturgical texts which emanate from the two leading oriental metropolises already mentioned, and the Mass formulas they contain differ considerably from the later authorized forms. From the sphere of Alexandria-Egypt we have the *Euchologion* of Bishop Serapion of Thmuis. From the sphere of Antioch-Syria we have the liturgy in the eighth book of the *Apostolic Constitutions,* also called the Clementine liturgy. A closer inspection of both these documents will be rewarding.

Serapion, bishop of Thmuis, a little town in lower Egypt, is well-known as a friend of St. Athanasius and of the hermit St. Anthony. He was a bishop between 339 and 362. The *Euchologion* authored by him, first dis-

been vigorously propounded by F. Probst (d. 1899) in several of his works, but tied in with a rather unhappy reference to the so-called Clementine liturgy (see the chapter following). In opposition to this notion, Baumstark, *Vom geschichtlichen Werden,* 30, makes the emphatic statement: "The historical progress of the liturgy is not a growth from an ancient unity to an ever larger local diversity, but rather from the latter to an accretive unification." But this can only be understood to mean that originally the text of the prayer and other details differed from place to place and from case to case, not the general plan or outline; cf. Baumstark's own detailed explanation, *ibid.,* 29-36.

[1] Synod of Hippo (A.D. 393), Can. 23 (Mansi, III, 884; cf. 850 C, 895 D). The precept is repeated in subsequent African synods (Mansi, III, 884 B, 922 C).

covered in a monastery on Mt. Athos in 1894, contains amongst other things the liturgy of the Mass, but unfortunately with no explanatory rubrics.[3]

The list of Mass prayers begins with a prayer for a fruitful reading of the Scriptures. There follows a prayer "after standing up from the homily," then a group of formulas for the general prayers for the Church: for the catechumens, for the people, for the sick. To each of these groups is appended a χειροθεσία, a blessing by the bishop—for a good crop, for the church, for the bishop and the Church, and finally a "genuflectional prayer," probably a closing benediction. These prayers—like the eucharistic prayer that follows—display a definitely theologizing trend, and, in their broad unfolding of parallel periods, the ornament of Greek oratory. Remarkable is the uniformly recurring doxology, which is characteristic of the third/ fourth century. The doxology is directed to God through Christ in the Holy Ghost. The prayer, for instance, will make mention of our Lord and then continue somewhat in this fashion: Through whom there is to Thee honor and power in the Holy Ghost now and forever!

More important for us is the eucharistic prayer. It begins: "Fit it is, and proper, to praise, to glorify and to exalt Thee, the everlasting Father of the only-begotten, Jesus Christ." Then is lauded the unsearchable being of God, made known to us through the Son. And praise turns to prayer for a right understanding and to the vision of the angelic choirs over whom God reigns:

> *Before thee stand a thousand thousand and ten thousand ten thousand Angels and Archangels, Thrones, Principalities, Dominations, and Powers. Before Thee stand the two six-winged Seraphim, with two wings hiding their face, two their feet, and flying with two, and they praise Thee. With them do Thou accept our praise, as we say: Holy, holy, holy Lord of Sabaoth, heaven and earth are full of His glory.*

Typical of this, as well as of all later Egyptian Mass-liturgies, is the passage from the *Sanctus* to the account of the Institution; peculiar is the interruption of the account with prayers—reminiscent of the usages of the primitive Church.

> *Complete this sacrifice with Thy power and with Thy participation, for it is to Thee we have offered up this living sacrifice, this unbloody gift. To Thee we have offered this Bread, the oblation [ὁμοίωμα] of the body of the Only-begotten. This Bread is the oblation of His holy Body; for on the night . . . [there follows the words over the bread, 1 Cor. 11:23-4.] Therefore we too, ratifying the offering of His death, have offered up the Bread, and we cry out through this offering: Be merciful to us all and be appeased, O God of truth! And as this Bread was scattered . . . so gather Thy Church together . . . into one living Catholic Church. We have also offered up the chalice, the offering of His Blood; for the Lord Jesus . . . [Here is inserted the passage from Matt. 26:27 ff.]. Therefore we have also offered up the chalice as the offering of Blood. May Thy holy Logos,*

---

[3] Text in Quasten, *Mon.*, 48-67. The exact   arrangement of the prayers is not certain.

O God of truth, come down upon this bread, so that it become the Body of the Logos. . . . and grant that all who partake may receive a medicine of life. . . .

This petition for a fruitful Communion passes over into an intercessory prayer for the dead (presupposing a reading of the names) and for the living. The prayer then closes with the doxology. Then follows the breaking of the bread, to the accompaniment of a prayer by the celebrant, and then the Communion of the clergy, a blessing of the people, their Communion, and finally a closing thanksgiving prayer spoken by the celebrant.

The Mass-liturgy found in the eighth book of the *Apostolic Constitutions*[3] is, in several respects, of a very different stamp. This is often called the Clementine liturgy because it is contained in the long, eight-book collection of Church legislation which posed as the work of Pope Clement I, a pupil of the Apostles. Actually it is a product of the late fourth century.

The eighth book of the *Apostolic Constitutions* is, in its structure and its legal regulations, little more in general than a revision of the *Apostolic Tradition* of Hippolytus. But as regards the Mass-liturgy the traces of Hippolytus' draft are faint. In its place we have the usage, by now somewhat fixed, of the Syrian capital. But the eucharistic prayer itself is textually a creation of the redactor, a model formulary that could be spun out to vast proportion, and must therefore be looked upon not as a real usage[4] but as a suggested source to which the celebrant could turn in freely composing his prayer. In this liturgy the service of reading is definitely combined with the sacrificial worship. The Clementine liturgy begins with the readings which here, as in the case of Hippolytus, precede the consecration of a bishop. It presupposes a fourfold reading. There is a reading from the Law and from the Prophets—the synagogue tradition, quite obviously—and then from the Apostles and the Gospels. Afterwards there is a homily. Then those who are not full members are dismissed—the catechumens, energumens, candidates for Baptism and the penitents—each group after an intercessory prayer of the congregation and a blessing by the bishop. Then there is a two-part prayer for the faithful. After the kiss of peace and the washing of hands, the gifts are brought in and the eucharistic prayer begins. We will do well to try to visualize at least its outline and sequence. The prayer begins with the introductory dialogue, and continues:

(VIII, 12, 6) Fit indeed it is, and proper, that we praise Thee above all, the true God, who wast before all creation, from whom all paternity in heaven and on earth takes its name, alone without becoming, without beginning, over whom there is no king and no lord, who needest nothing and grantest every good . . .

(7) . . . Thou hast called all things from nothing into being, through Thine only-begotten Son, and Him hast Thou conceived before all times. . . .

---

[3] *Const. Ap.*, VIII, 5, 11-15, 11 (Funk, I, 476-520; Quasten, *Mon.*, 196-233).   [4] Cf. Baumstark, *Liturgie comparée*, 22.

(8) ... Through Him hast Thou created before all else the Cherubim and the Seraphim, the eons and the Dominations, the Virtues and the Powers ... and then this visible world and all that is in it.

(9) Thou didst build up the sky like a vault and didst stretch it out like a hide. ...

(10) Thou who didst make the water for drinking and cleansing, the air for breathing and carrying the tone of the voice ... [praise is meted out for the fire, the sea and its tides, the earth with its changes of wind and rain; finally for man].

(17) Thou hast made him of an immortal soul and a decaying body, the former created from nothing, the latter from the four elements. ...

(18) Thou, almighty God, hast planted Paradise in Eden towards the east. ...

(20) [After the trial and fall] hast justly driven him from Paradise, but in Thy goodness didst not despise him who was entirely lost, since he was Thy creature [the stories of Cain and Abel, Abraham, Melchisedech, Job, Isaac, Jacob, Joseph, Moses and Aaron, and the wonders of the Exodus from Egypt are recounted[5]].

(27) For all this, glory to Thee, omnipotent Lord! Thee do the un-counted hosts of angels praise, the archangels ... who ... without ceasing and without becoming silent cry out:—*and all the people should say to-gether:*—Holy, holy, holy Lord of Sabbaoth, Heaven and earth are full of Thy glory. Praised forever! Amen.

(28) *And the bishop continues:* (29) Holy indeed art Thou and all-holy, the highest and most exalted in eternity;

(30) But holy, too, is Thine only-begotten Son, our Lord and God, Jesus Christ ... who did not disdain the race of men, that had perished, but ... [and another review of the history of Israel and its continued faithless-ness] ... according to Thy pleasure resolved to become man, He the creator of men. ...

(32) He lived holily and taught justly, and banished every sickness and every weakness from men. ...

(33) He was turned over to the Governor Pilate, and was judged, He the Judge, and was condemned, He the Saviour, and was nailed to the cross, He who was not subject to suffering, and He died, He the Lord of nature, and was buried, He who gave life, in order to conquer suffering and to tear away from death those for whose sake He had come, and to loose the devil's fetters and free men from his deceit.

(34) And He arose again from the dead, and after spending forty days with His disciples He ascended into heaven and sat down at Thy right hand, O God and Father.

(35) Remembering what He has suffered for us, we give thanks, omnipo-tent God, not in accordance with our debt but in accordance with our ability, and we fulfill His command.

(36) For on the night in which He was betrayed ...

After the words of consecration there follows the anamnesis in which, besides the death of our Lord and His resurrection, His second coming is

---

[5] This passage, 12, 21-26, is derived from the post-exilic Temple service; see A. Baumstark, "Das eucharistische Hochgebet und die Literatur des nachexilischen Ju-dentums," *Theologie u. Glaube,* II (1910), 353-370, esp. 364 ff.; *idem., Liturgie com-parée,* 54 f.

mentioned. The arrangement of the rest of the text is like Hippolytus', with this distinction, that an epiklesis and an intercessory prayer are added:

(38) Recalling . . . we offer Thee, King and God, according to His command, this Bread and this Chalice, by giving Thee thanks for having considered us worthy to stand before Thee and perform our priestly service,

(39) And we beg Thee, look with favor, O God of riches, upon these gifts that lie before Thee, and let them be pleasing to Thee, for the honor of Thy Christ, and deign to send down upon this sacrifice Thy Holy Ghost, the witness of the Passion of Jesus, that He might manifest (ἀποφήνῃ) this Bread as the Body of Thy Christ and this Chalice as the Blood of Thy Christ, so that all who partake might grow in devotion, obtain the forgiveness of their sins, be freed from the devil and his deceit, and, filled with the Holy Ghost, might be made worthy of Thy Christ and partakers of everlasting life, if thou be merciful to them, almighty Lord.

Then follows the intercessory prayer, the ten sections of which each begin with the phrase, "We ask Thee further." The final doxology ends with the Amen of the people. For the Communion, too, a special liturgical frame is provided.[6] True, the *Pater noster* is still missing, although it is elsewhere—a short time later—mentioned as a Communion prayer, but there is presupposed a long prayer of preparation to be said by the bishop after a litany by the deacon. Then is the cry raised: Τὰ ἅγια Τοῖς ἁγίοις, with the hymnic response of the people. During the Communion of the congregation Psalm 33 is sung. After a preparatory admonition by the deacon, comes the finish, a prayer of thanksgiving and the final benediction of the bishop.

Although the text of the Mass-liturgy in both cases is not yet that which is standardized in the later liturgies of Alexandria and Antioch, still the external outlines of the liturgical usages of the East are clearly discernible, especially in the Clementine liturgy whose prescriptions would soon be established and enlarged by that great preacher of Antioch, St. John Chrysostom.[7] If we compare these fourth-century liturgies with what is seen in the contemporary Roman Mass, we notice in them a longer list of readings and a richer development of the general prayer for the Church which follows. We also notice, in this general prayer for the Church—and elsewhere, too—the prominent role of the deacon, who introduces the celebrant's prayer with a dialogue between himself and the people, and thus insures the latter a closer bond with the course of the sacred action. The eucharistic prayer (preface and canon) has indeed introduced the first suggestion of petitions, but its lines are so firmly drawn that the whole is presented as a large unit. The *Sanctus* and the epiklesis appear in it as two climactic points. The Communion, too, is enriched in its surroundings.

[6] *Const. Ap.*, VIII, 13-15 (Funk, I, 514-520; Quasten, *Mon.*, 227-233).
[7] The material is gathered in Brightman, 470-481.
The appendix in Brightman's work, p. 459-522, contains all the text fragments concerning the Mass-liturgy and all the references of older writers in the Orient, arranged according to liturgical provinces or territories.

The fourth century, especially in the Orient, is still a time of lively development. But the fundamental liturgical texts are already beginning to take on a fixed shape. A new investigation of the Basilian formula of the Byzantine Mass, and of the formularies related to it,[8] permits us to get a clearer view of the manner in which the texts extant at that time were revised and expanded. A Greek redactor—there are good grounds to suggest St. Basil the Great (d. 379)[9]—came upon a prepared eucharistic prayer which was for him apparently too jejune, although it was not poor in scriptural allusions. He enlarged it, and enriched it with a stronger sifting of quotations from the Bible. The still extant basic text,[10] had this to say, for instance, right after the Sanctus: After we had transgressed Thy command in Paradise, "Thou hast not thrust us aside entirely, but hast watched over us through Thy prophets, and didst appear to us in these latter days through Thine only-begotten Son, who took flesh of the holy Virgin and became man and showed us the way of salvation." The redactor weaves into the text, after the mention of the Son, a number of phrases: the praise of His divinity, from Hebrews 1:2 f.; the quotation from Baruch 3:38 about the Wisdom that appeared on earth; the quotation about the nature of a slave, from Philippians 2:6 f.; and then the conquest of sin and of death, to which all had been condemned through Adam, in phrases from Romans 5:12 and 6:29.[11]

It was also Basil who first makes us aware of a new trend which, as it grew, became for all oriental liturgies a fundamental trait. This trend was a growing consciousness of sin and a mounting reverence in the presence of the great mystery—a trend which increased to almost gloomy proportions.[12] Those celebrating the liturgy describe themselves as "Thy lowly and sinful and unworthy slaves"[13] who should be tried "on the day of Thy just judgment."[14] This change in expression coincides clearly with the veering in theological attitude resulting from the struggle with Arianism, a struggle waged over the essential divinity of the Son. The noise of this battle penetrated even into the house of God and is reflected in the wording of prayers. In place of the doxology, customary up to then, which

---

[8] H. Engberding, O.S.B., *Das Eucharistische Hochgebet der Basileios-liturgie* (Münster, 1931).
[9] Engberding, p. lxxxiv, ff.
    A talk with P. Engberding in November 1942 convinced me that the author wished his chain of reasoning and his deductions to be considered merely an hypothesis.
[10] This is the Egyptian Basilian anaphora: Renaudot, *Liturgiarum orient. collectio*, I (1847), 57-85.
[11] Engberding, 10-21.
    This example shows how questionable is the basic thesis of F. Probst's book, *Liturgie des vierten Jahrhunderts und deren Reform* (Münster, 1893), that in the fourth century there was a general tendency to shorten the liturgy. Besides, Probst's thesis is founded on the repeated assumption that the Clementine liturgy—known at that time only from antiquity—was until the fourth century the basis of all liturgies.
[12] M. J. Lubatschiwskyj, "Des hl. Basilius liturgischer Kampf gegen den Arianismus," ZkTh, LXVI (1942), 20-38.
[13] Brightman, 317 Z, 12 f.; cf. *ibid.*, 329 Z, 13 f.
[14] Brightman, 320 Z, 15 f. Arguments for attributing this and similar expressions to Basil are found in Lubatschiwskyj, 33 f.

offered praise to the Father "through the Son in the Holy Ghost," Basil favored the new form, which offered praise to the Father "with the Son, at one with the Holy Ghost"[15]—a way of praying and of praising in which our vision is no longer cast upon Christ's humanity, by which He is our intermediary before God, but upon His divinity, in which He is one in nature with God. Emphasis is not on the grace which He brings but in the right that He exercises, His might as a fearsome judge, before whom we ought to tremble and be afraid.[16] And already in Basil the sentiment towards the Eucharist is altered. The pertinent chapter in his *Shorter Rule* is entitled: "With what fear . . . we ought to receive the Body and Blood of Christ."[17] The same attitude towards the Blessed Sacrament, even aside from the thought of communicating, is noticeable in various parts of the eastern world. It is especially strong in Chrysostom, who time and time again talks about "the terrible sacrifice," about the "shuddering hour" when the mystery is accomplished, and about the "terrible and awful table."[18] This attitude left its mark not only on the character of the oriental liturgies, but on the peculiar form of oriental piety.[19] Even Chrysostom gave vent to the complaint that few dared approach the holy table for Communion. The decline in the frequentation of Communion in the East was already remarked by Latin Fathers of the fourth-fifth century.[20]

It is therefore no mere accident that precisely in the Orient the celebration of the mysteries took on an ever greater splendor. The activities at the altar became the object of the awesome gaze and wonder of the assembled congregation. The clergy appear in splendid vestments, lights and incense are introduced into the service, an external ceremonial with bowings and Προσκύνησις is gradually evolved. Forms broaden out, following the pattern set by the Emperor and his highest officials on festive occasions.[21] The bearing of gifts to the altar and, of course, the procession

---

[15] Basil, *De Spiritu Sancto*, I, 3 (PG XXXII, 72 C). Cf. Lubatchiwskyj, 24; Jungmann, *Die Stellung Christi im liturgischen Gebet*, 155-163.

[16] Lubatschiwskyj, 25 f., 32 ff.

[17] Basil, *Reg. brev. tract.* 172 (PG XXXI, 1195 BC) ; Lubatschiwskyj, 34 f.

[18] E. Bishop, in an appendix to R. H. Connolly, *The Liturgical Homilies of Narsai* (Cambridge, 1909), 92-97 ; Jungmann, *Die Stellung Christi*, 217-222. Remarkable is the fact that a man friendly to the Arians, like Philostorgius, *Hist. eccl.* II, 13 (Bidez, 25) should use the phrase τὴν φρικτὴν θυσίαν.

[19] Cf. Karl Adam, *Christus unser Bruder*; English translation, *Christ our Brother* (London, 1931), 48-49. Against this line of thought already expressed by me previously, a number of considerations have been presented by, amongst others, O.

Casel, JL, VII (1927), 182 f., and by S. Salaville, *Eph. liturg.*, LIII (1939), 13. See also the latter's book, *An introduction to the Study of Eastern Liturgies*, trans. Barton (London, 1938), 96-7. But so far no scientific investigation of the question has been undertaken, aside from the work of Lubatschiwskyj already mentioned. Regarding Salaville cf. ZkTh, LXV (1941), 233 f.

[20] Cf. *Infra,* Vol. II, Ch. 3, 11.

[21] As Prof. Th. Klauser pointed out to me (in a letter of Oct. 18, 1942), the ceremonial rights were transferred to the bishops already under Constantine when they were raised to the rank of the official hierarchy. Amongst these ceremonial rights were the right to be preceded by lit torches and the προσκύνησις. Some of these ceremonies will engage us in the older Roman *Ordines*;

for their distribution in Holy Communion are turned into solemn parades of the clergy, who appeared like the legions of the heavenly spirits (as the festive hymns expressly declare).[22]

In addition the line of demarcation between the altar-sanctuary and the people became more and more pronounced. The railings which lay between the two grew higher until at last they became the ikonostasis, the picture-wall which fully hides the sanctuary from the gaze of the people.[23] Thus the action at the altar is all the more raised in dignity. It is enveloped in an atmosphere of holy awe. As a further result, the actions before the liturgy—that is, before the readings—are formed into a more important prelude.[24] And so the divine service is noticeably lengthened. Later on, it would seem they strove for more brevity here by having the celebrant say some of his prayers silently, for instance, reading his oration softly even while the deacon is still repeating with the people the litany which was intended as an introduction to the oration.

The details of the evolution in the oriental Mass do not fall within the scope of this book. However, in order to understand the various analogies which a comparative study of the liturgies of Rome and the East must necessarily draw between the two, it is imperative that we give at least a broad outline of the branching out of the eastern liturgies as this occurred since the fourth century.

Up till now we confined our attention exclusively to the liturgies in the Greek tongue, that great cultural language in whose ambit the Apostles themselves trod and within whose limits most of the liturgical evolution

---

cf. also the later discussion of incensing and the Gospel. Klauser is to assemble the material in the article "Hofzeremonial" in RAC. For handy reference see H. Leclercq, "Adoration," DACL, I, 539-546; A. Arnold, "Die Ausgestaltung des monarchischen Zeremoniells am römischen Kaiserhof," *Meitteilungen des Deutschen archäologischen Institutes, röm. Abt.* XLIX (1934), 1-118.

[22] The details mentioned are noticeable as a group for the first time in the Syrian explanation of the Liturgy which is ascribed to Narsai (d. about 502) ; R. H. Connolly, *The liturgical Homilies of Narsai* (Cambridge, 1909), and the appended discussion by E. Bishop, "Ritual Splendour," *ibid.,* 88-91. Bishop maintains that the pictures sketched by Narsai correspond to a wealth of cult such as the West reached about the thirteenth century. The later so-called "Great Entrance" with the offerings, is already described by Theodore of Mopsuestia (d. 428), *Sermones catech. V* (Rücker, 21 f.), who compares the solemn parade of

the deacons to the procession of invisible angel hosts. See F. J. Reine, *The Eucharistic Doctrine and Liturgy of the Mystagogical Catecheses of Theodore of Mopsuestia* (Studies in Christian Antiquity, 2; Washington, 1942), 90-94. For this growing splendor cf. further testimonies in Hanssens, III, 286 ff.

[23] There are great differences of opinion regarding the antiquity of the ikonostasis. For an early appearance, see Bishop, *op. cit.,* 91. On the other side, Braun, *Der christliche Altar,* II, 666 f.

[24] See *infra,* p. 263.

[25] The main texts of all Mass-liturgies in the Orient are found in Brightman, *Liturgies.*

The introductory questions, in Baumstark, *Die Messe im Morgenland* (Kempten, 1906) ; P. de Meester, "Grecques (Liturgies)", DACL, VI (1925), 1591-1662. A compendious introduction is A. Raes, S.J., *Introductio in liturgiam orientalem* (Rome, 1947).

of the first centuries occurred. But the liturgy of the primitive Church in Palestine was certainly not Greek but Aramaic. Aramaic—that is, Syriac —was, by force of necessity, also the language of the ecclesiastical liturgy which penetrated to the North and East beyond the bounds of the Roman Empire. The liturgy that thus evolved was the *East-Syrian*.

The East-Syrian liturgy is known also as the *Nestorian*, because of the desertion to Nestorius, or as *Chaldean*, with reference to the groups who returned to communion with Rome. It is still employed by the descendants of these Christian peoples: by the Syrians in Mesopotamia and by the Christians living on the Malabar coast (the most important mission territory of the East-Syrians). The East-Syrian Mass, as recorded in the oldest documents, gives indications of a period of Greek influence, but this soon came to an end as this part of Christendom became gradually isolated. For the sacrifice or anaphora three different formulas are in use.

In the Greek world, as was already noted, there were two outstanding metropolises, Antioch and Alexandria. The former became the center of the *West-Syrian* liturgy, also called the Liturgy of St. James; after the fourth century it was Jerusalem that took the lead in this sphere. We can get an idea of the radiating power of this liturgy of Jerusalem from the description of the Gallic pilgrim-lady, Ætheria, who had visited the holy places about 390 or (according to other interpretations) 417, and to whose account we will have occasion to return more than once, although it touches on the Mass itself only in passing. However, a lengthy description of the Mass is recorded in the last of the conferences known as the *Mystagogic Catecheses*, ascribed to St. Cyril of Jerusalem (d. 386). From Jerusalem, too, is derived the basic formulary for the sacrifice in the West-Syrian liturgy, the anaphora of St. James. After the Council of Chalcedon (451) the majority of the West-Syrians became Monophysites; their Church is called the Jacobite, after its tireless organizer (Jacobus Baradæus). The non-Monophysite Christians are the Maronites. A growing national consciousness provoked the introduction of Syriac as the liturgical language, although after the suppression of the Syriac by the Arabic, the vernacular Arabic was later adopted for the readings (lessons) and the litanies. The West-Syrian liturgy is distinguished for its numerous anaphora which were composed in the course of centuries after the pattern of that of St. James and of which the older are Greek in origin. There are over sixty, but the present-day Syrians use only a small portion of them.

Parallel to that of the West-Syrian liturgy is the development of the *Egyptian* liturgy known as the Liturgy of St. Mark. In the Patriarchate of Alexandria after the Council of Chalcedon there is the same sort of movement: mass desertion to Monophysitism and the adoption in the liturgy of the ancient national language now called Coptic (and later on, in part, the use of Arabic and, in the Abyssinian highlands, of Ethiopic [Géez]). But, besides the *Euchologion* of Serapion and the papyrus of Der-Balyzeh (containing remnants of a related Greek Mass-liturgy),[26] there survive also some documents of a Greek liturgy of St. Mark. The oldest of these are certain fragments of the basic anaphora of St. Mark, from the fourth-fifth century,[27] distinguished from the rest of the composition by the lack of many amplifications. The Copts possess only three anaphora formularies. The Ethiopian liturgy is known to have seventeen, but not all are in common use. The effect of the Monophysite attitude, which is inclined to view in Christ only His divinity, is noticeable in several anaphoras: the Coptic anaphora of St. Gregory Nazianzen, for instance, directs all prayers straight to Christ; the Ethiopian anaphora of Mary directs all to our Lady.[28]

At the time when the liturgical texts were beginning to be definitely fixed and determined, a third center of Greek liturgy was gradually asserting itself alongside the other two, a center destined to surpass the others in point of influence—Byzantium-Constantinople. All of the East-Slavic countries adhere to the *Byzantine* liturgy, in this case a liturgy vested in the Old Slavonic (Staroslav) tongue. The constant contact with the Eastern Roman imperial court brought about in this liturgy above all, a rich development of forms. Still only two formularies are extant, although these take in not only the anaphora but almost the whole Mass-service. These are the liturgy of St. John Chrysostom and the liturgy already noticed,[29] that of St. Basil. The pronounced unchangeableness of the priest's prayers has had repercussions of some consequence in the multiplication of hymns and other songs which for the most part vary with the Church year, not to mention the readings which, of course, comprise a variable element in all liturgies.

Byzantine and Syrian forms have been combined with primordial materials in the *Armenian* liturgy, the language of which—after a brief Syro-Greek beginning—became and remained the national tongue, classical Armenian. In addition, as a result of the return of the Armenians to union with Rome, the liturgy has been considerably modified by Latin influences; there is Psalm 42 *(Iudica)* at the beginning, and the St. John prologue at the end.[30] For the Mass-sacrifice proper there are extant several anaphoras.

Of all these Eastern liturgies the Byzantine is nowadays by far the most important. For that reason we shall meet with it often in the course of the following study. But for the present we must content ourselves with an outline of its structure, along with a description of some of the peculiarities that set it apart. In that way we shall see that its ground-plan was already to be found in the Antiochene Mass of the fourth century.

[26] Quasten, *Mon.*, 37-45.

[27] M. Andrieu and P. Collomp, "Fragments sur papyrus de l'anaphore de s. Marc," *Revue de science relig.*, VIII (1928), 489-515; also Quasten, *Mon.*, 44-48.

[28] Cf. Jungmann, *Die Stellung Christi*, 36 ff., 46 ff., 201 f.

[29] *Supra*, p. 38.

[30] Brightman, 416, 456.

The fore-Mass begins with two introductory rites of considerable length, which precede the readings. The first of these rites, developed during the course of the Middle Ages, is the *proskomide* or preparation of the offerings, which takes place at a special table, the πρόθεσις, at the north, or left, side of the altar—the churches are regularly oriented—amid many ceremonies. The second is the ἔναρξις, or opening, something like a condensed form of the Lauds in our Office, but supplemented by solemn incensations at the beginning and by the hymn Μονογενής at the end. The readings start with a solemn procession, the Little Entrance (μικρὰ εἴϛοδος) of the clergy, carrying the book of the Gospels (which had previously lain on the altar) through the nave of the church and back again to the sanctuary. Several songs with the trisagion ("Αγιος ὁ Θεός) at the finish, accompany this procession. There are only two readings, the "Apostle" and the Gospel. The fore-Mass closes with a general prayer for the Church, which passes into a special prayer for the catechumens—who are then dismissed—and a prayer for the faithful; each of these sections consists of a diaconal litany and a prayer by the celebrant—a typical arrangement in the Byzantine liturgy.

The Mass proper begins with the Great Entrance (μεγάλη εἴϛοδος,) the beautiful procession in which the offerings are carried from the πρόθεσις on through the nave of the church and then back to the altar. Meanwhile the Cherubikon or Hymn of the Cherubim is sung. The kiss of peace and the recitation of the Creed follow. After the usual dialogue the great eucharistic prayer begins. The priest says the invariable preface secretly while the choir is singing a prolonged *Dignum et justum est*. He raises his voice at the transition into the *Sanctus*, again at the words of consecration, and lastly after the anamnesis at the words of offering: τὰ σὰ ἐκ τῶν σῶν σοὶ προϛφέροντες. This is followed at once by the epiklesis and an intercessory prayer, and the reading of the diptychs by the deacon.

The train of thoughts in the eucharistic prayer is quite in line with the primitive tradition. In the liturgy of St. Basil it is much elaborated, in that of St. Chrysostom it remains very concise. The chief ideas of the latter —after the usual introduction and some references to the unfathomable greatness of God—are thanks for the creation and the Redemption:

> Thou hast called us out of nothing into being, and when we were fallen, hast lifted us up again, and hast done everything to lead us to heaven and to give us the Kingdom to come.

Words of thanks to the Triune God carry over into adoration, into an invocation of the heavenly hosts and into the *Sanctus* sung by the people. The priest then takes up the cry: "Holy":

> Holy art Thou, and holy is Thine only-begotten Son and Thy Holy Ghost. ... Thou hast so loved the world as to give Thine only Son. ... Who came and consummated the whole work of salvation for our sakes, and on the night when He delivered himself up, He took bread ...

The eucharistic prayer ends after the mementos with a doxology and the Amen of the people.

The *Pater noster* which follows is said in common by all. It is introduced by a deacon's litany and a prayer of the priest, and ends with the trinitarian doxology, "For Thine is the Kingdom." The priest blesses the people and elevates the sacred Host saying, "Holy things to the holy" (Tὰ ἅγια τοῖς ἁγίοις), the Host is broken and a particle is placed in the chalice and the deacon adds thereto a little warm water (ζέον.) After the priest and the deacon have received Holy Communion, the latter goes to the open doors and invites the faithful to communicate. The choir, which has just sung the κοινωνικόν, intones an ἀπολυτίκιον. A prayer of thanksgiving and a blessing by the priest—as usual with an introductory litany by the deacon—form the closing portion of the service, but there are added various ceremonies like the distribution of the bread (antidoron), which had been blessed during the *proskomide* but had not been consecrated.

5. The Latin Mass in Christian Antiquity.

A Latin Christianity makes its first appearance in North Africa about the close of the second century, at a time when in Rome itself Greek was still the standard·liturgical language. While for the Greek period of the Roman Mass we possess the valuable descriptions of Justin and Hippolytus, the incipient history of the Latin Mass in Rome, and in the West generally, is until the sixth century dim and uncertain. All we have are a few citations and the scanty light that can be thrown on the period by a reconstruction from later authoritative records. A close parallel can be drawn between the variegated history of oriental liturgies and that of the West; here, too, until well into the Middle Ages, there were various liturgies and therefore also various forms of the Mass. There is this distinction, however: in the West, Latin, which was the sole language of culture, was retained as the only language of the liturgy. Another feature which distinguishes the western liturgies as a whole from the eastern is the constant variation of the formulary—or at least of specific formulas—in the course of the Church year.[1]

From here on, we will consider the liturgies of the West other than the Roman, only in so far as such a consideration is requisite for a more complete exposition of the liturgy of Rome.

The Mass-liturgies of the West are broadly divisible into two families: the Roman-African and the Gallic. Although fixed forms were generally preserved, there were in both groups many local differences, consequent upon conditions in earlier times. No complete text of the African Mass

---

[1] The one exception for the Orient noted by Baumstark, *Vom geschichtlichen Werden*, 93 f., is the fragment of a peculiar Easter liturgy derived from ancient Christian Egypt (edited by H. Hyvernat).

Readings and chants are, however, determined by the church year calendar in the East as in the West.

has come down to us, but scattered references[2] give us sufficient grounds for believing that in many points it coincided closely with the Roman. The Gallic liturgies are further subdivided into four chief forms: the Gallican (in a narrower sense), the Celtic, the Old Spanish or Mozarabic, and the Milanese or Ambrosian.

The *Milanese* liturgy, still employed in the archdiocese of Milan, was from earliest times permeated with Roman forms, and to be more precise, right in the Mass itself, where the Roman canon was incorporated. But numerous details of pre-Roman usage survive, and even the parts taken over from Rome exhibit, to a degree, older forms than are found in the present Roman Mass.[3]

The *Old Spanish* or *Mozarabic* liturgy[4] is also in use, but only in one place, a chapel of the cathedral of Toledo which the great Cardinal Ximenes had established around 1500 to insure the perpetuation of this rite. The Mass book used here, the so-called *Missale Mixtum*, which Ximenes had had compiled from the manuscripts then at hand, shows Roman influence in several instances.[5] By using older manuscripts it has since been possible to regain a pure form of the Mozarabic Mass as it appeared before the Moorish invasion (A.D. 711).[6]

The term *Celtic* is applied to the Latin liturgies in use among the Celtic peoples of northwestern Europe, especially the Irish and the Scots. The chief propagators of this rite were the Scotch-Irish monks who in their pilgrimages and missionary journeys traveled through many countries. In the few documents that survive,[7] the liturgy reveals the character of this wandering monasticism. So far as the Mass is concerned, it is a liturgy generally composed of foreign elements: Gallican, Roman, Mozarabic and (not least) oriental patterns were borrowed and in some way or other woven together, so that it is only in a broad sense that we can speak of a distinct liturgy.

In contrast, the *Gallican* liturgy, used in the Frankish realm during the early part of the Middle Ages, shows a magnificent independence and exclusiveness.[8] Although it disappeared by the eighth century, at least the Mass from this liturgy is fairly well known. Amongst the documents that have come down, there is especially the work which originated near the

[2] E. Dekkers, *Tertullianus en de geschiedenis der liturgie* (Brussels, 1947); W. Roetzer, *Des hl. Augustinus Schriften als liturgie-geschichtliche Quelle* (Munich, 1930); F. Cabrol, "Afrique (Liturgie)", DACL, I, 591-657.
[3] P. Lejay, "Ambrosienne (Liturgie)", DACL, I, 1373-1442; P. Borella, "La Messa Ambrosiana," an excursus in Righetti, *Manuale*, III, 508-568.
[4] Cf. H. Jenner, "Mozarabic Rite," in CE, X, 611-623. See also Dom German Prado, *Historia del rito mozarabe* (San Domingo de Silos, 1928).
[5] *Missale mixtum*, with notes by A. Lesley, S.J. (1775) in Migne, PL, LXXXV.
[6] M. Férotin, *Le Liber mozarabicus sacramentorum* (Paris, 1912); idem., *Le liber ordinum* (Paris, 1904).
[7] L. Gougaud, "Celtiques (Liturgies)," DACL, II, 2969-3032. For the Mass, the Stowe Missal of the beginning of the ninth century comes to mind. The Missal of Bobbio is also often referred to.
[8] L. Leclercq, "Gallicane (Liturgie)," DACL, VI, 473-593.

end of the seventh century, the so-called *Missale Gothicum,*[9] a sacramentary which is supposed to have come from the monastery of Gregorienmünster in Alsace.[10] There are also authoritative records of the systematized list of pericopes.[11] In addition there are countless references to various particulars, especially in Gregory of Tours (d. 594), and in the seventh century *Expositio Missæ* at one time ascribed to St. Germanus of Paris.[12]

All the Gallic liturgies can be reduced to a simple basic type, especially in reference to two peculiarities in the priest's Mass prayers. These are composed, not as in the Orient—at least for the Mass proper—of a continuous prayer, not even for the anaphora, but of a series of individual prayers, even for the great (or eucharistic) prayer. Furthermore, not only are certain of these prayers subjected to the variations of the church year, but the whole series. Every feast of our Lord and every saint's feast had as a rule a distinctive formulary, although this did not exclude the possibility of having neutral formulas to be used at any time, of which the Masses discovered and published by Mone (the Reichenau fragments) offer fair samples.[13]

One question that up till now has been given no uniform answer is, where this liturgical type had its origin. How could such an important liturgical sphere arise in Western Europe without having the Roman mother-church, whose leadership was commonly accepted, as a center? How opposite to what we saw happening in the Orient, apparently without there being any such center at all. Msgr. Duchesne has suggested a solution[14]: he proposes Milan as just such a center. During the fourth century Milan was the residence of the Emperors. In ecclesiastical affairs Milan's influence later extended as far as Spain.[15] Accordingly, if we suppose that one of Milan's bishops who came from the Orient—like the Cappadocian Auxentius (355-374)—had established this liturgical type, then we can explain many of the coincidences with oriental usage, more particularly with Antioch—coincidences which are features of the Gallican liturgies and distinguish them from the Roman. Such points of coincidence are the offertory procession after the fore-Mass, the position of the kiss of peace,

[9] Amongst others, Muratori, II, 517-658; also Migne, PL, LXXII, 225-318. An edition in facsimile, with introduction by C. Mohlberg, appeared in Augsburg, 1929.

[10] G. Morin, "Sur la provenance du Missale Gothicum," *Revue d'hist. eccl.*, XXXVII (1941), 24-30.

[11] Above all, the Lectionary of Luxeuil (7th cent.), edited by J. Mabillon (PL LXXII, 171-216). Cf. P. Radó, "Das älteste Schriftlesungssystem der altgallikanischen Liturgie," *Eph. liturg.*, XLV (1931), 9-25; 100-115.

[12] *Expositio antiquæ liturgiæ gallicanæ Germano Parisiensi ascripta,* ed. J. Quasten (Opuscula et Textus, ser. liturg. 3; Münster, [1934]); also Migne, PL, LXXII, 89-98. The late date above assigned to the work is occasioned especially by the dependence on Isidore of Seville, *De ecclesiasticis officiis* (about 620); see Quasten, 5 f.

[13] F. J. Mone, *Lateinische und griechische Messen aus dem 2.-6. Jh.* (Frankfurt, 1850); Migne, PL, CXXXVIII, 863-882.

[14] Duchesne, *Christian Worship*, 90-95.

[15] Duchesne, *Ibid.*, 32 ff, 91 f.

the epiklesis. However, a great change must then have taken place even under St. Ambrose, for the canon of the Mass, as Ambrose describes it, is essentially Roman.[16] The opinion advanced by others, that the Gallic liturgy was originally the common liturgy of the West, abandoned later on by Rome and, particularly, by Milan, runs up against one big difficulty, namely, that the Gallic liturgical type itself exhibits a relatively late stage of evolution, so that, with all its complications and enrichments, it could hardly be earlier than the fourth century.[17]

The Gallic liturgy did not last long. In France the lack of any regulating center and the resulting multiplicity of forms brought on a growing distaste for this particular liturgy, so that by the eighth century the Roman rite was being substituted for it. On the British Isles it was the advance of the Anglo-Saxon element that forced the introduction of the Roman Mass. In Spain it was the recapture of the peninsula by the young kingdoms which had, in the interval, adopted the Roman system. We shall later come upon many details of the Gallic rites in our exposition of the Roman Mass. The following survey takes in the condition of the Gallic Mass in its final stage.[18]

The Mass begins with a fourfold song sequence. First there is a psalmody which, like the Roman introit, accompanies the entrance of the clergy. After the bishop has greeted the congregation (*Dominus sit temper vobiscum*) there follows the singing of the trisagion ("Αγιος ὁ θεός), in Greek and Latin. Then the *Kyrie eleison*, sung by three boys, and finally the canticle *Benedictus* (Luke 1:68-79), which is concluded with an oration. The service of readings consists of three lessons. The first is as a rule taken from the Old Testament, the second from the Acts or the Epistles, the third from the Gospels. After the first reading, the Canticle of the Three Young Men in the Babylonian furnace, *Benedictus es,* is interposed, along with a responsorial chant. The trisagion is again introduced, both before and after the Gospel. Before the Gospel there is a solemn procession led by seven torch-bearers. Following the reading of the Gospel there is a homily. And the fore-Mass is brought to a conclusion with the general prayer for the Church, which is in two parts: a prayer for the faithful and a prayer for the catechumens (who are then dismissed)—both parts, as in the East, introduced by the dialogue of the deacon in the form of a litany.

The Mass proper begins with a second solemn procession, in which the

---

[16] *Vide infra,* p. 52.

A solution along the same lines was suggested recently by G. Morin, "Depuis quand un canon fixe à Milan?", *Revue Bénéd.,* LI (1939), 101-108.

[17] Duchesne, 93 f.

This thesis was argued by F. Probst, *Die abendländische Messe vom 5. bis 8. Jh.* (Münster, 1896), 264-268. In earlier works also Cabrol; but cf. F. Cabrol, *La messe*

en Occident (Paris, 1932), esp. 37, 166 ff., where Cabrol no longer talks about a Gallic type which Rome had given up, but rather (by minimizing the peculiarities of Roman liturgy) about a common Western Mass.

[18] Cabrol, *La Messe en Occident,* 139-156; Duchesne, *Origines,* 200-240; A. Wilmart, "Germain de Paris (Lettres attribuées à) V, 1. La messe," DACL, VI (1924), 1066-1090.

clergy carry the offering-gifts to the altar—the offering of the gifts by the people had already taken place before Mass. This is the entrance of the triumphant Christ. The procession is accompanied by the chanting of what is called a *sonus*, and is brought to a close with another song. A kind of opening address (*præfatio missæ* or *missa* it is called) expounds in carefully contrived periods the motive and meaning of each particular festivity; an oration follows. Next comes the reading of the diptychs with the names of those who are offering the sacrifice, or for whom the sacrifice is being offered in a particular way. This closes with a prayer; then there is the kiss of peace, and another prayer. After that, at last the eucharistic prayer.

There is the customary introductory dialogue, then the first part or preface—called *immolatio* or *contestatio*, whose basic motif is thanksgiving but which frequently turns to petitions. This leads into the *Sanctus*. After the *Sanctus*, and usually linked to some word of it, comes the *Post Sanctus*, which forms a simple transition to the words of consecration. The next prayer is designated *Post secreta* or *Post mysterium* (in Spain, *Post Pridie*); it comprises mostly both an anamnesis and an epiklesis. What follows, the breaking of the Bread and the arrangement of the particles on the altar, is carefully regulated; an antiphonal chant accompanies the ceremony. A special prayer, variable like all the others, leads into the *Pater Noster;* this is said by the entire assembly, and ends in a frequently changing embolism. The culmination and climax of the Gallican Mass comes, at least at a pontifical service, just before Communion, when the deacon invites all to receive the blessing and the blessing is given; there are special collections of the formulas for this blessing, fitted to each changing feast. The Communion itself is accompanied by the chanting of Psalm 33 or appointed selections thereof or some other song; it is concluded with an oration.

Even this rough sketch makes one thing sure. The plan of the Gallican Mass, which reappears with slight changes in all the liturgies of the type, shows a definite leaning towards splendor and ceremonial. Even if we deduct some of the chants, which obviously belong only to the later stages of the liturgy, the trend is still discernible. The same impression is given by the rhetoric employed, ornamental and diffuse, often spinning its message out to such an extent that the form is lost and a prayer becomes an address, and an address becomes a prayer. The theological thought-structure reflects the constant upheavals provoked by christological battles; after all it was not only in Spain that the opposition to Germanic Arianism had an effect on Christian life. As an example, this excerpt from the *Missale Gothicum* will do; it is a *collectio ad pacem* for the feast of St. Clement. In it the favorite Gallican address to the Trinity becomes an address to Christ.

> *Concordator discordiæ et origo societatis æternæ, indivisa Trinitas, Deus, qui Sisennii infidelitatem ab Ecclesiæ unitate disiunctam per sanctum Cle-*

mentem antistitem et subdis catholicæ fidei et innectis perpetuæ caritati: exaudi preces nostras illamque nobis pacem tribue, quam quondam ætherem ascensurus Apostolis reliquisti, ut qui præsentium labiorum impressione inlegati fuerint osculo, tua custodia pacifici parmaneant in futuro. Quod ipse præstare digneris qui cum Patre.[19]

6. The Roman Mass from the Third to the Sixth Century

The beginnings of the Latin Mass in Rome are wrapped in almost total darkness. The oldest documents to register such a Mass are nearly all the work of diligent Frankish scribes of the eighth and ninth centuries, and even with all the apparatus of literary criticism and textual analysis, we can hardly reconstruct any records back beyond the sixth century, certainly not beyond the fifth. For the most part whatever is here transmitted as the permanent text—especially the canon, but likewise the major portion of the variable prayers of the celebrant, and the readings—is almost identical with present-day usage. We are thus brought face-to-face with a sharp contrast: the Latin Mass as it has been practiced ever since, and the Greek Mass to which Hippolytus attests—and a broad gulf between. In place of the earlier freedom within a given schema, there is now to be found a fast and solid rigidity of forms. Of these forms there is a veritable treasure, their variety conditioned by the course of the church year. Although well within the stiff limitations of the new outline, these forms seem to have explored every possibility of the newer arrangement. There are hundreds and hundreds of variable texts, especially for feasts of martyrs. There are one or two prayers by the celebrant in the fore-Mass, a prayer over the sacrificial gifts, an ever-changing text for the *præfatio* before the *Sanctus,* and a prayer after the Communion. This is the content of the older formularies of the priest's Mass prayers for each day's celebration.

The tendency to diversify the texts is set in bold opposition to the stability of what was later called (in a narrow sense) the canon, the essentially unchanging text of the prayer from the *Te igitur* to the concluding doxology, and its continuation from the *Pater noster* to the dismissal. In contrast to the smooth-flowing eucharistic prayer recorded by Hippolytus, the Roman canon, with its separate members and steps, and its broken-up lists of saints, presents a picture of great complexity. For the new science of liturgy, schooled as it was in philology, here was an alluring problem. The new science, as it developed till the turn of the century, had only the Clementine liturgy of the fourth century as the last link before the appearance of the Roman canon; how to fill in the hiatus, at least by hypotheses, proved an inviting question.

---

[19] Muratori, II, 554. For the theological bearing, cf. Jungmann, *Die Stellung Christi,*   78-93; 195-198.

Thus a number of theories were developed to explain the origin of the Roman canon, but as a result of their mutual disagreement little more is left of them now than ruins.[1] One of the boldest of these theorists, Anton Baumstark, not long ago, while making a new examination of the problem, himself summarized it in this very way.[2] That does not mean, however, that there is absolutely no hope of clearing up the history of this development. The only thing that seems doomed to failure is the attempt to gather from here and there bits of text that appear to be similar, and then expect to explain the whole configuration, for such similarities are to be found everywhere. The liturgy of Rome must have developed in Rome itself, although there may have been influences there from outside.

The first thing that was to be done during that interval between the third and the sixth century, was to translate the liturgy from Greek into the Latin tongue, the result, no doubt, of the changed composition of the Roman community. This transition was not a sudden one. The inscriptions on the papal tombs are found in Latin during the second half of the third century, beginning with Pope Cornelius (d. 253). If there were in Rome already before Constantine more than forty churches,[3] it is possible that Latin congregations had existed before Cornelius.[4] Yet even as late as the

---

[1] F. Cabrol, "Canon Romain," DACL, II (1910), 1847-1905, gives an extensive notice of this problem; likewise Fortescue, *The Mass* (1912), 138-171; idem., "Canon of the Mass," CE, III (1908), 255-267. The most important solutions proposed are: Chr. Bunsen (1854): in the canon two different parts have been shoved together, the main text of the priest and the the diaconal "diptychs"; P. Cagin (1896): the "diptychs" are an insertion which previously, in the older, ostensibly Gallican arrangement of the Roman liturgy, had had a place before the preface; P. Drews (1902): after the *Sanctus* there followed a continuation of the thanksgiving prayer, while the *Te igitur,* the *Memento* for the living, and *Communicantes,* after the model of the liturgy of St. James, originally had a place after the consecration as a resumption of the *Supplices*; Baumstark (1904): in addition, the prayers of oblation, *Hanc igitur, Quam oblationem, Supra quæ,* and *Supplices,* are to be traced from Alexandria by way of Ravenna; Buchwald (1906): the present-day text, aside from the "diptychs" is developed from what was left of an epiklesis, which in turn was bound up with the *Supra quæ*; and W. C. Bishop (1908): the clue to the original arrangement of the Roman canon

is to be found in the Roman prayers for the blessing of baptismal water, which must have been modelled on the original canon, now lost.

[2] A. Baumstark, "Das 'Problem' des römischen Messkanons," *Eph. liturg.,* LIII (1939), 204-243. Quite a number of liturgists have for a long time steered clear of the whole puzzle, e.g., Batiffol, *Leçons* (1927; first appeared 1918), 223 ff.

[3] Optatus, *Contra Parmen.,* II, 4 (CSEL, XXVI, 39).

[4] C. P. Caspari, *Ungedruckte, unbeachtete und wenig beachtete Quellen zur Geschichte des Taufsymbols,* III (Christiania, 1875), 303-466, esp. 456 f.

Cf. Eisenhofer, I, 151 f.; G. Bardy, "Latinisation de l'église d'occident," *Irénikon,* XIV (1937), 1-20; 113-130; idem., "Formules liturgiques grecques à Rome au IVe siècle," *Recherches de science relig.,* XXX (1940), 109-112, referring to Ambrosiaster, *In ep. I ad Cor.,* 14, 14 (PL, XVII, 255), according to whom many Latins had been overjoyed to join in the singing of the Greeks (*græce cantare*); it is rather questionable whether this refers to liturgical song.

Th. Klauser, "Der Übergang der römischen Kirche von der griechischen zur lateinischen Liturgiesprache," *Miscellanea G.*

year 360 the Roman rhetorician Marius Victorinus cites a Greek quotation from the Roman *oratio oblationis* of his day: σῶσον περιούσιον λαὸν ζηλωτὴν καλῶν ἔργων.[5]

While the variable formularies of the Latin Mass book could naturally arise only by a slow process, and even the principle of change and the method of its employment could not have been uniform all at once, there must have been from the start a requirement regarding the formulation of the great eucharistic prayer that could not be rejected. Was this first formulation already our Roman canon? The conjecture has indeed been put forth, and an attempt made to support it.[6] But it is more probable that the change-over from Greek to Latin produced many intermediary forms, particularly since in the third century we have not in general to reckon with any universally fixed texts. Besides, it is hardly likely that the sober temper of the Romans, which speaks so plainly even in the prayer-language of the canon, would have penetrated through and through immediately after such a transition.

On the other hand, at least the *core of the Roman canon* must have existed by the end of the fourth century. In an anonymous writing of this period a phrase is cited from the *Supra quæ*; the unknown author remarks in connection with his rather remarkable opinion that Melchisedech was the Holy Ghost:

> *Similiter et Spiritus Sanctus missus quasi antistes, sacerdos appellatus est excelsi Dei, non summus, sicut nostri in oblatione præsumunt*[7]

Mercati, I (Rome, 1946), 467-482, takes the stand that this change of language was much less simultaneous and quite a bit later (under Damasus). Cf. for an opposite view, B. Botte, *Bulletin de Théol. anc. et. méd.*, V (1948), 374.

[5] Marius Victorinus, *Adversus Arianos*, II, 8 (PL, VIII, 1094) ; cf. *ibid.*, I, 30 (VIII, 1063).

Cf. Frere, *The Anaphora*, 142 f. In this expression (which depends on Titus 2:14) there is question probably of an excerpt from a blessing which was spoken either before or after the Great Prayer ; cf. *Const. Ap.*, II, 57, 20; VIII, 41, 8 (Funk, I, 167, 552). A more external parallel in the East-Syrian Mass : Brightman, 264, 3.

[6] A. Baumstark, "Ein Ubersetzungsfehler im Messkanon," *Studia catholica*, V (1929), 378-382; idem., *Missale Romanum*, 13 f. In the phrase *summus sacerdos tuus Melchisedech* the word *summus* is somewhat surprising. According to Baumstark this is explained on the supposition that the fundamental Greek text read: τὴν προσφορὰν Μελχισέδεχ τοῦ ἱερέως σοῦ τοῦ ὑψίστου; in

the translation the words τοῦ ὑψίστου were erroneously construed with ἱερέως.

Cf. in opposition H. Engberding, "Einfluss des Ostens auf die Gestalt der römischen Liturgie," *Ut omnes unum* (Münster, 1939 ; 61-89), 67. C. Mohlberg has also voiced disagreement, *Theol. Revue*, XXVII (1938), 43. A decisive argument is that the word ἀρχιερεύς, which has much the same force as *sumus sacerdos*, was already used in reference to Melchisedech in *Const. Ap.*, VIII, 12, 23 (Funk, I, 502) ; cf. Botte, *Le canon*, 65. A word of like purport, *pontifex*, is also sometimes applied to him by Latins, e.g., Jerome, *In Ezech.*, c. 44 (PL, XXV, 429 B) ; Leo the Great, *Serm.*, 5, 3 (PL, LIV, 154 C).

[7] *Quæstiones Veteris et Novi Testamenti*, c. 109, 21 (CSEL, L, 268; PL, XXXV, 2329). The author is probably the Jew Isaac who had been a Christian for a time. O. Bardenhewer, *Geschichte der altkirchlichen Literatur*, (Freiburg, 1912), III, 520-525; G. Bardy, "Melchisédech dans la tradition patristique," *Revue Biblique*, XXXVI (1927), 25-37; Baumstark, *Missale Romanum*, 10.

The words of the canon that immediately adjoin these, namely the words which designate Melchisedech's gift as a sacrifice, are attested for the middle of the fifth century by the *Liber Pontificalis* which gives an account —here more trustworthy—of Pope Leo the Great's insertion *intra actionem sacrificii* of the words *sanctum sacrificium et cetera*.[8] Further, Jerome seems to play on the words of introduction to the Lord's Prayer, *audemus dicere*.[9] But it is above all St. Ambrose who, in his instructions to the newly-baptized, gives us an extensive excerpt from the Mass prayers, which differs very little from the respective prayers of the present Roman canon.[10] He is trying to show his listeners that it is Christ's creative word which turns the earthly gifts into the Lord's Body and Blood:

> *Accipe, quæ sunt verba. Dicit sacerdos: Fac nobis, inquit, hanc oblationem adscriptam, ratam, rationabilem, acceptabilem, quod figura est corporis et sanguinis Domini nostri Jesu Christi. Qui pridie quam pateretur, in sanctis manibus suis accepit panem, respexit in cœlum ad te, sancte Pater omnipotens æterne Deus, gratias agens benedixit, fregit fractumque apostolis suis et discipulis suis tradidit dicens: Accipite et edite ex hoc omnes, hoc est enim corpus meum, quod pro multis confringetur. Similiter etiam calicem, postquam cœnatum est, pridie quam pateretur, accepit, respexit in cœlum ad te, sancte Pater omnipotens æterne Deus, gratias agens benedixit, apostolis suis et discipulis suis tradidit dicens: Accipite et bibite ex hoc omnes, hic est enim sanguis meus.*
>
> *Vide quid dicat: Quotiescunque hoc feceritis, toties commemorationem mei facietis, donec iterum adveniam. Et sacerdos dicit: Ergo memores gloriosissimæ eius passionis et ab inferis resurrectionis et in cœlum ascensionis offerimus tibi hanc immaculatam hostiam, rationabilem hostiam, incruentam hostiam, hunc panem sanctum et calicem vitæ æternæ; et petimus et precamur ut hanc oblationem suscipias in sublimi altari tuo per manus angelorum tuorum, sicut suscipere dignatus es munera pueri tui iusti Abel et sacrificium patriarchæ nostri Abrahæ et quod tibi obtulit summus sacerdos Melchisedech.*

Certain details of this text will engage us elsewhere. Right now we must

---

[8] Duchesne, *Liber pont.*, I, 239.

[9] Jerome, *Contra Pelag.*, III, 15 (PL, XXIII, 585 A).

St. Jerome's authorship of a phrase which plays on the words of the *Nobis quoque* is questionable: *In psalm.* 72 (PL, XXVI, 109, *resp.* 1033): ". . . *ad capessendam futuram beatitudinem cum electis eius, in quorum nos consortium non meritorum inspector, sed veniæ largitor admittat Christus Dominus.*" Cf. Baumstark, *Missale Romanum*, 10, and note 11.

[10] Ambrose, *De Sacramentis*, IV, 5 f. (Quasten, *Mon.*, 160-162). Quasten, 137 f., has all the literature regarding the question of authorship, undisputed till a short while ago. The argument for Ambrose's authorship has meanwhile been continued by H. Frank, "Ein Beitrag zur ambrosianischen Herkunft der Predigten De sacramentis," *Theol. Quartalschrift*, CXXI (1940), 67-82, and O. Faller, "Ambrosius, der Verfasser von De sacramentis," ZkTh, LXIV (1940), 1-14, 81-101. According to Faller (99 f.) this work of Ambrose is a stenographic report of his preaching, which was not restricted by the laws of the *arcana*, in marked contrast to the *De Mysteriis*, and could thus give us such precious accounts. This explanation had already been suggested, but only as a conjecture, by F. Probst, *Liturgie des 4. Jahrhunderts und deren Reform* (Münster, 1893), 238 f. The same contention has been lately insisted on by R. H. Connolly, *The De Sacramentis a work of St. Ambrose* (Downside Abbey, 1942).

accept this as certain: the core of our Mass canon, from the *Quam obla-tionem* on, including the sacrificial prayer after the consecration, was already in existence by the end of the fourth century. We do not know for sure whether the slight differences in wording are to be traced to a divergent older text or are to be charged to the episcopal orator who, to be sure, was really concerned only with the words of consecration.[11] At least the first words, which have no real connection with anything preceding, would be a free rendering of the sense, since the prayer for the changing of the gifts, as thus introduced, is presumably the continuation of a previous presentation of the material gifts.[12] This fourth-century canon exhibits, by comparison with the eucharistic prayer of the third, only these new elements: a more pronounced expression of the prayer that the gifts will be graciously accepted, and the explicit prayer for a change in these gifts.

We might ask, are the intercessory prayers contained in our Roman canon, particularly the doubled *Memento*, part of the fourth-century contents? We saw how in the Orient these intercessory prayers, which had their roots in an earlier stage of the eucharistic prayer, had actually become part of it during the fourth century, and in part precisely in conjunction with the enumeration of the names.[13]

Another striking allusion to the Roman canon is to be found in the remark by which Ambrose introduces the quotation already given; everything, he says, that precedes the efficacious words of transubstantiation, is but human utterance:

> *reliqua omnia, quæ dicuntur in superioribus, a sacerdote dicuntur, laudes Deo deferuntur, oratio petitur pro populo, pro regibus, pro ceteris.*[14]

This could refer to prayers of intercession which would be inserted after the preface *(laudes)*. Still the intercessory prayers mentioned are such as the people would be invited *(petitur)* to make, and that is certainly unusual within the canon. Ambrose is probably telling off the prayers in reverse order, from the consecration backwards. His mind would recall the arrangement in which the general prayer for the Church preceded the Mass proper, the arrangement which was continued in the Gallican liturgies.

The question of arranging the diptychs was one that was at that very time much discussed so far as the Roman liturgy was concerned. In the year 416, Bishop Decentius of the Apennine town of Gubbio had consulted Pope Innocent I on this very point of usage. The bishop had been wont to

---

[11] Batiffol, *Leçons*, 215.
[12] By quoting Gallic canon-prayers, which are strikingly like Ambrose's, Botte, *Le canon*, 26, 37, 41, 43, builds up a more complete text and presents some noteworthy arguments that Ambrose was citing an existing text word for word. However, it still seems more probable that the original of the Gallic prayers was not Ambrose but

some other canon-text that was making the rounds.

[13] Serapion, n. 13 *(supra,* p. 35); *Const. Ap.,* VIII, 12, 40-49 *(supra,* p. 37); Cyril of Jerusalem, *Catech. mystag.,* V, 8-10 (Quasten, *Mon.,* 102 f.).

[14] Ambrose, *De sacramentis,* IV, 4, 14 (Quasten, *Mon.,* 158).

have the names read (by the deacon) before the celebrant, by his prayer, commended the gifts to God. But now some openly objected to this arrangement. Innocent replies to Decentius' question as follows:

> De nominibus vero recitandis antequam precem (al. preces) sacerdos faciat atque eorum oblationes, quorum nomina recitanda sunt, sua oratione commendet, quam superfluum sit, et ipse pro tua prudentia recognoscis; ut cuius hostiam necdum Deo offeras, eius ante nomen insinues, quamvis illi incognitum sit nihil. Prius ergo oblationes sunt commendandæ ac tunc eorum nomina, quorum sunt, edicenda; ut inter sacra mysteria nominentur, non inter alia quæ antea præmittimus, ut ipsis mysteriis viam futuris precibus aperiamus.[15]

The passage is not very clear, but despite a variety of interpretations, this much seems sure: according to Pope Innocent the reading of the names (on the diptychs) should not take place till after the gifts have been commended to God. The commendation must be understood to refer to the *secreta*. But the words that follow, that the names should be mentioned *inter sacra mysteria* indicate a recitation within the eucharistic prayer or canon,[16] perhaps after a prayer corresponding to our *Te igitur*.

That the continuation of the *Te igitur* was also in existence at this time, we can gather from papal letters of the years immediately following, which speak of a remembrance of the Emperor *inter ipsa mysteria*,[17] *oblatis sacrificiis*.[18]

We thus account for at least three formulas in the canon (before the consecration) at the start of the fifth century: *Te igitur* (with the continuation: *in primis quæ tibi offerimus*), *Memento Domine* (or some such formula for introducing the listing of names), and *Quam oblationem*. It is striking that the Spanish *Liber ordinum*, which in several other places contains a mixture of old Roman materials,[19] actually exhibits a Mass

---

[15] Innocent I, *Ep.* 25 (PL, XX, 553 f.).

[16] Cf. R. H. Connolly, "Pope Innocent I de nominibus recitandis," *Journal of theol. studies*, XX (1919), 215-226.

The *alia quæ antea præmittimus* are obviously the *secreta*, or more correctly, the general prayers for the Church of which the *secreta* at that time formed the last member. The closing phrase, *ut ipsis . . . aperiamus*, defies elucidation. The explanation on which P. Drews, *Zur Entstehungsgeschichte des Kanons* (Tübingen, 1902), 35, built his theories in good part, namely, that through the consecrated elements the way is readied for the intercessory prayers that follow, gives a new turn to this clause, which is apparently intended to present the purpose of the preceding prayers; according to this very unlikely suggestion, the *mysteria* have a subservient role over against the intercessory prayers. Batiffol,

Leçons, 219, is inclined to read *oblationibus* instead of *mysteriis*. Connolly, 219 ff., and with him V. L. Kennedy, *The Saints of the Canon of the Mass* (Rome, 1938), 23; cf. also F. E. Brightman, *The Journal of theol. studies*, XXIII (1922), 410, would construe *mysteriis* with *futuris* (dative: the prayer as preparation for the mysteries). But then the words have to be rearranged, and even so *futuris* is hard to fit in. The same sense is more easily attained by reading *fusis* for *futuris*.

[17] Boniface I (418-422), *Ep.*, 7 (PL, XX, 767).

[18] Celestine I (422-432), *Ep.*, 23 (PL, L, 544 C).

Cf. Kennedy, 21.

[19] For example, the notice of the use in Spain even before 580 of Roman formulas for penance of the sick; see Jungmann, *Die lateinischen Bussriten*, 110 ff., 113.

prayer which welds precisely these three elements into one.[20] Thus it would seem that these three prayers at one time actually existed alone, and the question then arises, whether the independent *Memento* had been from the beginning bound up with both the others.[21]

Only the following parts of our Roman canon could not be found at the beginning of the fifth century: *Communicantes, Hanc igitur,* and after the consecration, *Memento etiam* and *Nobis quoque.* However, these formulas too (with the exception of the *Memento* of the dead), are to be found in the oldest extant manuscripts of the Roman canon, in a form that must at all events belong to the sixth century. During the interval all these prayers came into being; and the others took on, where they differed, the form they have at present.[22] The authentic version goes back possibly to Pope Gelasius I (492-496), to whom the finished canon of the so-called Stowe Missal is ascribed: *Incipit canon dominicus papæ Gilasi,*[23] and to whom many other references point.[24]

But there is something distinctive even about the more ancient shorter version, in which the prayers mentioned above are missing. If we join to this version the preface and the *Sanctus,* and compare it then with the anaphoras of the Orient, we will notice the vast difference. Of course the difference is not so great but that in many spots a glimmer of the most antique tradition peers through, displaying again and again the resemblances to peculiarities of the Egyptian liturgy.[25] We have here to do with traditional material from a period when the congregations of Rome and Alexandria were linked not only by an intense sea commerce, but by the ties of a common language and culture, a period when there were still no

[20] Férotin, *Le Liber ordinum,* 321 f. Cagin, *L'eucharistie,* 62 f., was the first to refer to this prayer, a *Post-Pridie* formula; cf. Batiffol, 220 ff. It runs: *Per quem te petimus et rogamus, omnipotens Pater, ut accepta habeas et benedicere digneris hæc munera et hæc sacrificia inlibata, quæ tibi in primis offerimus pro tua sancta Ecclesia catholica, quam pacificare digneris per universum orbem terrarum in tua pace diffusam. Memorare etiam, quæsumus Domine, servorum tuorum qui tibi in honore sanctorum tuorum illorum reddunt vota sua Deo vivo ac vero pro remissione suorum omnium delictorum. Quorum oblationem benedictam, ratam rationabilemque facere digneris, quæ est imago et similitudo corporis et sanguinis Jesu Christi Filii tui ac Redemptoris nostri.*
Cf. Férotin, *Le Liber mozarabicus sacramentorum,* n. 1440.
[21] To the *Memento* we must append the second part of the *Te igitur: in primis quæ tibi offerimus,* which, in meaning, properly

belongs to it. In this way there is a smooth connection between *Quam oblationem* and the preceding section: *uti accepta habeas . . . hæc sancta sacrificia illibata. Quam oblationem.* This readjustment would give us the first form of the Roman canon, before the insertion of the names, which could have been made not long before Innocent I; the first evidence of the canon comes just a few decades sooner; cf. *supra,* p. 51 f.
[22] Leo the Great especially must have been at work here; see C. Callewaert, "S. Leon, le Communicantes et le Nobis quoque peccatoribus," *Sacris erudiri,* I (1949), 123-164.
[23] Botte, *Le canon,* 32.
[24] Kennedy, *The Saints,* 32-35; 58.
[25] The instances of relationship are collected in Baumstark, *Das 'Problem' des römischen Messkanons,* 212-232; some also in Brinktrine, *Die hl. Messe,* 22, Note 1, and Lietzmann, *Messe und Herrenmahl,* 45 f., 59 f. The following points of contact deserve special mention: A sort of *secreta* precedes

fixed texts but a living custom that sought uniformity with friendly sister-churches.

In an effort piously to preserve such traditions, someone in the fourth century must have worked out the basic text of the Roman canon. That this text, compared with the great eucharistic prayer of other liturgies, incorporated the lineaments of a greater antiquity, has already been demonstrated more than once.[26] To try to name the author would be a thankless undertaking.[27] But it will be well to point out a few of the author's stylistic peculiarities. He has a preference for word-doubles (the coupling of synonyms or related expressions):

> rogamus ac petimus; accepta habeas et benedicas; catholicæ et apostolicæ fidei; quorum tibi fides cognita est et nota devotio; sanctas ac venerabiles

the eucharistic prayer. The intercessory prayers stand just before a *memento* of the dead, after the consecration. Before the consecration there is a plea for the consecration (epiklesis).

There is also a whole round of agreements in the formulation of the prayers: In the introduction only Egypt has the form of greeting like our own: Ὁ κύριος μετὰ πάντων (ὑμῶν), while otherwise a longer formula from 2 Cor. 13, 13, is used here. There is almost the identical wording in the cry: Ἄνω (ἡμῶν or ὑμῶν,—both probably secondary addenda) τὰς καρδίας. Among parallels to *Vere dignum et iustum est æquum et salutare*, only Egypt has, for one thing, the simple wording of the initial words, Ἀληθῶς γὰρ ἄξιόν ἐστιν καὶ δίκαιον ... instead of Ὡς ἀληθῶς ... *et al.*; and for another, it employs the word *salutare* (ἐπωφελές). The connecting link *Per Christum Dominum nostrum per quem* has only one parallel, namely the equivalent in the anaphora of St. Mark: Ἰ. Χρ., δι' οὗ σοι.... εὐχαριστοῦντες προσφέρομεν. The same thing holds for the asyndetic and consecutive nàming of the angelic choirs: *Laudant angeli, adorant dominationes...*, and in the transition to the song of the angels, in the form of a plea for the gracious acceptance *(admitti iubeas)* of our song of praise, to which the congregation is expressly invited. And the fact that the oblation not only of the material but of the consecrated gifts is ascribed to the faithful *(qui tibi offerunt hoc sacrificium laudis)* is again reflected only in Egypt (Μνήσθητι ... τῶν προσφερόντων τὰ ἅγια δῶρα ταῦτα). There are also identical amplifications of the account of the institution, amongst others,

ad te Deum Patrem suum. To the Roman *offerimus præclaræ maiestati tuæ de tuis donis ac datis* there corresponds in Egypt not a simple Τὰ σὰ ἐκ τῶν σῶν σοὶ προσφέροντες, but the formal sentence τὰ σὰ ἐκ τῶν σῶν δώρων προσεθήκαμεν ἐνώπιον τῆς ἁγίας σου δόξης. —Strangest by far is the parallel in the prayer begging the Father's acceptance: διὰ τῆς ἀρχαγγελικῆς σου λειτουργίας God should take the gifts to the heavenly altar, ὡς προσεδέξω τὰ δῶρα τοῦ δικαίου σου Ἄβελ τὴν, θυσίαν τοῦ πατρὸς ἡμῶν Ἀβραάμ. The Egyptian counterpart belongs to the pre-consecratory intercessory prayers; there is an immediate connection with the text of Ambrose. The agreement has suggested the possibility that the entire canon is derived from Egypt; see *supra*, Note 1. Further discussion regarding the Egyptian links to the *Memento* of the dead and the *Nobis quoque*, infra.

Other points in common are found in the extra-eucharistic liturgy.

[26] Baumstark, *Vom geschichtlichen Werden*, 89 f., refers to the simplicity of the introductory dialogue and the lack of an epiklesis, in place of which there is a simple prayer begging acceptance.

[27] G. Morin many years ago suggested Firmicus Maternus, and more recently considered the conjecture well-founded; *Revue Bénéd.*, LI (1939), 103 f. The phrase of Gregory the Great, *Ep.* IX, 12 (PL, LXXVII, 957) regarding the *prex quam scholasticus composuerat*—which is considered as a good lead for this opinion—can really be referred to the canon only with difficulty; see *infra* in the discussion concerning the *Pater noster*.

manus; de tuis donis ac datis; respicere et accepta habere; sanctum sacrificium, immaculatam hostiam; omni benedictione cœlesti et gratia; partem aliquam et societatem; non æstimator meriti sed veniæ largitor; omnis honor et gloria.

Even in the prelude to the *Pater noster* that same trait is dominant: *præceptis salutaribus moniti et divina institutione formati.* Sometimes he employs a three-member phrase, and in the petition for the consecration (epiklesis) and in the prayer of blessing before the closing doxology there are even five members: *benedictam, adscriptam . . .* , and *creas, santificas . . .*[28]

In the same era in which the canon got its final shape other portions of the Roman Mass must likewise have been altered and amplified. The oldest sources of the Latin Mass of Rome exhibit, in every single Mass formula, along with the current expansion of the canon, by way of the preface, a regular tripling (or even quadrupling) of the priest's orations, as is still the rule: one (or two) at the beginning, one over the sacrificial offerings, one after the communion. Thus the communion obtained a conclusion in prayer, and the offering of the gifts, as its counterpart, is made grander in such wise that the gifts of the people are accented and emphasized. This latter is a peculiarity of the Roman liturgy. The valuation of the material gifts already insisted on by Irenæus has thus discovered a corresponding expression in ritual and prayer, more pronounced than in other liturgies. Besides these, there is also, just as nowadays, an oration before the readings.

The documents of the fourth century still show the Mass beginning abruptly with the lessons,[29] and these are followed—as in the oriental and Gallic liturgies of the following centuries—by the general prayer for the Church. With regard to both of these items the Roman Mass made changes.

The general prayer for the Church was still a part of the Roman rite under Pope Felix (483-492), and precisely with a division into prayer for the catechumens and prayer for the faithful.[30] After that there are no further records of it, and the oldest sources of the Latin Mass show it to have disappeared.[31] On the other hand an oration has appeared just before the lessons. This can be explained only as a part of some already existing introductory act, like those subsequently developed in other liturgies.[32] The adopting of such an introductory act, with the opening oration just spoken of, must be as old as the oldest examples of the Mass formularies which are regularly fitted out with such an oration. Now these reach back at

[28] Brinktrine, *Die hl. Messe,* 228-230; Cabrol, *La messe en Occident,* 76 f.
[29] Thus especially clear *Const. Ap.,* II, 57, 5 ff.; VIII, 5, 11 ff. (Funk, I, 161 ff., 476 ff.
[30] Felix II, *Ep.* 13 (Thiel, 263). Further details in the special discussion, *infra.*
[31] The probability that the second of the

four orations of the older sacramentaries belonged to this prayer for the Church, is discussed *infra,* p. 484.
[32] For the citation to show that this was the first part of the Roman fore-Mass, and for further details regarding the entrance rite, see *infra,* p. 263. ff.

least as far as the middle of the fifth century.[33] The introductory act was then filled out further with song and prayer. There is much to be said in favor of the view that it was under Felix II's successor, Pope Gelasius I (492-496), whose liturgical activity is celebrated in the *Liber Pontificalis*,[34] that here and elsewhere many important changes were introduced into the Roman Mass. It must have been Gelasius who introduced the *Kyrie*-litany, thus providing for the oration a preliminary dialogue after the oriental fashion, the prayer traditionally styled *deprecatio Gelasii*. Note, however, that the list of petitions in this litany coincides rather closely with the themes of the general prayer for the Church as it is to be found in Rome prior to Gelasius. We are justified in concluding that Gelasius had removed the general prayer for the Church, and had substituted the *Kyrie*-litany.[35] A concomitant factor in deciding to make this exchange might have been the thought that intercessory petitions had now been included in the canon —it might even have been Gelasius who gave them greater prominence[36] —and the further consideration that, since circumstances had voided the custom of separating catechumens from the faithful, there was no longer any reason for continuing a series of prayers, the apparent basis for which was gone.[37]

The framework of the Roman Mass—and this is the conclusion to be drawn from all the facts we have established—must therefore have been essentially determined by the turn of the fifth century, at least as regards the public utterance of prescribed prayers by the priest. Later on, in the course of our study of various Mass-elements, we will encounter only a few modifications by Gregory the Great (590-604)—chiefly in the *Kyrie*, *Pater noster*, preface and *Hanc igitur;* but these are for the most part a return to older simpler forms.

As far as the time of establishment or fixation is concerned, what was said about the arrangements for the prayers holds true similarly for the singing which served as an added embellishment to the prayers and readings. Not indeed that the texts were fixed this early, but the type had been determined and the scheme planned out. This is certain in regard to the old simple chants between the lessons, and probable in regard to the pro-

---

[33] Many formulas exhibit in their wording a striking resemblance to the style of Leo the Great (440-461) ; F. Cabrol, "Léonien (sacramentaire)," DACL, VIII (1929), 2552; cf. also C. Callewaert, *S. Léon le Grand et les textes du Léonien* (Bruges, 1948), ed. D. E. Dekkers. There are also indications that Damasus (366-384) was the first author of some of the Mass prayers handed down; F. Probst, *Liturgie des 4. Jahrhunderts und deren Reform* (Münster, 1893), 455 f.; R. Buchwald, *Das sogenannte Sacramentarium*

Leonianum (Vienna, 1908), 23 ff.
[34] *Liber. pont.* (Duchesne, I, 255) : *Fecit etiam et sacramentorum præfationes et orationes cauto sermone.*
   Cf. also *supra*, p. 55.
[35] Kennedy, *The Saints*, 7-38, esp. 33 ff.
[36] Kennedy, 38, 189, traces the respective form of the *Memento* for the living and the *Communicantes*, as well as the *Memento* for the dead along with the *Nobis quoque*, back to Gelasius.
   But cf. the opposite in Note 22 *supra.*
[37] Kennedy, 34,

cessional chants at the beginning, at the offertory and Communion. A more minute study will be provided later on in the chapters devoted to the particular chants. In any case, however, at this early period before the sixth century we have to reckon only with a very unpretentious type of singing, still affected by that timid attitude towards the musical arts which caused the Church to ban every instrument from divine service.[38]

The fifth century was for Rome a time of great calamity indeed, but the following century, with its Gothic threat and its Lombard invasion, was one long succession of disasters and oppressions. Yet it was in this very period that Roman worship unfolded into ever-increasing splendor. This development is closely linked with the extraordinary esteem in which papacy and Church were held in the Eternal City during these years. The papacy had become the one only glory and pride of the Roman population.[39] As the pope became more and more the only support of the afflicted city, and finally found himself burdened with the cares of civil administration, the papal church-service became the prime expression of civic life.

Gradually, along with the simple services held Sundays and feast days in the many titular churches of the city for the people attending, there arose also a community service, conducted by the pope himself in the church privileged as the day's *statio,* and attended not only by members of the court but by people from every quarter of Rome.[40] Stational worship of a similar sort is mentioned also in connection with other episcopal churches of the early Middle Ages.[41] These services must necessarily have been more modest in character. It was Rome that produced the most extensive results in setting down in writing this new type of service. Two

---

[38] J. Quasten, *Musik und Gesang in den Kulten der heidnischen Antike und christlichen Frühzeit* (LQF, 25; Münster [1930]), 84 ff.

[39] G. Schnürer, *Kirche und Kultur im Mittelalter,* (Paderborn, 1924), I, 322; cf. 257.

[40] Cf. J. P. Kirsch, "L'origine des Stations liturgiques du Missel Romain," *Eph. liturg.* XLI (1927), 137-150; idem., *Die Stationskirchen des Missale Romanum* (Ecclesia Orans, 19; Freiburg [1926]).

The stational services continued in Rome till the popes removed to Avignon. After their return the essential part, the celebration of Mass, was established as a *Cappella Papale* (nowadays as a rule in the Sistine chapel), in which the representation of the city was restricted to the highest circle of nobles: see G. Moroni, *Le Cappelle pontificie, cardinalizie e prelatizie* (Venice, 1841). On the other hand, the introductory *collecta* or *litania,* which was connected with the stational service more and more, especially

in Lent (see *infra,* p. 184) is still continued in Lent (under the name *stazione*) as an evening penitential procession at the church marked in the missal as the stational church of the day, people and clergy from all parts of the city participating.

[41] There are accounts for the fourth to the sixth century from Jerusalem, Antioch, Oxyrhynchus, and Tours; see A. Baumstark, in Mohlberg-Baumstark, *Die älteste erreichbare Gestalt des Liber sacramentorum,* 16* f.

For a somewhat later time and for Transalpine territory (Augsburg, Mainz, Trier, Cologne, Metz, Angers, *et al.*) pertinent notices are assembled in J. Dorn, "Stationsgottesdienst in frühmittelalterlichen Bischofstädten": *Festgabe A. Knöpfler zum 70. Geburtstag* (Freiburg, 1917), 43-55; L. Pfleger, "Frühmittelalterliche Stationsgottesdienste in Strassburg," *Archiv für elsässische Kirchengeschichte,* VII (1932), 339-350.

factors contributed: the greater splendor of the Christian capitol, and the Roman's native sense of order. The effect was not only to fix forms, but to fix them in such wise that they were regulated for the whole course of the year—*per circulum anni*, as the caption puts it. With this we come to the books of the Roman Mass over which we will tarry long enough to get to understand the references made to them in our later elucidations.[42]

7. The Oldest Books of the Roman Mass

What we get to know from the books of the old Roman liturgy is, as has been said, first of all the great festival services. This follows from the very character of the books themselves. They are divided according to the persons or groups performing the prescribed actions. For the celebrating priest or bishop there is the *liber sacramentorum* or *sacramentarium*, which contains the orations and prefaces that vary from feast to feast. Only in later times were the ordinary or fixed parts included, and among these the canon of the Mass, for the latter was anteriorly to be found on a special tablet[1] or was presumed to have been memorized by the celebrant.[2] For the lessons (readings), which were of course recited by two different readers, two separate books were prepared, the *apostolus* for the reader of the Epistle, and the *evangelium* for the deacon who read the Gospel. Further, a book was required containing the texts for the group of singers that now appear, the *schola cantorum*[3] who had to accompany the processions at the entrance, the offertory and the communion with their antiphonal singing. There was also a special book, the *cantatorium*, for the individual singer who took the lead in singing the old traditional responsorial chants between the lessons. And not to be overlooked, finally, there was the book of directions to help regulate the functions, in view of the great array of liturgical factors, especially for the rites that occur only on certain days of the year. This book even took into account the ordinary celebration of the stational services which took place each time at a different place and partly under diverse surroundings. The books which were composed for this purpose were the *ordines*, rubric-books for the cleric whose function it was to act as a sort of master of ceremonies in directing

---

[42] For a more detailed study, cf. above all A. Baumstark, *Missale Romanum* (Eindhoven-Nijmegen, 1929); Eisenhofer, I, 60-87; 103-111.
[1] Cf. H. Lietzmann, *Auf dem Wege zum Urgregorianum*, JL (1929), 136. Cf. the *rotulus* with the text of the canon sent by Pope Zachary to St. Boniface in 751; Zachary, *Ep.*, 13 (PL, LXXXIX, 953 B). A "canon tablet" from the 13th century in Ebner, 159. Cf. A. Manser, "Kanontafeln," LThK, V, 785.

[2] That the fixed main prayer of the Mass (*prex sacerdotis*) was recited by heart (*memoriter tenere*) is taken for granted in Augustine, *Contra litt. Petiliani*, II, 68 f. (CSEL, 52, 58 f.); Roetzer, 120 f.
[3] *Schola* here means not a school but only a group, a choir.
[3a] See Salavile, *An Introduction to the Study of Eastern Liturgies* (Trans. Barton; London, 1938), 185 ff.

the celebration. These older liturgical books are thus laid out like the actors' parts in a sacred play, as the share of each individual in a community performance. The oriental Churches to this day employ only liturgical books of this sort, while in the West, the liturgical books are ordinarily organized—for reasons which we shall consider later on—not on the basis of the participants but on the basis of the acts performed, so that everything for Mass is found in the missal, just as everything for the Office is bound into a breviary and everything for the dispensing of the sacraments is contained in the ritual.

Of the Roman Sacramentary, three different versions have come down to us, giving us three different plans for the priest's part of the liturgy, and thus furnishing us with another proof that as the period of Christian antiquity came to a close, there was little thought of a form for the Mass prayers that would be once and for all fixed and firm. These three sacramentaries—which were manifestly preceded by smaller collections of Mass formularies in various *libelli*[4]—were rather arbitrarily named, by the liturgists of the last centuries, after the three popes to whom they were ascribed, an assignment which proves to be at least partially confirmed.

The Leonine Sacramentary, *Sacramentarium Leonianum*, preserved in a single manuscript of the seventh century,[5] is a collection of Mass formularies arranged according to the Church year, and apparently finished about 540.[6] The first part, from Christmas to the middle of April, is missing. The Roman origin of the book is manifest in several places. The compiler seems to have drawn on every source at his disposal. Thus there are fourteen Masses for the feast of St. Lawrence, twenty-eight for SS. Peter and Paul. The Leonine is generally considered a private venture, and rightly, for some of the formularies are put together in part very casually, and some of the texts have a strikingly personal tone,[7] two things hardly compatible with a Mass book intended for general use. In fact one may well wonder whether at the time under consideration, namely the middle of the sixth century, a Mass book that would be the obligatory standard

---

[4] Cf. F. Probst, *Die ältesten römischen Sacramentarien und Ordines* (Münster, 1892), 78-80.

Here belongs also the type of short sacramentary which survived even in Carolingian times; see A. Dold, *Das älteste Liturgiebuch der lateinischen Kirche* (Beuron, 1936), 92 ff.

Similar *libelli* with a few formularies, but containing all the necessary parts already existed early for purposes of *private* Mass; see Ebner, 359 f. The best known example is the Stowe Missal (*supra*, p. 45, Note 7).

[5] The most important editions: C. L. Feltoe, *Sacramentarium Leonianum* (Cambridge, 1896); L. A. Muratori, *Liturgia Romana vetus* (Venice, 1748), I, 288-484; also in Migne, PL, LV, 21-156.

[6] H. Lietzmann, *Petrus und Paulus in Rom* (2nd ed.; Berlin, 1927), 30-35; idem., JL, II (1922), 101 f.

[7] The reference is especially to certain prefaces which are metamorphosed into noteworthy controversial speeches against personal enemies, chiefly false monks, e.g., Muratori, I, 301, 350 f. According to Duchesne, *Christian Worship*, 143, 144, they seem to presuppose conditions of the 4th/5th centuries.

text was even possible.[8] Conversely, it is quite thinkable that this compilation did have some official standing as an orderly arrangement of available liturgical materials.[9] Not a few texts—174 by actual count—have found their way from the Leonine Sacramentary into our present-day missal, and three of them are used daily in the Ordinary (*Aufer a nobis; Deus qui humanæ substantiæ; Quod ore sumpsimus*).

The Gelasian Sacramentary (*Sacramentarium Gelasianum*) is a real and proper Mass book. Two different forms of it have to be distinguished, an older and a later. The older form, *the* Gelasian,[10] preserved entire in only one manuscript, a text of the early eighth century which probably comes from St. Denis (Vat. Reg. 316), contains Mass formularies arranged in three books: the first book has the formularies for the Christmas and Easter cycles; the second for saints' feasts of the entire year from January to December, and, as a supplement, formularies for Advent-tide and the Advent Ember-week; the third book has a list of Sunday Masses and a selection of Votive Masses for the most diverse occasions and contingencies. The Gelasian is indeed a Roman Mass book in all essentials. But the special Roman local coloring is obscured by the fact that stational notices are missing and a large number of non-Roman saints' feasts are incorporated. Gallican materials are interspersed in several places—some prayers, some saints' names in the canon. The Good Friday oration for the Emperor has the wording, *Respice propitius ad Romanum sive Francorum benignus imperium*. And completely Gallican is the section devoted to minor orders (I, 95, 96), the texts of which crept into the Roman Pontifical, just as much of the other material of this sacramentary survives in our Roman Missal.

The Roman materials in the Gelasian Sacramentary, either in the form of a complete book or in small collections, got into France at the very latest in the first half of the seventh century. Previously, in the sixth century, the corresponding formularies must have been in use at Rome. There is no incontrovertible testimony that the book goes back to Pope Gelasius I (492-496), but this pontiff's reign coincides with the period to which we can assign the formation of the heart of the book. From the materials in this Gelasian Sacramentary, and from other liturgical materials meanwhile imported chiefly from Rome,[11] another type of Mass book

---

[8] Baumstark, *Missale Romanum*, 32 f.

[9] Cf. Th. Klauser, JL, XV (1941), 470: "Man findet hier die liturgischen Formularkonzepte der römischen Bischöfe vereinigt"—the Roman Bishops' ideas of a formulary are here brought together. Cf. also his remarks, JL, XIII (1935), 355 f. For the provenience of the texts, cf. C. Callewaert, "S. Léon le grand et les textes du Léonien," *Sacris erudiri*, I (1948), 35-122; B. Capelle, "Messes du pape Gélase dans le sacramentaire léonien," *Revue Bénéd.*, LVI (1945/6), 12-41.

[10] The most important editions: H. A. Wilson, *The Gelasian Sacramentary* (Oxford, 1894); Muratori, I, 493-776; also in Migne, PL, LXXIV, 1055-1244.

[11] The Roman material exists chiefly in a Gregorian Sacramentary of the time of Honorius I which will be mentioned presently.

was composed in France around the first half of the eighth century, the later or Frankish Gelasian. This sacramentary, often called the eighth-century Gelasian, is preserved in several manuscripts, the best known of which was written about 800 at St. Gall.[12] In this sacramentary the movable and immovable cycles are not separated but are confusedly intermingled.

The same is the case in regard to the third type of sacramentary, the *Sacramentarium Gregorianum* which brings us back once more to Rome. It is true the manuscripts are for the most part Frankish, and—except for some fragments—no earlier than the ninth century. But a comparative study has enabled us to reconstruct the exemplar sent by Pope Hadrian I to Charlemagne[13] in the year 785-786.[14] It is even possible to suggest the oldest attainable form of the sacramentary, as it appeared in the time of Honorius I (625-638)[15] or just a little later.[16] In fact, during the last few decades the conviction has grown that Gregory the Great actually produced this Mass book. Again, many of the prayer-texts still in use today stem from Gregory.[17]

The work was not thought of primarily as a book for the ordinary parish services; it was a papal feast-day and stational missal. That explains many of the omissions in the book—the customary Sunday service, for instance, which the Gelasian Sacramentary is so careful to provide. However, a second edition must have been put out for the use of the titular churches, although we have only indirect knowledge of such an issue.[18] Because the sacramentary sent to Charlemagne was incomplete—the Sunday Masses, amongst others, were missing—a supplement was added by Alcuin containing the requisite materials for parochial services and also mixing many Gallican traditions with the Roman.[19] In its further development, more and more material of the supplement—like so much of the Gelasian—was transferred to the sacramentary itself. And so a new type of the Roman Mass book was produced.[20]

For the liturgical lessons it was customary till far into the Middle Ages

[12] Edited by C. Mohlberg, *Das fränkische Sacramentarium Gelasianum in alamannischer Uberlieferung* (LQ 1/2; Münster [1918]; 2nd ed.; Münster [1939]).

[13] H. Lietzmann, *Das Sacramentarium Gregorianum nach dem Aachener Urexemplar* (LQ 3; Münster [1921]); corresponding to Muratori, II, 1-138; 241-271; 357-361.

[14] Th. Klauser, *Histor. Jahrbuch*, LIII (1933), 179.

[15] C. Mohlberg-A. Baumstark, *Die älteste erreichbare Gestalt des Liber sacramentorum anni circuli der römischen Kirche* (LQ 11/12; Münster [1927]).

[16] Klauser, *ibid.*, 173, Note 13, gives the earliest possible date as 642.

[17] E. G. the Christmas preface, the oration of Epiphany; B. Capelle, "La main de s. Grégoire dans le sacramentaire grégorien," *Revue Bénéd.*, XLIX (1937), 13-28. Even the present-day composition of the prefaces of Easter and Ascension must have been Gregory's work; B. Capelle, *Les Questions liturgiques et paroissiales*, XX (1935), 89-97; XXI (1936), 73-83.

[18] H. Lietzmann, "Auf dem Wege zum Urgregorianum," JL, IX (1929), 132-138, esp. 135 f.

[19] The texts in Muratori, II, 139-240; 272-356; 362-380.

[20] Of this sort is the Gregorianum printed in Migne, PL, LXXVIII, 25-240; it is the *Cod. Eligii* of the 10th century, edited in 1642 with valuable notes by H. Ménard.

to use not some special reading texts, but simply the Holy Scriptures, from which were read the excerpts which had already been appointed for a long time.[21] Later on we find lesson-indexes or catalogues, which marked the pertinent passages (chapters or *capitula*) ; hence they are called capitularies. These are the most extensive source for our knowledge of the old system which governed the liturgical readings, particularly the lessons of the Roman Mass. But even at an early period, there were special texts prepared for divine service, called lectionaries or *comes*[22] or (in accordance with their contents) *epistolarium, evangeliarium*. The most ancient lectionary of the Roman Church containing Epistles and Gospels is the *Comes* of Würzburg,[23] whose contents indicate the seventh century. Still such lectionaries are the exception until well beyond the year 1000.

The arrangement of the readings within the Mass from the earliest sources which make them known, has undergone fewer alterations than the prayer of the celebrant as transmitted in the sacramentary.[24] However, certain definite degrees of development, or types, can be distinguished, particularly as regards the changes of the calendar. Through the work of Theodore Klauser, the arrangement of the Gospel readings in the Roman Church has been fixed for the years 645, 740, 755, and an arrangement which was expanded in Frankish territory has been dated 750.[25] The last named arrangement indicates a final stage and it is, in all essentials, the order which survives in the Roman Missal. For the Epistle readings, besides the *Comes* of Würzburg and a *comes* worked on by Alcuin,[26] the most remarkable table is that of Murbach,[27] whose Church year is based on that of the later Gelasian, and which remained (along with the latter) more or less definitive.

A text book of some sort for the singing of the *schola cantorum* was a requisite from the very foundation of such an organization. Consequently, fragmentary remnants survive from even pre-Gregorian days.[28] But what comes to us as a complete work is a book that can also be traced to Gregory

[21] Cf. e.g., A. Dold, *Das älteste Liturgiebuch der lateinischen Kirche. Ein altgallikanisches Lektionar des 5./6. Jh.* (Beuron, 1936).
The whole matter is thoroughly discussed by G. Kunze, *Die gottesdienstliche Schriftlesung* (Goettingen, 1947), I.
[22] The name *comes* seems to have been used in civil life to indicate simply a book from which one drew instruction; Eisenhofer, I, 82. For the more strictly liturgical notion of *comes* see Th. Klauser, JL, XV (1941), 465 f.
[23] G. Morin, "Le plus ancien comes ou lectionnaire de l'eglise Romaine," *Revue Bénéd.*, XXVII (1910), 41-74, and the supplement *ibid.*, XXVIII (1911), 297-317.

[24] Baumstark, *Vom geschichtlichen Werden*, 89, cites an opposite trend in the Orient, with continually new creations; new arrangements of the pericopes are forever appearing among the Copts and the West-Syrian Jacobites.
[25] Th. Klauser, *Das römische Capitulare evangeliorum* (Münster, 1935), I.
[26] Critical edition by A. Wilmart, "Le lectionnaire d'Alcuin," *Eph. liturg.*, LI (1937), 136-197.
[27] A. Wilmart, "Le comes de Murbach," *Revue Bénéd.*, XXX (1913), 25-69. The *comes* contains also the Gospels.
[28] Cf. *infra*, in the discussion of the Offertory chants, Vol. II, Ch. 1, 2.

the Great, but which survives only in manuscripts of the Carolingian period, the *liber antiphonarius* or the antiphonal.[29] But by a process of collation, especially by the excision of formularies for newer feasts, we can arrive at the form of the Mass songbook in the time of Honorius I (625-638).[30] In these oldest manuscripts no melodies are given. It is not till the tenth century that we find the first witness to the melodies written in neums.[31] Before this time the songs must have been handed down by tradition in actual performance. That St. Gregory busied himself with ecclesiastical chant is a tradition which had wide vogue even in the early Middle Ages. Precisely in what his reform consisted we can only guess,[32] but this much is certain: the attribution of the "Gregorian Chant" to him is not groundless.[32a]

The antiphonal (antiphonary) which, properly speaking, contained only the antiphonal chants of the *schola cantorum*, was at this early period distinguished from the *cantatorium*, which contained the songs traditionally assigned to the soloist who intoned them from the ambo, while the people answered with a short verse of response—the songs called the gradual, the alleluiatic chant and the tract. Only a few such *cantatoria* have survived.[33] When the performance of these chants was turned over to a *schola* divided into soli and chorus, the text was likewise incorporated into the choir's antiphonal, so that, because of its new contents, the latter was also called a gradual.

The regulations of the external ceremonial of a papal stational rite were drawn up in books known as Roman *Ordines*. The list of these ancient documents begin with an *ordo* written down in England shortly after 680 by John the Chanter, arch-chanter of St. Peter's in Rome, who, at the request of Benedict Biscop, had been sent by Pope Agatho to help regulate the chant in the Anglo-Saxon church. John's writing is no longer extant in its original form,[34] but we do have two Frankish revisions, which are preserved in some eighth-century manuscripts,[35] both of which contain the order of the Mass.

[29] The six oldest manuscripts are printed in parallel columns by R. J. Hesbert, *Antiphonale missarum sextuplex* (Brussels, 1935).
[30] Th. Klauser, JL, XV (1941), 469.
[31] They have been issued since 1889 by the Benedictines of Solesmes in the volumes of *Paléographie musicale*.
[32] P. Wagner, *Einführung in die gregorianischen Melodien, I. Ursprung und Entwicklung der liturgischen Gesangsformen bis zum Ausgang des Mittelalters* (3rd ed.; Leipzig, 1911), esp. 188 ff.
[32a] Cf. G. Morin, *Les veritables Origines du chant Grégorien* (2nd ed.; Rome-

Tournai, 1904); E. G. Wyatt, *St. Gregory and the Gregorian Music* (London, 1904).
[33] The 8th century *Graduale of Monza* (printed in the first column of Hesbert, *op. cit.*) is such a *cantatorium*. The oldest Mass book with neums, the 9th century *Codex 359* of St. Gall, also belongs here; Eisenhofer, I, 78 f.
[34] A. Baumstark, "Johannes Archicantor und der römische Ordo des Sangall. 349," JL, V (1925), 153-158.
[35] Edited by C. Silva-Tarouca, *Giovanni "Archicantor" de S. Pietro a Roma e l'ordo Romanus da lui composto* (Atti della Pont. Accademia Romana di archeologia, Me-

The *Ordo* of St. Amand, which likewise preserves the picture of the Roman stational services, goes back at the earliest to the turn of the eighth century.[36] But the best known of all are the *Ordines* published by Jean Mabillon,[37] of which the first is for us particularly important. Its clear and detailed presentation of the course of the papal stational service, along with the preparations to be made for it, will be a good starting-point for much of our explanation of the Mass. The *Ordo Romanus I* is preserved in numerous manuscripts, sometimes with later adaptations of the rite and large additions. But in its oldest form it can be dated at least as early as the seventh century.[38]

How strong the influence of the papal stational service was as a pattern for solemn service can be gauged by the fact that in the lands of the North many revampings of this *ordo* appeared during the succeeding centuries. Sometimes they were simply illustrations of the papal Mass, like the eleventh century *Ordo Romanus III*, sometimes they were revised to suit the pontifical celebrations of a bishop, like the *Ordo Romanus II* (ninth and tenth centuries), or the *Ordo Romanus V* (tenth century) or the *Ordo Romanus VI* (tenth century). Wavering in its presentation between these two methods, we have the so-called *Ordo Romanus antiquus* (or *vulgatus*), which emanated about 950 from a monastery in Mainz as a part of the Romano-German Pontifical.[39]

morie I, 1; Rome [1923]). Of these two recensions, one, which has only Roman conditions in view, is called *Capitulare ecclesiastici ordinis*, continued in *Instructio ecclesiastici ordinis*, the other, revamped for monastic conditions, is called *Breviarium ecclesiastici ordinis*.

[36] Duchesne, *Christian Worship*, 455-480.

[37] J. Mabillon, *Museum Italicum*, II (Paris, 1689), recopied in Migne, PL, LXXVIII, 937-1372. A new critical edition was prepared by M. Andrieu, *Les Ordines Romani du haut moyen âge. I. Les manuscrits.* (Louvain, 1931).

[38] In Mabillon's text, n. 4-21. This section reproduces a text which was re-issued from a 9th century MS by R. Stapper, *Ordo Romanus primus* (Opuscula et textus, ser. liturg. 1; Münster [1923]).

[39] Edited by M. Hittorp, *De divinis catholicæ Ecclesiæ officiis* (Cologne, 1568), 19-85. M. Andrieu (*Op. cit.*, I, 494-506) has

done much to establish the origin and provenience of this *ordo*.

Of the later Roman *Ordines* of Mabillon we will encounter oftenest the eleventh, which was produced between 1140 and 1143 as a description of the papal service during the whole Church year. To the same period (before 1145) belongs the description of the liturgy in the Lateran basilica prepared by Prior Bernard; ed. by L. Fischer, *Bernhardi . . . Ordo officiorum ecclesiæ Lateranensis* (Munich, 1916).

Various accounts relative to the Roman Mass-*ordo* are found also in Mabillon's thirteenth *ordo*, which presents the ceremonial of Gregory X (d. 1276): in the fourteenth, composed by Cardinal Stefaneschi in 1311, but printed by Mabillon from a later recension, and in the fifteenth, written by Peter Amelii (d. 1403). Cf. Eisenhofer, I, 104-107.

8. The Roman Stational Services in the Seventh Century

The grand Roman stational worship, as it was developed up to about the eighth century, is especially important for the further history of the Mass-liturgy, and this for two reasons. For one thing, the service achieved a moment of stability, when all its component elements were set down in writing—as all codification entails a fixed arrangement, at least for some time. A certain interval must have ensued before the lineaments of such a form were again broken here or there. And secondly, by the very fact that this solemn service was written down in a definite and determined form and thus could easily be transmitted to other territories—by that very fact it became the model and standard for further shaping and forming the Mass generally. The effect of this example would be felt in the divine service of every village church and would even touch the ceremonial of low Mass.

On this account we must now glance at the stational services at least in their broad outlines.[1]

The pope comes mounted from his *patriarchium* on the Lateran to the appointed stational church.[2] In a later stage of development, in the eighth century, this trip has become a stately procession in which the entire papal court takes part[3]: first a group of acolytes on foot, and the *defensores* (the legal administrators of church properties in the whole city), then on horseback the seven deacons from the city's seven regions which they managed for the care of the poor, each with his appointed regional subdeacon. Behind the pope, and likewise on horseback, come the chief dignitaries of the Apostolic Palace, the *vicedominus, vestiarius, nomenclator,* and *saccellarius.* At the entrance to the appointed church the pope is met by those in charge of the place. The rest of the clergy have already taken their places on the benches which run the length of the semi-circle in the *presbyterium* (sanctuary) and around the altar, like the later choir-stalls. In

[1] A more minute study of the most important sections, along with reproductions of the text, will be found in the particular discussions of Part III. Here we must be satisfied with a summary, since we are interested chiefly in giving a general picture, in the main from *Ordo Romanus I* (PL, LXXVIII, 937-948). Archeological interpretations are found in Beissel, *Bilder aus der Geschichte der altchristlichen Kunst und Liturgie,* 296-328; Batiffol, *Leçons,* 65-96; Atchley, *Ordo Romanus primus* (London, 1905), 3-55. Cf. Card. Schuster, *The Sacramentary,* I, 66-71: "The Papal Mass at the Roman Stations."

[2] Only on specified days, days of penitence, especially in Lent, was there any other arrangement. On such days clergy and people from all parts of the city assembled with the Pope or his representative at one of the more centrally located churches (*collecta*), and from there, singing the litany and penitential anthems, they marched together to the stational church. Cf. R. Hierzegger, "Collecta und Statio," ZkTh, LX (1936), 511-554.

[3] *Ordo Rom. I,* n. 1-3, a passage recognized as a later addition, missing in many MSS, e.g., in the one published by Stapper. The changes incident to the arrival of the papal court for divine service, are noticed in E. Caspar, *Geschichte des Papsttums* (Tübingen, 1933), II, 785-787.

the middle, that is, at the vertex of the apse, is the slightly-raised *cathedra* or throne for the pope. At the right sit the six suburbicarian bishops, to the left the presbyters of the titular churches. The altar, a simple table, stands about the center of the semi-circle. Since there is no superstructure, it does not hinder the view from the back. The nave of the basilica has already filled with a large crowd, which has come in seven processions from the seven regions of Rome, each with its silver processional cross at the head.

The pope is first led to the *secretarium* which is built close to the entrance of the basilica. Here he is vested with the liturgical *paramenta*, a rather considerable number: *linea* (our alb), *cingulum*, shoulder cloth or scarf, *linea dalmatica* (our tunicle), and *major dalmatica*,[4] finally the *planeta*, the bell-shaped chasuble worn by all the clerics, even the acolytes. The last vestment put on by the pope is the pallium. Now the Gospel book is opened; it is held by an acolyte, not bare-handed but over the ruffled *planeta*; accompanied by a subdeacon he carries it to the altar, and meanwhile all stand up. The paraphonist then presents himself to the pope to announce which of the regional subdeacons will sing the Epistle and what choir soloist will sing the responsorial chants between the readings; one of the deacons has already been appointed for the Gospel.

When all is ready the pope reaches for his maniple and waves it as a signal.[5] The clerics who have been waiting in front of the *secretarium* with tapers and incense receive their command: *Accendite!*[6] And the singers who have lined up in a double row to right and left at the entrance of the *presbyterium* receive theirs: *Domni iubete!* The introit is intoned and the procession is on its way.

The signs of reverence which are given to the pope as he makes his entrance for divine service are noteworthy. It is evident that the *thymiamaterium* and the seven torches of the acolytes are in his honor; it is a reverence to which the emperor[7] and the higher state officials had been

---

[4] The *maior dalmatica* is not mentioned in the older text as printed in Stapper, 16.

[5] This gesture *(dum ei annuat pontifex)* appears to be connected with the taking up of the maniple *(mappula)*: the pope picks it up in order to give the signal with it, just as in ancient Rome the consul used the *mappa* to give the signal for starting the games.

[6] It is interesting to note that this initiating *Accendite* was still to be heard a thousand years later in French cathedrals on feast days. At Angers it was sung in polyphony. See de Moléon, 26, 67, 87, 129, 161; Martène, 1, 4, 2, 1 (I, 358).

[7] In the 2nd/3rd centuries it was part of the honor due the emperor and his spouse to

carry the fire ($\tau\grave{o}$ $\pi\tilde{u}\rho$) in front of them; several examples from Herodianus, *Historiæ*, are found in Atchley, *A History of the Use of Incense*, 51 f. Also some striking accounts (*ibid.*, 48 ff.) from Roman civil life where the use of incense played a role. Light (fire) and incense must have been considered as going together, even in the time of the Republic; *ibid.*, 56 f. Th. Mommsen, *Römisches Staatsrecht* (3rd ed. Leipzig, 1887), I, 423 f., speaks in the same sense of torch and brazier (a fire-pan for quickly relighting the torch), which must have been used at the solemn appearances of the magistrate.

The ceremonial survived in the Byzantine court. The victorious Heraclius was ac-

entitled.[8] The pope reaches out his hands to the two deacons accompanying him; they kiss them and continue to assist him in walking[9]—another custom which must derive from the ancient and originally oriental court ceremonial.[10]

companied into the city of Jerusalem in 619 *cum thuribulis et suffitu*; Eutychius, *Annal.* (PG, CXI, 1089 C) ; cf. Atchley, 53 f. In the discussion regarding the worship of images at the Second Council of Nicæa (787) the remark was dropped that even the pictures of the emperor were met outside the city with candles and incense (μετὰ χηρῶν καὶ θυμιαμάτων); Mansi, XII, 1014 D. Nicephorus Phocas was received in a similar manner in 963; *De cærem. antæ. byz.* (PG, CXII, 808).

In the West examples are to be found as late as the 12th century of lights (i.e., lights and incense) being carried before rulers (the Doge of Venice, Richard the Lionheart) on festive occasions; Atchley, 186 f. Corresponding to this are the prescriptions in the Ordo of Farfa (11th century.; *MGH Scriptores*, XI, 547; Biehl, *Das liturgische Gebet für Kaiser und Reich*, 168) for receiving the king; cf. Eichmann, *Die Kaiserkrönung*, I, 184 f.

Among noble Austrian families it was still customary even in our century to meet a member of the imperial house at the door with two burning candles (or, according to another communication, a servant stood at the foot of the steps with a candelabrum).

[8] Atchley, 55; E. Fehrenbach, "Encens," DACL, V. 14 f.; Batiffol, *Leçons*, 75 f.
    Cf. *supra*, p. 39.
[9] *Ordo Rom. I*, n. 8: *sustentantes eum*. Similarly at the offertory (n. 13 f.) and when going to distribute Communion (n. 20).
[10] Cf. 4 Kings, 7:2; 7:17; 5:18; Esther, 15:3.
    Hermas, *Pastor*, Vis. I, 4, 3.
    Gospel of St. Peter, n. 35-40 (L. Vaganay, *L'évangile de Pierre*, Paris [1930], 292-300), which includes the various previous attempts to explain the scene) : two angels support Christ, who appears heroic size, rising from the grave. Here possibly belongs the miniature in the Sacramentary of Henry II, a picture of the emperor holding in one hand a lance and in the other a sword, and supported at both elbows by a holy spirit; see the illustration in Eich-

mann, *Die Kaiserkrönung*, I, Frontispiece; the discussion of the picture (II, 105 f.) does not enter into this particular feature. This consideration will also help explain the depiction of God the Father in Raphael's "Vision of Ezechiel," of which Künstle, *Ikonographie*, I, 235 (cf. 238) remarks, that it appears "unsatisfactory that the arms of this 'God the Father' should have to be stayed up by angels."

The *sustentatio* by two clerics was subsequently transferred to the ceremonial of pontifical high Mass; see esp. *Ordo Rom. II*, n. 4, 9, 14 (PL, LXXVIII, 970 A; 973 A; 976A) ; *Ordo eccl. Lateran.* (Fischer 82 l., 21 ; 87 l., 21 ; cf. 886 l., 6) ; the Pontifical of Durandus (Andrieu, *Le pontifical Romain*, III, 638) ; cf. Durandus, *Rationale*, IV, 6, 10. It likewise stayed in the ceremonial of papal worship for centuries : *Ordo Roman. XI* (ab. 1142), n. 17 (PL, LXXVIII, 1032 B) ; an Ordo in Martène, 1, 4, xxxvii (I, 686 D), which can belong at the earliest to the 13th century. (See the stressing of *perfusio*) ; *Ordo Rom. XIV* (ab. 1311; here also in the recasting by Peter Amelii, d. 1403), n. 95 (PL, LXXVIII, 1220 C). It still survives in a diluted form; see Brinktrine, *Die feierliche Papstmesse*, 4, 7, etc., referring to two assisting cardinal deacons. Similarly the *Cæremoniale episc.* of 1600, still in force, provides for two canons to assist the bishop *in habitu diaconi*, and details their duties further : *procedente episcopo a secretario ad altare . . . ipsum medium facientes ac fimbrias anteriores pluvialis hinc inde sublevantes...et, si opus erit, eius brachia sustentantes deducunt* (I, 8, 2). Some of the ritual, like holding the edge of the *pluvialis* or chasuble by assisting levites, e.g., at incensing, was transferred to the ordinary high Mass of a priest, and is still demanded by rubricists ; Gavanti-Merati, *Thesaurus*, II, 4, 4 (I, 214 f.; 217 f) ; J. B. Mueller, *Zeremonienbüchlein* (13th ed.; Freiburg, 1934), 91 ; Fortescue, *The Ceremonies of the Roman Rite Described* (7th ed. rev. by J. O'Connell; London, 1943), 104.

The cortege pauses as two acolytes approach to show the pope an opened casket *(capsæ)* in which is reserved a particle of the Holy Eucharist. The pope adores, making a low bow.[11] When the procession reaches the place where the *schola* has its station, between the nave and the sanctuary, the torch-bearers part, four to the right and three to the left. The pope goes up before the altar, bows, makes a sign of the Cross on his forehead, and exchanges the kiss of peace with one of the bishops who has approached from his seat, as well as with one of the priests and the assembled deacons. At a sign from the pope, the *prior scholæ* brings the introit to an end with the *Gloria Patri* and the repetition of the antiphon. Meanwhile a carpet is spread out and the pope prostrates himself in prayer,[12] in silent homage to God—a rite with which divine service is opened even now on Good Friday and Holy Saturday. After a moment he rises, kisses the Gospel book and the altar. Meanwhile, during the interval of silent prayer, the deacons have come up to the sides of the altar two-by-two and kissed it. While the choir sings the *Kyrie eleison*, the pope goes to the *cathedra*, but remains standing with his face to the East, in an attitude of prayer.[13] Again he gives the signal to stop the singing of the *Kyrie eleison*, which is nothing more than the continuous repetition of the same unchanging strain. Then, if the day's festival appoints it, he intones the *Gloria in excelsis Deo*, and since it is an invitation and an address to the people, he momentarily turns to them (if he is not already facing them) but at once faces eastward again in the attitude of prayer.[14] At the end of the chant he greets the throng with *Pax vobis* and sings the oration to which all answer *Amen*.

This over, all in the half-circle of the sanctuary—the only place where there are seats—sit down. A subdeacon goes into a pulpit (ambo) and reads the Epistle. When he descends, a singer goes up into the ambo with his *cantatorium* and sings the gradual alternately with the *schola,* and (as

---

Although the formal *sustentatio* of the priest was not demanded as a rule even in earlier times, one medieval ritual, that of Soissons, does give explicit notice of it: The deacon reaches out his left hand, *super quam sacerdos dextram suam ponens statim ascendit ad altare pompatice*; Martène, 1, 4, xxii (I, 610 D); cf. *ibid.,* xix (I, 607 A).

[11] *"Salutat sancta."* The meaning of the ceremony, which *Ordo Rom.* I, n. 8 recounts, is not clear. Certainly the adoration of the Sacrament does not, as the context shows, exhaust the meaning. More details *infra*, Vol. II, Chap. 3, 5.

The word *sancta,* treated as an indeclinable noun, is occasionally used elsewhere for the Eucharist: *Ordo Rom. I*, n. 19 (PL, LXXVIII, 946 C); *Ordo* of St. Amand (Duchesne, *Christian Worship*,

461) ; a sacramentary of the 12th century in Ebner, 341.

[12] *Ordo Rom. I,* n. 8: . . . *ut ponat oratorium ante altare. Et accedens pontifex orat super ipsum.* By *oratorium* must be understood a carpet (*contra* Stapper and Batiffol) ; cf. *Ordo Rom. antiquus* (Hittorp, 52) : *prosternat se episcopus una cum pœnitentibus in oratorio.*

[13] In the "occidented" basilicas—thus most of the older churches of Rome—this meant looking towards the people. But this was not the precise point of view. In those churches where the choir faced east, the pope stood looking away from the people; Beissel, *Bilder,* 82-85. Cf. *infra,* p. 253.

[14] This direction is given very explicitly in the later text form printed by Mabillon (n. 9; PL, LXXVIII, 942).

the occasion demands) the alleluia or the tract. The chanting of the Gospel is attended by a flourish of ceremony. First the deacon goes up to the *cathedra* and kisses the foot of the pontiff,[15] who then pronounces a blessing over him. The deacon then takes the Gospel book from the altar, kisses it, and preceded by two subdeacons—one carrying a censer—and two acolytes with torches, he marches to the ambo from which he reads the sacred text. Then the papal subdeacon *(subdiaconus sequens)* takes the book, holding it with the ruffled *planeta*, reaches it to every one in the *presbyterium* to be kissed, and then hands it to an acolyte who immediately carries it back to the Lateran.

No sermon is considered. Nor is there any further mention of dismissal of the catechumens. With the disappearance of heathendom, the forms of an exclusion of those under instruction were no longer usable, and, except in the Orient, actually disappeared.

The pope again greets the throng with *Dominus vobiscum* and intones *Oremus*—but there is no prayer immediately following. Now the external preparations for the Mass-sacrifice begin. First there is the covering of the altar which up till now has stood there, a stately but empty table, decorated only with a costly cloth that hung from the edges[16]—the forerunner of the antependium. An acolyte approaches with a chalice over which he has laid the folded corporal. A deacon takes the latter, lays it on the right side of the altar and throws the open end to the second deacon at the other side in order to spread it over the entire top.[17] Then the offertory begins with the offering of the gifts of the people.[18] The pope starts proceedings by receiving the bread-offerings of the nobility, while the archdeacon accepts their offerings of wine. The other members of the clergy continue accepting the offerings, while the pope returns to his throne. After the people have presented their gifts, the archdeacon, at a signal from the pope, goes to the altar and, with the help of a subdeacon, arranges the breads that are to be consecrated. The chalice is placed on the altar and water is added to the wine by one of the members of the singing choir. After all this is done the pontiff leaves his place and kisses the altar and then himself receives the oblation of the assisting clerics. Lastly he lays his own obla-

---

[15] The kissing of the foot is a moderated form of the proskynesis stemming from the Orient. It was part of the court ceremonial as a prerogative of the senators in regard to the emperor; Eichmann, *Die Kaiserkrönung*, I, 189 f.

Just as the kissing of the foot was reserved to the emperor, so too it was, on transfer, reserved to the pope, and not to the bishops; cf. Th. Klauser, "Abendländische Liturgiegeschichte," *Eleutheria Bonner theol. Blätter für kriegsgefangene Studenten*, I (Bonn, 1944). 12 f. (translated in *Orate Fratres*, XXIII [1948/9] as

"A Brief History of the Liturgy in the West;" see p. 16).

[16] Cf. Braun, *Die liturgischen Paramente*, 192 ff., and the illustration, page 195.

[17] Only in the late Middle Ages did the corporal diminish to the small shape prevalent at present. Even in the year 1000 it still covered the entire mensa; Braun, 206. On the other hand, a number of altar cloths were used already in the Carolingian period. The use of three linen altar cloths besides the corporal became general only since the seventeenth century; Braun, 186.

[18] For details see *infra*, Vol. II, Chap. 1, 1.

tion (two small loaves brought for this purpose from the Lateran) on the altar. The *schola* has meanwhile accompanied the offertory with singing, but now a signal is given to stop so that the single offertory prayer—the prayer nowadays called secret—can be said.[19]

Then begins the canon, taking the word in the comprehensive meaning it then had. Each one has taken his appointed place. Normally that would mean that the pope, coming from his *cathedra*, would stand behind the altar facing the people—for the church usually was not oriented in our sense, but "occidented," the entrance towards the East. Behind the pope, and forming a row in the axis of the church back toward the throne, stand the bishops and perhaps the priests also. To the right and left of the pope and in front of the bishops, the deacons are ranged, and behind them the acolytes.[20] The subdeacons are on the other side of the altar opposite the pontiff.[21] During the canon there is no further change externally.

The pope begins the prayer in a loud voice. The subdeacons respond to the introductory versicles and take up the singing of the *Sanctus*.[22] The pope alone stands once more erect and continues the prayer, while the others remain bowed. The words of consecration, like all the other parts of the canon, are said audibly; otherwise there is nothing distinctive about them. At the *Nobis quoque*[23] the subdeacons straighten up and make ready for the ceremony of breaking the Bread; the paten for this has already been brought up to the altar at the start of the canon. At the *Per quem hæc omnia* the archdeacon too straightens up; when the pope elevates the Host in the sight of all and recites the final doxology, it is the archdeacon's duty to take the chalice by the handles—holding it with a cloth called the *offertorium*—and to lift it, too, on high. The canon is therefore quite simple and free of any other display. The *actio*, as it is termed, simply presents the pontiff's sacramental word, with no ornament other than his prayers. Even the succeeding *Pater noster*, with its appended embolism, does not break into the picture, at least since Gregory the Great had fixed it immediately after the canon.

External activity does not commence again until the *Pax Domini*, the signal for the mutual greeting with the kiss of peace, which the archdeacon gives first to one of the bishops and which the people, too, exchange. The pope initiates the breaking of the Bread, detaching a portion and laying it on a paten that is handed to him. Then he returns to his throne.

---

[19] Explicit testimony regarding this connection is first found in *Ordo Rom. II*, n. 9 f. (PL, LXXVIII, 973 C).

[20] Regarding these latter see *Ordo* of St. Amand: Duchesne, 461; cf. Batiffol, *Leçons*, 88.

[21] This position of the subdeacons continues to be mentioned and stressed in the following centuries. We will come across it again later as an element in the allegorical inter-

pretation of the Mass.

[22] This duty of the subdeacon is mentioned for the first time only in the later form of the text as printed by Mabillon, n. 16 (PL, LXXVIII, 944 f.).

[23] *Ordo Rom. I*, n. 16 in no way intimates that these words or those that follow are to be rendered in a louder tone of voice; they are, as a matter of fact, audible without this, as is the whole text of the canon.

The archdeacon advances to the altar while the *defensores* and the notaries take their station beside him to right and left like a guard of honor. First the archdeacon hands over the chalice with the Precious Blood to a sub-deacon standing at the right side of the altar; this is a safety measure. Next he places the consecrated breads in the small linen bags held by the acolytes. They are then taken to the bishops and the presbyters, who continue the *fractio* while the *schola* intones the *Agnus Dei*.

In the meantime, very inconspicuously, a more profane activity is going on, in reference to the papal court. The *nomenclator* and two other officials approach the pontiff to get the names of those who are to be invited to his table or to that of the *vicedominus*. They at once relay his invitations.

Then the paten with the Sacrament is carried to the throne. The pope communicates, but leaves a small particle which he places in the chalice, handed him by the archdeacon, meanwhile saying the words of commingling. Then he receives the Precious Blood, the archdeacon supporting the large chalice *(confirmatur ab archidiacano)*. Since those not communicating could now depart, the archdeacon first makes the announcements regarding service on the succeeding days.

Then follows the Communion of the clergy and people. The procedure is an almost exact duplicate of the reception of the gifts at the offertory. The pope and the archdeacon begin the distribution, others carry on. For the Communion of the chalice, a number of large vessels *(scyphi)* are used, filled with wine into which a few drops of the consecrated Blood from the pope's chalice have been poured. Meantime the *schola* is singing a Communion psalm. The Communion over, the pope goes once again to the altar and recites the postcommunion. Then a deacon appointed for this duty by the archdeacon, having received a nod from the pope, sings the *Ita missa est*, to which the answer is given, *Deo gratias*. The procession then forms for the return to the *secretarium*.

If we mull over this description in its entirety, we will get the strongest impression of a magnificent completeness. A great community exercise, heir of a thousand years' culture, had produced its final form in the church, lending to the divine service the splendor of its noble tradition. The person of the papal liturgist is surrounded by a court of many members. The ceremonial has absorbed courtly elements and has been filled out to the smallest detail. And still, through all this luxuriant growth, the bold outlines of the Christian eucharistic solemnity stand out clearly in all their essentials: the gorgeous pomp is suddenly quieted when the canon begins, and does not burst forth again until it is concluded. The old communal feeling, it is true, is no longer so strongly and immediately involved. The people apparently no longer answer the prayers, no longer take part in the singing, which has become the art-function of a small group, but the choir is not a profane intrusion into the texture of the service, but rather a connecting link joining the people to the altar. Prayer and song still sound in the language of the masses, and the people still have an important role in the action through their offering of gifts and their reception of Communion.

As new practices in the proper course of the liturgy, mention should be made of the commingling of the bread and wine before Communion and the introduction of the *Agnus Dei* chant in connection with the enriched build-up of the *fractio* rite. Both these elements the Roman liturgy derived from the Orient, the result of the constant flow during the seventh and eighth centuries of clerics from the East into places of importance in the Church of Rome—even to the papal throne.

The Greek influence, which for two centuries had also been felt in the Byzantine domain in Italy, forms at the beginning of the Middle Ages an important factor in the development of the Roman Mass. Even at an early period the *Kyrie eleison* and certain names of oriental martyrs in the canon —Cosmas and Damian, Anastasia—had already been introduced. The Roman Antiphonal shows a great many chants which were created at this time from Greek models,[24] and not seldom—according to the evidence of various *ordines* and also several manuscripts—songs in the West were sung in Greek.[25] The readings at a solemn papal Mass are still today sung in both Latin and Greek, following an old tradition.[26] Even greater was the influence of the Orient in other spheres of the liturgy, especially on the festival calendar. It was not without solid grounds that the statement was made that the Roman liturgy in the eighth century was seriously in danger of being intrinsically orientalized.[27]

But against this danger a counter-influence was at work in the very same period. The liturgy, which until then—except for the Anglo-Saxon missionaries—was in force only in Rome and its environs and claimed nothing more, soon rose up as the liturgy of a large kingdom.

9. The Roman Mass in France

Even before the eighth century some individual bishops of France must have been seeking a liturgical "annexation" to Rome. It was significant that St. Boniface, coming from the Anglo-Saxon Church, also strove for the same thing in his continental mission field. After 754, the year Pepin must have decreed the acceptance of the Roman liturgy,[1] the political

[24] Baumstark, *Vom geschichtlichen Werden*, 63, with the note 14.

[25] L. Brou, "Les chants en langue grecque dans les liturgies latines," *Sacris erudiri*, 1 (1948), 165-180.
Regarding Greek chants at St. Denis— which, to be sure, had a very different origin—see *infra*, p. 91.

[26] Brinktrine, *Die feierliche Papstmesse*, 14-16.

[27] Baumstark, *op. cit.*, 82 f.

[1] Th. Klauser, "Die liturgischen Austauschbeziehungen zwischen der römischen und der fränkisch-deutschen Kirche vom 8. bis zum 11. Jh.," *Hist. Jahrbuch*, LIII (1933), 169-189, esp. 170 ff.; H. Netzer, *L'introduction de la messe romaine en France* (Paris, 1910), 30 ff. As to the motives which determined this event, there is no unequivocal evidence. It might have been, as Baumstark, *Vom geschichtlichen Werden der Liturgie*, 61 f., maintains, that the

power likewise appeared on the scene, and from then on great progress was made in taking over Roman forms. Thus the Roman liturgy acquired a new home, a hothouse for a further growth that would be determined for more than two hundred years essentially on Franco-German soil.

Because of the difficulty of travel, one had to rely chiefly on books to achieve this transplanting of the Roman liturgy to its new ground, books which were obtained, not without trouble, from Rome.[2] Only in the very slightest degree was there any additional help from clerics who traveled to Rome to see with their own eyes how the services were conducted there. Amalar, the first great commentator on the Roman liturgy in the Carolingian kingdom, who made a trip to Rome in the year 831, prefaces the third edition of his work *De ecclesiasticis officiis* with a foreword[3] in which he points out a great many differences which he remarked between the liturgical praxis of Roman clerics and the practice as it had developed meantime in the North.[4] The fact, then, that books were practically the only means employed in transplanting this foreign liturgy, brought along as a matter of course the danger of misunderstanding; we will encounter such mistaken interpretations in not a few places in the Mass-liturgy.[5]

One of the big disadvantages in this system was that the books to be had from Rome, although they contained directions that went into the minutest details, really dealt only with the solemn form of the liturgy, the liturgy of the papal stational services. Of course in eighth-century Rome divine service was also conducted in another fashion. In the titular churches of the city and in the country towns of the vicinity, which as a rule had only one presbyter and one or the other extra cleric, the arrangement was necessarily quite different; the Mass was the Mass of a simple priest, not that of a bishop.[6] As a rule it was neither necessary nor possible to have a trained choir. And it is quite doubtful that the songs of the antiphonal,

Frankish rulers were influenced by political interest in a closer bond with Rome, which they had undertaken to protect, as well as by concern for a stronger internal unity in their far-flung realm. But Klauser, following Th. Zwölfer, *Sankt Peter Apostelfürst und Himmelspförtner* (Stuttgart, 1929), 64-151, esp. 96 ff., 130 ff., is right in placing the religious motive in the foreground, especially for Pepin: "The closer the juncture with St. Peter and with the Church in the city of Rome that is intrinsically bound to him, the surer appeared to the Germanic man of that day the entrance into everlasting welfare" (172). Ecclesiastical circles might also have been disgusted with a Gallican liturgy that often went to extremes, often emphasized the unusual, was most disorganized and frequently varied from place to place. They were thrilled, on the other hand, by the clear Roman arrangement; cf. Netzer, 18 f. This was especially true regarding the core of the Mass, where Gallic formulas often omitted such important elements as the anamnesis and the offering. This explains the appearance of the Roman canon in some books of the Gallic liturgies—the *Missale Francorum*, the Bobbio and Stowe Missals.

[2] On the lack at Rome of available books even in the 7th and 8th centuries, see Klauser, 172 f., 181 f.

[3] Amalar, *De eccl. off.*, præfatio altera (PL, CV, 987-992).

[4] See *infra*, Vol. II, Number of orations, incensing, place of chalice and paten, etc.

[5] Position of the deacon at the Gospel, meaning of preface and canon, *fractio*.

[6] Cf. *infra*, p. 208 ff.

with their variable texts—even prescinding from the melodies—were generally in use. In any case it was only at the turn of the seventh century that there was any obligation to begin every Mass—in town or country, Sundays and weekdays—with an introit, and to join to every Communion a psalm with *Gloria Patri* and an antiphon.[7]

Although filling out the lacunæ in the books sent from Rome, especially the Gregorian Sacramentary, and adapting and supplementing them as Alcuin had undertaken to do was hardly avoidable, it is nevertheless astonishing how devotedly the new texts were forthwith adopted in all other things. The Frankish sacramentaries which were now produced embodied many feasts of Roman martyrs whose very names must have been almost entirely unknown. All the native saints' feasts were displaced except Martin who was also in the Roman books. They kept even the notations regarding the Roman stations wherever they were found in the captions of the Mass formularies, even though they obviously had a practical meaning only for Rome.[8] Only a few Mass formularies, recognized as being post-Gregorian, would Alcuin allow the copyists to omit from the transcription. With similar fidelity the directions of the first Roman *Ordo*, directions which had in view Roman circumstances and presupposed the pope as celebrant, were copied and made the basis of local liturgical practice. It was not till the tenth century that anyone dared to work out a conscious revision and expansion of the Roman rubric book.[9]

Unconsciously of course, but nonetheless surely, profound alterations were made from the very outset in the Roman liturgy, especially in the Roman Mass—in fact, fundamental transformations. The exotic seedling, when planted in a new soil and in a new climate, was still pliant enough to be reshaped and modified by these influences. Still it was not primarily a Germanic world that it came face to face with, but rather a Romanized Celtic world, which had created for itself in the Gallican liturgy a religious mode of life all its own. The features which bring the Celt into bold contrast with the clear logical orderliness of the Roman, with his laconic brevity and stark realism,[10] are hardly to be distinguished from the features

---

[7] Ordo of John the Chanter (Silva-Tarouca, 204 f., 207). Further details *infra*, p. 208 and Vol. II, Chapter 3, 14. The pertinent sentences were not written in Rome, it is true, but the conditions of the writer's Roman homeland were clearly taken as a basis.

[8] On the contrary, *Cod. Reg. 316* of the older Gelasian has left out the stational indications.

Following not the letter but the spirit, Metz in the 8th century took over the Roman station arrangements for the Easter cycle. The list indicates churches in Metz and its vicinity for every liturgical day from Ash Wednesday to Easter Saturday, a clear but free imitation of the Roman pattern. See Th. Klauser, "Eine Stationsliste der Metzer Kirche aus dem 8. Jh., wahrscheinlich ein Werk Chrodegangs," *Eph. liturg.*, XLIV (1930), 162-193.

[9] So at least if the dating of *Ordo Romanus II* as a 10th century document is right.

The *Ordo* of John the Chanter had attempted an adaptation quite a bit earlier, but it was never widespread.

[10] Bishop, *Liturgica historica*, 1-19. The chapter also appears, expanded, as a special work, E. Bishop-A. Wilmart, *Le génie du rit romain* (Paris, 1920).

we are wont to emphasize in the German,[11] The restlessness and agitation, the strong passionate estheticism which mark the German character, must have been the Celt's too, but only in greater measure, and so were found already well suited to the Gallican liturgy. This liturgy continued in force and did not give way before the Roman till it had communicated to it something of its own stamp.

Going into the peculiarities which must have been anchored in the very temperament of the new people, we find two especially which had an effectual bearing on what we are considering: a predilection for the dramatic and a delight in endlessly long prayers. In both of these features the Gallic tradition is closer to the oriental mode than to the Roman; in some cases, in truth, we come across traces of direct oriental influence.

Take as an instance the *dramatic* build-up of the Mass-liturgy. Whereas the Roman system had a carrying of the censer only for the entrance of the pope and for the procession before the reading of the Gospel, the high Mass in the Gallic area introduced a number of incensations. With censer swinging, the altar was encircled according to an elaborate and fixed plan, first at the beginning of the Mass proper, soon also at the beginning of the fore-Mass. For the reading of the Gospel it was not enough that the incense envelop the book, but in conformity with a practice in vogue for quite a time, it was carried out into the midst of the assembled people, necessitating soon a multiplication of censers.[12] Then the parade to the Gospel-singing became Christ's triumphal march: to Christ resounds the *Gloria tibi Domine*, of which until then the Roman Mass knew nothing. The heightened dignity of the Gospel is further emphasized by the place in which the reading is done; the top of the ambo is reserved for it alone, while the Epistle and the intervening chants, particularly the gradual, must be satisfied with the steps *(gradus)*.[13] The appearance at this spot in the Mass of a poetic element, the sequence, was a related phenomenon.

The second basic change, the *multiplying of prayers*, was first of all noticeable in this, that, along with the one oration of the Roman tradition —we are concerned for the nonce with the collect before the Epistle— several others are introduced. Even strict upholders of the Roman manner do not seem to fret at this as long as the number seven is not overstepped. Again, at the high Mass of a bishop the solemn pontifical blessing, of Gallic tradition, is retained. And in a number of places in the Mass the private praying of the celebrant in a low voice is extended, with more and more texts appearing as the next few centuries go by.

The prayers which serve for this last-mentioned purpose are mostly

---

[11] See A. L. Mayer, "Altchristliche Liturgie und Germanentum," JL, V (1925), 80-96, esp. 83 f.; I. Herwegen, *Antike, Christentum und Germanentum* (Salzburg, 1932). [12] See below, pp. 317, ff.; 450 ff. and Volume II, Chapter 1, 5.

[13] Details below, pp. 432 ff.
For the dramatic propensities of the Gallican liturgy which were operative later on, cf. M. Boehme, *Das lateinische Weihnachtsspiel* (Leipzig, 1917), 7.

couched in the singular, unless some older specimens are utilized. No longer is it "we" but "I" that dominates. In phrasing and styling too they are far removed from the form of the Roman oration. The Sacramentary of Amiens,[14] which originated in the ninth century, contains in addition to the Roman textual contents a great variety of such prayers. A long series is placed even before the commencement of the Mass.[15] Then again several prayers for the offertory, five of them beginning with *Suscipe sancta Trinitas*, and the last the *Orate fratres*. Then prayers for Communion, including already the text *Domine Jesu Christe, Fili Dei vivi*. And finally the *Placeat* and a prayer while unvesting.[16] A large body of these prayers is already wholly or partly identical with the prayers still in use. There we find, besides the examples cited, several of the present-day vesting prayers and the *Quod ore sumpsimus*.

That all this silent praying was alien to the tenor of the old Roman scheme is noticeable even today in the external deportment of the priest while saying the prayers, for he stands not with arms outstretched, like the *orans* of the religious culture of antiquity, but with hands folded, a posture matching the usage of the northern countries.[17]

While most of the sacramentary manuscripts of the tenth century still display but few of these new accessions, they are to be found in bewildering profusion in the eleventh. What we have at the present is but a fraction of what was then developing. If there is one element in which this accretion of quiet prayers of a private stamp was made especially and emphatically prominent, and by which it showed most clearly how far removed it was from the spirit of the older Roman liturgy, that element is the *apologiæ*. These are the personal avowals of guilt and unworthiness[18] on the part of the celebrant, mostly of considerable length.[19] Usually they are conjoined to a prayer begging God's merciful favor.[20] They appear earliest in various documents of the Gallican liturgy[21] and have their parallels in

---

[14] V. Leroquais, "L'Ordo missæ du sacramentaire d'Amiens," *Eph. liturg.*, XLI (1927), 435-445.

[15] First Psalm 50 with versicles and orations, then prayers for washing the hands and vesting, then three *apologiæ* to accompany the walk to the altar, finally prayers for incensing; *ibid.*, 439-441.

[16] *Ibid.*, 441-444.

[17] This usage, with its symbolism expressive of submissiveness, of the resignation of one's own power to a higher one, is traced back to Teutonic culture. It is akin to the custom by which a vassal or liegeman vowed homage and fealty by placing his hand in that of his lord. Eisenhofer, I, 267; Heiler, *Das Gebet*, 103.

[18] The word *apologia* has here a meaning

analogous to the English "apology," an acknowledgment of guilt in a spirit of regret.

[19] Other Latin designations include *excusatio sacerdotis*; e.g., Leroquais, *Les sacramentaires*, I, 110; also *confessio peccatorum*, as in the 11th century Sacramentary of Echternach: *confessio peccatorum brevis sit inter missarum sollemnia*; Leroquais, I, 122.

[20] F. Cabrol, "Apologies," DACL, I, 2591-2601.

[21] In the *Missale Gothicum* (Muratori, II, 595 f.) is a formula headed *Apologia sacerdotis*; it begins: "*Ante tuæ immensitatis et ante tuæ ineffabilitatis oculos, o maiestas mirabilis, . . . vilis admodum precator accedo.*" In a variant version it was preserved

the contemporary and later sources of oriental liturgies.[22] Already in the ninth century they break into the Romano-Frankish liturgy, and by the eleventh century reach an ultimate of power and extent,[23] then disappear as at a blow,[24] with only a small remnant surviving, amongst others especially our *Confiteor* and the *oratio S. Ambrosii* in the preparation prayers of the Roman Missal.

The zenith in the development of the *apologiæ* is evinced in the Mass *ordo* which had its origin about 1030 and which Flacius Illyricus, the historian amongst the Reformers, published in 1557 from an old manuscript as an example of a Mass in use (he thought) about 700—before the Romish Mass!—in which there was no acknowledgment of the Real Presence; hence it is generally styled *Missa Illyrica* for short.[25] This Mass order, which assembles practically all the prayer formulas to be gotten anywhere at that time, contains *apologiæ* after vesting, before entering the house of God, a lengthy series after the kissing of the altar, one during the *Gloria*, again a long list during the chants between the readings, and another group during the offertory singing, during the preparation of the gift-offerings, after the *Orate fratres*, during the *Sanctus*, and during the Communion of the people.[26] A phenomenon akin to this is the tenth-century sacramentary from St. Thierry near Reims, which has seven formularies for a *Missa generalis*, each of which consists of collects, *Super oblata*, preface, *Hanc igitur* and *Ad complendum*—all having the form and mood of *apologiæ*, put in the plural.[27]

in the Romano-Frankish liturgical documents, e.g., in two revisions of the *Missa Illyrica*: Martène, 1, 4, iv (I, 499 E, 501 A).
[22] Cf. Jungmann, *Die Stellung Christi im liturgischen Gebet*, 223 f.
[23] Examples from the period in question in Martène, 1, 4, iv-xvi (I, 490-598).
[24] Still there are exceptions even in a later period. Thus the Seckau Missal of about 1170 (Koeck, 19 f.) has *apologiæ* during the *Gloria*, before the sermon, during the *Credo*, before the canon. And a Westminster Missal of about 1370 (ed. Legg; HBS, V, 495-498) still has six *apologiæ* during the *Gloria*.
[25] This dating follows the investigations of J. Braun, "Alter und Herkunft der sog. Missa Illyrica," *Stimmen aus Maria-Laach*, LXIX (1905, II), 143-155. Braun suggests Minden as the place of origin of this Mass *ordo* intended for a bishop. Flacius Illyricus himself soon realized his mistake but it was impossible for him to recall the copies already issued.

Cf. also F. Cabrol, "Flacius Illyricus." DACL, V (1923), 1625-1635. Cabrol's very conjectural transfer of the origin of the *Missa Illyrica* to the court of Charlemagne is based almost exclusively on a consideration of the *apologiæ* and on the attribution of a large portion of them to Alcuin (instead of to the 10th century Pseudo-Alcuin; cf. *infra*, Vol. II, Chap. 3, 12, Note 5). The study of the Mass *ordo* (*infra*, pp. 273, ff., 281 ff.) confirms Braun's dating. The text of the *Missa Illyrica* in Martène, 1, 4, iv (I, 490-518); also in Migne, PL, CXXXVIII, 1305-1336, and in Bona, *Rerum liturg. libri duo*, App. (913-954).
[26] There are in all some 35 formulas, filling altogether about nine folio-columns in Martène, and forming actually a third of the complete Mass *ordo*.
[27] Martène, 1, 4, x (I, 552-562). These are obviously Votive Masses for private celebration. See *infra*, p. 217.

It is not easy to comprehend the world of thought in which so remarkable a crop could be produced, a world which speaks to us in almost frightening fashion of the consciousness of sin and its attendant miseries.[28] Besides a popular factor which we cannot well grasp, there are two things we must take notice of. On the one hand, there was the Gallic tendency to confusing God and Christ, which obscured the concept of saving grace. On the other, the fact that up into the eleventh century sacramental penance was customary only once a year even in monastic institutions,[29] while for an acknowledgment or confession as such, because of the *erubescentia* attached to it, there was claimed an extraordinarily high power of forgiveness.[30] The disappearance of the *apologiæ* is bound up with the clarification of the notions of forgiveness and the growth of the practice of more frequent sacramental confession.

If there is here a tie-in with the history of dogma, the case is even clearer with regard to the apparently insignificant text-change which not a few of the variable prayer formulas of the Roman Mass underwent, a change which became more and more a determinative standard for the texts newly incorporated. The orations of the Roman Sacramentary were so constructed that they concluded, without exception, in a *Per*, that is to say, they were directed to God the Father and could come to a close with the well-known mediation formula. Not a few of these orations, wherever they offered the opportunity, now acquired the conclusion *Qui (vivis)*, that is, they were now considered as being addressed to the Son even if they perchance had the introductory greeting *Deus qui*. The inclination to make such a change derived from the style of prayer in the Gallican liturgy, whose earliest development in the atmosphere of the anti-Arian struggle had led to a similar rejection of this mediation formula and a similar stressing of the essential equality of the three divine Persons, just as the oriental liturgies have done.[31] A connected element, the Gallican emphasis on the Trinity, has had visible effect even on our present Ordinary of the Mass, in the two prayers addressed to the Holy Trinity, *Suscipe sancta Trinitas* and *Placeat tibi*. The same grounds have been effective in annexing to the liturgy the *Credo* which originated amidst the doctrinal battles of the East.[32]

---

[28] As an example of an unnaturally extended self-accusation this shorter formula, which in the *Missa Illyrica* is said after kissing the altar, will do: *"Suscipe confessionem meam, unica spes salutis meæ, Domine Deus meus, Jesu Christe, quia gula, ebrietate, fornicatione, libidine, tristitia, acidia, somnolentia, negligentia, ira, cupiditate, invidia, malitia, odio, detractione, periurio, falsitate, mendacio, vana gloria, levitate et superbia perditus sum et omnino cogitatione, locutione, actione atque omnibus malis extinctus sum; qui iustificas impios et vivificas mortuos, iustifica me et* resuscita me, Domine Deus meus. Qui vivis." Martène, 1, 4, iv (I, 496 B). The formula occurs again *ibid.*, v, vi, xiii, xv (I, 520 C, 531 B, 575 D, 588 B).

[29] Cf. Jungmann, *Die lateinischen Buszriten*, 172 ff., 282-285.

[30] See the bibliography *ibid.*, 268.

[31] Details below, p. 380 ff.

[32] A complete picture of this background in J. A. Jungmann, "Die Abwehr des germanischen Arianismus und der Umbruch der religiösen Kultur im frühen Mittelalter," ZkTh, LXIX (1947), 36-99, esp. 54 ff., 57 ff.

More profound and more enduring has been the effect of another circumstance on the basic character of the Roman Mass. When the Roman liturgy was brought into France it invaded an area where only a small layer of society—principally the clergy—knew the language of the liturgy. True, the Gallican liturgy was also a Latin one, but it was not till after its disappearance that the Romance popular dialect became so remote from the basic Latin that it was no longer possible for one not specially educated to understand the latter. But Latin was the universal literary language and consequently the only language considered for divine service. Even a translation of the Scriptures into the vernacular—whether Romance or one of the German dialects—so that the vernacular would actually become a "literary" language, and so capable of becoming a liturgical language, was at that time unthought of. And because even amongst the laity the leaders were so impressed by things Roman that they recognized and acknowledged therein the highest culture, there was therefore no wish or demand for the use of their own language.

Quite different was the course of affairs a short while later amongst the Slavs, where Sts. Cyril and Methodius from the very beginning conducted services—and at least by the death of St. Cyril (869) even the Roman Mass[33]—in the Slavic tongue. German clerics were their bitterest opponents, alleging that they dared conduct divine worship in a *lingua barbarica*, whereas in accordance with the inscription on the Cross, this should be done only *hebraice, græce et latine*. One could reply that Slavic was not a *lingua barbarica* since there were versions of Holy Scripture in that tongue and in at least a portion of Slavic territory the Roman liturgy has survived to this day in the Old Slavic, the Glagolitic, language.[34]

Thus in the Carolingian empire the Mass-liturgy, so far as understanding its language was concerned, became a clerical reserve. A new kind of *disciplina arcani* or discipline of the secret had developed, a concealment of things holy, not from the heathen—there were none—but from the Christian people themselves.

At the time the situation was not conceived of as a problem. Aside from the consideration that religion is always concerned with mysteries, and concealment and secrecy have ever been associated with mysteries—aside from this, the development also encountered a theological notion which led to the same conclusion from two different angles.

---

[33] This is proved by the Kiev fragments of a Roman Missal in the Old Slavic language; it is modelled on a Gregorian Sacramentary of the 7th century and could have been done only by Cyril himself while in Rome; see: C. Mohlberg, "Il messale glagolitico di Kiew," *Atti della pont. Accademia romana di archeologia, Memorie* II (Rome, 1928), 207-320, esp. 223 f., 280 ff. The same line of thought is suggested by

F. Ušenicnik in his study in *Bogoslovni Vestnik*, X (1930); see the review, JL, XI (1931), 326. Even earlier various things pointed to the fact that this had to do with Roman liturgy; see H. v. Schubert, *Geschichte der christlichen Kirche im Frümittelalter* (Tübingen, 1921), 520.
[34] Details in L. Rogic, "Glagolitische Schrift," LThK, IV (1932), 513-515.

In the concept of the Church, the foreground was no longer, as in earlier times, the communion of the redeemed bound together with a glorious Christ in one Mystical Body. In Spain and France the fight against Arianism had caused the thought of the glorified God-man, mediator and high-priest, to be brushed aside in favor of a stronger accentuation of His divine prerogative.[35] One necessarily became more clearly aware of the external earthly Church, its hierarchical structure of clergy and laity. The social position of the clergy—who were far and wide the governing class in society and practically alone in possession of a higher education—contributed no little to estranging them, lifting them above the people.

In addition a change had been taking place in the concept of the Eucharist. In the earlier periods of liturgical life we saw the emphasis placed on the Mass as a *eucharistia*, as a prayer of thanks from the congregation who were invited to participate by a *Gratias agamus*, and whose gifts, in the course of the Mass, were elevated by the word of the priest into a heavenly sacrificial offering. But now an opposite view was taking precedence in men's minds, swayed as they were especially by the teaching of Isidore of Seville.[36] The Eucharist is the *bona gratia*,[37] which God grants us, and which at the climactic moment of the Mass, the consecration, descends to us. Soon scholars were earnestly at work trying to discover when, precisely, in the Mass-liturgy this descent took place. According to St. Isidore it was the *oratio sexta*, that group of prayers in the Gallic liturgy which began with the *Post Sanctus* and to which the *Post Pridie* belonged.[38] Transferring this to the Roman liturgy, it is the series of prayers from the *Te igitur* to the doxology just before the *Pater noster*. By grasping suggestions that apparently led to this way of thinking, this portion of the Mass is explained as the canon in the sense of Isidor's *oratio sexta*,[39] to which the preface serves as a solemn but important introduction.[40] And this section is now enveloped in a second veil of mysterious isolation, being now spoken by the priest in a soft, low tone. The priest alone is to enter this inmost sanc-

---

[35] See *supra*, p. 38 ff.

[36] For his influence in the Frankish area see *supra*, p. 46., Note 12. According to a Freising account of things *quæ iussa sunt discere omnes ecclesiasticos* (n. 13) canons had to know Isidore's *De ecclesiasticis officiis* (MGH, Cap. I, 235 l. 26).

[37] Isidore, *Etymol.* VI, 38 (PL, LXXXII, 255 B).

[38] J. Geiselmann, *Die Abendmahlslehre an der Wende der christlichen Spätantike zum Frühmittelalter* (Munich, 1933), 180 ff.

[39] The Carolingian commentary on the Mass, "*Expositio Dominus Vobiscum*," explains the *hostiam puram*, etc., in the *Unde et mem-*

ores, as if the consecration had not yet taken place (PL, CXXXVIII, 1170 A). A later tenth-century exposition of the same title argues against this explanation (Gerbert, *Monumenta* II, 274). J. Geiselmann, *Studien zu frümittelalterlichen Abendmahlsschriften* (Paderborn, 1926), 88 f.

[40] The slighting evaluation of the preface (and indeed of the words of consecration) is revealed in this, that an opinion could be formed that the Apostles had actually consecrated with the Our Father, and immediately broke the bread and partook of Communion. Geiselmann, *Die Abendmahlslehre*, 210 f. Cf. *infra*, Vol. II, Chap. 3, 2.

tum, while the people stand praying without, as once they did when Zachary burned incense in the Temple sanctuary.[41]

The idea is extended and developed with conscious tenacity. At a spot where it was still thought that changes could be made, a new rite was introduced during the eighth century. When the priest has laid out and prepared the gift-offerings, before he steps into the sanctum of the canon he turns around once more at the altar and begs the bystanders for their prayers that he—as one commentator puts it—might be made worthy to offer up to God the oblation of the whole congregation.[42] Even in the text of the canon a slight emendation was permitted. If one thought about it, it seemed rather surprising that the *Memento* for the living should speak about the faithful as people *qui tibi offerunt hoc sacrificium laudis*—as offerers. Although no one in general dared to cross out these words, none-theless an addition was introduced, to make certain of the leading role of the priest; in the recension of the Gregorian Sacramentary emanating from Alcuin are prefaced the words *pro quibus tibi offerimus.*

The line of separation between altar and people, between clergy and laity, between those whose duty it was to perform the sacramental action and those who formed the celebrating congregation—a separation which was always taken for granted as essential to the Church's constitution, and which was never really forgotten—was now made into a broad line of demarcation, not to say a wall of division. This had its effect even on church architecture. The altar was moved back to the rear wall of the apse. In cathedrals, that necessitated transferring the bishop's throne[43]; it is now generally[44] placed at the side of the altar.[45] The choir-stalls of the assistants, which in the old arrangement formed a half-circle around the altar, following the line of the apse, are now set in two rows facing each other in front of the altar. The way was open for a further development, the rood-gallery or choir which somewhat later became in many places a

---

[41] For references see *infra*, Vol. II, Chap. 2, 1 and 2, 5.

[42] Amalar, *De off. eccl.* III, 20 (PL, CV, 1132 C).

Remigius of Auxerre, *Expositio* (PL, CI, 1252 D) puts the same construction on the words *Sursum corda;* the faithful, he says, should lift up their hearts *ut sacrificium, quod Deo offerendum mihi obtulistis, digne offere valeam.* Details *infra*, Vol II, Chap. 1, 7.

[43] According to the *Ecloga* (PL, CV, 1321 A), which in this matter obviously repeat the ideas of Amalar's *Expositio* of 813-814 (*infra*), the bishop after the collect still sits *versus ad populum.* Cf. also the *Expositio "Introitus missæ quare,"* ed. Hanssens, (*Eph. liturg.*, 1930), 44. In the

rest of the Carolingian sources there is no longer any clear reference to the matter.

Acc. to Amalar, *De eccl. off.* III, 10 (PL, CV, 1117) only the height of the bishop's throne signifies that the bishop should watch over the people.

[44] For the *cathedra* in the older position Martène 1, 4, iii (I, 364 f.) refers to the cathedrals of Lyons and Vienne. In Mainz, too, the choir is behind the altar and the *cathedra* forms its center.

[45] The new arrangement is made clear from the changes which *Ordo Rom. II*, n. 1, 5 (PL, LXXVIII, 969 A, 970 C) shows by comparison with *Ordo Rom. I*, n. 4, 8 (PL, LXXVIII, 939 B, 942 A): *pergit ad dexteram altaris ad sedem suam.*

real wall separating the *presbyterium* (sanctuary) from the nave of the church.

The function of the priest, by whose action the Eucharistic Presence was effected, and the reality of this Presence itself were brought more sharply into focus than heretofore. Even theoretically such questions were studied more thoroughly. About the middle of the ninth century (after 831) a controversy was waged in which Ratramnus maintained, against Paschasius Radbertus, that the Body of Christ was present in the Sacrament in all reality, not, however, in His earthly appearance but only in substance. Into the background recedes that interest in the symbolism of the Sacrament in which Augustine laid such great—perhaps too great—stock, and which is exhibited in the prayers of the Roman Sacramentaries, particularly in the post-communions. Forgotten is the relationship between the sacramental Body—the "mystical" Body, as it was then often termed—and the Body of Christ which is the church.[46] The same is true for the connection between the Sacrament and the death of Christ.[47] And so, too, the conscious participation of the community in the oblation of Christ is lost sight of, and with it that approach of the community towards God to which the Sacrament in its fulness is a summons or invitation. Instead the Mass becomes all the more the mystery of God's coming to man, a mystery one must adoringly wonder at and contemplate from afar. The approach to the Holy Table of the Lord in Communion is no longer the rule even on feast days; already the Eucharist had not been our daily bread for a long time.

Closely connected with such extinguishing of the Sacrament throughout all phases of every-day life was the change which took place about this time in the type of bread used, the change to unleavened bread. Alcuin and his pupil Rabanus Maurus are the first indisputable witnesses to this new practice,[48] which spread only very slowly. The increased reverence for the Sacrament probably helped to introduce the use of the pure white wafers which could be so much more easily broken without worry about crumbs.

The change in the type of bread brought in its train a whole series of further changes in the Mass-liturgy. The offertory procession is relegated to specified feast-days and by slow degrees becomes an offering of money. Likewise there was a gradual diminishing in the importance of the breaking of the bread within the Mass. The *Agnus Dei*, which had just been introduced in the seventh century as a song to accompany the ceremony of breaking the Bread, appears at the beginning of the ninth century in some of the Carolingian sources as a Communion song, or a song at the *Pax*. The ceremony which had previously been so carefully built up now disappears, either because the breaking has been taken care of beforehand

[46] Cf. H. de Lubac, *Corpus mysticum. L'Eucharistie et l'Eglise au moyen-âge* (Paris, 1944).
[47] See the amplifications of this in O. Casel, "Das Mysteriengedächtnis der Messlitur-gie im Lichte der Tradition," JL (1926), 113-204; esp. 177 ff., 185 ff.
[48] Geiselmann, *Die Abendmahlslehre*, 21-36; particulars *infra*, Vol. II, Chap. 1, 3.

(since with unleavened bread there was no longer any fear of a too-quick drying-up) or because the particles intended for the Communion of the faithful were already prepared in the desired shape and size—a thing which was not the rule till the eleventh century.

Then, too, there is a transformation in the paten hitherto in use. Some sort of large platter-like dish had been required for breaking the Bread into, and for distributing it. But now that type falls out of use and instead the paten becomes a tiny plate fitting over the cup of the chalice and used for the priest's host alone, while for the particles intended for the Communion of the faithful the container employed is a chalice-like ciborium. In the manner of distributing Communion, opportunities arise for giving in to the desire for a more reverent handling. The particles are no longer handed to the faithful (the particles are hardly suited to this), but are laid at once on the tongue, a thing more difficult in the case of the brittle pieces of leavened bread.[49] The next step—which, however, took quite a long time—was for the faithful to receive kneeling. And this, in turn, had a final effect on the church building: the low communion rail was introduced, a feature of which ancient church architecture knew nothing.

Still, despite all these features calculated to broaden the moat between the faithful and the sanctuary, during the Carolingian period there was at work an earnest endeavor to bring about an efficacious religious renewal in the whole population. This included a correspondingly organized participation of the faithful in divine service and especially in Holy Mass. Various prescriptions aimed at this very thing. The people were urged to join in singing the *Kyrie* and the *Sanctus*, and even the *Gloria Patri*—obviously the doxology which concluded the chants of the *schola*.[50] They were also encouraged, it seems, to respond to the greeting and the prayers of the priest.[51] The faithful were likewise admonished to take part in the offertory procession and in the kiss of peace.[52] And an attempt must even have been made to acquaint the faithful with the contents of the priest's prayers, those at least that were spoken aloud and that recurred time and again during the Mass. The Carolingian clergy were not only to know the liturgy themselves—to guarantee this there was a yearly examination in the liturgy, prescribed since 742[53]—but they were also to disclose to the

---

[49] For the connection mentioned there is this corroborative fact, that the first documents surely to vouch for the usage belong to the 9th century; see *infra*, Vol. II, Chap. 3, 13.

The ablution rite after the Communion of the priest is not expanded till about the 9th century. There was, for lay people, a washing of hands before Communion, but none after; see *infra*, Vol II, Chap. 3, 13 and 3, 16.

[50] Cf. G. Nickl, *Der Anteil des Volkes an*

der Messliturgie im Frankenreiche (Innsbruck, 1930), 15 ff.

[51] Cf. *infra*, p. 236.

[52] The Reform Synod of Mainz (813), can. 44 (Mansi, XIV, 74): *Oblationem quoque et pacem in ecclesia facere iugiter admoneatur populus Christianus.* Cf. Nickl, 44 f., 49 f.

[53] By agreement with St. Boniface, Carloman had enjoined in 742 *ut unusquisque presbyter in parochia habitans . . . semper in Quadragesima rationem et ordinem mi-*

faithful *totius religionis studium et christianitatis cultum.*[54] As a matter of fact, amongst the explanations of the Mass that appeared around the turn of the eighth-ninth century, there is one—the *Expositio "Quotiens contra se"*[55]—which is concerned only with the texts spoken aloud, and handles them with remarkable minuteness and detail. After a short survey of the fore-Mass, it takes up the words and phrases from *Dominus vobiscum* and *Sursum corda* to *Hosanna in excelsis*; then it skips over the canon and continues with *Præceptis salutaribus moniti*.

If, in the instance named, the pronouncement on the instruction of the faithful reveals nothing more than that the prayers which are not audible, especially the canon, are missing, a new and different sort of explanation soon evolves which is developed entirely from the viewpoint of the faithful, being concerned generally not with the words of the Mass, which are of course spoken in a strange tongue, but with the form and external actions that are perceptible to the eye. This is the allegorical interpretation of the Mass. It was known even in pre-Carolingian France. The seventh century *Expositio* of the Gallican Mass already mentioned is dominated by it,[56] and even earlier yet it was common in the Orient. Just as in pre-Christian times the olden myths of the gods were explained as meaning something else (ἄλλα ἀγορεύειν) than what their immediate sense indicated, and just as Philo of Alexandria had begun in a grand style to

nisterii sui, sive de baptismo sive de fide catholica sive de precibus et ordine missarum, episcopo reddat et ostendat (MGH, Cap. I, 25). The prescription was repeatedly inculcated in the following decades, in 769, 774 and 789, and was included in episcopal decrees, even as late as 852 by Hincmar of Reims. Andrieu, *Les ordines Romani*, I, 476-479; R. Stachnik, *Die Bildung des Weltklerus im Frankenreiche* (Paderborn, 1926), 23 f., 57 f.

A portion of the liturgical writings which appeared in the years to follow were conceived as aids to the liturgical study enacted here; Andrieu, 479 f. There were also little catechism-like writings for the related "Question and Answer play"; see for example the *ioca episcopi ad sacerdotes* in Franz, 342 f. and also the *Expositio "Introitus missæ quare,"* ed. Hanssens, *Eph. liturg.*, XLIV (1930), 42-46, already printed in extract in Franz, 410-412.

[54] Capitulary of 802, n. 5 (MGH, Cap. I, 106 1. 23).

A similar ordinance already at the Council of Cloveshoe in England (747), can. 10 (Mansi, XII, 398): *verba quæ in missæ celebratione et officio baptismi*

sollemniter dicuntur. Cf. Nickl, 7.

[55] *"Quotiens contra se"*: Martène, 1, 4, xi (I, 443-461); PL, XCVI, 1481-1502.

The most important of the Carolingian Mass interpretations are: *"Primum in ordine"* (about 800): Gerbert, *Monumenta* II, 282-290; PL, CXXXVIII, 1173-1186. For the manuscript tradition cf. A. Wilmart, "Un traité sur la messe copié en Angleterre vers l'an 800," *Eph. liturg.*, L (1936), 133-139.

"Dominus vobiscum": Gerbert, *Monumenta* II, 276-282; PL, CXXXVIII, 1163-1173 (and besides PL, LXXXIII, 1145-1154; PL, CXLVII, 191-200). Add to this another *expositio* beginning with the same words and controverting the other, in Gerbert, II, 269-276.

About the interpretations that trace back to Amalar, and about other Carolingian interpretations there will be discussion presently. Related to Amalar's writings is the catechism-like explanation *"Introitus missæ quare,"* ed. Hanssens, *Eph. liturg.* XLIV (1930), 42-46.

Further particulars in A. Wilmart, "Expositio missæ," DACL, V (1922), 1014-1027.

[56] *Supra*, p. 46.

give a philosophical turn to the accounts of primitive biblical history, so too in Christendom it early became the practice to put an allegorical interpretation on sacred texts whenever they appeared mystifying.[67] At first it was the Old Testament, where actual types were at hand to suggest the possibility of extending such prefigurements. Then, as liturgical life began to become fixed and standard, and thence to become obscure, the liturgy, too, received this treatment.[58] A preparatory step and condition for the introduction of allegorization was a delight in symbolism. Rites were in use that had been consciously introduced into the liturgy as indications of deeper things, like the washing of hands and the kiss of peace; there were others which had indeed a different origin but whose significance easily obtruded, like the mixing of water with the wine. Allegory went a step further and sought no longer for any apparent and actual signification.

One of the first to champion this liturgical allegorization at the start of the sixth century was Pseudo-Dionysius, whose neo-Platonic thinking inspired not only the method but, to a degree, also the content of his interpretation of the liturgy. However, he uses the allegorical system to explain only isolated moments in the Mass, as when he interprets the priest's coming from the altar to distribute Communion as an image of the Incarnation.[69] Before him others had already gone much further: Theodore of Mopsuestia (d. 428) and the Syrian Narsai (d. about 502), who understand, for instance, the carrying of the gift-offerings to the altar as the burial of Jesus, the transubstantiation as His Resurrection, and the breaking of the consecrated bread as the appearance of the risen Saviour.[60] Of a different sort are Sophronius (d. 638) and Maximus Confessor (d. 662), of whom the former finds in the Mass-liturgy representations of our Lord's life (the Annunciation, the Nativity, the Revelation on the banks of the Jordan, the Transfiguration) and especially of His Passion,[61] while the latter perceives predominant therein images of the relationships and activities of the spiritual life.[62]

In regard to the Roman liturgy, it was seemingly Alcuin who first applied the allegorical method.[63] But it was his pupil Amalar[64] who made the most

[67] J. C. Joosen-J. H. Waszink, "Allegorese," RAC, I, 283-293.
[58] The many intellectual associations out of which liturgical allegory arose are pointed out in an (unprinted) Innsbruck theological dissertation by P. Rusch, *Wurzeln und Anfänge der allegorischen Liturgieerklärung* (1933), esp. pp. 61 ff.
[69] Ps. Dionysius, *De eccl. hierarchia*, III, 3, 13 (Quasten, *Mon.*, 313).
[60] Theodore of Mopsuestia, *Sermones catech.*, V and VI (Rücker, 21 f., 31 ff.). Connolly, *The liturgical homilies of Narsai*, 3 ff., 11, 23 f., 55 f.

[61] Sophronius, *Commentarius liturg.* (PG, LXXXVII, 3981-4002) ; Franz, 336 f.
[62] Maximus, *Mystagogia* (PG, XCI, 657-718) ; cf. Franz, 337 f.
[63] Franz, 361 f.
[64] The first piece to be considered is the masterwork of Amalar of *Metz, De ecclesiasticis officiis* or, as the title reads in the manuscripts, *Liber officialis* (PL, CV, 985-1242). The work presupposes the author made a pilgrimage to Rome about 813; it was completed by 823. A revision in which a fourth book was added to the three already written appeared in 831. The manu-

extensive and thorough use of it. Although it was nothing new, still the type of explanation as handled by Amalar with such thorough logic appeared unwonted and strange. Pressed by one of Amalar's opponents, the deacon Florus of Lyons, the interpretation was condemned at the Synod of Quiercy in 838,[65] the allegation being that shadows and images might perhaps suit the Old Testament but certainly not the New, which claimed a *rationabile obsequium* without superstitions or nebulous fancies.[66] But this judgment was unable to halt the triumphal progress of Amalar's allegorical method, or to hinder the constant spread of his writings.[67] The following centuries do, however, exhibit expositions of the Mass that give scarcely any space to allegory. Florus (d. 860) himself composed an interpretation that relied essentially on quotations from the Fathers.[68] Following his example, Remigius of Auxerre (d. 908) worked hard at a good verbal explanation of the Ordinary of the Mass.[69] Rabanus Maurus (d. 856) was content to stress the chief ideas that course through the Mass.[70] Walafrid Strabo (d. 849) goes into details, and displays not only a great deal of interest but an astonishing insight into liturgico-historical matters.[71]

script tradition of this highly-esteemed work is consequently quite involved; see J. M. Hanssens, "Le texte du 'Liber officialis' d'Amalaire," *Eph. liturg.*, XLVII (1933), 113-125 and the continuation till XLIX (1935), 413-435; summary: XLIX (1935), 433 f. The critical text for which this study was a preparation has not yet appeared.

A second explanation of the Mass, imperfectly preserved, is one written by an Amalar of *Trier*, the first part of it while on a voyage to Constantinople 813-814; edited by J. M. Hanssens, "Le traité de la messe du ms. Zürich C 102," *Eph. liturg.*, XLI (1927), 153-185. The first part (in Gerbert, *Monumenta* II, 149-156) is also preserved in a later revision called *Expositio "Missa pro multis,"* ed. by J. M. Hanssens, "Le premier commentaire d'Amalaire sur la messe," *Eph. liturg.*, XLIV (1930), 24-42; also in Hittorp, 582-587 (interpolated). A similar recasting of the second part is found in the well-known *Eclogæ de officio missæ* (PL, CV, 1315-1332).

Following Hanssens, *Eph. liturg.*, XLI (1927), 158, we leave the question open whether Amalar of Metz and Amalar of Trier are identical. For this reason the author of the books is called simply Amalar. For the distinction, cf. Franz, 351 ff. A closer study of divergencies between the two allegorizings might actually produce evidence for a distinction.

[65] Franz, 359 f., 394 f.

[66] Florus Diaconus, *Opusculum de causa fidei*, n. 6 (PL, CXIX, 82 f.). Florus' further polemic concerns not so much the principle of allegory as rather the many seeming contradictions found in Amalar's practice. Franz, 359 f., 394 f.

[67] As early as 853 the *Liber de tribus epistolis*, c. 40 (PL, CXXI, 1054) complains that Amalar's writings had spread to practically every church in the land of the Franks.

But Franz, 395, goes too far when he summarizes his case for Amalar by saying, "The synod of Quiercy had found a correction in the almost unanimous votum of medieval theology and in church practice."

[68] Florus Diaconus, *De actione missarum* (PL, CXIX, 15-72).

[69] Remigius of Auxerre, *Expositio in celebratione missæ* (PL, CI, 1246-1271, as c. 40 of Ps.-Alcuin, *De divinis officiis*). Franz, 370, 405 f.

[70] Rabanus Maurus, *De inst. clericorum*, I, 33 (PL, CVII, 322-326). New edition by A. Knoepfler (Munich, 1900).

[71] Walafrid Strabo, *De exordiis et incrementis quarundam in observationibus ecclesiasticis rerum* (PL, CXIV, 919-966); new edition by A. Knoepfler (Munich, 1890).

But in the years that followed it was not these attempts that proved determinative, but rather Amalar's work, especially his chief opus, *De ecclesiasticis officiis*. Because of its heaping up of allegorical meanings, this book had given its opponents many opportunities for attack. Everything receives a significance — persons, vestments, church vessels and utensils, dates, actions and motions. Different types of signification are employed: ethical admonitions (moral allegory), fulfillments of the Old Testament (typological allegory), events in the economy of salvation (rememorative allegory) or allusions to the consummation at the end of time (eschatalogical or anagogic allegory). The shoulder-cloth of clerics signifies the *castigatio vocis* (II, 17); the seven torches carried by the acolytes signify the seven gifts of the Holy Ghost (III, 7); the two lights that go before the Gospel refer to the Law and the Prophets because these, too, preceded the Gospel (III, 18); when the bishop mounts his throne he images Christ sitting at the right hand of God the Father (III, 10). It was the rememorative meaning however, which was predominant in Amalar.

This appears almost exclusively in Amalar's shorter *Expositio* (813-814). A good view of the whole scheme is presented by the author himself in the summary of contents with which he prefaces the work:

> The *introit* alludes to the choir of the Prophets [who announced the advent of Christ just as the singers announce the advent of the bishop] . . . , the *Kyrie eleison* alludes to the Prophets at the time of Christ's coming, Zachary and his son John among them; the *Gloria in excelsis Deo*, points to the throng of angels who proclaimed to the shepherds the joyous tidings of our Lord's birth [and indeed in this manner, that first one spoke and the others joined in, just as in the Mass the bishop intones and the whole church joins in]; the *prima collecta* refers to what our Lord did in His twelfth year . . .[72]; the Epistle alludes to the preaching of John, the *responsorium* to the readiness of the Apostles when our Lord called them and they followed Him[73]; the *Alleluia* to their joy of heart when they heard His promises or saw the miracles He wrought . . . , the Gospel to His preaching . . . The rest of what happens in the Mass refers to the time from Sunday on, when the disciples drew close to Him [along with the multitude—shown in the Mass by the procession of the faithful making their gift-offerings], up to His Ascension or to Pentecost. The prayer which the priest says from the *secreta* to the *Nobis quoque peccatoribus* signifies the prayer of Jesus on Mount Olivet. What occurs later signifies the time during which Christ lay in the grave. When the bread is immersed in the wine, this means the return

[72] The link is this: the collect corresponds to the first (public) appearance of our Lord —the first time He "appeared before the public." This signification hardly ever recurs anywhere later on.
[73] In the corresponding chapter (Gerbert, *Monumenta* II, 151) we read: "*Responsorium ideo dicitur eo quod uno cantante ceteri respondeant. Cantavit unus Christus, id est vocavit Petrum et ceteros apostolos,*

et illi responderunt, quia Christum imitati sunt . . . Ipse idem qui inchoavit solus, solus versum cantat, quia Christus qui apostolos vocavit seorsum [et] pernoctans et solus orabat . . ."
The repetition (at that time customary) of the responsory by the choir has its correlative in the Gospel account. *Respondens autem Petrus dixit: Domine si tu es, iube me venire ad te.*

of Christ's soul to His body. The next action signifies the greetings offered by Christ to His Apostles. And the breaking of the offerings signifies the breaking of bread performed by the Lord before the two at Emmaus.[74]

Not all the points, but the more important, occur again in Amalar's greater work: the choir of Prophets, the sermon of Christ, the parade of the multitude, the prayer on the Mount of Olives, the breaking of bread in Emmaus. For the Mass proper, where the shorter work of 813-814 contains only the summary signification already quoted, the later Amalar proffers a whole series of supplementary details. Many of these additions by the later Amalar were not retained in the allegorical explanations of later years, e.g., the meaning of *Sursum corda* as the summons to enter into the cenacle, the preface as a reference to our Lord's speeches, and His prayer of thanks at the Last Supper, the communion antiphon as a *vox reciproca* imaging the mutual encouragement of the disciples at Emmaus and the Apostles when apprised of Christ's Resurrection (III, 33). Others, at least in main outline, become part and parcel of the standard Mass allegorization during the following centuries: The assistants stand bowed from the *Te igitur* till they hear the final petition of the Our Father, the *Sed libera nos a malo*, to signify the sorrow of the disciples over the suffering of Christ till they hear the news of His deliverance from the power of death (c. 23).

The deacons who stand behind the celebrant are a type of the Apostles who hid themselves in fear. The subdeacons who stand opposite the celebrant on the other side of the open altar are types of the holy women who remained standing near the Cross *(ibid.)*. The prayer after the consecration signifies the Passion of our Lord on the Cross. When the priest bows down (at the *Supplices*), our Lord bows His head and dies (c. 25). The slight lifting of the voice at *Nobis quoque* refers to the centurion's loud profession at the death of Jesus (c. 26). The deacons at this point straighten up and begin to busy themselves with the Body of the Lord, to signify the steadfast courage which seized the women and their work at the grave *(ibid.)*. At the concluding doxology the celebrant and the deacon elevate the Host and the Chalice and then set them down again, to signify Nicodemus' and Joseph of Arimathea's taking down our Lord's corpse from the Cross *(ibid.)*. The seven petitions of the Our Father typify the rest and quiet of the seventh day, that is, Holy Saturday (c. 28), while the division of the formula into three parts, introduction, prayer and subsequent embolism, typifies the three days our Lord lay in the tomb (c. 29). The division of the Host into three parts refers to the *corpus Christi triforme* (c. 35).[75] The commingling of the species refers to the reunion of Christ's soul and body at the Resurrection, the *Pax Domini* to the peace which the Resur-

---

[74] Gerbert, *Monumenta* II, 150. The portions in brackets are additional remarks extracted from the corresponding chapters in the body of the work.

[75] Further discussion of this in Vol. II, Chap. 3, 4. This was the main objection cited at Quiercy. Cf. Franz, 357, 359.

rection brought to mankind (c. 31). The last blessing and the dismissal remind us of our Lord's last blessing of the disciples on the Mount of Olives and of His departure from this world (c. 36).

In these allusions and references there is revealed a fancy that is without doubt remarkably perceptive. The transparency of the meanings, be it admitted, is often spoiled by the fact already pointed out that several methods of allegorizing are used side by side, as when at the offertory and the *Hosanna* the multitude represent Old Testament prefigurements, the altar is the sacrificial altar for burnt offerings on which we should offer up the mortification of the flesh and our good works, while the altar cloth is a symbol of the soul's purity, and the censer is the presentation of Christ's body through which we hope for God's grace (c. 19). But this juxtaposition is not meaningless. In one part of the moral allegories there is clearly disclosed the important notion that the Mass involves not only the oblation of Christ but at the same time the oblation of the Church. Therefore, Amalar maintains, the fore-Mass means the preaching of Christ and also the preaching of His followers to the end of the world, and the rest of the Mass means the Passion and glorification of Christ and also the sacrifice and glorification of His followers.[76] Therefore the altar is the Cross in reference to the mysteries of Christ, it is the altar for burnt offerings in reference to our own self-oblation.[77] Both meanings should be kept in mind.

On the whole, then, this way of explaining the Mass, as practiced by Amalar, marked out the trend for the future. The share of the Church was perhaps less prominently mentioned, but in other matters the majority of commentators, as we shall see, followed in Amalar's footsteps.

It can thus be seen that the transplanting of the Roman liturgy into Frankish lands was associated with many profound changes. These changes clearly bear witness to the intense spiritual life with which the Carolingian epoch was filled, a spiritual life which sparkled especially in the monasteries and in the cathedrals, whose clergy were organized in conventual life by means of chapters. It is to be noted that, in spite of difficulties of travel, distance put hardly a barrier in the way of mutual exchange and mutual stimulation. Thus at St. Denis they were studying Greek culture, rewriting a life of St. Dionysius from Greek sources[78] and adapting liturgical texts from the Antiochene liturgy.[79] Liturgical creativeness is to

---

[76] *De eccl. off.*, III, 18 (PL, CV, 1126).
[77] *op. cit.*, III, 26 (PL, CV, 1145 A).
[78] Abbot Hilduin, later chancellor of Louis the Pious, was the first to identify Dionysius of Paris with pseudo-Dionysius the Areopagite whose writings were at that time becoming known in France. On the cultivation of Greek at various Carolingian educational centers, see H. v. Schubert, *Geschichte der christlichen Kirche im Früh-*

mittelalter (Tübingen, 1921), 723-726; cf. 464. Greek studies in the Occident from the 9th to the 12th centuries are examined by A. Strittmatter, *Eph. liturg.*, LV (1941), 8, Note 11.
[79] The Mass *Ordo* of St. Denis in Martène, I, 4, v (I, 518-528; acc. to Leroquais, I, 142, the MS comes from the 11th century) contains not less than six formulas derived from the Greek liturgy of St. James, one

be traced at several points within the confines of the Frankish empire. At the outset of the period of accepting the Roman liturgy, the German monasteries—like St. Gall, Reichenau, Rheinau—stand out above all as the native places of more important liturgical manuscripts. But from the ninth century on, we can detect, through the manuscripts, a shift in the centers of Carolingian culture, first to places in the heart of French territory, like Tours, Corbie, Paris, Reims, but then also to some on the periphery, like Arles, Verona, Regensburg, Fulda or the episcopal cities of Normandy.[80]

For the enlargement of the Roman Ordinary by new prayers, the first important source, still in the ninth century, is the manuscript of Amiens already referred to,[81] with which two other pieces are partially connected, namely the tenth-century manuscript sacramentary of Abbot Ratold of Corbie (d. 986)[82] and the contemporaneous sacramentary of Fulda,[83] the last, however, distinguished from the other two by a greater reserve in admitting new creations, for example, the apologiæ.

10. The Romano-Frankish Mass as a New Basic Type, and Its Differentiation

Out of all this shaping and shifting of liturgical forms in the Carolingian area a new Mass rite of the Romano-Frankish type was produced. It was at once rich and sharply outlined and soon had won wide acceptance. The evidences are scattered over broadly separated parts of a Carolingian realm which had meanwhile disintegrated. The episcopal city of Séez in Nor-

---

for the entrance to the sanctuary, one for the washing of hands before the offertory, and four for incensing (519 C, 523 D, 525) ; cf. Brightman, p. liv, and infra, Vol. II, Chap. 1, 5.

At St. Denis, too, during the following centuries they used to sing Greek songs at Mass on certain occasions, especially Epiphany and Pentecost ; this was done at several monasteries, but St. Denis was the chief. The songs in question were as a rule chants from the ordinary : Κύριε, Δόξα, Πιστεύω. This wonderful monastic culture continued to blossom at St. Denis till the outbreak of the French Revolution. Ursprung, Die kath. Kirchenmusik, 92 f. Cf. also the accounts in Martène, I, 3, 2, 8-10 (I, 281) ; de Moléon, 263.

Sacramentaries containing these chants in Greek are noticed in L. Delisle, Mémoire sur d'anciens sacramentaires

(Paris, 1886), 103, 107, 263, 398. Further discussion in Netzer, L'introduction de la messe romaine en France, 214-216, 223 f
[80] Cf. the sketch in Lietzmann, Das Sacra mentarium Gregorianum, p. xvii-xxvi, or the discussion of the sacramentary manuscripts in Leroquais, I, 1 ff., and of the ordines manuscripts in Andrieu, I, esp. 467 ff.
[81] Supra, p. 77.
[82] PL, LXXVIII, 239-245; cf. ibid., 19. Also in Martène, I, 4, xi (I, 562-568). According to Leroquais, I, 79, Ratold must have gotten the MS. from Arras. The vesting prayers are composed for the most part in hexameters.
[83] Ed. By G. Richter and A. Schoenfelder (Fulda, 1921). On the typography of this sacramentary, all examples of which come from Fulda itself, and all of which are distinguished by excellent miniatures, cf. Baumstark, Missale Romanum, 123 f.

mandy,[1] and Minden on the Weser, (which is considered the place of origin of the *Missa Illyrica*)[2] the monastery of Gregorienmünster in Alsace,[3] and St. Lawrence in Liége[4]—these are the principal places where this Ordinary was to be found. It appears in various settings and was soon transferred also to Italy.[5]

The nearest thing to a basic form of this Ordinary is in general apparently the Mass *ordo* of Séez[6]; accordingly we can speak about a Séez group. However, it cannot be the basic form itself since—to instance one point — the *apologiæ* which are inserted here are replaced in the other manuscripts by different *apologiæ*.[7] The basic form must have developed somewhere in Franco-German territory before the year 1000, since there are extant several derivatives to be dated about this period.[8]

[1] The Mass *ordo* designated *ex codice Tiliano*, edited by H. Ménard, in Migne, PL, LXXVIII, 245-251; cf. *ibid.*, 20 f.

Also in Martène, 1, 4, XIII (I, 574-580), with the misleading superscription *Ex ms. pontificali Salisburgensi*. This label is probably to be explained by the fact that the Mass *ordo* belongs to a supplement which was added at Séez during the second half of the 11th century to a pontifical which actually came from Salzburg (at present in Paris, Bibl. Nat. Lat. 820); see Andrieu, *Les ordines*, I, 351-355.

[2] *Supra*, p. 79.

[3] Martène, 1, 4, XVI (I, 594-600).

[4] *Ibid.*, XV (I, 582-594). Martène's reference to Stablo in Belgium is erroneous; see M. Coens, *Analecta Boll.*, LVIII (1940), 48 ff.

[5] Cod. Chigi in Bona, altera app. (955-964); Martène, 1, 4, XII (I, 568-574). This is only partly preserved. It is related to the more important Mass *ordo* in the Missal of St. Vincent's Abbey at Volturno (Cod. Vat. lat. 6082), a work of the end of the 11th century, only recently published by V. Fiala in *Beiheft z. 23. Jahrg. d. Benediktinischen Monatschrift* (1947), 180-224. Likewise incomplete is the *ordo* preserved in the Pontifical of Halinardus which was meant for Langres and was sent in 1036 to Dijon; Martène, 1, 4, XIV (I, 580-582). Also in the Missal of Troyes in Martène, 1, 4, VI (I, 528-534), originally about the middle of the 11th century; see G. Morin, *Revue Bénéd.*, XXXIV (1922), 288; it breaks off after the offertory.

A late example is found in the Sacramentary of Seckau, originally about 1170, of which excerpts are given in Köck, 17 ff.,

95 ff., etc. Another in the Sacramentary of Boldau in Hungary, originally 1195, described by Radó, 31-58.

[6] Proof in the citations given below for the various parts; see, for example, the prayers at accession and vesting.

[7] Also the first acts, washing the hands and putting on the sandals, with the respective companion prayers, reappear (in reverse order) only in the Missal of Liége and in Cod. Chigi, but these books show secondary additions, e.g., aside from the rubrics, the insertion of Ps. 25 before Ps. 42 on the way to the altar. The rubric for the *mixtio* is inverted, being found unchanged in Liége and Gregorienmünster, but preserved at Séez in a curtailed form; see below, Vol. II, Chap. 3, 5. Nor is the entrance-rite at Séez entirely original; see below, p. 291 ff.

[8] Leroquais, *Les pontificaux*, I, 142, dates the *Pontificale* of Halinardus as the second half or end of the 10th century. According to Browe, JL, XIII (1935), 47, Note 11, a Mass *ordo* from Münster i. W. belonging to the "10th/11th century" agrees "almost word for word" with that of St. Lawrence in Liége (first half of the 11th century)—and proofs presented by Browe confirm this. The date for the *Missa Illyrica* is about 1030, yet in this the schema is already much expanded; cf. *supra*, p. 79.

The Cod. Chigi is dated by Bona, 1, 12, 4 (149 f.) as 10th century, but the evidence of the Lombard script makes a different date possible; the MS. seems to have disappeared, since it is not mentioned in Ebner, 167. The contents suggest rather the middle of the 11th century (the rite of high Mass, see below, II, 3; the *Confiteor*, see below, III, 5).

Amongst the peculiarities to be found in the Mass *ordo* of the Séez group is the insertion in four places of psalm prayers. While the sacramentary of Amiens adds Psalm 50 right before vesting, this Ordinary includes along with a fully developed series of vesting prayers,[9] an independent group of prayers, the kernel of which is composed of Psalms 83, 84, and 85, with the versicles and the oration *Aures tuæ pietatis*. Here, too, Psalm 42 appears for the first time, to be said upon entering the House of God; it begins with the antiphon *Introibo ad altare Dei*, and concludes with the oration *Aufer a nobis*, and only after that follow the avowals of sinfulness or, *apologiæ*, which are different in the various redactions. At a high Mass, at least, these continue all through the fore-Mass. Only one short, oration-like *apologia*, *Omnipotens (sempiterne) Deus qui me peccatorem*, seems to belong to the original form of this group of prayers, recurring as it does in the same form in all the manuscripts. Just before bringing the gift-offerings to the altar, there are a number of sacerdotal oblation prayers, of the Gallican type *Suscipe sancta Trinitas*, like those that already appear in the sacramentary of Amiens. The offertory itself is accompanied by some new texts. At the mixing of the water with the wine the formula *Deus qui humanæ substantiæ* is used. The incensing that follows is accompanied by all the prayers still in use today. The assisting clergy respond to the bidding *Orate fratres* with a prayer which is taken up again after the *Sanctus*, a whole series of appropriate psalms being said in common; thus the quiet of the canon is again undermined. The communion series is composed of most of the prayers still in use.[10] A psalm prayer—namely the canticle of the Three Young Men, with Psalm 150 and corresponding conclusion—follows at the end, on the return to the sacristy. The obligation to say this final series—just as with the entrance prayers—was far less strict than the obligation with regard to the other parts of the Mass.

As can be seen, in this Mass Ordinary which hails from Franco-German territory, there are not a few elements that are still to be found in today's Roman Mass or at least appear as preparation and thanksgiving.

Soon after its origination, this Ordinary was on its way to Italy where its further development was again decided. In many Italian Mass books of the eleventh and twelfth centuries we find not only the elements still retained at present but also other peculiarities, some of them trivial, which have since disappeared.[11] Some of the items of this *ordo*, like Psalm 42

---

[9] The prayers differ from those of Amiens *(supra*, p. 78), from which the formulas customary today stem for the most part.

[10] Namely *Domine Jesu Christe Fili, Perceptio, Panem cœlestem, Quid retribuam;* the order in which they follow varies.

The *Missa Illyrica* also contains the Prayer for Peace, the formula at the sumption and the *Quod ore sumpsimus*.

[11] Amongst these (aside from certain texts which already appeared in older arrangements of the Mass, even in part in the Sacramentary of Amiens) are: the prayer previously mentioned as attached to the *Aufer a nobis*, an oration having the character of an *apologia: Omnipotens Deus qui me peccatorem*; the formula which follows for kissing the Gospel-book, *Pax Christi quam nobis*; the words with which the deacon hands over the chalice, *Immola Deo*; the

and its oration, or the prayer for incensing, appear from this time on in all the Italian Mass books. We could refer particularly to some manuscript witnesses which either present us with the complete *ordo* unaltered, as does Codex Chigi,[12] or at least give us the greater part with more or fewer additions. Among these latter are especially two Mass books of the eleventh century, from the Benedictine center of Camaldoli,[13] a somewhat later book from Monte Cassino,[14] another Benedictine sacramentary from the vicinity of Verona,[15] the sacramentary of Modina which was finished before 1174,[16] and two pontificals of the eleventh and twelfth century.[17]

Thus we come to that episode which proved to be of such incalculable importance for the entire subsequent history of the Roman liturgy. About the middle of the tenth century the Roman liturgy began to return in force from Franco-Germanic lands to Italy and to Rome, but it is a liturgy which meanwhile had undergone radical changes and a great development. This importation entailed supplanting the local form of the Roman liturgy by its Gallicized version, even at the very center of Christendom. A Romano-Germanic pontifical compiled at Mainz about 950—the basic model of today's *Pontificale Romanum*—at that time found its way to Lucca and to Rome, as we learn from manuscripts which were written about this period at both the places mentioned.[18] It was likely the frequent journeys to Rome of Otto the Great, in whose company a large number of German clerics made the trips, that brought the book into Italy.[19] The earliest copies of the pontifical[20] contained the so-called *Ordo Romanus VI* which provides an arrangement for the bishop's Mass that is in extraction and content very similar to our own Ordinary.[21] Some usages had already got to Rome from the North at an earlier period.[22] A great many others were

formula for offering up the chalice, *Domine Jesu Christe qui in cruce*; the formula for blessing both the offerings, *In nomine D.N.J.C. sit sacrificium*; the psalm-prayer after the *Sanctus*; the formula at Communion: *Communicatio et confirmatio*; the formula attached to the *Placeat: Meritis*. A second *apologia*-like oration, *Fac me quæso*, is missing in the Séez text, but in most other texts is found near the oration *Aures*.

A more detailed study of the sources of these prayers can be gotten (with the help of the Index) in the explanations which follow in Parts III and IV.
[12] See *supra*, note 5.
[13] Ebner, 297 ff., 300 ff.
[14] *Ibid.*, 309 ff. The *ordo* begins with the *Kyrie*.
[15] *Ibid.*, 306 f.
[16] Muratori, I, 86-95; cf. Ebner, 97 f.
[17] Ebner, 311 ff., 327 ff.
    Cf. still another missal of the 12th/

13th century: Ebner, 321 ff.
[18] Andrieu, *Les ordines*, I, 511 ff.
[19] Klauser, *Die liturgischen Austauschbeziehungen* (*Hist. Jahrbuch*, 1933), 186 f., concludes that the years 962-964, in which Otto I was in Rome, were the years during which this transfer to a Franco-German liturgy took place. This would hold true in the first place for the rites retained in the Roman Pontifical.
[20] MS. of Lucca, probably written about 962-964 (Andrieu, *Les ordines*, I, 156 ff., as n. X); also the two MSS. from Monte Cassino and Rome-Vallicellana, which were copied from an original written ab. 1000 (*ibid.*, 176 f., 199).
[21] Before the entrance procession the clergy pray *VII psalmos*; this is presupposed also —in fact doubly—in the *Missa Illyrica*. After the *Orate pro me* the Gradual Psalms are said. *Ordo Rom. VI*, n. 1, 10 (PL, LXXVIII, 989 C, 993 B).
[22] Klauser, 183 f.

soon to follow, as northern liturgical books replaced those locally in use and thus crowded out the customs hitherto obtaining.

At the time, this displacement was unfortunately not very difficult. In matters liturgical (as in other matters) the tenth century was for Rome an era of collapse and demoralization. It would seem that at that time new manuscripts were simply not being produced.[23] In the scriptoria of the North, on the contrary, there was bustling activity; in particular there flourished at the time in German monasteries the art of manuscript illumination.[24] It is worthy of note that Pope Gregory V made an agreement in 998 with the abbey of Reichenau, stipulating that in return for certain privileges accorded on the occasion of the blessing of a new abbot, the monks were to send, amongst other things, a new sacramentary.[25] It goes without saying that this would mean only the style of Mass book then current in the North.[26]

Of course there were many different ways in which this revamped Mass book from Carolingian territory, with its new *ordo,* could get to Italy. In the instance cited in the last paragraph the path led from a German monastery directly into the Lateran. But in other cases it could be easily the road from one monastery to another. Amongst the examples of places on Italian soil where this new Mass *ordo* clearly made its appearance, the Benedictine share looms very prominent. Even Codex Chigi, one of the earliest witnesses, is of Benedictine origin.[27] Recall the early shift of the Cluniac reform to Italy. Abbot Odo (c. 942) was able to draw into the reform a great number of monasteries of Rome and its environs, and even Monte Cassino.[28] In 1000 Abbot Odilo was at Ravenna to meet St. Romuald, founder of the Camaldolese,[29] from whose ranks we already mentioned two witnesses of the new Mass *ordo.* On the other side, Cluny also had won great power and influence in France even during the tenth century, so extensive that it came into contact with the new Mass *ordo* at many points and could thus become its "carrier,"[30] if it had not already assisted at its birth.[31]

[23] Klauser, 183.
[24] U. Berlière, *L'ordre monastique des origines au XIIe siècle* (Paris, 1924), 150.
[25] A. Brackmann, *Germania pontificia II,* (Berlin, 1923), I, 152; Andrieu, 515 f.
[26] Andrieu, 516, Note 1, refers to the fact that in the canon of the Mass books used in the papal chapels from the 11th/12th centuries on, the extra-Roman practice of naming the bishop is followed: *una cum famulo tuo papa nostro N. et antistite nostro N.*
[27] Bona, *op. cit.,* 955.
[28] E. Sackur, *Die Cluniacenser,* (Halle, 1892), I, 93-114.
[29] *Ibid.,* 346-349.
[30] Around the year 1000 both Verdun and

Dijon, among others, were involved in the movement. From Verdun comes one of the texts of the Mass *ordo* published by Martène (*supra,* note 4). Another such reached the reformed monastery of S. Bénigne in Dijon at least in the year 1036 (*supra,* note 5).
[31] Abbot William of Dijon, who came from Cluny, took over in 1001 the monastery of Fécamp, which from then on, because of its school, became the center of reform not only of the monasteries but also of the secular clergy. Sackur, (Halle, 1894) II, 44-48; G. Schnürer, *Kirche und Kultur im Mittelalter,* (Paderborn, 1926), II, 185, 213 f. Some such point of departure would best explain the uniform spread of the

The chief factor for ensuring the penetration, through and through, of this new fashion in Roman liturgy and its arrangement of the Mass, was the political power of the Romano-German empire. Although this influence was indirect it was considerable, for since Otto the Great, the Emperor had interfered in the affairs of Rome and Italy and had time and again put his own candidates in the chief positions. In one case, in fact, we are told of a direct interference by a German ruler in the shaping of the liturgy of Rome; when Henry II came to the Eternal City for his imperial coronation in 1014, he asked as a favor that at Rome also the *Credo* be sung at Mass as was long the case in the North.

So, for a second time in the West, liturgical unity was achieved but this time it was not the members that yielded to the head, but rather the head accommodated itself more and more to members grown meanwhile strong and wilful. The refined clarity of the old forms was no longer present in the newer growth, nor were latent there the inner forces that might have reformed it in the olden spirit.

Fundamentally the new Mass *ordo* from the North was only one type out of many. Open suggestions were offered therein for new elements in the Mass-liturgy as demanded by the trend of the times, but none of these had any real binding force. Such elements were left on principle to local or at most regional regulations. Indeed the new silent prayers, which formed a goodly part of the recent acquisition, could be changed or even extended by the priest himself, since they were purely the expression of private devotion. Many details of external deportment, especially in a non-solemn Mass, such for instance as the manner of preparing the chalice, and the precise moment of the Mass that this was to be done, were left more or less free, since the rubrics were concerned only with a high Mass where many assistants took part. Thus we find throughout the later Middle Ages a great variation in all those parts of the Mass-liturgy which were not fixed as a heritage of the ancient Roman sacramentaries—variation not only from country to country but from church to church, in fact, from Mass book to Mass book. Amongst the Mass books from the latter half of the Middle Ages which are still in existence—there are thousands of them —there are seldom (to judge from descriptions at hand) two Mass books that agree to such an extent that the later copy does not add a prayer text or a rubric, or leave one out, or consciously alter it.

A special case, all through the Middle Ages, is the variation in the wording of many prayers, particularly the shorter ones. The shorter the formula, the greater the diversity. The formula for the distribution of Communion, the text accompanying the offering of host and chalice, or the *Suscipiat*— only with great trouble can one arrive at a fixed basic text. A phrase is

Mass *ordo* both in episcopal and abbey churches. The Norman episcopal city of Séez was not the home of these original witnesses by mere accident. From Nor-mandy, half a century later, when liturgical writing was still scarce elsewhere, came the work of John of Avranches, *De officiis ecclesiasticis*.

enlarged here or there, it is doubled, it is enhanced with emotional high-lights, or it is even changed to something else or left out entirely. This is understandable, for such texts were mostly handed down, not in writing, but by word of mouth, and were spoken by heart till such time as they were again taken down, somewhere, somehow, in writing.[32] In many Mass books they were not to be found at all, or they were inserted only as an appendix. They were on the very verge between official prayers and private prayers. And so there was sometimes no hesitation in inserting absolutely private prayers in the course of the Mass, as did a certain twelfth century Bishop Gondulph of Rochester, who daily said a second Mass in the presence of his monks, and after the Gospel, while the choir-boys sang the offertory, he sat down and gave himself over entirely to his devotions, and sighed and wept.[33]

The direction of all this lay as a matter of principle in the hands of the metropolitan.[34] But there was no stopping the continual procurement of books (and consequently of ritual customs) from other church provinces, if the books were not obtainable from one's own. Nor was there any special aversion to a conscious difference of usage. Over and over during medieval times the phrase of St. Gregory is reiterated: *in una fide nil officit Ecclesiæ consuetudo diversa*,[35] sometimes word for word,[36] sometimes only in substance.[37]

It was the monasteries that first introduced a more rigid discipline. The customs of the larger reformed abbeys, which were written down chiefly

---

[32] A parallel from the present day might help to establish this point. The verse *Adoramus te, Christe, et benedicimus tibi, quia per crucem tuam redemisti mundum* has become a popular prayer among the people, being frequently used at the Way of the Cross. But little changes have crept in; in my own South Tyrol, for instance, instead of *Christe* they say "Lord Jesus Christ," and in the second part usually "by Thy holy cross and Passion Thou hast redeemed us and the whole world."

[33] Berlière, *L'ascèse bénédictine*, 153 f.

[34] In this sense we must interpret many of the decrees of synods of the 5th/7th centuries, some of which were included in medieval collections of canon law; see Franz, *Die Messe im deutschen Mittelalter*, 149, 296. Cf. also the fifth Synod of Arles (554), Canon 1 (Hardouin, III, 328 B). A similar demand is made by Burchard of Worms, *Decretum III*, 66 (PL, CXL, 687): *ut institutiones missarum sicut in metropolitana ecclesia fiunt, ita . . . in omnibus comprovincialibus ecclesiis . . . serventur*. The same basic notion is still enunciated at the

close of the Middle Ages by Gabriel Biel (d. 1495), *Canonis expositio*, lect. 80. The lectures contained in this work were delivered at Tübingen, and the author therefore —following the argument already indicated —submits the use of Mainz.

[35] Gregory the Great, *Ep. I*, 43 (PL, LXXVII, 497). The far-reaching advice which the same pope is supposed to have given to St. Augustine in England, *Ep. XI*, 64, 3 (PL, LXXVII, 1187), agrees with this trenchant axiom; choose, he said, the best of the various customs that you get to know on your trip through Gaul, and introduce them into England. This letter, however, is not genuine, as S. Brechter, *Die Quellen zur Angelsachsenmission Gregors d. Grossen* (Münster, 1941), 13-111, proves quite conclusively.

[36] The Trier *Liber officiorum* (11th cent.; in Franz, *Die Messe*, 374); Anselm, *Ad Waleranni querelas*, c. 1 (PL, CLVIII, 552 D); Bernhard von Waging (d. 1472; in Franz, 571).

[37] Fulbert of Chartres (d. 1029), *Ep. 3* (PL, CXLI, 192 D).

since the eleventh century, contain in good measure prescriptions for divine worship and, amongst these, exact and detailed regulations of the Mass *ordo*. This is true, first of all, of the catalog of the customs of Cluny as set down in the middle of the eleventh century by the monk Bernard,[88] and in a stricter arrangement around 1080 by the monk Udalrich.[89] Therein everything is carefully regulated that concerns the handling of the Eucharist, from the preparation of host-bread to the ablution after reception, for which a series of new regulations are introduced.[40]

The new branches of the Benedictines too, soon after their establishment, prescribed fixed liturgical arrangements for their churches. Amongst these were also a peculiar regulation of the Mass *ordo* which was afterward altered very little. A concomitant factor was—as in similar cases—the local tradition of the home diocese of the mother-house. Take the case of the Cistercians whose rite was regulated in the *Liber usuum* shortly after 1119,[41] incorporating the usage of Chalon-sur-Saône. As regards singing and architectural appointments, the Cistercian service is very simple, a conscious contrast to Cluny. For an external portrayal of this special rite —outside Castile[42]—which was given up in 1618, the most significant point was this: almost nothing except the preface and canon was said at the center of the altar; the *Gloria* and the greeting that followed were said on the Epistle side, the *Credo* and the secret on the Gospel side.

The liturgical arrangement for the Carthusians was compiled in the *Statuta antiqua* just shortly before 1259,[43] but it belongs substantially to

---

[88] *Bernardi Ordo Cluniacensis* (Herrgott, *Vetus disciplina monastica*, 133-364).

[89] *Udalrici Consuetudines Cluniacenses* (PL, CXLIX, 635-778). A further development of these customs is extant in the *Constitutiones Hirsaugienses* of Abbot William of Hirsau (d. 1091), in PL, CL, 927-1146. But even before Cluny itself, these customs were fixed in writing by other monasteries affected by Cluny's reform ideas. Thus especially the *Consuetudines* of Farfa (PL, CL, 1193-1300; Albers, I, 1-206), written down about 1040, but containing adaptations to local conditions.

For a survey of the inter-relationships of the various *Consuetudines*, see P. Polk, *Der Liber ordinarius des Lütticher St. Jacobsklosters*, p. xiii-xxi; cf. also U. Berlière, *L'ascèse bénédictine* (Paris, 1927), 24-36; E. Tomek, *Studien zur Reform der deutschen Klöster im 11. Jh.*; I. Die Frühreform (Vienna, 1910), 173 ff.

[40] A synopsis of the liturgical prescriptions according to Udalrich and a partial commentary on them in Tomek, 184-232. A general evaluation of the sources is found

in a pertinent chapter of G. de Valous, *Le Monachisme Clunesien*, (Paris, 1935), I, 327-372.

[41] Critical text in Ph. Guignard, *Les Monuments primitifs de la Règle Cistercienne* (Dijon, 1878); H. Séjalon, *Nomasticon Cisterciense seu antiquiores ordinis consuetudines* (Solesmes, 1892). I use a text which is apparently only slightly different, in Migne (PL, CLXVI, 1421-1442).

R. Trilhe, "Citeaux (Liturgie de l'ordre de)", DACL, III, 1787-1811; F. Schneider, "Vov alten Messritus des Cistercienser Ordens," *Cistercienser-Chronik*, XXXVII (1925), 145-152, with 30 further articles till XL (1928), 77-90; in the last there is an index (88-90); there is a French edition, slightly revised: *L'ancienne messe cistercienne* (Tilburg, 1929). Cf. A. A. King, *Notes on the Catholic Liturgies*, 62 ff.

[42] B. Kaul, "Auf den Spuren des alten Cistercienserritus in Spanien," *Cist.-Chronik*, LIV (1947), 226-235; LV (1948), 218 f.

[43] In the chapter (I, 43) *De officio sacer-*

the twelfth century.⁴⁴ The Savoyard origin of the first Carthusians explains the similarities to the rite of Lyons. The Mass ceremonial, in use even today, is distinguished by its archaic character. In this rite the Mass still concludes with the *Ite missa est*. The liturgy of the Premonstratensians was also put in order by the twelfth century.⁴⁵ But the ancient form of the *Liber ordinarius* which was then compiled, unlike the corresponding books of the Cistercians or the Dominicans, was altered in the course of years, until in the seventeenth century the Missal of Pius V was finally adopted.

If the old orders, living on the basic principle of *stabilitas loci*, found it necessary to secure uniformity in liturgical regulation, this was true in a higher degree even with regard to the itinerant orders of the thirteenth century. The Dominicans had their first Mass book determined even before 1244. This was fixed by the *Ordinarium iuxta ritum sacri Ordinis Fratrum Prædicatorum*,⁴⁶ and was produced under the General, Humbert de Romans, and enacted into law in 1256.⁴⁷ As far as the rite of the Mass is concerned —there was a special chapter on the *missa privata*—this extremely careful regulating had its repercussions far beyond the confines of the order itself. Various monastic groups, like the Teutonic Knights, adopted the Dominican rite. The Mass ceremonial of the *Liber ordinarius* of the Benedictine abbey of St. James in Liége, which in its turn had an extensive influence, was nothing else than a slight modification of the Dominican.⁴⁸ The same is true of the ceremonial established by the Carmelites in the General Chapter of 1312,⁴⁹ a ceremonial still used by the Calced Carmelites. While the Dominican rite in some details displays certain antique traits, as for instance the shortness of the prayers at the foot of the altar, in others it exhibits an energetic progress and development. Thus, for the first time, the repetition at the gradual is underlined, the customary ablution rite

---

dotis, diaconi et subdiaconi: Martène, 1, 4, XXV (I, 631-635).

⁴⁴ A. Degand, "Chartreux (Liturgie de)," DACL, III (1913), 1045-1071.

⁴⁵ Pl. F. Lefèvre, *L'Ordinaire de Prémontré d'après des mss. du 12. et du 13. siècle* (Louvain, 1941) ; M. van Waefelghem, *Le liber ordinarius d'après un ms. du 13./14. siècle* (Louvain, 1913). Wherever there is no question of text variants, I cite from the latter book, since it is accompanied by a thorough-going commentary giving indications of later changes in the rite. I am also indebted to a finished study, still in manuscript, by Dr. Hermann Joseph Lentze, O.Præm. (Wilten), "Die Liturgie des Prämonstratenserordens."

Cf. also B. Luykx, "Essai sur les sources de l'Ordo missæ Prémontré," *Analecta Præmonstratensia*, XXII-XXIII (1946-47), 35-90.

⁴⁶ Newly edited by F. Guerrini (Rome, 1921). The prescriptions for conventual Mass according to an English MS. of the 13th century, also in Legg, *Tracts*, 73-87, with further remarks, pp. 87-96.

⁴⁷ M. H. Lavocat, "La liturgie dominicaine," *Liturgia*, ed. by Aigrain (Paris, 1935), 860-864; further bibliography cited there. The liturgical arrangement before Humbert is thoroughly discussed by G. G. Soelch, *Hugo von S. Cher, O.P., und die Anfänge der Dominikanerliturgie* (Cologne, 1938). Cf. also William R. Bonniwell, *A History of the Dominican Liturgy* (N. Y., 1944), 28-35; and esp. 118-129.

⁴⁸ P. Volk, *Der Liber ordinarius des Lütticher St. Jakobs-Klosters* (Münster, 1923). For geneological relationships see p. lxxii.

⁴⁹ B. Zimmermann, *Ordinaire de l'Ordre de Notre Dame du Mont Carmel par Sibert de Beka (Bibliothèque liturgique* 13)

makes its first appearance, and likewise the St. John Gospel at the end of the Mass. The dramatic moments are visibly high-lighted—the extension of the arms after the consecration, and the signing of the chalice at the end of the canon.

Even more extensive in its effect on the history of the Mass-liturgy was the conduct of the other mendicant order, the Franciscans. They too at first took up the liturgical usage of the order's native place, but afterwards, prompted by the many diversities of the Mass-liturgy which they met with in their early wanderings, they chose for themselves the *Missale secundum usum Romanæ curiæ*. The papal curia, which already by that time had grown into an organization of quite considerable range, had formed for itself, out of the various designs of the contemporary city liturgy, especially along the lines of the old patriarchal basilicas, a special type of Roman Mass book.[50] This was done chiefly, it appears, under Innocent III. This type is characterized by a sanctoral calendar cataloging many old popes, and by a Mass *ordo* that is really simple,[51] as the unsettled life of the papal court at that time indeed required. The new enlargement by multifarious greetings and blessings and petitions, versicles and responses, as we find them in the Mass books of Northern lands, especially in the compass of the offertory and the communion, are omitted, and continue to be omitted during the succeeding centuries. In fact in some places there is a noticeable attempt at simplification.[52] Here especially the change from sacramentary to missal which we will investigate in a moment, had been comparatively swift.

This missal the sons of St. Francis made their own, but without renouncing the right to make changes—the trend of the time.[53] But from this period on, the Franciscan missal and the *Missale secundum consuetudinem Romanæ curiæ* (also called *Missale Romanum* for short) are almost identical.[54] This missal type was carried all over the world by the wandering mendicant Friars. It was soon the predominant type of Mass book in

(Paris, 1910); *idem.*, "Carmes (Liturgie de l'orde des)," DACL, II (1910), 2166-2175. Cf. King, *op. cit.*, 75-85.
[50] M. Andrieu, "Le missel de la Chapelle papale à la fin du XIIIe siècle," *Miscellanea Ehrle*, II (Rome, 1924), 348-376; Baumstark, *Missale Romanum*, 144-148. According to this the *ordinarium* used in the papal chapel service must have been composed already under Innocent III. However, there is question here of an arrangement quite different from the one Innocent used as a basis in his work, *De sacro altaris mysterio*, written before he was elected Pope (1198). Batiffol, *Leçons*, 6.
[51] *Ordo et Canon missæ* (Cod. Vat. Ottobon. lat. 356; about 1290), ed. J. Brinktrine,

Eph. liturg., LI (1937), 198-209. Excerpts from the same MS. also in Ebner, 347 f.
[52] In the Mass *ordo* of *Ordo Rom. XIV* (about 1311), which represents a revision of that of Innocent III (see note 50 *supra*), the prayer said while spreading out the corporal *(In tuo conspectu)*, still extant in the Mass *ordo* about 1290, is no longer found; n. 71 (PL, LXXVIII, 1186 C).
[53] Cf. A. van Dijk, "Il carattere della correzione liturgica di Fra Aimone da Faversham O.F.M.," *Eph. liturg.*, LIX (1945), 177-223.
[54] Other orders also followed the example of the Franciscans; Ebner, 251, cites a *Missale fratrum ordinis s. Augustini sec. consuet. Rom. curiæ* (of the year 1314) and

Christendom.[65] And after the inauguration of printing it won public prevalence in the whole Latin Church.[66] It paved the way for the reform under Pius V.

Also in other churches of the later Middle Ages were found special rites clearly designed. This was true of solemn pontifical service in the cathedrals; several *ordines* of such churches, especially in France, give us further knowledge of them.[67] For a non-solemn Mass, however, there was seldom if ever any written regulation, and in fact the tendency was toward utter simplicity. Local tradition and living custom had to suffice. However, certain centers were the exception, amongst them the church of Lyons, which developed its own definite rite and has retained it, with some modifications and restrictions, to this very day.[68]

In England too, where since William the Conqueror liturgical life had been determined to a great extent by that of Normandy, the rite of Salisbury or Sarum was gradually developed as a distinct and, up to the Reformation, an essentially conservative and fixed arrangement, both for the entire service and more especially for the Mass.[69] It was the standard not only in a great portion of the English Church but also here and there on the Continent.

In general, however, the right to regulate and supervise the liturgy by dioceses and ecclesiastical provinces appears to have produced very little.

---

a *Missale fratrum servorum s. Mariæ sec. consuet. Rom. curiæ* (14th century).

[65] Ebner, in the index p. 479 under the *Missale (M. sec. consuet. Rom. curiæ)*, cites 33 source-places for important manuscripts amongst Italian libraries alone, and for the Minorite Missals (*Missale fratrum minorum sec. consuet. Rom. curiæ*), ibid., 478, 18 other source-places. But the missals themselves must be far more numerous than these registered sources; see, e.g., Ebner, 22, Note 1.

[66] Baumstark, *Missale Romanum*, 149. Substantial additions in R. Menth, O.F.M., "Ein Missale Romanum von 1481," *Franziskan. Studien*, XX (1933), 89-129; according to him during the period 1474-1570 more than 320 printings of the *Missale Romanum* appeared in various presses, chiefly in Italy and France.

A new printing of it which appeared in Milan in 1474, with collations of various other later printings in R. Lippe, *Missale Romanum 1474*, 2 vols. (HBS, 17, 33; London, 1899, 1907).

[67] See, e.g., in Martène the excerpts from Ordinaries of Laon, Soissons, Bayeux, Chalon-sur-Saône.

[68] B. Buenner, *L'ancienne liturgie romaine. Le rite Lyonnais* (Lyon o. J., 1934). Cf. the pertinent remarks of Th. Klauser, JL, XIV (1938), 455-458.

See Archdale King, "The Rite of Lyons," *Orate Fratres*, XIII (1938-9), 450-454.

[69] The Mass *ordo* of Sarum according to an older (13th century) and a more recent (14th century) version in Legg, *Tracts* (HBS, 27). Further examples in Martène and in W. Maskell, *The ancient liturgy of the Church of England*, 3rd ed. (Oxford, 1882) ; the latter has parallel columns containing the arrangements of the Mass at Hereford and York. A survey of the Sarum *ordo* important peculiarities of the Sarum *ordo* in Fortescue, *The Mass*, 202-205 ; see also F. Thos. Bergh, "Sarum Rite," CE, XIII (1912), 479-481.

There are two more recent editions of Sarum Mass books; the latest is J. W. Legg, *The Sarum Missal edited from three early manuscripts* (Oxford, 1916). Regarding manuscripts of the Sarum Missal that were brought to Spain before 1472 and continued to have an influence there, see Ferreres, p. xcii f., 72, Note c.

In German territory it was rather the literary work of one liturgist that produced big results in directing, coordinating, and simplifying the liturgy. This work was the *Micrologus* written about 1085 by Bernold of Constance,⁶⁰ a champion of the reform of Pope Gregory VII, who had traveled much in Italy. His short explanation of the Mass, distinguished by its calm clarity, contained a special chapter (c. 23) with the text of the *Ordo Missæ* which he considered correct. While the psalmodic prayer of the *Præparatio Missæ* and at the end the Song of the Three Young Men, with the pertinent prayers, form a single series with the other parts of the Mass *ordo*, still, as regards adopting the prayers within the Mass that had long been in circulation, a great amount of discretion and conservativeness is exercised. For instance, both the prayers at the offering of host and chalice are missing. Between *Agnus Dei* and communion only one prayer, *Domine Jesu Christe Fili*, was adopted. Bernold expressly states (c. 12) that in the canon nothing was allowed to be added, not even the names of saints.

Thus out of the great amount of prayer material that had grown up, a fixed core was lifted out, to become the basis, at least in Germany, for further development.⁶¹ In Hungary about 1100, the bishops, by explicit decree, prescribed the arrangement laid out in the *Micrologus* as the obligatory norm.⁶²

A similar importance for France, if not a similarly extensive influence, might be attached to the short and predominantly rubrical portrayal of the Mass which Bishop John of Avranches, who died in 1079 as Archbishop of Rouen, offers in his explanation of the liturgy.⁶³

11. The Gothic Period

Someone has said, and rightly, that Gothic is in a special degree not only an art style *(Kunststil)* but a period style *(Zeitstil)*. Because up till now the younger peoples of the North had studied zealously in the school of the older order of things, propriety and proportion, as they appeared in Romanesque, could become the expression of their life. But their growing powers were beginning to spring the old grooves on all sides, seeking newer designs. The individual and subjective, seeing and feeling on one's own personal activity and personal capability—these came to the fore, and led to a stressing of the concrete and realistic, and consequently to a multiplicity of forms which could be kept together and coherent only by a renewed desire for organization. This new spirit did not call a halt even

⁶⁰ Bernold, *Micrologus* (PL, CLI, 977-1022). Regarding the question of Bernold's authorship, see Franz, 414. Cf. also Schwertner in CE, II (1907), 512-513.
⁶¹ Cf. Franz, 415 f.
⁶² D. Kniewald, *Eph. liturg.*, LIV (1940), 221.

It is significant that the MS. which contains the oldest sacramentary of Hungary (12th/13th centuries) also offers the *Micrologus;* see C. Mohlberg, *Eph. Liturg.*, XLI (1927), 67 f.; Radó, 31-36.
⁶³ John of Avranches, *De off. eccl.* (PL, CXLVII, 27-62).

with regard to divine service[1]; the arrangement of the Mass felt its influence in a most profound manner. Already there was talk of that multiplicity of forms which had developed after the year 1000, but an effort was also made to codify the new forms; we can see in this a parallel to an attempt at mastering the heaped-up resources of knowledge by means of the *summas* which have been ranged side by side with the daring architecture of the Gothic cathedrals.

At least in the eleventh-century community, forces still held the balance of power in ecclesiastical life and the life of divine worship. Beside the cathedral chapter there was in every larger place, and often also in the country, a collegiate chapter in which clerics under the leadership of a provost or dean led a life in common, and above all conducted a community service of worship. In contrast to them the clerics who were individually in the service of the nobility remained absolutely in shadow, especially since most of them lacked any higher education. For these capitular churches, and for Roman church architecture in general, a characteristic was the roomy choir with its stalls, no longer set in a half-circle around the altar but arranged in several parallel rows between altar and people. The daily conventual Mass, which was celebrated, as in the monasteries, in the presence of the assembled clerical community, formed the crown of choir prayer and the very climax of divine service. In the Mass regulations and in the rubrics of the liturgical books this community service is almost the only one considered; there the celebrant appears nearly always accompanied by deacon and subdeacon, even though private celebration is not unknown. Above all, however, the entire setting of the liturgical texts is still always predicated on the cooperation of a plurality of officials and ministers. The priest needs only the sacramentary. Lectionary and antiphonary continue to be separate books for the use of those who are to read or sing. This situation continues to prevail till about the start of the twelfth century.

But then a new arrangement of the liturgical books breaks into the picture; on the strength of this the priest can take over the roles of lector and chanter and thus discharge the duties of his office independently of them. The ties of the individual are thus loosed in the liturgy, just as in this same period the organization of the canonries had slackened or even dissolved with the trend towards personal prebends and separate residences. In the thirteenth century the *Missale Plenum* displaces the sacramentary.[2] Presages of this new arrangement were the many silent prayers which, as we have seen, had begun to appear in the sacramentaries, at first (since the ninth century) only here and there, but since the eleventh almost universally. These prayers the priest did not have to perform with the community, but softly by himself.

There are isolated instances, especially within the confines of monas-

[1] Cf. A. L. Mayer, "Die Liturgie und der Geist der Gotik," JL, VI (1926), 68-97.   [2] Ebner, 359-363; Baumstark, *Missale Romanum*, 132-143.

ticism, where even at an earlier period the priest's Mass book was fitted out with the lessons, so that the service of a lector could be dispensed with.[3] Such books were very likely intended for the convenience of wandering monks, as may also be judged, in the case of the Missal of Bobbio, from the smallness of the book. In the church of Milan too, the oldest sacramentaries almost all incorporate the readings.[4] Since the ninth century there appeared at various places sacramentaries in which, appendix fashion, a number of Masses with readings are inserted, sometimes also with the chant-texts. As a rule, in fact, the Masses of the *commune* and the *Missæ diversæ*, along with the Votive Masses, including the Masses for the Dead, were thus distinguished.[5] Votive Masses and Masses for the Dead were employed essentially in the interests of individual families and persons, and especially if they followed each other in rapid succession, were held in the simplest form, often without the lector whose presence was, as a rule, still presumed.

But cases occur at least as often, in which the song-texts are inserted all through the sacramentary. Frequently all that was done was to indicate the first words on the margin—in an age that knew all the psalms by heart this was more than sufficient.[6] In other instances an antiphonary was bound up in one volume with the sacramentary.[7] Especially since the eleventh century, Mass books which contain the song-texts but (outside of the *commune* and the Votive Masses) not the readings, occur more often.[8] There again the first thought must have been private celebration,[9] in which John the Arch-chanter's[10] notion prevailed, that these texts were never to be left out. They had to be in the Mass books even when the lessons were left out, because a lector always cooperated, reading the Epis-

---

[3] Here belong the Missal of Bobbio (7th century) and, as the earliest example of a Roman "Lection-Sacramentary," the palimpsest text of Cod. 271 of Monte Cassino (8th century) ed. A. Dold, *Vom Sakramentar, Comes und Capitulare zum Missale* (*Texte und Arbeiten*, 34; Beuron, 1943).
[4] Examples, beginning with the 9th/10th century: Ebner, 71, 73, 87, 91, 92, 93. Also a sacramentary from the suffragan see of Brescia, from the middle of the 9th century: Ebner, 22.
Later examples from other churches, *ibid.*, 362, Note 6.
[5] Two examples of the 9th century from Verona: Ebner, 286 ff., 290 f.; one from the 9th/10th century: *ibid.*, 286. Further examples from the same period in Leroquais, I, p. xii, f. From a later period, see Ebner, 192, 293 ff.; cf. 15 ff., 33 f., 47.
[6] Already found, written by a second, almost contemporary hand, in the well-known

MS. of the Gregorianum, Cod. Ottobon. 313 (first half of the 9th century) ; these marginal notations reprinted in Muratori, II, 7 ff.
More recent examples are cited by Ebner, 362, Note 3.
[7] Several examples from the 10th/13th centuries mentioned in Ebner, 361, Note 3. On the contrary, cases in which a lectionary (*ibid.* Note 4) or a lectionary and an antiphonary (Notes 5 and 6) are added are less frequent.
Cf. also Baumstark, *Missale Romanum*, 133.
[8] Examples in Ebner, 47, 134, 141, 224; Köck, 3.
[9] In the early Middle Ages the song texts might be missing even in a *missa cantata*; see *infra*, p. 209. All the more does this hold for private Mass.
[10] *Supra*, p. 65.

tle and perhaps sometimes the Gospel also, if he did not have to hand the evangeliary to the priest[11] or if the priest did not have the pertinent Gospel pericope in his own Mass book.[12]

Since the thirteenth century simple sacramentaries were very seldom produced.[13] The *Missale Plenum* or complete missal, which had at first predominated only in monasteries,[14] has become the rule. The cleric to read the Epistle disappears from private Mass. If there are no deacon and sub-deacon, both readings are done by the ·priest himself, and are therefore indispensable in the Mass book, just as the chant-texts, too, cannot be omitted from it.

At high Mass the chant-texts are to be read by the celebrant (and the assistants) ; this we find stipulated for the first time in 1140 in regard to the introit, and the prayers the priest intones, *Gloria, Credo, Sanctus* and *Agnus Dei.*[15] This is expressly ordered for all the chant-texts for the first time, about the middle of the thirteenth century,[16] although a similar rule for the readings is not yet prescribed.[17] Here in this approach to the private Mass we find a sensitive loosening of the liturgical texture, corresponding in general to the centrifugal tendency of the Gothic period. The priest makes himself, to a certain extent, independent of the singing choir. What the latter is doing is no longer considered as a complementary part of the community celebration. Thus the trend to secular song instead of ecclesiastical can grow all the more powerful. But another factor may have had some influence with regard to the priest himself. Right into the twelfth century it had been customary for the celebrant to fill every pause in his prayers at high Mass with *apologiæ*. Were people finally getting tired of them? It was at any rate a step forward to admit that it would be

[11] Amongst the Cistercians in the case of a (conventual) Mass *cum uno ministro*—and the same thing held, no doubt, for a private Mass—the missal was laid on the altar to the right, the evangeliary to the left; the latter was then removed after the Gospel: *Liber usuum,* c. 54 (PL, LXVI, 1429 A). According to the Augsburg Missal of 1555 (Hoeynck, 372), the priest at the beginning of Mass kissed the evangeliary at the left of the altar, the missal at the right.

[12] Not a few of the sacramentaries since the year 1000 contain the Gospels along with the prayers, but omit the Epistles and the chant texts. Amongst these are the so-called *Vetus Missale Lateranense* (11th/12th century) in which the Epistles and chant texts were added later; Ebner, 168. Other examples, *ibid.,* 13, 96 f., 174, 185, 280; cf. 39.

[13] Amongst the latest examples we must list the sacramentary of the papal chapel (c.

1290) mentioned in the last chapter, note 51 (cf. Ebner, 234 f.) and a 15th-century sacramentary from SS. Apostoli in Rome (Ebner, 146 f.). Another 15th-century sacramentary (Autun) is cited by Leroquais, III, 84.

[14] Examples since the 10th century in Baumstark, 134 f. A newly recovered fragment, probably done at Monte Cassino about 1000, is edited by A. Dold, JL, X (1930), 40-55.

[15] *Ordo eccl. Lateran.,* ed. Fischer, 80, 82 f., 85 ; *officium* = Introit.

[16] Ordinarium O.P. of 1256 (Guerrini, 235, 237, 239, 244). This could not have been the usual thing much earlier, since the Mass regulations of the preceding years, otherwise rather full and exact, make no mention of it.

[17] But the Epistle is indicated in the *Ordo* of the Lateran church (Fischer, 81, line 12).

much more fitting if the priest would replace those endless self-accusations with the biblical texts which were being sung by the choir.

The complete missal is therefore the product not indeed of the predominance of the private Mass (which had long been in use), but at least of its general extension and its increased acceptance.[18]

For the participation of the faithful, the Mass celebrated as a service with or without sacred ministers, with its Latin chanting and its mystery-filled ceremonies, continued during the years to follow as the standard form. The manner of explaining also remained the same, namely allegory, as we saw in Amalar. The Mass is looked upon as a holy drama, a play performed before the eyes of the participants. But meanwhile the graphic ceremonial has been enriched. The signs of the Cross in the canon, most of them of pre-Frankish origin, were multiplied till far into the eleventh and twelfth centuries—at the *Supplices* and at the closing doxology. In addition there were in many churches signings with the Cross, and corresponding blessing formulas at the offertory, after the presentation of the gifts[19]; and the priest blessed himself a number of times, especially at the Gospel. The Gothic principle of cumulation, the repetition of the same detail, the heaping up of ornament, had its effect on the kissing of the altar. Although up to the twelfth century, this was customary—in line with tradition—only when first approaching the altar and again when leaving, since the end of the thirteenth century it was performed every time the celebrant turned around at the altar.[20] The kiss at high Mass when handing the celebrant any object, and the kiss of greeting for the celebrant are also added at various places.[21] The extension of the hands after the consecration became, since the thirteenth century, a vivid imitation of the outstretched arms of the Crucified. For a time, too, the ceremonial was built up further; the priest at the anamnesis, on recalling the Resurrection and Ascension of our Lord, was supposed to mimic these movements with his hands.[22] Bowing the head at the end of the *Memento* of the dead, and

[18] For a more detailed discussion cf. *infra*, p. 212 ff.
[19] *Infra*, Vol. II, Ch. 1, 4.
[20] *Infra*, p. 317.
A Hungarian missal of the 13th century demands a threefold kissing of the altar at *Veni sanctificator* and *Supplices;* Radó, 62.
[21] Cf. the *Ordo eccl. Lateran.* (c. 1140), ed. Fischer, 80-87 and in the Index under the word *osculum* (p. 181); the numerous places at which the kiss is expressly prescribed make it clear that this is not an old tradition taken for granted. Cf. however the trend manifested already about 1100 in the Missal of St. Vincent; Fiala, 201 ff. Innocent III, *De s. alt. mysterio*, VI, 6 (PL, CCXVII, 909 f.), has a special chapter "*De diversis osculis quæ dantur in*

missa"; he mentions, amongst other things, seven ways in which the pope receives the kiss.
[22] According to Hugh of St. Cher, *Tract. super missam* (ed. Soelch, 37), the priest was to *extendere* [*manus*] *in modum crucis* —*parum erigere in signum quod Christus —parum erigere in signum quod Christus invictus leo resurrexit—erigere in signum quod Christus Deus et homo ascendit*. Similarly the Missal of Riga (about 1400; v. Bruiningk, 85) and Hungarian Mass books of the 15th century (Jávor, 116). Cf. Sölch, *Hugo*, 93 f. In like manner it was customary among the Premonstratensians for the priest at the *Credo* to wait till the *Et resurrexit* before he rose from the genuflection; see JL, IV (1924), 252.

striking the breast while saying *Nobis quoque* in a loud voice—these actions appear to have been introduced as a vivid presentation of our Lord's death and the impression it made on the bystanders.[23]

And the dramatization of the readings[24] took a new turn since Ivo of Chartres (d. 1117); where there was no single ambo to determine the place for the readings, older memories were recalled and so the Gospel was read at the right side (reckoned from the viewpoint of the ancient position of the episcopal throne) and the Epistle at the left. This led to the distinction between the Gospel side (church or altar) and the Epistle side.[25]

All these usages, making a bid for the curious and fascinated eyes of the Christian people, obtained an allegorical significance. Less and less did the spoken word project its own contents; one concentrated rather on the alternation between the loud and the soft tones of prayer.[26] The meaning of ceremonies was often a synthetic one, abstracting entirely from the course of the sacred action, and giving a fixed significance to each repeated ceremony just as a fixed significance was given to the visible appurtenances. Ever since Amalar the priestly vesture had been treated allegorically,[27] and in the years that followed this treatment was extended to the church building.[28]

In the same way, the ceremonies that were oft repeated acquired a fixed meaning, with little thought given to their particular status here and now in the liturgical action. Often enough, besides the picture which presents

---

Ceremonies of this sort of imitative symbolism were developed in great number, as is well known. And they often turned into something quite playful, as (for instance) when the boy-abbot in the monastery schools on the Feast of Holy Innocents (Dec. 28) at Vespers, when the words *deposuit potentes de sede* were sung, was summarily shoved from his chair. The same dramatic instinct was at work here which produced the mystery plays.

Cl. de Vert, *Explication simple littérale et historique des cérémonies* (Paris, 1706-1708), wanted to use this imitative symbolism of the late Middle Ages as the main principle for the explanation of the ceremonies.

[23] Such attempts to create a symbolism that would push the allegory of existing ceremonies even further and produce new ones, were at work quite early. St. Anselm, who died 1109, in a letter, *Ad Waleranni querelas,* ch. 3 (PL, CLVIII, 553 f.), chides those priests for leaving the chalice uncovered during Mass on the plea that Christ had hung naked on the cross of suffering.
[24] Cf. *supra*, pp. 77 ff.

[25] In greater detail *infra*, p. 414 ff.
[26] Cf. the anonymous explanation of the Mass in the Graz Cod. 730 (about 1300; in Franz, 631): *Ea autem quæ laici noscere et quæ eis dici possunt, quæ ad missam pertinent, in tribus comprehenduntur, videlicet in gestibus—ut sunt VII oscula, V versiones, IV inclinationes, XXV cruces sive benedictiones, locorum mutationes, manuum extensiones—in verborum prolationibus....*
[27] Perhaps it would be more correct to say "symbolically," since, to be exact, the vesture does not of itself express or signify anything and therefore it cannot rightly be said to "say something else." But in reality we are dealing here not with any original symbolism (the sort of thing found, for instance, in the washing of hands), but only with a secondary symbolism subsequently connected with it—which is hardly to be distinguished from allegory; cf. J. Braun, *Liturgisches Handlexikon* (2nd ed., Regensburg, 1924), 333 f.
[28] J. Sauer, *Symbolik des Kirchengebäudes* (2nd ed., Freiburg, 1924). Sauer follows especially the meanings developed in Honorius Augustodunensis.

itself, the number of repetitions offered a solution. Thus the triple silence in the Mass proper—at the secrets, during the canon and after the *Pater noster*—represents the three days our Lord rested in the tomb.[29] The five-fold turning of the priest toward the people[30] refers to the five appearances of our Lord after the Resurrection.[31] Similarly the number of crosses made over the *oblata* received by preference a numerological meaning. The three crosses after the *Te igitur* typify the three times our Lord was mocked before the high priests and Herod and Pilate, the five crosses in the *Unde et memores* typify the five wounds, and so forth.[32] The signs of the Cross within the canon are, since the eleventh century, the main theme for instructing the people about the Mass.[33] A didactic poem of this period outlines the minumum that each priest must know about the Mass; what is the sacrifice, and what the altar and chalice, water and wine, and the crosses signify.[34]

With few exceptions[35]—among them the straightforward and objective exposition by the Parisian doctor, Jean Beleth (d. about 1165), deserves a prominent place[36]—the explanation and interpretation of the Mass remains strictly within the bounds initiated by Amalar. The Mass is understood as a dramatic presentation of an action in the divine economy, especially of the suffering, death and resurrection of Christ, beginning with the longings and sighs of the patriarchs and prophets and concluding with our Saviour's ascension into heaven.

The newly developed and newly added ceremonies had also to be considered in this allegorizing. Keeping the book at the altar and moving it from Epistle side to Gospel side—this did not fit easily into the plans heretofore in vogue. It led, as a consequence, not only to an architectonic enlargement of the measurements of the altar, up to now rather modest,[37]

---

[29] A rhymed explanation of the Mass (12th century) ed. by A. Leitzmann, 2nd ed. (*Kleine Texte*, LIV), 19, l. 30.

[30] The number, but without its meaning, already in Jean Beleth, *Explicatio*, ch. 37 (PL, CCII, 45).

[31] A preacher of the 13th century draws this oft-repeated meaning out still further: the the third turning around, at the *Orate*, is a "secret" greeting and refers to the appearance to Peter which is not known to us in detail. Franz, 643 f.

[32] Thus several interpreters, according to the account by Albertus Magnus; cf. *infra*, p. 113. Moreover it was precisely in the field of number-symbolism that the most widely diversified solutions were offered. Durandus, IV, 36, 8, for example, gives five different explanations for the three crosses after the *Te igitur*.

[33] *Infra*, Vol. II, Ch. 2, 5.

[34] Ps-Hildebert, *De s. eucharistia* (PL, LXXI, 1209).

[35] Amongst these are Richard of Weddinghausen (12th century), who throughout his explanation of the canon carries out a symbolism built on the number three, but without any rememorative allegory (Franz, 418 f.), and Odo of Cambrai (d. 1113), who creates his exposition on the basis of word meanings and theology (*ibid.*, 426 f.).

[36] Jean Beleth, *Explicatio divinorum officiorum*, also known as *Rationale div. off.* (PL, CCII, 13-166).

[37] Until the 11th century the altar tables were rarely more than 3 or 4 feet square. (But by the 15th it was not unusual to find them 12 feet long.) At this time, too, the altar began to be built up beyond the simple *mensa*; not only temporary and occasional reliquaries were placed over it, but permanent altar-pieces as well—the start of the

but also to a revamping of the Mass-allegory. Even the first sure evidence of the term ‟Gospel side"—in Ivo of Chartres—refers to it as the *sinistra pars ecclesiæ*[38] and the author is then faced with the riddle, why the Gospel should be given the less honorable side; he solves it by explaining that this signifies how when the Jews refused the faith, the apostles turned to the Gentiles (Acts 13:46).[39] Thus in the rememorative allegory of the Mass the preaching to the Jews—in contrast to Amalar's plan—had to come before the reading of the Gospel. The collects, too, since they preceded, had to get a new interpretation. Ivo explains them as typical of how our Lord taught His disciples, especially how He taught them to pray. The Epistle then signifies the mission of the disciples.[40] The intervening chants refer to the joyous response of those who were well disposed.[41]

The same interpreter, taking a cue from older projects, sketches for the first time a well-rounded explanation of the canon and its silence as a fulfillment of Old Testament prefigurements. His is therefore a typological allegory intermixed with rememorative elements. Like the high-priest on the great day of Atonement, so the celebrant walks alone into the Holy of Holies, carrying the memorial of the Blood of Christ, and on his breast the names of the twelve patriarchs (the naming of the twelve Apostles), and with the Blood of the Saviour he sprinkles it. When he returns, the scapegoat is chased into the wilderness in the *Jube haec perferri*. Then, instead of changing his garments, he changes his voice and speaks the *Pater noster* aloud.[42] This attempt at an explanation was carried on by later interpreters and deepened theologically, ultimately to the better un-

---

immense reredoses of a later date; Braun, *Der christliche Altar*, II, 253 ff., 277 ff. Moreover, cross and altar candles appear on the table; Braun, *Das christliche Altargerät*, 466 ff.
[38] Ivo of Chatres, *De conven. Vet. et Novi Test* (PL, CLXII, 550 A).
[39] *Ibid.*
This interpretation recurs constantly down to the present; cf., e.g., Paul Bussard, *The Sacrifice* (St. Paul, 1939), 84.
A second meaning in Innocent III, *De s. alt. mysterio*, II, 35 (PL, CCXVII, 820): hereby is represented the truth that Christ came to call not the just but sinners to repentance (Matt. 9:13; cf. 25:33). Durandus, IV, 23, repeats both significations.
[40] Ivo of Chartres, *op. cit.*
A similar meaning of the Epistle, but for other reasons, is already found in Remigius of Auxerre, *Expositio* (PL, CI, 1250 A).
[41] *Loc. cit.*
Ivo's interpretation of the pre-Gospel pieces reappears in Hildebert of Le Mans,

Versus de mysterio missæ (PL, CLXXI, 1178) and likewise in some other later expositors. Still even near the end of the 12th century, Robertus Paululus, *De cæremoniis*, II, 17 (PL, CLXXVII, 421 f.) interprets the Epistle as the preaching of John the Baptist. Innocent III, *De s. alt. mysterio*, II, 29 f. (PL, CCXVII, 816) also gives the preference to this signification.
In addition, Ivo also suggests a new interpretation of the start of the Mass-sacrifice which is frequently repeated later: the quiet prayers during the offertory refer to the prayer of our Lord on Olivet; at the preface he interrupts them and goes to his disciples to exhort them to pray; *op. cit.* (PL, CLXII, 553 f.).
[42] *Op. cit.* (PL, CLXII, 559 B). In some details the interpretation is not always in taste. Cf. also Franz, 429-431.
Hildebert, in his verses, has made an acceptable selection; *op. cit.* (PL, CLXXI, 1182 f.).

derstanding of the sacrificial character of the Mass.[43]

New images of Old Testament origin were introduced into the allegorizing of the Mass by Honorius of Augustodunum (d. about 1125).[44] In the Mass the exodus from Egypt, the revelation of the commandments, the conquest of Amalec at the prayers of Moses pleading with arms outstretched, the entrance into the Promised Land under the leadership of "Jesu"—all these are re-enacted in a new manner. The bishop, accoutred in his sacred garments as in the armor of war, is the general; the lector is the herald, bells and chants are the fanfare of battle. Even the struggle between David and Goliath is rehearsed in the Mass. Since Honorius adds other pictures, includes audacious number-symbolism, and embraces also much of the traditional allegory of Christ's Passion, the result is a bewildering wealth of variegated meanings, to which one could scarcely apply the title of an explanation. Sicard of Cremona (d. 1215) wanders along the same pathway, but adds to the confusion with a plethora of quotations.[45]

In general, however, the work of the medieval Mass commentators is wedded to the extension of the rememorative type of allegory. Rupert von Deutz (d. 1135) expands it to include the sacerdotal vestments, in which he perceives the person of Christ outlined; the humeral reminds one of the concealment of Christ's divinity by His humanity; the alb, of His purity; the stole, of His obedience unto death; the chasuble, of His raiment which is the Church.[46]

A healthy reaction to this increased overloading of the interpretation of the Mass with so many diverse elements, and at the same time a high point of rememorative allegory is found in the work composed by Innocent III, at that time still Cardinal Lothar, just before his election as Pope (1198).[47] Except for an abundantly practical number-symbolism, he restricts himself almost entirely to the traditional meanings derived from Christ's life and Passion, which he presents distinctly in simple words. His work, therefore, became the basis for the Mass interpretations of the later Middle Ages, which are often content to repeat the words of the great Pope, either cutting them down or broadening them out.[48]

The great compiler of medieval liturgical allegory, William Durandus (d. 1296), acknowledges—in his *Rationale divinorum officiorum* which we

---

[43] In this category is the work at one time attributed to Hugh of St. Victor, *Speculum de mysteriis Ecclesiæ* (PL, CLXXVII, 335-380), which expounds the Mass from offertory on as a fulfillment of the Old Testament types; the *iube hæc perferri* in his explanation realizes the sprinkling of the Holy of Holies; ch. 7 (368 ff.).

The interpretation of the canon proposed by Isaac of Stella (d. c. 1169) will be treated later, Vol. II, Chap. 2, 15.

[44] Honorius Augustodunensis, *Gemma animæ* (PL, CLXXII, 541-738). Whether the word Augustodunum refers to Autun or to Augsburg is still in dispute; Franz, 420-425.

[45] Sicard of Cremona, *Mitrale seu de officiis ecclesiasticis* (PL, CCXIII, 13-434).

[46] Rupert of Deutz, *De divinis officiis* (PL, CLXX, 11-332).

[47] Innocent III, *De sacro altaris mysterio* (PL, CCXVII, 773-916).

[48] Cf. Franz, 459, 565, 493, 509, 523, etc.

must come back to time and again because of its opportune mention of the rites then in use—that he took Innocent III as his guide for the explanation of the Mass.[49]

In Innocent we find for the first time a determination of liturgical colors for specified days,[50] along with the respective significance thereof. His rules are more or less those still in force today: white as the festive color (and he tries to discover a reason for the white—even in the white of the clouds on Ascension Day!), red for martyrs' days and Pentecost, black for days of penance and for Masses for the Dead, green for days without a festal character.[51] The sensuous interest in colors and the zeal in explaining their significance were alike manifestations of the spirit of the Gothic period.

A new trend is manifest also in the understanding and meaning of the various liturgical vestments. Innocent himself[52] finds chiefly a moral meaning like that which Amalar offered; in particular, he is familiar with the spiritual battle (I. 64), although this is better developed in other writers.[53] But Innocent also avails himself of a christological explanation somewhat similar to Rupert von Deutz who saw relationships between the priestly garments and the properties and attributes of Christ's person. But by the middle of the thirteenth century this had turned to a form of rememorative allegory, which here too perceived symbols of the Passion of Christ.[54]

Development is also to be found in practical paramentics. The Gothic chasuble is still broad and mantle-like, but the two ornamental stripes falling down from the shoulder and joined as a line down the middle became in time a forked cross and this in turn became (on the back of the chasuble) a regular cross with horizontal cross-beam. This development means that the allegorical presentation of the Crucified could be imaged even in the external figuration,[55] but it also led not only to a richer and richer ornamentation but also, because of the need for a stiff surface, to the later misshaping of the garment. Similar forces were at work in changing the shape of the altar. The altar screens (polyptych retables or "wing-

---

[49] Durandus, IV, 1, 2.

[50] About the same time the *Liber ordinarius* of the Premonstratensians (Lefèvre, 6, 1. 18) not only pays no attention to a rule regarding colors, but even insists that chasubles all be *unius coloris*, a regulation which is missing in later sources. Cf. Waefelghem, 28.

[51] Innocent III, *op. cit.*, I, 65 (PL, CCXVII, 799-802). Cf. Braun, *Die liturgische Gewandung*, 729-736. Cf. E. G. Atchley, "Liturgical Colours," in V. Staley, *Essays on Ceremonial* (London, 1904), 89-176.

[52] Innocent III, *op. cit.*, I, 11-64 (PL, CCXVII, 781-799). In a Klosterneuburg MS. of the 13th century, there is a poetic elaboration of this section of Innocent; H.

Maschek, "Eine metrische Symbolik der Sakralgewänder aus dem 13. Jh.", *Eph. Liturg.*, XLVII (1933), 368-377.

[53] Braun, *Die liturgische Gewandung*, 705 f.

[54] This meaning, along with the moral one, is found in a Franciscan writer who is otherwise generally very dependent on Innocent, William of Melitona, *Opusculum super missam* (ed. A. van Dijk), in *Eph. liturg.*, LIII (1939), 219-349; see 312-14. William sees in the shoulder-cloth the scornful blind-fold, in the alb the white robe of ridicule, in the cincture, maniple and stole the cords, and in the chasuble the purple mantle. Similarly also Hugh of St. Cher, *Tractatus super missam* (Sölch, 8-10).

[55] Braun, *Die liturgische Gewandung*, 209-219.

altars") offer us the very best in Gothic from the viewpoint of artistic performance, but from the viewpoint of the liturgy they were definitely an aberration.

The allegorical method of contemplating and explaining the liturgy had to face a crisis in the thirteenth century, and it is really a matter of wonder that it was able to weather the storm and that the old method should survive unscathed in the period to follow. In a century when medieval Scholasticism reaced a peak, the very basis of all allegory was naturally called into question. For allegory is founded entirely on a conception of the world which is interested in the sensible and visible phenomena only insofar as they are mirrors and symbols of an invisible, intangible higher world. Even in the book of nature, attention was focused not on the forms of individual things, not on the shapes of the "letters," but only on the hidden meaning which, one thought, could be read therein. It is the spirit within the writing, the spirit within the liturgy—especially in its space-visible appearance—that is sought, every effort being made to grub out the thought that must lie hid there.[56] Art in this period, whether concerned with animals and plants, or the attributes of the saints, or geometrical patterns, seeks principally to enlarge and explain this world of symbols. This is nothing more, really, than the logical consequence of carrying through Plato's theory of knowledge, with its sharp separation of the world of sense and the world of ideas. But with the switch to Aristotle and the new basis for a theory of knowledge—*Cognitio incipit a sensibus* —the world of sense, and the concrete phenomena of forms in divine worship along with it, at once appears in a new light. It deserves to be studied and appreciated for its own sake.

Albertus Magnus was the pathfinder who led the Scholastics along the new way of explaining Holy Mass.[57] First of all, he presents an enlightened and theologically grounded explanation of the course of that Mass that is for the most part derived from the text of the Mass *ordo*. Besides he makes repeated thrusts at the allegorical exposition, especially at the rememorative. He says it is *mirabile* to refer the silence of the Mass proper to events in the story of our Lord's Passion—things in no way touched upon in the text of the Mass.[58] In fact, in reference to the explanation that the kissing of the altar at the *Supplices* signified Judas' traitorous kiss, and the signs of the Cross that follow signify the bonds and ropes by which our Saviour was led to Annas, he says scornfully: *omnino profanum est et omnibus fidelibus abominandum.*[59] The different signification attached to the signs

---

[56] E. Mâle, *Die kirchliche Kunst des 13. Jahrhunderts in Frankreich* (German trans., L. Zuckermandel; Strassburg, 1907), 24-34; P. Pourrat, *Christian Spirituality*, II (trans. S. J. Jacques; N. Y., 1924), 109-117: "The Symbolistic Conception of the Universe" (in the 12th century).
Cf. also A Dempf, *Sacrum Imperium*

(Munich, 1929), 229-268: "Der deutsche Symbolismus des 12. Jh."

[57] Albertus Magnus, *De sacrificio missæ* (*Opera omnia* ed. Borgnet, 38, 1-189). See in this connection Franz, 466-473.

[58] *Op. cit.*, III, 2, 5 (80).

[59] *Op. cit.*, III, 15, 2 (130).

of the Cross at the *Quam oblationem* he termed: *deliramenta et hominum illiteratorum.*[60] But Albertus' objections made little headway. Allegory continued to hold the field. Even St. Thomas' *Summa Theologica* contained an interpretation of the Mass that made many concessions to allegory.[61]

One result of Scholastic thought must be acknowledged, the consideration given to the organization of the Mass into parts following one after the other. Allegorical thought was concerned mostly with a series of pictures, and either took their order for granted or considered the division a mere external.[62] Now, however, intrinsic and theological viewpoints became paramount. Albertus Magnus had distinguished three parts: *introitus* (up to the collects inclusive), *instructio* (up to the *Credo* inclusive), and *oblatio*, with appropriate subdivisions for the last. This division recurs in the *Expositio missæ* of Nicholas Stoer, written about 1412.[63] Another outline derives from Alexander of Hales (d. 1245).[64] It is found in a bettered form in Bernard de Parentinis, O.P. (about 1340)[65] and in Henry of Hesse (d. 1397)[66]; Henry heads the sections: *præparatio, instructio, oblatio, canon, communio, gratiarum actio.* Hugh of St. Cher, O.P. (d. 1263), like so many medieval authors, takes the Augustinian interpretation of the words of St. Paul, *obsecrationes, orationes, postulationes, gratiarum actiones,*[67] and applies them to the Mass, thus distinguishing four parts, of which the first embraces everything up the *Sanctus*, the second takes in the canon, the third begins with the *Pater noster* and the fourth with the postcommunion.[68]

In these new attempts at a division of the Mass, the segment before the Epistle, as is remarked more than once, is (even today) instructive. But the weakest point in the outline is the placing of the preface. Since the Mass is viewed chiefly from the standpoint of the consecration and the canon is reckoned as beginning with the *Te igitur*, the prayer of thanks, which had such great importance in the ancient Church, no longer presents a problem. Albertus Magnus, and also Alexander of Hales and his

[60] *Op. cit.,* III, 10, 2 (118).
The examples mentioned, and others cited by Albert, are also found word for word in Innocent III, *De s. alt. mysterio,* III, 12; V, 5.

[61] Thomas Aquinas, *Summa theol.,* III, 83, 5. The section under consideration is not the work of Thomas himself, as is well known.

[62] Franz, 460.
It is significant that Honorius Augustodunensis—and similarly Sicard—gives a seven-fold division, in which the fifth part is the canon, the sixth the blessing of the bishop (cf. *infra,* Vol. II, Ch. 3, 3) and the seventh the kiss of peace. Franz, 422, 450 f.

[63] Franz, 529. Also in the *Compendium doctrinæ catholicæ* of Petrus Soto (1549);

see Ch. Moufang, *Katholische Katechismen des 16. Jh.* (Mainz, 1881), 352-362.

[64] Franz, 640 f. Its value is to be found not in the main divisions (*illuminatio, immolatio, rememoratio accepti beneficii*—the last meaning from the post-communion on), but in the detailed subdivisions. Slightly altered in William of Melitona, *Opusc. super missam* (ed. van Dijk), in *Eph. liturg.,* LIII (1939), 317-349.

[65] Franz, 505 f.

[66] That is, Henry of Langenstein, author of *Secreta sacerdotum*; Franz, 518.

[67] I Tim. 2:1; Augustine, *Ep.* 149, 16 (CSEL, XLIV, 362 f.).

[68] Hugh of St. Cher, *Tract. super missam* (Sölch, 11). The same division in Durandus, IV, 1, 50.

school, considered the preface a part of the offertory, a sort of conclusion to it. According to Beleth, the second of the four Augustinian portions begins with the *secreta*; the preface is thus drawn closer to the canon, but makes of it a very secondary member in the series.[69] Others take a middle course—like Hugh of St. Cher[70]—by placing the preface in the first part of the Mass without further ado, and thus it becomes accidentally one of the preparatory acts for the consecration.

That is about all that Scholastic thought effected in the interpretation of the Mass. As for the development of the Mass-liturgy, or for all that, the development of an understanding of the Mass-liturgy, Scholasticism left scarcely a trace—a rather surprising thing. The *Rationale* of Durandus which is constructed entirely on the basis of allegory, continued to be the liturgical handbook for the late Middle Ages and beyond.[71] And the later interpreters, whose number is not without weight, follow more or less along the same paths.[72]

A further evolution was gradually effected. The vestments which the priest wore to the altar had been interpreted as signifying Christ's Passion. The next step was certain—to conceive of the Mass, not only from the canon but from the beginning on, as a presentation of Christ's suffering. An anonymous interpreter of the fifteenth century does just that.[73] According to him, when the priest goes to the altar our Lord is taken away captive, at the *Confiteor* he stands before Annas and Caiphas, etc. A more pronounced extension of this type of consideration does not however come to notice till the post-medieval Mass expositions.[74] A broadening-out of

[69] Jean Beleth, *Explicatio*, ch. 43, ff. He calls the preface a *prælocutio quæ est ad ministerium præparatio* (ch. 45; PL, 202, 53 B), thus like Amalar, *De off. eccl.*, III, 21 (PL, CV, 1133 A), who had simply rendered the name as *præparatio*.
[70] The same is true of Innocent III, *De s. alt. mysterio*, II, 61 f. (PL, CCXVII, 835-840).
[71] This is shown by the countless manuscripts and even more by the fact that by 1500 there were already 43 printings of the work.
[72] As works of greater importance, though in part not printed, Franz lists and describes, amongst others: the interpretations of the Mass by Guido of Mont Rocher (circa 1333; Franz, 490 ff.), Henry of Hessen (circa 1390; *ibid.*, 517 ff.), Bernard of Waging (1462; *ibid.*, 566 ff.), Balthasar of Pforta, O.Cist. (circa 1494; *ibid.*, 584ff.), John Bechofen, Erem. S. Aug. (circa 1500; *ibid.*, 592 ff.).
The *Expositio canonis missæ* of Magister Egeling Becker (circa 1450; *ibid.*, 537 ff.),

which grew out of a series of lectures, did not find a wide circulation until it was revised in 1488 by Gabriel Biel and reappeared in print under his name (*ibid.*, 550 ff.). This extensive work is essentially a study of the wording of the canon; sometimes the treatment of the more important ideas is built up into a theological tractate.
Nor was the number of smaller studies of the Mass at the end of the Middle Ages inconsiderable. How well-liked the discussions on this matter were is shown by the example of a university instructor, probably from Vienna, who used to spend his vacation with the Benedictines at Mondsee and repaid them for their hospitality by lecturing on the Mass. Franz, 565 ff.
[73] Surviving in a Stuttgart MS.; Franz, 740 f.
[74] Franz, 735 f.
Those who were affected by the *devotio moderna* towards the end of the 15th century sometimes engaged in a type of devotion for Mass based on the contemplation of Christ's Passion but freed more or

the allegory of Christ's Passion resulted also from the elevation of the species at the consecration, a custom which grew, as we will see, from the thirteenth century on. This ceremony naturally suggested the raising of Christ on the Cross.[75]

Besides, allegorical interpretation of the Mass again went awry in the late medieval period. Elements of different types of explanation were thrown together. The oft-changing explanation of the sign of the Cross did not fit well into the course of the Mass. In the last analysis, all that was needed was a little imagination to invent more arbitrary explanations for the various liturgical details which were already explained quite arbitrarily. So, besides the exclusive Passion interpretation there were other plans—seeing exemplified in the Mass the forty *opera* of Christ's life,[76] or his thirty-three years.[77] With the eclectic methods then in vogue this could lead only to further confusion.

That is precisely what happened, and since no one seemed able to manage any other form of devotion or interpretation, attempts were again made towards the end of the Middle Ages to bring order into the allegorizing by trying to establish a clear and neat series built up on a time basis. Of this sort are the explanations of Simon van Venlo[78] and Franz Titelmans (d. 1537).[79]

Despite this vacillation, the fundamental theme of all Mass allegory was the suffering, or at least the life and suffering of Jesus. Our Lord's command, "Do this for a commemoration of me," was never lost sight of even in the plain and simple devotion of these centuries; rather it had been fulfilled in a sort of figurative fashion. Significant in this respect is the picture of St. Gregory's Mass, a theme repeatedly utilized by artists of the late

---

less from any consideration of the ceremonies; this devotion, however, was for clerics and religious. Franz, 26-28.

[75] Thus already explained by Berthold of Regensburg (d. 1272) in the first Latin sermon on the Mass, printed in Franz, 744. Likewise later interpreters like Ludolf of Saxony (d. 1377), *Vita D. N. Jesu Christi*, II, 56, 8 (Augsburg, 1729, p. 558), and John Bechofen, *Quadruplex missalis expositio* (Basel, 1500; no page numbering). The latter relates the elevation of the sacred host to the *Ecce homo*, and the elevation of the chalice to the raising of our Lord on the Cross.

Moreover Radulphus Ardens (d. 1215), *Hom.* 47 (PL, CLV, 1836), had already explained the older elevation at the words *accepit panem* as referring to Christ's being raised on the Cross.

[76] An interpretation of the Mass found in an Andechs MS. of the 15th century, in Franz,

609 f. Here are represented the entrance into the Virgin's womb, the flight into Egypt, etc.

[77] The Minorite Michael de Hungaria distinguishes 33 acts in the Mass which he refers to the 33 years of Christ's life. Franz, 675.

[78] M. Smits van Waesberghe, "Die misverklaring van Meester Simon van Venlo," *Ons geestlijk Erf*, XV (1941), 228-261; 285-327; XVI (1942), 85-129; 177-185; see esp. XVI (1942), 116 ff.

[79] Fr. Titelmannus, *Mysteriorum missæ expositio* (Lyons, 1558). Here are some new suggestions that fit nicely into the full picture: the priest's sitting silently during the singing of the interposed chants after the Epistle is related to Christ's stay in the wilderness; the praise of God in the preface is related to the meal at Bethany, when the whole house was filled with the fragrance of the ointment.

Middle Ages. While Gregory is at Mass our Lord appears to him above the altar as a man of suffering, with the instruments of His Passion.[80] On the other hand, the notion of sacrifice as such, and of the sacrifice which is here consummated and which the Church here co-offers—that stays surprisingly in the background, even though the theologians hand on the traditional doctrine.[81] The offertory procession is still the practice on many occasions, but in the various explanations of the Mass there is hardly any mention of the fact that the assembled people have a part in the oblation or at least participate in praising and honoring God. By the gifts which the faithful present at the offertory *"kauffent (sie) sich und frument sich in die marter Christi und in das verdienen seines leidens, das da wirt bedacht in der mess"* [82]—they purchase and make available to themselves the sufferings of Christ and the merits of His Passion which is commemorated in the Mass. The Mass is viewed almost exclusively as an action of God. In the liturgical unfolding of the celebration of Mass, the action of the Church, its prayer of thanks, and its gift-offerings are no longer perceived as in former ages; only the work, the redeeming work of God. The priest alone is active. The faithful, viewing what he is performing, are like spectators looking on at a mystery-filled drama of our Lord's Way of the Cross. It is no accident, then, that Calderón in his *autos sacramentales* should employ the traditional medieval allegory to present a drama in which the whole economy of salvation, from Paradise to world's end, is hinged to the Mass; and yet never a word, either at the offertory or at the Communion, of the concelebration of the laity. The *eucharistia* has become an *epiphania*, an advent of God who appears amongst men and dispenses His graces. To gain a share in these graces, we are gathered before the altar, in an attitude of wondering contemplation that bespeaks our longing to take part in the Mass as often as possible.

It is no wonder that the allegorical method which reigned supreme through so many centuries should leave its traces on the Mass-liturgy which has come down to us. The Middle Ages inserted certain rites to make the sacred drama more potent. Amongst these, as we shall see, is the ceremony of hiding the paten under the corporal at the offertory—to signify our Lord's self-abasement and the hiding of His divinity in His Passion; the bowing of the head at the end of the *Memento* of the Dead— to signify our Saviour's death; the lifting of the voice at *Nobis quoque*—to

---

[80] R. Bauerreiss, "Gregoriusmesse," LThK, IV, 689 f.; Braun, *Der christliche Altar*, II, 453-455.
[81] How little and how seldom the idea of sacrifice entered into the liturgical thought of the 12th century is seen rather pointedly in the reasons given for daily Mass in Honorius Augustod., *Gemma an.*, I, 36 (PL, CLXXII, 555); daily Mass is celebrated, he says, so that (1) the laborers in the vineyard—that is, the priests only—might be able to communicate; (2) that neophytes might be included in the Body of Christ (by the Baptismal Communion; cf. A. Landgraf, ZkTh, LXVI [1942] 119-131); and (3) that the *memoria passionis* might remain alive amongst the faithful.
[82] The explanation of the Mass in a Stuttgart MS. of the 15th century; Franz, 705.

signify the cry of the captain of the guard; the five crosses at the doxology concluding the canon—to signify the five wounds; the anticipation of the commingling—as symbol of the Resurrection—so that the greeting *Pax Domini* might appear as the greeting of the risen Saviour; the lifting of hands and eyes before the last blessing—after the model of our Lord before the Ascension.[83]

This consideration of the Mass as an epiphany, although brought to the fore by the allegorizing pattern, received, at one point at least, a further impetus and enforcement when, at the turn of the twelfth century, the practice of elevating host and chalice after the consecration came into being.[84] All our bodily eyes can see of Christ in the Eucharist is the sacramental covering and wrapping beneath which His Body and Blood are concealed, but medieval man was so eager[85] to view even this, that various devices were employed to render possible this perception of the Sacrament.[86]

Out of the distant past, eucharistic thought had gradually taken a new turn, so that from the time of Isidore and the controversies of the ninth century it began little by little to look upon the Sacrament (omitting its symbolism) almost entirely from the viewpoint of the Real Presence.[87] This Presence and the mode of its achievement were the topics on which theologians focused their attention more and more. Since Anselm of Laon (d. 1117) and William of Champeaux (d. 1121) theological teaching had become more clear and precise, namely that in the Sacrament not only were the Body or the Blood of Christ present, but the whole Christ, *totus Christus*, was present.[88] Thus a formula was attained which blended well with the popular eagerness, nursed by allegory, to look at the Eucharist. The people had learnt that at Holy Mass the Blessed Sacrament was not so much a *thing*, Christ's Body and Blood as sacrificial gift and sacrificial meal, to be offered up prayerfully and received devoutly, but rather a *person*, the person of the Lord, to be accompanied thoughtfully on His path of redemption. Thus the contemplation of the Christ of history and His earthly-ethical appearance (thoughts which had grown more and more prominent in the popular consciousness since the time of St. Bernard)[89] could mingle with the contemplation of the Eucharist, and strengthen interest therein.[90]

A like trend was produced by the defense against heretical agitation

[83] For further details see *infra*, Parts III and IV.
[84] The records of the origin and development of the rite will be studied in Vol. II, Chs. 2, 13.
[85] Cf. A. L. Mayer, "Die heilbringende Schau in Sitte und Kult," *Heilige Uberlieferung, IId. Herwegen zum silbernen Abtsjubiläum* (Münster, 1938), 234-262.
[86] E. Dumoutet, *Le désir de voir l'hostie* (Paris, 1926); P. Browe, *Die Verehrung der Eucharistie im Mittelalter* (Munich,

1933), 26 ff., 49 ff.; Mayer, *op. cit.*, 255-262.
[87] Cf. H. de Lubac, *Corpus mysticum* (Paris, 1944), especially the comprehensive meditation, "du symbole à la dialectique," pp. 255-284.
[88] Geiselmann, *Die Abendmahlslehre*, 80 ff.
[89] Cf. the deductions regarding St. Bernard's delineation of Christ in W. Kahles, *Radbert und Bernhard* (Emsdetten, 1938).
[90] Still the older forms of speech continued to prevail. We still say *festum Corporis*

during the same period. The heresy of Berengarius of Tours (d. 1088), whose rationalistic explaining-away of the Real Presence had been condemned by various synods, was only a remote attack. The controversy raised by him had hardly gone beyond theological or clerical circles. Here, in any case, and especially in the monasteries, the greatest care was from this time on devoted to the forms with which the Sacrament was surrounded; prescriptions about the choice and preparation of the materials, the custom of keeping the fingers together which—after a special cleansing —had touched the Sacrament, the detailed rules for the ablution of the fingers and of the vessels after Communion.[91]

But in the wider ranks of the people a deep impact was first caused after the rise of the neo-Manichean heresy of the twelfth century which had been aroused over the wealth of a Church become a feudal institution. The heresy had grown particularly conspicuous and rank as Albigensianism. Along with its almost complete denial of the hierarchy and of the sacraments, it had rejected belief in the Eucharist.[92] Here indeed was a struggle for the souls of men! The very word for heretic in German, *Ketzer* (Cathari), which originated at the time, suggests this very pointedly. The new teaching, with its ideal of a poor church and the primitive simplicity of its statements, was indeed alluring. It explained the Blessed Sacrament outright as simply bread, *purum panem*[93]; it regarded its own blessing of bread as an equivalent substitute for the Eucharist.

On the Catholic side, however, even in the twelfth century, we begin to hear accounts of eucharistic miracles.[94] In place of the species of bread, our Lord was seen in His own human appearance. Even if these accounts cannot withstand critical examination, still they are professions of faith all the more emphatic because couched in the realistic language of the people.[95] Here again is a clear expression of that longing to see what is concealed in the Sacrament. Even if the ordinary Christian acknowledges his unworthiness to be favored by the visible appearance of the Redeemer, he will at least want to see the outward veil beneath which He lies hid.

Christi and the new elevation hymn uses the words *Ave verum Corpus* (*infra*, Vol. II, Ch. 2, 13). On the other hand see the formulas used to designate the Sacrament before Communion, e.g., in the *Rituale* of Bishop Henry I of Breslau (*infra*, Vol. II, Ch. 3, 12).

Another usage, very widespread in the later Middle Ages, substituted simply "God" for "Christ." Even Berthold of Regensburg (d. 1272) had already preferred the term *Gottesleichnam* (God's body); cf. his sermons, ed. Pfeiffer, II, 87 ff.

[91] *Infra*, Vol. II, Chap. I, 3; 2, 13; 3, 16.

[92] G. G. Grant, S.J., "The elevation of the host a reaction to twelfth century heresy," *Theological Studies*, I (1940), 228-250.

[93] Radulphus Ardens (d. 1215), *Serm. in dom. 8 post Trin.* (PL, CLV, 2011).

[94] Grant, 247 f. Cf. P. Browe, *Die eucharistischen Wunder des Mittelalters* ("Breslauer Studien zur hist. Theologie," N.F. 4; Breslau, 1938).

[95] Abbot Eckebert of Schönau (d. 1184), *Serm.* 11, 15 (PL, CXCV, 93 f.) confronts the Cathari with the story of St. Gregory's Mass (cf. *supra*, p. 116). Alanus ab Insulis (d. 1203), *Contra hæreticos*, I, 62 (PL, CCX, 365) speaks about a great number of eucharistic miracles which had occurred *propter infirmitatem quorundam.*

That was for him, at the same time a substitute for sacramental communion which was then seldom permitted him.

For such a view of the host the first opportunity was offered by an old traditional rite, when at the words *accepit panem* the priest took the bread in his hands, as once our Lord himself had done, and lifted it slightly. Urged by the desire of the people, the priests emphasized and augmented the rite. But since the interest of the people was centerd not only on the outward act of oblation but on the presence of our Lord (which was not yet at this moment actual), many bishops were greatly concerned lest the people adore the bread, and so about 1210 a decree of the Bishop of Paris introduced the regulation which determined everywhere that the priest should elevate the Host only after the words of consecration, and so high then that all might see and adore.

Thus the Mass acquired a new center, a new focal point, and the devotion of the people acquired an object which corresponded to their understanding and to which they thenceforth clung tenaciously. To see the celestial mystery—that is the climax of the Grail-legend in which, at this same period, the religious longing of the Middle Ages found its poetic expression.[96] And as in the Grail-legend many grace-filled results were expected from seeing the mystery, so too at Mass.[97] Esteem for this opportunity to look upon the Host went to such lengths that it was placed side by side with Holy Communion, and the question was asked, would sinners commit a new mortal sin by looking at the sacred Host?[98]

To look at the sacred Host at the elevation became for many in the later

---

[96] Even in the oldest poetic version of the Grail story, that of Chrétien de Troyes (circa 1168-1190), the Grail procession formed a culmination, a climax. Here the Grail appears as a mysterious, jewel-studded vessel in which the Eucharist is brought to the ailing King (v. 3220 ff.; cf. v. 6423). In the brilliance that emanates from it the light of the accompanying candles fades away as do the stars before a bright moon. Cf. K. Burdach, *Der Gral* ("Forschungen zur Kirchen- und Geistesgeschichte," 14; Stuttgart, 1938), 415 ff. See also A. E. Waite, *The Holy Grail, Its Legends and Symbolism* (London, 1933).

While in Chrétien the miraculous, life-giving effects are still traced to the host contained in the Grail, in the work attributed to Robert de Borron (about the turn of the 12th century) and in that of Wolfram von Eschenbach, these effects are ascribed to the Grail itself, and are produced by looking at it. Burdach, 456 f., 475, 516.

But about Burdach's attempt to trace the main elements of the Grail legend to the Greek liturgy we must say what M. Lot-Borodine said about the more precise thesis outlined by E. Anitschkof in three articles in *Romania,* LVI (1930) to LIX (1933); cf. the notice in JL, XIII (1935), 402 f.

[97] It is in the first decade of the 13th century that mention is first made of the wonderful effects of gazing at the Eucharist; see Dumoutet, *Le désir de voir l'hostie,* 18 f. There is a startling parallel here, but the notion that the efficacy of the vision of the Grail was transferred to the Eucharist is rightly repudiated by Dumoutet, *op. cit.,* 27 f.

[98] Dumoutet, 18-25; Browe, *Die Verehrung der Eucharistie im Mittelalter,* 59-61. The question was answered by theologians in the negative. Still those who were under excommunication or interdict were sometimes expressly forbidden even to look at the Eucharist; it was to get around this prohibition that now and then the persons concerned made holes in the church walls. Browe, 61 f.

Middle Ages the be-all and end-all of Mass devotion. See the Body of Christ at the consecration and be satisfied! In the cities people ran from church to church, to see the elevated Host as often as possible,[99] since rich rewards could be expected from such a practice.[100] People even started lawsuits to ensure their getting a favorable view of the altar.[101] There are examples of congregations where the majority of the faithful waited for the sance-bell signalling the approach of the consecration before they entered the church and then after the elevation they rushed out as quickly as they had come in.[102]

Of course such abuses were discountenanced, but the underlying usage itself gradually obtained ecclesiastical approval.[103] Great preachers knew how best to inculcate the right attitude. Berthold of Regensburg in one of his sermons on the Mass cried out: "At the elevation of the Sacrament the priest seems to be saying three things to you: See the Son of God who, for your sakes, shows His wounds to the Heavenly Father; see the Son of God who, for your sakes, was thus lifted on the Cross; see the Son of God who will come to judge the living and the dead."[104] For this reason some wanted the elevation of the sacred Host at this spot to be not a mere momentary lifting but an actual "showing" lasting some time, so that the congregation could greet and worship the Body of the Lord in prayerful song. The ceremony might even be repeated at other places in the Mass—at the end of the canon[105] or after the Agnus Dei[106]—and it was not to be omitted even on Good Friday.[107] On the other hand, naturally, warnings about moderation had to be given, since some priests seemed to know no bounds.[108]

[99] Browe, 66-68

[100] A Graz MS. of the 15th century indicates that on that day, among other things, one will not lose one's eyesight, will not starve, will not meet a sudden death; that heedless words will be forgiven, etc. Franz, 103; cf. 70.

[101] Dumoutet, 67 f.

It could happen—as it did in England—that if the celebrant did not elevate the host high enough, the people would cry out: "Hold up, Sir John, hold up. Heave it a little higher." Fortescue, *The Mass*, 341 f.

[102] They rush out of the church *quasi diabolum vidissent*, is the moan of the Franciscan Michael de Hungaria, *Sermones dominicales* (Hagenau, 1498), Serm. 74; Dumoutet, 69. A similar complaint is registered by a Westphalian preacher; Franz, 18.

[103] Theologians manifested a certain reserve as early as the end of the 14th century; the people's interest lagged after the 16th. Dumoutet, 29 ff.

[104] Franz, 744. Cf. Bridgett, *A History of the Holy Eucharist in Great Britain* (London, 1908), 100-102.

[105] Thus the ancient elevation of host and chalice grew into a sort of "showing," tied in often with the *Pater noster*; see *infra*, Vol. II, Chap. 3, 2.

[106] Thus for a time the Dominicans; Browe, 63. This was but an augmentation of the custom they still have at present of holding the host over the chalice from the *Agnus Dei* to the Communion; see *infra*, Vol. II, Chap. 3, 7.

The *Officiarium curatorum* of Autun, printed in 1503, opposes such customs with the injunction that the host is to be shown only once, because Christ was crucified only once, but it adds: *quamvis secundum aliquos trina fiat ostensio propter crucifixionem linguarum Judæorum dicentium, Crucifige*; Dumoutet, 55.

[107] Browe, 64. The practice is retained to this very present.

[108] Browe, 63 f. There were even ecclesiastics who took a stipend for these longer "showings"; Dumoutet, 70 f.

However, it was not long before this "showing" was freed from its connection with the Mass, and, with the introduction of the monstrance, was transferred to other occasions. From the beginning of the fourteenth century it became customary to carry the Blessed Sacrament, unconcealed, in solemn procession through the streets on the feast of Corpus Christi, a feast which had come to the fore since 1246 as a result of the new movement.[109] Then, during the high Mass that followed, It was allowed to remain on the altar; this was continued through the entire octave, and sometimes the solemn exposition was extended through the whole period of the choral office in this festival season.[110] During this same fourteenth century it even became customary to leave the Blessed Sacrament exposed on other feast-days of the year, especially on Maundy Thursday, in connection with the Votive Mass of the Blessed Sacrament.[111]

Mass before the Blessed Sacrament exposed, which then became customary and which, after the Reformation, along with the rest of the exposition cult—again as a protest against heresy—was given a new impetus, was from then on the most striking expression of the fact that in the whole course of the Mass-liturgy interest and understanding was still centered mostly on the moment of consecration. There was still a desire that this moment and the corresponding elevation of the Host might be stretched out through the whole Mass.[112] Roman legislation had always held aloof from these efforts which had, in the years to follow, grown to great proportions particularly in the south; for such things Rome allowed very little leeway.[113]

Towards the end of the Middle Ages there arose, out of the same zeal for honoring the Blessed Sacrament, a rite which penetrated everywhere

[109] Browe, 98 f.
[110] Ibid., 154 f.
[111] Browe, 141-154. In Klosterneuburg a weekly solemn Votive Mass in honor of the Blessed Sacrament was instituted as early as 1288; Schabes, Alte liturgische Gebräuche, 71.

In my own native parish, Taufers in the Pustertal, during my youth it was still customary every Thursday to celebrate this Votive Mass, the so-called "Pfinstagamt," as a missa cantata with exposition. The practice was discontinued in 1910. While here the choice of Thursday makes it plain that the reason for the custom was thankfulness for the institution of the Blessed Sacrament, there are to this day parishes in the Alpine countries where every day there is celebrated either a Requiem or a "Segenmesse," that is, a German Singmesse before the Sacrament exposed.
[112] The notion that the whole liturgy was

properly only a decorative framework for the accomplishment of the Sacrament was given rather unreserved utterance in the metrical Pastorale novellum of the Beromünster choirmaster, Rudolf von Liebenegg (d. 1332) : Missa sacramento servit specialiter isti, Cuius ad ornatum patres hanc constituerunt, Præcipue Jacobus et Basilius venerandi. Franz, 488. Cf. in a similar vein Heinrich von Hessen (d. 1397) ; ibid., 518.
[113] See Codex Jur. Can., c. 1274 and the numerous sources noted there. Cf. J. Kramp, Eucharistia. Essays on Eucharistic Liturgy and Devotion (trans. Wm. Busch; St. Paul, 1926), 111-157.

Nicholas of Cusa (circa 1400-1464), when sent by Nicholas V as papal legate to Northern Germany and the Netherlands, 1450-1452, took a very determined stand against the practices of long expositions and exposition Masses (outside of Corpus Christi). Browe, Die Verehrung, 170-172.

and changed the outward picture of the Mass-liturgy between consecration and Communion, ornamenting and enlivening it in remarkable fashion—the genuflection before and after every touching of the Blessed Sacrament. This was not known before the fourteenth century.[114] Thus at this very late date there was transferred to the Blessed Sacrament a token of honor which—like the use of lights and incense, and throne and baldachin—originated in princely ceremonial and from thence had long ago been taken over into the liturgy as an honor to persons.[115]

A clear parallel to the conception and presentation of the Mass-liturgy as a dramatic play which appeals primarily to the eyes of the onlooker was to be found in the efforts made to enrich also the audible side of the liturgical action.

Gregorian Chant had already achieved a great height in the eighth century, especially in Rome itself. Not a few Frankish and Anglo-Saxon clerics, coming to Rome, had taken the trouble to procure from Rome books and teachers of the ecclesiastical chant. It was an art-song rich in melodies, demanding a *schola* properly trained, but—save for the accompaniment of boy voices singing an octave higher—strictly built on the principle of unison. But even in the last years of the Carolingian period the first waves of ornamental enrichment had risen. At that, it affected chiefly only the text.[116]

The long melismas or series of notes, often built upon a single syllable, seemed to have had little appeal to Germanic tastes. So new texts were created in which each syllable corresponded to a note of the given melody. This is the original form of the so-called *tropes*. They were sung as decorative covering by one part of the choir, while the rest of the singers sang the foundation text to the same melody. In the tenth century they had spread everywhere, on festive occasions accompanying first the Proper parts of the Mass, later on also the Ordinary, from introit and *Kyrie* right through to the end of the Mass, sometimes including also the *Ite missa est*. At the same time, corresponding phrases were inserted in the traditional melody along with the corresponding text, or—especially in the introit—introductory phrases preceded the melody. A very special case was the sequence which arose out of the many-toned melodies of the alleluia. It then acquired an independent existence, was developed far and wide during the Middle Ages, and produced thousands of poems. It is noteworthy that Rome and Italy, which showed the greatest reserve towards Gothic art, were also very reluctant to admit the sequences which

---

[114] See *infra*, Vol. II, Chap. 2, 13.
[115] A genuflection is still prescribed for the clergy whenever they pass before the bishop; *Cæremoniale episc.*, I, 18, 3. The relation to the ancient προϲϰύνηϲιϲ is made clear in *Ordo Rom. VIII* (8th century), n. 7, which enjoins upon the candidate for episcopal

consecration a triple *prostratio* before the pope.
[116] Ursprung, *Die kath. Kirchenmusik*, 67-75; Wagner, *Einführung*, I, 248-299; Gustave Reese, *Music in the Middle Ages* (New York, 1940), 185-193. The exact origin of the tropes and sequences has not yet been determined with sufficient clarity.

were the very first metrical productions to be introduced into the Mass. Since as a rule only new texts were under consideration, this enrichment of the liturgy was generally of value only to clerics who understood Latin.

But new melodies too, were composed, especially after the year 1000, melodies for those texts which were repeated at every Mass, the texts of the Ordinary. Up to this time the chants of the Ordinary had the same simple recitative character as the altar chants of the priest; in fact, they were often only continuations of these[117]—or like the acclamations and responses from which they differed only in length.[118] They were little more than elevated speech, relieved by certain cadences. Everyone could therefore take part in them.

A corroboration of what has been said is found in the fact that only by way of exception is the *schola cantorum* mentioned as carrying these melodies.[119] It is true that even in the Carolingian period they were not as a rule sung by the people—excepting perhaps the *Sanctus*—but they were at least at this time and, in general, also in the twelfth and thirteenth centuries, reserved for the clerics in the sanctuary who formed the choir.[120] The trained singers who sang the chants of the *Proprium* would naturally take the lead here, and as the chants of the Ordinary grew more ornate, gradually take over. This was the case with the *Kyrie* as early as the tenth and eleventh centuries. The songs of the fore-Mass thus assumed a greater importance than those of the Mass proper.[121] Richer melodies for the

[117] In this class belongs the Gregorian Mass numbered XVIII in the *Kyriale*, still used at present on ferias in Advent and Lent and, with changes, at Requiems.

[118] Actually not only the *Kyrie*, but also the *Sanctus, Benedictus* and *Agnus Dei* have an acclamatory quality at least in a wider sense, and even the *Gloria* is composed in good part of acclamatory materials.

[119] This is the case, in part, in the Roman *Ordines,* especially clear in that of St. Amand (Duchesne, *Christian Worship,* 456, 458) and in the Roman city *Ordo XI,* n. 18 (PL, LXXVIII, 1032 f.).

[120] Wagner's opinion, expressed in *Einführung,* I, 61, that by the 11th/12th century the choir displaced not only the people but also the clergy at singing, cannot be sustained, at least in this general form. True, the authors do usually ascribe the singing to the *chorus,* but as a rule this included not only the *schola cantorum* but all the clergy present in "choir." This is especially plain in John of Avranches, *De off. eccl.* (PL, CXLVII, 38; cf. 36 ff.) : the kiss of peace is given *in utroque choro,* and then at once the *chorus* sings the *Agnus Dei.* Sicard of Cremona, *Mitrale,* III, 2 (PL,

CCXIII, 96 f.), in describing the singing of the *Kyrie,* uses *chorus* and *clerus* as synonymous.

But there is another terminology, to be noticed in Honorius Augustod., *Gemma an.,* I, 6, 7, 16, 19, 23, etc. (PL, CLXXII, 545, etc.), where a distinction is made between the *chorus* as a singing choir and the *clerus.*

In our study of the individual chants of the Ordinary we will have the occasion to note that the clergy still undertook them as late as the 12th and 13th centuries. Of a lay element in the choirs the liturgists of this period as yet make no mention.

[121] This distinction, in which the considerations that led to the silence of the canon continue to function, was consciously kept in view for a long time. Even polyphony was restricted at first to the texts of the fore-Mass; Ursprung, *Die Kath. Kirchenmusik,* 121. Likewise Nicholas of Cusa, in the course of the reform he undertook as papal legate, wanted to restrict the use of the organ to the Mass of the Catechumens; *ibid.,* 163 f. He made the same demand as bishop of Brixen; G. Bickell, *Synodi Brixi-*

Sanctus and *Agnus Dei* were not created until somewhat later. The *Gloria* and *Credo* retained a simple, psalmodic-recitative character even in the new forms they now acquired.[122] Still the musical ornamentation of the chants of the Ordinary had become so elaborate by the time of St. Bernard (d. 1153) that, under the reform of church music begun with his cooperation, it was thought these forms would have to be banned from use in churches of his order.[123] At that time the chants of the Ordinary were not conceived as units. The oldest example of a chant Mass comprehending all its parts as a unit is one originating about the end of the thirteenth century, a Mass still frequently sung, the *Missa de Angelis*.[124]

Gradually *chorus* begins to mean something new. It turns into a choir of singers separated from the clergy, often composed of laics, and independent even as regards its place in the church. First it rambled to the rood-loft, the high reading- and singing-gallery often found in Gothic structures in place of the sanctuary enclosure between the choir and the nave, and elevated in its entire width. Later it finally wandered to the upper gallery which was built at the back of the church.

Polyphony begins to take on some importance in Church music. The first attempts at counterpoint, starting in the ninth century, affected only the songs of the *Proprium*. These attempts resulted from the use of a second voice singing an accompaniment to the main melody at the interval of a fourth or fifth. The text might be with a trope or without. And the accompanying voice—*vox organalis*—might be an instrument.[125] In the twelfth century it is the cathedral of Notre Dame in Paris that takes the lead. On festive occasions the gradual or alleluia was sung not to the chant melody alone, but a second or even a third or fourth voice was added here and there in a free independent movement. And sometimes, where an over-elaborate melisma presented the opportunity, a special text, often even one in the vernacular, was added to the proper one.[126] Of a similar sort, but of course not so high a rank was the song art of the travelling singers who, we are told, were wont to sing their verses at Mass *super Sanctus et Agnus Dei*.[127] Such music seemed to suit the time which liked this type of light

nenses sæc. XV (Innsbruck, 1880), 34.

The same idea, in a new dress, is proposed today by E. Drinkwelder, O.S.B., *Die Grundfunktion der Gesänge im Amt: Heiliger Dienst*, II (Salzburg, 1948), 143-145.
[122] Ursprung, 57 f.
[123] *Ibid.*, 93.
[124] *Ibid.*, 58.
[125] *Ibid.*, 116 ff.; cf. also Eisenhofer, I, 231-233. Further notes on organum and discant in G. Reese, *Music in the Middle Ages* (N. Y., 1940), 249-330.
[126] The so-called "motets"; see the tables in Ursprung, 129 f., with examples from MSS. of the 13th/14th centuries. A late German

example is presented in a Klosterneuburg MS. of 1551; here the Easter Mass *Resurrexi* has a polyphonic setting with an upper voice accompanying the Latin text with the German Easter hymn, *Christ ist erstanden*; Schabes, 150. See the discussion in Gustave Reese, *Music in the Middle Ages* (New York, 1940), 311 ff.
[127] The Synod of Trier (1227), can. 9 (Mansi, XXIII, 33). Other synods which forbade the appearance of *ioculatores, trutanni* or *goliardi* in Browe, *Die Pflichtkommunion*, 97.

There was even some consideration of refusing players and ballad-singers Com-

embellishment. But it was a dangerous road to take. So warning voices were raised to safeguard the seriousness of the traditional ecclesiastical chant and even to induce the ecclesiastical authority to take a definite stand.[128]

As a matter of fact the art of Church music did again confine itself to stricter bounds during the last centuries of the Middle Ages. It was satisfied—especially in Germany—to accompany the Gregorian Chant melodies at holyday services, even (and later, especially) the music of the Ordinary, with a form of falso bordone, as it was the practice to do—and is still done today in many churches—in psalmody.[129] By the fourteenth century the organ had been perfected enough to make its entrance everywhere in the larger churches, provided no stricter principles stood in the way, and could perform a like duty.[130] About this same time in France the first example of Mass composition in our modern sense begins to appear— compositions in which all the parts of the Ordinary of the Mass, from *Kyrie* to *Agnus Dei* are set to polyphony and are no longer bound down to the Gregorian Chant, even though chant melodies are used as a *canto fermo* or are interwoven with the harmony.[131] When, in 1377, the papal court returned with Pope Gregory XI from Avignon to Rome, the papal singers brought the art of polyphony with them to Italy. Slowly the new art spread to other countries. It did not get the same joyous reception everywhere; thus Swiss monasteries were very reserved in their attitude, and at St. Gall it was banned from divine service even as late at 1560.[132] But all in all a new period had begun in the history of Church music and in the history of the external embellishment of the liturgy.[133]

munion; *ibid.,* 93 ff. Cf. W. Bäumker, *Zur Geschichte der Tonkunst* (Freiburg, 1881), 106-122.
[128] In this connection an enactment of the II Ec. Council of Lyons (1274) is often cited (but hardly with right); amongst other things it forbids *publica parlamenta* (Mansi, XXIV, 99 A); a reference to singing *(quod ... ars cantus melius doceretur)* is found in the Appendix, III, 1 *(ibid.,* XXIV, 130 B). More emphatic is one of the decretals of John XXII of 1324-5, which does not condemn polyphony outright but does expressly forbid that the plainsong melodies be smothered *triplis et motetis vulgaribus; Corpus Jur. Can., Extrav. comm.* III, I (Friedberg, II, 1256). Cf. Ursprung, 138 f. This decretal and other references to church music conveniently available in *Oxford History of Music,* ed. H. E. Wooldridge, (2nd ed., 1929), I, 290 ff.
[129] Ursprung, 141 f. For a study of fauxbourdon and English discant see Reese, 398 ff.

[130] Ursprung, 163 f.

[131] Ursprung, 147 f.; P. Wagner, *Geschichte der Messe,* I (Kleine Handbücher der Musikgeschichte, XI, 1; Leipzig, 1913). A study of Machaut's Mass and the *Messe de Tournai* in Reese, 356.

[132] Wagner, *Geschichte der Messe,* 27, note.

[133] How sweeping this change was is seen, for instance, in the choice of the patrons of music. In the high tide of the Chant it was St. Gregory the Great; at the start of the polyphonic era it was John the Baptist (at whose birth his father had been given back his speech). But now the heavenly patronage is switched to St. Cecilia, on account of the words *cantantibus organis* in her Office, although amongst the Irish her musical association had long been cultivated. All in all the development in the musical world as well as in the entire later medieval culture was from unity and simplicity to plurality and multiplicity. B. Ebel, "Die Kirchenmusik als sinnbildlicher Ausdruck

During the years that followed, the chants of the *Proprium*, whose texts were built up on the lyrical materials of the psalms and which had been knowingly inserted into the "rest" periods of the service as an artistic element, retained the archaic simplicity of their ancient traditional Gregorian melodies.[134] But the unassuming acclamatory phrases, in which originally the people were able to frame their cries of prayer and praise, or in which at any rate, represented by the clergy, they professedly resumed and continued the altar chants of the priest—these were fitted out in the pomp of polyphony.[135] Even if these latter texts (with the exception perhaps of the *Credo* which arose out of the doctrinal struggle of the East, the recitation of which was in part at least quite prosaic), because of the pithiness of the words, proved favorable to an artistic handling and were not ill-fitted for the musical development of their contents, still it was precisely this artistic elevation above the ordinary plane that put them beyond the reach of the people who were called upon to cooperate, and so to a certain extent the texts departed from their proper function.

In view of the foreign language of the liturgy, the only possible pathway was again the stressing of the *Ordinarium*, since there was no question, in general, of creating new texts.[136] Through the development of these various choral Masses, a road was opened to getting away from the traditional melodies. The texts were always the same, and their meaning could easily be explaind even to people not knowing Latin; hence these texts lent support to the propagation or spread which came about through their new musical setting. Their constant repetition made their performance rather easy. And if the *Sanctus* and *Benedictus* especially filled in with their sound the vacancy left in the canon, this was a compensation to the hearing of the congregation for whom the basic tone of the *eucharistia* was thus once more rightfully restored where it had been barred by the silence of the canon and, fundamentally, by the insertion of the intercessory prayers.

12. The Close of the Middle Ages and the Tridentine Reform

The designation of the fourteenth and fifteenth centuries as the "autumn of the Middle Ages" (Huizinga) proved to be exceptionally apt in the history of the liturgy and not least in that of the Mass. There is indeed a rich and manifold growth, as we have just seen exemplified in Church music.

der Gemeinschaft der Heiligen im Wandel der Zeiten," *Liturg. Leben*, V (1938), 223-233, esp. 230 ff.

[134] The only exception was the *Requiem* which still incorporates both Ordinary and Proper.

[135] Wagner, *Einführung*, I, 61, arrives at this judgment from a different viewpoint: "This evolution of things brought about no special gain."

[136] An exception is to be found in the songs at the consecration and, partly, in the new Communion songs (*infra*, Vol. II, Chap. 2, 13 and 3, 14).

New forms, new inferences are continually being developed. But the inferences are developed only from what is already at hand. There is no cutting back to the living roots, no springing forth of new, healthy growths. Scholastic theology produced nothing for the liturgy of the Mass or for a better understanding of it. So the forms appear over-ripe, the growth becomes dry and withered.

But all this does not hold so true for the text of the Mass *ordo*. Even though here too, especially outside Italy, the preparatory prayers, the versicles and invocations of the prayers at the foot of the altar, the blessings at the offertory, the hymnic greetings before the Communion have become prevalent, still, since they are all the silent prayers of the priest, this is all more or less in the background. However, within the ambit of the Ordinary there were some things that fit more surely into the description we have given—the musical expansion mentioned in the last chapter and the increase in the forms by which the Sacrament is venerated.

Reverence for the Sacrament led to a change in policy regarding the handling of the sacred Host by lay people. No lay hand was allowed to touch it, even if that meant depriving a dying person of Viaticum. It was a very special favor when Popes of the fourteenth century gave to princes in certain instances the permission to touch the chalice on Communion days with their bare hands.[1] In the late Middle Ages the corporal was often shown honor that amounted to superstition.[2] For the washing of the corporal special prayers were composed.[3] In this same connection we might note that the chapters on the *pericula* or *defectus* which might occur in the Mass grew larger and larger. The early medieval period had already considered certain contingencies, like spilling the chalice or dropping a particle, and had prescribed stern punishments for them.[4] Now pertinent mistakes and defects are discussed and decided with reference to theology and from the practical viewpoint of what to do so that due reverence will be shown towards the Sacrament in every instance. Innocent III had considered certain cases at some length[5] and St. Thomas devotes an Article of his *Summa* to them.[6] But new *pericula* were constantly being discovered —even such as: what if the Lord should appear in *specie carnis vel pueri!*[7] —and for each, corresponding instructions were given.[8]

---

[1] Browe, "Die Sterbekommunion im Altertum und Mittelalter," ZkTh, LX (1936), 13.

[2] Franz, 88-92.

[3] Breviarium of Linköping of the year 1493 (J. Freisen, *Manuale Lincopense*, Paderborn, 1904, p. XIX).

[4] P. Browe, "Liturgische Delikte und ihre Bestrafung im Mittelalter," *Theologie u. Glaube*, XXVIII (1936), 53-64.

[5] Innocent III, *De s. alt. mysterio*, IV, 11; 16; 24; 31 f. (PL, CCXVII, 863; 873; 877 f.). Cf. also the work attributed to Odo

of Paris, *Præcepta synod.*, c. 22 ff. (Mansi, XXII, 681 f.).

[6] Thomas Aquinas, *Summa theol.*, III, 83, 6.

[7] Franz, 474, note 1; Beck, 330.
Bernard de Parentinis devotes to the *pericula* the third of three main sections of his exposition of the Mass (ab. 1340); Franz, 505 f. Cf. also *ibid.*, 491, 605.

[8] A selection of the useful portion has been inserted in our Missal as the chapter *De defectibus in celebratione missarum occurrentibus*.

Of course here it was often only a lack of proportion—too much of a good thing! But considerable consequences were to be feared from the one-sided discussions and the unenlightened and isolated popularizing of another phase in the teaching of the Mass, the phase of the effects of the Mass. That the Mass not only offers God due honor but also redounds to the welfare of living and dead was already a conviction of Christian antiquity. But now this side of the sacrifice comes to the fore. In the declining Middle Ages it becomes the main theme of sermons on the Mass.[9] Formal enumerations of the fruits of the Mass are compiled, especially of those fruits which derive from a devout hearing of Holy Mass.[10] Such enumerations first appear in the thirteenth century. People were satisfied then with four or five or six points, with the spiritual effects foremost.[11] But soon it became ten fruits, finally twelve. The editor of a German version of them made the remark that "the formulas for the fruits of the Mass take on a more gross appearance the nearer they stand to the end of the Middle Ages."[12] For each of the spiritual effects a Father of the Church is cited in support—no matter how incredible the effect may sound.[13] Although contemporary theology did not approve such exaggerations, still they were able to flourish unimpeded in the homiletic and devotional liturature of the day. That meant the people were encouraged to zealous attendance at Holy Mass, but also they were lulled into a false security, as though the salvation of their souls could be assured by merely hearing Mass.[14]

With this exaggerated description of the effects of the Mass, another fact is intimately connected, the Votive Mass. Towards the end of the Middle Ages there appear numerous new formularies.[15] And they are ar-

---

[9] Franz, 738 f.

[10] A considerable portion in Franz, 36-72: The "Fruits" of the Mass, is devoted to this matter. Cf. also *supra*, p. 117.

[11] Franz, 37 f. The heart of the matter is found in the following assurances: One returns from Mass *quasi deificus, minor peccato, confortatus contra diabolum, felicior quam prius.*

[12] Franz, 40.

[13] Thus Augustine is saddled with the statement that during the time one hears Mass one does not grow older; Franz, 51; cf. 57. Other fruits are these: after hearing Mass one's food tastes better; one will not die a sudden death; the souls in Purgatory will not have to suffer while one is hearing Mass for them, etc. In a poetic rendering which appeared about the 14th century, the first of the fruits of the Mass is thus described: If one owned all that sun and moon shone upon, and he gave it all to the poor, and if he wandered over the face of the earth, in heat and cold, in hunger and thirst,

that would not do his soul as much good as the hearing of one Mass; Franz, 48 f.

Similar presentations of the *virtutes missarum* circulated in England; see examples in Simmons, *The Lay Folks Mass Book*, 131 f.; 366-371.

As a rule the emphasis was laid on a devout attendance in the state of grace. A portion of these assurances was transferred to the devout looking at the Host; see *supra*, Chapter 11, note 100.

[14] See the conclusion in Franz, 71 f. Also *ibid.*, 61-71, a theological discussion of each of the medieval "fruits of the Mass."

[15] To those already at hand are added formularies of Masses against various sicknesses, against dangers to right and property, against attacks by an enemy, and especially formularies in honor of those saints who were honored as patrons and protectors in these various situations; see the thorough treatment in Franz, 115-217; numerous examples also in Ferreres, *Historia del Misal Romano*, 350-376.

ranged in marked and defined series, the particular order of the Masses being thought to obtain certain specified results. The start of this custom of a series of Masses is traced to the *Dialogues* of St. Gregory the Great, where we read—though without a particular significance being attached to the numbers—that Mass was said for a deceased person in one case for seven days in a row, in another for thirty.[16] This example had successors all through the medieval period.[17] But it was not till the last few centuries that any arrangement was decided upon and carefully planned out. Series are stipulated for 3, 5, 6, 7, 9 and 30 Masses, even for 41, 44 or 45, for the benefit of the dead and also for the wishes and intentions of the living. For each Mass a specified formula, independent of the day's Mass, is prescribed; sometimes, too, a specified number of candles and a specified number of alms-gifts are stipulated.[18] What was really questionable in this practice of Mass series and Votive Masses was the assurance—recurring time and again—of unfailing results. Such assurance could even be seen in Mass books; *Si quis positus in aliquo necessitatis articulo has triginta missas celebraverit vel celebrare petierit, liberabitur sine mora.*[19]

It is hardly to be wondered at that the faithful seized upon an easy means like this which coincided with their own mania for miracles. And so there arose during the last centuries of the Middle Ages an unnatural multiplication of Masses and, along with it, an unnatural increase in clergy of whom a part, at least, derived their entire income from Masses either through endowments (foundations or chantries) or by way of Mass stipends.[20] For the most part they celebrated Votive Masses or Masses for

[16] Gregory the Great, *Dial.* IV, 55 (PL, LXXVII, 416-421).

[17] K. Eberle, *Der Tricenarius des hl. Gregorius* (Regensburg, 1890), 20-38.

[18] Franz, 218-291; L. A. Veit, *Volksfrommes Brauchtum und Kirche im deutschen Mittelalter* (Freiburg, 1936), 26 ff.

Thus, for example, a septenary for each day of the week included on the first day a Mass *de Trinitate* with three candles and three alms; on the second *de angelis* with nine candles and nine alms, etc.; Franz, 254, 255, 258 f., 265 ff. Other examples of the Gregorian trentals and votive lists in Bridgett, *A History of the Holy Eucharist in Great Britain*, 131 ff.

[19] Missal of St. Lambrecht of 1336: Köck, 34. Similar assurances in other Styrian missals, *ibid.*, 27; 36 f.; 41 f.; 74; 81; 83; 137; 138; 139. Cf. Franz, 250, 262, 266, 270, 278, etc. For Hungary, see Radó, 171 f.

[20] Towards the end of the Middle Ages every town had countless "altarists" ("altarthanes") who had no other duty except to say Mass and the Office. Strassburg, for instance, in 1521 had 120 Mass foundations; L. Pfleger, *Kirchengeschichte der Stadt Strassburg* (Colmar o. J., 1941), 172. Further details in F. Falk, "An der Wende des 15. Jh.," *Hist.-pol. Blätter*, CXII (1893, II), 545-559. In England Henry VIII suppressed 2,374 chantries just before his death; Bridgett, *History of the Eucharist*, 136.

The rise of this spiritual proletariat was a source as well as an effect of these curious views. W. Neuss, *Das Problem des Mittelalters* (Colmar o. J., 1943), 26 f., shows that the increase of these city clerics who were unemployed was associated with the fact that in many of the guilds only a specified number of craftsmen and laborers were given entry. This gave the impulse to find some security for the other young people of the town in the clerical state, sometimes by means of established foundations, but more often on the chance of making something out of the various Mass bequests.

the Dead, since these the people wanted most.[21]

This multiplicity of Masses had its effect on the rites and ceremonies. Some of the Masses were celebrated with chant. But since in churches only one Mass could be sung, a solution was worked out by which several such Masses could be celebrated in close succession. These were the so-called "Boxed Masses" which followed each other in this way: one Mass was sung to the offertory or to the *Sanctus*, then continued as a low Mass while at another altar a second Mass was begun.[22] But the most pronounced result of the multiplying of Masses was the increase in low Masses, since most of them were for private requests and had no public character. This trend to the private and the subjective, to an independence from the grand order of things was also displayed in another abuse, namely, setting aside the arrangement of the ecclesiastical year and confining oneself to Votive Masses either chosen at will or arranged according to the rules of the Mass series.[23]

Even while these various conditions were setting in, Peter Cantor (d. 1197) was inveighing against the evil he saw coming; there would have to be fewer churches, fewer altars, fewer and better priests.[24] Several later German mystics spoke in a similar vein.[25] John Gerson comes out publicly against the nuisance. He says: Preachers who attach extravagant promises to the Mass are misleading the people into Judaism and promoting superstition.[26] In Germany too, voices were raised in like denunciation.[27] Nicholas of Cusa gave the example of practical reform. As Bishop of Brixen, he ordered in 1453 and 1455 that all Mass books in his diocese should be

[21] The Provincial Council of Florence in 1517 imposed a penalty of two ducats upon priests who out of avarice celebrated anniversary Masses even on Sundays and feasts in place of the Mass of the day (Mansi, XXXV, 240).

[22] J. Greving, *Johann Ecks Pfarrbuch* (Reformationsgeschichte. Studien u. Texte, 4-5; Münster, 1908), 81-83; J. B. Goetz, *Das Pfarrbuch des Stephan May in Hilpoltstein vom Jahre 1511* (same series, 47-48; Münster, 1928), 65, 95; cf. 24, 27; A. Gümbel, *Das Messnerpflichtbuch von St. Lorenz in Nürnberg im Jahre 1493* (Munich, 1928).

Berthold von Chiemsee, *Keligpuchel* (Munich, 1935), Ch. 20, 9, mentions this method of celebration as an "unbecoming custom" which is to blame that many think they can leave after the consecration.

The custom continued even down to modern times, especially at funerals; the diocese of Brixen had to forbid it as late as 1900; *Synodus Brixinensis* (Brixen,

1900), 33 f.; and in some parishes in the Salzburg diocese the practice lasted even into the present century.

[23] There were complaints that often only the *missæ favorabiliores*, which were likewise *missæ obolariæ*, were chosen; Franz, 149 ff. There is an account of priests who never said any Mass except that *de beata Virgine* and whose action was guarded against ecclesiastical authority even by miracle; *ibid.*, 152 f.

[24] Petrus Cantor, *Verbum abbreviatum*, c. 28 f. (PL, CCV, 102-107). A further demand, which is rather startling to us, was that the offertory procession be reduced to three or four times a year.

[25] Franz, 298 f. Amongst other warnings is this remark of Meister Eckhart: "Note that neither blessedness nor perfection consist in saying or hearing a lot of Masses."

[26] John Gerson, *Opera* (Antwerp, 1706), II, 521-523; Franz, 299 ff.

[27] Franz, 301-308; 312 f.

assembled at certain centers, Stams, Wilten, Neustift and Innichen, and corrected according to one stipulated unobjectionable examplar.[28] The use of uncorrected books was sternly forbidden. Unfortunately men of such energy were not to be found elsewhere. In general, the evil continued to flourish. The holiest of the Church's possessions remained, it is true, the center of genuine piety. But alas, the clouds and shadows surrounding this center brought matters to such a pass that the Institution of Jesus, that well of life from which the Church had drawn for fifteen-hundred years, became an object of scorn and ridicule and was repudiated as a horrible idolatry by entire peoples.

The complaints raised by the Reformers, especially by Luther, were aimed accurately and quite relentlessly against questionable points in ecclesiastical praxis regarding the Mass; the fruits of the Mass, the Votive Masses with their various values, the commerce in stipends.[29] But the complaints went far beyond that. Taking as his principle the Bible alone, Luther denied the sacrificial character of the Mass and thought in this way to have reached the root of the trouble. The Eucharist was only a "testament," a bequest and benefit handed us, and as such—this is Luther's rash conclusion—in no wise a *"bene-fit"* or good work that we can offer God in order to "merit" from Him something for ourselves or especially for others. Therefore, the Mass cannot be read either for the living or for the dead.[30] All prayers in the Mass-liturgy in which there is any mention of this, particularly of sacrifice—like the canon—are bad human additions and must be dropped. A special work of Luther's deals with "the abomination of the low Mass called the canon" (*Von dem Greuel der Stülmesse so man Canon nennet,* 1524). Very effective were the charges made that Masses, especially Masses for the Poor Souls, were a means of fleecing the people. The result was felt even in sections of Europe which remained staunchly Catholic, so that as early as 1528 we are told that in the church of Salzburg a hundred *gratiani* (priests who lived on stipends) could formerly be maintained more easily than now even a single one.[31]

The reference to self-interest and superstition had made an impression. And considering the low state of religious training, this adverse criticism threatened to destroy in people's minds not only the excess foliage but the very branch and root. The Mass was disregarded, despised. And nothing was done about it. The Council of Trent did indeed accomplish one thing; in its doctrinal definition the Council clearly distinguished between truth

[28] G. Bickell, *Synodi Brixinenses sæc. XV* (Innsbruck, 1880), 37, 39 f., 53; Franz, 308.

[29] Examples in Franz, 316-322.

[30] M. Luther, *Eyn sermon von dem newen Testament.* The passages in Franz, 314 f. Cf. L. Fendt, *Der lutherische Gottesdienst*

des 16. Jh. (Munich, 1923), 78-81; N. M. Halmer, "Der literarische Kampf Luthers und Melanchthons gegen das Opfer der hl. Messe," *Divus Thomas,* XXI (1943), 63-78.

[31] Berthold von Chiemsee, *Tewtsche Theologey* (Munich, 1528), ch. 66, 6; Franz, 324.

and error and declared the objective character of the Sacrifice of the Mass as something more than a mere reminder of the Sacrifice of the Cross or a mere Communion rite. Thus the foundations of Catholic liturgy were secured. But a reform was also needed, a reform which would attack the ecclesiastical praxis of the celebration of Mass and, not least, take cognizance of the Mass books which had in many ways become a jungle.[32]

According to the law then in force, the diocesan and ecclesiastical provinces were called upon to undertake such a reform provided only they did not touch the ancient traditional Roman core of the Mass book, particularly the canon. Thus the provincial synod of Trier in 1549 commanded that in all the dioceses of the province the diocesan missal alone should be standard, or if there was none, the Trier missal should.[33] Something similar was prescribed in Mainz, along with the demand that every diocese have its missal checked and corrected by experts, so that some common arrangement might be reached in the whole province.[34] But neither here nor in any other church province was a program, so carefully circumscribed, ever put through. The demand for the reform of the Mass book itself was expressed in the German Reichstag at Speyer in 1526, long before any synod even thought of it. The demand could not be refused.

About the same time there was hue and cry for a unified missal in which only the special diocesan saints' Masses would be added as a sort of appendix. The first such recommendation was made in Italy in 1546, and then later, more strenuously, in Spain and Portugal.[35] But the idea was not shared everywhere. The proposals sent to the Council from France preferred internal regulation within each country, and the attitude of England during the brief period of Mary Tudor was much the same.[36] But in the last analysis, as previous experiences had demonstrated, some sort of initiative on the part of the Church as a whole was quite indispensable.

So the Council of Trent took up the matter. In 1546-1547, while considering the use and misuse of Holy Scriptures, it had touched on the question of the Mass book. And in 1562, in connection with the discussions regarding the doctrine of the Sacrifice of the Mass, the subject was finally taken up. A special commission was to assemble the *abusus missæ*. This task was not difficult, since sore points had been constantly marked out not only by the innovators but by the Council itself, by synods, in memorials and reform programs. Saints' sequences and prefaces with legendary content, prayers for peace, prayers in need, and various chants after the consecra-

---

[32] Cf. H. Jedin, "Das Konzil von Trient und die Reform des Römischen Messbuches," *Liturgisches Leben*, VI (1939), 30-66. Most of what is said in this chapter is based on this article of Jedin's or his other in *Eph. liturg.* noted below.

[33] Hartzheim, VI, 601.

[34] Hartzheim, VI, 579.

[35] Jedin, *loc. cit.*, 34, 37 f.
    This point is illustrated more clearly in another article by the same author, "Das Konzil von Trient und die Reform der liturgischen Bücher," *Eph. liturg.*, LIX (1945), 5-38; esp. 8, 11, 28, 37.

[36] Jedin, in *Liturg. Leben* as above, 40.

tion,[87] new Mass formularies of questionable origin, especially the abuses regarding Votive Masses, Mass series, and the setting aside of the order for Sundays and the Church year in favor of privately chosen formularies —these were all pointed out. Add to the list the great variety of Mass rites which, as Cardinal Hosius charged, sometimes went so far that, to the surprise and bewilderment of the people, not even in the same Church did all follow the same rite.[88]

The commission did not neglect any of this and even added to its collection,[89] which was "the most comprehensive accumulation of reform ideas,"[40] a long list of minutiæ which, because they were theologically controvertible, would have to be examined and tested. They included certain expressions like *Hostia immaculata, calix salutaris* at the offertory, the crosses after the consecration, the prayers at the commingling which in Italian Mass books began with *Fiat commixtio*, the offertory of Masses for the Dead. Likewise the custom of saying private Masses in church while high Mass was going on, and the practice of saying private Masses without at least two participants present were placed amongst the disputable points. Without imposing a complete uniformity, the commission desired chiefly for the secular clergy a certain consistency, at least for the beginning and conclusion of Mass, where the greatest differences were to be found, and a certain consistency in the rubrics, especially in external ceremonial.

It stands to reason that the Council, already assembled overly long, could hardly discuss details of this sort, about which there could be many opinions. The plan of the commission had to be drawn in a second, a third and finally a fourth draught, each one shorter and more likely to obtain general acceptance.[41] The *Decretum de observandis et evitandis in celebratione missæ*, which was passed on September 17, 1562, in the twenty-second session, as a supplement to the teaching and the canons regarding the Sacrifice of the Mass, is concerned only with the most obvious abuses and evil conditions which could be lined up under the notions of avarice, irreverence, and superstition. The bishops should be vigilant about stipends. Mass should be celebrated only in consecrated places. Disturbing and irreverent conduct and frivolous music must be banished. The capriciousness of

---

[87] Thus at Hilpoltstein about 1511 an antiphon was daily sung after the consecration, usually *Gaude Dei Genitrix*; Goetz, *Das Pfarrbuch des Stephan May*, 28 f.

Customs of this sort existed in other countries besides the north. As late as 1677 the Congregation of Rites was asked by Seville whether it was permissible to interrupt the Mass after the elevation of the chalice or just before the *Pater noster* and to insert prayers for various needs, the priest participating; *Decreta authentica* SRC, n. 1588, 9.

[88] Jedin *(Liturg. Lebens)*, 34-5.

The confusion grew all the more with the start of the Reformation era, since many priests took it upon themselves to start their own reforms. In Austria many priests even left out the canon. *Ibid.*, 44.

[89] *Concilium Tridentinum*, ed. Soc. Goerres., VIII, 916-921.

[40] Jedin *(Liturg. Leben)*, 47.

[41] *Concilium Trid.*, VIII, 921-924; 926-928; 962-963. See Schroeder, 144-152 for the pertinent chapters on the Eucharist.

priests regarding rites and prayers at Mass, and the superstitious observance of numbers for fixed Masses would have to cease.[42] There was no mention of the reform of the missal. By a decree in the twenty-fifth session this was left—along with the reform of the breviary—to the pope.

Pius IV at once (apparently in 1564) set about carrying out this decree by creating for this purpose a commission which his successor, Pius V, enlarged.[43] Unfortunately there are no detailed reports of what the commission did. Only the product of their activity, *Missale Romanum ex decreto ss. Concilii Tridentini restitutum, Pii V. Pont. Max. iussu editum* which by a Bull of July 14, 1570, was made binding, with certain reservations, on the whole Western Church, gives us some ideas, for by comparing this composition with what was then in existence, and adding the few occasional remarks that have been handed down, we can learn something of the work done and of the aims that directed it.[44]

The task of reform was not therefore solved by a number of ordinances and decisions by which the abuses were branded and the proper lines for creating new missals pointed out. One of the proposals sent to the Council had suggested that the regional differences in the Roman Mass and the episcopal right to regulate them be left unrestricted. But the commission took another course, by establishing the wished-for uniform missal. This uniform missal was in truth a Roman Missal, for as its basis they chose the *Missale secundum consuetudinem Romanæ Curiæ* which already had the greatest vogue. However, this choice could not have been taken for granted, since not only was Pius V a Dominican, but members of the Dominican order, which had its own well-integrated rite, had been in the commission even before this Pope ascended the throne.[45]

As far as the calendar and the collects and Gospels of each Mass were concerned, the new missal agreed very closely with the *Breviarium Romanum* which the same commission had produced and published just two years before—an agreement hardly to be found in previous books. For the exact rules about the choice and arrangement of each Mass formula and for the directions regarding the ritualistic aspect of the Mass, the *Rubricæ Generales Missalis* and the *Ritus servandus in celebratione Missæ* were prefaced to the new Mass book. These were taken almost bodily from the *Ordo Missæ* of the papal master of ceremonies, John Burchard of Strassburg, a work which appeared in 1502 and had meanwhile circulated widely.[46]

[42] Only the Gregorian series for the dead has finally been allowed to continue.

In our own day a new series of 44 Masses (and the usual superstitious promises) has turned up in Poland; it was immediately condemned by Roman authorities; *AAS*, XXVI (1934), 233.

[43] Jedin (*Liturg. Leben*), 52-54.

[44] *Ibid.*, 54-66.

[45] *Ibid.*, 53.

[46] Printed in Legg, *Tracts*, 124-174. Another edition, prepared by F. Ravanat, appeared as a supplement to *Eph. liturg.*, XXXVIII (1924).

Cf. K. Schrod, "Die Rubricæ generales des Römischen Messbuches. Eine literarhistorische Notiz," *Der Katholik*, LXIV (1884), I, 314-316.

By this means Votive Masses were restricted to proper limits.[47] Besides, only a few of these Masses were retained, a small selection of formularies where the danger of superstition was less likely, mostly those for each day of the week, Sundays excepted. The fear that greed might induce abuses prompted the dropping of the offertory procession which was still provided for in Burchard's *Ordo*.[48] One practical innovation was a *Commune Sanctorum* in which not only a number of texts were included for introit, collect, etc., but complete Mass formularies were provided.[49]

Other viewpoints which guided the reform come to light in the study of the festal calendar of the new missal. First of all, the Church year is freed somewhat from the overburden of saints' feasts which in the later Middle Ages had increased immensely. The new missal had, in round numbers, 150 days free of feasts, not counting octaves. This was achieved by retaining only those feasts which were kept in Rome itself up to the eleventh century.[50] Of the countless feasts later introduced, especially under the influence of the Franciscans, only a small number were preserved, and few of these of saints outside Italy.[51]

The commission's ideal, therefore, was a return to the liturgy of the city of Rome, and indeed, the liturgy of that city as it was in former times. With this coincides the stern opposition the commission showed toward the sequences which abounded in other Mass books and amongst which— even apart from the four kept—there were genuine pearls which might have heightened the splendor of many a solemnity. But they were a modern growth and had never taken hold in Rome or Italy. Besides, their unclassical rhythm might not have suited the humanist taste of the era.[52]

In many places there was the intention of putting through a real reform in the sense of disengaging the basic "form" from all distorting accretion. This can be seen from the fact that already in 1563, when the correction of the missal was still being taken up by the Council, a Vatican manuscript of the Gregorian Sacramentary was sent from Rome to Trent. This was not a solitary instance. The commission, too, had investigated the ancient sources. In the Bull of July 14, 1570,[53] introducing the new missal, Pope Pius V expressly attests that the scholars on the commission had discharged their work *diligenter collatis omnibus cum vetustis Nostræ Vaticanæ Bibliothecæ aliisque undique conquisitis, emendatis atque incorruptis codicibus, necnon veterum consultis ac probatorum auctorum scriptis*, and that they had thus brought the missal *ad pristinam sanctorum Patrum normam ac*

---

[47] *Rubr. gen.*, IV, 3.

[48] See *supra*, p. 129 ff.

[49] A *Commune Sanctorum* is to be found even in some of the earliest sacramentaries, lectionaries and antiphonaries; cf. Righetti, III, 99-101.

[50] E. Focke and H. Heinrichs, "Das Kalendarium des Missale Pianum und seine Tendenzen," *Theol. Quartalschrift*, CXX

(1939), 383-400; 461-469.

[51] Germany, for instance, was represented only by St. Ursula (*loc. cit.*, 466).

[52] An attempt was made to re-introduce a portion of these old sequences; see G. Mercati, "Un tentativo d'introdurre nuove sequenze sotto Gregorio XIII," *Rassegna Gregoriana*, VI (1907), 141-145.

[53] Printed in every missal.

ritum. The self-evident idea, that the development which had taken place meanwhile, separating the present from the *pristina sanctorum Patrum norma* should not be put aside as long as it did not disturb the ground-plan but rather unfolded it—that idea was never once expressed.[54]

No one need be surprised that this high aim should have been attained only in a very limited way. Even if there had been further sources for research, one could not expect a commission composed of a few men and entrusted with a practical job, to anticipate in two years the liturgico-historical knowledge which would be attained only by the continued efforts of many students during several centuries. So much in the Mass book and in the Mass *ordo* remained unaltered and perhaps even unexamined—much that during the Franco-German period had been overlaid inartistically upon the austere form of the Mass of the city of Rome, or that had during the Gothic period found a place in the Mass books *secundum usum Romanæ Curiæ.*[55] The Mass book of this type, and therefore the traditional practice in Italy, remained the standard, in general, for the *Ordo Missæ.* But whatever could be done with the tools of the period, was done substantially. In particular the humanistic period had an opportunity to leave its own trace on the work.[56] The newer appraisement of the Church Fathers was shown in the fact that, besides the memorial days of the four Latin Fathers who were alone acknowledged in the Middle Ages, those of the Greeks were also included. Here and there in the literary style the humanist touch was added.[57] Besides the whole task of purifying the Mass book of disturbing accessories was itself in line with the "love of humanism for the clean, the unadulterated form."[58] This work of purification was accomplished with remarkable energy. The members of the commission were not held back from doing away with added trimmings which the pious mind considered untouchable, like the already traditional Marian insertions in the *Gloria in excelsis.*[59] Finally, it was because of the humanist artistic spirit that the Council did nothing to hinder the polyphonic Church music

---

[54] Similar principles, aiming at a return to ancient models, were at work some decades later in the reform of the *Rituale Romanum*; see B. Löwenberg, "Die Erstausgabe des Rituale Romanum von 1614," ZkTh, LXVI (1942), 141-147, esp. 142.

[55] Obviously the Commission did not want to go as far as Radulph de Rivo (d. 1403), *De canonum observ.,* ch. 22, f. (Mohlberg, II, 124-156) had sought. He deplored, especially in the Office, the use of the rite of the papal court, which the Franciscans had spread everywhere, preferring the older rite of the Roman basilicas. In the Missal the Mass order of Micrologus (see *supra,* p. 103) appears as the ideal. Cf. Baumstark, *Missale Romanum,* 148 f.

[56] Cf. A. L. Mayer, "Renaissance, Humanismus und Liturgie," JL, XIV (1938), 123-171.

[57] Amongst these the careful insertion of *eundem, eodem* in the conclusions of orations. There are slight differences, too, in many prayers; the text of Burchard still has in the *Suscipe s. Trinitas*: . . . *memoriam facimus*; in the *Suscipiat*: . . . *et totius Ecclesiæ*; in the Memento for the living: *circumstantium*; in the prayer for peace: *pacem meam do vobis, pacem relinquo vobis* Cf. Jedin *(Liturg. Leben),* 58, note 87.

[58] Mayer, 158.

[59] See *infra,* p. 359 f.

which meanwhile had become strong and flourishing, and so left the road open for the great masterpieces of Church music.[60]

To have gone farther and deeper, say in the direction of a restoration of a stronger communion between priest and people, would have demanded different spiritual conditions amongst the faithful. It was understandable that a preference was felt for things which even in their traditional form had a meaning and a solid foundation, and not for exorbitant and often heretical pretensions of reformational polemics, particularly since their supporters had refused to take part in the Council.[61] Clear limits were here the thing that was essential. One exception was made in the case of the chalice for the laity; the experiences were not favorable. For that reason the dogmatic chapters of the Council did not confine themselves to putting down errors. They tried to focus attention once more on the grand outlines of the Christian sacrificial celebration, even to the point where they recommended that the faithful receive Communion each time they came to Mass, a notion far removed from the practice of the day.

The greatest and most consequential innovation of the Mass book of Pius V was the enactment, clearly expressed in the Bull of introduction, that this book was to be, from then on, the standard in every church and that no changes were to be made therein. Only churches which could demonstrate a two-hundred years' custom for their own usage, were permitted to retain that usage. This was the case with the ancient orders which since the eleventh century had produced their own variants of the Romano-Frankish Mass-liturgy and which have kept them, for the most part, till the present.[62] Many dioceses also took advantage of this stipulation, among them—besides Milan and the remnant of the Mozarabic rite —Trier, Cologne,[63] Liége, Braga and Lyons, of which only the last two have kept their own rite until now.[64]

Such a broad and sweeping unification could never have been completely accomplished before the day of the printing press. Even as things stood,

---

[60] The compositions of the Fleming, Jacques de Kerle, which were sung at the Rogations during the last period of the Council, seem to have been decisive; Ursprung, 182-186. Palestrina's first works were also becoming known. Ursprung, 186, designates the new vocal polyphony which blossomed at this time as "a musical style closely related to the Tridentine liturgical reform."

[61] Still some of the more pertinent questions were the occasion of debate in the Council. Several bishops advised that those who wanted to say the canon aloud be left undisturbed; *Concilium Trid.*, ed. Goerres, VIII, 756, 1. 27; 757, 1. 52; 768, 1. 25; 771, 1. 40. Many likewise were anxious that the use of the vernacular be not condemned;

ibid., VIII, 757, 1. 51; 758, 1. 12; 766, 1. 20; 768, 1. 25; 780, 1. 3.

[62] *Supra*, pp. 98 f.

[63] See the writing, issued anonymously, *Die Liturgie der Erzdiözese Köln* (Cologne, 1868). A special Cologne Missal appeared as late as 1756 (*ibid.*, 105).

[64] Cf. J. Schmid, "Weitere Beiträge zur Geschichte des römischen Breviers und Missale," *Theol. Quartalschrift* (1885), 472 ff.

Details about the gradual change to the Missal of Pius V in P. Guéranger, *Institutions liturgiques* (Le Mans, 1840), I, 445-476.

Regarding the Braga rite see Archdale A. King, *Notes on the Catholic Liturgies,* 153-207.

there were bound to be many doubts and problems resulting from such widely diverse conditions and local customs, not to speak of the difficulties of making the change. To handle these doubts and problems, Pope Sixtus V, by the Constitution "Immensa" of January 22, 1588, founded the Congregation of Rites. Its charge was to see to it that everywhere in the Latin Church the prescribed manner of celebrating Mass and performing the other functions of the liturgy were carefully followed. It had to settle doubts, to give out dispensations and privileges, and, since there was always a chance of introducing new feasts, it had to provide the proper formularies for them. On the other hand it was not in the ordinary power of the Congregation to change the rubrics or alter the wording of prayers.[65] Thus the Congregation of Rites was not to be an organ for liturgical evolution.[66] In so far as such a devolopment might occur within the narrow limits left for it, the Congregation was to act as a regulator, charged with the duty of seeing that the status of things established by the Missal of Pius V be in no way altered or endangered. To regulate new questions in accordance with existing ordinances, that was the task fulfilled by the decrees of the Sacred Congregation of Rites which have appeared since 1588.[67] Almost half of these have to do with the Mass-liturgy and its requisite concomitants.[68] Few of these decrees, however, provide any new regulations for the rites of the Mass itself. The chief ones are the stipulation of certain reverences, the decree that the chalice be covered after the Communion just as it was at the start of the Mass, the casuistic regulation of the order in which various saints are to be mentioned in the oration *A cunctis*, and who is the *antistes* to be named in the canon.

A greater number of the decisions dealt with the various circumstances around the Mass; the proper hour for celebrating it, consideration of locale in choosing the formulary, the *applicatio pro populo*, bination, removal of defects. Many decrees refer to special questions about high Mass or pontifical Mass, or to peculiarities incident to services with celebrants of various ranks, or to the reverence to be made when handing the celebrant the sprinkler *(aspergillum)*, or when offering the Gospel book to be kissed, or at the incensings or at the *pax*. Or they refer to the function of the assistant priest and other assistants, or to the choir rules at a conventual Mass, or to the limitations regarding the use of chant and organ. Many are devoted to the various kinds of Votive Masses and to the Requiem and how the conflicting wishes of those who set up the foundation or ordered the Masses might be reconciled with the arrangements of

[65] See M. Gatterer, *Annus liturgicus, cum introductione in disciplinam liturgicam,* (5th ed., Innsbruck, 1935), 45-55.
[66] This is shown, for example, in the word *tuendis* which is still often used in the official headings of the documents: *Patres sacris tuendis ritibus præpositi.*
[67] The older collection, begun in 1807 by A. Gardellini, had grown by 1887 to 5993 numbers. The new *Collectio authentica* published at Rome 1898-1900 contains but 4051, about a third of the older decrees being dropped; Gatterer, 80-87. Since 1909 the decrees of the Congregation of Rites also appear in the *AAS*.
[68] See the systematically arranged work of

the Church year. And finally, the changes in the Mass rite occasioned by the course of the Church year. Very many of the decrees settle an open abuse or decide an anxious question with the simple reply: *serventur rubricae.*[69]

Some real changes since the sixteenth century in the rubrics and in the text of the Missal of Pius V have resulted in certain instances from papal orders. For instance, in the new edition of the missal under Clement VIII (1604), the biblical chant pieces, which in some printings had been arbitrarily changed in favor of the new Vulgate, were restored to their original state, and new regulations were made regarding the final blessing.[70] In another new edition of the Mass book under Urban VIII (1634), the wording of the rubrics was greatly improved and the revision of the hymns already accomplished in the breviary was carried out also in the few hymns of the missal.[71] No new edition with any notable changes came out till that of 1920 which contained the revisions based on the reform of Pope Pius X.[72] For the rest, excepting the increase in saints' feasts, very little was done to affect the arrangement of the Mass. Pope Clement XIII prescribed the Preface of the Holy Trinity for Sundays, and Pope Leo XIII ordered the prayers said after low Mass.

On the other hand, despite the force of general regulation, some rubrics, under pressure of custom, have dropped out of practice—the use of the *Sanctus* candle, for instance, and the rule that at the distribution of Communion each communicant should partake of the *purificatio.*[73]

All in all, the changes thus made within the Mass-liturgy are very few indeed. After fifteen hundred years of unbroken development in the rite of the Roman Mass, after the rushing and the streaming from every height and out of every valley, the Missal of Pius V was indeed a powerful dam holding back the waters or permitting them to flow through only in firm, well-built canals. At one blow all arbitrary meandering to one side or another was cut off, all floods prevented, and a safe, regular and useful

---

P. Martinucci, *Manuale decretorum SRC* (4th ed., Regensburg, 1873).

[69] Gatterer, 84-86, holds, not without good grounds, that even the *decreta particularia,* even though they answer questions of a particular church, have a universally binding force.

[70] Slight changes regarding the vesture of the Mass-server and the time of preaching; see *infra.*

Further details enumerated in J. O'Connell, "A sixteenth century Missal," *Eph. liturg.,* LXII (1948), 102-104. See also the introductory Bull of July 7, 1604 which is printed in all the modern missals.

[71] Cf. Baumstark, *Missale Romanum,* 152-154.

Regarding the revision under Leo XIII (1884), see Fortescue, *The Mass,* 209.

[72] The changes are, in substance, found in a special chapter added to the general rubrics, *Additiones at variationes in Rubricis Missalis;* they are concerned especially with the new regulations regarding the use of ferial Masses in Lent.

[73] *Ritus serv.,* X, 6, 9.

Further examples in Kramp, "Messgebräuche der Gläubigen in der Neuzeit," StZ, II (1926), 212, Note 1. Cf. the thorough discussion in C. Callewaert, *De s. liturgia universim* (3rd ed., Bruges, 1933), 139-146.

flow assured. But the price paid was this, that the beautiful river valley now lay barren and the forces of further evolution were often channeled into the narrow bed of a very inadequate devotional life instead of gathering strength for new forms of liturgical expression.

13. The Mass in the Baroque Period, the Enlightenment and the Restoration

Due to the reform of 1570, the divine worship of the Church became refined and purified. Since the new Mass book was not only declared binding everywhere, but also withdrawn from all regional initiative,[1] the Roman Mass entered into a condition of rigidity and fixation, even though this stiffening was not set down as necessarily permanent. To take the place of a development of existing things, prominence was given to the juristic and casuistic discussion of established norms. A special branch of knowledge was developed for this purpose, the science of rubrics. In fact someone has styled this period of liturgical history beginning with Pius V as the epoch of inactivity or of rubrics![2]

However, it is hard to say whether in the period to follow, this circumstance was good fortune or bad. What would have happened to the Roman liturgy if the various irenic tendencies had taken a path of development closer to that trodden by Protestant worship? Or if the creative spirit of the Baroque had been allowed to tamper with the rite of the Mass as fully

---

[1] However, the notion that one could work out new formularies for Masses needed in a particular diocese or religious congregation, without getting a special approbation, continued for long. There are examples of formularies newly devised or revised in the 17th century in Bremond, *Histoire litt. du sentiment relig.*, II, 410, 510. The oldest formularies for the feasts of the Sacred Heart of Jesus and the Heart of Mary originated and spread in this private fashion; cf. N. Nilles, *De rationibus festorum ss. Cordis Jesu et purissimi Cordis Mariæ*, (5th ed., Innsbruck, 1885) II, 1-42.

[2] Theodor Klauser, "A Brief History of the Liturgy in the West," *Orate Fratres*, XXIII (1948-9), 7-17, 61-67, 116-121, 154-160. His fourth epoch is styled "The Period of Codified Liturgy and Rubrical Rule" (p. 154). Klauser further points out the dangers that lurked in this view of the rubrics (pp. 157-159) and the wisdom of Pius XI's move in setting up (Feb. 6, 1930) a special historical department within the Congregation of Rites.

[3] Cf. G. Rietschel, *Lehrbuch der Liturgik* (Berlin, 1900) I, 396-441; L. Fendt, *Der lutherische Gottesdienst des 16. Jh.* (Munich, 1923); P. Graff, *Geschichte der Auflösung der alten gottesdienstlichen Formen in der evangelischen Kirche Deutschlands*, I, (2nd ed., Göttingen, 1937). The attitude of the Anglican High Church was hardly less conservative; after making the great change in liturgical tradition to the Book of Common Prayer, it stood pat and made few other changes; see the survey by H. Zettel, "Das anglikanische 'Book of Common Prayer'," *Liturg. Leben*, III (1936), 177-197.

The greatest distinction between the Protestant and the Catholic tradition lay in the sacrificial character of the Mass; hence the canon was the part most affected. But even a Catholic bishop, Friedrich Nausea of Vienna, proposed a change in the canon at the Council of Trent; *Concilium Trid.*, XII, 420 f.

as did the Middle Ages, handling it according to its own conceptions of sacrament, sacrifice and solemnity?

In reality, the Baroque period was but little concerned with the liturgical form of the celebration of Mass. The contrast between the Baroque spirit and that of the traditional liturgy was so great that they were two vastly different worlds.[4] The new life-spirit which would wrap earth and heaven in one whirling tempest—how different from the quiet dignity of the old Roman orations. More than this: theological and religious thought, caught up in the swirl of the Counter-Reformation, was as different from the old Roman tradition as it is possible to be, granted the basis of the same Catholic faith. No one who learns to know the intellectual situation of the time will make it a matter of reproach that the period had found no closer tie to the liturgy.

Through the controversy with the Reformers, the whole stress of thought on the Eucharist was directed to and bound down to the Real Presence, almost to the neglect of other aspects. Even for the scientific treatment of the liturgy which now began, how much the defense of the eucharistic mysteries stood in the foreground is seen in the fact that Muratori, who issued a careful edition of the older sacramentaries, devoted the greater part of the introductory study to a discussion of this dogma as revealed in the liturgical texts.[5] A detailed re-evaluation of the sacrificial character of the Eucharist resulted from the efforts of a new blossoming of Scholastic study. But these studies were likewise aroused by the Protestants' impugning of the dogma and consequently more or less determined by it. Since the greatest concern was Christ's oblation which is constantly realized and re-realized without hurt to the singleness of the Christian sacrifice, and since no interest was felt for the offering through the Church, of which the prayers of the Roman Mass speak, these studies too merely skirted the edge of the liturgy. Thus the spirit of the times forced into the background any notion that the faithful had a part to play in the prayer of the priest or that they should co-offer in closer union with him. For, since the Reformers had denied a special priesthood, it seemed necessary to stress not what was common and connective between priest and people, but rather what was distinctive and separative. This was certainly the case in the Society of Jesus whose theologians were leaders in the intellectual movement of this period; its members had no close contact with the liturgy and did nothing towards a pastoral development of liturgical possibilities. True, the Ignatian *Exercises*, with their definite theocentricity and their conscious alliance to Christ, appeared to harmonize most favorably with liturgical prayer and thought, but the circumstances of the time did not permit this germ to bud forth—in fact, they acted quite the contrary.

But an important step toward realizing what the Mass had to offer was

[4] Cf. A. L. Mayer, "Liturgie und Barock," JL, XV (1941), 67-154.   [5] L. A. Muratori, *Liturgia Romana vetus* (Venice, 1748), I, 101-288.

taken in the French Oratory of Cardinal Pierre de Bérulle (d. 1629). On the basis of meditation on the Word made flesh and of His complete life-long dedication to the Father, worship was established from the start as the center of piety.[6] Private prayer was deliberately allied to public liturgy.[7] In fact participation in the oblation of Christ gradually became the fundamental concept of piety in the school of Bérulle, of Condren (d. 1641) and of Olier (d. 1657).[8] Thus in regard to the Mass, the sacrifice of the Church and with it the liturgical side of the sacrifice became more prominent.[9] During this period, one of the best explanations of the Mass came from the circle of the Oratory.[10] The invitation was given to the people to draw closer to the priest's action.[11] Similar attempts, be it said in passing, were not absolutely lacking in Germany.[12]

But efforts of this sort did not at the time gain a favorable reception. Apparently fearing that an effort was being made to introduce the vernacular into the Mass, Alexander VII had in 1661 condemned a translation of the Roman Missal into French and had forbidden any further translations under pain of excommunication.[13] The strict idea which had already obtained in the Middle Ages was thus increased.[14] Rome took, and continued

[6] Bremond, *Histoire litt. du sentiment relig.*, III, 22 ff., 155 ff.

[7] *Ibid.*, 118, and note 2.

[8] *Ibid.*, 359 ff., 491 ff.

[9] Lepin, *L'idée du sacrifice de la Messe*, 485 f., 494-496.

[10] P. Lebrun, *Explication littérale, hist. et dogm. des prieres et des cérémonies de la Messe* (Paris, 1716-1726). The first volume contains a detailed explanation of the Mass; the other three are devoted to other discussions. Lebrun even studies the question, how the Church and the faithful take part in the sacrifice (I, 22-26, ed. 1860).

[11] N. Letourneux, *De la meilleure manière d'entendre la sainte Messe* (Paris, 1680). The so-called Montpelier Catechism, by the Oratorian F. A. Pouget, *Instructions générales en forme de catéchisme*, contained several thorough instructions on the Holy Mass, but the book was put on the Index in 1721 for its Jansenist leanings. Cf. E. M. Lange, "Vergessene Liturgiker des 17. Jh.," JL, XI (1931), 156-163. See also an account of the liturgical materials in the work named above, JL, XIV (1938), 523-543.

[12] A. G. Volusius, *Catechismus biblicus* (Mainz, 1660), devotes fully a third of the book to an explanation of the sacrifice of the Mass and presents a careful instruction on how to unite one's prayer at Mass with

the priest. Cf. J. Hofinger, *Geschichte des Katechismus in Osterreich von Canisius bis zur Gegenwart* (Innsbruck, 1937), 167 f., 334.

A forerunner of these efforts to get the people to join in the prayers and offering of the priest was the Strassburg priest who became papal master of ceremonies, John Burchard, whose Mass order appeared 1502 (Legg, *Tracts,* 135).

[13] H. Vehlen, O.S.B., "Geschichtliches zur Ubersetzung des Missale Romanum," *Liturg. Leben,* III (1936), 89-97. The undertaking in question, by Joseph de Voisin, was branded as *vesania.* The prohibition was eventually explained in many different ways, and was not everywhere accepted as binding.

Further studies in P. Bussard, *The Vernacular Missal* (Washington, 1937), 10-39. Cf. also Ellard, *The Mass of the Future,* 125-132.

[14] Even in the late Middle Ages translations of the missal, with or without the canon, appeared. Vehlen, p. 89, mentions two manuscripts and one printed translation from the century before Trent. The little exposition of the Mass published in 1480, *Messen singen oder lesen,* included the canon; later editions left out just the words of consecration; Franz, p. 632. Johannes Busch, the reformer of northern German monasteries

to take,[15] the stand that the Latin Mass prayers were not to be given to the faithful in any way, although nowhere was this formulated in a general Church law. In harmony with such a misconception, was another fundamental notion, that the faithful would reverence the liturgy of the Mass more if the veil of mystery were kept around it.[16] The old idea of the canon as a sanctuary which only the priest could enter thus survived and was in fact extended to the whole Mass. There was therefore little chance of encouraging a closer participation in the priest's celebration,[17] and in any case this approach was left to the devotion of each individual. All these endeavors made hardly any impression on the general picture of the divine service at this time.

On the other hand, it is the heritage of the Middle Ages, purified and refined by the Tridentine reform, which really determines the religious picture of the Baroque period as well as the picture of its religious service. The great abuses have all disappeared. But still the Mass remains a service in which only the priest and his assistants have an active role. The faithful follow the divine action only from a distance. As in the late Middle Ages, an effort is made to foster their devotion by bringing certain more general features of the Mass closer to them—its worth, its fruits, its imaging of the Passion of Christ. The old themes are thus the standard.

But there are plain traces of a deepening effected by the theology of Trent. The essence is more distinctly laid in the sacrifice and by preference unfolded on the basis of the four aims of sacrifice. The fruits of the Mass are spiritualized and the representation of our Lord's life and sufferings is no longer culled from the individual ceremonies but connected with the celebration only in their great phases.[18] Allegorizing is not yet dead,[19] but in an age already nearing empiricism and scientific

---

(d. circa 1479), bemoans the fact that lay people had *missale cum canone . . . in teutonico*; he himself found, and burnt, copies that nuns had; *ibid.*, 632, note 3.

A French translation of the Paris Missal is found as early as 1370; Batiffol, *Leçons* (1927), p. xix. Various translations of the Mass order also appeared long before Voisin—in 1587, 1607, 1618, 1651; Bremond, IX, 176 f.

[15] In a notice to a Chinese missionary, Sept. 15, 1759, it was made clear that the prayers to be said in the vernacular by the people at Mass were not to be those said by celebrant or deacon or altar boy (servente) or choir; *Collectanea S. C. de Prop. Fide* (Rome, 1907), I, p. 267, n. 422; cf. X. Bürkler, *Die Sonn- und Festtagsfeier in der katholischen Chinamission* (Rome, 1942), 96, note 24.

[16] Cf. Bremond, IX, pp. 164 ff.

[17] But it grew and grew, as a statement of Claude Judde, S.J. (d. 1735) indicates; he would not recommend the method, but he timidly admits "the Church tolerates it; it can now be made use of without scruple" (*Oeuvres Spirituelles*, V, 397). See Lange, JL, XI (1931), 162; also G. Chevrot, *Unsere hl. Messe* (Einsiedeln, 1946), 25 f.

[18] This description is certainly true of the commentary which was most widespread in Germany and German-speaking countries, the work of the Capuchin Martin von Cochem (d. 1712), *Medulla missæ germanica*, which aimed at gathering all the best and most useful material on the Mass into one book.

[19] A noteworthy continuation of the Amalar ground-plan is seen in Bellarmine, *Christianæ doctrinæ latior explicatio* (1598; Kempten, 1711), 206-209; taken in relation

study it has lost most of its strength. No longer does it satisfy the people. It can no longer so shackle the minds of the faithful that they are able to follow the action in silence. Those who during the Counter-Reformation attempted to rebuild religious life had to look for other ways and means to enable the faithful to participate in a devout manner. Of course, judging from what we have said, these ways and means could only be stop-gap measures, filling in what the Middle Ages had to offer, since there were too many obstacles in the way of a closer approach to the priest's prayer.

Amongst these ways and means was the prayer book which, after the advent of the printing press, had gained in importance at least for people with some education. It is true there is at first only a slight inducement to any participation in Holy Mass, since the prayer book originated chiefly from the Book of Hours with its extra-eucharistic prayer material. In the early stage it generally appears in the form of one of the traditional allegorical explanations of the Mass,[20] but formulated prayers are also offered.[21] Aside from the elevation of the species at the consecration, these prayers for the most part[22] follow the course of the Mass along very general lines,[23] and even when the prayers are more or less faithful to the missal text, the fundamental rule still holds that the canon must be excluded.[24]

The masses, however, were not reached by the prayer book. A genuine interest in souls, however, did hit upon a plan of overcoming the estrangement of those who attended Mass without really taking part in it—namely, common prayers and singing. This method had often been chosen since the beginning of the eigtheenth century, especially during the popular missions

with his theory on the Mass we find: The *Pater noster* represents our Lord's words on the Cross; the fraction is the piercing by the lance; the Communion is the burial; etc.

Besides the prayerbooks, the allegorical exposition played a role also in religious instruction. In his catechetical missions in the Passau diocese in the latter half of the 18th century, Father Karl Helbling, S.J. was accustomed to explain the Mass from the pulpit while another read the Mass at the altar; he would relate the mysteries of Christ's Passion to the ceremonies and add an exhortation; B. Duhr, *Geschichte der Jesuiten in den Ländern deutscher Zunge* (Regensbrug, 1928), IV, 2, p. 243.

Of course, in some form or other the method reached down to our own days.
[20] Cf. Franz, 709 f., 719 f.
[21] F. Falk, *Die deutschen Mess-Auslegungen von der Mitte des 15. Jh. bis zum Jahre 1525* (Cologne, 1889). For the 16th to the 18th centuries see A. Schrott, "Das Gebetbuch in der Zeit der katholischen Restauration," ZkTh, LXI (1937), 1-28; 211-257.
[22] But there were always exceptions; Falk, p. 34, describes a prayerbook with prayers at the *Kyrie*, collect, preface, canon, consecration, communion. Two other samples *ibid.*, pp. 11, 31.
[23] Falk, 27, 32, 35 f.; also 34 f.

Peter Canisius, too, in his prayerbook. *Rechte und katholische Form zu beten* (2nd ed., Augsburg, 1563) inserts for the devotion at Mass long prayers of preparation to awaken faith, hope and love, and a prayer at the elevation of the Host; then follow prayers to Christ's Passion; Schrott, p.214. Most prayerbooks contain, besides a devotion of this type, also an allegorical exposition of the Mass; Schrott, pp. 237, 243, 248. But the tie with the priest's prayers is apparently quite loose.
[24] Schrott, 244, 248.

of the Jesuits.[25] Thus they started, in certain instances even on the occasion of a common celebration, to have a low Mass but accompanied by prayers said out loud. In the prayer texts employed in such cases, one cannot expect any closer approach to the liturgy than was to be found in the prayer books. Quite often, it appears, the rosary was used,[26] with or without additions.[27] Inadequate as such an attendance at Mass might seem to us in the light of our own superior methods, it must be conceded that, in common with the allegorizing of the Mass, it offered the contemplation of the mysteries of Redemption, and offered it, moreover, in a way comprehensible to the people, and with the advantages of congregational participation.

There is somewhat more consideration of the course of the liturgy in the German Mass-songs which begin to gain in significance about this time. In their beginning in the Middle Ages, these songs did not manifest any close regard for the liturgy; a continued series of verses unfolded the meaning of the Mass as a memorial of the Passion and as a sacrifice, and interspersed appropriate petitions.[28] A short time later the custom appears of singing a song at the *Credo* and at the sermon, and of inserting into the sequence strophes in the German tongue.[29] The cultivation of German ecclesiastical song by the Reformers could not remain without its repercussions on the Catholic side. Canisius continually spoke out warmly for German church song.[30] In the sixteenth century we again find not only the song at the sermon but likewise (since the sequence had practically disappeared) a song in the vernacular at the gradual.[31] Besides these, there was also a song at the offertory and at the communion,[32] or one after the *Sanctus*[33] or after the consecration.[34] These do not appear to be anything but pre-Reformation growths which at that time sprang up into stronger life and spread out over a wider area.[35]

The Cantual of Mainz (1605) contains a fixed plan for singing in German in churches in which non-Latin song had long been customary. The Cantual first makes a reference which is very significant for the changes in men's minds, namely, that many of the laity had a greater desire to sing than to meditate on Christ's Passion, as they did of old, by praying from their prayer books or on their rosaries; and because it often happens that there are not enough singers for the chant, the Cantual goes on to outline a plan for the sung-Mass *(Singampt)*. According to this arrangement, German hymns could be inserted even at a Latin Mass, especially in place of the chants of the Proper, namely, instead of the gradual, the offertory, and likewise after the *Agnus Dei* and—*"wann viel Communicanten seyn"* —also during the Communion. Besides, one could also insert a hymn in honor of the Blessed Sacrament after the consecration. The Cantual also gives directions for singing German hymns during a low Mass: The singing should stop at the Gospel, at the elevation, and at the final blessing.[36] From then on, these directions are repeated in various places.[37]

epistolæ et acta, ed. Braunsberger, III, 650-652; cf. IV, 889 f.; V, 569. In his letter of Oct. 2, 1566 he mentions the German hymn as *causam piam et Ecclesiæ salutarem*; *ibid.,* V, 327.

[31] According to the Breslau Synod of 1592 (Hartzheim, VIII, 395), wherever Latin singing was not customary a song in the vernacular was to be inserted at the gradual and after the consecration.

[32] So Joh. Leisentritt, *Geistliche Lieder und Psalmen* (Bautzen, 1567), Introduction (printed in W. Bäumker, *Das Katholische Kirchenlied,* I [Freiburg, 1886], 189).

[33] According to an injunction of the Würzburg Cathedral chapter of the year 1564, for the parish of Ochsenfurt, the priest was directed to have the people sing in German the Act of Faith, right after the *Patrem* and before beginning the sermon; and to keep the people till the elevation he should have the *Media vita* sung in German right after the *Sanctus*; this, they maintain, was customary in the Catholic church. A. Amrhein, *Reformationsgeschichtliche Mitteilungen aus dem Bistum Würzburg* (Reformationsgeschichtl. Stu-

dien u. Texte, 41-42; Münster, 1923), p. 154.

[34] See *supra,* note 31.

[35] It is striking that Luther, in his *Formula missæ et communionis* of the year 1523 (ed. Lietzmann: Kleine Texte, 36 [Berlin, 1936], p. 22) speaks of the possibility of inserting songs in the vernacular in his Mass (still in Latin) *iuxta Gradualia, item iuxta Sanctus et Agnus Dei,* either after the Latin chant or in place of it.

As a matter of fact, even German synods of the 15th century—among them the Synod of Schwerin (1492) which is often understood in a different way—were struggling against the obviously repeated attempt to introduce vernacular songs into the High Mass; see W. Bäumker, *Zur Geschichte der Tonkunst* (Freiburg, 1881), 128 f.; J. Janssen, *Geschichte des deutschen Volkes* (20th ed., Freiburg, 1913), I, 289, 291 (with note 3), 298.

[36] Text reproduced in W. Bäumker, *Das katholische deutsche Kirchenlied* (Freiburg, 1886), I, 198-200.

[37] Ursprung, *Die Katholische Kirchenmusik,* 225.

If certain starts were thus given to a communal celebration of Mass that reached down to the people, still in all these instances, as can be plainly seen, there was little thought of following the course of the Mass except within very modest limits. The liturgy of the Mass stands before the faithful in all its splendor, but it is a splendor whose greatness is self-contained and whose arrangement is as immutable as it is puzzling; and in the midst shines the Blessed Sacrament, a precious jewel for which this traditional setting appeared just, right, and necessary.

Indeed, the Mass was actually treated as self-contained even where it appeared in its festive form and where a Baroque culture could share with it its own riches. The mighty Baroque sermon was extended before the Mass whenever it did not—as it might rightfully have—lay claims to its own hours. And when it did find its way into the Mass, it seemed to burst beyond its limits, so that it seldom had any connection with the Gospel. Since the Middle Ages the site of the pulpit had gradually been altered, moved generally away from the altar and further into the nave. Like the sermon, it grew independent. The Communion of the faithful took place as a rule *after* the Mass, and *not* after the parochial Mass but rather— because of the law of fasting—after one of the early Masses. As far as frequency went, this was once more on the increase. But Communion was an independent, self-contained exercise, looked upon not as a participation in the sacrifice but simply as a reception of our Lord present continually in the Sacrament.

What has been said holds true also for church music at this time. Here, too, the Mass was treated as self-contained. Music spread its gorgeous mantle over the whole Mass, so that the other details of the rite scarcely had any significance. Encouraged by the moderate attitude of the Council of Trent, it had developed into mighty proportions. The seventeenth and eighteenth centuries are marked by a plethora of new musical forms. Besides the organ, there were accompaniments by other instruments, growing ever richer, more gorgeous. And often a single many-voiced choir was not sufficient, but use was made of several choirs either answering each other or even blending together. The history of music, therefore, makes mention of a particular "splendid" style which was formed during this period.[88] The victorious temper of the post-Tridentine age, which once more felt the courage to absorb the entire wealth of the contemporary culture into the Catholic cosmos—that temper found its triumphal voice in this music.

It is significant that the princely courts, both great and small, were the first places where this type of church music was cultivated and where it

[88] Ursprung, 204 f.
 At the consecration of the cathedral of Salzburg, 1628, a festival Mass by Orazio Benevoli (d. 1672) was sung, requiring two eight-part choirs and corresponding orchestras—in all 53 voices or parts; *ibid.*, 207.

reached its splendor.[39] Because of the religio-cultural situation it sometimes happened that this church music, which had fallen more and more into the hands of laymen, forgot that it was meant to subserve the liturgical action. As a result of this, the music often fitted very poorly into the liturgical setting. And since this latter was but little understood, and because esthetic consideration began to hold sway, the liturgy was not only submerged under this ever-growing art but actually suppressed, so that even at this time there were festive occasions which might best be described as "church concerts with liturgical accompaniment."[40] Even the connection with a text was taken very ill by music such as this. Texts which could be chosen at random—as was permitted after the elevation—were transferred to other places in the Mass,[41] and the Proper especially was replaced by some such songs.[42] On the other side, the celebrant often tried to continue with the offertory even while the choir was still singing the *Credo*,[43] or to restrict the singing of the preface and *Pater noster* to the initial words so as to leave the rest for the music and the organ.[44] Thus singing, too, had freed itself from the liturgical bonds and achieved independence.

The place taken by the choir corresponds to this new situation—not in the *choir* from which it derives its name, but far away, on the boundary between the world and the church, in the organ-loft.[45]

The development in the field of music made it really possible to "hear" the Mass. In fact on festival occasions the hearing of polyphonic pieces—

[39] Ursprung, 220.
Right down to the present the court churches and palace chapels were in the forefront in the cultivation of church music, e.g., at Vienna, Munich, Dresden.
[40] Ursprung, 219.
[41] As far as Rome was concerned this attempt was frustrated in 1657 by Alexander VII, who insisted on the use of approved texts. Ursprung, 219; cf. F. Romita, *Jus Musicæ Liturgicæ* (Rome, 1947), 77-79. The pertinent paragraphs are reproduced in the *White List* of the Society of St. Gregory of America (New York, 1947), 4.
[42] Ursprung, 219.
[43] Even before the reform of the missal St. Francis Borgia had, on the occasion of the first General Congregation of the Society of Jesus, 1558, urged this procedure for all High Masses in the Society. *Monumenta hist. S.J., S. Franciscus Borgia* (Madrid, 1908), III, 346 f.; cf. 356.
But such a practice must have become widespread in France even after the reform of the missal, since Letourneux expressly combats it; JL, XIV (1938), 537. The Congregation of Rites replied in the

same tenor against similar attempts in answers to Beneventum, Sept. 13, 1670, to Besançon, April 3, 1677, and to Genoa, Dec. 17, 1695; Martinucci, *Manuale decretorum SRC*, n. 631, 700, 709. Similar practices of telescoping are not unheard of even nowadays!
But even more revolutionary things were to be met with. The Cologne Provincial Synod of 1536 had to enjoin that the Epistle, symbol, preface or *Pater* were not to be omitted or shortened on account of the music; can. 12 (Hartzheim, VI, 255). Likewise a Synod at Trier (1549), can. 9 (Hartzheim, VI, 600).
[44] Lebrun, I, 337, who had encountered this abuse during a trip through Germany, 1714; a condemnation at the Council of Basle, 1431, shows how early this practice had crept in.
[45] This change appears to belong to the 17th century; Ursprung, 219 f. For its previous position, see *ibid.*, 208-9; 215. Ursprung, p. 220, correctly points out that the chants of the Ordinary of the Mass were by rights the congregation's but had been taken over gradually by the clergy.

which demanded no activity whatever on the part of the congregation—cast all other sensations into shadow. But in ecclesiastical Baroque the eye, too, was satisfied. Looking at the Host at the consecration no longer possessed the attraction and significance that it had towards the end of the Middle Ages." The new age sought not the sight of the holy, but the sight of the beautiful in art and universe. And so the church became a great hall, its walls shimmering with marble and gold. The paintings on the ceilings, which grew right out of the plaster of the entablature, made the room appear to fade away into heavenly glory. The *presbyterium* is hardly any longer distinct from the nave, and along with the latter it mounts upwards, by force of the cupola or dome, into a higher unity. At its base the glance falls on the mighty structure of the high altar in which the design of the Gothic altar-piece has been reconstructed architecturally. The prominent thing in this structure is the altar-piece itself, perhaps also the exposition throne for the Blessed Sacrament, and finally the tabernacle which has become part and parcel of the plan. By contrast, what really makes the altar an altar, the *mensa*, is not given the prominence it deserves. Its significance appears to have suffered, just as in Baroque polyphony the liturgical action suffered." The interior of the church has become a great hall filled with sensuous life. Even the galleries and boxes are there. And the liturgy itself is conceived of as a play, to be looked at and listened to. But it is no longer—as it was in the Middle Ages—the Mass itself with its succession of ceremonies which bears this dramatic character. Only the adoration of our Lord at the consecration retains its position as the dominating climax. Indeed, the adoration and glorification of the Sacrament, which had been so outrageously attacked by the Reformers, now stands so prominently in the foreground that one is almost bound to look upon the Mass in general chiefly from this point of view. The catechism of J. M. Kettler which appeared at Würzburg in 1734 treats the Mass as one of the five ways in which to worship Christ in the Sacrament." It is no wonder, then, that eucharistic devotion, especially the Forty Hours and the grand processions, vied with the Mass in splendor and in the fervor of attendance, and that in many countries it became the rule more and more to expose the Blessed Sacrament during Mass as an enhancement of the celebration,

---

⁴⁶ Dumoutet, 72-74; 102-104.

⁴⁷ Mayer, "Liturgie und Barock," JL, XV (1941), 142 ff.; Braun, *Der christliche Altar*, II, 288 f. See the description of Baroque in H. Lützeler, *Die christliche Kunst des Abendlandes* (Bonn, 1932), where its relation to liturgy is carefully weighed (152 f., 160 ff.).

A very good description of the Baroque church is presented by Paul Claudel, *Ways and Crossways* (trans. Fr. J. O'Connor;

London, 1935), "On Art," p. 132.

⁴⁸ J. Hofinger, *Geschichte des Katechismus in Osterreich*, 168. Martin von Cochem, too, in his two chapters on devout attendance at Mass, deals mostly with the consecration; till the elevation, say your daily prayers, after that worship the divine Lamb (*Medulla*, 3rd ed., Cologne, 1724, p. 439). However he gives instructions about paying attention to the *Confiteor* and the *Sanctus* (ibid., p. 433).

especially on feast days.[49] This type of piety achieved at this very time its highest artistic manifestation and, at the same time, the proof of its power in the *autos sacramentales* of Spanish poetry.[50]

That the manner of celebrating Mass in the post-Tridentine era did not correspond in every respect to the deep mystery and especially to the faithfully guarded form of its Roman vesture could not even then remain hidden from everyone. The advent of the Reformers had not only awakened a theology of controversy but had also necessitated a closer and deeper study of the writings of the Fathers and of the life of the ancient Church. Along with the writings of the Fathers the old liturgical texts came to light—the sacramentaries, the *ordines*—and with them a picture of a divine service which, far and wide, had embraced the entire Christian people in the community of celebration.[51] This picture easily became a pattern and model. Knowledge became a spur to make some attempt—on one's own initiative —in the direction which was deemed, or at least poetically painted, as the ideal. There were few restraints in the way of this attempt, at least where the relationship to the government of the Church Universal had become slack either because of dogmatic differences as in the circles of Jansenism, or because of canonical and legal disagreements as in Gallicanism, or finally because of a novel view of Christendom which de-emphasized the supernatural in favor of the natural, as in the Enlightenment. So various attempts were made at improvement, but even in the good and worthwhile things that they contained they were burdened by this double difficulty, that they worked on their own and that they were stimulated by questionable motives, so that they were from the outset bound inevitably to fail.

It was not a good omen when one of the first to take up the slogan that simple people were not to be deprived of the consolation of lifting their voices in union with the voice of the entire Church, was Pasquier Quesnel.[52]

---

[49] The fact is attested especially by the efforts made to oppose it in the period of the Enlightenment; see *infra*, p. 153.

[50] In Germany the Corpus Christi play developed to a high degree during the era of the Baroque; see R. Hindringer, "Fronleichnamsspiele," LThK, IV (1932), 216; A. Dörrer, *Bozner Bürgerspiele* (Leipzig, 1941), I, 107-239.

[51] Of the liturgico-historical publications of this period only the few need be mentioned which are still of value in the study of the Mass: the editions of the Roman *Ordines* and of medieval explanations of the liturgy by M. Hittorp (1568); the work of three Benedictines of the Congregation of St. Maur: the edition of a Gregorian Sacramentary, with a goodly supply of notes by H. Ménard (1642), the collection of the Roman *Ordines* with a commentary by J.

Mabillon (1687-89), and the texts assembled from numerous MSS. and accompanied by a discussion in the important work of E. Martène (after 1700); further the edition of Roman and Gallican Sacramentaries by L. A. Muratori (1748) and the collection of ancient liturgical source-materials in German libraries by Abbot M. Gerbert (1779). Add the various drafts of an historical appraisal of the Roman Mass, especially those by Cardinal J. Bona (1671), by Cl. de Vert (after 1707), by P. Lebrun (after 1716) and by the learned Pope Benedict XIV (1748).

Further bibliography in Eisenhofer, I, 134-141.

[52] In his *Reflexions morales* (1691; the work appeared earlier but in a different form); cf. the 86th of the propositions condemned in 1713 (Denziger-Umberg, *En-*

Soon after his appearance the endeavor was made in France to have the canon prayed aloud, but an episcopal prohibition was passed against this for the first time in 1698.[52] In a new printing of the Missal of Meaux in the year 1709 there suddenly appeared in the canon and in some other places a red-printed R just before the Amen; the people were thus expected to respond to each prayer section, and this presupposed that the praying was done aloud. A lengthy battle ensued regarding this inconspicuous but yet not unimportant innovation.[54] The ominous letter had to disappear. In the year 1736 a Missal of Troyes carried this notice regarding the praying of the canon: *submissa voce*; it sought thus to retain the rubric in a mitigated form. According to the same authority, the prayers before the distribution of Communion, from the *Confiteor* to the *Domine non sum dignus*—which had formerly been said in the Mass—were to be left out. And the priest was no longer obliged to repeat softly to himself the chants and readings which had formerly been performed aloud. There were also in this Mass book as in the Paris Mass book of 1684, attempts along another path, to substitute biblical texts for the non-biblical song texts. The former directions had to be rescinded, in accordance with a governmental decree which the then archbishop of Sens obtained in 1738.[55] But editions of the missal which made changes in the texts of the *Proprium* continued to appear and, following the example of Paris, were finally adopted in more than fifty dioceses.[56]

Later, but more pretentiously, the feeling of dissatisfaction with the traditional forms of the divine service found expression elsewhere. In Germany especially, where the Baroque had had its greatest development in ecclesiastical life, the reaction in that same ecclesiastical life—after this development had exhausted its strength — was the strongest. This occurred during the Enlightenment. The desire was to get free from all excess of emotions, free from all surfeit of forms; to get back again to "noble simplicity." As in contemporary art, where the model for this was sought in antiquity and attained in classicism, so in ecclesiastical life the model was perceived in the life of the ancient Church. And so a sort of Catholic classicism was arrived at, a sudden enthusiasm for the liturgical forms of primitive Christianity, forms which in many cases one believed could be taken over bodily, despite the interval of a thousand years and more, even though one was far removed from the spirit of that age.[57]

chiridion, n. 1436) : *Eripere simplici populo hoc solatium iungendi vocem suam voci totius Ecclesiæ, est usus contrarius praxi apostolicæ et intentioni Dei.*
[53] Prosper Guéranger, *Institutions liturgiques* (Le Mans, 1841), II, 180 f.
[54] Guéranger, *op. cit.*, 181 ff.
The defense of silent prayer was taken up by Lebrun (see note 10 above), who devoted half of his fourth volume to the problem; IV, 226-520. He thought he was able

to prove silent prayer was to be found even in the earliest centuries of the Church.
[55] Guéranger, *op. cit.*, 188 ff.
[56] Guéranger, *op. cit.*, 365 ff.
The liberties taken with the Breviary were even greater; see F. Cabrol, "Liturgies neó-gallicanes," *Liturgia* (Paris, 1935), 864-870. The Holy See did not take any stand whatever regarding these activities.
[57] A. L. Mayer, "Liturgie, Aufklärung und Klassizismus," JL, IX (1929), 67-127.

One group of liturgists in the Enlightenment absolutely misjudged the essence of the liturgy and wanted to make of divine service a human service designed for instruction and moral admonition.[58] Others desired only to set aside disturbing non-essentials and to bring into prominence an outline of the celebration of the Mass which would consolidate the congregation. The whole community should assemble in the parish church; here one Mass, and only one Mass should be celebrated. After the Gospel there was to be a sermon, and after the priest's Communion the Communion of the faithful. Instrumental music was not to be allowed, or at most only on great feast-days. As much as possible the people themselves were to accompany the sacred ceremony with singing in the vernacular or even with prayer, which, however, should correspond to that of the priest. The common recitation of the rosary during Mass was censured. These demands are repeated in the pastoral theology of the period with almost wearisome uniformity.[59] They are demands in which one would hardly say an ecclesiastical spirit was wanting.[60] Other wishes which often reappear are for an increase in the frequency of Communion,[61] for a decrease in altars,[62] for the turning of the altar towards the people,[63] for greater restraint in the exposition of the Blessed Sacrament.[64] The offertory procession,[65] the kiss of peace,[66] and concelebration[67] are also proposed as the objects of reform.

B. Thiel, *Die Liturgik der Aufklärungszeit. Ihre Grundlagen und die Ziele ihrer Vertreter* (Breslau, 1926).

A very thorough and detailed survey is presented in W. Trapp, *Vorgeschichte und Ursprung der liturgischen Bewegung* (Regensburg, 1940), 14-189.

[58] Trapp, 19-68. A leading part was played by Canon Winter of Eichstätt; see A. Vierbach, *Die liturgischen Anschauungen des V. A. Winter* (Munich, 1929).

[59] See the proofs in Trapp, 85-189. Most of these demands are found repeated by the extremists amongst the Enlightened; *ibid.*, 21 ff.; Vierbach, 102-151.

For reforms that were actually put into practice see Vierbach, 32-44. For a general idea of pastoral work in this period see E. Hegel, "Liturgie und Seelsorge in der Zeit der Aufklärung," *Theologie u. Glaube,* XXXV (1943), 103-107.

[60] The proper notion is conveyed in a reform-writing which appeared in 1812, which points to the need of giving the liturgy "full play" in religious life, since, owing to the secularization which had occurred, so many external aids had been withdrawn; Trapp, 117.

[61] Trapp, 90, 157 f., 166 ff.

[62] Trapp, 102, 134.

Like so many of the points already mentioned, this part of the program was also taken up at the Synod of Pistoia (1786); the demand was made that in every church there be but one altar. This proposition was characterized as *temeraria* by Pius VI in the Bull *Auctorem fidei;* similarly other propositions requiring the use of the vernacular and the discontinuance of Mass-stipends and of private Masses (Denziger-Umberg, *Enchiridion,* n. 1528, 1530 ff., 1566). Cf. R. Pilkington, "La liturgia nel Sinodo Ricciano di Pistoia," *Eph. liturg.,* XLIII (1929), 310-424; the author points out that not everything the synod did was bad, and that some of its liturgical notions contained "delle cose buone" (p. 410). The same must be said of the more conservative program developed in that same year, 1786, at the Congress of Ems; see Mayer, "Liturgie, Aufklärung und Klassizismus," 102 f., 111 f.

[63] Trapp, 122 f., 162 f., 219; cf. 25; also Vierbach, 149.

[64] Trapp, 90, 98, 103, 131, 136, 158.

[65] *Ibid.*, 126.

[66] *Ibid.*, 122, 222.

[67] *Ibid.*, 126 f., 165.

In all of these desires for change, one point plainly recurs time and again, and that is that the participation of the faithful had reached a certain critical stage. The faithful ought not only to be present at Mass but ought to be able to follow along. Concern over this matter was practically as old as the split between the vernacular and the liturgical language. The solution adopted for many centuries, the allegorical interpretation, is no longer considered; it is not even mentioned.[68] The ornamentation of the Mass with rousing music is hardly a more practical remedy than the common praying of the rosary, which appears to have become quite extensive at the daily celebration of Mass.[69] So new ways had to be sought. One substitute would be the thorough instruction of the faithful.[70] Prayer books would have to be distributed in which the Mass prayers are offered in faithful translation.[71] For a similar reason, praying and singing in common should be practiced. But ultimately one had to acknowledge that for a closer coordination between the people and the liturgy the language was the great stumbling-block. This was a time when Latin, which had already for a long time ceased to be the means of communication between the cultured, no longer served as the language of learned literature. Therefore the desire was expressed time after time for a more or less extensive use of the vernacular, especially where the priest turns to the people. A reference to 1 Cor. 14:16 f. often recurs. Still no one was blind to the value of Latin, any more than to the limits of the advantages which a language change could produce.[72] Indeed there were continual warnings against any arbitrary procedure and a demand for deference to ecclesiastcal superiors.[73]

While other points in the program of the liturgists of the Enlightenment left no traces in the devotional life of the subsequent period, their work in one field was crowned with lasting success, namely, in the field of German church-song. As we have already seen, it had been customary even in the previous centuries under certain circumstances to accompany the celebration of Mass with singing in the vernacular. But now there was inaugurated a certain systematic promotion of popular church singing, which led eventually to the formation of the German *Singmesse*. German

[68] But cf. note 19 above.
[69] Cf. Trapp, 24 f., 115, 134, 147 f., 157, 178; Vierbach, 75, 109.
[70] Trapp, 90, 92, 106 f., 164.
[71] *Ibid.*, 92, 119 f., 146, 159 f.
This demand was fulfilled to some extent by the Constance hymnbook of 1812: *Christkatholisches Gesang- und Andachtsbuch*; Trapp, 148. A complete translation of the Mass prayers was offered in J. M. Sailer, *Vollständiges Lese- und Betbuch* (Munich, 1783), I, 1-69.
[72] Trapp, 106, 119, 161. Sailer especially, while emphasizing the seriousness of the question, also points out the preliminaries

that must be investigated before any change to the vernacular was feasible. Amongst these difficulties he names the incoherence that is to be found in many of the Scripture texts used; *ibid.*, 214-216. Similarly, K. Schwarzel; *ibid.*, 108.
[73] The "episcopalism" of the era is shown by the fact that usually only ordinariates and synods seem to come to mind; see Trapp, 106, 108 f., 130.
In the years that followed, two others especially sued for a German liturgy, F. A. Staudenmaier (*ibid.*, 248) and, with particular zeal, J. B. Hirscher (218, 222 f., 225 f.).

songs replaced not only the variable chants of the Proper but also those of the Ordinary which up till now had continued current here and there in their Latin text and with their ancient chant melodies even amongst the people.[74] The Paderborn Hymnal of 1726 contains German songs for the *Gloria, Sanctus, Agnus Dei*; finally the Speyer Hymnal of 1770 contains a *Singmesse* with German selections for all parts of the Ordinary.[75] The best known example from this period is the *Singmesse "Hier liegt vor deiner Majestat"* (Here before thy majesty lies), which appears with a first melody in the Landshut Hymnal of 1777 and which, after acquiring a new set of melodies by Michael Haydn (d. 1806) continues in use even today.[76]

Just as the first attempts to introduce German singing into the Mass-liturgy dealt with a service in which the priest continued to sing his part at the altar, so also in the eighteenth century no one had any misgivings about combining the new *Singmesse* with a chanted Mass as well as with a low Mass. That is plainly to be seen especially from the prefaces in the hymnals.[77] A circumstance which might have urged some such solution was the situation in which country choirs found themselves at that time—a situation even now not entirely overcome. The many-voiced church music performed at the court churches and the large city churches had become the fashion, a fashion which was followed even in the country, although with inadequate resources. Therefore a simple song in the vernacular actually appeared to deserve the preference, more especially since the ecclesiastical prescriptions regarding the language of the accompanying singing were not then so precise and the liturgical books generally left the question quite open.[78] Thus a German high Mass came into common use and

[74] W.Bäumker, *Das katholische deutsche Kirchenlied* (Freiburg, 1891), III, 13 ff.; (1911), IV, 13.

That the singing of the Chant was still alive amongst the people in the 18th century is seen by the fact that many proponents of the Enlightenment opposed it as vehemently as they opposed the rosary; Trapp, 178; cf. 59. The resistance of the people in the diocese of Mainz to the introduction of the German High Mass rested largely on this fact that the Chant would be ousted; see JL, VI (1926), 425. Gregorian chant did not disappear from Mainz until 1837.

[75] Ursprung, 225. A midway sample is found in the *Singmesse* in the *Lobklingende Harfe* published 1730 by the Jesuit missionary Anton Koniass (*ibid.*, 225, 227).

[76] Ursprung, 259 f.

[77] The hymnbook which appeared at St. Blaise in 1773 under Abbot Gerbert expressly proposed that the German songs be substituted for the Latin ones which the

farmers hardly used. Similarly the Catholic songbook of Ignaz Franz (1778) was intended as a replacement in villages and small towns for the figured music commonly employed. Trapp, 176 f.

In Mainz and Paderborn episcopal decrees commanded the substitution of German songs for the Chant. Ursprung, 257. Further evidence in Trapp, 88, 136, 147, 156.

[78] The Paderborn Hymnal of 1726 refers to a decree of the Roman Provincial Council of 1725 under Benedict XIII ordering that at High Mass catechetical hymns be sung in the vernacular right after the sermon; Ursprung, 225.

On the other hand, the singing of vernacular songs at Mass was forbidden—in 1639 in a reply to Rimini (Gardellini, n. 1129), and on March 22, 1862, in a reply to Valencia *(Decreta Authentica SRC,* n. 3113). An admonition to get rid of the custom *sensim sine sensu* was addressed to the bishop of St. Hyacinth in Canada

as a result of a custom already in vogue it remained in use, especially in North German dioceses, all through the nineteenth century and right down to the present.[79]

This type of service employed at sung Mass appears to have been carried over to the low Mass only secondarily. As a matter of fact the German *Singmesse*—the term was now by preference applied to this latter case—gave somewhat the impression of a one-sided conversation, for not only the orations but the readings (or at least the Epistle) and the preface and *Pater noster*, none of them unimportant parts in the structure of the Mass, do not receive any kind of expression. That there was no mention of any of the changeable chants of the *Proprium* was again a carry-over from the high Mass that was then current and is to a great extent still current. But, this much must be conceded, that in the German *Singmesse* a form of celebrating the Mass had been found which was both popular and dignified, a form moreover which was nowhere in contradiction to existing legal prescriptions; for with regard to the method of accompanying a *missa lecta* with prayer and song the fullest liberty reigned, and still reigns. It was a form by which the people could not only understand the action of the priest but also to a certain extent actively follow. It was a form in which, through singing in common, the community consciousness was aroused, and indeed imbued with a certain degree of solemnity. No wonder that in many dioceses the German *Singmesse* gradually won great popularity.[80] That this did not occur more quickly was due in part to the violent methods by which its introduction was effected in many places, in part also to the weaknesses of content which the creations of the period of Enlightenment so frequently displayed.[81]

The weaknesses and mistakes with which the Enlightenment proved to be burdened, in other fields more plainly perhaps than in the liturgy, turned out to be the reason why a reaction was bound to set in, a return to the complete affirmation of dogma and the supernatural, to a respect for the hierarchic structure of the Church and for tradition. A Catholic *Restoration* was bound to come.[82] The excessive enthusiasm for reform reached an end. The older arrangements were once more honored, including the arrangement of the celebration of Mass, just as a former generation had

on Dec. 10, 1870 (*ibid.* n. 3230). The first *decretum generale* to forbid the mingling of vernacular singing with the Latin at High Mass did not appear till May 22, 1894 (*ibid.*, n. 3827). Since then several particular decrees (*ibid.*, 3880, 3994) and the *Motu Proprio* of Pius X (*ibid.*, n. 4121, 7) have confirmed this legislation.

[79] Its toleration for Germany has been affirmed by the Holy See by a letter of the Cardinal Secretary of State dated Dec. 24, 1943.

[80] In Lower Austria it appears to be a valid substitute even for the parish Mass on Sundays in many of the country churches, so that the Latin service (except for the *Requiem*) is heard only on feasts.

[81] Cf. Ursprung, 258 f.

[82] A. L. Mayer, "Liturgie, Romantik und Restauration," JL, V (1930), 77-141. Mayer maintains that Romanticism, because of the independence of its views, had little or no connection with the liturgy (104 f.); still certain Romantic elements did enter

found it, with all its excellencies and, to a great extent with all its deficiencies. No one wanted to listen to critical voices.[83] Even the healthy reform aims of the older period—many of which were to be taken up, a century later, by the highest authority in the Church—were looked upon with suspicion because they had emanated from the epoch of the Enlightenment.

Still by teaching respect for the existing liturgy, this period of Catholic Restoration did begin the necessary preparation for a healthier and more blessed resumption of these former strivings at a later time. The beauty of the Latin prayers, the dignity of the ceremonies, the harmony of the whole conglomerate—all these were extolled. Enthusiasm developed once more for Gregorian Chant and for all vocal art based on the chant after the manner of Palestrina.[84]

It was in the field of church music that the Restoration set to work most visibly to remodel the divine service. The works of the Baroque period which had found in the liturgy only an occasion for unfolding a musical splendor that was all too worldly and which often bore no relationship to the seriousness of the liturgical text and the liturgical mystery—from these one turned aside. An effort was made to bring the unabbreviated words of the sacred songs into their rightful place. War was declared on the amalgamation of songs in the vernacular with the Latin service, which now frequently returned in its pure unadulterated form. The Cæcilian movement made the relevant demands and principles common property of the widest circles, and succeeded in introducing even in country churches many-voiced Latin singing in place of the German Mass-songs.[85]

But this movement had one drawback; the people at Mass were once more—and this time more consciously than ever—reduced to the role of spectators, and the attempt to reveal the Latin liturgy to the faithful was turned aside partly as a matter of principle.[86] The Mass-liturgy was, for the leaders who espoused this tendency, a monument, finished and fixed once and for all, a monument which in its mystery-filled objectivity not only did not take the faithful into consideration but even shut off their

into the restoration, especially, e.g., the attraction of the Middle Ages.

[83] Cf. the views of M. v. Diepenbrock regarding the opposition of Hirscher; Trapp, 270.

[84] Ursprung, 280.

[85] Ursprung, 277 ff.; O. Rousseau, *Histoire du mouvement liturgique* (Paris, 1945), 151-166.

In many places, however—as in the Provincial Council of Cologne, 1860—Gregorian Chant was prescribed except on feastdays.

For the decision of the Third Plenary Council of Baltimore (1884) regarding Chant, and for other early evidences of an American "liturgical movement" see Wm. Busch, "The Voice of a Plenary Council," *Orate Fratres*, XXI (1946-47), 452-458.

[86] This was the stand taken by H. Bone in the preface to his hymnal *Cantate* (Mainz, 1847); the temple of God, he maintained, would lose none of its sublimity even if no congregation ever assembled there for worship, for the living principle is not the congregation but the sanctuary and the sacrifice. The earlier attempts to introduce the vernacular and a participation of the faithful he tags as "devotional communism"; these attempts, he felt, went too far. Trapp, 271-273.

every approach. Therefore the liturgy is praised as a finished art-product, as a wondrous work of the Holy Spirit, and it is almost forgotten that in the service of this higher master, human hands had been at work through the centuries, probing and fumbling and not always very happily, endeavoring to make the eternally incomplete as fit for its purpose as they possibly could.[87]

In such a treatment of the liturgy we recognize the expression of a time grown tired, a time which is accustomed, with every technical skill, to measure the tasks of intellectual culture, not by an independent judgment of things themselves but by comparison with certain finished patterns which thus passed muster as an unalterable canon. This was the age which started out in classicism, following the traces of classical antiquity, an age which in matters ecclesiastical considered Gothic the ideal in architecture, Raffaele and Perugino in painting, and Palestrina in music. It is an age in which our churches began to be filled with imitations and in which the liturgy of the Mass, by and large unquestionably wonderful, was crystallized in a framework that was utterly unworthy of it.

The intellectual backgrounds of this phase of evolution will be made more plainly visible by a consideration of the parallel phenomena in the French area. In Abbot Prosper Guéranger, founder of Solesmes (1833) and renovator of the monastic ideal, there arose an implacable adversary of the so-called neo-Gallican liturgies, or to speak more exactly, of the arbitrary changes introduced into the Roman Missal and Breviary. He demanded an uncompromising return to the books of the pure Roman liturgy,[88] and was so successful in carrying this out all along the line that in many dioceses even the Propers which were ancient and traditional were swept by the board. By 1860 the Roman Missal and the Roman Breviary without any additions had once more been reintroduced nearly everywhere.[89]

Here, too, it is the spirit of the Catholic Restoration which stands behind the movement. At the same time, however, the opposition to the previous generation's deification of reason took on, in one strong group, the form of traditionalism. This became the teaching that, in general, man can achieve all higher knowledge, not through the labor of his own reason, but only from tradition, and in the last analysis from an original revelation. Tradi-

---

[87] See the survey in Trapp, 319-324. The most striking thing is the effort to compare the liturgy thus conceived (as a work finished and complete) with other products of spiritual culture. According to J. B. Henninger (d. 1892) the Church possesses in the prayers of the liturgical books a treasure "which would of itself suffice to prove its divine origin" (p. 320, note 244). According to F. Hettinger (d. 1890) the contents of the liturgy, especially the missal,

are amongst "the most perfect possessions of literature" (p. 323).
[88] P. Guéranger, *Institutions liturgiques,* 3 vols. (Le Mans & Paris, 1840-1851). The second volume especially is devoted to this struggle. Miscellaneous polemic papers were assembled after his death (1875) in a fourth volume of the 2nd edition (1878-1885).
[89] F. Cabrol, "Guéranger," DACL, VI (1875-1879); H. Leclercq, CE, VII (58-59); Rousseau, 1-43.

tion and authority, as opposed to every individual project and all private initiative, thus acquired an unconscionably great importance. This attitude was prominent already in the case of Joseph de Maistre. And young Guéranger, too, paid homage to this spirit. He had picked it up in the circle of Lamennais and in his work with him. After Lamennais' condemnation Guéranger definitely broke with him, but the unsparing fight against the liturgical independence of the French bishops which he had opened up in Lamennais' publication, he continued to the end in the same spirit in which he had started it.[90] Guéranger therefore stood squarely for the persistence of the existing Roman liturgy and a veneration for it that set aside any critical consideration. In spite of his great work on the Church year he did not favor an unrestricted elucidation of liturgical texts and practices for the people; for the Christian multitude the liturgy should instead remain wrapped under a veil of mystery.[91]

14. The Mass since Pius X

Notwithstanding the shadows that envelop even a figure like Dom Prosper Guéranger, it was from him and from what he established that the most momentous impulses proceeded for that intense rapprochement of the liturgy to the people and for that far-reaching reorganization of divine service which we witness today. Reverent and loving submersion in actualities has at last proved to be a blessing, thanks to the wealth that lies buried deep in the liturgy. It led to a knowledge of the ways and means to bridge, at least in some scant manner, the thousand-year old cleft between the Mass-liturgy and the people, without using allegory and also without any fundamental changes.

First of all, the *opus Dei* as performed in the new centers of monasticism, dignified, replete with the spirit of adoration, became a drama in the best sense of the word, drawing to itself the eyes of all. The products of Beuronese art soon gave it a visible background. Gregorian Chant, too, was refurbished. There were many differences to be found in the various editions and even at Rome there was no obligatory norm regarding the use and execution of the chant,[1] but at Solesmes it was made the object of learned study, so that its true form in the flourishing period, as discovered in the manuscripts, was once more re-established. These studies received the highest recognition under Pius X, who had already in early life been influenced by the Benedictine movement for the renewal of chant,[2] and

---

[90] E. Sévrin, *Dom Guéranger et La Mennais* (Paris, 1933); see the review, with further references, by A. Schnütgen, JL, XIII (1935), 442-444. For similar and related matters in Germany see Trapp, 268 ff.
[91] Guéranger, *Institutions*, III, 210 ff.; cf. II, 230, 245.

[1] The *Editio Medicea* of the Roman Graduale, printed 1614-1615, was first declared authentic by Pius IX in 1868, and this only in the form of a privilege for 30 years to the publishing firm of Pustet (Regensburg) which edited the work. Ursprung, 279, 286.
[2] Ursprung, 283, 286.

who, as Pope, utilized the results of the labors of Solesmes as the basis of his efforts for the restoration of chant and for the new authentic editions of the chant books *(Editio Vaticana).*[3] The chants of the *Ordinarium missæ* appeared in 1905, the complete *Graduale* by 1907. Already in the very first year of his pontificate, on November 22, 1903, the *Motu Proprio* on church music had appeared,[4] calling attention to the dignity of Gregorian Chant, encouraging the participation of the people in its rendition, but also developing the norms for a polyphony and a harmonized music that is ready to serve in the sacred celebration.

Under Pius X, too, other endeavors, which in the nineteenth century had resulted in a deeper search into the treasures of the Church's heritage, began to bear fruit in the life of Christian worship. Not in vain had the life of the ancient Church been lifted out of the darkness of the catacombs. Not in vain had a more intense study of patristic literature been inaugurated. Not in vain had a revival of Scholasticism brought honor once more to an uncurtailed affirmation of dogma and of the Sacrament. Since the middle of the nineteenth century voices had been raised more and more confidently to seek for a return of the practice of the ancient Church regarding Communion, and to point to the natural conclusion of the Mass in the Communion of the faithful.[5] Thus the ground was somewhat prepared for the decree *On frequent and even daily Communion* which appeared in 1905,[6] marking a milestone in liturgical history even more important than the decrees of the same pope which were more directly liturgical.

At first glance the decree seemed to have little relation to liturgical affairs. It had indeed in its very first words *(Sacra Tridentina synodus)* alluded to the wish of the Council of Trent that the faithful receive Communion at Mass not only spiritually but also sacramentally. But for the rest, it had not gone into the connection between Mass and Communion at all, but had restricted itself to setting forth and analyzing the value and the conditions of freqeunt Communion. If you read through the religious periodicals in the years following the publication of the decree, conning the articles that urged frequent Communion, you will see that at first the liturgical connection hardly played any role at all in their arguments. For generations men had been accustomed to regard Communion as an exercise complete in itself, and everywhere, in town and country, in the convent and in the parish church, Communion was distributed each day, perhaps, but always before or after Mass. After a few years had passed, however,

---

[3] A brief but satisfactory survey of the history and results of this work in Léon A. McNeill, "Sacred Music: Its Restoration," *The American Ecclesiastical Review,* LXXVIII (1928), 276-288, esp. 280 ff.; cf. also Sablayrolles' article on Gregorian Chant in *Liturgia* (Paris, 1935), 446 ff.

[4] Printed in *Decreta authentica SRC,* n.

4121; in English in *The American Ecclesiastical Review,* XXI (1904), 113 ff. and in the *White List of the Society of St. Gregory* (New York, 1947), 7-11.

[5] Trapp, 297-306.

[6] *Acta S. Sedis,* XXXVIII (1905-6), 400-406. See *The American Ecclesiastical Review,* XXXV (1906), 75-81.

the realization began to grow that this Communion movement could last only if Communion were fitted into some larger entity and became fully integrated in the organization of Christian life—if it took its rightful and natural place within the Mass.

Here it was, then, that the Communion movement came into contact with the liturgical movement, a decade or so after the appearance of the decree. And the latter kept making these facts plainer and more manifest: the offering to God in the sacrifice is the proper preparation for Holy Communion; the sacrificial meal belongs to the sacrifice, God invites us to it; all the prayers of the Mass lead up to it; and this meal is at the same time the meal of the Christian community. The Eucharist once more appears in a new light. The ancient and more complete symbolism gradually creeps back into Christian consciousness; the simple cult of adoration, already shaken by the decree on Communion[7] loses its dominance.[8] After another decade these realizations begin to have an effect on parochial life: Communion once more stands in its natural liturgical relationship as a conscious participation in the Holy Sacrifice. From the viewpoint of liturgical history that was a very important step, and it was not the only one.

The liturgical movement, which, especially in its first beginnings was almost entirely a movement promoting the Mass, had come closer to the Mystery of the altar also from another angle. When the movement—a closed movement embracing wider circles—suddenly came into being in Belgium only to spread at once into Germany and other countries, it made itself manifest, above all, by a new way of participating in the celebration of Mass.[9] Growing out of the intellectual movement of the past decade, it had still to overcome many obstacles. The first thing that demanded solution, even if it was not formally expressed, was the question whether the separation between people and celebrating priest, maintained for more than a thousand years, was to be continued. It was certainly continued in law by the prohibition to translate the Mass books. Efforts had been made to shake this prohibition, but even as late as 1857 the prohibition to translate the Ordinary of the Mass was renewed by Pius IX, although, to be sure, its enforcement was no longer seriously urged.[10] However, it was not openly and definitely rescinded until near the end of the century. In the revision of the *Index of Forbidden Books*, issued under Leo XIII in 1897, the prohibition was no longer mentioned.[11] After that the spread of the

---

[7] By the reference to the fact that the Eucharist is intended to sanctify the faithful, *non autem præcipue, ut Domini honori ac venerationi consulatur*; *op. cit.*, p. 401.

[8] The transition is signalized somewhat by the booklet of J. Kramp, S.J., *Essays on Eucharistic Liturgy and Devotion*, trans. Wm. Busch (St. Paul, 1926).

[9] Regarding the beginning see Rousseau, 217-229; Trapp, 362-367; A. Manser,

"Liturgische Bewegung," LThK, VI (1934), 615-617.

See also vol. 6 of the *Cours et Conférences* (Louvain, 1931), with the theme, "Le mouvement liturgique dans les différents pays."

[10] Vehlen (*Liturg. Leben*, 1936), 95 f. Cf. 182 f.

[11] Vehlen, *op. cit.*, p. 96.

For that reason Schott's missal did not

Roman Missal in the vernacular took on greater and greater proportions.[12] Ever-widening circles of the laity began to read the prayers of the Mass along with the priest. And thus the separation between people and priest was closed in at least one definite point: in their prayer the faithful used the same words as the priest at the altar.

But now a new wish stirred, to do collectively and in common what many were already doing by themselves individually, and with this wish the liturgical movement brushed against the picture of divine worship which had prevailed up till now. Thus arose the problem of the community Mass—or as it is called in some places, the *missa dialogata* or *missa recitata*. The argument ran something like this: If reading along with the priest was to be something more than reading from a textbook, as is customary at the opera or at the production of an oratorio, there must be, in some measure at least, an external speaking along with the priest, especially since the rubrics of the missal in several places seem to expect some such response from the *circumstantes*.[13] The first steps in this direction were taken in academic circles, and then by societies of young students. It was only later that parochial worship followed suit. At first there was no clear norm.[14] But in the German area the threatening disorder was held off in some places by private projects.[15] And finally, in 1929, a uniform text of all the prayers to be read in common was agreed on for Germany and this was used as a basis by most publishers.

Gradually the various principles on which the dialogue Mass is to be based became clearer. It is a fact that the history of liturgy must take into account, that at the beginning of the twentieth century the low Mass had

carry a translation of the canon till 1900, and the words of consecration were missing even in the 7th edition of 1901.

[12] The most popular missal in the German tongue was the *Messbuch der hl. Kirche* by Anselm Schott, O.S.B., which first appeared in 1884; in 1906, in its 10th edition it had reached 100,000 copies and by 1939, in its 45th edition some 1,650,000 copies. Predecessors were the translations of Ch. Moufang (1851; 19th ed., 1905) and of G. M. Pachtler, S.J. (1854; 9th ed., 1890); cf. Trapp, p. 363. But all these are surpassed by the popular American missals of J. A. Stedman, *My Sunday Missal*, of which 15 million copies sold in the years 1939-1945. Another popular English missal is the *Leaflet Missal* published in St. Paul, Minn.; see Ellard, *The Mass of the Future*, 129.

[13] *Rit. serv.*, III, 9; IV, 2; VII, 7.

[14] This was really but another step in a long, gradual process. For it was already cus-

tomary in many places for the youngsters at the "Children's Mass" to pray aloud either prayers of a private character or even devotions more or less liturgical. As early as 1883 V. Thalhofer had advocated the people's answering the priest. In one diocesan hymnal, that of Königgrätz (1897), liturgical prayers were included along with the songs; the people were to say the *Confiteor*, an offertory prayer, etc., in German. Trapp, 293, 331; cf. 163 ff., 290 ff.

[15] The earliest attempts included: R. Guardini, *Gemeinschaftliche Andacht zur Feier der hl. Messe* (1920); J. Kramp, *Missa* (1924). Greater success attended the work put out by Pius Parsch, *Klosterneuburger Chormesse,* and the version of the dialogue Mass in the *Kirchengebet* issued by L. Wolker which has reached five million. In the U. S. the greatest success followed the introduction of a version by the Sodality of our Lady (The Queen's Work).

gained such a great preponderance over the various forms of high Mass that without further ado it was used as the groundwork for the development of the dialogue Mass. No one seemed to notice that in this sort of Mass the alternation of functions between priest, lector, singing choir and people had been leveled off to a uniform speaking by the priest alone, and this more or less quiet. Now it was recognized that in essentials the high Mass had to set the norm, and that therefore at a *missa recitata* the people would answer and pray along in those parts that had been taken over by the choir, thus to some extent recovering these parts for themselves, while the old chants of the *schola*, the readings, and the prayers spoken aloud by the priest would be read aloud in the vernacular by a special reader or leader.[16] In Germany the development reached a certain definite shape when in 1940 the whole problem of the liturgical movement, and along with it the question of the dialogue Mass, was taken over by the assembled episcopate[17] and thus brought to some kind of clarification. In many dioceses, therefore, directions for the celebration of the dialogue Mass—which left no little room for variations—were published.

A most significant variant of the dialogue Mass grew out of the inclusion in it of elements proper to the German *Singmesse*.[18] The so-called *Betsingmesse*—"Pray and sing" Mass—has very quickly gained recognition since its first trial use at the Vienna Catholic Day in 1933, and since it is at once liturgically inspired, popular, and solemn, not only has it often replaced the simple *Singmesse*, but it is even being used with increasing frequency as the Sunday parish Mass.[19]

A similar development was taking place about the same time in places where French is spoken,[20] and elsewhere it is still in process.

---

[16] Cf. J. Gülden, "Grundsätze und Grundformen der Gemeinschaftsmesse in der Pfarrgemeinde," *Volksliturgie und Seelsorge* (Colmar o. J., 1942), 98-122. Cf. G. L. Dieckmann, O.S.B., in *Orate Fratres*, XXIII, (1948-9), 472 ff.

[17] Encouragement was given the movement towards using this dialogue Mass when the Fulda episcopal conference of 1936 issued directions for aiding youth (*Volkslit. und Seelsorge*, 151) ; in Belgium the Provincial Council of Malines had urged it in 1920 especially for educational institutes and religious societies (see Lefebvre, p. 189, as below) ; in the U. S. inspiration came not only from individual bishops but from the Sodality of our Lady and the Liturgical Conference (see Ellard, *The Mass of the Future*, 202-210).

[18] Gülden, 122.

[19] Thus in the diocese of Salzburg in 1937 it was prescribed once a month as Sunday parish Mass in those parishes that had more than one priest.

[20] B. de Chavannes, "La messe dialoguée et ses réalisations," *La vie spirituelle*, LVIII (1939), 307-317 ; see also *Orate Fratres*, XII (1937-8), 225, 469, 517. G. Lefebvre, "La question de la messe dialoguée," *Cours et Conférences*, XI (Louvain, 1933), 153-196. (This whole volume is devoted to the topic of "Active participation of the faithful in worship.") The French form of the dialogue Mass is an outgrowth of the popular chant service, with a substitution of recitation for singing; it does not usually include any vernacular elements. A particularly festive form has been developed for the circles of Jeunesse Ouvrière Catholique, including a symbolic decking of the altar and presentation of offerings. For the U. S. see G. Ellard, S.J., *The Dialogue Mass* (New York, 1942).

In all of these changes—some of them not unimportant—not one letter of the *Missale Romanum* was touched, not a word, not a rubric[21]; for in no case was there any tampering with the priest's performance of the Mass for which the norms of the *missa lecta* continued to serve always as unimpaired principles. All these changes had to do only with the participation of the people, for which there were nowhere any exact regulations. Therefore no objections were raised by the highest authority in the Church,[22] especially since the new forms match the fundamental instructions of the popes with regard to the active participation of the faithful in the liturgy.[23] And yet something very important was achieved. In this setting—even though in a still imperfect form—our celebration of the Mass was assured, at least to some extent, an advantage which the liturgy of the Eastern Church appears to have retained all along by means of its accompanying interchange of prayers between deacon and people.[24] The old distance between altar and people was to a great extent broken down at the opportune moment. From the dialogue Mass the faithful gain a living knowledge of the actual course of the Mass and so they can follow the low Mass as well as the solemn Mass with an entirely new understanding. To have been deprived of such an understanding much longer would not have been tolerable even to the masses in this age of advanced education and enhanced self-consciousness. But what is even more important, now that the faithful answer the priest and concur in his prayers, sacrifice with him and communicate with him, they become properly conscious for the first time of their dignity as Christians and at the same time they achieve an awareness

[21] The rubrics themselves take cognizance of the presence of people attending Mass, by regulating the use of the voice. The *clara voce* parts of the *missa recitata* correspond to the regulations of the *Rubricæ generales*, XVI, 2.

[22] The common response of the people was given a reluctant approval by the Congregation of Rites, August 4, 1922; *Decreta authentica SRC*, n. 4375. For a detailed study of this decree see: J. Pauwels, "De Fidelibus qui Celebranti Respondeant," *Periodica*, XI (1923), 154-157; I. M. Hanssens, "Vetera et Nova de Missa Dialogata," *Periodica*, XXV (1936), 57-89; cf. also *Eph. liturg.*, XLVII (1933), 181-184; 390-393; and W. J. Lallou, "The Status of the 'Missa Recitata,'" *The American Ecclesiastical Review*, CIV (1941), 455.

[23] Pius X, Motu proprio of Nov. 22, 1903: The people assemble in God's house *ad eundem spiritum ex primo eoque necessario fonte hauriendum, hoc est ex actuosa cum sacrosanctis mysteriis publicis sollemnibusque Ecclesiæ precibus communicatione*

(*Decr. auth. SRC.*, n. 4121). The same thought in Pius XI, Constitution "Divini Cultus Sanctitatem" of Dec. 20, 1928 (AAS, XXI [1929], 35) and again, with greater emphasis on concrete methods of participation, in the encyclical of Pius XII, "Mediator Dei" (AAS, XXXIX [1947], 521-595, esp. 554 ff., 560, 589 f.).

[24] In view of the system in the Orient, where the faithful do (and always did) have numerous opportunities to play an active part in the liturgy, but where the texts used are limited and the connection with the action of the priest is, to say the least, reserved, it may be questioned whether the ideal form of participation is achieved when the people say all the prayers along with the priest whether by means of a lay leader reading aloud or by silently following the prayers in the missal. Or should the prayers for the people be specially fitted out for them? On the other hand, the use of such newly-created texts always involves a great deal of bickering and is hardly ever free from justified objection. Regarding the special

that they are the Church, that they stand in corporate relationship to all those whom God has graciously drawn to Himself in Christ.[24] If in this way a start has been given to a broad and comprehensive cure of souls fed on the very basic forces of the Church, it is not hard to estimate what weight all this will have not only for the individual's confirmation in faith and for his mode of life, but also for the stabilization of the Church at a time when nearly all external props have fallen down.

The community or dialogue Mass achieves its goal by superimposing its own form like a shell over the fixed, permanent structure of the *missa lecta* or low Mass. The price it must pay is high, namely that the first *liturgus*, the priest, is wholly in the background during the audible part of the Mass, the greetings and summonings excepted. For this reason, the Mass which is adorned with the altar songs of the priest—the *missa cantata*—must and will take the first place. The questions about the proper form of the celebration of Mass all come back to this, and chiefly to the priest's celebration. The ideal which Pius V had in view, to give the Mass a purity and clarity such as it possessed in the time of the Fathers *(ad pristinam sanctorum Patrum normam ac ritum)* will always stand before the Church. Not, indeed, as though ancient forms should be or could be merely brought back—even the church architecture of the last century does not simply revive the ancient basilica—but in the sense that in the celebration of the Christian mysteries the inner wealth of the Church comes to light as of old and the children of the Church constantly renew their joy and gladness because of their possessions and their blessings.

The monumental greatness of the Roman Mass lies in its antiquity which reaches back to the Church of the martyrs, and in its spread which, with its Latin language, spans so many nations. Nowhere else is it so plain that the Church is both apostolic and catholic. But this double advantage of the Roman Mass also involves weaknesses. The Latin tongue has nowadays become more and more unfamiliar even to cultured people. Will there ever be any relaxing in this matter in the setting of the Mass? As a matter of fact, Latin is by no means the only liturgical language within the Catholic Church, even abstracting from the diocesan rituals in which the vernacular already occupies a large space. The Catholic Mass is celebrated not only in the ancient languages of the Orient and of the Slavic peoples, but also in several modern languages.[26] Even within the Roman Mass tendencies in this direction are to be found: in Glagolitic congrega-

form the people's prayer should have, see Jungmann, *Liturgical Worship*, 122-124.
[25] For a moderate discussion of the desire for the vernacular in the readings, see E. Dolderer, "Die Volkssprache in der Liturgie," *Theol. Quartalschrift*, CXXVII (1947), 89-146.
[26] The Byzantine Mass, for instance, is cele-

brated by the Roumanians, even Catholics, in Roumanian. See the survey by W. de Vries, "Die liturgischen Sprachen der katholischen Kirche," StZ (1940-41), 111-116; and the chapter "de linguis liturgicis" in Raes, *Introductio*, 207-227; cf. also Ellard, *The Mass of the Future*, 146-158, and a pertinent bibliography, 159-160; cf. 257.

tions the Old Slavonic has been in use for centuries.[27] When at the beginning of the seventeenth century the Chinese missions began to flourish, the question was very seriously posed, whether the language of the liturgy should not be Chinese, for, unlike the early medieval mission to the Germans, here a people was being dealt with who already had a literary language of its own.[28]

The Latin language is only one of the peculiarities of the Roman liturgy that, due to its venerable age, has to some extent become a problem. As we already saw in the exposition so far, each succeeding cultural epoch has overlaid the original plan of the Mass-liturgy with its own layer. Not always has this been a harmonious, progressive, organic growth. In our explanation of the various parts of the Mass we shall have to point out continually how in the process of development, displacements, intermixtures, contractions occurred which sometimes left nothing more than a remnant of the expression of the original idea. In other cases the basic idea itself has become strange to us.

Thus in the present shape of the Roman Mass, forms and practices have been retained which are no longer comprehensible to the ordinary onlooker and for which an adequate explanation can sometimes be found only after a tiresome search into history. And when this does not concern some inconspicuous, subordinate rite, it is really very irritating.[29] Still this venerable heritage, which took centuries to produce, should not be discarded lightly. Even so, it is clear that at a time when one unified missal is appointed for nearly all Christendom, it is no longer possible—as it was possible, perhaps, and self-evident in the era of manuscript missals—to make the changes that one recognizes ought to be made, or to make them all at once. A great deal of patient waiting is certainly needed.

And yet, because the Church is eternally young, it will not shrink back from a task however big. When Pius X determinedly undertook the revision of the psalter in the breviary, he remarked that he was thereby taking

[27] *Supra*, p. 81.

Benedict XV, on May 21, 1920, also approved the use of Old Slavonic at Mass on certain feasts in the many sanctuaries within Czecho-Slovakian territory; see *Bibel u. Liturgie*, X (1935-6), 113 f.

[28] The permission to use Chinese was actually given in 1615 by Paul V, but it never reached the petitioners. When, in 1631, after the new missal was finished, the request for permission was renewed, it was no longer granted; Benedict XIV, *De s. sacrificio missæ*, II, 2, 13 (Schneider, 85); A. Vaeth, *Das Bild der Weltkirche* (Hannover, 1932), 96-98.

H. Chirat, in *Etudes de liturgie pastorale* (Paris, 1944), 227, tells of Pius XI's approval of a project to use the Roman liturgy, translated into Estonian, in Estonia.
[29] Cf. P. Simon, *Das Menschliche in der Kirche* (2nd ed., Freiburg, 1936), 52 f.

What H. Mayer, *Religionspädagogische Reformbewegung* (Paderborn, 1922), 141 wrote is not at all impertinent: At one time, he remarked, liturgy was the interpreter of religion, acting as a sort of sermon or catechism. Nowadays we are in the uncomfortable position of having to interpret what should be the interpreter, and of tuning up what should have been able to give us life and spirit.

only the first step towards a correction and reform of breviary and missal.[30] When at the same time he revamped the position of the Sunday Masses and the weekdays in Lent, making them privileged, he was but following a plan which Trent had followed, to emphasize the essentials and to repress what is merely rank overgrowth.[31] The same line was traced in the years after Pius X when, for the first time in nearly a thousand years, new prefaces were composed for the Universal Church—arrangements of the prayer of thanksgiving which once more brought into renewed prominence the central themes of all *eucharistias*, the pierced heart of our Redeemer and His eternal Kingship. Great changes, like the sanctioning of evening Masses and the easing of the law regarding the eucharistic fast, are witnesses to the courage to make bold reforms when they are required. In the last analysis, the revival of elementary liturgical thinking, as it was ushered in, in such a magnificent fashion, by the encyclical letter of Pope Pius XII, *Mediator Dei* of November 20, 1947, is the foundation—supporting but also necessary—for any and every renovation in the matter of external forms.

[30] In the Bull "Divino afflatu" of Nov. 1, 1911 (printed at the beginning of the missal and of most copies of the breviary: *nemo non videt . . . primum nos fecisse gradum ad Romani Breviarii et Missalis emendationem.*

[31] The rubrical formulation of this and other changes followed in the new edition of the missal which appeared in 1920 under Benedict XV.

Still shortly before efforts were made to add other unessentials even to the Ordinary of the Mass. Under Leo XIII, as the result of a postulatum of many Frenchmen, it was almost certain that the name of St. Joseph would be added to the *Confiteor, Suscipe s. Trinitas, Communicantes* and *Libera nos*; see E. Springer in *Pastor Bonus*, XXXIV (1921-22), 20 f.

Part II

THE NATURE AND FORMS
OF THE MASS

1. Names of the Mass

THE NAMES BY WHICH THE EUCHARISTIC CELEBRATION HAS BEEN designated at various times do not give us an idea of its essence. They do not even suggest what that essence was thought to consist in. But they do show us certain aspects, whether purely on the surface or deeply intrinsic, by which the Mass was principally known to the faithful. These names are like a shadowy outline which permits certain characteristics of the essence to appear.

The earliest names we meet with are taken from outstanding details in the rite. The Acts of the Apostles uses the term "the breaking of (the) bread," referring thereby to the act by which the presiding person, following the ancient custom and the example of our Lord Himself at the Last Supper, opened the meal.[1] But perhaps the idea behind the "breaking of bread" was not the material meal which was associated with the ceremony, but rather the sacramental bread itself: "Is not the bread we break a participation in Christ's body?"[2] This is all the more certain if—as seems probable—the consecration of the bread was bound up with this rite of breaking. St. Paul himself calls the celebration "the Lord's Supper," Κυριακὸν δεῖπνον (1 Cor. 11:20) and thus places its character as a meal all the more plainly in the foreground.

Since the turn of the first century the term "Eucharist" has been employed, and thus is brought into prominence a spiritualizing word which had been connected with the meal from the outset. Εὐχαριστία is first of all the prayer of thanks with which, after the manner of our Lord himself, the sacred action was surrounded. The word was used by Catholic writers as well as by the Gnostic groups from which the apocryphal histories of the Apostles stemmed.[3] In the Fathers of the second century this is the word which suggests a precise phase of the celebration; it is a celebration

---

[1] Κλάσις ἄρτον, fractio panis: Acts 2:42, 46; 20:7. Cf. supra, pp. 9-11.
[2] 1 Cor. 10:16; cf. Acta Johannis, 110

(Quasten, Mon., p. 341); Acta Thomæ, c. 27 (ibid., p. 343).
[3] Cf. e.g., Acta Thomæ, c. 27, 49, 158 (Quasten, 343-5).

in which the thanks of the redeemed rises up to God.[4] In the *Didache*[5] at least by inference, and plainly in Justin the consecrated gifts themselves are called Εὐχαριστία.[6] And in this last meaning especially, the word is adopted by Tertullian and Cyprian as part of the vocabulary of the Latin Church,[7] and has so remained till the present.

As we saw, the celebration of the Eucharist was very early designated as an *offering* or *sacrifice*. And the designation became a name then and there. In the Latin area there appeared, in this sense, the words *oblatio* and *sacrificium*, respectively from *offerre* and *sacrificari*—again first of all in the writings of the two Africans already mentioned. In Africa the word *sacrificium* appears to have prevailed as the usual name. Cyprian[8] and Augustine[9] use it regularly for the celebration of Mass. How strongly it was impressed on the literary usage of the Middle Ages we can learn from the fact that in the penitential books offenses against the eucharistic species are denominated as offenses against the *sacrificium*.[10]

But in other sections of the Church the word *oblatio* prevailed. Thus the pilgrim lady Aetheria, whenever she refers to the celebration of Mass on her pilgrimage, regularly uses *oblatio* and *offerre*.[11] Until the sixth century *oblatio* continued to be the usual name for the Mass.[12] To describe the action, *offerre* (even without an object) continued in use even later[13]; *sacerdotem oportet offerre* is what the bishop still says at ordination.

---

[4] Cf. *supra*, pp. 20-22.

[5] *Did.*, 9, 5.

[6] Even Philo already calls the meal connected with the thanks-offering εὐχαριστία: Th. Schermann, "Εὐχαριστία und εὐχαριστεῖν" (*Philologus*, 1910), 391.

[7] Dekkers, *Tertullianus*, 49, where it is at once apparent that Tertullian had no fixed term to designate the celebration; for Cyprian see Fortescue, *The Mass*, 44.

[8] Citations in Fortescue, 398.

[9] See the index, PL, XLVI, 579 ff.

[10] *Pœnitentiale Vallicellanum I* (8th century), n. 21: *si quis non custodierit sacrificium*; cf. n. 123-125 (H. J. Schmitz, *Die Bussbücher und die Bussdisciplin der Kirche* [Mainz, 1883], 344 f.; cf. 386 f., 425 f., etc.). The terminology seems to hark back to Scottish penitentials: *Pœnitentiale Cummeani*, c. 13, 5-23 (*ibid.*, 641-643). As Prof. W. Havers wrote me in reference to R. Atkinson, *The Passions and the Homilies from Leabhar Breac* (Dublin, 1887), 6360, the word is also to be found in Old Irish in the form *sacarbaic*. In England the word was still in vogue in the late Middle Ages; see the Sarum

Missal: (Martène, 1, 4, XXXV (I, 667 A): *calicem cum patena et sacrificio*.

The word was also used in German; in the rhymed explanation of the Mass (12th century, edited by A. Leitzmann (*Kleine Texte*, 54), 19, l. 22, we read of the little elevation: the priest "daz sacrificium ûf heuet" (the priest lifts up the sacrificium).

[11] *Ætheriæ Peregrinatio*; see the index in the edition of Geyer (CSEL, XXXIX, 408).

[12] H. Kellner, "Wo und seit wann wurde Missa stehende Bezeichnung für das Messopfer?" (*Theol. Quartalschrift*, 1901), 429-433, 439. Prof. Havers tells me that in Middle Irish the word *oifrenn*, from the word *offerendum*, had become the common term for Mass; but a Celtic word with the same meaning, *idpart* (the root means "to offer up") was also employed. In modern Celtic languages the only term used is one equivalent to "offering": Irish, *an t'aifreann*; Welsh, *yr offeren*; Cornish, *an offeren*; Scots, *an aifrionn*; see D. Attwater, *The Christian Churches of the East* (Milwaukee, 1948), 30, footnote.

[13] Citations in Batiffol, *Leçons*, 174 ff.

In the Greek Orient the corresponding word προσφορά was used only in passing.[14] A word of similar import, ἀναφορά was generally employed only in the narrow sense of the Mass proper, and to designate the formulary used therein.[15] On the other hand, the Syrians, both East and West, commonly used the word *Kurbono* or *Kurbana*, "gift"[16] as the name for the Mass.[17] The Armenians, too, use a word that means offering.[18]

We need not be surprised that, besides those names which go to the very core of the matter, other words are to be met with which—in accordance with a rule of sacral speech—designate the sacred action only with a certain reserve, as though from a distance. Several denominations of this sort are to be found.

Thus the West Syrians use, besides the word already referred to, another which expresses only the reverential and awe-filled "approach" to God, *Korobho*. It is generally used not for the whole Mass, but only for the Mass proper—the anaphora—and for the variable anaphora formulas.[19]

Elsewhere the Mass is called simply "the Holy," *sacrum*, just as we use it in modern Latin. Thus in one portion of the Semitic language-group various derivatives of the word *kadosh*, "holy," are employed. Amongst the Abyssinians (Ethiopians) the Mass is called *keddase*,[20] amongst the Arabs, *kuddas* or *takdis*.[21] Amongst the Syrian Nestorians (and the Catholic Chaldeans) the corresponding word *kuddasha*, "the hallowing," is commonly used for the Mass formula.[22] Of a similar sort is the Greek ἀγιασμός, which, however, designates more precisely the sacred—or better, the sanctifying—action. The word has become and has remained the usual name for the Mass amongst the Copts, obviously as a result of the influence of Alexandria.[23]

Another name originated by considering the personal source from which the sacredness of the celebration springs—Christ our Lord. So the Mass

---

[14] Synod of Laodicea, can. 58 (Mansi, II, 574).

[15] So chiefly in the non-Byzantine rites, and usually in the respective national tongue.

This narrower use of ἀναφορά is quite appropriate, for while προσφέρειν means in a general way "to bring along," ἀναφέρειν means "to lay upon" (the altar) ; Brightman, 569, 594 f.

Cf. A. Baumstark, "Anaphora," RAC, I, 418-427.

[16] Cf. Mark 7:11: κορβᾶν, ὅ ἐστιν δῶρον. Similarly the Coptic liturgy is sometimes called *korban*.

[17] Brightman, 579; Hanssens, II, 22.

[18] Brightman, 580: *patarag*.

[19] Brightman, 579; but see the letter of James of Edessa (d. 708) who places the two words *kurobho* and *kurbono* as equivalents; *ibid*, 490, line 25. The two names are

etymologically connected, for *kurbono* (*kurbona*) is derived from the same stem, *kerabh*, "to approach"; that with which we approach, a gift.

[20] Brightman, 579.

[21] Brightman, 580; Attwater, *loc. cit.*

[22] A. J. Maclean, *East Syrian daily offices* (London, 1894), 295.

[23] Hanssens, II, 22.

In the *Euchologion* of Serapion ἀγιασμός is used for the praise contained in the *Sanctus* (13, 10) and for the blessing of baptismal water (19, tit.; Funk, II, 174, 180). In this word, therefore, two allied notions are inherent, two different meanings of the term "hallow": "to call holy," that is, to worship God; and "to make holy," that is, to bless some creature. Which of these notions applies in the case of the designation of the Mass has yet to be investigated.

is called *dominicum,* "the Lord's," a name which was current in North Africa and Rome around the third and fourth centuries.[24] During the Diocletian persecution the martyrs of Abitina declare: *sine dominico non possumus . . . Intermitti dominicum non potest.*[25] This formation of a name which calls the Mass the celebration of Christ is parallel to that which calls Sunday the day of Christ (*dominica,* κυριακή), and the Christian place of worship the house of Christ, the house of the κύριος (κυριακόν = church). Nor is the creation of either term far apart in time.

In other instances, the name for the Mass is derived from the fact that it is a *service* which those who are invested with the fulness of the Church's power perform for the believing congregation. That is, as we know, the sense of the word λειτουργία, liturgy,[26] which in church terminology designates primarily ecclesiastical functioning in general, then secondarily divine worship, and, amongst the Greeks since the ninth century, simply the Mass.[27] Even outside the Greek-speaking area of the Byzantine rite— especially amongst the Slavic peoples and the Roumanians—the same Greek word is in use as a name for the Mass.

There are other instances of a similar practice elsewhere. In German, for example, the solemn Mass is called *Amt* and *Hochamt* (service and high service, respectively), the latter corresponding to the Latin *summum officium* of the decadent medieval period.[28] In the closing years of Christian antiquity the common terms in Latin were *actio,* and the related *agere.* In Ambrose the expression for "to celebrate Mass" was either *agere* or *offerre.*[29] This expression designates the "consummation" of the sacred action.[30] This is brought out by the fact that later the word *actio* is taken in the narrow sense of the sacrifice proper, the canon, which is designated

[24] Batiffol, *Leçons,* 171 f.

[25] *Acta Saturnini,* etc., c. 10 f. (Ruinart, *Acta Martyrum* [Regensburg, 1859], 418 f.) ; cf. in Tertullian, *De fuga,* c. 14 PL, II, 141 A) : *dominica sollemnia.* The Pauline term *dominica cœna* (1 Cor. 11 :20) also belongs in this category.

[26] E. Raitz v. Frentz, "Der Weg des Wortes 'Liturgie' in der Geschichte," *Eph. liturg.,* LV (1941), 74-80; H. Strathmann-R. Meyer, λειτουργέω etc., *Theol. Wörterbuch z. N. T.,* IV (1938), 221-238.

[27] Eisenhofer, I, 5 ; Hanssens, II, 33-36.

[28] J. Greving, *Johann Ecks Pfarrbuch,* 79.

[29] F. J. Dölger, *Antike und Christentum,* I (1929), 54-65.

In Gelasius I, *Ep.* 14, 6 (Thiel, 365) the Mass is called *actio sacra.*

[30] Dölger, *Sol salutis,* 295-299, derives the word from the usage in ancient sacrificial rites where the sacrificing minister, before

giving the fatal stroke, used to ask, *agone?* But it seems difficult to admit an immediate transfer of such a usage to Christian sacral speech. Rather we are dealing here with an emphatic *agere,* such as was in use in ancient sacral language, along with *facere* and *operari,* to designate a sacral deed (even in the general sense of "celebrating a feast") ; see O. Casel, "Actio in liturgischer Verwendung," JL, I (1921), 34-39; *idem,* "Actio," RAC, I, 82 f. In any case we could complement the word with an object in the sense of the full expression *missas agere,* a phrase which actually appears, e.g., in Victor Vitensis, *Historia persec. Afric.,* II, 2, 13 (CSEL, VII, 25, 39) ; cf. Leonianum (Muratori, I, 401 ; Feltoe, 101) : *actio mysterii; Liber pont.* (Duchesne, I, 239) : *actio sacrificii.*

On the other hand the derivation from *gratias agere* proposed in Batiffol, *Leçons,* 170, is very unlikely.

the *canon actionis.*[31] The word *agenda* is also 'used,[32] so that the full expression for "celebrating Mass" was *agere agendam.*

While in these designations the point of view is the activity of the spiritual officiants, Christian antiquity also recognized names which view the celebration of Mass as an assembly of the Christian people—an assembly that was centered on the mysteries of the Eucharist. A Latin appellation of this kind was actually used for the Mass—the word *collecta*—but its use was only passing.[33] Since it was soon employed in the liturgy in another sense, the word did not endure. But it was different with regard to a Greek word having the same meaning, the word σύναξις which from the fourth century on, was for a long time the prevailing name[34] until it was displaced by the term λειτουργία. However, it still lives in modern Latin as a substitute for Eucharist: *sacra synaxis.*[35] A word of the same type was also developed amongst the Syrians.[36]

That the celebration of the Eucharist which Augustine lauded as *signum unitatis* should have taken its name from a *coming together* is something we could very well understand. But it is puzzling indeed that, as a matter of fact, it has been designated by a *separating*, a *going apart.* Such, however, appears to be the case in regard to the word which both in Latin and in the modern languages of the West has practically supplanted all other names, the word *missa*, "Mass." For today there is no doubt at all as to the original and basic meaning of the word: *missa = missio = dimissio.* It meant, in late Latin, a dismissal, the breaking up or departure after an audience or public gathering.[37] Thus too in the language of the Christian liturgy, it was used both to announce the closing of the assembly in the *Ite missa est* and to designate what preceded this close. In this latter signification the word emerges around the end of the fourth century.

---

[31] A special feast-day text of the *Communicantes* will therefore carry the heading, to be inserted *infra actionem.* As we all know, this heading now stands, very unsuitably, even above the basic text of the *Communicantes* in the *Missale Romanum.*

[32] Du Cange-Favre, *Glossarium*, I, 138.

[33] In the Acts of the Abitina martyrs the word appears time and again along with the word *dominicum*, sometimes as an extension of the latter, sometimes as its equivalent, e.g., c. 12 (Ruinart, 419), where, in connection with the proconsul's question, *Si in collecta fuisti*, the narrative remarks: *Quasi christianus sine dominico esse possit.* Cf. Eisenhofer, II, 4 f.

[34] Hanssens, II, 24-33; *ibid.*, 24 f., citations of a transient use of another word derived from the same root and used in a similar sense: συναγωγή

[35] The word appears to have been given currency first by the Humanists. In the Middle Ages it was used only in the wider sense of a worshipping assembly; Du Cange-Favre, VII, 688.

[36] Brightman, 581: *cenushyo.*

[37] Avitus of Vienne, *Ep.* 1 (PL, LIX, 199): *in ecclesiis palatiisque sive prætoriis missa fieri pronuntiatur, cum populus ab observatione dimittitur.* For textual criticism of the passage see Dölger, *Antike u. Christentum*, VI (1940), 87 f.

Cf. for the following Jungmann, *Gewordene Liturgie*, 34-52 (on the history of the meaning of *missa*); here will be found an extensive bibliography and the citation of sources. Among the latest untenable meanings suggested we must mention here the conjecture of C. M. Kaufmann, *Handbuch der altchristlichen Epigraphik* (Freiburg, 1917), 221, that *missa* is to be educed from *mesa* (actually

This closing did not consist simply in a mere prosaic announcement, as we have it in the phrase *Ite missa est*. It regularly comprehended (whether at Mass or at some other service) a definite ecclesiastico-religious act, a dismissal in which the Church once more drew her children to herself with motherly affection before sending them on their way with her blessing. That is the way it was even in the early Church. Already in the church order of Hippolytus the catechumens are sent away each time with a laying-on of hands. And thus it continued for centuries both in the Mass and outside. In a different form this arrangement has remained alive, even today. Nor need that surprise us. For the arrangement is found in the very essence of the Church, which, as the holy Church, is for her members essentially a refuge of grace and blessing. Just as the word *missa*, when we first encounter it as a name for the close of divine service, often implies the blessing just mentioned,[38] so also the word *missa* became a designation for the concluding blessing, and then for the blessing in general.

In a more modern extension of the meaning, a custom grew up of calling every divine service as a unit a *missa*, because it included a blessing, much as we today style every evening devotion briefly as a benediction. This usage had already appeared about 400. Soon there was talk of a *missa nocturna*, of *missæ vespertinæ* and *matutinæ*. The celebration of Mass, too, was such a *missa*. The usage took hold all the more easily because the same posture of body—standing bowed—which was perceived when the priest or bishop stretched out his hands in blessing was to be seen frequently also at the high points in the various functions—at the priest's orations and especially at the preface and in the canon of the Mass. In a sense the

found in inscriptions), and this in turn from *mensa*, altar-table.

A recent explanation, without knowledge of the derivation I have proposed, comes from F. Bömer, *Ahnenkult und Ahnenglaube im alten Rom* (Leipzig, 1943), 128 ff., who makes the suggestion that *mittere inferias* or simply *mittere* was a sacrificial term of the Roman cult of the dead, with the original meaning; to send the dead in the grave a gift; from this we get *missa patella* as the designation of the corresponding sacrificial plate. On this Bömer builds the hypothesis that the Christian *missa* must have stemmed from this *mittere* of the cult of the dead (132, note 1). However, the connection with the cult of the dead is hard to demonstrate. The Mass was never "sent" to the dead Christ, still less to a dead martyr; it was always an offering made to God, commemorating the Risen Christ who overcame death. The regular connection

of the Christian altar with the grave of a martyr belongs to the beginning of the Middle Ages, and in Rome itself is not prior to the 7th/8th centuries, while *missa* already appears even here as early as the 5th century, and precisely with our signification. See *infra*.

[38] See especially *Ætheriæ Peregrinatio*, c. 24, 2, 6 (CSEL, XXXVIII, 71 f.), et al. In the oft-cited passage in Ambrose, *Ep.*, 20, 4 f. (PL, XVI, 1037) the word has this meaning; after Ambrose had dismissed the catechumens, following the fore-Mass, he turned to explain the symbol to some candidates for baptism (*competentes*); then the sudden invasion was announced to him: *Ego tamen mansi in munere, missam facere cœpi. Dum offero. . . .* By *missa* is here meant the dismissal of the *competentes* (which was done by means of a blessing), for they had to be sent out just as the other catechumens were, before the *traditio symboli; cf. infra*, p. 480, note 33.

priestly praying was always a sort of *missa*, for it always drew down God's favor and blessing upon all who bowed down before Him in adoration; but especially was this true where Christ's Body and Blood became present through the word of the priest. So the name *missa* was gradually appropriated to the Eucharist, not (for a long time) exclusively, but at least by preference. Since the middle of the fifth century, examples are to be found in the most widely separated parts of the Latin area—Italy, Gaul, North Africa—examples in which *missa* is used univocally for the Mass celebration. The oldest extant example is in a decretal of Leo the Great in the year 445, in which he inveighs against certain instances in which divine service was held only once on Sundays, *si unius tantum missæ more servato sacrificium offerre non possint, nisi qui prima diei parte convenerint.*[39]

At the outset, the word used in this narrower sense was employed mostly in the plural, *missæ*, or with some addition, *missarum sollemnia.*[40] Only by exception, however, was there any adjective appended like *sanctæ missæ.*[41] Even to day in the official language of the Church such adjectives are as a rule left out; it is simply *fit missa* or *celebratur missa*. It is as though the word *missa* has in it so much splendor that it can well do without extra ornament.[42] At the time of origin and development it must have approached, in content and mood, the Græco-Coptic ἁγιασμός, for it is *the* celebration in which the world is sanctified.

2. Meaning of the Mass. The Mass and the Church

If we put together such meanings as we derive from the names of the Mass we glean nothing more than a very superficial sketch. The Mass is a celebration for which the Church assembles, a celebration which occupies the center of her charge and service, a celebration which is dedicated to the Lord. It is a celebration which presents God with a thanksgiving, an offering, indeed a sacrifice. And it is a celebration which reacts with blessings upon those who gather for it. Other essential features have been revealed to us by the course of history, for we have learnt the various aspects which were given special prominence as time went by. But we must

---

[39] Leo the Great, *Ep.* 9, 2 (PL, LIV, 627). Further citations in Jungmann, *op. cit.,* 40-42.

[40] This last expression is employed as a rule by Gregory the Great; see, for instance, the Christmas lesson in the breviary. In the early Middle Ages the expression is quite frequent; see, e.g., *infra,* p. 196, note 7. It answers to the consciousness that the Mass had to be "celebrated" or "solemn-

ized," and to the fact that a solemn Mass was then the usual type.

[41] Thus once in Cassiodorus, *Expos. in ps. 25* (PL, LXX, 185 B).

[42] The other names of the Mass already described are used as a rule without any qualifying additions, with the exception of those used in the area of the Byzantine rite, where the term is regularly "the divine liturgy."

now inquire what the Church herself has said in her formal pronouncements, whether by direct teaching or in theological discussion, regarding
the meaning and the essence of this celebration.

It will not be out of place to present this question in a book which has
as its primary subject-matter the variety of forms that the Christian celebration possesses. For the discussion should serve not only to establish or
prove this variety but also to understand it in its development and growth
from its roots, from the very core of its nature. So it is necessary, first of
all, to have this essential core before our eyes to see what it is. Naturally
it is not our task to excerpt and to rewrite the pertinent treatise in dogmatic theology as an isolated and self-contained chapter or even one related
to the full-rounded theological structure or more particularly to the doctrine of the Sacraments. We must rather realize the liturgical connotations
of the problem, and try to pose the questions and construct the answers
with an eye to religious life and ecclesiastical service.

Let us first orient ourselves with regard to the liturgical facts hitherto
established, making them the starting point for a broader excursion into
the field of theology. These facts show that we cannot make the notion of
sacrifice a basis absolutely and exclusively, otherwise we would leave no
room for many other important and essential features. We must start off
from one of the broader and more general ideas which find an application
in an examination of the essence of the Mass solemnity. Such a notion is
the one by which our Lord himself indicated the meaning of what He
instituted: "Do this for a commemoration of me." The Mass is a solemnity
dedicated to the memory of Christ; it is *dominicum*. And further, it is not
merely a remembrance of His person, but a recollection of His work—
according to the word of the Apostle: "For as often as you shall eat this
bread and drink the cup, you proclaim the death of the Lord, until he
comes" (1 Cor. 11:25).

The consideration of the Mass must therefore commence with the mystery of our Lord's Passion and death. This is what is continually being
made present and actual—in the institution of the Last Supper. However,
neither can this mystery be exhausted with one simple idea. In this mystery our Lord sealed with His blood His testimony to truth (John 18:37),
to the Kingdom of God which had come in His own person, and thus had
"borne witness to the great claim" (1 Tim. 6:13). With a heroic obedience
that was steadfast even to the death of the Cross (Philippians 2:8), He
had in this mystery fulfilled the will of His Father against whom the first
Adam had set himself with defiant disobedience. With free resolve our
Lord had put himself into the hands of His enemies, silently, making no
use of His wondrous might, and had offered up His life as "a ransom for
many" (Mark 10:45). He had taken up the warfare against the invisible
enemy who held mankind imprisoned in sin, and as one who is stronger
still, He had been victorious (Luke 11:22): He had cast out the prince of
this world (John 12:31). He took His place at the head of mankind, strid-

ing forward through suffering and death, thus entering into His glory (Luke 24:26). As high priest He has offered up in the Holy Spirit the perfect sacrifice; with His own blood He has entered the sanctuary and set a seal upon the new and eternal covenant (Heb. 9:11 ff.). He himself became the Paschal Lamb, whose blood procured our ransom out of the land of bondage, whose slaughter inaugurated our joyous Easter feast (1 Cor. 5:7 ff.), the Lamb that was slain and yet lives, the Lamb for whose wedding feast the bride has clothed herself (Apoc. 5:6 ff.; 19:7 ff.).

By all these notions, by all these pictures the attempt is made in the writings of the New Testament to circumscribe and to illustrate the great occurrence by means of which Jesus Christ effected the re-establishment of mankind.

All that is characteristic of the redeeming death of Jesus is clearly contained in some way in the institution of the Last Supper. There, in a manner that is full of mystery, this suffering is made present, this suffering that is at once testimony and obedience and atonement and struggle and victory and stainless sacrifice. It is made present under the signs of bread and wine, the elements of a simple meal, which are transformed by the hallowing words into Jesus' Body and Blood, and thus changed, are enjoyed by all who partake of them. But what is the more precise meaning of the Presence that is consummated day after day in a hundred thousand places? Does that meaning rest in the very Presence as such?

When Christ on the Cross cried out His *Consummatum est*, few were the men who noticed it, fewer still the men who perceived that this phrase announced a turning-point for mankind, that this death opened into everlasting life gates through which, from that moment on, all the peoples of earth would pass. Now, to meet the expectant longing of mankind, this great event is arrested and, through Christ's institution, held fast for these coming generations so that they might be conscious witnesses of that event even in the latest centuries and amongst the remotest nations, and might look up to it in holy rapture.

The Middle Ages actually did turn to this side of the eucharistic mystery with special predilection. What takes place on the altar is above all the *memoria passionis*. The suffering of Christ was seen represented in the breaking of the bread, in its distribution to the faithful, in the partaking of the Chalice whereby the Blood of the Lord is poured into the mouth of the faithful.[1] From this obvious symbolism the step to an allegorical interpretation of the whole rite was easily made; particularly after the ninth century the whole Mass was explained as a comprehensive representation of the Passion of Jesus. In the action of the assisting clerics, who step back at the start of the preface, is seen the flight of the disciples. In the celebrant's extended hands our Lord is seen agonizing on the Cross

---

[1] M. Lepin, *L'idée du sacrifice de la Messe d'après les théologiens depuis l'origine jusqu'à nos jours* (Paris, 1926), 87-90, 112-129.

with arms outstretched. In the commingling of the species is seen His glorious Resurrection. In fact, the whole life of Christ, the whole history of Redemption is seen represented in the Mass. The sacred action at the altar becomes a play, in which drama and reality are intermixed most mysteriously. How strong an impression this viewpoint made can perhaps be gauged by the fact that even today we use the expression "to hear Mass,"[2] as if we were an audience.

We must perceive that even in these explanations of the medieval interpreters, a primary essential trait of Christ's institution is given expression; this institution is a memorial ceremony, a sacred action which recalls into the midst of the congregation a redemptive work which occurred long ago, a "mystery-action."[3]

Another aspect of Christ's institution which was prominent from the very outset and which in earlier times was made visible through its liturgical form, was the fact that a holy meal was being held—a meal and a memorial. The Eucharist is a memorial instituted by our Lord for a remembrance of Himself. A table is set; it is the Lord's table. For a long time Christian speech avoided—or at least refrained from using—the term for altar derived from pre-Christian religion and even today still employs the simple name *mensa*, ἁγία τράπεζα.[4]

At this table the faithful community is gathered in holy society. Here the Lord himself is given them as nourishment, His Body and His Blood handed to them under the species of bread and wine, as a spiritual food, a spiritual drink (cf. 1 Cor. 10:3 ff.).

[2] The expression "to hear Mass" is already found in the 13th century *Lay Folks Mass Book* (ed. Simmons), 6; cf. 4. The Germans speak of "hearing Mass": *die Messe hören*.

Decretum Gratiani, III, 1, 64 (Friedberg, I, 1312): *missas totas audire*; cf. *ibid.*, 62 (1311), but here the MSS. disagree. Even in Regino, *De synod. causis*, II, 5, 64 (PL, CXXXII, 285) one of the questions is whether the shepherds come to church on Sunday and hear Mass (*missas audiant*). The Carolingian explanation of the Mass, "*Dominus Vobiscum*" (PL, CXXXVIII, 1167) considers the *circumadstantes* of the priest's prayer to refer to those who have come *ad audiendam missam*, and that he then prays also for those *qui oblationes suas offerunt*.

An Albanian confrere informs me that the Albanians speak about "seeing Mass." On the other hand the indeterminate expression "to attend Mass," or at least the concept corresponding to it, is much older; cf. Tertullian, *De or.*, c. 19 (CSEL, XX,

192): *de stationum diebus non putant plerique sacrificiorum orationibus interveniendum*. Tertullian commends this *intervenire* in which one can, even without communicating, bring the body of the Lord home; cf. Elfers, *Die Kirchenordnung Hippolyts*, 293.

[3] Nothing is here said about the details of the nature of the *mysterium*; cf. the use of the word "*mysterium*" in W. Goossens, *Les origines de l'Eucharistie*, 246 f. It is this locution, however, that is borrowed by O. Casel, JL, XI (1931), 271.

[4] In older English usage the altar is often called God's board, and this expression is especially (though not exclusively) used when reference is made to Holy Communion; cf. Bridgett, *A History of the Holy Eucharist in Great Britain*, 191. In the Greek-speaking East at the present day the usual expression for altar is *hagía* or *hiéra trápeza* (the holy or sacred table); cf. Salaville, *An Introduction to the Study of Eastern Liturgies* (London, 1938), 133.

Thus the eucharistic institution does more than commemorate our Saviour. In it the communion and society of the faithful with their Lord is continually renewed. The meal is a sufficiently striking proof of that. And we can therefore safely say that, aside from the external activity, the meal is still in our own time the basic form of the eucharistic celebration.[5] However, even in the biblical sources, this meal is distinguished as a sacrificial meal. The table of the Lord which is prepared in the church in Corinth is contrasted to the tables of the demons, the tables at which the meat offered up to the heathen gods is eaten.[6] Already in the primitive Church it was recognized that in the celebration of the Eucharist a sacrifice was offered up, and that therein was fulfilled the prophecy of Malachias who foretold a clean oblation which would be offered up in all places.[7] The thought of a sacrifice, of an oblation to God, taking place in the Eucharist, occurs time after time in the works of the Fathers. That thought has definitely figured in every text of the eucharistic celebration which is known to us.

The Middle Ages, too, whose devotion to the celebration of the Mass had drawn the remembrance of the Passion so much into the foreground, did not on that account lose sight of the idea of oblation and sacrifice. In fact the later medieval period did so much to emphasize the sacrificial aspect and stressed in so many forms and fashions the value of the Mass for gaining God's grace and favor for the living and the dead, that not only did the Reformation find herein a subject for its immoderate indictment but even Church authorities, both before and after the storm, found reasons for making certain corrections.

The Council of Trent, therefore, was careful to clarify this very phase of the eucharistic mystery. The Council stressed the doctrine that the Mass is not a mere meal nor only a memorial service recalling a sacrifice that had taken place of yore, but is itself a sacrifice possessing its own power of atonement and petition.[8] Christ had offered this sacrifice at the Last Supper and had given His Apostles and their successors the commission to offer it. Indeed He himself makes the offering through their ministry. Thus He left to His beloved spouse, the Church, a visible sacrifice.[9] The Mass is therefore a sacrifice which is made by Christ and at the same time by the recipients of His commission; it is the *sacrifice of Christ* and the *sacrifice of the Church*. In our liturgical study we may not treat the sacrifice of the Church as a matter of secondary moment.

[5] R. Guardini, *Besinnung vor der Feier der heiligen Messe* (Mainz, 1939), II, 73 ff. Cf. *supra*, p. 21, note 63.

[6] 1 Cor. 10:14-22. Cf. the discussion of the passage in Goossens, 202-208.

[7] *Didache*, 14, 2 f.

[8] Sess. XXII, can. 1 (Denziger-Umberg, n. 948) : *S. q. d. in missa non offerri Deo verum et proprium sacrificium aut quod offerri non sit aliud quam nobis Christum ad manducandum dari, a.s.*; can. 3 (*ibid.*, 950) : *S. q. d. missæ sacrificium tantum esse laudis et gratiarum actionis aut nudam commemorationem sacrificii in cruce peracti, non autem propitiatorium . . . , a.s.*

[9] *Ibid.*, c. 1, 2 (Denziger-Umberg, n. 938, 940).

In the theological controversies of the Reformation period and in subsequent theology, the sacrificial notion did indeed stand out as central, but the Church's sacrifice played only a minor role. For the main concern was over a much deeper presupposition, whether the Mass was a sacrifice at all, and—opposing Calvin especially—whether believing that it was contradicted the teaching of the Epistle to the Hebrews regarding the *one* sacrifice of Christ. Thus, above all else, the Mass had to be safeguarded as the sacrifice of Christ.

But when apologetic interests receded and the question once more arose as to what is the meaning and the purpose of the Mass in the organization of ecclesiastical life, it was precisely this point, the sacrifice of the Church, which came to the fore. The liturgies themselves are quite emphatic in the matter. One has only to scan the text of the Roman Mass, or of any other Mass-liturgy for that matter, to see that there is nothing plainer than the thought that in the Mass the Church, the people of Christ, the congregation here assembled, offers up the sacrifice to Almighty God. What is happening at the altar is called, in one of the most venerable texts of our liturgy, an *oblatio servitutis nostrœ, sed et cunctœ familiœ tuœ*. And, corresponding exactly to this, there are the phrases to be read right after the words of consecration, at the very climax of the whole action: *nos famuli tui, sed et plebs tua sancta . . . offerimus prœclarœ maiestati tuœ*—and the gift mentioned is the *hostia pura*, the sacred Bread and the Chalice of salvation. The same notion finds expression in a phrase incorporated into the Mass some thousand years later, when the priest speaks of *meum ac vestrum sacrificium* which should be acceptable to God. That the Mass is also the sacrifice of Christ is, in the Roman Mass *ordo*, only assumed, but never directly expressed.

There is actually a definite contrast between this language of the liturgy and the language we are used to nowadays in sermons, catechisms, and other religious writings. We prefer to insist on the fact that on our altars Christ renews His Passion and death in an unbloody manner. We talk about the renewal of the sacrifice of the Cross, about an oblation in which Christ gives himself to His heavenly Father. But it is only in very general terms that we mention the sacrifice of the Church,[10] and for this reason even our theological textbooks in discussing the ensuing problem as to precisely where Christ consummates His sacrifice, refer without much reflection to His presence in the sacred Host.

If, by way of contrast, we skim through the pertinent writings of the

[10] This is true not only of German-language catechisms, which are satisfied with a statement that "Jesus Christ offers himself in holy Mass"; the New Baltimore is equally vague ("Christ gives us His own body and blood . . . to be offered. . . .," q. 356) and equally one-sided ("The Mass is the sacrifice of the New Law in which Christ, through the ministry of the priest, offers Himself to God in an unbloody manner under the appearances of bread and wine." Q. 357); cf. G. Ellard, " 'Mediator Dei' and Catechism Revision," *The American Ecclesiastical Review*, CXX (1949), 289-309.

Fathers even casually, we are surprised to note that they use similar terms in reference to Christ's oblation in the Eucharist and in reference to our own. They emphasize with equal stress the fact that we (or the Church or the priest) offer up the Passion of the Lord, indeed that we offer up Christ himself.[11] This is likewise true of the pre-Scholastic Middle Ages. Seldom, it is true, do they use words of their own to express the traditional teaching, but when they do they are especially clear in pointing out that it is the priest at the altar, who, in place of Christ, offers up our Lord's Body,[12] that in so doing he is the *coadiutor Redemptionis*[13] and *vicarius eius*.[14] And at the same time they declare that the Church offers up the sacrifice through the ministry of the priest.[15] Even the theologians of earlier

---

[11] Irenæus, *Adv. hær.*, IV, 17 f.; esp. IV, 18, 4 (al. IV, 31, 3; Harvey, II, 203): *hanc oblationem Ecclesia sola puram offert fabricatori.*

Cyprian, *Ep.*, 63, 17 (CSEL, III, 714): *passio est enim Domini sacrificium quod offerimus.*

Athanasius, *Ep. heort.*, 2, 9 (PG, XXVI, 1365): We offer up not a material lamb but the true Lamb that was already offered, our Lord Jesus Christ.

Chrysostom, *In Hebr. hom.*, 17, 3 (PG, LXIII, 131): our priest is he who offered up the cleansing sacrifice; it is this same sacrifice that we now offer up ..., not another.

Passio Andreæ (5th century; *Acta ap. apocr.*, ed. Lipsius-Bonnet, II, 1, p. 13 f.): *Omnipotenti Deo ... immaculatum agnum cotidie in altare crucis sacrifico.*

Augustine, *Ep.*, 98, 9 (CSEL, XXXIV, 531): *Nonne semel oblatus est Christus in seipso et tamen in sacramento non solum per omnes paschæ sollemnitates, sed omni die populis immolatur?*

Cyril of Jerusalem, *Catech. myst.*, V, 10 (Quasten, *Mon.*, 103): When we are offering up our prayers to God for the dead, we do not plait a wreath but we offer up the Christ slain for our sins.

According to Theodoret, *In ps.*, 109 (PG, LXXX, 1773) "the Church offers the mystery of the body and blood," even if Christ were not active at all.

[12] Remigius of Auxerre (d. 908), *In ep. ad Hebr.*, 8 (PL, CXVII, 874 C; Lepin, 139): *Dum enim nos offerimus sacramenta corporis eius, ipse offert.*

Pseudo-Alcuin (9th/10th century, *Confessio fidei*, IV, 1 (PL, CI, 1087; Lepin,

139). *quamvis corporeis oculis ibi ad altare Domini videam sacerdotem panem et vinum offerentem, tamen intuitu fidei et puro lumine cordis inspicio illum summum sacerdotem verumque pontificem Dominum Jesum Christum offerentem seipsum.*

Hugo of Amiens (d. 1164), *Contra hær.*, II, 2 (PL, 192, 1276; Lepin, 140): *Quapropter manus illæ, manus ad hoc sacratæ, quibus Christi corpus et sanguis in altari sacro habet confici, manus utique sunt Christi. ... Consecratus itaque sacerdos stat vice Christi coram patre summo.*

The idea that behind the activity of the visible priest stands everywhere the activity of the High Priest Christ is also strongly emphasized by Paschasius Radbertus, *De corpore et sanguine Domini*, 12, 2 (PL, XII, 1312).

[13] Peter Comestor (d. 1178), *Sermo 47* (PL, CXCVIII, 1837 C; Lepin, 140).

[14] Stephen of Baugé (d. 1136), *De sacramento alt.*, c. 9 (PL, CLXXII, 1280; Lepin, 140).

[15] Lepin, 141.

Early Scholastic theologians incline towards the view that an excommunicated priest or one publicly heretical can no longer validly consecrate because he can no longer speak the *offerimus* of the prayer in the Canon in the name of the Church (Lepin, 141, note 3). Even Peter Lombard still subscribes to this opinion (Lepin, 157).

Similarly, Cyprian had denied to priests outside the pale of the Church the power to consecrate; C. Ruch, "La messe d'après les Pères," DThC, X, 939 f.

St. Thomas, *Summa theol.*, III, q. 83, answers with a distinction: only the prayers which are to be said in the name of the

Scholasticism[16] and the great teachers of the flourishing schools of the thirteenth century use the same language,[17] without, however, going into any deeper discussion of the topic. Only Duns Scotus lays any great emphasis on the sacrifice of the Church. The Eucharist, he says, is accepted by God, not because Christ is contained in it, but because He is offered up in it, offered up by the Church.[18] The theologians of the declining Middle Ages stress the activity of the Church with such one-sidedness and partiality that the sacerdotal function of Christ himself is to some extent obscured.[19]

Even the Council of Trent itself pointed out, as we already remarked, that it was our Lord's intention at the Last Supper to leave "to His beloved Spouse, the Church, as human nature requires, a visible sacrifice." [20] The Church, therefore, was to have this sacrifice, and through it was to be able to satisfy the desire of human nature to honor God by means of sacrifice. For any theological view which would also do justice to liturgical reality, this statement of fact is fundamental.

Our next question therefore follows along this direction. We want to know *how* Christ's institution is to be understood as a sacrifice of the Church, in what relation it stands to the life of the Church in all its fulness, and especially what principles of liturgical formation are taken for granted in it.[21]

To be more precise, how is this sacrifice which the Church is supposed

---

Church lose their efficacy, not the consecration, which is performed in Christ's name and by virtue of the inamissible power of ordination. Adrian VI (d. 1523), *In IV Sent.*, f. 28 (Lepin, 230) adheres to the conviction that even the power to offer up the sacrifice (which is not taken away by the sinful state of the priest) is always exercized in the name of the Church and for this reason retains its efficacy *ex parte Ecclesiæ committentis.*

[16] Lepin, 148 ff.

[17] Lepin, 180, 210 f.

Albert the Great, *De s. Euch.*, V, 3, forms an exception: *solus Filius est sacerdos huius hostiæ,* says he.

[18] Duns Scotus, *Quæst. quodlibet,* 20, 22 (Lepin, 231).

Scotus even contests the notion that Christ here himself, *immediate,* offers up the sacrifice, because of the wording of the Epistle to the Hebrews and because otherwise the Mass would be equal in value to the Passion. Because it is the Church that essentially makes the offering, it is also needful that someone answer the priest *in persona totius Ecclesiæ;* Duns Scotus, *In IV. sent,* 13, 2 (Lepin, 238).

[19] A. Gaudel, "La messe: III," DThC, X, 1082 f.

[20] Sess. XXII, c. 1 (Denziger-Umberg, n. 938). See *ibid.,: novum instituit pascha se ipsum ab Ecclesiæ . . . immolandum* (see Schroeder, 144-5). This makes it plain that the words of the Council about *idem offerens* (c. 2) are not to be pressed to the point of excluding the cooperation of the Church, which really represents a subject not at all independent of Christ. Besides, in the same passage the words *offerendi ratio diversa* also leave room for this extension of the subject: Christ here offers along with His Church.

[21] In recent times the sacrifice of the Church has been given theological emphasis by M. de la Taille, S.J., *Mysterium Fidei* (Paris, 1921). Of the three sections of this work the first deals with the Lord's sacrifice, *De sacrificio Dominico,* the second with the Church's, *De sacrificio ecclesiastico.* Insofar as the Mass, contrasted with the Cross, is a new sacrifice, it is so (according to de la Taille) exclusively as the sacrifice of the Church. The offering which Christ made on the Cross she makes her very own by performing it on His commission and through His power (299). A detailed dis-

to offer up—how is it brought about? By the fact that the Church joins in the sacrifice of her Lord and Master, so that His oblation becomes her oblation. Therefore, in the Mass the one sacrifice of Christ, the one oblation of Golgotha by which He redeemed the world, is in mysterious fashion made present. Because of St. Paul's letter to the Hebrews, the oneness of the sacrifice of Christ is a matter which cannot be assailed.[22]

But how is this presence of the sacrifice of Christ to be understood? There must be something more here than just a representation of the oblation that took place once upon a time, something more than the *memoria passionis* as we see it commonly exhibited by the separate presentation of the Body and the Blood of Christ. On the altar a sacrifice truly takes place, but it is a sacrifice which in many respects coincides with the sacrifice of the Cross. For the Council of Trent says of it: "There is the same oblation, and the same Person who now makes the oblation through the ministry of the priests and who once had made an oblation of himself on the Cross. Only the manner of offering is different."[23] It is here that the speculations of theologians take their start; the result has been a variety of explanations which, since the sixteenth century, have continued to multiply.

The simplest solution seems to be one that was not proposed till our own day. According to this explanation the *memoria passionis* is intensified into an objective remembrance in the sense of a *Mysteriengegenwart*— a mystical presence. In the celebration of the Eucharist not only Christ himself but His one-time act of redemption are made present under cloak of the rite, "in the mystery."[24] The past happening, Christ's Passion and Resurrection, is re-enacted in time, not indeed in its historical course but "in the Sacrament." So, from the very nature of the case, there is present an oblation—the same oblation which once took place. This, however, is a supposition which is not found in tradition in the precise form it here takes, but is rather the result of reasoning from tradition,[25] a deduction which must enlist the aid of certain hypotheses which are themselves quite questionable.[26] According to this theory the one oblation of Christ achieves

cussion of de la Taille's theory of the Mass in Lepin, 659-720, and in most theological manuals.
[22] Hebr. 9:24; 10:18.
[23] c. 2 (Denziger-Umberg, n. 940).
[24] The concept is presented by O. Casel in countless publications. Prominent are "Das Mysteriengedächtnis der Messliturgie," JL, VI (1926), 113-204, and his later article, which sets out his position fully, "Glaube, Gnosis und Mysterium," JL, XV (1941), 155-305.
[25] G. Söhngen, *Symbol und Wirklichkeit im Kultmysterium* (2nd ed., Bonn, 1940), 132-135. A brief introduction to the study of the mysterium is provided by P. Botz,

O.S.B., "The Mysterium," *Orate Fratres*, XV (1940-41), 145-151. Of this theory, aside from its detailed application, Th. Klauser, "A Brief History of the Liturgy in the West: I," *Orate Fratres*, XXIII (1948-9), 15, has this to say: "The conception of various liturgical acts as 'mystery-deeds' is clearly demonstrable in certain ecclesiastical regions, particularly eastern ones, and in the writings of some Fathers, but it has never become a general and common teaching of the Church."
[26] Cf. J. Pohle-M. Gierens, *Lehrbuch der Dogmatik*, III, 9 (Paderborn, 1937), 361-363.

simply a new presence by means of the consecration. The disparity of the actual oblation would thus be reduced to the barest possible minimum, so small that it is hard to see how there could be any new *ratio offerendi* or how the Eucharist could still be called *our* sacrifice, or how we would be linked to Christ's oblation in any relationship except a very external one.[27]

The older explanations, on the contrary, generally sought to find the new and "different" manner of offering, of which the Council speaks, in the act of consecration itself. By means of the consecration, the Body immolated on the Cross and the Blood shed thereon are presented to the Father once again at this point of time and space. In this re-presentation which Christ fulfills through the priest—*ministerio sacerdotum*, says Trent—we have the oblation in which, according to the testimony of Christian tradition, the great high-priest offers himself at every Mass. This new offering is necessarily also a sacrifice in its own right, but not one that has independent redemptive value, since it is nothing else than a sacramental extension of the one and only redemptive sacrifice on Calvary which the Epistle to the Hebrews had in view.[28]

There appeared to be only one difficulty. This re-presentation is indeed some sort of offering (*offerre*), but is not properly a sacrificial offering (*sacrificari*), an *immolation*. Pre-Tridentine theology was not at all agitated over this distinction, the sacrificial character of the Mass being supplied by the *oblatio* which took place in it.[29] But the pressure of controversy seemed to demand a search for the precise sacrificial act within the Mass. And especially in view of the sacrifices of the Old Testament, it seemed necessary to acknowledge that a destruction of the gift was essentially required, so that, in the case of a living thing it had to be killed (destruction theory), just as Christ himself consummated His redemptive sacrifice by His death. The post-Tridentine Mass theories are concerned for the most part with demonstrating this "destructive" sacrificial activity in the Mass.[30] However, no agreement over the solution has ever been reached.[31]

Some theologians wanted to substitute for this destruction a mere altera-

---

[27] Cf. A. Stolz, O.S.B., *Manuale theologiæ dogmaticæ* (Freiburg, 1943), VI, 173-175.
[28] The above formulation is the result of numerous discussions I have had with a confrere of mine, P. Karl Rahner.
[29] See the succinct presentation of statements for the chief periods in the history of the theology of the Mass-sacrifice in the comprehensive article "Messe" in DThC, X (1928), 795-1403, the first three centuries; from the 4th to the 15th by A. Gaudel, 1036 f.; 1081-1083.
St. Thomas distinguishes the two concepts *oblatio* and *sacrificium* when he says (*Sum. theol.*, II. II[ae], 85, 3 ad 3) : *sacrificia proprie*

dicuntur, quando circa res Deo oblatas aliquid fit, but he places no special importance on it; see Gaudel, *loc. cit.*, 1061 f., 1081.
[30] See the survey in Lepin, 337-770; A. Michel, "La Messe, V," DThC, X, 1143-1289; F. Renz, *Die Geschichte des Messopfer-Begriffes*, II (Freiburg, 1902).
[31] The first generation of post-Tridentine theologians tried to be content to find in the Mass some kind of image of a sacrificial destruction. They were satisfied to refer to the commemoration of the Passion as represented in Communion and, in a limited way, even in the fraction (M. Cano), or finally also in the consecration under sepa-

tion of the gifts, which, added to the offering, would suffice for a sacrificial act.[32] Others finally thought they could ignore any special act of immolation that would require the destruction or alteration of the gift, and following the lead of pre-Tridentine tradition they explained that the simple presentation of the gifts was sufficient. Christ, they declared, is made present under the species which by their separation are a sign of His bloody sacrifice of old; thus He presents himself anew to the Father.[33] There could not, of course, be any thought of an oblation of Christ that takes place here and now if this presentation were to consist simply in the interior resignation, in Christ's sacrificial sentiment which is present in this moment of time and space (because enclosed in the sacramental pres-

rate species (Salmeron). But under the pressure of controversy, an actual destruction occurring here and now was looked for: Bellarmine (d. 1621) sought it ultimately in Communion, which he likened to the consumption of the sacrificial victim by fire; Gregory of Valencia (d. 1603) in the consecration, fraction and Communion together.

Soon it was acknowledged more and more that the destroying sacrificial act could only be looked for in the double consecration, which was the only thing requisite for the completion of the eucharistic sacrifice. Lessius (d. 1623) saw—as several others had already seen before him (Lepin, 413) —that the double consecration which produces, *vi verborum*, the separation of body and blood, was an act in itself suited to achieve the actual death of the sacrificial Lamb if the latter were still liable to death; it was therefore equivalent to a real sacrificial act (later designated *mactatio virtualis*). Vasquez (d. 1604), whose theory was supported in the last century by Perrone, found that this double consecration would not in itself acquire the status of an independent sacrificial act, but in view of the relative character of the Mass, reverting as it does to the sacrifice of the Cross —for it is really a commemorative sacrifice —the image of death, the representation of the former slaying inherent in the double consecration, the *mactatio mystica*, would suffice; later adherents to this thesis added that, even abstracting from the relativity, the *mactatio mystica* would do, because Christ appeared each time under the image of death (Bossuet, Billot).

Cardinal de Lugo (d. 1660) maintained that an actually destructive change was in-

admissible as an homage to God, the master of life and death; according to his theory, the words of consecration placed Christ before men's eyes in a *status declivior*, in the condition of food, and this even by the single consecration; the double consecration was required not for the sacrifice but for the representation of Christ's Passion. This theory of de Lugo was revived by Cardinal Franzelin (d. 1886), and J. Brinktrine, *Das Opfer der Eucharistie* (Paderborn, 1938), has endeavored to extend it by the notion that the humanity of Christ, through this reduction to the state of food, experiences a dedication or hallowing; see in this connection F. Mitzka, ZkTh, LXIII (1939), 242-244.

[32] St. Thomas is here cited as the authority (see *supra*, note 29). Thus R. Tapper (d. 1559) refers to the fact that in the Mass the glorified Christ assumes a sacramental form of existence (DThC, X, 1107, 1109 f., 1116). This theory has been taken up again more recently by N. Bartmann, *Lehrbuch der Dogmatik* (4th ed., Freiburg, 1921), II, 369 f.

Akin to this is the theory of Suarez (adopted to some extent by Scheeben), according to which the sacrificial transformation is referred not to Christ directly but to the eucharistic elements, the bread and wine; see *infra*, note 38.

[33] Thus especially, several German theologians since the 19th century, above all Moehler and Thalhofer. Lepin, who himself adheres to this theory, cites in its favor the representatives of the French Oratory since Cardinal Bérulle (d. 1629); Lepin, 462 ff., 543 ff. But see in opposition A. Michel, "La messe," DThC, X, 1196-1208.

ence) and enduring (because also retained permanently in heaven). For an interior sacrificial sentiment, the will to sacrifice is not itself a sacrifice. Sacrifice demands some sort of action which moreover must be expressed in an external sign. Those who hold this opinion are therefore forced to assume that Christ in heaven makes a sacrifice which fulfills these conditions, and which is made present in the consecration[34]—an assumption which cannot easily be confirmed.[35]

Christ does, however, make the presentation of His one-time sacrifice before the face of God in an externally perceptible action, namely in the consecration which He performs through His priests. The consecration not only stems from Christ, in so far as the commission and powers are derived from Him, but it is in its very performance His work in the first degree, a work of His priestly office.[36] And it is a work which—unlike the other sacraments, aimed in the first place at the sanctification of souls—is directed immediately to the glorification of the Father. It is a presentation or offering to the heavenly Father in the very here and now, in an act which enshrines in itself the core of every sacrificial activity: *dedication*.[37]

---

[34] This profound notion was developed especially by Valentin Thalhofer; see Lepin, 575 f. In his own statement of his standpoint Lepin believes it possible to admit a heavenly sacrifice without any external act (737-758; see 747).

[35] F. A. Stentrup, *Prælectiones dogmaticæ de Verbo incarnato*, II, 2 (Innsbruck, 1889), 278-347.

This notion of sacrifice, constructed as it is exclusively on the concept of oblation, is plainly distinguished from the pre-Tridentine notion in this one essential point, that the latter thought in this connection almost entirely of an offering by the Church while the former speaks of the oblatory activity of Christ and ascribes it to the Christ present in the Eucharist. From this conception a new mode of eucharistic piety derived, directed towards the life of Christ's soul in the Eucharist. It is to be found exemplified amongst the members of the French Oratory; some citations in Lepin, 482 ff., 491 f., 546.

[36] Cf. St. Thomas, *Summa theol.*, III, 83, 1 ad 3: *Sacerdos gerit imaginem Christi, in cuius persona et virtute verba pronuntiat ad consecrandum. . . . Et ita quodammodo idem est sacerdos et hostia.* Thomas (and with him apparently the Tridentinum, which alludes to his formulation) sees the sacerdotal activity of Christ at work especially

in the effective consecrating act of the priest.

According to one trend of theological thought, we would have to postulate a physical activity of Christ in each and every consecration—not only knowing of each one but willing it and, as *instrumentum coniunctum divinitatis*, producing it. However, no new act is demanded for each consecration; it is sufficient that there be a continuation of the affirmation and determination of all future oblations, made by Christ during his life on earth in virtue of His foreknowledge. Cf. R. Garrigou-Lagrange, O.P., "An Christus non solum virtualiter sed actualiter offerat missas quæ quotidie celebrantur," *Angelicum*, XIX (1942), 105-118. Differently in W. Lampen, O.F.M., "De Christo non actualiter, sed virtualiter offerente in Missa," *Antonianum*, XVII (1942), 253-268.

New light on the question in G. Söhngen, *Das sacramentale Wesen des Messopfers* (Essen, 1946), especially, pp. 25 ff.

[37] Basically what is requisite for a sacrifice over and above the oblation is nothing more than an expression of dedication. While with regard to a gift by which we wish to honor a man, we do nothing more than hand it to him: in regard to a gift to the invisible God it is possible to make such an offering only by removing it from our own posses-

This dedication is consummated upon a thing which is still profane, still the world, is in fact the world and human life in the intensest sense, since men prolong their life through it; but it is altered and transformed into the holiest thing between heaven and earth, into the sacrificial gift offered up on Golgotha, an image of which is set forth in the species after the transubstantiation.[38] In the "holy and venerable" hands of the Lord the earthly gift has become a heavenly gift in the very act of giving.[39] Thus the oblation of Christ is again on our altars, and as an oblation which He himself performs anew before our very eyes. But He does not perform it in order to present us a drama, but in order to include us and His Church

sion and designating it as belonging to God and "dedicated" to Him. The form this designation will take is dependent on the nature of the gift. The history of religions brings to light oblation-gifts that are merely set down in some holy place and are thus hallowed by reason of the place, the "altar." Thus the Old Testament had a sacrifice of this sort in the bread of proposition. The dedication and appropriation to God is best secured, however, when the gift is entirely removed from human use—the incense burnt on the charcoal, the wine-offering poured out, the animal slaughtered, the flesh consumed by fire. On the sacrifices as found in the history of religions see W. Koch, "Opfer," LThK, VII, 725-27.

[38] That the bread and wine were also to be included in the sacrificial act was long maintained by renowned theologians: Suarez, De missæ sacrificio disp., 75, I, 11 (Works ed. Berton, XXI, 653); Bellarmine, Disp. de controv., III, 3, 5 (De sacrif. missæ, I), c. 27 (ed. Rome, 1838: III, 734); lastly M. J. Scheeben, The Mysteries of Christianity (trans. C. Vollert, S.J.; St. Louis, 1947), 507-511.

The corresponding ideas are found expressed in many passages in the Fathers since Irenæus: The layman who presents the bread and wine for the Eucharist is considered a (co-) offerer; see supra, p. 27.

[39] That there should be a distinction between the gift as it is alienated by men and the gift as it is determined for God's service, that the point of expropriation and appropriation should not exactly coincide, is seen even in pre-Christian sacrifices, for instance, the presentation of the smoke of sacrifice which is common in ancient hea-

thendom as well as in the Old Testament (Gen. 8:21, et al.). The eucharistic sacrifice, too, was so instituted by Christ that it should start as bread and wine and not till afterwards become the gift properly so-called.

The favorite argument, that the reference of the sacrificial action exclusively to Christ fits the wording of the Tridentinum (eadem hostia) better, really proves nothing; for the conception explained above in no way contradicts it, any more than the inclusion of the sacrifice of the Church contradicts the words of the Council about idem sacerdos. Since no problem regarding these ideas had been proposed to the Council, there was no call for a more precise statement.

Please notice, however, that in the above demonstration we are not saying—as does Jos. Kramp, S.J., Die Opferanschauungen der römischen Liturgie (2nd ed.; Regensburg, 1924), 109 ff.; idem., The Liturgical Sacrifice of the New Law, trans. L. F. Miller (2nd ed.; St. Louis, 1927), 34-35—that the core of the sacrificial action is the fact that bread and wine are consecrated; what we claim is that the core of the sacrifice is to be found in the fact that, by the consecration, Christ once more presents to His Father the gift of the body and blood He had already sacrificed to Him. But this in no way hinders our perceiving in the sacrifice actually instituted by Christ a further symbolism in the consecration of earthly gifts; for Christ did not institute just any kind of sacrifice, but a determined sacrifice rich in many relationships, the sacrifice of His Passion as the sacrifice of the Church. Cf. in a similar vein G. Söhngen, Das sakramentale Wesen des Messopfers (Essen, 1946).

everywhere on earth and in every century in His *pascha*, His passage out of this world to His Father. His sacrifice becomes each time *the sacrifice of the Church*.[40]

Our Lord offered up the sacrifice on the Cross not for its own sake but that He might therein give His life as "a ransom for many" (Matt. 20:28). In this way He concluded for us that everlasting covenant with God which was promised in the prophets (Is. 61:8; Jer. 33:20 f.; Bar. 2:35) that covenant by which God receives mankind into His favor so that He no longer remembers their misdeeds (Jer. 31:31-34; cf. 33:8), but rather wishes them every good (Jer. 32:40), in the hope that the destined heirs obtain, forever, their promised inheritance (Heb. 9:15). But because it is a covenant, a compact, obedience and fidelity are expected also on our part. It was at the very time of its institution, at the Last Supper, that Christ spoke of the covenant. He speaks of His body "which is to be given up for you" (1 Cor. 11:24; Lk. 22:19). He designates His blood as "my blood of the new Testament, which is to be shed for many" (Mark 14:24; Matt. 26:28), and points to the chalice as "the new testament in my blood" (1 Cor. 11:25; Lk. 22:20). As if to say, this institution has a special meaning within that testament, and in the commission to do this perpetually as a memorial, something more is intended than merely a theoretical commemoration in connection with the repetition of this transubstantiation. Much more is accomplished than that. In it is created an opportunity for all the faithful of all times to ratify[a] in conscious manner this covenant which He had concluded in their name. At Baptism we are already taken up into this covenant and its goods are portioned out to us, without our having to do anything except receive them. In the Eucharist, Christ sets before us the Passion by means of which He inaugurated this covenant; now it is up to us to step forward with a willing "yes" to protest our adherence to the law of Christendom. His sacrifice should become our sacrifice, the Church's sacrifice, so that it might be offered up in her hands "from the rising of the sun to its going down" and the name of the Lord of hosts "be made great amongst all the peoples" (Mal. 1:10 ff.).

The Church received a sacrifice from Christ because it is in man's very nature to honor God by sacrifice. More especially is this true where all religion is not to be limited to the inwardness of the individual, that is to say in a social union like the Church, in the divine service of the community. Here the need to glorify God by outward gift, by the visible emblem of an interior subjection or an internal giving of oneself to God— this need naturally arises of its own accord. The inner thought has to be

---

[40] Anscar Vonier, O.S.B., *A Key to the Doctrine of the Eucharist* (Westminster, 1948), "Man's Share in the Eucharistic Sacrifice," 223-240.

[a] There can be no question of a ratification in the fullest sense, since this "covenant" is essentially a one-sided favor on God's part; cf. J. Behm, *Theol. Wörterbuch z. N. T.* (1935), II, 106-137; especially διαθήκη, 132 ff. But for its effectiveness an acceptance by each adult and a corresponding performance are constantly demanded.

the starting-point and the driving force of every sacrificial service if this service is not to be turned to mere pharisaism, for sacrifice is and must always remain only the symbol and sign of something else, an indication of what the soul intends.[42]

But why could not a simpler gift suffice to express this intention?[43] Because this intention, this inner sentiment towards God, is in Christianity a species all its own, at least as an ideal to which our striving is constantly pointed. The Sermon on the Mount, the Gospels, all the books of the New Testament speak of it. It is plainly put in St. Paul's *Hoc sentite in vobis quod et in Christo Jesu* (Philippians 2:5) It means entering into the thoughts of Jesus, rising to His mind and sentiment. In the life of our Lord himself the peak and triumph of that sentiment was reached on the Cross—a Cross which was erected as the wood of shame, and which our Lord willingly embraced in order to give himself wholly to His Father and at the same time to stretch out His arms over all the world and mercifully bring it back to the grace of God. The great commandment on which the Law depends and the Prophets, to love God with one's whole heart and soul and strength, and one's neighbor as one's self, this commandment of which He gave the living model, He also exemplified in death. That is the height to which He beckons His disciples. That is the fulness, the maturity of Christ to which they must grow.

So it is understandable—and yet remains a mystery!—that our Lord should choose as the token of His followers' glorification of God the very last and greatest thing that He himself had to give God the Father—His body that was offered and His blood that was shed. But this sacrificial gift is presented in such a way that each time it actually grows out of His followers' own gift, out of the produce of their own clay and sweat, out of a tiny piece of bread and a sip of wine by which they live. And it actually grows out thus by their own doing, by the words of consecration which someone from their midst is empowered to utter. So the Church is able not only to join in some extrinsic fashion in Christ's oblation which is made present in her midst, but she actually offers it as her own gift, as a gift which, in its natural state, is expressive of her own life and leads that life back to God, along with all that God's creative hand apportions to it along the way. This gift in its supernatural state manifests and confesses what the Church has become by God's grace and what she knows she is

[42] St. Augustine, *De civitate Dei*, 10, 5 (CSEL, XL, I, p. 452, l. 18) : *Sacrificium ergo invisibilis sacrificii sacramentum, id est sacrum signum est.* Modern theologians are unanimous in stressing the fact that sacrifice is *in genere signi*; cf. E. Masure, *The Christian Sacrifice*, trans. Dom. I. Trethowan (New York, 1943), 66-77 and *passim*. Unfortunately few authors pay any

attention to the content of what is signified. [43] The idea that it is incumbent upon the Church to offer not just any gift but precisely the sacrifice of Christ still forms for Protestant theology even today the greatest obstacle in Catholic teaching concerning the Mass-sacrifice; see, e.g., the report by E. Stakemeier in *Theologie u. Seelsorge* (1944), 91-99.

called to be. Thus the Church is enabled truly to offer up her very self["]; as St. Augustine says, she learns to sacrifice herself in His sacrifice.[45] This self-oblation of the Church is the precise object which the eucharistic mystery serves. Never is the Church so closely bound to her Master, never is she so completely Christ's spouse as when, together with Him, she offers God this sacrifice.

By the term "Church" is here meant—as everything we have said goes to show—not only the Church Universal and the priest representing her at the altar, but likewise the assembly of the faithful gathered around the priest at each celebration of the Mass. That the faithful offer the sacrifice was taken for granted in the more ancient theological tradition. *Plebs tua* explicitly stands in juxtaposition to *servi tui* in the Roman canon. Now, as an understanding of the priesthood of the faithful[46] reawakens, the thought once more comes consciously to the fore. It is announced with complete clarity in the great encyclicals of Pope Pius XII.[47]

And now, looking at it more closely, how is this self-oblation of the Church accomplished? The action which brings this about precisely is—again—the consecration. The same act which realizes the sacrifice of Christ also realizes the sacrifice of the Church, but with this difference, that the Church's sacrifice begins to take shape from the very start of the Mass and then receives the divine seal and acceptance when at the consecration Christ takes it in hand and, after richly ennobling it, offers it to His heavenly Father as His own. For the priest who performs the consecration in Christ's name and with Christ's power is always at the same time acting on commission from the Church. This commission he received at his ordi-

[44] Cf. Scheeben, *The Mysteries of Christianity*, 509-510.

[45] Augustine, *De civitate Dei*, 10, 20 (CSEL, XL, I, p. 481) : . . . *ipse offerens, ipse et oblatio. Cuius rei sacramentum quotidianum esse voluit Ecclesiæ sacrificium, quæ cum ipsius capitis corpus sit, se ipsam per ipsum discit offerre.*
Cf. *ibid.*, 10, 16 (CSEL, XL, I, p. 475, l. 23).

[46] E. Niebecker, *Das allgemeine Priestertum der Gläubigen* (Paderborn, 1936) ; R. Grosche, "Das allgemeine Priestertum," *Liturgisches Leben*, IV (1937), 1-33 ; Paul F. Palmer, S.J., "The Lay Priesthood: Real or Metaphorical," *Theological Studies*, VIII (1947), 574-613, esp. 610 ff.
Niebecker equates "priest" with "a man who offers sacrifice" ; 74 ff. Here we could insert many passages from Christian tradition where the offering of the Mass is predicated of the faithful. For the early Scholastic period see F. Holböck, *Der*

eucharistische und der mystische Leib Christi in ihren Beziehungen zueinander nach der Lehre der Frühscholastik (Rome, 1941), 225-229. As late as 1453 Nicholas of Cusa founded his demand that people attend Mass while still fasting on this concept, *quia . . . simul cum ipso sacerdote hostiam offerunt* ; Franz, *Die Messe im deutschen Mittelalter*, 63. But by the time Luther came into prominence such ideas were no longer current and had then to be revived.
See also Sebastian Tromp, S.J., "Quo sensu in sacrificio missæ offerat Ecclesia, offerant fideles," *Periodica*, XXX (1941), 266 ; Godfrey Diekmann, O.S.B., "With Christ in the Mass," *Christ's Sacrifice and Ours* (National Liturgical Week, 1947 ; Boston, 1948), 42-48, esp. 44 ff.

[47] "Mystici Corporis," AAS, XXXV (1943), 232 f., and with even greater emphasis in "Mediator Dei," AAS, XXXIX (1947), 554-556.

nation, for it was the Church that appointed him and ordained him as a priest of Christ. And he receives this commission for this precise situation by his office or at least by the fact that, in his celebration of the Eucharist, he fits himself into the Church's pattern and thus places himself at the head of the faithful who, as a portion of the Church Universal, have here and now gathered round him.[48] As their representative he stands at the altar. He consecrates the bread and the chalice to present Golgotha's sacrifice to almighty God as their own. And since all through the course of the Mass he acts and speaks not simply in his own name but on commission from the Church, this authorization does not cease at the moment of transubstantiation merely because Christ's commission is superimposed, for it is the Church that calls on him to accept this second commission so that she, as the Bride of Christ, might once more enter into His sacrifice.[49]

This sacrifice is present on the altar under the form of gifts which are emblems of our life-support and are at the same time manifestations of unity, of the combining of many into one. The ancient Church was vitally conscious of this symbolism of the eucharist species to which even St. Paul had already alluded[50]: "As this broken bread was scattered upon the mountain tops and then, being harvested, became one," as the wine has flowed out of many grapes into this chalice, so the faithful should, through this sacrament, become one in Christ.[51]

Another thing. This oblation was instituted with the express determination that the participants be fed with it: "Take and eat." The sacrificial meal is not something plainly included in the notion of sacrifice. There were sacrifices in the Old Testament which were entirely consumed in the fire, with nothing remaining for the offerers to eat—the sin-offerings, for instance; the offerers were not worthy to enter into so close a community with God. But the sacrifice of the New Covenant is essentially constituted as a meal, so that the offerers might gather around the sacrificial table, the table of the Lord, to eat. They are in communion with Christ who had undergone His sufferings and is now exalted; they become anew one body with Him.

This element of the symbolism of the species, which is emphasized in

---

[48] Or who have asked him for this celebration, e.g., by a stipend. In the extreme case of a private Mass the priest himself, with or without the server, represents the collective Church. The relationship of the priest to the Church Universal is further elucidated by G. de Broglie, "Du rôle de l'Eglise dans le sacrifice eucharistique," *Nouvelle Revue théologique*, LXX (1948), 449-460.

[49] The priest's representing Christ and his representing the Church are not parallel; they are disposed one behind the other. This destroys the contention of J. B. Um-

berg, ZkTh, XLVII (1923), 287, that the admission of the Church as *offerens* contradicts the words of consecration, *Hoc est corpus meum*.

[50] I Cor. 10:17.

[51] *Did.* 9, 4; *Const. Apost.*, VII, 25, 3 (Funk, I, 410 f.); Cyprian, *Ep.*, 69, 5 (CSEL, III, 754); cf. *Ep.*, 63, 13 (*ibid.*, 712); Augustine, *Sermo* 227 (PL, XXXVIII, 1100); 229 (1103), et al. Regarding the continuance of this knowledge during the early Middle Ages, see F. Holböck, *Der eucharistische und der mystische Leib Christi*, 192 f.

the words of consecration—this element above all must be taken in earnest. Every sacrament serves to develop in us the image of Christ according to a specified pattern which the sacramental sign indicates.[52] Here the pattern is plainly shown in the double formation of the Eucharist; we are to be drawn into the sacrifice of our Lord on the Cross. We are to take part in His dying, and through His dying are to merit a share in His life.[53] What we here find anchored fast in the deepest center of the Mass-sacrifice is nothing else than that ideal of moral conduct to which the teaching of Christ in the Gospel soars; the challenge to an imitation of Him that does not shrink at sight of the Cross: a following after Him that is ready to lose its life in order to win it[54]: the challenge to follow Him even, if need be, in His agony of suffering and His path of death, which are here in this mystery so manifestly set before us.

If the Church's gift of homage to God is thus changed by the priest's words into the immolated Body and the spilled Blood of our Lord, and if the Church, firm and unafraid, then offers it to God, she thereby stamps her "yes" upon the chalice which her Master has drunk and upon the baptism which He experienced. And by that same oblation which she bears in her hands, she is dedicated and sealed for the same road that He traveled on His entrance into glory (Luke 24:26). The sacrifice of Christ is renewed sacramentally not only *in* His Church but *upon* the Church,[55] and is renewed daily because it is daily demanded of her (Luke 9:23). The Mass-sacrifice is not only a presentation of the redemptive Passion and, with it, of the whole collection of Christian doctrine on salvation. It is also an epitome of Christian life and conduct. The height on which Christ lived and died comes before our gaze each time as an ideal, admonishing and alluring, as a towering peak which we can only reach by tremendous try-

---

[52] In comparison with the treatment accorded the causality in the sacraments, Scholasticism was chary in its dealing with the symbolism of the sacramental salutary effects and even (to take in a detail) of the Christ-formative efficacy of sacramental grace. This failure has been rectified in the work of G. Söhngen, *Symbol und Wirklichkeit im Kultmysterium* (first publ. 1937; 2nd ed. Bonn, 1940), esp. 43-109; see also the same author's *Der Wesensaufbau des Mysteriums* (Bonn, 1938).
[53] Cf. Karl Rahner, "Eucharistie und Leiden," *Zeitschrift f. Aszese und Mystik*, XI (1936), 224-234.
[54] Matt. 10:38 f.; 16:24 f., and parallels.
[55] It is, however, quite another question whether (with Söhngen, *Symbol und Wirklichkeit*, 152-157) we are to see exclusively in this the sacrificial character of the Mass;

see the criticism by F. Lakner, ZkTh, LXVI (1942), 60.

It was in the course of explaining how his notions differ from Casel's that Söhngen arrived at his thesis. He altered Casel's idea to this extent, claiming that the spiritual reality of the sacramental action is present not *in se* but only in the recipient of the sacrament. Transferring this to the sacrifice of the Mass, Söhngen opposes Casel's concept that the sacrifice of Christ was to be considered as pre-existent to the sacrifice of the Church in the *mysterium*. Söhngen's theory is this: The sacrifice of Christ on the Cross is "sacramentally present when Christ consummates His sacrifice as the sacrifice of the Church" (139).

In any and every case Söhngen has given a fecund turn to the theology of the mystery.

ing, along the ascent of Christian asceticism.[56] All this puts Communion in a new light. Communion, too, is stamped with the Cross and the death of the Lord.

At the consecration, the Church as a society affirms the oblation of Christ and makes it her very own, but the individual Christian might feel satisfied to follow from afar, more of an onlooker than an actor in the sacred drama. In Communion, however, it is the individual participant who really wants to co-celebrate the Mass—it is his word that counts. Everyone must be seized with the impulse to be swallowed up in the mystery of Christ's Passion. Thus and only thus can the partakers hope to meet Him who had already entered into His glory; thus and only thus can they be embraced by Him and hallowed by the fire of His godhead.

Just as the participation of the Church in Christ's oblation at the consecration is a sacramental proceding, so too the completed incorporation of the individual in Communion is a sacramental proceeding. The recipients of the Eucharist become participants in the oblation *ex opere operato.*[57] But it is somewhat different with sacrifice as such. Since this is a moral activity, a free and humble homage before God, a genuine and essential consummation of the sacrifice cannot be produced in the mere reception of a divine operation, as is the case with the sacraments in which God sanctifies man. Therefore the sacrifice, in so far as it is the oblation of the Church, is not completely concluded with an *opus operatum*; the *opus operantis* must join in, and not merely as an addition to the completed work, but as a requisite belonging to the very structure at least as an integrating part.[58] True, Mass is not simply man's good work—as Luther pretended to explain Catholic teaching on the subject—but neither is it simply the result of God's activity, as, for instance, Baptism is. The Church is not drawn into Christ's Passion under compulsion, but enters into it freely, consciously, deliberately. That is the Mass.

In a higher measure and in another way than in the sacraments, therefore, there is required beside the passive moment also an active one. Were Mass only the *mysterium* of Christ's Passion or only a memorial meal, then—with the addition perhaps of a consentient anamnesis to cast a glance at the redeeming sufferings—the account of the Last Supper, with the consecrating words over bread and wine, and the reception of the Sacra-

[56] To this thought ample expression was given by Gregory the Great, *Dial.*, IV, 59 (PL, LXXVII, 428) : *Sed necesse est, cum hæc* [the sacrifice which represents the Passion of Christ] *agimus, nosmetipsos Deo in cordis contritione mactemus, quia qui passionis dominicæ mysteria celebramus, debemus imitari quod colimus. Tunc ergo vere pro nobis hostia erit Deo, cum nos ipsos hostiam fecerimus.*
[57] Cf. J. Bütler, "Die Mysterienthese der Laacher Schule im Zusammenhang scholastischer Theologie," ZkTh, LIX (1935), 555.
[58] We are not answering here the question, what minimum is demanded to bring about the sacrifice. For this question cf. J. B. Umberg, "Die wesentlichen Messopferworte," ZkTh, L (1926), 73-88. As we know, neither sense organs nor members *(partes integrantes)* are required in order to have a "man."

ment would suffice. Mass, however, is also and primarily an immolation to God, an expression of the self-offering of the Church. The Church does not wait for the redemptive grace that pours down on her anew; having long ago obtained the favor of her Lord, she takes the initiative, she sets out on her own to offer God her gift, a gift which, at the height of her ascent, is changed for her into the oblation of Christ.

We therefore find that it is a common phenomenon in the history of the Mass-liturgies that some action of the Church precedes the consecration, a movement toward God which gains its essential utterance in the great prayer of thanksgiving but which is also expressed in many customs that, even during the preparation of the elements, suggest the προς-φέρειν, the presentation, the *oblatio*, the gift, just as they continue to express the same thoughts after the transubstantiation. According to its essence, therefore, Mass-liturgy is accomplished in three steps—not very sharply defined: the submissive and laudatory approach to God, the sacramental performance of Christ's sacrifice, and the reception of the sanctified gift.

The institution of Christ thus once more implies that the Church realizes this active moment of the sacrificial proceeding not only in her official representative who stands at the altar but also in the participating congretion. The "we" in the priest's prayers and the spatial assemblage of the participants around the officiating priest already tend in this direction. It follows that an interior immolation is required of the participants, at least to the extent of readiness to obey the law of God in its seriously obligatory commandments, unless this participation is to be nothing more than an outward appearance.[59] A participation that is right and justified in its essentials should, of course, involve the desire to tread again the pathway of the Master and to make progress on it. To such an interior attitude, however, corresponds an exterior expression which exhibits a connection with the essentially significant sacrificial proceedings by means of tokens or words that have the presence of the participants as their starting point. All the liturgies have developed for this a wealth of expressive elements, but of these only a portion have stayed in living practice. The ideal condition would be if the sacred activity conducted by the priest would evolve from the ordered activity of the congregation and all its members, just as it does evolve from their will.

Since the Mass is a sacrifice of the Church, it normally presumes a larger or smaller assembly of the people. The different types of this assembly gave rise, in the course of history, to a principle of formation; it will be our task in the next few chapters to study the development of this principle more closely. In its most complete development we have the assembly

---

[59] The Sunday precept is concerned immediately only with the external act in the sense of a conscious attendance, the limits of which are detailed by the moralists; see J. J. Guiniven, *The Precept of Hearing* *Mass* (Washington, 1942), 79-86; 103-107; cf. 108-109. However, the purpose of the precept is, of course, to secure the inner participation, a coordination of mind and heart in the action at the altar.

of all the people in the place; in early times this occurred mostly under the leadership of the bishop, while later on the priest, especially the pastor, was appointed for this. The bishop's Mass and the priest's Mass, therefore, form two of the basic tyes of the Mass. But the assembly can also shrink to just a few persons, and finally—as an irreducible limit—to the single person of the celebrating priest, who, indeed, can also offer up the Mass in his own name. However, we find the Church constantly trying to avoid this extreme case, to such an extent in fact that in none of the rites, either East or West, did any form of Mass develop in which at least the etxernal outlines of community participation were left out. The forms of private Mass are always only diluted forms of public celebration.

3. From the Episcopal Collective Service to the *Missa Solemnis*

The primitive and original form of Mass celebration is that in which the bishop surrounded by his clergy offers up the sacrifice in the presence of the congregation. Nearly all the accounts of the Mass which we have from the end of the first century until well into the fourth presuppose this arrangement. This sort of thing was to be expected from the fact that Christianity was then predominantly an urban religion. Ignatius of Antioch is quite pointed in his reference to this common service: "Take care, then, to partake of one Eucharist; for one is the Flesh of our Lord Jesus Christ, and one the cup to unite us with His Blood, and one altar, just as there is one bishop assisted by the presbytery and the deacons, my fellow servants."[1] The Roman *ordines*, too, give the same picture in regard to papal services.[2] In fact in Rome, as also in other localities,[3] there is a further development insofar as the principle of a roving assembly-place makes it possible even in a large city to retain, at least in its fundamental outlines, the system of gathering the whole community together. Since the Roman *ordines* became for centuries the norm for regulating the episcopal services in almost the whole West, this arrangement remained in vogue elsewhere.[4]

---

[1] Ignatius of Antioch, *Ad Philad.*, 4 (ed. Kleist; Westminster, 1946; p. 86). Cf. *Ad Smyrn.*, 8, 1 f. (*ibid.*, 93); *Ad Ephes.*, 20, 2 (*ibid.*, 67-8).
The full assembly of the congregation, including the clergy under the leadership of the bishop, is presupposed in Justin, *Apol.*, I, 65; 67; *Didascalia*, II, 57; Hippolytus, *Trad. Ap.* (Dix, 6; 40 ff.); *Canones Hippolyti*, c. 3; *Const. Ap.*, II, 57; *ibid.*, VIII, 5 ff. (cf. esp. VIII, 11, 7 ff., 15, 11); Pseudo-Dionysius, *De eccl. hierarch.*, III, 2; Narsai, *Homil.*, 17 (Connolly, 4).

Some accounts in Martène, 1, 3, 8, 2 (I, 329 f.).
[2] *Supra*, pp. 67-69.
[3] *Supra*, p. 61.
[4] Cf., e.g., Theodulf of Orleans (d. 821), *Capitulare*, I, c. 45 (PL, CV, 208).
The outlines are still maintained in the *Decretum Gratiani*, III, 1, 59 (Friedberg, I, p. 1310 f.). At the second Synod of Seville (619) the dominant position of the episcopal service was secured by forbidding the presbyters *eo* [episcopo] *præsente sacramentum corporis et sanguinis Christi con-*

Thus the ideal form for uniting the whole community of the episcopal see in one service and promoting the complete self-oblation of the community remained alive for long in the consciousness of the occidental Church. In the Orient this is still the case even today.

The position taken by the clerics, particularly the priests, in this common service is expressed in the principle of *concelebration*.[5] This principle implies, for all the participants, a proper share in the community service, but not necessarily a co-consecration on the part of the priests present.[6] For priests as well as for the rest of the faithful—to whom even late medieval sources quite unabashedly ascribe a *celebrare missam*, a concelebration[7]—the essential thing in this participation was to answer the chief

---

ficere (can. 7; Mansi, X, 559). Cf. de Puniet, *Das römische Pontifikale*, I, 235 f. A similar injunction was already to be found in Martin of Braga, *Capitula*, c. 56 (PL, LXXXIV, 582): *Forasticis presbyteris præsente episcopo vel presbytero civitatis offerre non liceat.*

[5] P. de Puniet, "Concélébration liturgique," DACL, III (1914), 2470-2488; A. Fortescue, "Concelebration," CE, IV, 190.

[6] The proofs are marshalled in J. M. Hanssens, "De concelebratione eucharistica," *Periodica*, XVI (1927), 143*-154*; 181*-210*; XVII (1928), 93*-127*; XXI (1932), 193*-219*.

On the basis of Hanssen's distinction between *concelebratio cæremonialis* and *concelebratio sacramentalis* (that is, with the words of consecration said in common), H. v. Meurers, "Die eucharistische Konzelebration," *Pastor Bonus*, LIII (1942), 65-77; 97-105, presents a summary view of the historical development and the legal status of the rites. According to this article, sacramental concelebration was still to be found at Rome in an addition (8th century) to *Ordo Rom. I*, n. 48 (PL, LXXVIII, 958 f.): on five great feasts of the year each of the Cardinal priests who surround the altar of the pope carries three hosts on a corporal and, together with the pope, speaks over these the entire Canon including the words of consecration. Cf. the same custom in the Ordo of St. Amand (Duchesne, *Christian Worship*, 460), where, however, the pope alone says the Canon aloud; and, as early as the 6th century, a remark, not very clear, in the *Liber pontificalis* (Duchesne, I, 139; see also Duchesne, 175, note 2). But even in Rome the custom no longer obtained after the

13th century. Prior to this it is cited still by Innocent III, *De s. alt. mysterio*, IV, 25 (PL, CCXVII, 875 f.).

Aside from this practice in the city of Rome, sacramental concelebration came into use between the 8th and the 12th centuries on the occasion of the ordination of priests and the consecration of bishops, the bishop and the newly ordained (*resp.* consecrated) participating; for a time, too, it was in use at the consecration of abbots. Since then concelebration at ordination and consecration has continued as a fast rule within the limits of the Roman rite. In the Orient (ceremonial) concelebration was customary and common from time immemorial, but it is only in the Uniate groups that the joint pronouncing of the words of consecration was added, apparently not till the start of the 18th century and then under the influence of Rome, which recognized no other type than the sacramental concelebration in use at the administration of Orders. In fact, as we gather from Benedict XIV, *De s. sacrificio missæ*, III, 16 (Schneider, 437-444), the co-consecration by all celebrating was considered a necessary requirement, and the concelebrants were permitted to take a stipend therefor (*ibid.*). It is only within the Byzantine rite that this sort of thing has become customary even outside the Uniate groups, the words of consecration being spoken on certain occasions by all together, in addition to the usual praying (softly) of the other prayers; cf. de Puniet, "Concélébration," 2479 f.

[7] Gregory of Tours, *De gloria confessorum*, c. 65 (PL, LXXI, 875 C): *[mulier] celebrans quotidie missarum sollemnia et offerens oblationes pro memoria viri sui.*

celebrant, to join him in prayer at certain stated times, and to receive with him the Holy Sacrament. Still the dignity of the service demanded that suitable recognition be given each hierarchic rank.[8] The presbyters took their place in the *presbyterium* along with the other clerics; they wore the liturgical garment proper to them—in early medieval Rome this was the *planeta.*[9] At the papal stational Masses they also assisted in receiving the gift-offerings, in breaking the species and distributing Holy Communion. Naturally this assistance was subject to variations in degree. In the Oriental rites the incensings are distributed among the concelebrants.[10] Quite early we meet the custom of dividing the various orations—outside the canon—among the participating priests or bishops.[11] There is mention, too,

Of a woman whose son had been waked from the dead by St. Gertrude of Nivelles (d. 659), the biographer says, *in crastinum missam celebravit in honore virginis Christi Gertrudis; Acta SS. Mart.,* II, 596.

Of Alcuin, who was only a deacon, his Vita says (n. 26; PL, C, 104 C): *Celebrabat omni die missarum sollemnia.*

A Paris document of 1112 relates: The faithful of a new chapel of ease went on six feast days *missarum sollemnia ibi* (in the mother-church) *celebraturi et offerendas ex more oblaturi;* quoted in Schreiber, *Untersuchungen zum Sprachgebrauch des mittelalterlichen Oblationswesens,* 30 f. Further examples in F. de Berlendis, *De oblationibus* (Venice, 1743), 256.

Patently what is here thought of is a participation along with the making of an offering.

Cf. also Hanssens, *loc. cit.,* XVI (1927), 143*.

[8] Similar rules on how to honor a bishop present at Mass are still in force; see *Cæremoniale episc.,* I, 30; II, 9.

Amongst the earliest regulations of this sort committed to writing are those of the *Ordinarium O.P.* of 1256 (Guerrini, 245 f.), where place is given to the bishop even more than at present: he is invited to say the *Confiteor* and to give the final benediction; he blesses the water to be mixed, and the incense; he receives the Gospel-book to kiss, is the first to be incensed and the first to receive the *pax.*

[9] *Ordo Rom. I,* n. 4 f. (PL, LXXVIII, 639 f.). Cf. *supra,* p. 68 ff. In the pontifical service of the church of Lyons, when there is concelebration—which is not infrequent even today, although only on Maundy Thursday are the words of con-

secration spoken in common—there are, besides seven acolytes and an equal number of deacons and subdeacons, also six priests, vested in chasubles. They stand and sit next to the episcopal throne. Formerly they also received Communion from his hand. Buenner 261, 269 f., 283 f.; Archdale A. King, "The Rite of Lyons," *Orate Fratres,* XV (1940-41), 66; de Moléon, 47, 73. A description of a present-day service for Maundy Thursday at Lyons in *La Maison-Dieu,* n. 8 (1946), 171 f. De Moléon, 11, 28, relates a similar service at Vienne.

According to medieval sources, there were assistant priests, vested in chasuble, at pontifical functions in other churches, too: at Chalon there were seven, at Soissons and Sens, twelve; Marténe, 1, 3, 8, 2 (I, 331); cf. *ibid.,* XIX, XXI, XXX (I, 604, 609, 647). Twelve priests are required by Bonizo of Sutri (d. c. 1095), *De vita christiana,* II, 51 (ed. Perels; Berlin, 1930, p. 58).

[10] Hanssens, "De concelebratione," *Periodica,* VII (1928), 104*.

[11] The *Canones Hippolyti,* c. 3 (Riedel, 202) lay down the following injunctions regarding the blessing of oil which could be conjoined to the eucharistic prayer: "If there is oil there, let him likewise pray over it; if several are present, let him distribute the various sections; it is however one power."

At the crowning of the pope, according to *Ordo Rom. XIV,* n. 27, 30 (PL, XLVIII, 1135 f.), three cardinals each said an oration right after the prayers at the foot of the altar; then after the *Gloria* the pope himself recited the oration of the day. Cf. *ibid.,* n. 45 (1145 C). A

of pronouncing certain texts, even the preface, together,[12] so that it was but a slight step to the joint pronouncing of the words of consecration as in the present-day rite of ordination.[13]

However, in the Western Church the genuine remnants of ancient Christian concelebration are not to be found in the ordination Mass, but rather in the Mass on Holy Thursday with its priests' Communion,[14] and in the regulation for the last day of Holy Week that all private Masses are to be omitted and that the assembled clergy are to participate—informally —with the rest of the faithful in the one public celebration. Another trace of it is the *Ordo ad synodum* of the Roman Pontifical which presupposes that the bishop alone goes up to the altar and that the assembled clergy receive Communion at his hands. A similar prescript holds for the cardinals gathered for the papal election.[15] For the first thousand years, such a method was taken for granted in all cases where a number of priests were assembled and where they individually had no other religious duties—an

similar program was followed at the coronation of the Emperor; *ibid.*, n. 105 (1239 f.).

In the Byzantine liturgy the various orations are today recited softly by the chief celebrant while the deacon is still announcing the corresponding ektenes, but the concluding doxological ekphoneses which are said aloud are allotted to the various concelebrants. Hanssens, *Institutiones*, III, 536.

[12] At Orleans toward the end of the Middle Ages six canons sang the Maundy Thursday Mass along with the bishop, excepting only the words of consecration; de Moléon, 196. A similar practice obtained at Vienne; *ibid.*, 17. At Chartres as late as the 18th century, on this same day six archdeacons concelebrated with the bishop, singing the preface and *Pater noster* along with him, and with him turning to the people to say *Dominus vobiscum*; J. Grancolas, *Commentarius historicus in Romanum Breviarium* (Venice, 1734), 304.

Even today at the beginning of the ceremonies of the consecration of a bishop, while the consecrator addresses the examination questions to the candidate, the co-consecrators pronounce the same lines in a semi-audible tone; *Pontificale Rom., De cons. electi in episcopum.* A similar practice already in the 12th century; Andrieu, *Le Pontifical Romain*, I, 142.

[13] In our present-day rite of concelebration at the ordination Mass, the most striking

thing is the fact that the newly ordained disregard the architectonics of the Mass, saying all the prayers right through with the bishop, even those otherwise said quietly. Here is an indication that this joint utterance had a different basis than the concelebration otherwise attested in the history of liturgy, for the latter patently sought only a proper arrangement and disposition of all the participants according to hierarchical rank. In the case of ordination the fundamental idea obviously was to put the order just awarded to practical proof, in the same way that the foregoing ordinations were put into practice. The respective rubric, without the prescription of kneeling, is found in the Roman Pontifical since the 13th century; Andrieu, II, 349; cf. III, 370 f. The desire for a more select form has been uttered more than once; see v. Meurers, 67; L. Beauduin, "La concélébration," *La Maison-Dieu*, n. 7 (1946), 7-26, esp. 20 f.

[14] The pontifical function of Maundy Thursday preserves still another example of primeval concelebration: at the blessing of the oil twelve priests—as representative of all the city clergy—appear in *paramentis* and, as an old Ordo of Rouen (PL, LXXVIII, 329 A) puts it, *simul cum pontifice verbis et manibus conficiunt*, a word which Amalar had used of the co-consecration at Mass, *De eccl. off.*, I, 12 (PL, CV, 1016 C).

[15] Cf. v. Meurers, 100.

arrangement which is still today normal in the Orient.[16] When St. Paulinus of Nola (d. 431) on his deathbed was visited by two bishops, he begged *ut una cum sanctis episcopis oblato sacrificio animam suam Domino commendaret.*[17] For a long time the custom obtained in the monasteries, especially on feast days, for the whole community, including the priests, to gather together not only for the conventual Mass but for a general Communion.[18] Amongst the Carthusians this is still the rule on Christmas, Easter and Pentecost.[19] St. Francis of Assisi spoke in very general terms when he expressed the wish "that the brethren in their foundations celebrate only one Mass a day, as is the custom in Holy Church. And if there are several priests at home, for the love of God let one be satisfied to assist at the celebration of the other."[20]

For the rest this arrangement was maintained longest in the case of the sacred ministers at high Mass.[21] What had previously been taken for granted was prescribed at least for them on certain occasions, and the arrangement was thus kept up for a long time during the later Middle Ages. In the eleventh century the rule is cited more than once that one or even two of the particles into which the Host was broken should serve for the Communion of deacon and subdeacon.[22] Subsequently, Communion each time for deacon and subdeacon was stipulated only at the Mass of the bishop[23] and of the abbot,[24] or for high Mass on Sundays and holy days,[25] or for the first day of the weekly duty of the respective sacred ministers,[26] or finally in monasteries for the days when Communion was

[16] For examples from the present-day oriental colonies in Rome see v. Meurers, 66, note 5.

Illustrations from earlier times in Martène, 1, 3, 8, 2 (I, 330).

[17] *Acta SS.*, Jun., V., 171.

[18] The monastic *Breviarium eccl. ordinis* of the 8th century (Silva-Tarouca, 196, 1; 11), in describing the entry at the feastday Mass at which all communicated, named in the first place *presbyteri, qui missas publicas ipso die non celebrant* [*ur*].

For the Benedictine monasteries of the early Middle Ages see Berlière, *L'ascèse bénédictine*, 156 f.

Amongst the Cistercians there were four great feasts in the year at which the whole convent was present at the services, including the priests, and Communion was obligatory for all, as is plain from the *Liber usuum*, c. 66 (PL, CLXVI, 1437). Cf. for this v. Meueres, 104, note 78.

Also amongst the Dominicans the Ordinarium of 1256 seems to take for granted that on Communion days the

priests as a rule received along with the rest, since it notes that no one may stay away from Communion *nisi celebret missam ipsa die* (Guerrini, 248).

[19] v. Meurers, 102 f.

[20] Cf. P. Robinson, *The Writings of St. Francis of Assisi* (Phila., 1906), 115. This injunction appears to have been inspired by a high regard for community life and also lest frequent celebration might diminish the reverence due to the mystery. Cf. v. Meurers, 104 f.

[21] Browe, *Die häufige Kommunion im Mittelalter*, 45-51.

[22] See *infra*, Vol. II, Chap. 3, 4, note 43.

[23] *Ordo eccl. Lateran* (Fischer, 85 f.).

[24] This is reported by Bernard Ayglerius (d. 1282), Abbot of Monte Cassino; E. Martène, *Commentarius in Regulam S. Benedicti* (PL, LXVI, 580 A).

[25] Thus at Cluny; *Udalrici Consuet. Clun.*, I, 9 (PL, CXLIX, 653). Further evidence from the 12th to the 14th centuries in Browe, 47 f.

[26] Thus according to the regulations in the

prescribed for all.[27] Only in isolated instances did the later Middle Ages continue the usage of Communion for both sacred ministers at every Mass (outside of Mass for the Dead).[28] The Council of Trent contented itself with making a warm recommendation to this effect.[29]

The direct descendant of the bishops' collective service is the pontifical service, especially in its most elaborate form, the papal Mass,[30] although it is true that in these cases the participation of the people has become a matter of fact rather than of principle. Even the solemn high Mass of a simple priest, which one might well have expected would be explained as an elaborated growth of the presbyter Mass,[31] proves rather to be a late simplification of the pontifical service. For that reason the difference between a pontifical Mass and the sacerdotal high Mass in the Roman liturgy is today comparatively slight.[32] This fact is closely connected with the circumstances under which the Roman liturgy was taken over by the Frankish Church, for at that time the only directions in the *ordines* for the external solemnization of the service were the rubrics for a pontifical rite. In consequence, not only were these used in cathedrals, but they had to serve as the basis elsewhere, too. The first Roman *ordo* itself offered a handy pretext for this very thing, for one Roman addition[33] not only suggested that the bishops *qui civitatibus præsident* should perform everything like the pope, and that the bishop who replaced the pope at the Roman stational service had to make just a few changes,[34] but it remarked that this latter direction held good also for a presbyter *quando in statione facit missam* (aside from

Augustinian monastery at Dontinghem; Browe, 49.

[27] Browe, 48 f.
Amongst the Augustinians at Seckau, Communion was enjoined upon the levites for Sundays and feasts even as late as 1240, but in the reformed statutes of 1267 it was prescribed only once a month; L. Leonhard, "Stand der Disziplin . . . im Stifte Seckau," *Studien u. Mitt. aus dem Ben.- und Cist.-Orden*, XIII (1892), 6, 9.

[28] Thus Odo Rigaldus in 1256 in the reform-statutes for St. Stephen in Caen (ed. Bonnin, 262). Amongst the Castilian Cistercians the practice still held in 1437 when it was repealed by Eugene IV as *plerumque damnosum;* Browe, 48 f.

[29] Sess. XXIII, De reform., c. 13: *sciantque [diaconi et subdiaconi] maxime decere, si saltem diebus dominicis et sollemnibus, quum altari ministraverint, sacram communionem perceperint.* Cf. *Concilium Tridentinum*, ed. Goerres., IX, 482, 1. 17; 527, 1. 34; 533, 1. 2; 559, 1. 4; 627, 1. 8.
This recommendation was taken over into the *Cæremoniale episc.*, II, 31, 5. A like

norm appears now and then in some of the 16th century reform statutes, those of St. Charles Borromeo, for instance; Browe, 50 f. The communion of deacon and subdeacon as a practice still alive in the Vatican basilica is attested by J. Catalani, *Cæremoniale episcoporum,* I (Paris, 1860; first publ. 1747), 195.

[30] On this last item see J. Brinktrine, *Die feierliche Papstmesse und die Zeremonien bei Selig- und Heiligsprechungen* (Freiburg, 1925); A. Hudal, *Missa papalis* (Rome, 1925).

[31] Thus, e.g., Brinktrine, *Die heilige Messe*, 43 f., note.

[32] Even plainer is the distinction in the Byzantine liturgy, where in an episcopal rite, especially in the fore-Mass, there is an extensive allotment of the functions amongst the concelebrants and repeated blessing with Trikirion and Dikirion. Something like this is true also in the West-Syrian rite. Hanssens, *Institutiones*, III, 535-543.

[33] *Ordo Rom.* I, n. 22 (PL, LXXVIII, 948 f.).

[34] He was not allowed to occupy the cathe-

the rule that he might not intone the *Gloria* except on Easter).[35] It did not require any bold exegesis to turn this slight suggestion into a definite direction for every case when a priest had to conduct a solemn service in larger surroundings like those to be found (in the centuries to follow) not only in monasteries but also in numerous other capitular churches.

In any case this was the principle that was presently followed. Ample proof is to be found in the arrangement for Mass as outlined in an eighth century *Breviarium ecclesiastici ordinis* adapted to the circumstances of a Frankish Scots monastery; compare this with the prescriptions in the *Capitulare ecclesiastici ordinis*, which goes back to the Roman arch-cantor John and describes a papal stational Mass.[36] Aside from the papal court—which is not prominent in the *Capitulare* either—and the rite of *sustentatio* which is proper for the pope,[37] nearly everything of ritual splendor has been transferred to the monastic *sacerdos*: he is surrounded by priests (*sacerdotes*), deacons, subdeacons, and clerics; the seven candles[38] and the censer are carried before him; he steps up to the altar amid the same greetings as the pope; like the pope he employs the *Pax vobis*; during the whole fore-Mass he remains at his place *retro altare* and washes his hands before the offertory.[39]

The same sort of solemn Mass is encountered in Frankish sources of the ninth and tenth centuries. Most of the time it is distinguished as a bishop's Mass, but sometimes the presbyter appears explicitly as the celebrant.[40] Then, too, the new Mass arrangement which is noticed about the year 1000 in the documents of the Séez group[41] is drawn up first of all for the bishop's Mass, but is soon allotted to the priest also.[42]

The outlines of the present-day form of the *missa solemnis* become distinct and clear after the tenth or eleventh century. Whereas before—and

---

dra; the oration he said at the right side of the altar; at the fraction he remained at the altar and helped along and then put the *fermentum* of the pope in his chalice.
[35] Cf. also the Ordo of St. Amand (Duchesne, *Christian Worship*, 464).
[36] In parallel columns in the edition of Silva-Tarouca, 196-200.
[37] *Supra*, p. 68 ff.
[38] But there is an addition: (*aut septem) aut duo*. Silva-Tarouca, 196, 1. 14.
[39] This washing of hands was at the time no peculiarity of the papal or episcopal rite. The *Gloria*, too, is intoned by the *sacerdos*, although Christmas is substituted for Easter (cf. *infra*, p. 356, note 43). Still the *Breviarium* contains certain divergencies from the papal rite, as the result of the encroachment of Gallic traditions, like the *Dominus vobiscum* before the Gospel, the carrying of the offertory-gifts from the

sacristy, the plea for prayer on the part of the celebrant (*Orate*).
[40] This is the case in the description of Remigius of Auxerre, *Expositio* (PL, CI, 1248 ff.), but details about the ritual are missing. Amalar's explanations of the Mass regularly refer to the bishop, but the *Expositio "Missa pro Multis"* (ed. Hanssens: *Eph. liturg.*, 1930, 31, line 27), in its first mention of the celebrant, does say *episcopus aut presbyter*. In Rabanus Maurus, *De inst. cleric.*, I, 33 (PL, CVII, 322-326) the priest as well as the bishop is included in the designation *sacerdos;* cf. *ibid.*, I, 3-5 (301 C).
[41] *Supra*, pp. 74-75.
[42] This is plain in the Mass-ordo of St. Vincent (Fiala, 187, 196 ff.), in Cod. Chigi and in Gregorienmünster: Martène, 1, 4, XII; XVI (I, 568 ff., 595 f., 599): *sacerdos, presbyter*. In the Missal of Liége the

sometimes also later—there is mention of a number of deacons and sub-deacons,[43] now there appear only one deacon and one subdeacon to accompany the priest as he proceeds to the altar and to perform their duties there. Amongst the first indisputable testimonies of this arrangement is the writing of John of Avranches which dates about 1065. It still includes for the priest certain details from the episcopal rite which today are no longer retained,[44] but it definitely states that the bishop's *cathedra* is to be more prominent.[45] The conventual Mass at Cluny at the same time also displays the same type of Mass with deacon and subdeacon.[46]

In general the rite of high Mass has not changed much since the eleventh century, if we except the peculiar usages of certain regions and certain monasteries. In the twelfth century there appear, in addition to the other reverences, numerous kissings when handing over or receiving things—kisses which are still prescribed.[47] About this time likewise occurs the rule that the celebrant (and his assistants with him) were to read softly the texts sung by others.[48] The careful description of the priestly high Mass which is presented in the 1256 *Ordinarium* of the Dominicans[49] reveals in all essentials the present-day arrangement, and also the same differences

celebrant is *episcopus aut presbyter; ibid.*, XV (I, 582).

The rubrics regulating the ritual are quite scanty in the common basic text.

[43] The Synod of Limoges (1031) still enjoins (Mansi, XIX, 545 B) : Abbots and other priests are not to have more than three deacons on feast-days, while bishops are allowed to have five or seven.

The documents of the Séez group still mention a plurality of deacons in different ways.

The assertions in the Sacramentary of Ratoldus (d. 986; PL, LXXVIII, 239-245) are discrepant. Isolated stands Remigius of Auxerre (d. 908), who in his *Expositio* (PL, CI, 1247 f., 1250, 1271) speaks only of deacon and subdeacon.

[44] John of Avranches, *De off. eccl.* (PL, CXLVII, 32 ff.) : When the priest reaches the altar after the *Confiteor*, he kisses deacon and subdeacon. The deacon thereupon kisses the altar at both the narrow sides, hands the priest the Gospel-book to be kissed; then the priest kisses the altar. Several taper-bearers are among the assisting group, on feast-days seven. When the subdeacon begins the Epistle, the priest sits down, but *iuxta altare*. The subdeacon hands bread and wine to the deacon after the Gospel; the water is brought by a cantor. The incensing follows. Then the

subdeacon takes the paten, but turns it over to an acolyte. At the Communion deacon and subdeacon receive a portion of the large host.

[45] *Ibid.*, (PL, CXLVII, 33 A) : *Sessio episcopi . . . ceteris celsior debet fieri.* See the remarks on this matter by H. Ménard, (PL, LXXVIII, 331 f.)

[46] *Udalrici Consuet. Clun.*, II, 30 (PL, CXLIX, 716 ff.).

Cf. also the Mass arrangement of Cod. Chigi, Martène, 1, 4, XII (I, 569 f.), in which the description of the entry bears a striking resemblance to that of John of Avranches and at the same time plainly marks a transition to the type we are accustomed to: *Deinde cum clerici inceperint Gloria post Introitum, procedat, antecedente eum diacono et ante eum subdiacono cum libro evangelii et ante subdiaconum acolytho cum thymiamate, ante quem duo alii acolythi præcedant cum candelabris et luminaribus, et sic ordinate exeant secretario.* One variation from John of Avranches is to be noticed; instead of the two taper-bearers John has only one *ceroferarius* who follows the censer-bearer.

[47] *Supra*, p. 107 f.
[48] *Supra*, p. 106.
[49] Guerrini, 233-246.

Cf. also the off-shoots of this *Ordinarium* cited on p. 100.

from the arrangement of the pontifical service as it was finally fixed in the *Ceremoniale episcoporum* of 1600. The solemn vesting program is dropped, two to four candles are found sufficient, and they stand on the altar.[50] The priest no longer employs the phrase *Pax vobis* but only *Dominus vobiscum*, he says the oration, and likewise the *Gloria* and the *Credo*, at the altar, and washes his hands only after the incensing. The most impressive distinction, which for years had marked the pontifical service in northern countries, was the solemn pontifical blessing after the canon, which endured all through the Middle Ages and which the priest never dared to assume.[51] Likewise the *presbyter assistens*, substitute for the older college of priests,[52] who was still clearly in the foreground in the twelfth century,[53] has now by universal law been reserved to the pontifical rite.[54]

Many peculiarities of the medieval high Mass and pontifical Mass which were of a more technical sort have since disappeared,[55] or have survived

[50] At quite an early period the number of candles began to be adjusted according to the rank of the feast; cf. Eisenhofer, I, 286 f.

[51] For details see *infra*, Vol. II, Chap. 3, 3. The pontifical blessing is not mentioned in the *Ordinarium O.P.* but it is specially cited in the derivative *Liber ordinarius* of Liége as a main distinction. Volk, 97.

[52] *Supra*, p. 201. But even today it is customary in the churches of the archdiocese of Vienna to signalize specially solemn occasions by having two other clerics, dressed in tunicles, at the altar, although they perform no functions; such a service is humorously styled a "five-team high Mass."

[53] *Ordo. eccl. Lateran* (Fischer, 80-87). A transitional form is seen in the arrangement of the 10th century *Ordo Rom. VI*, n. 1 ff. (PL, LXXVIII, 989 ff.); here there are two priests who take over, in part, the *sustentatio*, as the assisting deacons do otherwise, but later one of them serves at the book (n. 4).

Even later some French cathedrals had, besides the seven deacons and seven subdeacons, not one but six or more priests; cf. *supra*, note 9.

[54] *Cod. Iur. Can.*, c. 812. The presence of an assistant priest is an honor reserved to bishops and other prelates who have the use of pontificals. Some religious orders claim the privilege for their higher superiors on the ground of long-standing usage. For the simple priest the presence of an assistant priest is now permitted only by indult. True, there are two nebulous references to an assistant priest in the Missal

rubrics (*Rit. serv.*, VII, 11; VIII, 8), but by universal law the only exception is the case of a newly-ordained priest; at his first Mass such an assistant in cope is "tolerated" (*Decr. auth.* SRC, n. 3564), not so much as an honor, but as an aid.

[55] Thus it was the deacon's duty, stressed more than once, to fold back the celebrant's ample chasuble, especially when he turned around to the people: *deorsum eam in anteriori parte trahendo; Ordo eccl. Lateran* (Fischer, 83; cf. 81 f.). Cf. *Ordinarium O.P.* of 1256 (Guerrini, 236, 239 f., 244); *Liber ordinarius* of Liége (Volk, 93, 1.17); *Ordo Rom. XIV*, n. 47 (PL, LXXVIII, 1151), et al. There is evidence for the practice among the Premonstratensians since the 12th century (Waefelghem, 47, 67, 96); a vestige of it is still to be found in the repeated kissing of the chasuble (*ibid.*, in the notes; also other examples). Cf. also *Ordinarium Cartusiense* (Chartreuse, 1932), c. 29, 13; 32, 13.

During the Canon the deacon was to have a fan (*flabellum*) handy, *tempore muscarum*, to safeguard priest and offerings; *Ordinarium O.P.* (Guerrini, 240); *Liber ordinarius* of Liége (Volk, 93 f.). In *Udalrici Consuetudines Cluniacenses*, II, 30 (PL, CXLIX, 719) this task is entrusted to two acolytes. In the Orient, where the liturgical fan (*rhipidion* or *hexapterigon*) is still much in use, but now primarily with symbolic meaning, the same original purpose is attested in the *Apostolic Constitutions*, VIII, 12, 3 (Quasten, *Mon.*, 212, with note). Further details in Braun, *Das christliche Altargerät*, 642-660.

only in monastic rites.[56]

The greatest change in solemn high Mass since the Middle Ages is in regard to its frequency. For centuries the high Mass was the prevailing form of public worship in those churches which held the leadership in liturgical life—and these were, besides the cathedrals, the monastic churches and the capitular churches, that is, the churches of collegiate chapters which were organized on a monastic pattern.[57] In all these churches the daily conventual Mass sung after Terce, with deacon and subdeacon, was part of the fixed order of the day.[58] From this time on,[59] it formed the climax of the liturgical office.[60] Indeed, at Cluny and in its orbit already since the eleventh century, a second conventual Mass had been said each day, a *missa matutinalis* in addition to the *missa maior*. And at this second Mass there were a deacon and subdeacon. But it was distinguished from the other by a slight diminishing of solemnity[61]; the altar was incensed at the offertory but not at the beginning of Mass, the interposed chants were shortened, and the *Credo* was regularly dropped. On days that had no spe-

The *Liber ordinarius* of Liége places upon the sacristan the job of providing the *flabellum* for the private Masses of the brethren during the insect season, and during the intense cold providing for a pan of coals *(carbones in patello;* Volk, 49, 1.23). The latter provision is also included in the *Ordinarium Cartusiense,* c. 29, 7.

[56] Such is the practice of having the two acolytes stand on either side of the deacon and subdeacon whenever these are standing behind the celebrant, so that the group is arranged *in modum crucis; Ordinarium O.P.* (Guerrini, 235). The custom is still in force in the present Dominican rite; it is frequently attested in the Middle Ages; cf. Arens, 19.

The custom of deacon and subdeacon turning with the celebrant to greet the people is witnessed among others by *Cod. Chigi: Martène,* 1, 4, XII (I, 570 D), and in the *Ordo eccl. Lateran.* (Fischer, 83, 1. 30); it is still practiced in Benedictine monasteries.

[57] Cf. *supra,* p. 103 f.

[58] P. Sawicki, *De Missa conventuali in Capitulis et apud Religiosos* (Cracow, 1938). The expression *missa in conventu* or *missa conventualis* since the 12th century. Besides these, other designations were used, like *missa canonica, missa capitularis;* Sawicki, 7, note 6.

Carolingian authors called it also *missa*

legitima, missa generalis; Bona, *Rerum liturg.,* I, 13, 1 (175 f.)

[59] In the earlier monasteries, wherein the canonical hours developed to the form they latterly possess, daily Mass was still, as we know, strange. The mention of Mass in St. Benedict, *Regula,* c. 35 and 38, presupposes that the monks assembled for it only on Sundays and feasts. The same is seen in the *Regula Magistri,* c. 45 (PL, LXXXVIII, 1007 f.) and in Fructuosus of Braga (d. c. 665), *Regula,* II, c. 13 (PL, LXXXVII, 1120 f.). Reg. St. Columban (d. 615) his *Vita* tells us that he read Mass only on Sundays; I, 26; III, 16 (PL, LXXXVIII, 740 and 765).

[60] Only the Carthusians present an exception. In their first stage (they were founded in 1084) the conventual Mass took place only on Sundays and feasts; Bona, I, 18, 3 (256); P. Goussanville in the notes to Peter of Blois, *Ep.,* 86 (PL, CCVII, 266). Besides, both amongst the Carthusians and in part amongst the Cistercians, there was no subdeacon; see *infra,* p. 209.

[61] There was, in addition, a scaling of the solemnity in the rites of the High Mass on Sundays: at the introit the semi-verse was repeated even before the *Gloria Patri;* the *Gloria in excelsis* was inserted; there was but one collect; gradual and Alleluia were chanted by two soloists; all received the kiss of peace. *Udalrici Consuet. Clun.,* I, 8 (PL, CXLIX, 653).

cial feast the formulary of the Mass for the Dead was chosen,[62] since this second Mass was for the benefit of the souls of deceased benefactors for whom Cluny had developed an extended solicitude.

A similar arrangement became customary amongst the Premonstratensians,[63] and was soon adopted elsewhere.[64] In France at the time of Honorius III there appeared a tendency to be satisfied with the daily service for the dead, especially since it had some advantage as regards time, and so the Mass which was due *ratione diei vel festi* was omitted. This was the occasion of a decree issued by this pope in 1217, in which the fulfillment of one obligation as well as the other was required.[65] From this decree many canonists drew the conclusion that all collegiate chapters and even monasteries were bound to the double conventual Mass, so that the frequency of solemn Mass was, where possible, still further increased.[66] In an effort to stem the swell of Masses for the Dead, and to promote as much as possible a correspondence between Office and Mass, the Missal of Pius V took this legislation as the basis for its regulations for cathedrals and collegiate churches regarding the double Mass, of which in the cases given one was to be *de feria*, the other *de festo*,[67] and also for the rules regarding the substitution of Votive Masses and Masses for the Dead.[68] In general the double conventual Mass has in modern times been restricted to days of a double liturgical character (in the sense just indicated). And more often it has

[62] *Op. cit.,* I, 6; 9 (PL, CXLIX, 651; 653); II, 30 (718).

[63] Waefelghem, 29-32. Only in the more urgent harvesting time were they content with just one conventual Mass (29). Amongst the reductions of solemnity that signalized the early Mass for the Dead was the attendance of only one acolyte; *ibid.,* 98-101.

[64] John of Avranches, *De off. eccl.* (PL, CXLVII, 32 B).
Amongst the Cistercians, too, there was a Mass *pro defunctis* (to correspond to the Office for the Dead) every day, even on Sundays and feasts, with just a few exceptions; it was said at a special altar, apparently without the whole community being present; *Liber usuum,* c. 51 (PL, CLXVI, 1420); cf. R. Trilhe, "Citeaux," DACL, III, 1795.

[65] *Decretales Gregor.,* III, 41, 11 (Friedberg, II, 642 f.).

[66] Sawicki, 34 ff.
Sawicki shows that in reality the ecclesiastical obligation to a conventual Mass for religious with choir did not exist till Pius X; this was the last stage in the development of the principle that Mass was

part of the obligation of choir (64 f.; cf. 68 ff.). But the Church has been reluctant all along to impose a new obligation regarding a conventual Mass for the Dead (45 f.) Even in the Middle Ages the praxis remained quite diversified. At Klosterneuberg there was always a Low Mass for the Dead, but it was said at a special altar only during the singing of High Mass; besides there was always an early Mass after Prime (mostly *de Beata*); Schabes, 59 f.; 64.
On the contrary, at the Benedictine monastery of St. James in Liége there was as a rule only one conventual Mass; it was only from time to time that a *missa matutinalis* was said, and this was sometimes dedicated to the dead; Volk, 53 and the index under *missa matutinalis*.

[67] This basic principle already in Bernold, *Micrologus,* c. 58 (PL, CLI, 1019 B), and in Honorius Augustod., *Gemma an.,* IV, 117 (PL, CLXXII, 736).

[68] Roman Missal, *Rubr. gen.,* III ff. Later the canonists interpreted the law to mean that the second Mass was to be applied to the dead but the formula was not specified; this solution received the sanction of law under Benedict XIV. Sawicki, 52-55; 58.

been reduced in solemnity so that, outside of Sundays and Feast-days, it is no longer a *missa solemnis* but a *missa cantata*[69]—this latter probably the form of the monastic Sunday Mass in the beginning.

The real high Mass has again become rarer, the result of various concurring forces. In the cities the collegiate chapters, whose first occupation was solemn divine service, have long since been dissolved. In cathedrals and to some extent also in the surviving monastic establishments, other activities have loomed larger. The independent life of clerical communities, a cloistered and Godward life as it flourished in the later Middle Ages, is rarely possible since the secularization of the past few hundred years. Its outward expression in the daily high Mass has therefore disappeared with the disappearance of that life.

There is another point to notice. This Mass was no longer the collective act of worship of a congregation like the old Roman stational Mass from which it derived. As a rule it took place at a choir altar, situated in a chapter choir or sanctuary that had gradually gotten farther away from the nave and had become almost an independent clerical church, and so even from this viewpoint the Mass was truncated and withered-looking. But more than this, in monastic churches the people had been absolutely excluded since the early Middle Ages. *Missæ publicæ* were generally not allowed, so that the monastery would not unnecessarily mix into the hurly-burly of the world, and the people, on the other hand, would not be drawn away from their parish churches.[70] The very architecture of the older monastic churches is proof of this—as a rule an immense choir and a very small nave.[71]

In modern times, the interests of the care of souls once more became a focal point in worship and therefore the congregation once more came to the fore. In fact the new orders in the sixteenth century showed a decided opposition to solemn services of the late medieval type, since the liturgical duties left hardly any time for other pastoral tasks which were then growing so urgent.[72] The materialistic and prosaic intellectuality which had

[69] Sawicki, 86.
Amongst the Capuchins the conventual Mass is generally a *missa lecta*; *ibid.*, 71; see note 72 below. As far as church law is concerned, nothing more is demanded even of other orders with choral obligation; Sawicki, 86.
[70] Public Mass in monasteries was forbidden more than once under St. Gregory the Great; see *Ep.*, II, 41; VI, 46; etc.; Roman Synod of 601 (PL, LXXVII, 1312). The first Lateran Council (1123) also forbade monks *missas publicas cantare*; can. 17 (Mansi, XXI, 285); cf. Bona, I, 13, 3 (178 ff.).
On the other hand, the 8th century

Breviarium eccl. ord., in its disposition of services distinguishes monasteries *ubi populus* [read -o] *vel feminis licitum est introire* from those *ubi non ingrediuntur feminæ* (Silva-Tarouca, 198, l. 10). At the *Sanctus* it directs the clergy *cum omni populo* to bow and sing (*ibid.*, 198 f.).
[71] As high as four-fifths of the space was occupied by the monastic community; G. Dehio, *Geschichte der deutschen Kunst* (3rd ed.; Berlin, 1923), I, 72 f.
[72] The several groups of Discalced Augustinians that made an appearance in the 16th century have one regulation in their Constitutions that is peculiar but yet common to all the groups: they are never to sing

become more and more widespread since the eighteenth century, and the increasing independence of the masses had dampened that joy in princely splendor with which the high Mass encompasses the celebrant as the successor of a pope who had become something of a secular ruler and had been surrounded with the pomp of secular courts.[73] The high Mass has been retained only for great feast days when, enriched with musical values that spring from a cultural level very close to us, it continues to function as the expression of highest festive joy and as the self-assertion of a Church happy in its possession.[74]

4. From the Presbyter Mass to the *Missa Cantata*

Besides the episcopal collective service, even Christian antiquity found another type of Mass necessary, since in the territory of each individual bishop there were many churches with their own clergy.[1] This was the Mass of the presbyter,[2] which we must look upon as a second original basic type

high Mass. M. Heimbucher, *Die Orden und Kongregationen* (2nd ed.; Paderborn, 1907), II, 188.

The Society of Jesus, too, not only had no choral Office but also no high Mass, since for the latter the contemporary arrangements usually presupposed the presence of the community to take care of the singing. *Constitutiones S. J.* (finished in essentials by 1550), VI 3, 4; see *Institutum S. J.* (Florence, 1893), II, 99 f.: *non utentur Nostri choro ad horas canonicas vel missas et alia officia decantanda.* In the years that followed some exceptions were allowed in the matter of singing Mass; *ibid,* II, 527, 533, 539.

The Capuchins retained the choral Office but at the same time refused to have a (sung) conventual Mass, substituting a Low Mass; in addition private Mass was permitted the brethren (in this early stage of the reform) but only on feast-days. *Cæremoniale Romano-Seraphicum ad usum O.F.M.Cap.* (Rome, 1944), 327 ff.

[73] This seems to be true not only in Germany but in other countries, too.

[74] The Communion of the whole congregation had in most instances already disappeared.

[1] According to Eusebius, *Hist. eccl.,* VI, 43, there were at Rome even in the time of Pope Cornelius (d. 253) 46 presbyters (be-

sides 7 deacons and 7 subdeacons, as well as 42 acolytes and 52 other minor clerics), and according to Optatus, *Contra Parmen.,* II, 4 (CSEL, XXVI, 39) even during the period of the Diocletian persecution there were more than 40 basilicas. Among these there were in the 5th/6th centuries the 25 titular churches where regular congregational services were conducted; see Duchesne, *Liber pont.,* I, 164 f. Since the 5th century there appear on synodal records the signatures of Roman presbyters with mention of their titular churches. Cf. Mabillon, *In ordinem Rom.,* c. 3 (PL, LXXVIII, 858 f.) ; Batiffol, *Leçons,* 34. Even the figures furnished by Eusebius, *loc. cit.,* regarding the number of poor in the Roman Christian community who received support —1500—shows that a division of services (for worship) was already a self-evident necessity.

Cf. for details V. Monachino, *La cura pastorale a Milano Cartagine e Roma nel secolo IV* (Rome, 1947), 279-406.

[2] There is, however, but little express evidence that in the early era the presbyters actually conducted the eucharistic services: Cyprian, *Ep.,* 5, 2; cf. 15, 1 (CSEL, III, 479; 514) ; Athanasius, *Apol. c. Arianos,* c. 85 (PG, XXV, 400 C).

Cf. however, Ignatius, *Ad Smyrn.,* 8, 1 (ed. Kleist, 93) : "Let that celebration of

for the celebration of Mass, a type which survives in the *missa cantata*, the simple sung Mass. Although this second basic type must even then have been much more frequent than the grand stational service, there are practically no accounts of it extant. Perhaps precisely because of its frequent recurrence and because of its greater simplicity, there was no special call to put its description in writing. We can, however, reconstruct it in general outline. We grasp its essential form when we realize that at such a service, besides the congregation, only the presbyter and a second cleric were present as a rule.

The second cleric was generally a deacon. Chrysostom speaks on one occasion of wealthy Christians who possess entire villages but who do not build any churches; he demands that they erect churches and provide for a *priest* and a *deacon* so that divine service might be conducted and Sunday Mass might be celebrated.[3] In the Orient the deacon as a general rule stands next to the priest even today. This was also the case to some extent in the West well into the Middle Ages. Cyprian presupposes that the presbyters who sought out and visited the imprisoned Christians in order to celebrate the Eucharist with them, were each time accompanied by a deacon.[4] In the correspondence of St. Gregory the Great mention is often made of the need to ordain presbyters and deacons for orphaned churches which had no bishop.[5]

However, in the Roman liturgy a cleric of a lesser rank took the place of the deacon at a very early period.[6] This was all the easier since the deacon's proper functions were but little in demand even at a bishop's Mass, for his duty as prayer-leader for the people was never much developed and the various invitations to prayer and to the kiss of peace were proclaimed by the celebrant himself. In the city of Rome there was an additional reason, for the number of deacons was limited, as it was in other towns too, to the biblical number of seven (Acts 6:3). Thus it appears

the Eucharist be considered valid which is held under the bishop or anyone to whom he has committed it."

[3] Chrysostom, *In Acta ap. hom.*, 18, 4 f. (PG, LX, 147 f.).

Amongst the Syrians the indispensability of the deacon is declared by Ischojabh I (d. 596), *Canones ad Jacobum*, c. 3 (Hanssens, II, 465).

[4] Cyprian, *Ep.*, 5, 2 (CSEL, III, 479) ; cf. *Ep.*, 34, 1 (*ibid.*, 568). See also the question which Ambrose, *De off.*, I, 41 (PL, XVI, 84) puts in the mouth of St. Lawrence speaking to Pope St. Sixtus II; irrespective of its intrinsic historicity, it is indicative of the relationship of deacon to priest or bishop: *Quo, sacerdos sancte, sine dia-*

cono properas? The bishop, too, might celebrate with a smaller group; cf. *infra*, p. 214.

[5] Gregory the Great, *Ep.*, I, 15; 78; II, 43; IV, 41, etc.

Even Remigius of Auxerre, *Expositio* (PL, CI, 1247 D) makes the axiom of St. Isidore (*De eccl. off.* II, 8, 3: PL, LXXXIII, 789) his own: *presbyter sine diacono nomen habet, officium non habet.*

[6] Such a cleric could indeed be present along with a deacon. Thus the inscriptions found at Grottaferrata witness to the presence in that country congregation of a presbyter, a deacon, a lector (who was also an exorcist) and an exorcist; see J. P. Kirsch, *Röm. Quartalschrift*, XXX (1922), 99; Brinktrine, *Die hl. Messe*, 43, note 1.

FROM PRESBYTER MASS TO *MISSA CANTATA*   209

that at the titular churches in olden times a lector[7] usually served at the
altar, and later usually an acolyte.[8] He went with the priest to the altar.
He took over at least one of the readings. The priest probably, even in
earlier times, retained the Gospel for himself, no doubt in order to indicate
its higher dignity.[9] The assistant helped at the offertory procession of
the faithful and at the arranging of the gift-offerings, at the breaking of
the bread and at the distribution of Communion. The larger outlines of the
liturgical function remained the same. The text of the sacramentary was
used in its entirety. But, because a special choir was demanded only for
pontifical services, the chants of the *schola* dropped out, that is, besides
the introit (which, from the situation itself, was unnecessary), also the
offertory and communion.[10] Thus the more ancient arrangement survived,
somewhat in general like the arrangement nowadays on Holy Saturday.
If it was necessary because of a lack of other assistance, the cleric sang
the psalmody between the lessons, to which the congregation responded;
that is to say, he took over the duties of the *psalmista*.[11] The responses to
the altar chants of the priest were, of course, the right of the congregation,
and likewise the chants of the Ordinary—of which, till the sixth century,
only the *Sanctus* existed.

Some such Mass celebration must have fitted most naturally into the
circumstances of the early medieval monasteries. As long as the individual
monks were not as a rule ordained, it was the type that was taken for
granted. But even the conservative branches of the Benedictine order in

---

[7] Grave inscriptions of lectors in the 4th and
5th centuries with mention of the titular
church to which they were attached (among
them the churches of Eusebius, Fasciola,
Pudentiana, Velabrum) in E. Diehl, *Lateinische altchristliche Inschriften*, II (Kleine
Texte, 26-28; Bonn, 1913), 8 f. In the
country the services of the lector continued
longer; see Synod of Vaison (529), can. 1
(Mansi, VIII, 726). Cf. W. Croce, "Die
niederen Weihen und ihre hierarchische
Wertung," ZkTh (1948), 269 f., 282.

[8] In contradistinction to the deacons, subdeacons, notaries and defensors, and (on
the other hand) like the lectors, the acolytes were assigned to a certain titular
church; in fact in the time of St. Gregory
they became real "assistant clergy"; B.
Fischer, "Der niedere Klerus bei Gregor
dem Grossen," ZkTh (1938), 64. Cf. Diehl,
p. 10 f.: Acolytes of Vestina, Clemens,
Capua.

[9] In the Ordo of St. Amand (Duchesne,
Christian Worship, 477) it is said that at

the first Mass which the newly-ordained
priest celebrates in his titular church (with
the privilege of having his seat next to the
altar and of intoning the *Gloria*) the Gospel
is read by the *paranimfus presbyter*.

[10] Thus also Mabillon, *In ordinem Rom.*,
c. 4 (PL, LXXVIII, 866); Eisenhofer,
II, 9.

For Masses for the Dead no chants
were provided even in the 9th century;
see *infra*, p. 219, note 48.

That they could be missing in other instances too is indicated by the 11th century
order for the sick in the Pontifical of Narbonne: Martène, 1, 7, XIII (I, 892); it
does contain the fore-Mass and the Communion section, but without the chants.

[11] There is at least a recollection of this in
John of Avranches, *De off. eccl.* (PL,
CXLVII, 32 C): of the two acolytes who
are presumed for the High Mass it says:
*unus qui cantet Graduale et deferat cande-
labrum, alter qui Alleluia et ferat thuribulum*. Similarly in Rouen as late as 1651
(PL, CXLVII, 73 D).

the eleventh century had a conventual Mass in which the basic type of the presbyter Mass can be recognized. The liturgy of the Carthusians, for example, does not even today have a subdeacon as a special functionary; only the deacon assists the priest. For the singing of the Epistle a monk especially appointed steps out of the choir.[12] A similar usage occurred, and occurs even nowadays, amongst the Cistercians, at least for the ferial rite of the conventual Mass[13] and perhaps elsewhere too.[14]

This same manner of celebrating Mass was the only one possible in country churches and in churches on large estates. But that Mass was actually performed in this way, and especially that a cleric served at it—of these things the traces in the older sources are not very clear; there are traces, however. The ninth century *Admonitio synodalis*[15] orders: *Omnis presbyter clericum habeat vel scolarem, qui epistolam vel lectionem legat et ei ad missam respondeat, et cum quo psalmos cantet.*[16] Plainly what is meant here in the first place is the parochial service, a Mass celebrated with chant. The word *respondeat* seems to suppose that even in parish churches the people no longer themselves gave the answers in a loud voice. Besides, of course, no such responses were needed as yet at the prayers at the foot of the altar, although they were probably at the *Orate fratres.*[17] There is express mention of divine service in *parochiis ruralibus* in a Mainz synod of 1310 which censures the abuse of priests celebrating *sine ministri suffragio* because of lack of assistants, *propter defectum clericorum.* Against this custom, the synod legislates that even in rural places the priest should not celebrate without the cooperation of some responsible persons who

---

[12] A. Degand, "Chartreux (Liturgie des)", DACL, III, 1047.

[13] See the chapter "Die Konventmesse cum unico ministro" in Schneider (*Cist. Chr.* [1927]), 298-303; cf. *Liber usuum,* c. 53 (PL, CLXVI, 1423 C): the subdeacon after the Epistle *eat in chorum cantare cum aliis, si necesse fuerit.* Cf. Schneider (*Cist. Chr.* [1926]), 316. Something similar is also found in the *Ordinarium O.P.* of 1256, where both *ministri* are expected to help the choir *maxime in parvis conventibus* (Guerrini, 237). This was also the rule amongst the Benedictines of the Bursfeld Union; Schneider, *loc. cit.*

In the Cistercian rite on feast-days a special *subminister* (in addition to deacon and subdeacon) served at the altar for certain duties, coming up to the altar as occasion demanded; R. Trilhe, "Citeaux," DACL, III, 1792.

[14] Cf. John of Avranches, *De off. eccl.* (PL, CXLVII, 33 f.), where there is a similar direction: *subdiaconus vero, excepto tempore ministrationis suæ, in choro maneat.*

In this instance, however, the ministrations of the subdeacon are more in demand.

[15] Also called Homilia Leonis, with reference to Leo IV (d. 855). On its diffusion see P. Browe, ZkTh, LVI (1932), 389, note 60; cf. H. Leclercq, DACL, VI, 576-579.

[16] PL, CXXXII, 456 B; cf. 96, 1376 C.

A similarly worded injunction is ascribed to the Council of Nantes (9th century): Mansi, XVIII, 173 f.

[17] The requirement of the *Admonitio* indicates at the same time how during the Middle Ages recruits were trained for the clerical state. Express mention is made of this at the Council of Vaison (529), can. 1 (Mansi, VIII, 726 f.) which requires the parish priest to keep and instruct *iuniores lectores.* See also Anton De Waal, "Liturgical Chant in Early Christian Rome," *The American Ecclesiastical Review,* LXVI (1922), 465 ff., esp. 468-471. For a later period cf. R. Stachnik, *Die Bildung des Klerus im Frankenreiche* (Paderborn, 1926), esp. 56 f.

could read and sing.[18] Here, in case of necessity, the assistance of a capable layman is declared sufficient, but even the present-day missal considers it quite normal that, at a Mass celebration without sacred ministers, *aliquis lector superpelliceo indutus* should read the Epistle.[19]

So the *missa cantata*, which in most dioceses today is the predominant form of parish service, is seen to be the unbroken continuation of the presbyter Mass of Christian antiquity.

It, too, has been subjected to the trend of borrowing as much as possible from the episcopal service. For one thing, since the sacramentaries intended for the episcopal service were generally also standard for the titular churches, the opening rite of *Kyrie* and oration before the readings must have become customary in the presbyter Mass even in Christian antiquity. Soon, too, at a very early period the antiphonal chants were included,[20] but this can only mean that the texts were spoken by the priest, since any musical performance—if the priest himself did not undertake it[21]—was in most instances impossible[22] and even today is still in most instances impossible.[23] And also during these centuries of the Middle Ages the presbyter Mass must have shared in the whole development of the Mass-liturgy: the inclusion of the *Gloria, Credo, Agnus Dei,* the silent prayers, the incensing, and finally the *pax*-usages. It could really not be otherwise, because Church law demanded that all churches conform, in the

---

[18] Mansi, XXV, 312.

A similar decree at the Synod of Cologne held that same year, can. 17 (Mansi, XXV, 23): use may be made only of *litterati qui in defectu respondentis ad altare cum camisiis lineis assistant.*

[19] *Rit. serv.,* VI, 8.

Several synods at the end of the 16th century that still made more or less stringent demands for the use of a cleric as server even at private Mass are cited by R. Saponaro, "Estne munus in missa privata ministrandi, clericorum proprium?" *Periodica,* XXVIII (1939), esp. 380 f.

[20] *Supra,* p. 105.

[21] In many places the practice must have developed of the priest himself singing these pieces at the altar. P. Wagner, *Einführung,* I, 194, note 1, speaks of "numerous manuscripts" which contained, beside the sacramentary text with the priestly orations, also these chants with their melodies noted. As a matter of fact, examples of this sort from the 11th to the 13th century have been catalogued, e.g., by Ebner, 134, 268, 270, 278; Köck, 3. References to extra-Italian sources in Ebner, 361 f. An example where only the Wedding Mass has the neums, *ibid.,* 48.

[22] Toward the end of the Middle Ages a method of simplifying matters had gained ground, namely the introduction of votive Masses even on Sundays, their melodies growing familiar by constant recurrence. The Synod of Mainz, 1549 (c. 61; Hartzheim, VI, 579) did not want to cross those *qui peculiaria singularum dominicarum officia propter cantorum, paucitatem observare non valentes, officia, de Trinitate et de Spiritu Sancto, aut, quod decentissimum erat, de Domini resurrectione.diebus dominicis servaverint.* Cf. Franz, 151.

For the same reason, many churches today, both in the country and in the city, resort to week-day Requiem Masses, day in and day out, since the tunes are simple and there is further no worry about *Gloria* or *Credo.*

[23] Since recent decrees of the Congregation of Rites expressly demand that all the prescribed texts be sung at a *missa cantata,* recourse has been had of late to substitutes in place of the lengthy planesong melodies, either a Psalmodic formula or some sort of recitation. Cf. F.A. Brunner, *Cæcilia,* LXXV (1947-8), 106 and LXXVI (1948-9), 72.

institutiones missarum, to the pattern of the cathedral or the metropolitan church.[24]

Even the more solemn ceremonies of these latter were copied by the smaller churches; especially in the later Middle Ages the services in the larger parishes were very similar to those in the chapter churches. The common choir prayer of the clergy was combined with the repeated celebration of public Mass.[25] Of these a daily *summum officium* was distinguished, a Mass like the *missa maior* of the chapters, marking the climax of the morning service and capable of many varying degrees, reaching a high-point in a solemn Mass with deacon and subdeacon and an introductory procession of the clergy carrying relics of the saints.[26] Taking over polyphonic music in city and country churches was the last step in this development.

5. From Domestic Eucharist to Private Mass

Even though in the early days of the Church it was a fundamental principle that the Eucharist was to be celebrated only for the sake of the faithful and not as a personal devotion of one endowed with the powers

---

[24] *Supra*, p. 98.

[25] The parochial clergy were also expected to conduct the canonical hours publicly; this was insisted upon, e.g., by the Synod of Trier (1238), can. 30 (Hartzheim, III, 560) : *In parochialibus ecclesiis pulsentur [et cantentur] horæ canonicæ*. (The bracketed words are uncertain.)

A prescript issued at Rouen in 1245 enacted *quod quilibet sacerdos in parochia sua seu capellanus in capella sua dicat matutinas de nocte et omnes horas horis competentibus, vid. Primam mane, post Tertiam missam, et post Sextam et Nonam, et pulset horis debitis ad quamlibet horam.* A. Roskovány, *Coelibatus et Breviarium* (Budapest, 1861), V, 62.

The parish priest who was alone could not sing the hours himself at the proper time, but he had to see to it that his "scholars" did; *Decretales Gregor. III*, 41, 1 (Friedberg, II, 635).

A gesture in the same direction was already to be found in an early capitulary (801) : The parish priests are to train their *scholarii* to be able to perform in their stead the hours of Terce, Sext, None and Vespers when necessary (MGH, Ch. I, 238). Likewise in a letter of Alcuin to

Arno in 799 (MGH, Ep. Carol. 9 Aevi, II, 278) and in Regino, *De synod. causis*, I, 208 (PL, CXXXII, 229). Further traces, some of them older, in H. Leclercq, "Gallicane (Liturgie) : XIV. Paroisses rurales," DACL, VI, 561 f.; cf. among others the Synod of Tarragona (516), can. 7 (Mansi, VIII, 542 D). Even in the 18th century Matins, Lauds and Vespers were often considered part of the Sunday parochial services; see E. Hegel, "Liturgie und Seelsorge in der Zeit der Aufklärung," *Theologie u. Glaube* (1943), 105.

[26] Greving, *Johann Ecks Pfarrbuch*, 78 ff.; Goetz, *Das Pfarrbuch des Stephan May*, 27 (where other references are given).

By *summum officium* (Greving, 79; Goetz, 27) is meant only the main service of the day. Cf. also *summa missa* in *Liber ordinarius* of Essen (Arens, 1 ff., 136). Even today, as I am given to understand, the chief Sunday service is still called *summa* in Lithuania. If the word "High Mass" (German: *Hochamt*) is taken as more or less the equivalent, this would explain why in ordinary parlance the word is used to refer not to a *solemn* Mass but to an ordinary *sung* Mass, a *missa cantata* without deacon or subdeacon.

of priesthood, still it was not seldom the case in this era when "they broke bread in this house or that" (Acts 2 : 20), that only a small domestic group gathered around the holy table. This domestic celebration of the Eucharist in the primitive Church was the forerunner of its later celebration in more or less private circles, and finally also of the private Mass. Aside from the texts of the *Didache* which have always been taken in this sense,[1] other unmistakable evidences of this usage are to be traced, all of them also of the second century. In the various apocryphal histories of the Apostles we find, along with many vulgar and heretical additions, indubitable testimonies regarding the ecclesiastical customs in this matter, an array of examples where the legends picture the Apostles as "breaking bread" before a small group, of "giving thanks" over bread and wine in the presence of only a few participants.[2] Tertullian includes in his account of the era of persecution the celebration of the *dominica sollemnia* at which only three persons were present.[3] In Cyprian, too, there is mention not only of a morning Mass in the presence of the congregation, but also of an evening Eucharist for a small circle.[4] Basil speaks of priests who, because of a fault, are permitted to perform their priestly office only in private homes.[5] Gregory of Nazianzen cites the eucharistic celebration in his sister's home.[6] However, in the Orient in the fourth century, the Synod of Laodicea issued a general prohibition against such celebrations of the Eucharist.[7] In other

---

[1] *Supra*, p. 13, Note 28.

[2] The passages in question in Quasten, *Mon.*, 339-345.

[3] Tertullian, *De fuga*, c. 14 (PL, II, 142 A). Further reports about Mass in the era of persecution, when the Christians celebrated the mysteries *qualiter poterant et ubi poterant*, as Victor of Vita put it, *Historia persec. Afric.*, I, 18 (CSEL, VII, 9), are gathered in Martène, 1, 3, 5 (I, 299 ff.).

[4] Cyprian, *Ep.*, 63, 16 (CSEL, III, 714) : *cum cœnamus ad convivium nostrum plebem convocare non possumus, ut sacramenti veritatem fraternitate omni præsente celebremus.* For an interpretation of the passage see Zimmermann, *Die Abendmesse*, 58-62; E. Dekkers, "L'Eglise ancienne a-t-elle connu la Messe de soir?" (Miscellanea Mohlberg, I, 231-257), 246-249. To this celebration of Mass with a small group must be referred the remark of St. Cyprian, *Ep.*, 57, 3 (CSEL, III, 652), about the daily Mass: *sacerdotes, qui sacrificia Dei cotidie celebramus.* Of his testimony regarding the celebration of Mass in the prisoners' cells mention was already made, *supra*, 208. Cf. Augustine, *Breviculum coll., III, 17, 23*

(PL, XLIII, 644). Here also we must insert the Mass of Lucian of Antioch (d. 312) who, while lying in prison, spoke the wonted prayers with the σύμβολα τῆς ἱερουργίας on his breast; see Philostorgius, *Vita*, ed. Bidez, c. 14 (GCS, Philostorgius, 196; cf. *ibid.*, 25).

[5] Basil, *Ep.*, 199 (PG, XXXII, 716 f.).

[6] Gregory of Nazianzen, *Or.*, 8 (al. 11), 18 (PG, XXXV, 809). On the other hand what Gregory relates regarding his ailing father was hardly a real eucharistic celebration; *Or.*, 18, 29 (PG, XXXV, 1020 f.; cf. *ibid.*, 983-986).

[7] Can. 58 (Mansi, II, 574) : Ὅτι οὐ δεῖ ἐν τοῖς οἴκοις προσφορὰς γίνεσθαι παρὰ ἐπισκόπων ἢ πρεσβυτέρων. A similar proscription was issued by the synod of Seleucia-Ktesiphon (410), can. 13 (O. Braun, *Das Buch der Synhados* [Stuttgart, 1900], 21) : The sacrifice is not to be performed in houses. Baumstark, *Vom geschichtlichen Werden*, 8, connects this prohibition with the cessation of the persecutions first in Rome and then in Persian territory. Nestorius, too, while patriarch of Constantinople (428-431) had reprimanded one of his priests for celebrating Mass in

places it is simply required that for this the bishop's permission be asked; this was the case in the Byzantine area,[8] where in the ninth/tenth centuries every family in easy circumstances had its house chapel, which was used especially for memorial Masses for the Dead.[9]

At an earlier date in North Africa the second Synod of Carthage (about 390) was content to demand an episcopal permission.[10] This fits in with what Augustine has to tell about one of his priests who was once called to the country estate of a former Roman officer, Hesperius. Here the slaves and cattle were suffering from demoniacal molestations, but the priest offered up the sacrifice of Christ's Body, and the molestations ceased.[11]

In Rome, too, the house Mass was not unusual. Here in many places since the beginning of the third century there were domestic oratories dedicated to the memory of certain martyrs.[12] It might have been in one such oratory that St. Ambrose, at the invitation of a prominent Roman lady, once offered up the sacrifice.[13] It is told of Melania the Younger that she had Mass said daily by her chaplain Gerontius, at her cloister-like home on the precipice of the Mount of Olives, "as was the custom of the Church of Rome."[14] Paulinus of Nola, as we saw above, offered up the holy sacrifice with the visiting bishops in his own sick-room.[15] Gregory the Great admonishes the Bishop of Syracuse to allow Mass to be celebrated in the house of a certain Venantius.[16]

In Frankish territory and later on generally throughout the northern lands, where the manorial estates of the nobles were scattered wide over the country, the house chapels, with their Masses celebrated by the house chaplain or manor priest *(Burgpfaffe)*, became permanent institutions. But it was not easy to legislate against the abuses, which could hardly be

a home, but received the reply from his clergy that it was here a common practice (Hardouin, I, 1322).

[8] Trullanum (692), can. 31 (Mansi, XI, 956).

[9] This is testified in an enactment of Emperor Leo the Philosopher (886-911) who simply declares domestic Masses are allowed (PG, CVII, 432). Cf. Hardouin, II, 16-19.

[10] Can. 9 (Mansi, III, 695).

[11] Augustine, *De civ. Dei*, 22, 8 (CSEL, 40, II, p. 602). As the context makes plain, there was as yet no church in the place.

[12] J. P. Kirsch, "I sanctuari domestici di martiri," *Rendiconti della Accademia Romana di Archeologia* (1924), II, 27-43; cf. JL, V (1925), 246.

H. Grisar, *Geschichte Roms und der Päpste* (Freiburg, 1901), 168-170.

[13] Paulinus, *Vita Ambrosii*, c. 10 (PL, XIV, 20): *cum trans Tiberim apud clarissimam quamdam invitatus sacrificium offerret*.

[14] In R. Raabe, *Petrus der Iberer. Ein Charakterbild zur Kirchen- und Sittengeschichte des 5. Jh.* (Leipzig, 1895), 36. From this we must distinguish the Eucharistic service which Melania caused to be celebrated for her whole convent community every Friday and Sunday and on feasts; *Vita* of St. Melania, c. 48 (M. Card. Rampolla, *Santa Melania giuniore* [Rome, 1905] 27, 68).

[15] *Supra*, p. 198 f.

[16] Gregory the Great, *Ep.* VI, 43 f. (PL, LXXVII, 831 f.).

avoided under the circumstances.[17] At first, stress was laid on the obligation of attending the bishop's church or the parish church on all higher feasts,[18] but later on this was reduced to just the feast of Easter.[19] The Carolingian reform sought to reaffirm the canon of Laodicea forbidding all divine service in the home, but eventually had to tolerate a practice less strict.[20] A capitulary of Haito of Basel (807-827) permitted Mass to be said in the homes of the sick.[21] But finally, after much hesitation and change of policy in medieval legislation, the Council of Trent forbade Mass in private dwellings.[22]

From these Masses said in private homes, on an estate or at a graveside where at least a group of people, however small, attends the service, we must carefully distinguish the *private* Mass strictly so called. This we understand as a Mass celebrated for its own sake, with no thought of anyone participating, a Mass where only the prescribed server is in attendance, or even where no one is present, as was once the case in the so-called *Missa solitaria*. These are the Masses—contrasted to the conventual Mass and the parochial Mass—which are most generally referred to in medieval documents as *missæ privatæ* or *speciales* or *peculiares.*[23]

---

[17] Archbp. Agobard of Lyons (d. 840), *De privil. et iure sacerd.*, c. 11 (PL, CIV, 138) complained that there was hardly a moneyed man who did not have a palace chaplain whom he then employed sometimes as a table-waiter, sometimes as a stablegroom.

[18] Synod of Agde (506), can. 21 (Mansi, VIII, 328).

[19] IV Synod of Orleans (541), can. 3 (Mansi, IX, 113 f.).

Further indications of the gradual but continued decrease in the demand are outlined in Browe, *Die Pflichtkommunion im Mittelater*, 48.

The Missal of Bobbio (Muratori, II, 916) contains a special formulary: *missa in domo cuiuslibet.*

[20] Evidence supplied in Browe, *Die Pflichtkommunion*, 47 f. The reform Synod of Pavia (850) desired only that the priests in question be approved by the bishop, and even lauded regular domestic worship; can. 18 (Mansi, XIV, 936 f.).

[21] N. 14; MGH, Ch. I, 364.

In England this permission was still retained in law collections around the year 1000, e.g., in that of King Edgar (967), can. 30 (Hardouin, VI, 662 B), but otherwise it was soon restricted to bishops and

abbots. Still even as late as the 16th century there are individual instances of a general permission for Mass in the sickroom; P. Browe, "Die Sterbekommunion im Altertum und Mittelalter," ZkTh (1930), 26-30. Cf. *ibid.*, 27, for references to liturgical books (like the older Gelasian, III, 69) which contain a special Mass *super infirmum in domo.* There is such a formulary in the Sacramentary of Moissac, 11th century; Martène, 1, 7, XI (I, 879 f.); this contains texts also for the proper chants and for the readings, as well as a special *Hanc igitur: H. i. oblationem, Domine, famuli tui ill. in hac domo consistentis.*

[22] Sess. XXII, *Decretum de observ. et evit. in celebr. missæ.*

The result of further evolution in the law is to be found today in canons 1188-1196 of the official *Cod. Iur. Canon.;* service is much restricted in private chapels, but is accorded in semi-public oratories and public chapels.

[23] G. Schreiber, "Mittelalterliche Segnungen und Abgaben," *Zeitschrift d. Savigny-Stiftung, kan. Abt.* (1943), 243.

Regarding the various concepts of *missa privata* to be discovered later in the controversies with the Reformers, cf. Bene-

Without doubt there is no intrinsic contradiction in such a performance of the Christian sacrifice. Apart from any consideration of parallels outside revealed religion, the very first sacrifice cited in Holy Writ is one which two individuals, Abel and Cain, offered up, each by himself. Further, in the levitical cult the possibility was not excluded that at a sacrifice requested by someone absent, the priestly officiant alone should be present.[24] Both cases are conceivable also in the New Covenant, all the more when the consciousness grew that in the Eucharist all the sacrifices of former times find their fulfillment and consummation,[25] even those which the individual was wont to offer up or to have offered up. In other words, the sacrifice of the New Testament was not only a Eucharist of the redeemed community, but an oblation which one could present as a prayer or as an expiation in certain difficulties.[26] In this sense the Council of Trent defined the propitiatory character of the Mass sacrifice.[27] Since a public celebration at which the congregation assembled was at first provided only on Sundays and the infrequent feast-days, it was quite easy to assume that a bishop or priest might, on one of the other days, offer up the sacrifice in his own name, urged on by personal gratitude and petition. He could then say Mass at his own home in much the same way as he would say it elsewhere when asked to do so.

Evidences of such Masses survive from at least the sixth century. Gregory the Great says that Cassius, Bishop of Narni, was accustomed to offer God the holy sacrifice every day.[28] John the Almoner (d. 620) reprimands the people who were less zealous, saying that he could just as well have offered Mass at home for himself as in the public Church.[29]

Personal devotion must likewise have induced the individual priest-monks to say private Masses in their monasteries. Although St. Benedict himself showed no inclination to countenance having a number of priests in his convents,[30] St. Gregory the Great already appears to favor the ordi-

dict XIV, De s. sacrificio missæ, III, 22, 7 (Schneider, 257 f.).

But Eisenhofer's notion, II, 10, that the essence of private Mass consists in the absence of levites and singers and in the fact that the prayers are not spoken in a singing tone, is to be discounted, for these are merely secondary features which result from its private character. Cf. W. H. Freestone, The Sacrament Reserved (London, 1917), 24-31.

[24] Here we must cite the sacrifice which Judas Maccabæus had offered in Jerusalem for the slain, 2 Macc., 12:43.

[25] Cf. the appeal to Mal. 1:11 in the Didache, 14, 3.

[26] Cf. the growing prominence of the designations oblatio, sacrificium, etc.; supra, p.

170. The link between certain Votive Masses and various sacrifices of the Old Law was already exploited by Amalar, De eccl. off. III, 19 (PL, CV, 1127). Cf. Franz, Die Messe, 117 f.

[27] Sess. XXII, c. 2; can. 3 (Schröder, 146, 149).

[28] Gregory the Great, Dial., IV, 56 (PL, LXXVII, 421).

In Ev. II, hom. 37, 9 (PL, LXXVI, 1281 A) Gregory remarks that shortly before his death Cassius had celebrated Mass in his house-chapel (in episcopii oratorio); the previous references must therefore have likewise concerned this oratory.

[29] Leontius, Vita, c. 41 (PL, LXXIII, 375 f.).

[30] St. Benedict, Regula, c. 60.

nation of monks, and the Roman Synod of 610 under Boniface IV, which approved the ordaining of monks, seems to have marked the turning-point.[31] From that time on, the number of priests in monasteries begins to grow.[32] Even if this did not itself give the first impetus to the desire for personal celebration, the latter did soon follow more or less frequently.[33] An indication of this is the increase in the number of altars in the monasteries; at first they are erected, one apiece in all the oratories of the monastery,[34] later on they are all brought together in the main church as side-altars.[35] In eighth-century accounts of the lives of various holy monks mention is made time after time of their celebrating Mass almost daily,[36] and in the ninth century this is already accepted as a permanent rule.[37]

The personal devotion of the celebrant was not, however, whether in the monasteries or elsewhere, the only source of this increase in private Mass, nor was it even the strongest source. Stronger by far was the desire of the faithful for Votive Masses; that is to say, for Masses which took care of their earnest concerns (vota), not the least important of which was regard for the dead.[38] The domestic celebration of the Eucharist had also in great measure served such interests. And as these Masses which were devoted to special interests were detached from the domestic congregation and were transferred to the oratories connected with the church or monastery, the occasions when the priest stood at the altar alone were multiplied. Thus from this angle too, impetus was given the private Mass.

A great importance attached even in ancient times to the Mass for the Dead. As early as 170 there is evidence from the apocryphal Acts of St. John that in Asia Minor a eucharistic memorial for the dead was conducted on the third day after burial[39]; this took place at the grave. The anniversary

---

[31] Mansi, X, 504 f. Also in Decretum Gratiani, II, 16, q. 1, c. 25 (Friedberg, I, 767).

[32] A larger number of priest-monks must be presupposed for the missions in England and Germany; statistical data in Berlière, L'ascèse bénédictine, 40.

[33] In the legendary life of the Irish St. Brendan (d. circa 576) it is recounted that he and his companions had often read Mass on week-days; C. Plummer, Vitæ Sanctorum Hiberniæ, (Oxford, 1901), I, 133.

[34] Bede, Hist. gent. Angl., IV, 14 (PL, XCV, 195), relates that after an epidemic had subsided, Mass was said in thanksgiving in all the oratories of the monastery. Further references in Bona, I, 14, 1 (191).

[35] Benedict of Aniane gave four altars to the church of the Saviour which he had built in 782. The monastery church of Centula, which was finished in 798, has

eleven altars. In the plans drawn up in 820 for the reconstruction of the monastery church at St. Gall seventeen altars were projected. Braun, Der christliche Altar, I, 372, 389.

[36] Berlière, L'ascèse bénédictine, 40, with references to Boniface, Ceolfrid and Winnebald.

[37] Abbot Angilbert of Centula (d. 814) laid down the injunction that, besides the two conventual Masses, there should be said daily at the various altars at least 30 other Masses; Hariulfus, Chron. Cent., II, 7 (PL, CLXXIV, 1250).

[38] The expression missa votiva is already found in the Bobbio Missal (Muratori, II, 911-914) but it seems to be taken in a much narrower sense than here.

[39] Acta Johannis, c. 85 f. (Acta ap. apocr., ed. Lipsius-Bonnet, II, 1, p. 193). Cf. Dölger, Ichthys, II, 555-569.

commemoration is no more recent.[40] In the fourth century the commemoration on the seventh day and on the thirtieth day became known; elsewhere it is the ninth day and the fortieth day that are observed. All of these fixed days for the memorial of the dead, along with the ritual solemnization of the day of burial,[41] derive from pre-Christian tradition,[42] with the celebration of the Eucharist taking the place of ancient sacrifice for the dead and sometimes perhaps of the *refrigerium* too.[43]

It was precisely this *refrigerium* or memorial meal, eaten at the graveside of a deceased person, probably without reference to any particular day, and attested in the third/fourth century even for the burial sites of the Apostles Peter and Paul, that could be replaced by Mass when the Church began to take an adverse stand because of abuses that crept in— Mass in the sense of Votive Masses at the graves of Apostles and martyrs,[44] and intercessory Masses for the Dead at the graves of relations.

About the turn of the sixth century it was not unusual for a priest to read Mass for a dead person on a series of days one after the other, with no one participating. This can be deduced from a story of St. Gregory the Great about the priest John, who wanted to give his attendant at the public baths two offering breads, whereupon the latter made himself known as a soul doing penance and asked the priest rather to offer up the sacrifice for him, which the priest John therefore did daily for a whole week.[45] Towards the end of the seventh century there developed various prayer confraternities pledged to offer suffrages from church to church and monastery to monastery, and especially a number of Masses for the Dead. At the Synod of Attigny (762) the attending bishops and abbots bound themselves to say, among other things, a hundred Masses for each of the group who would die.[46] A cooperative agreement entered into in 800 between St. Gall and Reichenau stipulated, *inter alia*, that for each deceased monk every

---

[40] The congregation at Smyrna makes mention in 155-156 of its purpose to hold an annual memorial service for Polycarp; *Martyrium Polycarpi*, 18, 3.

Tertullian, *De corona mil.*, c. 3 (CSEL, LXX, 158) : *oblationes pro defunctis, pro nataliciis annua die facimus*. Cf. *De monogamia*, c. 10.

Without any time arrangement also *Didascalia*, VI, 22, 2 (Funk, I, 376).

[41] Cyprian, *Ep.*, 1, 2 (CSEL, III, 466 f.).

[42] E. Freistedt, *Altchristliche Totengedächtnistage und ihre Beziehung zum Jenseitsglauben und Totenkultus der Antike* (LQF, XXIV; Münster, [1928]).

[43] A series of studies regarding *refrigerium* (memorial meal for the dead) and related concepts is enumerated and expounded in JL, VIII (1928), 347-353. Cf. also Botte, *Le canon* 68 f. and J. Quasten,

"Vetus superstitio," *Harvard Theol. Review*, XXXIII (1940), 253-266. Other data regarding funerary banquets in C. Zammit, "I triclini funebri nelle catacombe di Malta," *Rivista di Archeologia Christiana*, XVII (1940), 293-297.

[44] In this sense J. P. Kirsch, "Die memoria apostolorum an der Appischen Strasse zu Rom und die liturgische Feier des 29. Juni," JL, III (1923), 33-50, esp. 49 f.

[45] Gregory the Great, *Dial.*, IV, 55 ·(PL, LXXVII, 417). Also *ibid.* (PL, LXXVII 421), the case of the Masses for the deceased monk Justus on 30 consecutive days. In this latter instance there could possibly have been some sort of distribution of the Masses amongst the brethren, but this was not to be thought of in the other case.

[46] A. Ebner, *Die klösterlichen Gebetsbrüderungen* (Regensburg, 1890), 52.

priest was to say three Masses on three successive days after the report of the death was received, and also another Mass on the thirtieth day; at the beginning of each month, after the Office for the dead of the convent, each priest was again to read a Mass; and finally every year on November 14 a general commemoration of the dead was to be held, again with three Masses by each priest.[47] From this time on, private Masses for the Dead is an established arrangement, especially in monasteries.[48]

Votive Masses for other purposes and in favor of individual persons or groups were also initiated in Christian antiquity. About 370 a Roman writer tells of repeated eucharistic celebrations for *peregrini et incolæ*.[49] Augustine pities the ladies and maidens who had fallen into the hands of barbarians because they do not have the eucharistic sacrifice and, in consequence, they themselves can neither take part in the public celebration nor have Mass said for them.[50] The *Leonianum* contains a great number of formularies which obviously have in view the private petitions either of the priest himself or of other offerers: among others are those marked *post*

[47] MGH, *Libri confraternitatum*, ed, Piper, 140. Also in Gerbert, *Vetus liturgia Alemannica*, I, 368 f. Regarding the fraternity at Reichenau see the studies by K. Beyerle in the memorial "Die Kultur der Abtei Reichenau" (Munich, 1925), 291-304; 1107-1217.

[48] Amalar, *De eccl. off.*, IV, 42 (PL, CV, 1239 D) speaks of places where Mass for the Dead takes place daily. But only later did such a daily Mass for the Dead become partially public; see *supra*, p. 205.

As far as ritual was concerned, the Mass for the Dead was at that time not as differentiated from other Masses as is the case nowadays, even aside from the color of the vestments; see Amalar. *De eccl. off.*, III, 44 (PL, CV, 1161): *Missa pro mortuis in hoc differt a consueta missa, quod sine Gloria et Alleluia et pacis osculo celebratur.* In pre-Frankish times it was distinguished above all by the insertion of the Memento of the Dead—otherwise absent—and a suitable *Hanc igitur.* Still there were special orations for the dead even in the Leonianum (Muratori, I, 451-454) and in the older Gelasianum, III, 92-105 (*ibid.*, 752-763).

There is an indication of the smallness of the attendance at these more ancient Masses for the Dead—just the circle of mourners—in the fact that in the six oldest Mass-antiphonaries (8th-9th centuries)

published by Hesbert, the chants are wanting. These chants, beginning with *Requiem æternam,* appear first in the antiphonary published by the St. Maur monks (PL, LXXVIII, 722-724). Proper lessons are found, for the Epistle in the *Comes* of Alcuin (ed. Wilmart; *Eph. Liturg.*, 1937, 163 f.), for the Gospel in the index of pericopes for the palace chapel of Charlemagne (Beissel, *Entstehung der Perikopen,* 141), and also in the Gospel-capitulary for the city of Rome, 645 (Klauser, p. 45 f.).

An index to the increasing number of Masses for the Dead in the later Middle Ages is the burgeoning stock of special formularies created for this type of Mass; there is an enumeration of such in B. Opfermann, "Notizen zur Missa defunctorum in der zweiten Hälfte des Mittelalters," *Liturg. Zeitschrift,* IV (1931-2), 167-172.

[49] Ambrosiaster, *Comment. in Tim.,* 3, 12 f. (PL, XVII, 471): *Omni enim hebdomada offerendum est, etiam si non cotidie peregrinis, incolis tamen vel bis in hebdomada.* According to Batiffol, *Leçons,* p. XXI, who discusses this somewhat obscure text, the reference is obviously to private Mass.

[50] Augustine, *Ep.*, 111, 8 (CSEL, XXXIV, 655): *nec istæ possunt vel ferre oblationem ad altare Dei vel invenire ibi sacerdotem per quem offerant Deo.*

infirmitatem[51] and several against the menace of evil tongues.[52] The Votive Masses in the older *Gelasianum* are fully developed; they form the main contents of the third of the three books of which the sacramentary is composed.[53] They have reference to private concerns like a journey, unjust threats, sickness, various afflictions, wedding, childlessness, birthday, anniversary of ordination, growth in charity, and we might add the Masses for the Dead; and likewise public concerns like mortality, plague, drought, good weather, war and peace, the welfare of the king, and such. The low state of medicine and hygiene and in general the small knowledge of natural remedies, as well as the widespread uncertainty of legal rights in the early medieval states, to some extent explain the large number of external petitions in these Votive Masses and the strong appeal they had for the people.

Of Gallic Mass books, the Missal of Bobbio is especially rich in Votive Masses, here fitted out with readings.[54]

The high tide for Votive Masses is the Carolingian period. Alcuin himself had not only prepared from older sources an important assortment of Votive Masses for his supplement to the Gregorian Sacramentary,[55] but he had compiled a special collection which has come down to us as a *liber sacramentorum*.[56] Here for the first time we find Masses expressly assigned to certain days of the week, three formularies for each day. Of these, the first is concerned with a particular theme from the Christian economy of salvation appropriated to each day of the week[57]; this section more or less approaches the Proper Masses of the Church year. The second group regards, as a rule, the greater ascetical needs; the formula for Thursday, to instance one case, is headed *pro tentatione cogitationum*. The third group

[51] Muratori, I, 335 f., 339.
[52] Muratori, I, 350 f., 442; cf. *supra*, p. 62.

Also the older Gelasianum, III, 67 (*ibid.*, I, 734; Wilson, 279 f.) contains a Mass *contra obloquentes*. Regarding the Votive Masses in the Leonianum, cf. Franz, 119 ff.
[53] III, 24-106 (Wilson, 245-314).

Some of the MSS. of the later Gelasianum also contain a collection of Votive Masses that accord to a great extent with those mentioned; see the survey in de Puniet, *Le sacramentaire Romain de Gellone*, 272*-307*; 314*-333*, and his commentary, *ibid.*, 95 ff. (=*Eph. liturg.*, LI [1937], 128-135; 278-305; LII [1938], 9-27; resp. LI [1937], 270 ff.). Also G. Manz, *Ein St. Galler Sacramentarfragment* (LQF, XXXI; Münster [1939]), 10-39.
[54] See the analysis in Franz, 126 f.
[55] Muratori, II, 187 ff.; cf. Franz. 132 f.

[56] PL, CI, 445-466.

Cf. Franz, 136-139, wherein the Alcuinian origin is still questioned. But see G. Ellard, "Alcuin and some favored Votive Masses," *Theol. Studies*, I (1940), 37-61.
[57] Sunday: *De Trinitate;* (Monday: *Pro peccatis*) ; Tuesday: *Ad postulandum angelica suffragia;* Wednesday: *De s. Sapientia;* Thursday: *De Caritate;* Friday: *De s. Cruce;* Saturday, *De s. Maria*.

Regarding later adjustments and additions for the week-days see Franz, 139-145; Eisenhofer, II, 15-17.

A group of six Masses which are patently intended for the several days of the week were a part of the original Sacramentary of St. Gregory the Great; see Mohlberg-Baumstark, 69-71; cf. C. Mohlberg, "Il messale glagolitico di Kiew," *Atti della pont. Accademia romana di archaeologia. Memorie* II (Rome, 1928), 222 f., 311-315.

called the *Missa s. Augustini,* is written in a tone of penitence and plea for pardon.[58] A considerable part of them was composed by Alcuin himself.[59] from this time on, the Mass books contain a superabundance of Votive Masses. In the Sacramentary of Fulda there are more than a hundred.[60]

In many cases the very topic theme or subject of the prayers shows that the celebrant alone was busy with the sacrifice. Typical in this regard is the formula of a *missa quam sacerdos pro semetipso debet canere*[61]; Masses of this sort appear already in the Missal of Bobbio[62] around 700 and after that with ever-increasing regularity in the Mass books of the Gallo-Carolingian area,[63] sometimes in several variant forms.[64] These formularies concentrate exclusively on the celebrant's own salvation and therefore all prayers—orations, preface and *Hanc igitur*—are written in the singular.[65] But Masses for the concerns of others also begin to be contrived in such a fashion that the presence of the faithful would be at most incidental. This must have been the case when, in some monasteries, a *missa quotidiana pro rege* became usual[66] or when synods of the tenth and eleventh centuries bound priests, on short notice, to ten or thirty Masses for king and kingdom.[67]

The ninth century is the time in which the celebration of Mass takes on an increase. Many celebrate two or three times a day,[68] and the report is circulated—as an encouragement and comfort—that Pope Leo III occa-

---

[58] Cf. the seven *missæ generales* in the Sacramentary of St. Thierry (10th century); Martène, 1, 4, X (I, 552-562).

[59] On the basis of his analysis of the sources, Ellard, *op. cit.,* 53, designates the following as "Masses that show no borrowings" because for them Alcuin appears to have been indebted to no extant sources: *De gratia S. Spiritus, Pro tentatione cogitationum, De Sapientia, Missa cotidiana sanctorum, Pro inimicis, Pro salute, S. Maria in Sabbato.* The majority of the others are taken, in whole or in part, from Mozarabic Mass books.

[60] Richter-Schönfelder, 202-329.

[61] Thus in an appendix (written before 850) to the Cod. 348 of St. Gall: Mohlberg, *Das fränkische Sacramentarium Gelasianum,* 249-252 (cf. *ibid.,* pp. LIV f., XCIX).

In the older Gelasianum, too, a formulary of this sort was inserted about 830 after III, 37 (Wilson, 254); see A. Wilmart, *Revue Bénéd.,* L (1938), 324-328.

[62] Muratori, II, 905-907.

[63] Text of the St. Gall Mass mentioned, with further sources and variants in Manz, *Ein St. Galler Sacramentarfragment,* 32-37; cf. 58.

For further ties with the general his-

tory of liturgy, see Baumstark, *Vom geschichtlichen Werden,* 116.

[64] The Sacramentary of Fulda (Richter-Schönfelder, 248-257) contains not one but eleven formularies of a Mass for the celebrating priest *(missa sacerdotis propria).*

[65] The formulas in the present Missale Romanum, *Pro seipso sacerdote*—No. 20 among the *Orationes diversæ* in the appendix—derive from a formulary of this type. It must be remarked that the singular is not altogether unheard of even in Masses of more ancient origin and public in character. Thus the formularies *In natali episcoporum* in the Leonianum (Muratori, I, 425 ff.) contain several phrases in the singular, but they are carefully adapted to the temper of a community celebration; e.g., *Hanc igitur oblationem quam tibi offero ego tuus famulus et sacerdos pro eo quod me . . . tribuisti sacerdotalem subire famulatum . . . Qua[m] oblatione[m] totius mecum gratulantis Ecclesiæ tu Deus . . .*

[66] Alcuinian appendix: Muratori, II, 188. Cf. Biehl, *Das liturgische Gebet für Kaiser und Reich,* 78, 150.

[67] Biehl, 78.

[68] Cf. *supra,* p. 218.

sionally offered the sacrifice seven and nine times in a day.[69] Daily celebration by each individual priest seems to have become at this time if not (by far) the general rule, at least the prevailing one. On Sundays and feasts it is said for the congregation, just as even today the *applicatio pro populo* is demanded of the pastor on these days. On weekdays it seems to have been, by and large, a Votive Mass for his own intention or that of others, even though the formulary chosen is one specified for the day,[70] as later on this was actually demanded.[71] This meant a momentous augment in the frequency of celebration. The appropriation of the sacrifice to the diverse concerns of the faithful had really aroused the desire of the faithful and so led to a multiplication of the celebration. This is made manifest in the fact that everywhere that a number of priests were together—not only in monasteries, that is, but also in cathedral churches and in the larger centers—altars started to increase in number. In the whole of Christian antiquity every church had possessed but one altar. In North Africa this continued so till the fall of Christianity in the seventh century,[72] and in the Orient, at least in churches of the Byzantine rite, it is still the rule.[73] At Rome about the sixth century, oratories in honor of the Apostles and

---

[69] Walafrid Strabo, *De exord, et increm.*, c. 21 (PL, CXIV, 943) ; Honorius Augustod., *Gemma an.*, I, 114 (PL, CLXXII, 582).

[70] At least for the circumstances of the city of Rome in the first millenary it can be said that public Mass, with the use of the corresponding formularies, was customary only on the days outlined in the *Proprium de tempore* and also, as a rule, on the days indicated in the *Proprium sanctorum* but then only at the respective shrines. All other days were therefore free for Votive Masses. That votive formularies and freely-chosen saints' formularies were preponderantly used for private Masses also in the northern lands can be gathered from the fact that at first the lessons and later even the chant texts were added to the formularies; see *supra*, p. 105. This preponderance continued all through the Middle Ages; cf. Franz, 149-154. And it was still the case in the sixteenth century. St. Ignatius, for instance, marked down what Mass he chose on 64 days in the year 1544; of these 41 were votive formularies, and only 23 were the Masses for the day; Jedin, *Liturg. Leben*, 1939, 64, quoting the saints' spiritual diary: *Constitutiones S.J.*, (Rome, 1934), I, 86-130. Even for Sundays a special Votive Mass, usually that of the Trinity, was prescribed in the weekly

series of formularies—and was often used; cf. *supra*, p. 211, note 22; *Franz*, 149-151. Not till the Missal of Pius V was the Sunday left open. The only controversy raged for a time around Masses for the Dead—whether it was right to say them on Sundays, as many did; ranged in opposition were, among others, the Arch-chanter John (Silva-Tarouca, 205) ; Theodulf of Orleans, *Capitulare*, I, c. 45, (PL, CV, 208) ; the *Consuetudines* of Farfa (Albers, I, 202).

[71] Synod of Würzburg (1298), can. 3 (Hartzheim, IV, 25 f.).

The Synod of Seligenstadt (1002), can. 10 (*ibid.*, III, 56) had merely warned against a superstitious preference for certain Votive Masses (Trinity, Michael), suggesting that the Mass *de eodem die* be used instead, and he added: *vel pro salute vivorum vel pro defunctis.* Cf. Franz, 150 f.

[72] Braun, *Der christliche Altar*, I, 373.

[73] Braun, I, 383-385. This single altar is appointed for public service. For the non-public celebration of the liturgy on week days there are often extra oratories or chapels (παρεκκλησίαι), more or less loosely connected with the main church. See Bona, I, 14, 3 (196) ; Salaville, *Eastern Liturgies*, 114.

martyrs, along with the altars pertaining to them—hitherto scattered all over the city—were erected inside the churches. But we come across this increase of altars on a larger scale in Gaul, where Bishop Palladius of Saintes about 590 had thirteen altars constructed in one church.[74] Similar instances are not uncommon after that.

From the ninth century on, side altars are part of the structure of every larger church.[75] A contributing factor was the worship of saints and their relics; it was thought that this could be done best in connection with a special altar. Another factor was the desire on the part of both faithful and priest for Votive Masses for which the path was now free and which could take place inside one's own church. Finally a third element entered in, this one a limitation; it was the practice to celebrate but once each day at any one altar and more especially it was forbidden that a priest should use an altar which had been used by the bishop previously on the same day.[76]

About the era of the Ottos, however, the dark side of this all too frequent celebration began to be remarked. Episcopal and synodal decrees gradually permitted only a triple celebration on any one day. Others even forbade bination outside the case of necessity,[77] as did Alexander II in 1065[78] and Innocent III even more positively in 1206[79]; since then it has continued as the general norm. As a consequence the number of altars in churches newly built since then, shrinks back to more reasonable proportion.[80]

But in the thirteenth century a new increase in private Masses sets in, this time not through the plural celebration of the same priest but rather as the result of the growth of the clergy in larger cities,[81] an element that contributed in no small way to the ecclesiastical crisis of the sixteenth

---

[74] Gregory the Great, *Ep.*, VI, 49 (PL, LXXVII, 834).

[75] Braun, I, 368-373.
Cf. *supra*, note 35.

[76] Braun, I, 373-377.
In this regulation the operative factor was apparently an aversion to any multiplication that ill befitted the greatness of the mystery, and particularly the basic axiom that in any one church the Sunday celebration of the Eucharist should take place but once only. This principle was then transferred to every altar (which originally had its own special chapel).

[77] K. Holböck, *Die Bination. Rechtsgeschichtliche Untersuchung* (Rome, 1941). Eisenhofer, II, 23.

[78] *Decretum Gratiani*, III, 1, 53 (Friedberg, I, 1308).

[79] *Decretales Greg.* III, 41. 3 (Friedberg, II, 636) ; Cf. Holböck, 30.

[80] Braun, I, 377 f.

[81] *Supra*, p. 130. Admonitions to celebrate daily also begin to make their appearance, intended to assure at the same time the worthy disposition of the priest. The writing ascribed to St. Bonaventure, *De præparatione ad missam*—which does not however appear in MSS prior to 1375 (Franz, 462)—has this to say about the priest who without reason fails to celebrate (the words are frequently quoted even today) : *quantum in ipso est, privat Trinitatem laude et gloria, angelos lætitia, peccatores venia* . . . (c. 5; *Opp.*, ed. Peltier, XII [Paris, 1868], 281). In this connection we might also mention Matthew of Cracow (d.1410), *Dialogus inter Rationem et Conscientiam*, and the work of the younger Henry of Hessen (d. 1427), *Exhortatio de celebratione missæ*. Cf. Franz, 515-517.

century. This increase was naturally accompanied by a new increase in the number of altars. Churches with thirty-five to forty-five altars were no rarity. The church of St. Mary at Danzig and the cathedral at Magdeburg each had forty-eight of them around 1500.[82]

Meanwhile church architecture had been successfully endeavoring to fit the side-altars into the building properly, worthily. In France the Romanesque period had already created the circle of chapels surrounding the choir of the church, and in the Gothic period this was taken up also in other countries. In other cases Gothic produced a number of altar niches in the aisle of the nave by making use of the buttresses as part of the inner structure; this solution corresponds to the double row of chapels opening onto either side of the nave, which Baroque architecture employed.[83] But that was hardly enough to supply the demand for side-altars which in the late Middle Ages served as church symbols of the guilds and the richer patrician families. In the age of the ecclesiastical reform, when limitations were again set on private Masses and a greater part of the formularies developed for this purpose were reduced to shrunken existence amongst the *orationes diversæ*, St. Charles Borromeo ordered the removal of all altars which had been built near the organ loft or next to the pulpit, in front of the columns and pillars,[84] and many other churches in the course of time followed his example.

In this swaying back and forth one can trace the problem that the private Mass gives rise to. In its favor is the acknowledgment that the holy sacrifice is an offering of impetation and propitiation, and in this sense has a special value for the anxieties and desires of individuals; as the well-known formula puts it, it is offered for the living and the dead.[85] On the other hand, however, society also has its high worth. The ideal of a single Eucharistia embracing all, once uttered by Ignatius the Martyr, should not be needlessly disowned or enfeebled. We saw how in the monasteries of the early Middle Ages and, in part, even much later the stipulation of worship in common and, on Communion day, of common Communion even for

---

[82] Braun, I, 378-382.

[83] Braun, I, 378, 380.

[84] Braun, I, 383.

[85] The formula occurs in Isidore, *De eccl. off.*, I, 15 (PL, LXXXIII, 752) : the third one of the Mass prayers he distinguishes (in the antique Spanish sacramentaries, *Post nomina*) is said *pro offerentibus sive pro defunctis fidelibus*. The same formulation *pro offerentibus et defunctis*, reappears—this time in reference to the Mass—in the introductory words, "Missa pro multis" which is the title usually given to an *expositio* dependent upon Amalar, ed. *Hanssens (Eph. liturg.* [1930]), 31.

In the 9th century *Ioca* [that is, a game

of cross-questions] *episcopi ad sacerdotes* (printed in Franz, 343) the first question, *Pro quid es presbyter ordinatus?* is answered . . . *hostiam offerre Deo omnipotenti pro salute vivorum ac requie defunctorum*. Cf. also the second question and answer.

In the Romano-German Pontifical written c. 950 the bishop hands the newly-ordained priest a chalice and paten with the words, *Accipite potestatem offerre sacrificium Deo missamque celebrare tam pro vivis quam pro defunctis in nomine Domini* (Hittorp, 95). These words, which occur here for the first time, are still part of the ordination rite, as we all know.

the priests—we saw how this stipulation was safeguarded. For a long time private Mass was not generally required, but only tolerated within certain limits.[86]

Thus a distinct form for the private Mass was evolved only slowly and gradually. In the first period, comprising the eighth and ninth centuries, there was a tendency to force the private character of the celebration even to extremes. At this time the so-called *missa solitaria*, without any server, was formed. The exclusive singular in the prayers of several Mass formulas bears this out.[87] If the ground-plan of the Roman Mass and particularly of the canon had not been regarded by tradition as beyond the reach of change, we would, in the ninth century, surely have experienced in the Roman liturgy what actually almost happened to the Gallic liturgy (which has no fixed canon)[88]; that is, the entire wording would have been rewritten in the "I" manner.

Luckily this result did not really occur. On the contrary, in the ninth century there is some new legislation aimed directly at stopping priests from celebrating alone.[89] For how can a priest say *Dominus vobiscum* or *Sursum corda* when no one else is there?[90] Others refer to *Oremus* or *Orate*

[86] The restrictions were quite various. At Cluny in the 11th century the priests were allowed to celebrate daily, even without special permission, either before Prime or in the interval before and after Terce and also after None. By way of exception it was also permitted after the Gospel of the conventual Mass. *Udalrici Consuet. Clun.*, II, 30 (PL, CXLIX, 724 f.). Similarly also *Bernardi Ordo Clun.* I, 71 (Herrgott, 263).

Among the Cistercians private Masses were allowed during the time devoted to reading and also after the offertory of the conventual Mass. Trilhe, "Citeaux," DACL, III, 1795; Schneider (*Cist.-Chr.* [1927]), 338-342.

Amongst the Sylvestrines the priests were permitted to leave the conventual Mass *incepta Epistola,* unless they were needed for the singing. P. Weissenberger, "Die ältesten Statuta monastica der Silvestriner" (*Röm. Quartalschrift* [1939]), 73.

Elsewhere they were more conservative. Amongst the Carthusians it was still an extraordinary privilege even in the 12th century for anyone to say Mass daily; Peter de Blois (d. c. 1204), *Ep.* 86 (PL, CCVII, 264). On the basis of medieval sources it is related of Klosterneuburg that "whoever wanted to celebrate private Mass

could do so in summer before Terce, in winter after Sext or after the Gospel of the conventual Mass. But to do so the priest had to get permission from the dean." Schabes, 65.

The Synod of Ravenna (1317), rubr. 1? (Mansi, XXV, 611 f.) disapproved of private Masses during a High Mass *(cum missa celebratur in nota),* and desired the presence of all clerics in choir. Similarly the Synod of Trier (1549), can. 9 (Hartzheim, VI, 600) and the Synod of Reims (1583), c. XI, 14 (Hardouin, X, 1284).

[87] *Supra,* p. 221 f.

[88] See, e.g., the Missal of Bobbio (Muratori, II, 905 f.); *Missale mixtum* (PL, LXXXV, 987 ff.). Still in the latter instance the responses of an assistant are stipulated for the prayers of the Ordinary, and in the other instance they are presupposed.

[89] Theodulf of Orleans (d. 821), *Capitulare,* I, c. 7 (PL, CV, 194) : *Sacerdos missam solus nequaquam celebret . . . Esse enim debent qui ei circumstent, quos ille salutet, a quibus et respondeatur.*

Similarly in the canonical collection of Archbishop Rötger of Trier (927), ed. by M. Blasen, c. 10 (*Pastor bonus,* 1941), 67 f.

[90] Synod of Mainz (813), can. 43 (Mansi, XIV, 74).

pro me or to the mention of *circumadstantes*—all of which would be meaningless if no one but the priest were present.[91] More than once the demand is made that, besides the priest, at least *two* persons must be present since he does say: *Dominus vobiscum*.[92] More precisely, mention is made of *ministri*,[93] of *cooperatores*[94] who should be on hand. But the emphasis is not on the function of serving. Walafried Strabo calls it a *legitima missa* if, besides the priest, there are present *respondens, offerens atque communicans*.[95] The minimum required in the case is therefore not so much that someone cooperates at the altar in the capacity of a serving deacon, but rather that someone is present as a co-celebrant,[96] so that the social, plural character which is so distinctly revealed in the liturgy we actually have, and which in some way or other issues from the very essence of the New Testament sacrifice, might be safeguarded. This is the direction taken in all the attempts to vindicate the position assumed; that the *Dominus vobiscum* might be able to be understood as a greeting of all Christendom, with whom the priest knows himself to be conjoined, and so on.[97]

[91] The passages are assembled by J. M. Hanssens, "Fungiturne minister missæ privatæ diaconi et subdiaconi vicibus?" *Eph. liturg.*, XLVIII (1934), 406-412, esp. 410f.

[92] Thus a decree accredited to Pope Soter in the *Decretum Gratiani*, III, 1, 61 (Friedberg, I, 1311) : *nullus presbyterorum missarum sollemnia celebrare præsumat, nisi duobus præsentibus respondentibus ipse tertius habeatur*. The prescription is first found in Burchard of Worms, *Decretum*, III, 74 (PL, CXL, 689) and from then on is repeated by the canonists; see the passages in Hanssens, 411, note 2. The gist of the injunction is reproduced by Bernold of Constance, *Micrologus, c.* 2 (PL, CLI, 979), by the Synod of Regensburg, 1512 (Hartzheim, VI, 94) and again by the Tridentine commission for the *abusus missæ (supra,* p. 133 f.).

A penitential written under Bishop Thorlak of Iceland (d. 1193) mentions amongst the prerequisites for the celebration of Mass the presence of two *viri ieiuni;* H. J. Schmitz, *Die Bussbücher und das kanonische Buss verfahren* (Düsseldorf, 1898), 712 f.

[93] Synod of Paris (829), c. 48 (Mansi, XIV, 567) : the practice of many priests of celebrating Mass *sine ministris* had slipped in *partim incuria, partim avaritia*.

[94] Thus an otherwise unknown Council of Nantes cited by Regino, *De synod. causis,* I, 191 (PL, CXXXII, 225). After a sharp

condemnation of an abuse found especially in monastic establishments, it demands : *Prævideant autem prælati ut presbyteri in cœnobiis cooperatores habeant in celebratione missarum.*

[95] Walafrid Strabo, *De exord. et increm.,* c. 22 (PL, CXIV, 951).

This ideal is still clung to tenaciously in William of Hirsau (d. 1091), *Const.* I, 86 (PL, CL, 1017) : if the brother serving at Mass does not want to communicate, someone else can then *ibi offerre* (and afterwards communicate).

Even in later times there is mention amongst the Cistercians of the Communion of the participants at a private Mass, for the General Chapter of 1134 grants permission for the Mass servers and others besides to receive on Communion days ; J. M. Canivez, *Statuta cap. gen. O. Cist.* (Louvain, 1933-4), I, 23; 33 (cited by Browe, *Die häufige Kommunion,* 47). Outside of the general Communion days it was customary to receive at private Masses; see Schneider (*Cist.-Chr.* [1928]), 8-10.

[96] Cf. Hanssens, *Eph. liturg.,* XLVIII (1934), 407 ff.

[97] Odo of Cambrai (d. 1113), *Expositio,* x. 2 (PL, CLX, 1057) ; Stephen of Baugé (d. 1136), *De sacramento alt.,* c. 13 (PL, CLXXII, 1289).

In the Summa of St. Thomas, III, 83, 5, ad 12, the decree of Pseudo-Soter is also explained in this way; cf. Hanssens, 412.

Since the thirteenth century, however, there are extant other statutes in which *one cleric*[98] is demanded also for private Mass: *nullus sacerdos celebrare missam præsumat sine clerico respondente,*[99] a demand which was no longer made in the Missal of Pius V[100] but which was repeated in many diocesan decrees in the sixteenth century.[101] The Liége statutes of 1286 regulate this cleric's clothing: *qui clericus habeat tunicam lineam vel superpelliceum vel cappam rotundam et calceatus incedat.*[102]

The requirement of having a cleric present could only be considered an ideal, especially after the sacerdotal recruits were derived chiefly from the Tridentine seminaries, and it was an ideal that even earlier could not be everywhere realized even for public Mass.[103] The monasteries could most easily make some corresponding provision. At Cluny in the eleventh century a lay-brother *(conversus)* was summoned to serve any priest-monk who wanted to celebrate.[104] But there is mention also of the *puer,* which probably refers to the young oblates.[105] If a cleric was at hand, he was allowed to exercise the duties of his order, that is, read the Epistle[106] if he

---

[98] Almost the same thing was already sought by the Synod of York (1195), can. 1 (Hardouin, VI, 1930) when it demanded a *minister litteratus.*

[99] Synod of Trier (1227), can. 8 (Mansi, XXIV, 200).

Further evidences cited in R. Saponaro, "Estne munus in missa privata ministrandi clericorum proprium?" *Periodica,* XXVIII (1939), 369-384.

[100] *Ritus serv.,* II, 1; *De defectibus,* X, 1.

[101] Saponaro, 379-381. The synod of Aix (1585) even demanded written permission from the bishop for any necessary exception; *ibid.,* 381.

[102] V, 13 (Mansi, XXIV, 896).

The Missal of Pius V originally had no such prescription in the pertinent rubrics (*Ritus serv.,* II, 1); but in the revision under Clement VIII (1604) to the words *ministro cum missali . . . præcedente* were added *superpelliceum induto.*

[103] Cf. *supra,* p. 210 f.

[104] *Udalrici Consuet. Clun.,* II, 30 (PL, CXLIX, 724).

Also in the *Consuetudines* of Farfa, which represent Cluniac usage in 1040, the *conversus* appears as Mass server (Albers, I, 161 f.).

In a monastic missal from Norcia two 14th century references to ministrants have been inserted: *Isti serviunt ad missam quilibet in septimana sua;* a *C* precedes the name each time; Ebner, 201, note 2.

[105] *Consuetudines* of Farfa (Albers, 1, 163; see the following footnote).

In the late medieval Mass-*ordo* of the monastery of Bec, the priest turns after the Communion and with the greeting from Apoc. 7:12 he addresses himself *ad ministrum puerum;* Martène, 1, 4, XXXVI (I, 675 A).

[106] In some isolated instances there was a certain vacillation. But even here the prototype of the public presbyter Mass remained the standard (*supra,* p. 208).

In the canonical collection of Bishop Rütger of Trier (927), ed Blasen, c. 10 (*Pastor bonus* [1941], 67 f.) with reference to the prohibition to celebrate alone, the point is stressed that no layman may read the Epistle, but only the subdeacon; is this restriction to the subdeacon a later addition? In the *Consuetudines* of Farfa (Albers, 1, 163) it is taken for granted that the reading is done by a "boy" who certainly was no deacon: *Puer qui legit Epistolam, ipse portat et calicem si valet et bene scit facere.* Cf. *Liber usuum O. Cist.,* c. 54 (PL, CLXVI, 1429 A).

In the *Ordinarium O. P.* of 1256 (Guerrini, 249), with reference to the *servitor* at private Mass, who could not have received any major orders, we read simply: *meliusque est ut Epistolam relinquat sacerdoti dicendam.* The practice of the server's saying it must therefore have existed still in the 13th century.

was in orders, and prepare the chalice and purify it after Communion.[107] Amongst the Cistercians the priest was supposed to have two Mass-servers, a cleric to serve him and answer the prayers, and a laic to present the water and light the candles.[108]

Whereas in most monastic constitutions there is only passing reference to serving, in the Dominican *Ordinarium* of 1256 the *servitor* at a private Mass is given greater attention.[109] The pertinent rubrics are still found—naturally somewhat developed—compiled in a special chapter of the Dominican Missal.[110]

In the *Ordinarium* of 1256 these rules for the server belonged to a special chapter which also contains more detailed directions for the priest at private Mass.[111] Of these a noteworthy one is the rule that the sequence, otherwise so frequent, should be dropped at private Mass. Other regulations for the priest, insofar as they did not regard the special Dominican usages, were already extant, scattered in older statutes. Thus it was almost a general custom that the priest vested at his respective side-altar.[112] Nor was the warning that he was to speak only in a medium loud voice anything new. To it corresponds, in the prescriptions of Cluny, the obviously necessary direction that the priest should read the song portions *in dire-*

---

[107] Thus still in the *Liber ordinarius* of Liége (Volk, 100), in agreement with the *Ordinarium O.P.* (Guerrini, 249). Cf. also *Liber usuum O. Cist.*, c. 54 (PL, CLXVI, 1428 f.).

[108] *Liber usuum*, c. 59 (PL, CLXVI, 1433 C). Thus also the very late *Rituale Cisterciense* (Paris, 1689), 91. Cf. Schneider (*Cist.-Chr.* [1927]), 374 f.

[109] Guerrini, 249 f. Among other things the Mass server had to spread the altar cloths and refold them at the end of Mass, had to transfer the book and the candle at the proper time, and help with the preparation of the chalice. For the rest he was to keep his eyes open and always be ready to wait on the priest or answer his prayers; therefore *parum autem vel nihil stet prostratus in tota missa*. This last was a reference to the bowed posture then customary at the orations and during the Canon. In this regard the *Consuetudines* of Farfa (Albers, I, 162) had enjoined: *Conversus ad primam collectas* [probably to read: *ad primam Collectam*] *et secreta*[s] *sit adclinis, ad canonem genua flectat vel stans oret*.

The *Liber ordinarius* of Liége (Volk, 100 ff). expands the suggestions of the *Ordinarium O.P.* in several points: at the start it prescribes a hand-washing for the

server; it has him receive the *pax* from the priest and pass it on (even though the heading is: *De privatis missis*). At the conventual Mass a signal of the bell is mentioned: *Alter acolythus ante tempus elevationis paucis ictibus campanulam pulset* (ibid., 94, 1. 29). The rubric about passing on the *pax* is also found in the Mass-Ordinary of John Burchard (1502); Legg, *Tracts*, 162. On the other hand there is no mention of a bell signal to be given by the ministrant either in Burchard or, apparently, in any other medieval ceremonial for private Mass.

Franz, 710 f, refers to two 15th century manuscript guides to serving.

[110] *Missale iuxta ritum O.P.* (1889), 24: *De servitoribus missarum privatarum.*

[111] Guerrini, 249-251: *De missis privatis.* To be exact, this chapter does not derive from the Ordinary itself but rather from the *Missale minorum altarium* which is linked with it, just as the directions for the High Mass belong to the *Missale conventuale;* Guerrini, p. VII. The same chapter, from a MS of the 14-15th centuries in Köck, 93 f.

[112] *Udalrici Consuet. Clun.,* II, 30 (PL, CXLIX, 724): On the way to the altar

ctum but that he certainly should not sing them.[113] Thus out of the private Mass grew the read Mass—the *low* Mass.

That the Mass is only read and not sung has at last become in the Roman liturgy the most prominent particular, in fact, the only actual difference to distinguish the rite of the private Mass from that of the public Mass, if we except the vernacular prayers which have recently been added to the conclusion. Wherever in the oriental rites, as a consequence of union, the private Mass has become usual, the differences are essentially greater.[114]

With us the private Mass has, in the last analysis, almost completely doffed its private character, gaining public recognition and in fact becoming simply *the* Mass. Not only do rubricists nowadays consider it the basis of any presentment of the external actions of the Mass, but even the Roman Missal itself, departing from a custom in vogue till late in the Middle Ages,[115] presents the rite of the *missa lecta* as the basic form, describing the special ceremonies of the solemn high Mass as a sort of appendix and devoting only a short notice to the peculiarities of the simple sung Mass.[116]

This strange phenomenon is on a par with the fact that at the beginning of the modern period the older solemn forms suddenly begin to lose some of the stateliness and the simplified forms partly replace them.[117] Besides a low interest in liturgy which this seems to show, another factor behind this is the unfamiliarity of the faithful in regard to the Latin, the strangeness of which was felt with growing keenness and the loud use of which, in prayers and readings, except insofar as it added to the splendor of the proceedings, was less and less appreciated. Thus it became increasingly easy to discontinue the singing at the altar. The read Mass became the ground form. And if it was found undesirable to follow the Mass in quiet devotion or if, at a larger gathering, it was thought agreeable to

the priest holds in his right hand the chalice, on which are the paten and the host (which had been placed thereon with a little ladle), in his left the cruets filled with wine and water, the server carries the chasuble and Mass book. Similarly *Bernardi Ordo Clun.* I, 72 (Herrgott, 263).

Amongst the Cistercians the custom of putting on the vestments in the sacristy even for private Masses was first introduced in 1609 "for greater reverence." Trilhe, "Citeaux," DACL, III, 1793 f.

[113] *Udalrici Consuet. Clun.* II, 30 (PL, CXLIX, 724 C) ; also William of Hirsau, *Const.,* I, 86 (PL, CL, 1016 D).

Something similar is recounted at the present time with regard to some Russian priests who, after their return to the unity of the Catholic Church, took up the practice of private Mass, but felt constrained to sing the portions chanted in their rite at least softly.

[114] They consist chiefly in certain shortcuts, different according to the different rites. The Ukrainians leave out the incensations ; the Little and the Great Entry are merely indicated, the latter by the priest's turning around at the altar with chalice in hand; etc. The Italo-Greeks shorten the introductory section and the litanies. The Melchites again have other abbreviations. Pl. de Meester, "Grecques (Liturgies)," DACL, VI, 1641-1643.

Donald Attwater, *The Christian Churches of the East* (Milwaukee, 1948), 30-31, points out that in few of the rites is the "low" Mass systematized.

[115] *Supra,* p. 103 f.

[116] Ritus serv., VI, 8.

[117] *Supra,* p. 206.

emphasize the social side of the celebration, the solution was more frequently in common prayer or song in the vernacular, accompanying the low Mass. And finally, in our own century, a form of community Mass, the dialogue Mass, was devised, built up on the *missa lecta* but recapturing in great part some of the simple beauty of the *missa cantata* and combining therewith the advantage of the vernacular.[118]

To this development another circumstance contributed no little, namely the fact that less and less stress was laid on the demand that the faithful take part on Sunday in a public celebration. The obligation had already been broken down somewhat during the later Middle Ages and was finally set aside entirely. Thus the low Mass, whether with singing in the vernacular or without, could be the Sunday Mass even in parish churches and it could thus easily attain that position of authority at the high altar which it had surely not enjoyed in previous years.

The rubrical convergence of the two forms of celebration to the point where the only distinction lay in the singing or speaking of the text was therefore only the consequence of a legal assimilation. However, this rubrical convergence was not the result only of the fact that the private Mass retained as much as possible of the high Mass, but also that the latter gave up many of its privileges. Already in the twelfth and thirteenth centuries the priest at a high Mass began to read from the Mass book the texts which were handled by others, just as he did at a private Mass.[119] Other privileges, while continuing as rubrics,[120] are practically abandoned. Scarcely ever does one see a cleric in attendance to read the Epistle, or the special server who tends the book and, if a cleric, brings the chalice to the altar, and after Communion covers it and carries it back. At most there is a second server who shares the duties of the first.

The problem of the server is today identical for both sung Mass and private Mass.[121] Whereas in the early Middle Ages a cleric was ordered for the former but not for the private Mass,[122] we see that later a cleric was

---

[118] *Supra,* p. 162 f.

[119] *Supra,* p. 106 f.

[120] Gatterer, *Praxis celebrandi,* 97 f., 260-264; A. Fortescue, *The Ceremonies of the Roman Rite Described* (7th ed., rev. J. O'Connell; London, 1943), 126-133.

[121] The duties of the server are touched upon very scantily in the rubrics of the Roman Missal (unlike the Dominican). For that reason, aside from the responses and the essential assistance with the book and the cruets, they vary from place to place. Thus a signal of the bell, prescribed for the *Sanctus* and the Consecration, is also inserted at other times: in Germany and Austria and parts of the U. S. at the offertory and the Communion *(Domine*

non sum dignus), in France and elsewhere at the Little Elevation *(omnis honor at gloria),* in Central America at the *Pax Domini,* etc. In some places (France and Alsace, for instance) the server mounts to the priest's side at the offertory and receives and folds the chalice veil, and after Communion he hands it to him again when he covers the chalice. The transfer of the book is usually the server's duty, despite. *Rit. Serv.,* V, 1 f. (According to *Ordinarium Cartusiense* (1932), c. 26, 12, the priest himself carries the book even at high Mass.) The Missal presupposes that the server extinguishes the candles before the priest leaves the altar (*Rit. serv.,* XII, 6), but this is not the usage in most places.

[122] *Supra,* 210; 226.

demanded for both and finally in either case a layman was permitted.[123] The practical solution, in fact, follows what was doubtless the tradition of former clerical schools in monasteries and chapters, and chooses young boys whose innocence can, in a measure, substitute for the clerical character.[124] Still that spiritual character cannot be entirely lacking if, in addition to the technical training, there is a spiritual commitment and, under favorable circumstances, even formal enrollment, as is actually being done in many places nowadays under orders of the bishop.[125]

The fact that the boundaries between private Mass and public Mass have gradually disappeared is connected also with the fact that in the last few centuries daily celebration by every priest has been taken more and more for granted.[126] On the one hand, this daily celebration by the priest

---

[123] *Supra*, p. 210 f.; 226 f.

Although the prime activity of the server is to be present and make the responses—substituting, therefore, for the people—and although this duty can be entrusted to lay people and, in case of need, can even be fulfilled by women (cf. *Cod. Iur. Can.*, c. 813, 2), still, viewing the server's work in its fullness as "serving," it must be considered a clerical function, in the last analysis the function of the deacon with whom, in fact, he even has his title in common (διακονος =*minister,* server). Reminiscent of this latter office is the oft-repeated designation of the server's vesture, as found in medieval inventories—clothing of various hues; *dalmaticæ puerorum,* they are called, or *tunicæ, albæ puerorum;* Braun, *Die liturgische Gewandung,* 60 f. Hanssens and Saponaro, in the problem they posed for themselves (*supra,* footnotes 91 and 99), both have only the first activity in view, and therefore come to quite a different conclusion—although this answer was necessary in order to demolish certain objections to the "community" Mass.

[124] However, objections continued to pile up against this solution of the problem. In his edition of the works of St. Gregory the Great, P. de Goussanville (d. 1683) called it an abuse which might possibly be excused on the ground of custom (PL, LXXVII, 1336 D). Martène, 1, 3, 9, 10 (I, 344) is equally severe in his declaration. Bremond, *Histoire littéraire,* VI, 220, relates that Claude Martin, who was prior of Marmoutier from 1690 on, wanted to banish children as well as married men

from the sanctuary. Even in the 18th and 19th centuries voices were raised against the use of altar boys; Trapp, 165, note 923; 295 f. along with note 97.

For our own day see, e.g., A. Mayer-Pfannholz, "Das Laientum im werdenden Kirchenbild" (*Theologie u. Glaube* [1941]), 91.

[125] Cf. F. K. Debray, *Dienst am Altar. Werkbuch für Ministrantenseelsorge* (Freiburg, 1942), 153-159. A formula for the "Consecration of the Altar Boy," approved for the diocese of Limburg, is reviewed in Th. Mathyssek, *Leitfaden der Pastoral* (4th ed.; Limburg, 1940), 299. If there is no formal "consecration" there should at least be a systematized method of enrollment; see the helpful suggestions in G. Johnson, "The Priest and His Sanctuary Boys," *American Ecclesiastical Review,* LXXXVI (1932), 7-28.

It is worthy of note that in Rome even in the 8th-9th centuries the young clerics were ordained first as acolytes (they had the privilege of carrying the little bag with the Eucharist); this ordination was performed by the pope or a bishop. Before that they just received a blessing at the hand of the archdeacon; *Ordo Rom. IX,* n. 1 (PL, LXXVIII, 1003): *accipient primam benedictionem ab archidiacono.* See M. J. Metzger, *Zwei karolingische Pontifikalien vom Oberrhein* (Freiburg, 1914), 68 f. But cf. M. Andrieu, "Les ordres mineurs dans l'ancien rit Romain" (*Revue des Sciences religieuses* [1925]), 36 f.

[126] In the early Middle Ages the Synods of Pavia (850), can. 2 (Mansi, XIV, 930)

himself has become, along with the breviary, part and parcel of his spiritual life. The ground for this is the consideration that personal celebration, even from the viewpoint of one's own religious life, has greater value than participation in another's Mass.[127] On the other hand, this personal desire of the priest coincides with the good of the cure of souls. The people are thus offered opportunities to attend Holy Mass every day in churches and chapels, and in large churches, especially on Sundays, also at various hours. At the altar not only the *festa fori* but also the *festa chori*, the individual saints' feasts, are celebrated. Thus the personal and public factors go hand in hand, leading in many cases to a regular semi-public celebration of the Mass.

There is still another influence at work, one that was efficacious already in Christian antiquity and which continually gives rise to the private Mass properly so called. There should be some way of satisfying the demands of the faithful who request the priest to offer the sacrifice for their special wants and who tender him the offering for this in the form of a stipend. That these offerings form, for a large number of the clergy, an important part of their income, especially at a time when richly endowed foundations are a thing of the past, cannot be denied. But that there is also peril here is equally beyond doubt. Church legislation, as the result of sad experiences which it has had in the course of history, seeks to counter it. Of

---

and of Compostella (1056), can. 1 (Mansi, XIX, 855) desired that bishops, *resp.* bishops and priests, celebrate daily. But the praxis in the later Middle Ages, in Spain and elsewhere, was far different from today's. Although the common esteem for Votive Masses drew many priests who had no other means of support and who literally lived from the altar, to celebrate daily, there were many others who seldom said Mass. For that reason a minimum had to be enjoined. Toledo synods from 1324 to 1473 set down the requirement at four times a year at least (Mansi, XXV, 734; XXXII, 392); and a Ravenna synod (1314) demanded at least one celebration a year (*ibid.*, XV, 546 c). A Synod of Bourges, 1336, demanded that priests with the cure of souls celebrate once or twice a month (can. 3; Mansi, XXV, 1060). Elsewhere a weekly celebration was prescribed; see the examples from the 13th to the 16th centuries in Browe, *Die häufige Kommunion*, 57, 67, 68; cf. 74.

Even as late as the 18th century it is said that many pastors in the Moselle region were not accustomed to celebrate daily;

unless there was a special occasion many of them would celebrate only once or twice a week *ex devotione*. The increase which subsequently took place is traced in great part to the influence of P. Martin von Cochem; A Schüller, "Ein Moselpfarrer" (*Pastor bonus* [1928]), 190.

[127] Theological discussions usually have had in view a different question, namely, whether it is better to celebrate daily than not to celebrate; see the pertinent chapter in Benedict XIV, *De s. sacrificio missæ*, III, 2 (Schneider, 304-313), and the authors there mentioned.

In regard to the question remarked above, reference should be made (in favor of celebrating oneself) to the so-called *fructus specialissimus* which, as theological opinion has it, is the celebrant's very own. Even more important is the fact that, by his more intense sharing in the Mass, the priest as a rule finds it easier to celebrate Mass with devotion. Still we must not overlook the fact that on the other side are the great values of unity and charity which, *suppositis supponendis*, a community celebration not only represents but actually cultivates.

course the legitimacy of celebration on this title is not at all questionable.[128] In fact, although the votive formularies do not—and rightly—play the same role as of yore, still the Votive Mass, or the sacrifice which is appropriated to a person or a family for their special intention, exhibits that title of private Mass which gives it most obviously the right and power to be, especially since it is anchored in the tradition of the Church since earliest times. But the personal factor which binds the offerer with such a celebration ought to be restrengthened as much as possible. The faithful who request a Mass must be conscious of the fact that they ought to participate as co-celebrants at such a Mass if at any. And besides care must be taken that such a votive celebration does nothing to hinder the development of public worship which must always be our first concern.

6. Forms of Popular Participation

The picture of divine worship in Christian antiquity, with the faithful crowded around the altar, offering up the sacrifice together with the priest and joining in the prayers and singing, turn and turn about—that picture is familiar to everyone nowadays. In fact the present arrangement of the Mass can be understandably explained at many points only by reference to that primitive picture.

From what has been said above, much can be seen of the many vicissitudes that popular participation at Mass underwent—its ebb and flow insofar as it has been impressed on various periods of liturgical history. Numerous particulars will be called to our attention later in our study of the various parts of the Mass-liturgy. Here we will endeavor to put together in a short sketch the most important factors, complement them with evidence of a more general nature, and, out of the see-saw of history, let certain supratemporal viewpoints come to the fore.

Christian antiquity therefore made a choice of the second solution, and even today it is preferred on those occasions—like large assemblies of the clergy—where individual celebration could not take place in worthy fashion. Cf. *supra*, p. 196 f. It has always been considered fitting and proper that the individual priest should exercise his power of Orders at the altar from time to time, even abstracting from the requirements of others. This viewpoint certainly played a part in producing an increase in private Masses in the early medieval monastic establishments. It must likewise have had a part in the legislation mentioned in the last footnote, legislation preserved in can. 805 of the Code. The rotation of the celebration of the conventual Mass in monasteries and other conventicles is also probably due to this notion. The same viewpoint was without doubt at work in the regulation of Byzantine monasteries where it is ordered that if more than five fathers are living in an establishment, the liturgy is held twice a week, where more than ten, three times, and where more than twenty, daily. K. Lübeck, *Die christlichen Kirchen des Orients* (Kempten, 1911), 189.

[128] *Cor. Iur. Can.* c. 824-844.

One fundamental condition for the formation of important types of general participation in the Mass celebration was that the assembled faithful should form a community tied together by the same faith and the same love. In the centuries of Christian antiquity that was to a great extent the case. Only at the fore-Mass was an outer circle of guests or candidates to the society admitted, but in the consciousness of the congregation these people were clearly distinguished from the narrower circle of fully authorized members. We thus encounter forms which were composed for their dismissal at the end of the Mass of the Catechumens. Far into the Middle Ages these rites for dismissing the catechumens were used for the children during Lent in the weeks of preparation for Baptism.[1] Even to the very threshold of modern times those who, as public sinners, were no longer worthy to take part in the worship of the community were expelled on Ash Wednesday.[2] The excommunicated, too, were very strictly excluded all through the Middle Ages. But aside from these very unusual cases the Middle Ages had no recognized outsiders. Just as in church building the old-time atrium and the parts in between became simply the open portion of the church, and the doorway was like an invitation to the whole town to come into the holy place, so all forms of banishment and dismissal fell into disuse. All the townspeople were Christians and all Christians were children of the house.

It was precisely the obviousness of the open doors to the Church, standing unlocked to all, that hindered a return to a more ancient severity when, at the start of modern times, circumstances grew so fundamentally different. For decades larger portions of the people wavered between the old Church and New Learning. In the hope of winning them back it was necessary not to turn them away at the door. And the suggestion that was brought up at the Council of Trent, to ban public sinners (prostitutes, concubinaries, usurers et al.) from the Church or at least to order them out after the Gospel,[3] was recognized as impracticable. Thus for our own time a situation has arisen which would have been incomprehensible to Christian antiquity, even aside from the laws of the *disciplina arcani*—a situation where at our divine service every sharp boundary between Church and world is broken down, so that Jew and heathen can press right up to the steps of the altar and can stand in the very midst of the faithful at the most sacred moment. Such a situation is possible and tolerable so long as the faithful are only onlookers and listeners at a sacred drama, and it will be substantially and actually overcome whenever and insofar as they take up a more active role.

---

[1] Durandus, VI, 56, 11, still speaks of this dismissal. In several churches the practices of the catechumenate were retained even much later; Eisenhofer, II, 255.

[2] Jungmann, *Die lateinischen Bussriten*, 67 f.

[3] *Concilium Tridentinum*, ed. Goerres, VIII, 921, 1. 27; 923, 1. 14; 928, 1. 1; 929, 1. 53; etc.

One of the first forms of expression by which a closed society reveals itself is a fixed order of coming and going; everyone gets there on time and no one leaves until the meeting is adjourned. A noteworthy severity with regard to late-comers was displayed in the fifth century Syrian *Testamentum Domini*. The deacons were directed to keep the doors locked when the sacrifice was being offered. If some of the faithful came late and knocked at the door they were not to be admitted; but for these tardy brethren a special prayer was included, that God might give them greater zeal and love.[4] At the end of the meeting we find in all the liturgies a formal dismissal. It happened of course that some individuals, even communicants, did not wait for this.[5] Little by little a special order became necessary for those who did not communicate, who already, towards the end of the ancient period, formed the greater proportion by far.

As we will see more in detail later, it was the practice in the city of Rome as well as in Gaul to let them depart before the distribution of Communion and this departure of many was not only countenanced but was even taken into account in the setting up of the liturgy; at Rome the announcements for the following week were made at this point,[6] and in Gaul those who were going to leave were given a solemn blessing right after the *Pater noster*.[7] The faithful were thus implicitly admonished to stay at least until then. For already in the sixth century many were under the impression that they had fulfilled their obligation if they heard the readings.[8] Therefore Cæsarius of Arles makes clear to his audience that the minimum required to fulfill one's Christian duty is to be present at the *consecratio Corporis et Sanguinis*, the *oratio dominica* and the *benedictio*.[9]

In the Carolingian reform, too, following the lead of tradition, the blessing is considered the conclusion prior to which no one was allowed to leave; but now it is the blessing of the newly introduced Roman liturgy that is meant, which is given in some form or other at the end of Mass.[10] The prev-

---

[4] *Testamentum Domini*, I, 36 (Rahmani, 89 f.): *Propter fratrem qui sero venit, supplicemus, ut Dominus ei diligentiam et laborem concedat, relaxet ab ipso omne ligamen mundi huius, tribuatque ei voluntatem dilectionis, caritatem et spem.*
[5] *Infra*, Vol. II, Ch. 3, 17.
[6] *Infra*, Vol. II, Ch. 3, 8.
[7] *Infra*, Vol. II, Ch. 3, 3.
[8] Cæsarius, *Serm.* 73, 2 (Morin, 294; PL, XXXIX, 2276 f.): *Cum enim maxima pars populi, imo, quod peius, pæne omnes recitatis lectionibus exeunt de ecclesia, cui dicturus est sacerdos: Sursum corda, aut quomodo sursum habere corda respondere possunt, quando deorsum . . . descendunt?* The same complaint rings out again in the 13th century; Franz, 17 f.

An analogous misconception is remarked by Walafrid Strabo, *De exord. et increm.*, c. 22 (PL, CXIV, 948 B), although here it regards a participation in Mass dictated by devotion only: *sæpe in illis transeunter offerunt missis, ad quas persistere nolunt,* that is, they leave after the offertory procession.

Another abuse, significant of a third popular misunderstanding of the Mass, was the practice of the later Middle Ages of rushing to church only for the elevation; see *supra*, p. 120.
[9] Cæsarius, *loc. cit.;* also *De Vita, c.* 2 (PL, LXVII, 1010 C), which tells how he often had the doors of the church locked after the Gospel.
[10] *Infra*, III, 6, 4.

alent rareness of the reception of Holy Communion had perhaps forced such a change of attitude. Therefore, Amalar, taking up a question often asked by the *vulgus indoctum*, at what parts of the Mass must one be definitely present, answers: from the offertory to the *Ite missa est*,[11] for here the sacrifice is being offered. Later moral theology also included the fore-Mass, whose independence was perceived less and less.[12] But Church legislation, whether during the Middle Ages or later, did not make any special declaration regarding these precise limits.[13]

In the liturgical action the participation of the people was manifested especially by the fact that they did not merely listen to the prayers of the priest in silence but ratified them by their acclamations. The custom of using such acclamations was inherited by the Church from the Synagogue; the very style and language in part betrays this: *Et cum spiritu tuo, Amen.* That the people in Christian antiquity actually spoke these answers is obvious from the occasional remarks of the Fathers. Even Justin testified to it.[14] Jerome mentioned one time that the Amen in the Roman basilicas reverberated like a heavenly thunder.[15] Augustine in his sermons and writings often made reference to the responses of the people.[16]

The only question is, how long during the Middle Ages did the practice continue. Cæsarius of Arles still takes it for granted.[17] It is also otherwise ascertained for the Gallican liturgy of the sixth and seventh centuries.[18] Even in the early medieval liturgy of the city of Rome, which had become quite pretentious as the result of the added *schola* and the presence of a numerous clergy, there was still a constant mention of the responses by the people.[19]

---

[11] Amalar, *De eccl. off.*, III, 36 (PL, CV, 1156). The same answer is given by Rabanus Maurus, *De inst. cleric.*, c. 33, *additio* (PL, CVII, 326).

[12] It is worth noting that moralists nowadays do not consider the Last Gospel as pertaining *ad integritatem missæ;* all else, from the prayers at the foot of the altar to the priest's blessing, does. H. Noldin-A. Schmitt, *Summa theol. mor.*, II (20th ed.; Innsbruck, 1930), 245; Aertnys-Damen, *Theol. Moral.*, I (14th ed.; Turin, 1944), 422: *Ita constat ex communi sensu et consuetudine totius Ecclesiæ.* This attitude reflects the circumstances of the 16th century when the Last Gospel was not yet linked fast to the Mass; see *infra*, Vol. II, Ch. 4, 5. Moralists of the 17th century sometimes even included this in the Mass obligation; see J. de Lugo, *De eucharistia,* 22, 1 (*Disput. schol. et mor.*, ed. Fournais, IV, 349).

[13] *Cod. Iur. Can.*, c. 1248.

The *Decretum Gratiani* III, 1, 63 ff. (Friedberg, I, 1311 f.) contains little more than the general injunction imposed by synods of the 6th century, that one must hear the entire Mass.

[14] *Supra*, p. 22 f.

[15] Jerome, *In Gal. Comment.*, 1, 2 (PL, XXV) : *ad similitudinem coelestis tonitrui Amen reboat.*

[16] Roetzer, 99, 115; 117 ff.; 124; 131; 236 f. Some of this we shall see later.

Other evidences from the Fathers will come to our attention in the places noted.

[17] *Supra*, p. 235, note 8.

[18] Nickl, *Der Anteil des Volkes*, 8 f. Cf. especially the data mentioned below, p. 365, with regard to *Et cum spiritu tuo.*

[19] Clearest of all in the Mass-*Ordo* of John the Arch-chanter who in every instance where an answer is expected inserts a phrase like *respondent omnes, respondentibus omnibus* (Silvia-Tarouca, 197-201). The *Ordo* of St. Amand makes a similar

The Carolingian reform appears to have insisted on this with a certain doggedness. In Charlemagne's *Admonitio generalis* of 789 there is a decree regarding the people' part.[20] Amalar advises those who do not understand the Latin Gospel lesson, at least to pronounce the *Gloria tibi Domine* with the rest.[21] Other Carolingian authors talk about these responses as something taken for granted.[22]

In his penitential lists, Burchard of Worms (d. 1025) mentions the neglect to respond as an example of unbecoming behavior in church.[23] And even later the responses are referred to as at least the ideal requirement.[24] After that, however, the practice falls into such oblivion that in our own century the right of the people to make these responses has had actually to be proved.[25]

remark for the *Deo gratias* after the announcements: *respondet omnis clerus* (Duchesne, *Christian Worship*, 473). The fact that the *Ordo Romanus I* makes no mention of the people is hardly to be taken as an absolute contradiction of what is said here; see Nickl, II f. The manuscript sacramentaries seldom give any indication as to who makes the responses (usually the sign R. is used); an exception is the Gregorianum in Cod. Pad. 47 (9th century), which is in substance a 7th century text, and which time and again prefaces he answer with *Respondet populus;* Mohlberg-Baumstark, n. 874, 889 f., 893. Similar rubrics occur frequently in later books, but they are probably not to be taken literally, as corresponding to reality.

[20] c. 70 (MGH, Cap., I, 59) : The people should sing *Gloria Patri* and *Sanctus*. Cf. Rudolf of Bourges (d. 866), *Capitulare*, c. 10 (PL, CXIX, 708).

[21] Amalar, *De eccl. off.*, III, 18 (PL, CV, 1125 f.). For the dialogue before the Preface, cf. *ibid.*, III, 19 (PL, CV, 1128 A, 1131 f.).

[22] The *Expositio 'Primum in ordine'* remarks in passing that the response to the *Dominus vobiscum* before the Preface and likewise to the *Pax Domini* of the priest is made by *et clerus et plebs* (PL, CXXXVIII, 1175 B, 1185 B). Rabanus Maurus, *De inst. cleric.*, I, 33 (PL, CVII, 323) informs the priest about the oration : *populum salutans pacis responsum ab illo accipiat . . . Amen hebraeum est, quod ad omnen sacerdotis orationem seu benedictionem respondet populus fidelium.*

Remigius of Auxerre, *Expositio* (PL,

CI, 1252 f.), also expressly mentions the counter-greeting and *Amen* of the people and their response in the dialogue before the Preface.

[23] Burchard of Worms, *Poenitentiale Eccl. Germ.*, n. 145 (Schmitz, II, 441 ; PL, CXL, 970 C) : *Fecisti quod quidam facere solent . . . cum eos presbyter salutat et hortatur ad orationem, illi autem ad fabulas suas revertuntur, non ad responsionem nec ad orationem?*

[24] Bernold, *Micrologus*, c. 2, 7 (PL, CLI, 979 ; 981 f.). Radulph de Rivo (d. 1403), also desiderates the ancient traditional *Amen* of all those present *(omnes adstantes)* as a *signum confirmatonis.*

Even in the *Ordo missae* of Burchard of Strassburg (1502), which has in view chiefly the Low Mass, the answer of the *interessentes* is sought along with the Mass server, even in the prayers at the foot of the altar and at the *Suscipiat;* Legg, Tracts, 135 ff. ; 152. In Italy it seems the people at that time actually made these responses; see the references in Ellard, *The Mass of the Future*, 103.

The Missal of Pius V does not have any unequivocal direction regarding the responses; cf. Kramp, "Messgebräuche der Gläubigen in der Neuzeit," (StZ [1926], II), 209, footnote 2.

[25] A. Barin, "Circa missam quam dialogatam appellant," *Eph. liturg.*, XXXV (1921), 299-313, had defended the view that at a *missa lecta* the duty of responding had been turned over by the Church to the server exclusively; that therefore the congregation's joining in was a presumption which violated can. 818 *(cave-*

Besides these short acclamations, the people's share in the Mass since earliest times also included a certain ever-increasing number of hymnic texts. The most venerable of them is the *Sanctus* along with the *Benedictus*, which also remained the people's song the longest. Of a similarly venerable age was the refrain in the responsorial chants, namely, in the Roman liturgy, the chants between the readings[26]; but these, with their ever-varying texts, were at an early period turned over to the *schola* in their entirety. Similar in character to the refrain was the *Kyrie eleison* in the introductory litany which came substantially later. After that the *Agnus Dei* was added. The two larger chants, the *Gloria* and the *Credo* (which appeared quite early in the northern countries), were perhaps intended principally for the clergy assembled around the altar. The individual fortunes of all these songs will occupy our attention in connection with the detailed explanation to come. Taken together—aside from the refrains of the interposed chants—they form the chants of the so-called Ordinary of the Mass which, along with the ancient acclamation, were taken over from the people by the choir of clerics and finally by the church choirs.[27]

Besides the words by which the participation of the people in the celebration was made manifest, we have to add also some activity, *doing* something. The "Partaking," simply, the κοινωνία, which consists in receiving the Sacrament, we see gradually disappearing, its early bloom shrivelled, shrunk into well-defined and all too few occasions. This receptive participation stands in contrast to the contributive, the upsurging motion of the offertory procession which grew increasingly strong near the end of the ancient period and remained a living practice for over a thousand years. As an introduction either to the Mass proper or to the reception of Communion, we have the kiss of peace, already known to the primitive Church and still remaining at the present in a residue of stylized forms. We will also come across traces of a transient handwashing by the people.[28]

---

atque [*sacerdos*] *ne alias cæremonias at preces proprio arbitrio adiungat"*). The articles of Hanssens and Saponaro noted above pp. 226 and 227 were written to controvert this opinion.

[26] In other liturgies responsorial chants were also used particularly at the Communion. In connection with the directions for Communion we read in the *Canones Basilii*, c. 97 (Riedel, 275) the express charge: The congregation should answer lustily after all the psalms.

[27] Whereas in the transfer of the chants from the people to the choir of clergy scarcely a trace of the chant has remained with the people, in the subsequent transfer from the clerical choir to the church

choir the direction was retained that the clerics should recite the chants of the Ordinary in a half-audible voice while they were being sung. This prescription was recalled as late as July 22, 1892, by a decree of the Congregation of Rites, *Decreta auth. SRC*, n. 3786. Cf. *Cæremoniale episc.*, II, 8, 36; 39; 52. Essentially the same thing is already to be found in *Ordo Rom.* XIV, n. 61 (PL, LXXVIII, 1175 f.), in the regulations for the cardinal who is assisting at the Mass of his chaplain: he is supposed to recite the chants and the introit (while they are being sung) with his assistants, *sine cantu, sine nota*.

[28] *Infra*, Vol. II, Ch. 3, 13.

Most especially, however, the inner participation of the faithful at the holy action has to be exhibited in a suitable bodily posture. The principal posture (aside from the early period with its meal celebration) has always been a posture of standing. Before the higher Being whom he wishes to honor, a person stands erect, particularly when he realizes his obligation of service. Just as the priest at the altar stands before God in reverential readiness, so also the faithful; they are the *circumstantes*. In line with this, it was an understood norm in olden times that the people followed the motions of the bishop or the priest when he said the prayers and, in general, in all the rest of his deportment, so that like him they stood with hands uplifted and facing east.[29] Standing was the ordinary posture of prayer even among ancient peoples,[30] in fact, standing with uplifted hands[31] and with eyes fixed in the direction of the rising sun. This posture of prayer was continued by the Christians, both people and *liturgi* together, with only this variant: they saw in the orient sun which they faced, an image of the Risen Christ.[32] Only when the celebrant pronounced a blessing over the congregation, to whom he turned standing erect, was there any change

[29] That the faithful also raised their arms while praying is manifest from the frequent depiction of the *orantes* in the catacombs. Literary evidences from the 3rd to the 5th century are assembled in Quasten, *Mon.*, 174, note 4, in the commentary on Ambrose, *De sacr.*, VI, 4, 17. It is precisely this passage from Ambrose that shows that the lifting of the hands (following 1 Tim. 2:8) was observed by the faithful especially at worship. Cf. also Chrysostom, *In Phil. hom.*, 3, 4 (PG, LXII, 204). In Switzerland it was still customary in 1500 for the faithful at High Mass to pray with arms outstretched from the Consecration to the Communion.

In the Orient, in the Egyptian liturgies, the bodily posture of the worshipers, especially at service, was carefully regulated by continuous directions from the deacon. Right after the *Dignum et iustum est* the deacon ordered them to stretch out their arms Πετάσατε, Brightman, 125; *contra* Brightman, 601, this seems to be addressed, like the following, to all the faithful), at a later spot to stand up (Οἱ καθήμενοι ἀνάστητε, *ibid.*, 131, 174, 231), and finally, just before the *Sanctus*, to turn to the east (Εἰς ἀνατολὰς βλέψατε, *ibid.*, 131, 174, 231).

For the orientation at prayer the most important evidence in Quasten, *Mon.*, 35; 184 (in the notes to *Didascalia*, II, 57 and

Const. Apost., II, 57, 14) and the basic researches in Dölger, *Sol salutis*, 136 ff.

Apparently the turning to the East was expected, no matter what the position of the church building. But we may suppose that this orientation at prayer had something to do with the subsequent change in the method of construction, having the apse to the East instead of the front of the building (which was the more ancient fashion), so that when the *liturgus* prayed the faithful did not have to turn their back to him and the altar.

[30] F. Heiler, *Das Gebet* (4th ed.; Munich, 1921), 100. In ancient Jewish usage the word "to stand" also meant "to pray." With this we might link the conjecture that *statio* (in the sense of the primitive Christian stational fast) originally meant prayer, place of prayer. Schümmer, *Die altchristliche Fastenpraxis*, 136 ff.

[31] Heiler, 101 f.

[32] Dölger, *Sol salutis*, 1-258. Already in the 2nd century it was customary to indicate the orientation by a cross on the wall in the proper place (cf. Matt. 24:30); the proofs in E. Peterson, "La croce e la preghiera verso oriente," *Eph. liturg.*, XLIX (1945), 52-68; cf. *idem.*, "Die geschichtliche Bedeutung der jüdischen Gebetsrichtung," *Theol. Zeitschrift*, III (1947), 1-15.

in the bearing of the congregation; now it differed from his in accordance with the shouted command, *Humiliate capita vestra Deo*[33]—they stood with heads bowed.

But later in the Middle Ages the bodily posture of the faithful grew more and more unlike that of the priest. The bow of the head, as at the blessing, gradually became a sign of the congregation's humility in the sight of God, and was used during the orations and especially during the canon.[34] On the other hand, kneeling was still generally limited during the first millenary to days without festive character and even here it was limited to the fore-Mass. First, kneeling was proclaimed by the deacon's *Flectamus genua* for the people's meditative prayer which introduced the orations. Then, for the people, kneeling was transferred to the respective orations themselves,[35] and on non-festive days the bowed but standing posture, hitherto in vogue during the canon and other orations, was also soon changed to kneeling.[36] Already by 813 the Synod of Tours represents this attitude as the fundamental characteristic posture of the faithful (always, of course, excepting the days when, in honor of Christ's Resurrection, one prayed standing).[37] On Sundays and feast-days (taking this latter word in its widest sense) the standing position was retained. It was not till the eucharistic movement of the thirteenth century that any inroad was made here, namely, by kneeling at the consecration. The *Ordo missæ* of John Burchard which appeared in 1502 still directed the participants at a Mass celebrated with singing to use the standing posture as a general rule; the only variations were kneeling at the *Confiteor* in the prayers at the foot of the altar, and at the consecration[38]; there was no longer any mention of bowing.

[33] This bow at the blessing also in other liturgies; cf. *infra*, Vol. II, Ch. 3, 3 and 4, 1.

[34] For this and what follows see *infra*, p. 370 f. and Vol. II, Ch. 2, 5.

[35] *Ordo Rom. antiquus* (Hittorp, 66).

[36] Kneeling during the Canon is prescribed for the priests around the altar in the *Ordo* of St. Amand, at the start of the 9th century (Duchesne, *Christian Worship*, 461); and later for the choir in the *Ordo eccl. Lateran.* (Fischer, 29). As the idea of how long the Canon lasted changed, the duration of the kneeling also changed. Kneeling (or the *prostratio*) was prescribed during the *Pater noster* as early as the 9th century; see *infra*, Vol. II, Ch. 3, 2. By the 13th century we begin to see a growing tendency to stretch out the kneeling (resp. *prostratio*) as long as the Blessed Sacrament was on the altar; see the *Ordo Rom. XIII* which comes from the time of

Gregory X (d. 1276), n. 19 (PL, LXXVIII, 1116).

An unusual extension of the kneeling is mentioned by Fr. Titelmans (d. 1537), in his explanation of High Mass, *Mysterii missæ expositio* (Lyons, 1558), 18, where he supposes that the faithful fall on their knees as soon as the priest approaches the altar, wherein he sees represented the shepherds adoring the divine Infant.

[37] Can. 37 (Mansi, XIV, 89).

[38] Legg, *Tracts*, 134. A genuflection is here prescribed also at the *Et incarnatus est; ibid.*, 135.

Similarly the Low German "Laienregel des 15. Jh" (Fifteenth century Rule for Laymen), c. 6 (R. Langenberg, *Quellen und Forschungen zur Geschichte der deutschen Mystik* [Bonn, 1902], 86-88), which prescribes it also for the collects and the last blessing, but leaves it free during the Canon.

Sitting, as a posture for the faithful, was hardly thought of seriously in the churches of the Middle Ages, since there was no provision made for seats.[39] Only for the choir of clerics in capitular and monastic churches were choir stalls erected and for this narrower circle of participants new choir rules were devised.[40] Established on the same basis as that which held for the faithful, these rules became constantly more detailed and began to include sitting, just as the bishop and *presbyter* had been doing previously in accordance with the oldest Roman *ordines*.[41] The choir sat at the Epistle and, provided the whole group did not sing, also during the following chants.[42] But it was not till near the end of the Middle Ages that any localities began to consider the possibility of the people's sitting down.[43] But now in many countries it is regularly taken into account in the erec-

---

[39] There is a record here and there of sitting on the floor, but it appears not to have been customary; cf. Dekkers, *Tertullianus*, 77. It was different, however, in those countries where it is still customary to sit on the floor. In the place-plan outlined in the Syrian *Didascalia*, II, 57 (Quasten, *Mon.*, 35 f.), there is constant reference to sitting for each of the groups of the faithful till the time for prayer.

Even today in African and Asiatic mission lands squatting seems to be the basic posture for the faithful; cf. Kramp, "Messgebräuche der Gläubigen in den ausserdeutschen Ländern" (StZ, [1927], II), 365 f.

[40] An example of exact rules for choir at Mass and Office is presented about 1285 in the *Liber ordinarius* of St. James' monastery in Liége (Volk, 102-109; regarding the conventual Mass, 102 f.). The rules now in force for choir assistance at Mass, rules frequently modified and detailed by local custom, are collected in the Roman Missal, *Rubr. gen.*, XVII, 5; *Cæremoniale episc.* II, 8, 69; 11, 5; 7; for details see P. Martinucci, *Manuale sacrarum cæremoniarum*, (3rd ed.; Regensburg, 1911), I, 9-88; J. O'Connell, *The Celebration of Mass* (Milwaukee, 1940), III, 64-74.

[41] *Supra*, p. 68 f.

[42] *Liber ordinarius* of Liége (Volk, 102 f.; cf. 105).

In the *Liber ordinarius* standing remains the primary posture; bowing is prescribed only for the collects, the *Sanctus*, the *Pater noster*, the first *Agnus Dei* and the

post-communion, and also, with capuche thrown back, at the blessing. Kneeling is done only at the Consecration (and at *homo factus est* in the *Credo*). But *tempore prostrationum* everyone knelt from the *Sanctus* to the *Agnus Dei*, that is, during the time when previously bowing was prescribed.

Similarly detailed choir regulations are contained . in the essentially older *Liber usuum O. Cist.*, II, 56 (PL, CLXVI 1430-1432). From this work the *Liber ordinarius* has taken, for instance, the direction that at certain times the brethren are to stand facing the altar, whereas otherwise they stand *chorus contra chorum;* also the mention of certain places at which they are to bow, like at the *adoramus* te in the *Gloria*.

[43] German preachers in the 15th century directed the people to sit during the Epistle, gradual and the sermon; Franz, 21 f.

The Low German "Rule for Laymen" which was produced in 1473 (Langenberg [above, note 38], 87) expected the people to sit at the Epistle and during the offertory.

The *Ordo missæ* of John Burchard (Legg, *Tracts*, 134 f.) also has in mind the provision of seats for the faithful; in this case they are to sit at the *Kyrie* and *Gloria* (after the celebrant has finished reciting them and the choir is still singing), at the Epistle and the interposed chants, at the *Credo* (as before), after the offertory chant till the Preface, and after the Communion till the post-communion.

tion of churches, especially when, as a consequence of the Reformers' agitation, the sermon began to take on greater importance.[44]

The benches or pews used in church also make provision for kneeling. This ties in with the ever-increasing importance of low Mass and the rules set down for it. It would seem that in the later Middle Ages the rules for posture at low Mass and at Masses conducted with less solemnity were basically the rules which held outside of feast-days and festal seasons.[45] That means, as a rule, kneeling at the orations and during the canon, to which must be added kneeling during the *Confiteor* at the beginning.[46] Standing was expressly required only during the Gospel.[47] To retain these regulations regarding kneeling and standing and at the same time to avoid a frequent and, in last analysis, disturbing change of posture during the short space of a low Mass, some simpler rule had to be devised for low Mass, namely, that aside from the Gospel one would kneel all the way through.[48] This rule, however, was never very strictly insisted on.[49]

[44] Cf. *infra,* p. 459 f.

In many countries outside Germany, especially those influenced by French, English and Spanish culture, sitting at the offertory is taken as much for granted as standing at the Gospel. In several places (e.g. the U. S.) people usually stay seated till the start of the Canon or even (as in the diocese of Namur and many parts of Spain) till the Consecration; Kramp, "Messgebräuche der Gläubigen in den ausserdeutschen Ländern" (StZ [1927], II), 355 f.

The Carthusians are accustomed to sit in choir even during the singing of the offertory chant; *Ordinarium Cart.* (1932), c. 31, 6.

[45] Even at the less solemn *missa matutinalis* different choir rules obtained than at the conventual Mass; thus in the 12th century among the canons of St. Victor in Paris: E. Martène, *De ant. Eccl. ritibus,* App. (III, 791 f.).

[46] The *Lay Folks Mass Book* (ed. Simmons, 6 ff.), which was compiled with the 13th century Anglo-Norman conditions in view, orders the participants to kneel (and then in each case to stand, since sitting is not provided for) at the *Confiteor,* at the collects and Epistle, at the *secreta,* during the Canon, at the *pax* and the priest's Communion, and at the post-communion; see the editor's commentary, 191, 307. Analogous but less detailed directions are found in the Vernon MS. (c. 1375); *ibid.,* 128 ff., especially 143 ff.

For the bishop who assists at the Mass of a priest, the Pontifical of Durandus has the rule: kneel at the collects, from the *secreta* to the communion of the chalice, and again at the post-communion (during the prayers at the foot of the altar the bishop stands next to the priest); Andrieu, III, 643-647. Similarly the *Ordo Rom.* XV, n. 35 (PL, LXXVIII, 1291).

[47] Cf. the details *infra,* p. 447 f.

[48] Thus already in the Mass-*Ordo* of John Burchard (Legg, *Tracts,* 134). This regulation has gone into our present Missal, *Rubr. gen.* XVII, 2.

[49] German preachers in the 15th century usually stress only the kneeling at the Consecration; Franz, 21 f. At the Council of Trent a Portuguese complained that in Italy the faithful stood up right after the elevation of the chalice; they ought to stay kneeling as long as Christ's body was on the altar, as is customary elsewhere; Jedin (*Liturg. Leben,* 1939), 35; cf. *supra,* note 36. Still in Brazil the men (not the women), who occupy the pews usually remain standing all during the Mass except at the Consecration.

Kneeling met with certain difficulties: especially the aristocrats found it hard, because they would get their clothes dirty and because their long turned-up shoes got in the way; Franz, 31.

In the U. S. kneeling is the characteristic posture not only at Low Mass but also at High (except for standing at the Gospel and sitting at certain other times). But

The forms of external participation, however, fulfill their meaning and purpose only when they are props and stays for an interior concurrence on the part of the faithful. The different forms of bodily demeanor are indeed an index to the distinction between prayer and reading, and even in prayer they bring the important thing to the fore. The acclamations help to accentuate this fact.[50] If the faithful of the earlier Middle Ages took part in the offertory procession, sang the *Sanctus* and the *Agnus Dei*, received the Sacrament or at least the *pax*, it is obvious that the grand lineaments of the sacred ceremony must have to some degree continually entered their consciousness. They could not, it is true, follow the wording of prayers and lessons when the language was different from their own, and this was a disadvantage, but it was by no means an absolute hindrance to devout participation. That the faithful were to pray silently by themselves during the sacrifice was also insisted on from early times.[51]

The natural pattern was, of course, for this inward devotion to adjust itself to the actual course of the liturgical function insofar as this was attainable, and to accompany the priest at least at a distance. This ideal had evidently inspired those who, in the Carolingian reform and even later in the Middle Ages, strove for the observance of the olden forms of outward participation. The prayer book of Charles the Bald presents prayer-texts of offering at the offertory, of intercession when the priest asks for prayer for himself, and of preparation for Communion[52]; they are texts which square thoroughly with those of the priest. An English prayer book from the thirteenth century[53] also sets great store on the liturgical collaboration of whoever used it.[54] Joining with the prayers of the priest occurs in many places, often, it may be, quite extrinsically.[55] Just on the threshold

it is worthy of note that Father J. O'Connell, at the request of many American bishops, included in his ceremonial rules for the laity that differ in little from the ordinary choir rules, and hence insist on a standing posture as basic; J. O'Connell, *The Celebration of Mass*, I. appendix.

[50] At the same time it cannot be denied that the juncture of the closing *Per omnia sæcula sæculorum* with the start of the new act is hardly conducive to a clear understanding of the structure of holy Mass. The problem will be met later on again.

[51] Cyprian, *De dom. or.*, c. 4 (CSEL, 3, 269); Const. Ap., II, 57, 21 (Quasten, *Mon.*, 186).

[52] See the pertinent sections in Vol. II, ch. 1, 4; and Ch. 3; 9.

[53] Simmons, *The Lay Folks Mass Book*, 1-60.

[54] Regarding the bodily posture, see *supra*,

note 46. Gestures at prayer included a sign of the cross at the Gospel and, in many places, kissing the book at the end of the Gospel, along with another cross. Mention is made of praying with uplifted hands at the elevation (and also, *ad libitum*, during the secret prayers); the offertory procession was considered optional.

[55] Prayers akin to the priest's prayers and similiar considerations are suggested at the *Confiteor*, *Gloria*, Gospel, *Credo*, *Sanctus*, both mementos, the elevation, *Pater noster* (answer: *Sed libera nos a malo*— the only response mentioned), *Agnus Dei*. In several places, however, like the collects and the Epistle, the *secreta*, the first memento, the Consecration, the only suggestion made is that the participant say the *Pater noster*, to which in some instances the Creed is added and in one case the *Ave*.

of modern times Burchard of Strassburg, in a similar vein, makes a rather comprehensive remark regarding the faithful's participation: Even if people do not understand the priest's words or the Latin tongue, they should not say any other prayers but should pay attention to what the priest is saying and doing and should in spirit offer up, supplicate and plead along with him except during the time when the Sacrament is adored, and at that place in the canon where he (at the *Memento*) prays softly by himself; then one could likewise freely pray for oneself and for all those whom one wishes to commend to God.[56] It is this same Burchard who wanted to inaugurate once more the responses by the *interessentes*.[57]

In the period of humanism such extravagant proposals might possibly have been suggested for educated groups. But for the broad masses of the faithful the simplest premises for such plans were entirely lacking, particularly the ability to learn the priest's prayers or even the Ordinary of the Mass.[58] Following the prayers of the priest was, and continued to be, beyond the reach of the average Catholic,[59] and so the external forms of particiation were also long ago lost. The great stress of popular liturgical leadership has therefore gone in other directions since the ninth century, as we saw. It was enough to point out to the faithful what they could follow with their eyes and to explain the details of these sensible images as representations of Christ's redemptive Passion, extracting as far as possible every last meaning out of our Lord's institution. Allegory dominates the scene till well into modern times.[60] A long intellectual preparation was

[56] Legg, *Tracts*, 135.
[57] *Supra*, p. 237, note 24.
[58] Near the end of the Middle Ages the secrecy of the Canon was kept less and less rigorously, not observed as absolutely as either before or afterwards; cf. *supra*, p. 143, n. 14; however, in the long run it continued unabated; Franz, 631 ff.
[59] The aporia inherent in this problem is aptly illustrated by an example which Simmons presents in his commentary in *The Lay Folks Mass Book*, 158. In these notes Simmons reprints an anecdote illustrative of manners in the 16th century—a supposed conversation, written down in 1527, between the Lady Mary (afterwards Queen of England) and her almoner or chaplain. The lady remarks on the chaplain's advice that "we ought nat to pray at masse, but rather onely to here and harken"; but then, she asks, why does the priest say: "Pray for me"? What I told you, the chaplain replies, is applicable espe-

cially up to this admonition of the priest's. But the lady retorts: "I can nat se what we shall do at masse, if we pray nat." Chaplain: "Ye shall thynke to the mystery of the masse and shall herken the words that the preest say [and those who do not understand] shall behold, and shall here, and thynke, and by that they shall understande."
[60] In the *Mediator Dei* of Pope Pius XII the Holy Father develops at length the idea that in holy Mass the people offer together with the priest, and bases his teaching on that of the great theologians and above all on the Mass prayers themselves. The pertinent sections (paragraphs 80-111, on "Participation of the Faithful in the Eucharistic Sacrifice") are a wonderful step to a fuller appreciation of the part the faithful must play, in heart and body, in offering the sacrifice. Cf. G. Ellard, "At Mass with My Encyclical," *Orate Fratres*, XXII (1947-8), 241-246.

required, and many intermediate steps had to be taken before it became possible once more to establish a closer spiritual bond with the praying and sacrificing at the altar, and thus to go back again to more ancient forms of expression. It was only after chant and the *Singmesse* and the spread among the laity of the use of the missal paved the road, that an opening was gradually made for a fuller participation in the celebration and offering of the Holy Sacrifice.

7. The Time of the Celebration of Mass

As we turn to inquire about the time arrangements made for the celebration of Mass we must be careful to keep our eyes mainly on its public celebration, especially in the centuries in which there was a clear distinction between private Mass and public Mass.

The day for the community celebration of the Eucharist was Sunday, even in the primitive Church. On a Sunday, Paul was with his congregation at Troas where he at night "broke bread."[1] Sunday is unequivocally designated in the *Didache*[2] and in Justin.[3]

What was till then more or less a matter of course, was at the beginning of the fourth century formulated as a sanctioned command at the Council of Elvira: *Si quis in civitate positus tres dominicas ad ecclesiam non accesserit, pauco tempore abstineat[ur], ut correptus esse videatur.*[4] After that, the precept of Sunday Mass was often repeated, both in the East[5]

---

[1] Acts 20:7; possibly it was the night of the Sabbath, not of the Sunday; see E. Jacquier, *Les Actes des Apôtres* (2nd ed.; Paris, 1926), 589. Cf. 1 Cor. 16:2.

[2] *Supra*, p. 18, note 54.

[3] *Supra*, p. 23.

The pertinent data in Hippolytus' *Traditio Ap.* (Dix, 3; 43) is not quite certified.

In the Syrian *Didascalia*, II, 59-61) Funk, 170-176) the faithful are emphatically admonished to appear for Sunday service, for the word of salvation and for the divine nourishment, and not to curtail the body of Christ in its members (II, 59, 2 ff.). Explicit, too, is the so-called *Doctrina Apostolorum*, which derives from the 3rd-4th century. According to Monachino, "La cura pastorale a Milano, Cartagine e Roma," 54-57, the people of Milan in St. Ambrose's time were content with the one episcopal service on Sunday, but by that time spatial limitations restricted attendance to only a portion of the Milanese Christians. A similar opinion for Carthage (*ibid.*, 186-191) rests on even stronger considerations; cf. ZkTh, LXX (1948), 377.

[4] Cf. J. J. Guiniven, C.Ss.R., *The Precept of Hearing Mass* (Catholic University Canon Law Studies, Washington, (1942) No. 158), 17-22, who argues that this legislation of Elvira is vague and inconclusive.

[5] The canon of Elvira recurs at the Synod of Sardica (Sofia, 343), can. 11 (Mansi, III, 19) and at the Trullanum (692), can. 80 (Mansi, XI, 977); as a Communion obligation it also occurs in the West; see W. Thomas, *Der Sonntag* (Göttingen, 1929), 110. Limited to attendance at the parish Mass the same punitive sanction reappears as late as 1624 at the Synod of Bordeaux, III, 3 (Hardouin, XI, 66B; cf. *ibid.*, 1331), which legislates regarding those missing three Sundays in a row.

and in the West.[6] From the decrees of the Synod of Agde (506)[7] it was copied into the general law of the Church.[8] Still in the carrying out of the obligation, especially in country places, there were many difficulties that had to be contended with all through the Middle Ages.[9]

Besides Sundays, other days began to be reckoned as days of public worship on which one counted on the attendance of the congregation or even demanded it; these were the feast days, including the martyr feasts of the respective church, and also the days after a great festival, especially Easter week, and the days of preparation for such festivals, especially Lent. During Lent daily attendance at divine service was considered of obligation for many centuries from Carolingian times on, and was so enjoined in the penitential books.[10] Besides it was the custom since the fourth century in nearly all Christendom on the stational days, Wednesday and Friday, to conclude the fast in the afternoon with a prayer-meeting. Except in Egypt and probably also in Rome, this was nearly everywhere joined to the celebration of Mass.[11] In Rome the same rule was followed, at any rate during the ember weeks, the Mass formulas for which have been preserved till our own day. And even in Rome it became customary after the outset of the Middle Ages, to celebrate Mass publicly at least on Wednesdays each week, as we are bound to conclude from the Scripture lessons appointed for this purpose.[12] Each Ember week ended in the night between Saturday and Sunday with a long vigil, and the Mass of this vigil counted for the Sunday. However, about the seventh century a special Mass was formulated for this Sunday and the vigil Mass was moved back to Saturday morning so that Saturday too, at least in Ember week, received a distinction like that of Wednesday and Friday.

In the Orient, ever since the fourth century, Saturday had gradually been invested with the privilege of public Mass week after week, but for entirely different reasons. As a defensive parry against Manichean doctrine, Saturday, the day when creation had ended, was in time looked upon as "Sunday's brother"[13] and was therefore fitted out in like manner with divine service.[14]

[6] Franz, 11.
[7] Can. 47 (Mansi, VIII, 332); cf. Guiniven, 23-25.
[8] Decretum Gratiani III, 1, 64 (Friedberg, I, 1312).
[9] Franz, 11-15.
[10] Theodulf, Capitulare, I, c. 39 (PL, CV, 204); Burchard of Worms, Decretum XIX, c. 5 (PL, CXL, 962 C). Likewise in the somewhat later Summa de indiciis omnium peccatorum; H. J. Schmitz, Die Bussbücher und das kanonische Bussverfahren (Düsseldorf, 1898), 492 f. Decretum Gratiani III, 1, 50 (Friedborg, I, 1307).

[11] Schümmer, Die altchristliche Fastenpraxis, 117. In Africa, at least in Tertullian's time, the celebration of the Eucharist appears to have taken place on these days early in the morning; ibid., 120; Dekkers, Tertullianus, 109 ff., 140 f.

[12] Infra, pp. 400-402.

[13] Gregory of Nyssa, Adv. eos qui castigationes aegre ferunt (PG, XLVI, 309 B).

[14] Const. Ap., II, 59, 3; V, 20, 19 (Funk, I, 171 f., 301 along with the pertinent notes). Cf. Bladau, Die Pilgerreise der Ätheria, 102 f.

A daily celebration of Mass with the character of a public service must, however, have remained unknown to the ancient Church until well in the fourth century. More comprehensive expressions are to be understood either of a private celebration[15] or even merely of Communion at home. But in the time of St. Augustine a daily Mass to which all the faithful could come must have been very widespread, at least in Africa.[16] When it became the prevailing rule to transfer Votive Masses to the public church, the sharp distinction between public and private celebration began to disappear in the churches of the West and there arose some transitional forms. The faithful were now able to attend Mass in church daily.[17]

Still, public Mass on Sundays and feast days continued to retain its special prerogatives. All through the Middle Ages it had its appointed hour. And since the Church was free and (after renouncing the evening meal) no longer bound to choose an early morning hour, a time was set for common worship that appeared to be fitting for such a momentous task. On Sundays and feast days it was the third hour,[18] which was designated at Rome[19] about 530,[20] as well as in Gaul,[21] and this hour it is which consistenly recurs in the writings of both the liturgists[22] and the canonists.[23] Since the Middle Ages it was regularly preceded by Terce, not only

[15] For Cyprian, *Ep.*, 57, 3, see *supra*, p. ???, note 4. Cf. Schümmer, *Die altchristliche Fastenpraxis*, 117 f.

[16] Daily Mass is mentioned in Augustine, *Ep.*, 54, 2, 2; 228, 6; *In Joh. tract.*, 26, 15; *De civ. Dei*, X, 20, etc. Cf. Roetzer, 97 f.; Monachino, "La cura pastorale a Milano, Cartagine e Roma," 191-193.

Cf. Chrysostom, *In Eph. hom.*, 3, 4 (PG, LXII, 29).

[17] This altered situation also necessitated a change in the arrangement of the church building and the altar, particularly the setting up of a special week-day altar to accommodate the smaller week-day congregation; see *Gottesdienst* (ed. R. Schwarz; Würzburg, 1937), 72.

[18] The "third hour" did not, of course, coincide precisely with our "nine o'clock," for the older reckoning was based on an apportionment of daylight into twelve parts from sunup to sundown; in winter these portions started later, were necessarily shorter; in summer they began earlier and were lengthened out. For that reason the Synod of Cambria (1586), III, 10 (Hardouin, IX, 2157) stipulated: in summer at 8 o'clock, in winter at 9. See H. Grotefend, *Zeitrechnung des deutschen Mittelalters*, (Hanover, 1891), I, 183 ff.; cf. also G. Bilfinger, *Die mittelalterlichen*

Horen und die modernen Stunden (Stuttgart, 1892), 1 ff.

[19] *Liber pont.* (Duchesne, I, 129): Pope Telesphorus, it relates, ordered that no one presume to celebrate *ante horæ tertiæ cursum*. The statement is, of course, unauthentic, but it indicates the attitude of the early sixth century.

[20] The choice of the third hour was already anticipated in Hippolytus, *Trad. Ap.* (Dix, 63), where this hour is commended to the faithful as the hour the bread of proposition (shewbread) was offered up (to which some of the sources add: "as a type of the body and blood of Christ").

[21] Synod of Orleans (538), can. 14 (Mansi, 16): *De missarum celebritate in præcipuis duntaxat sollemnitatibus id observari debet ut hora tertia missarum celebratio in Dei nomine inchoetur.*

[22] Among others: Amalar, *De eccl. off.*, III, 42 (PL, CV, 1160); Walafrid Strabo, *De exord. et increm.*, c. 23 (PL, CXIV, 951); Bernold, *Micrologus*, c. 58 (PL, CLI, 1019).

[23] Regino of Prüm, *De synod. causis*, I, inqu. 29 (PL, CXXXII, 188); Burchard, *Decretum*, III, 63 (PL, CXL, 686); *Decretum Gratiani*, III, 1, 48 (Friedberg, I, 1307).

in monastery and chapter churches but also as far as possible even in parish churches,[24] and Sext usually followed.[25] Therefore, in the still extant directions for ringing the church bells[26] a special peal—rung two or even three times—was provided.[27] The arrangement developed for Sundays and feasts was shifted also to week days when daily conventual Mass became common in monastery and chapter churches.[28] But it must also have been adopted at quite an early period as the order of worship in parish churches.[29] "Mass time" was an unambiguous time-designation all through the Middle Ages and even after, and it meant the third hour of the day.[30]

Already in Ambrose there is evidence of an evening celebration of Mass, but only on fast days.[31] In the Carolingian era a Mass at the ninth hour on fast days was as much a matter-of-course as the Mass at the third hour on other days.[32] This remained the custom in the centuries to follow, especially for Lent.[33] On other days that were midway between strict fasting days and feasts properly so called, the *dies profesti*, a middle course was taken from the eleventh century on, with Mass at the sixth hour.[34] It was not till near the end of the Middle Ages that any tendency was shown to push

[24] Cf. *supra*, pp. 211-212.

[25] John of Avranches, *De off. eccl.* (PL, CXLVII, 38 D) : *Diebus omnibus excepto ieiunii tempore Sexta missam sequatur.*

[26] Eisenhofer, I, 395 f.
Durandus, I, 4, 9-15.
A thoroughly detailed and exactly graded program for ringing the bells is contained in the *Missale Romanum* printed at Venice in 1501 (reprinted in Legg, *Tracts*, 175-178).

[27] According to Durandus, I, 4, 12, at Terce a first stroke of the bell was given *ad invocandum*, a second *ad congregandum*, and a third *ad inchoandum*.

[28] A notable early attestation is found in Bede (d. 735), *Hist. gent. Angl.*, IV, 22 (PL, XCV, 206 f) : The bonds of a prisoner were very often *(sæpissime)* loosened *a tertia . . . hora* because, as the story later reveals, his brother who was priest and abbot offered the sacrifice for him.

[29] According to Regino of Prüm, *De synod. causis*, I, inq. 33 (PL, CXXXII, 188) the parish priest should be examined *si tempore statuto, id est circa horam tertiam diei, missam celebret, et post hæc usque ad medium diem ieiunet, ut hospitibus atque peregre venientibus, si necesse fuerit, possit missam cantare*. The context shows that this refers to more than just Sundays and feasts.

[30] St. Ignatius of Loyola, in his Book of Exercises, still regularly employs the ex-

pression *ad horam missæ* as an indication of the time for meditation (*Exercitia spiritualia*, etc.). Notice that the *Directorium* for the Exercises, published in 1599, substitutes *paulo ante prandium* (c. 3, 7; *ibid.*, 348).

[31] Ambrose, *In ps.* 118 *serm.*, 8, 48 (PL, tualia [Regensburg, 1911], 151; 155; 173; XV, 1314). Cf. Paulinus of Nola, *Carmen* XXIII, v. III ff. (PL, LXI, 610 C).
F. Zimmermann, *Die Abendmesse in Geschichte und Gegenwart* (Vienna, 1914), 74 f., 82 f.

[32] Walafrid Strabo, *De exord. et increm.* c. 23 (PL, CXIV, 951).
The source material from the Gallic synods of the 6th century in J. Mabillon, *De liturgia gallicana*, I, 6 (PL, LXXII, 142 f.) ; repeated in Zimmermann, 114 f.

[33] Zimmermann, 117-132.
The *missa quadragesimalis* or Lenten Mass was probably celebrated at 5 o'clock in the 6th century; see the reference to *vespertina* in III Council of Orleans (558), can. 32 (*MGH, Conc.*, I 82) : *sacrificia vero matutina missarum sive vespertina*. But by the opening of the 9th century the time had been advanced; see P. Browe in *Theologische Quartalschrift*, CII (1921), 43.

[34] First occurrence in Bernold, *Micrologus*, c. 58 (PL, CLI, 1019). Zimmermann, 119 f. Further attestations up to the 13th century, *ibid.*, 120-132.

these later hours ahead by saying Mass as usual right after Sext or None, but anticipating these hours before noon.[35] Taking a cue from this, John Burchard, in his *Ordo missæ* (1502), expanded the existing tradition and thus developed the more exact regulations that were then taken over into the *Rubricæ generales* of our Mass book. Its most important stipulation is that the *missa Conventualis et solemnis* on Sundays and feasts (semi-duplex and upward) ought to take place *dicta in choro hora tertia*, on simple feasts and ferial days *dicta Sexta*, and on days of penance *post Nonam*[36]; that is, the Mass on feast days could, like the meals, continue to be attached to its usual hour of the day: it always takes place at the "third hour."[37]

However, this holding to an appointed time for public worship has quite generally lost its importance since the later Middle Ages. That fact is connected with what we have already seen regarding the gradual breakdown of the distinction between public and private Mass.[38] For a long time no particular hour was stipulated for private Mass,[39] and therefore no connection with a canonical hour.[40] True, the faithful, in accordance with ancient law, were not so free to attend the *missæ peculiares* on Sundays and holy days as to be drawn away from public Mass[41]; in fact, the faithful were obliged to fulfill their Sunday obligations not just in any public church but precisely in their own parish church.[42] But with the

[35] Thus in the middle of the 14th century according to P. Boeri; see E. Martène, *Regula s. Benedicti commentata*, c. 48 (PL, LXVI, 710 d).

[36] *Rubr. gen.* XV, 2.
At what time of day the hours were to be recited is not specified. Gottschalk Hollen (d. after 1481), however, in a sermon for the consecration of a church, repeats the old rule: third, sixth and ninth hours; but he emphasizes the fact that this holds only *de missis popularibus et conventualibus in quibus fit concursus populi* (cited by R. Cruel, *Geschichte der deutschen Predigt im Mittelalter* [Detmold, 1879], 210).
Zimmermann, 177 f., makes it appear probable that even in the 16th century the old-time regulations were still observed in many localities.

[37] Thus, to cite an instance that seems to correspond, in Ingolstadt in the time of Johann Eck (d. 1543) the daily *summum officium* took place in summer at 8.00, in winter at 9:00; Greving, 84.

[38] *Supra*, p. 229.

[39] See the accounts in Martène, 1, 3, 4, 10 (I, 297 f.).

Amalar, *De eccl. off.*, III, 42 (PL, CV, 1160), feels obligated to defend the freer treatment of the hours for private Mass; at that rate there must have been a certain easing of the rules; cf. Eisenhofer, II, 25.

[40] Not till the 13th century (first in the Statutes of the church of Rouen) is there any general regulation that Matins, Lauds and Prime are to be said before Mass; Zimmermann, 171. The same injunction is also found in German synods of the 13th century (Hartzheim, III, 646; 662; cf. IV, 25). Also in the *Liber ordinarius* of Liége (Volk, 100 f.).
In Burchard's *Ordo Missæ* (Legg, *Tracts*, 126), Prime is no longer demanded absolutely; in our Roman Missal (Ritus serv., I, 1; cf. De defect., X, 1) only Matins and Lauds are enjoined. There is no longer any distinction here between public Mass and private.

[41] Theodulf of Orleans, *Capitulare*, I, c. 45 (PL, CV, 208); *Decretum Gratiani* III, 1, 52 (Friedberg, I, 1308).

[42] Numerous decisions of this sort from 9th to 12th century in Browe, *Die Pflichtkommunion*, 49-51. Later ordinances, in in part with threats of excommunication, in Martène, 1, 3, 9, 4 f. (I, 337-340).

coming of the Mendicants this law was slowly relaxed even though synod after synod took a firm stand in opposition.[43] In the fifteenth century it had become in many places a right sanctioned by usage that the Sunday duty could be fulfilled in any church of one's choosing[44] and, in consequence, at any Mass of one's choosing[45] and this right soon obtained papal approbation, beginning in 1517 with a decree of Leo X.[46]

Thus on Sundays we continue to have, at the customary hour, a service which we usually style the main service, but besides this, service has long since been conducted also at other hours, particularly in cities. Of these the early hours with their Communion Mass, at which there is a homily, are from the pastoral viewpoint as important as the main service, though this latter is perhaps richer at least musically.[47] Even if the social aspect —the idea of community—is thus somewhat obscured, there is some compensation in the fact that so many of the faithful are offered the opportunity to take part in Sunday Mass, a viewpoint which was not entirely absent even in Christian antiquity.[48] And likewise service on weekdays has not for a long time been conducted along the pattern of a monastic community that is independent and self-contained and can therefore follow the old rhythm of the Office hours, but the determining factor has been rather the people's work day.

The decree of the Council of Nantes (Mansi, XVIIIa, 166-167), obliging the parish priest to inquire at the start of Sunday Mass whether anyone was present who belonged to another parish, and asking any such to leave unless they were on a journey or had due permission, is still repeated in the 13th century where it has become part of the *Corpus Iuris Canonici: Decretales Greg.* III, 92, 2 (Friedberg, II, 554).

[43] Franz, 15-17. Among the synods cited here the first is that of Prague, 1349, the last that of Hildesheim, 1539. The Council of Arles (1260) had already strictly prohibited religious to receive lay people into their churches and chapels on Sundays; can. 15; Mansi, XXIII, 1010. And the Council of Budapest, 1279, was even more severe, inflicting various penalties; can. 33; Mansi, XXIV, 285-6. See Guiniven, *The Precept of Hearing Mass.*, 30-34.

[44] Thus attests St. Antoninus (d. 1459), *Summa theol.*, II, 9, 10 (Verona [1740]: II, 1001).

[45] Nicholas of Cusa, when Bishop of Brixen, had admonished parish priests to instruct the people *quod non sufficit audire peculiares missas.* Franz, 16, note 4.

[46] Benedict XIV, *De synodo diœcesana,* VII, 64 (= *De s. sacrificio missæ;* ed. Schneider, 320 f.).

Still the Council of Trent advised the bishops to admonish their people *ut frequenter ad suas parochias, saltem diebus dominicis et maioribus festis, accedant;* Sess. XXII, *De observ. et vit. in celebr. missæ.*

The present legislation no longer makes mention of this; *Cod. Iur. Can.,* c. 1249.

[47] An even less favorable criticism of the Sunday's service in towns and cities is to be found in Parsch, *Volksliturgie,* 188.

[48] Leo the Great, *Ep.,* 9, 2 (PL, LIV, 627): *Necesse est autem, ut quædam pars populi sua devotione privetur, si unius tantum missæ more servato sacrificium offerre non possint, nisi qui prima diei parte convenerint.* This decision, which was sent to Alexandria, seems to presuppose a second, later Mass; however, it is not concerned primarily with tthe ordinary Sunday Mass, but rather with the unusual case of a gathering at a certain church where, because of a memorial service for a martyr, people from all over town have assembled; cf. Monachino, "La cura pastorale a Milano, Cartagine e Roma,"354 f.

Considerations of a similar sort under the conditions of World War II prompted the extensive approbation of evening Masses, and this exclusively as public Masses, celebrated in the interests of the faithful but without being confined to Sundays and holydays.[49] This is no unqualified innovation, even apart from the primitive Church,[50] and even when we have only divine service of a festal nature in view. For far into the medieval period the services for Easter and Pentecost and for the Ember Sundays were conducted on the eve or vigil at a late evening hour; even in modern times an analogous custom regarding the Christmas midnight Mass, which had its origin in Venice, became quite widespread.[51]

Besides the public Masses on Sundays and holydays with the corresponding assemblage—at least successively—of all the members of the congregation, attendance at weekday Mass also has been on the increase. In the early Church the only ones who attended weekday Mass were as a rule those for whose benefit the sacrifice was being offered. The celebration of Mass on the stational days must, no doubt, have gathered a larger crowd of the faithful. In North Africa where daily celebration was customary earliest of all, Augustine gives us to understand that this was very necessary for the faithful in days of peril, that they might be able to continue steadfast.[52] However, this is no evidence of a daily Mass attendance by a wider circle.[53]

[49] These indults were granted to the military ordinariates of Germany as well as the United States, etc. Since then various other indults for public evening Mass have been vouchsafed. See the discussion of the recent Roman grants in G. Ellard, "How Near is Evening Mass?" *American Ecclesiastical Review*, CXXII (1950), 331-340.

[50] Cf. in this connection E. Dekkers, "L'Eglise ancienne a-t-elle connu la Messe du Soir?" *Miscellanea Mohlberg* (1948), I, 231-257; according to this article the evening Mass of the Corinthians was more or less an exception. The author multiplies proofs that in the very earliest Christian age Mass was normally celebrated *ante lucem*, while in the patristic period even week-day Mass was said *sub vesperam diei*.

[51] Zimmermann, 146-157; 190-198.

It was this book, published in 1914, that gave the first impetus to this whole question of a post-noon Mass. In it he describes, 201-244, "the modern movement for evening Mass," but his own historical discussion of the question was the first great impulse this movement received. The more extended concession of evening Mass in our times began with indults granted to certain countries pressed by persecution (Mexico, 1927; Russia, 1929) and with the permission to celebrate Mass continually for three days and nights at Lourdes in 1935; see Ellard, *The Mass of the Future*, 331 ff.

A new problem has been pressing for authoritative discussion: the question, whether it is not more appropriate to fulfill one's Sunday obligation at a *Saturday*-night Mass instead of a *Sunday*-night Mass. The Church has already begun the Sunday observance with First Vespers; the method follows the ancient model of the vigil service. And the Sunday evening Mass would involve an impoverishment of divine service, since evening service over and above the Mass could hardly be developed.

[52] Augustine, *Ep.*, 228, 6 (CSEL, LVII, 489): those of the faithful especially had become recreant *quibus cotidianum ministerium dominci corporis defuit*. Cf. *supra*, p. 213, note 4.

[53] Augustine, in his *Confessions*, V, 9 (CSEL, XXXIII, 104, 1. 6) remarks of his mother, St. Monica, that on no day had

It was not till the late Carolingian era, in the writings of Regino of Prüm, that there are any traces of the faithful attending daily Mass.[54] Daily attendance at Mass in the castle chapel was part of the order of the day amongst the Norman nobility of twelfth-century England[55]; elsewhere too, the knights appear to have followed a similar practice.[56] The people were encouraged in sermons to attend Mass daily, even in the days before the widespread desire to see our Lord which went to such excesses during the late Middle Ages.[57] As a matter of fact daily attendance at Mass was a prevalent practice amongst all ranks of the people in the later Middle Ages.[58]

8. Accommodations of Space

One of the wonderful manifestations of the inner strength, power, and extent of Christian worship is the fact that it is so spiritualized that it seems to be almost indifferent to conditions of space and yet it has produced, in every century, masterpieces of architecture and the other structural arts such as no other of man's ideas has been able to produce. We cannot here go into very great detail in showing, as we have done with other questions, how the construction of buildings and other spatial accessories has developed as an outer frame surrounding the celebration of Mass. All we can do is sketch a general outline and lay bare certain underlying trends that are closely connected with the celebration, pointing out especially the genetic line of these tendencies.

she missed the *oblatio ad altare.*

Regarding pre-Carolingian Gaul there are some interesting remarks in Henry Beck, "A Note on the Frequency of Mass in Sixth-Century France," *American Ecclesiastical Review*, CXX (1949), 480-485; little is said, however, about the attendance of the people.
[54] *Supra,* note 29. It must be remarked that even in the eleventh century the daily conventual Mass in the monasteries was a rule, but not an absolute one; cf. p. 204, note 60.
[55] See the proofs in Simmons, *The Lay Folks Mass Book,* p. 38 f.
[56] In the Grail poem of Chrestien de Troyes (v. 6450 ff.). Parcival receives from a hermit the advice to go to church every morning. If Mass is said, he should remain till the priest has said everything and sung everything. Cf. the Grail legend, *Perceval le Gallois,* ed. Potvin (Mons. 1866), p. 261. Time and again Mass appears as part of the daily order for the knights in Wolf-

ram von Eschenbach, *Parzival* (ed. Lachmann; 6th ed.), III, 169, 17 ff.; IV, 196, 12 ff.; XV, 776, 25.
[57] Berthold of Regensburg, *Predigten,* ed. Pfeiffer, I, 458-460 ("at least once a day," 458 l. 7); 503; see Franz, 33 f.

A sermon ascribed to St. Ambrose (PL, XVII, 656 B) contains this admonition: *Moneo etiam, ut qui iuxta ecclesiam est et occurrere potest, quotidie audiat missam.* It is not clear whether this counsel was meant for the whole year or only for the Lenten season. This sermon must have been written some time about the end of the 8th or the start of the 9th century since in it a regular confession at the beginning of Quadragesima (n. 1) and Communion during Lent at least on Sundays (n. 6) is presupposed; both these had gone out of use entirely during the 9th century.
[58] L. A. Veit, *Volksfrommes Brauchtum und Kirche im deutschen Mittelalter* (Freiburg, 1936), 172.

One of the most revolutionary innovations which Christianity produced was the departure from a cultus of place-worship connected with certain localities—holy mountains, mystic groves, even the sacred Temple in Jerusalem. Worship can take place wherever a holy people are gathered before God, for this people is the true Temple of the Lord (2 Cor. 6:16; 1 Cor. 3:16). Therefore in every place, from the rising of the sun to its going down, the new sacrifice is offered up (Mal. 1:11). The true sanctuary is to be found neither in Garizim nor in Jerusalem, but in every place where true adorers worship God in spirit and in truth (John 4:21 ff.).

If, therefore, in the first centuries of Christianity there is but little mention of the place for divine worship and even that little is only incidental, the reason is to be sought in something more than just the circumstances of the persecutions. People assembled for their Sunday celebration wherever some member of the congregation could manage to set up the room for its performance. But the Eucharist was also celebrated in the burial places of the dead and even in the prisons of those held captive.[1] This basic freedom and mobility of divine service has been retained all through the succeeding centuries right down to the present. Today, too, whenever it is necessary, that sacrifice can be offered under the open sky or in any suitable place, and no other barricade against the profane world is exacted excepting the altarstone on which the sacred species can rest; and even this requirement is in our days set aside with the permission to use instead an *antimensium* like that traditional in the Eastern Church.[2] But two things continue to be indispensable for service: a resting place for the sacred species and a place for the assembling of the people. And thus, as soon as circumstances allowed Christianity to unfold and develop with less restraint, the history of church architecture and church art, already in embryo before Constantine's time, began its marvellous course.

It is significant that in the Romance languages the prevalent word used to designate the church building is the one which signifies an assembly, *ecclesia*, while in other languages, on the contrary, the word which is primarily intended for the church building, χυριαχόν, "church," has been transferred to the assembly. As a matter of fact the building is nothing else than the material surrounding of the living temple of God, a substantial shell which has formed and will continue to form even though human foolishness or the forces of nature may have destroyed it.[3] For that reason it seems in its design to mirror the idea and structure of the living temple.

[1] *Supra*, pp. 208, 217.
Cf. also Eusebius, *Hist. eccl.*, VII, 22, 4.
[2] Permission was granted to chaplains during World War II.

[3] Cf. H. Sedlmayr, *Architektur als abbildende Kunst* (Österr. Akad. d. Wiss. Phil.-hist. Kl., Sitzungsbericht, 225, 3; Vienna [1948], 4-13.

Just as the Church of God is built up of people and clergy, so too the presbytery or choir, in whose vertex stands the *cathedra* of the bishop, is separated from the nave of the church. Just as the ecclesiastical assembly, following ancient custom, was wont to pray facing East, toward the Orient from on high,[4] so too the ecclesiastical building is turned into a "ship" (nave=*navis*) voyaging towards the East,[5] and the orientation of the church is in fact carried out in such a way (first in the East and later also in the West) that the apse is to the East, and so the direction which the praying congregation faces coincides with the lie of the building.

Finally, the consecration of the living temple is, in a way, carried over to the material structure[6]; church and altar are consecrated and themselves become holy. There is something to be learnt from the fact that in this consecration ceremony—the old Gallican rite, revitalized with Roman traditions and still retained in today's *Pontificale Romanum*—church and altar are "baptized" and "confirmed" almost like human beings; they are sprinkled on all sides with holy water and are anointed with holy oil[7]; only after that is the first Eucharist celebrated.

The heart of the church, the focal point at which all lines converge, is the place of the sacrifice, the altar.[8] We nowadays take such a thing for granted, but actually a certain development lies back of this. In the church of Christian antiquity the personal element in the assembled congregation was so much to the fore that it was the seat of the bishop or rather the bishop himself who was the central figure; he is the *liturgus* who offers up the Eucharist to God. The material side of the gifts is, if anything, hidden rather than emphasized.[9] The table on which they lie is looked upon merely as a technical aid. It is, you might say, not an altar at all, in the sense of pre-Christian religions where the gift is hallowed and dedicated to God only when it touches the altar; our Gift is intrinsically holy, dedicated to God by its very nature and in the last analysis does not really require an altar. All the references we possess from the third and fourth centuries agree in their account of the altar; they regard the altar not as a part of the permanent structure of the church but only as a simple wooden table which is carried into position by the deacons as occasion dictates.[10] But the new appreciation for the material gift by which the sacrifice of the New Testament burgeons out of and beyond this earthly space and hallows it, and the deeper rooting of the Church in this world of time, were the

[4] Cf. *supra*, p. 301.
[5] For this cf. H. Rahner, "Antenna crucis, III," ZkTh, LXVI (1942), 196-227, especially 201.
[6] R. Grosche, "Versuch einer Theologie des Kirchbaus," *Betendes Werk*, ed. R. Schwarz (Würzburg, 1938), 113-121.
[7] Duchesne, *Christian Worship*, 406 ff.; 410-412.

[8] J. Braun, *Der christliche Altar in seiner geschichtlichen Entwicklung* (2 vols.; Munich, 1924) ; Geoffrey Webb, *The Liturgical Altar* (2nd ed.; Westminster, 1949).
[9] *Supra*, p. 24 ff.
[10] Eisenhofer, I, 344 f.

cause, or at least the occasion, for the altar's assuming a more fixed form. Often in the fourth century—and regularly thereafter—it is made of stone. But it remained a plain simple table. Even today its name in the Orient is still ἡ ἁγία τράπεζα.[11]

To this table the *liturgus* came at the beginning of the Mass proper, the sacrificial offering. On which side should he take his place—facing the people or facing away? History indicates that both practices were in use from the very start, at least in the vicinity of Rome. Even today they are both countenanced in the *Missale Romanum*.[12] One way, the priest stands turned towards the altar facing in the same direction as the people; this is at present the general rule both East and West, and appears to have always been the rule in the East. The other way, he stands on the side opposite, facing the people, and this is the position presupposed in some of the older Roman churches. However, this latter position appears to have been chosen only where there was some special reason for it.[13] The rule which grew ever more important, that at prayer all should look to the East —and naturally this included the celebrant first of all—led even in the early Middle Ages to the priest's assuming a place almost without exception[14] like the one he assumes today, on the side of the altar nearest the people, for he is the leader of the people in their prayer and at their head offers up to God their prayer and sacrifice.[15]

[11] Salaville, *Eastern Liturgies*, 133. This term is used even beyond the Greek-speaking areas; Brightman, 569.

[12] *Ritus serv.*, V, 3.

[13] Braun, I, 412 f., suggests three reasons: (1) If the altar was linked to a martyr's grave *(confessio)*, the side facing the people had to be open to give them access to the grave. (2) If in episcopal churches the *cathedra* stood in the apse (as it does in all the Roman stational churches), it was most convenient (although not imperative) that the side nearest the apse be chosen for celebrating. (3) Especially if the apse was built on the western side of the church, this method of celebrating had to be adopted, for the law that prayer be said facing East demanded such a solution. Cf. for Augustine's time, Roetzer, 89.

[14] An exception which literally confirms the rule is to be found in the altar in the west choir of Rhenish churches and others; so that even here the priest might stand properly oriented he had to take the side towards the nave. Braun, I, 415; cf. 387 ff.; G. Malherbe, "L'orientation des autels dans les églises à double chœur," *Les Questions liturgiques et paroissiales*, XXI (1936), 278-280.

[15] See the plans by R. Schwarz, *Vom Bau der Kirche* (Würzburg, 1937), esp. 56 f. Orientation at prayer and the symbolism it entails has lost much of its meaning for us. But the basic principle that at prayer all— including even the celebrant—should take a God-ward stance, could easily be at work here too, in establishing the celebrant's position at the altar. If Mass were only a service of instruction or a Communion celebration, the other position, facing the people, would be more natural. But it is different if the Mass is an immolation and homage to God. If today the altar *versus populum* is frequently chosen, this is the result of other considerations that come into play—considerations which are rated as of paramount importance particularly as a reaction to earlier conditions. It serves to narrow down the distance between priest and congregation and to highlight the instructive items contained in the prayer and the rite. In certain circumstances—like the services for young people—these reasons appear to be well-founded.

The same basic relationship is the reason for the position which the altar occupies in the space of the church. It is a striking fact that in the history of Christian church architecture the axial type appears in various localities, but that even here the altar is hardly ever placed in the center; both in oriental churches (with cupola and shaped like a Greek cross) and in the circular churches of the West (a style frequently used during the Baroque period), the altar stands in a niche or apse which was added to the circular structure, as a rule toward the East.[16] But during ancient times an effort was always made to set up the altar in such a way that it seemed to belong both to the nave and to the choir, being placed at the intersection of the two or even brought out a little into the nave itself.[17]

Then in the early Middle Ages a new movement set in, which gradually moved the altar into the background in the rear of the choir.[18] This is but the architectonic expression of an intellectual movement which stressed more and more the sacredness and aloofness of the mystery and restricted immediate access to it to the clergy.[19] In the Orient the altar stands free and open in the sanctuary but, by means of the ikonostasis, it is withdrawn from the people's gaze.[20] In the West, the altar itself was moved closer to the rear wall of the sanctuary and at the same time the sanctuary or choir in Romanesque architecture was vastly increased in size; in monastic and capitular churches it became a formal clerical chapel, specially designed for the clerical services which continually became more richly developed.[21] Here too, the railing which marked the limits of the choir often turned into a dividing wall, although intended to separate the clergy, rather than the altar, from the people.[22] Therefore, a second main altar (often called the "rood altar") was sometimes built in the church in front of this (choir) screen, to serve the people.[23] But when the chapters began to disappear the screen likewise disappeared, first from the leading churches and then soon everywhere. Baroque architecture restored the unity of place without, however, making any changes regarding the placement of the altar.

[16] Braun, I, 390-393.
[17] There are authenticated instances in many places in the ancient Church where the plan of building involved an altar in the center of the nave. For the old churches of Tyre, Zebed and Menas, *Vide* K. Liesenberg, *Der Einfluss der Liturgie auf die früchchristliche Basilika* (Diss.; Freiburg i. Br., 1928), 39 f.

This plan of construction was used quite generally in North Africa; J. Sauer, "Der Kirchenbau Nordafrikas in den Tagen des hl. Augustinus" (*Aurelius Augustinus*, ed. Grabmann and Mausbach; Cologne [1930]; 243-300), 286 f.

The same holds true of ancient Christian architecture in Greece; see the review of a pertinent discussion by G. A. Sotiriu in JL, XI (1931), 290.

[18] In Syria, for example, this development had already been completed by the time of the Islamic invasion; Liesenberg, 64.

[19] Cf. *supra*, p. 82 f.

[20] *Supra*, p. 40. Cf. also Salaville, *Eastern Liturgies*, 105-111.

[21] Cf. *supra*, p. 103 f., 205 f.

[22] Braun, II, 665 f.

[23] Braun, I, 401-406.

Regarding the history of side altars we have already given a brief resumé, *supra*, p. 222 ff.

The altar, too, saw a great development from the simple table of olden times to the elaborate forms of recent centuries; but a clear idea of the purpose of the altar was not always kept in view. As the place where the sacred mystery was celebrated, it was fitting that the altar should receive every mark of respect possible. Even in the pre-Constantine era people were conscious of this.[24] The altar was decked and decorated like a table; precious cloths were spread over it. Chrysostom had to give a warning about an excess of zeal in this matter that left other tasks undone.[25] The frontals *(antependia)* of our day which now cover usually the front of the altar only, are the last vestiges of this sort of reverence. The next move was to add railings and steps. The altar of the church in Tyre which was dedicated in 314 was surrounded by an artistically wrought railing.[26] The elevated position of the altar, standing as it did in a sanctuary which was raised somewhat above the level of the church, already lent special significance to the altar, but—in the Western Church—special steps were constructed in front of the altar itself, though this did not become a general rule till the eleventh century and after.[27] But the most prominent of the marks of distinction given the altar was the special shelter or canopy which surmounted it either by way of a *baldachin* or *testa* or by way of a fixed *civory (ciborium)*.[28] This covering over the altar served to emphasize the special character of the table.

The closer the altar was put to the rear wall, the more necessary it became that this wall itself should be connected with it in significance and importance. The wall of the apse had long been specially ornamented. Preferably they were decorations that expressed those matters which formed the core and kernel of Christian consciousness, very much as the thanksgiving prayer of the Mass did by means of words—the glorified Cross, the Lamb triumphant, the Good Shepherd, or finally Christ enthroned and surrounded by the saints or by the Apostles or by the ancients of the Apocalypse.[29] Later the representation of the Crucified was more often substituted for these others. Even in places where—as was not seldom the case in the Gothic period—a decorative wall-painting was introduced over the altar, the choice dictated by old tradition fell by preference on a crucifixion group either as the only representation or at least as the principal one.[30]

But about the eleventh century quite other rules were formed as the result of the introduction of a decorative structure ornamented with paintings, built either on the altar-table itself or immediately behind it, the

---

[24] Origen, *In Jesu Nave hom.*, 10, 3 (PG, XII, 881).

[25] Chrysostom, *In Matth. hom.*, 50, 4 (PG, LVIII, 509).

[26] Eusebius, *Hist. eccl.*, X, 4 (PG, XX, 865 f.).

[27] Braun, II, 178 ff.

[28] Peter Anson, *Churches: Their Plan and Furnishings* (Milwaukee, 1948), 100-103.

[29] C. M. Kaufmann, *Handbuch der christlichen Archäologie* (3rd ed.; Paderborn, 1922), 422-430.

[30] Braun, II, 533. Examples (several of them from churches in Cologne and southern Tyrol), *ibid.*, 532 f. More often this concerns side altars.

258 THE NATURE AND FORMS OF THE MASS

so-called retable. In the choice of subjects for these pictures the widest variety prevailed; all of Christian iconography was brought into play.[31] Strikingly enough, it is seldom the mystery of Redemption depicted in any shape or form. Where the crucifix did appear it was generally a quite realistic representation, with a host of strange figures around it.[32] Completely forgotten was the essential notion that a picture over the altar is not a pictorial record of the past but primarily an instrument for professing our Catholic faith and acknowledging our Christian hope. Most often the picture was one of the saint in whose honor the church was dedicated and whose relics—according to ancient principle—were buried there. Next to this, figures of other saints were frequently placed. Here is the key to the understanding of the iconographic phenomenon alluded to. It is explained, in the last analysis, by the connection which the altar had during the early Middle Ages with the grave of the martyr to which the devotion of Christian people had turned quite early with great zeal. The tension and strain which was naturally bound to develop between the shrines of the martyrs and the churches destined for congregational worship[33] was thus finally eased when the relics of martyrs (in a broad sense) were brought into the congregational churches and the latter then became martyr-shrines in their own right.[34] By the sixth/seventh century these relics were dismembered and inclosed in the altar itself, just as is prescribed for every altar today.[35]

The high honor paid to the relics led to another step in the ninth century, namely, that something was permitted on the altar which was not required for the performance of the Eucharist—a thing unthinkable previously, and still avoided in the East. For at this time an exception was made in favor of reliquaries or relic-shrines.[36] Again, as a result, the altar was built up, just as had happened in the case of the saints' pictures. The way was opened to the development of the massive structures we have come to know, the Gothic polyptych altars and the Baroque architectural masses, in which the *mensa* or table often seems to sink into the insignificance of a mere appendage.[37] But there was some compensation to be found

---

[31] Braun, II, 445 ff.

[33] Braun, II, 456.

[33] This is made plain in a document of the Egyptian Church stemming from the end of Christian antiquity, the *Canones Basilii*, c. 33 (Riedel, 250) : "When uncultured people venture to deny the Catholic Church and its law at the very graves of the martyrs, and no longer desire to remain under its power, the Catholic Church cuts them off as heretics. Just as the sun does not need the lamplight, so the Catholic Church [= the Church as a congregation] does not need the corpses of martyrs . . . The

name of Christ is enough for the honor of the Church, because the Church is the Bride of Christ which he bought at the price of his sacred blood." The sermon written down after 431 by the Egyptian monk Schenute appears to regard the same kind of conditions; this is referred to in Braun, I, 652, 654 f.

[34] Braun, I, 525-661, esp. 656 ff.

[35] *Cod. Iur. Can.*, c. 1198 § 4.

[36] Eisenhofer, I, 370.

[37] It was only in width that the measurements of the altar increased, since a distinction was made between Epistle and Gospel side. Cf. *supra*, p. 109.

for the splitting of the idea of the altar which was thus introduced, when in the eleventh century the crucifix was brought to the altar,[38] a prescription of law still maintained in our own day.[30]

[38] Braun, *Das christliche Altargerät,* 469 ff.

[30] *Missale Romanum, Rubr. gen.,* XX.

The present-day legislation does not distinguish whether or not there is on the wall behind the altar or on the altar-structure itself some adequate representation of Christ, so that, for example, on the Sacred Heart altar we will see a rather unpretty duplication.

Regarding other altar furnishings we will hear more in connection with the pertinent practices. For the rest, cf. the books by Braun already referred to and the more cursory presentation in Eisenhofer, I, 342-376. For present-day legislation regarding church, altar and furnishings, see Msgr. H. E. Collins, *The Church Edifice and Its Appointments* (2nd ed., reprinted, Westminster, 1946).

Part III

THE MASS CEREMONIES IN DETAIL

I. The Opening or Entrance Rite

1. Fore-Mass and Opening as a Unit

THE EUCHARISTIC CELEBRATION COULD HAVE STARTED WITH THE preparation of the sacrificial offerings and the prayer of thanksgiving. But at the very outset it had become an inviolable rule to have an introductory section composed of readings. First of all an atmosphere of faith had to be created before the great mystery of faith was performed. This introductory section is called the fore-Mass in contradistinction to the Mass proper or the sacrifice-Mass.[1]

As we shall see more in detail later, the fore-Mass—or, more precisely, the older portion thereof which began with the lessons—was originally an independent liturgical entity. The consciousness of a certain independence of this older fore-Mass remained alive for a long time. For it other regulations held than for the eucharistic service in the narrow sense. Sometimes the fore-Mass was conducted in one church, the Mass proper in another;

---

[1] The terms "Mass of the catechumens" and "Mass of the faithful" are also used to designate these parts respectively, but these expressions did not come into use till the 11th century. Florus, *De actione missarum*, n. 92 (PL, CXIX, 72), in the 9th century, still uses both expressions, *missa catechumenorum* and *missa fidelium*, in their original sense of dismissal of catechumens and faithful. After the Gospel, we read, *clamante diacono iidem catechumeni mittebantur, i.e. dimittebantur foras. Missa ergo catechumenorum fiebat ante actionem sacramentorum, missa fidelium fit post confectionem et participationem.* It must be noted in passing that the implications of the phrase "Mass of the catechumens" do not coincide exactly with those of "fore-Mass," for the catechumens were not allowed to stay till the very start of the Mass-sacrifice. The

readings were followed by common prayers for the various wants of the Church and its several classes of members. The last part of this was the prayer of the faithful, but before its start the catechumens were told to withdraw if they had not already done so. Compare the vacillation in the limits between pre-anaphora and anaphora in Oriental liturgies, due to the same causes; Hanssens, *Institutiones*, II (1930), 2 f. Indeed at Rome, from about the sixth century it became the custom to send the catechumens away even before the Gospel, because the Gospel was considered as much a matter of the *disciplina arcani* as the Our Father and the symbol; *Ordo Rom. VII*, n. 3 (PL, LXXVIII, 996 B). Cf. P. Borella, "La missa o dimissio catechumenorum", *Eph. liturg.* (1939), 67-72.

this was the custom in Jerusalem at the turn of the fourth century,[2] and also in North Africa.[3] There is, for example, an account of the monastery of St. Sabbas (Mar Saba) in the vale of Cedron, where monks of different nationality, Georgians, Syrians and Latins, lived together; they first performed the introductory service of readings and prayers in separate oratories and in their own vernacular, and then assembled for the sacrifice at which Greek was used.[4] Even today the independence of the fore-Mass is intimated in our pontifical service, for here during the fore-Mass the service hinges not around the altar, but around the *cathedra* of the bishop.

In olden times the fore-Mass began abruptly with the lessons or readings. This was certainly the case in the Orient,[5] and must also have been true in the West until far into the fifth century. St. Augustine gives us an account of the beginning of the Mass on a certain Easter day which was signalized by an unusual event. Before service began, a sick man who had been praying in the *cancelli* of St. Stephen was suddenly cured. There was a great deal of excitement amongst the people already assembled, loud cries of thanks and joy filled the house of God. Augustine, who was in the sacristy, ready to make his entrance into the church, was informed. But what is of real interest to us is that when the tumult had gradually died down, the bishop greeted the people *(salutavi populum)* and then without further ado began the reading of the lessons.[6] At that time, therefore—the story comes from the year 426—the fore-Mass began with the readings without any preliminaries. Even in the present-day Roman liturgy there is still one instance of an abbreviated fore-Mass starting with the readings, namely on Good Friday, although it is true no sacrifice-Mass follows, but only the reverencing of the cross and a Communion service; worship on this day begins with a lesson from Osee, after which there are two other readings, followed by the great intercessory prayers.

[2] *Aetheriæ Peregrinatio,* c. 25 (CSEL, XXXIX, 74 f.), et al.; cf. Hanssens, *Institutiones,* II, 4 f.

[3] Augustine, *Serm.,* 325 (PL. XXXVIII, 1449).

[4] Typikon of St. Sabbas (Hanssens, II, 6 f.); text compiled in the 12th century (Latins = Φράγγοι), so that even then similar conditions must have prevailed. Two older narratives regarding a similar separation and re-union between Greeks and Armenians; v. Hanssens, II, 5 f.

About 600 we hear about other monasteries where the Scripture reading, the very heart of the fore-mass, was generally skipped because the monks were already otherwise occupied with Holy Writ; Hanssens, II, 7 f. There is another reminiscence of the older plan to

be found, namely, the fact that Isidore of Seville, *De eccl. off.,* I, 15 (PL, LXXXIII, 752) begins his enumeration of the Mass prayers only after the Gospel. And in the Roman liturgy one instance of a Mass without a fore-mass still existed in the 7th-8th century, the exceptional case of Mass on Maundy Thursday: see *Breviarium eccl. ord.* (Silva-Tarouca, 209); cf. *Gelasianum,* I, 38; 40 (Wilson, 63; 72); Dix, *The shape of the liturgy,* 439-442.

[5] *Const. Ap.,* VIII, 5, 11 (Funk, I, 477). Likewise in the somewhat more recent *Canones Basilii,* c. 97 (Riedel, 273), but here with the notation, "while they [the faithful] are coming in they should read over the Psalms."

[6] Augustine, *De civ. Dei,* 22, 8 (CSEL, XL, 2, p. 610 f.).

Further details regarding the course of this more ancient fore-Mass in all liturgies included, as a rule, the following items. The individual readings were generally followed by a song of some sort, usually derived from one of the lyrical passages of Scripture. The last reading was a portion of the Gospels. And finally the series of readings concluded with a prayer. This fore-Mass was therefore nothing else than a Bible lesson, in which the words of Holy Writ were followed by some sort of scriptural echo and in which the last section was always a prayer.

The part preceding the lessons is the result of a less ancient development which ran more or less parallel in the various ecclesiastical provinces, but without following any common ground-plan. However, some sort of common basic idea was everywhere at work. This was the notion that the lessons should have a preliminary, an introduction. But the introduction did not come into full being at a stroke; rather it is here precisely that many different stages can be distinguished in the growing structure. There is one archway after the other, one ante-room after the other, each tacked on as the zeal and reverence of successive centuries dictated. The oriental liturgies have generally evolved a preliminary whose proportions far exceed those of our Roman liturgy. For not only do they interpose at the start, before the readings, some type of entrance ceremonial, but they preface this with a formal hour of canonical office, and in fact the Byzantine Mass even ushers this latter in with the *proskomide* during which the sacrificial gifts are prepared and pre-hallowed at a special offertory table—the *prothesis*—with a whirl of ceremonies and prayers that are in turn wonderfully rich and extensive.

The one peculiarity that the oriental fore-Masses have in common is the preparatory prayer hour which is always incorporated in it; in the East Syrian it is a variant of Vespers, in the other liturgies a creation corresponding to our Lauds.[7] This is the prayer ceremony which Aetheria, in Jerusalem about 390, came to recognize as the first morning service on Sundays. After the bishop had entered the Church of the Resurrection, a priest, a deacon, and another cleric, each in turn, intoned a psalm, to each verse of which the people responded with a refrain; the psalm was followed in each case by an oration.[8] This plan of prayer is most plainly evident today in the Byzantine Mass.

This forms the heart of the so-called ἔναρξις, or Opening. Here we find, one right after the other, three antiphonal songs composed mostly from the psalms (the three "antiphons"), to each of which is attached an oration by the priest along with the deacon's *ektene*. It is not till after this prayer-act that (in the Byzantine Mass) the so-called Little Entrance follows. The clergy participating in the liturgy form a procession, marching from the sanctuary through a side door of the ikonostasis or picture-wall into

[7] Baumstark, *Die Messe im Morgenland*, 78-86.   [8] *Aetheriæ Peregrinatio*, c. 24, 9. (CSEL, XXXIX, 73).

the nave of the church, and back again through the center door into the sanctuary. This is the entrance with the Gospel-book, to be distinguished from a later procession, the Great Entrance, with the sacrificial offerings. The introit of the Roman Mass corresponds to this first entrance, for in an earlier stage of development the clergy used to make their entry into the house of God in procession.[9] Even in the liturgical formation of this entrance the analogy to the Roman type cannot be mistaken. For this Little Entrance is accompanied by a special chant (εἰσοδικόν = introitus), which is usually followed, depending on the festival, by some other hymns (troparia) and finally by the trisagion, the same that the Roman liturgy also has on Good Friday. Both at the entrance and at the trisagion the priest softly recites a lengthy prayer; the lessons begin after that.

Turning now to the Roman entrance rite, the thing that strikes us about the whole ceremonial, from the prayers at the foot of the altar to the collect, is its lack of coherence; we do not get the impression of something unified. For that reason interpreters of the Mass scarcely ever treat it under one title. Each individual portion, prayers at the foot of the altar, Kyrie, Gloria, collects—each has its own individual explanation without much connection with the others. And precisely for that reason we must try to consider the whole section as a unit, in order to gain the right background for the various component parts.

Usually the collect is the part selected as a hub for the several connecting lines. But hardly anything could show more clearly than this how much in the dark we are regarding the whole subject. Some have suggested that the oration belongs by right to the reading service; originally its place was after the first reading and not till later was it shifted, owing perhaps to the influence of the introit psalm.[10] Others explain that the oration was originally a part of a special assembling ceremony which preceded the Mass. The reference here is to the old Roman custom of gathering at a different church; after all had convened, ready to start the procession to the church where Mass was to be celebrated, an oration was said over the assembled congregation. After this practice was abandoned, the oration was transferred to the church of the Mass, and placed after the processional litany which still survives in the Kyrie.[11]

Such opinions rest on the assumption that otherwise there is no reason for the oration being where it is. Is that really so?

With good cause other commentators maintain that the Kyrie, at least in its original form as a litany, required a priestly oration as its conclusion, just as the oriental ektene shows today[12]; putting it another way, the

[9] Hanssens, III, 104 f.

[10] P. Alfonso, L'Eucologia romana antica (Subiaco, 1931), 132-137; similarly Eisenhofer, II, 97.

[11] C.f. P. Parsch, The Liturgy of the Mass, trans. F. C. Eckhoff (St. Louis, 1936), 112.

[12] Fortescue, The Mass, 252.

Brinktrine, Die hl. Messe, 79, raises some objections against the originality of

oration in the Roman Mass has the character of a conclusion, and must therefore represent in this connection a stopping point after the litany already mentioned.[13]

As a matter of fact there can hardly be any doubt that the oration and the *Kyrie* belong together. This becomes all the clearer when we take cognizance of liturgical prayer outside of Mass. For the prayers of the congregation, the litany type, with its petitions intoned by a deacon and with its *Kyrie eleison* as the response of the people, has been the characteristic form since the fourth century. But the ancient Church was conscious of the fact that the litany demanded a concluding prayer by the priest.[14] This manner of concluding with prayer Ætheria, the pilgrim lady, remarked in the congregation of Jerusalem, especially amongst the monks, and for this reason a priest or deacon was always present at their common prayer to recite the oration at the end.[15] In particular, the litany at Vespers was concluded by the bishop with an oration.[16] In our own Office, too, each hour even now closes with the oration.

To be sure the *Gloria*, which is so often interposed between *Kyrie* and oration, and seemingly to no purpose, seems to put this whole matter of a connection between the two once more in serious doubt. For a grasp of the basic plan, however, this can really have very little significance, because originally the *Gloria* was inserted only by way of exception, and even later only on those feasts on which the *Kyrie* appeared to invite a more joyous supplement. Besides, it is not unheard of that some further popular prayers or even hymns were added to the litany and, in general, to all the alternating prayers of the congregation. In the *preces* of the breviary the *Kyrie* is followed by a long series of prayers and psalm verses and on some days even by a formal hymn (namely, the *Sanctus Deus*), and only after that

---

this arrangement, but they do not seem overwhelming. The question regarding the structural laws governing the enarxis is wholly independent of that other question, just when did the pertinent complexity of prayers become tightly joined to the fore-Mass.

[13] Batiffol, *Leçons*, 120.

So, too, Schuster, *The Sacramentary*, I, 88; but the author compromises with the other theories, p. 89.

[14] Cf. the decree of the emperor Justinian, *Novellæ*, 123, c. 32 *(Corp. Jur. civ.*, ed. Schoell, III, 617) : *qualiter enim est litania* [an impetrative procession, but probably involving a litany-prayer] *in qua sacerdotes non inveniuntur et sollemnes faciunt orationes?*

Cf. also Rabanus Maurus, De *inst. cleric.*, I, 33 (PL, CVII, 323 A) : *Post*

introitum autem sacerdotis ad altare litaniæ aguntur a clero, ut generalis oratio præveniat specialem sacerdotis.

[15] *Aetheriæ Peregrinatio*, c. 24, 1 (CSEL, XXXIX, 71).

[16] *Ibid.*, 24, 5 f. (CSEL, XXXIX, 72). The same tie-in is found in *Const. Ap.*, *VIII*, 6-11 (Funk, I, 478-494). Cf. also the Synod of Agde (506), can. 30 (Mansi, VIII, 329 f.).

This close connection between the prayer of the congregation and the oration seems to quash the suggestion put forth by Dix, *The Shape of the Liturgy*, 452-458, who would trace the introduction of the oration at Rome to an Egyptian model, and the introduction of *Kyrie* and *Gloria* to a later Syro-Byzantine one. The connection itself is vainly contested by Dix, p. 479.

is there a conclusion with the oration. Something of the kind can have happened in the case of the *Gloria*. Moreover, the *Gloria* does not interfere with the *Kyrie's* concluding in an oration, for it too seems to demand such a conclusion. The story is told that when Leo III and Charlemagne met in the year 799, the pope intoned the *Gloria* which was taken up by the entire clergy, whereupon the pope recited a prayer.[17] We are forced, therefore, to conclude that *Kyrie*, *Gloria*, and oration are part of a unified plan which is patterned on an ascending scale, the oration forming the high point. But how does it happen that the Mass is opened with such a schema of prayer? This question leads to still another: What about the prayers that precede, that is, the prayers at the foot of the altar, and the introit?

First the introit. Our introit, as everyone knows, is an entrance song, a processional, and to appreciate its meaning and form we must transport ourselves to one of the larger basilicas of Rome for the splendid and solemn ceremonial of a papal Mass, with its numerous clergy and its specially trained choral group.[18] Here we are confronted for the first time by a picture that we shall meet again in two other places in the Roman Mass: an external event which is sufficiently important to warrant some external expression. The people participating do not say a prayer, but the choral group, who are ready precisely for this occasion, sing a psalm, an entrance psalm, exactly as they afterwards sing the offertory psalm and the communion psalm. This external event is concluded with a prayer, as is proper in an assembly gathered for worship. As the *secreta* is said after the offertory, and the *post communio* after the communion, so here the collect (but in this instance with the people's *Kyrie* and *Gloria* intervening). In other words, the act or prayer is introduced by a procession into the basilica. This procession ought not only to be enhanced by the chanting, but it ought also to be distinguished as a movement to prayer, as an approach to God's majesty, as is done when the assembled congregation shouts out the petitions and the priest takes these up, and brings the proceeding to a conclusion with an oration. As a matter of fact, Amalar in the ninth century actually connected the introit and the oration in this manner.[19] Rupert of Deutz, too, includes all the proceedings up to the collects under one heading as *initium quod dicitur Introitus*,[20] and we have found the same thing even in Albertus Magnus and other commentators of the period.[21]

What is left to explain now is the group of prayers at the foot of the altar, a thing of much later date. But this is a very secondary structure

[17] Hardouin, IV, 935 D.
[18] *Supra*, pp. 68-70
Cf. Parsch-Eckhoff, *The Liturgy of the Mass*, 83.
[19] Amalar, *De off. eccl.*, III, 5 (PL, CV, 1108): *Officium quod vocatur Introitus habet initium a prima antiphona, quae*

dicitur Introitus, et finitur in oratione quae dicitur a sacerdote ante lectionem. Cf. also the declaration of Rabanus Maurus quoted in Note 14 above.
[20] Rupert of Deutz, *De div. off.*, I, 31 (PL, CLXX, 28 B).
[21] *Supra*, p. 114.

added to the already completed fabric as a further embellishment. It thus happens that the entire complex of prayers and rites antecedent to the readings, in particular the prayers following the introit, are all governed by the entrance procession. We can therefore rightly speak of an entrance or opening rite.

A confirmation of this reconstruction is to be found in parallel phenomena of the Roman liturgy. Take the *Ordo* of St. Amand, which reproduces the customs of the Roman church after 800. In it are presented the practices usual at a *collecta*, that is, at a penitential procession of the Roman community under the leadership of the pope, with which it was customary to introduce the stational services on certain days. These *collecta* took place in the following manner. The people gathered at a conveniently located church, generally St. Adrian's at the Forum, and from there marched to the church at which Mass was to be celebrated. The procedure was this: The pope and his attendant deacons, vested in dark *planetæ*, waited in the sacristy (which was usually near what we call the rear of the church). When it was time to start, the *schola* intoned the *antiphona ad introitum*. While the psalm was being sung, the pope and his deacons proceeded through the church up to the altar. As the pope passed the *schola* he gave a signal to skip to the end of the psalm and sing the *Gloria Patri*. Arriving at the altar, he bowed low in silent prayer. Then he kissed the altar, the deacons following his example. After the antiphon had been repeated in the usual fashion, the pope spoke the greeting, *Dominus vobiscum* and, after the *Flectamus genua* of the deacon, recited an oration. Then everyone left the church and set out in the penitential procession.[22] Here we have the Roman rite of opening a service clearly separate and carried out for its own sake. The only thing missing from the comparable portion of the fore-Mass is the *Kyrie* before the oration.

But it is significant that the scribe felt called upon to make a special note regarding the missing part: "When the antiphon at the close of the introit has been sung to the end, the *schola* does not sing the *Kyrie*."[23] The *Kyrie* therefore normally belongs to this rite. The reason it is left out here is obvious; it is intoned at the very beginning of the penitential procession. This procession is likewise the reason for the insertion of *Flectamus genua*. Almost the same procedure is repeated at every church visited on the way, and lastly at the stational church itself.[24]

[22] Duchesne, *Christian Worship*, 473-4; cf. 480. This same plan, somewhat abbreviated, also in the appendix to *Ordo Rom. I*, n. 23 f. (PL LXXVIII, 949).
Cf. Hierzegger, "Collecta und Statio," ZkTh (1936), 528 f., 533 f.
[23] Duchesne, 474, 480.
[24] Duchesne, 474; cf. *Ordo Rom. I*, n. 23 f. The only difference is that at the churches visited on the way the *schola* does not sing an introit-psalm but instead finishes the litany which was begun shortly before. In the church of the stational service the litany is again brought to a finish, but thereupon the introit is sung, to be followed, as at the first church, by an oration without any intervening *Kyrie*.

One could therefore, in a way, talk about a *rite of visiting churches*. The present-day *Pontificale Romanum* presumes this arrangement in all essentials when a visiting prelate is to be received ceremoniously in a church. Accompanied by singing he marches into the church and kneels down to pray before the main altar. While the versicle in honor of the patron of the church is chanted, he kisses the altar at the middle and then recites the pertinent oration at the Epistle side.[25] Here, too, the entry into the church, the visiting of a church, has been given a liturgical form. In the case of the Mass-liturgy, the visiting of the church has been transformed into an entrance or opening ceremonial.[26]

Although we have used the procedures of the *collecta* to explain the fore-Mass, we must yet take issue with a certain common misconception of the relationship between the two. Some interpreters have been too prone to draw a connection between the litany chant accompanying the procession on its way and into the stational church, and the *Kyrie* of the Mass, as if the latter was derived from the former. In like manner—something we have already touched on—the oration of the Mass, often called the *collecta*, is often derived from the oration recited at the church where the *collecta* took place. Both notions are untenable. The *collecta* as a gathering of the Roman community was not a stable and constituent part of the stational service, but only the prelude of a penitential procession which took place before the stational service on certain days—in olden times not very frequent—especially in Lent and the ember-tides, but never on Sundays or feasts.[27] The *Kyrie* could not therefore have intruded into the Sunday or feast-day service in this wise. As for calling the first oration *collecta*, we shall see further on that the term had a very different origin, and really means a gathering together, by the priest, of the preceding petitions of the people.

In this sense the term *collecta* is quite appropriate for this first oration of the Mass, for it seems to blend together all that has gone before. The congregational praying and singing and even the entry with its accompanying chant serves only to draw us nearer to God to honor Him in the holy sacrifice. Since the lessons are meant to be introduced before the beginning of the sacrifice, it would appear only proper to indicate the meaning of this common approach by means of a preliminary solemn prayer in much the same way as the Roman congregation did when it assembled at some

---

[25] *Pontificale Rom.*, p. III, *Ordo ad recipiendum processionaliter prælatum*. Similarly the other plans for reception contained in the Pontifical.
[26] At the basis of all this lies what I have elsewhere called the liturgical groundplan, namely the series: reading, singing, prayer of the congregation and prayer of the priest; there is only this difference, the external activity of the reception is substituted for the reading; cf. J. A. Jungmann, *Liturgical Worship* (New York, 1941), 65-81.
[27] R. Hierzegger, "Collecta und Statio," ZkTh, LX (1936), 511-554.

church for the start of a penitential procession, or when it stopped in at a church on the way. "We come to pray," is the basic motto of this first part of the Mass.[28]

Nowadays, however, this notion is no longer so apparent. The rite of entry has to a great extent lost its meaning, owing in the main to the fate which the entry has suffered in the course of centuries. Up till about 1000 it continued to be a fully-developed ceremonial, and so it was easy to survey the liturgical transformation which it was undergoing. Not only in the Roman stational service[29] but even in the Frankish Church, the entrance of the clergy had been a ceremony of capital importance, and in the descriptions and the allegorical explanations of Carolingian interpreters of the liturgy it assumed a formidable amount of space.[30] But in the years that followed a change set in. John Beleth (d. about 1165), in explaining the introit, had to make the remark that the bishop on feast days sometimes vested outside the choir.[31] In harmony with this, Durandus too felt compelled to note that the bishop—in whose regard, to be sure, every effort must have been made to retain the more solemn formalities—might take up the *paramenta* either *longe ab altari* or *juxta altare*.[32] All the more quickly, then, would the vesting of the priest be transferred to the sanctuary or its environs.[33]

This change is easily explained by the medieval evolution of choir prayer and the development of the fixed regulation that the conventual service, which for centuries simply meant the Mass, should each day immediately follow Terce or the other corresponding hour, for which the clergy were already assembled.[34] An entrance procession was therefore superfluous. Often the celebrant and his assistants were already clothed in the Mass vestments, as, for instance, when in monastic churches of the eleventh and twelfth centuries all priest members of the choir wore alb, maniple, and stole.[35]

---

[28] A similar schema was in recent years worked out for pedagogical purposes, to facilitate understanding the beginning of the Mass. The pertinent five-step plan was first devised by Dr. Pius Parsch in 1924 (as he was good enough to tell me), and was then circulated by means of wall charts and leaflets; see P. Parsch, *Kurze Messerklärung* (Klosterneuburg, 1930), 33; (2nd ed., 1935), 52. The schema then recurs in its essentials in Schott's *Messbuch der hl. Kirche* (37th ed., 1934), 26*, with the first step divided: We come —We beg. Cf. Parsch-Eckhoff, *The Liturgy of the Mass*, 43; Parsch, *Study the Mass*, trans. Wm. Busch (Collegeville, 1941), 19 ("We offer our prayer"); R. Bandas, *The Mass and the Liturgical*

Year (St. Paul, 1936), 19 ("We speak to God").
[29] For the entry in extra-Roman churches of Christian antiquity see several references in Bona, II, 2, 1 (553 f.).
[30] Thus, e.g., in Amalar, *De eccl. off.*, III, 5 (PL, CV, 1108-1113): *De introitu episcopi ad missam.* Cf. supra, p. 89.
[31] John Beleth, *Explicatio*, c. 35 (PL, CCII, 44 B).
[32] Pontificale of Durandus (Andrieu, III, 635).
[33] But the case is not often attested; *vide*, however, the Missal of Evreux-Jumièges: Martène, 1. 4, XXVIII (I, 642 D); here we have a Mass in which a deacon assists (644 E).
[34] *Supra*, pp. 204, 247.
[35] *Infra*, pp. 280, 284.

Usually, it is true, the vesting in the Mass vestments or—when choir dress and Mass dress were once more distinguished—the putting on of the *paramenta* was transferred to the sacristy.

But in Romanesque structures the sacristy was not built near the entrance of the church but somewhere close to the choir. In these cases the entry called for in the ancient Mass regulations could be reinaugurated. Sometimes, in fact, it was consciously revived and given a greater development by marching the long way through the nave of the church[36] (as was done in the late Middle Ages on great feast days),[37] or at least a procession down the aisle on Sundays in the course of blessing with holy water, as was customary all through the Middle Ages and still is in some residual form.[38] The liturgical reform of the sixteenth century permitted only the bishop to vest at the altar and this both as a privilege and as a prescription, perhaps because the various formalities which had developed meanwhile gave it the character of a dramatic introduction to the pontifical service.[39] The natural consequence of all this evolution was a change in the role of the introit; the introit would have to be sung, but not as an accompaniment to the few steps which as a rule were all that had to be taken to reach the altar. Instead of a processional, the introit became an introductory chant which in Rome already in the fourteenth century was not begun till the priest reached the altar steps.[40]

[36] According to the ancient rite of the Cistercians, the procession of the clergy first went to the south transept, where all remained bowed while the choir intoned the *Gloria Patri* of the introit. Schneider (*Cist.-Chr.* [1926], 252 f.

A similar entrance procession is still to be seen on festive occasions, sometimes starting from outside the church, sometimes starting from the sacristy but proceeding down the aisles and up the center. Such occasions as a First Mass, for instance.

[37] In the parochial services of the 16th century a procession was always included as part of a special solemnity; at the start of the celebration all the assembled clergy marched solemnly through the church and on occasion carried the relics which were displayed on the altar. See Greving, *Johann Ecks Pfarrbuch,* 85.

[38] Eisenhofer, I, 478 f.

This procession is still to be seen (or was a few years ago) in Lithuania; Kramp, "Messgebräuche der Gläubigen in den ausserdeutschen Ländern," (StZ [1927], II), 359.

[39] But Durandus, in his Pontifical (Andrieu, III, 635, 1. 11), pays no attention to the place of vesting, and in either case has the bishop stride to the altar *processionaliter et sollemniter.* Cf. *Cæremoniale episc.,* II, 8, 23 ff.

[40] *Ordo Rom. XIV,* n. 14; 27 (PL, LXXVIII, 1129 B; 1135 B).

The rubric of the present-day Vatican Gradual apparently takes the stand that the introit should again assume its rightful place as the entrance song of the Mass, for it expressly orders that the introit be intoned as the celebrant approaches the altar: "When the priest starts towards the altar, the cantors begin the introit." There are liturgists who insist that the Vatican Gradual introduced no change, that the introit is to be intoned only after the priest arrives at the foot of the altar. But actually the wording adopted is different from that in the older rubrics, substituting *accedente sacerdote ad altare* for the other reading, *cum . . . pervenerit ante infimum gradum altaris* (the rubric based on the Ceremonial of Bishops). The plain and ob-

The decline of the entrance ceremony entailed some other transformations at which we ought to look briefly. The lights which had previously been carried in procession and then placed next to the altar[41] were now more frequently set on the altar from the very start.[42] Since Carolingian times there was no longer any hesitancy about putting on the altar things other than those required for the sacramental celebration[43]; so in the new circumstances it was taken for granted that when no procession was held the candles should stand on the altar even before Mass and should stay there. Their previous significance as an honor to the celebrant —in the first instance a bishop[44]—was lost (so long as the other attendants at the more solemn feasts were not, in their turn, accompanied by candles). In place of honoring the celebrant was thus substituted a very becoming honor to the mystery that was consummated on the altar. A similar change took place with regard to the censer. It is not used so much as formerly, on the way to the altar or in the procession to read the Gospel,[45] but at the altar itself which is incensed.

Finally the psalm *Iudica*, which about the year 1000 was introduced into pontifical services as a part of the entrance procession, was definitely transferred to the foot of the altar, after a very diversified career; sometimes its few short verses had been said on the way to the altar, sometimes during the vesting, sometimes at the altar—and often not at all.

2. *Præparatio ad Missam*

That the soul must be prepared for the celebration of the Eucharist is one of those self-explaining requirements which were already insisted upon in the primitive Church.[1] This requirement applies not only to the priest

vious direction of the rubric is: Start the introit as soon as the celebrant appears in the sanctuary.

[41] *Supra*, pp. 68 and 201. Regarding this and also regarding the changing position of the candles (torches) in the sanctuary the Carolingian interpreters have presented very thorough discussions; e.g. Amalar, *De eccl. off.*, III, 7 (PL, CV, 1114 f.); Remigius of Auxerre, *Expositio* (PL, CI, 1248; 1250).

[42] The first literary notice of this arrangement is not to be found till Innocent III, *De s. alt. mysterio*, II, 21 (PL, CCXVII, 811). But various pictorial illustrations since the second half of the 11th century display candles on the altar. On the other hand the older system of placing them next to the altar did not disappear entirely until the 17th century

Braun, *Das christliche Altargerät*, 492-498. See also Edm. Bishop, "Of Six Candles on the Altar: an enquiry," *The Downside Review*, VI [XXV] (1906), 189 ff.

Peter Anson, *Churches, Their Plan and Furnishing* (Milwaukee, 1948), mentions the Cathedral of Chartres as still having its six candles on the steps of the high altar, not upon it; 113, note 21.

[43] *Supra*, p. 258.

[44] *Supra*, p. 68.

[45] Acc. to the Pontifical of Durandus (Andrieu, III, 635) the censer is also carried when the bishop has vested next to the altar, but in this case no incense need be placed in it. No immediate significance is therefore attached to it any more.

[1] *Supra*, p. 18.

but to whole Christian people. Nevertheless, within the liturgy itself special forms for this preparation were in general fashioned only for the priest, just as special service garments were prescribed for him alone. Only in the Sunday services of the congregation was any special rite of preparation created for the people, a rite involving the cleansing of the soul. This is the sprinkling with holy water at the *Asperges* or *Vidi Aquam*, two chants, one—with the beginning of Psalm 50—implying contrition and penance, the other—with the beginning of Psalm 117—suggesting the springs of grace gushing forth from the Easter mystery.[2]

Special prayer for the priest, to prepare himself for the holy action even before he puts on the liturgical garments, is outlined also in the oriental churches at quite an early period.[3] But most of the time this prayer is inserted into the rite of the Mass itself as a prayer upon entering the sanctuary. In the West there is no evidence of any preparatory prayer before going to the altar, other than the canonical hours, until in the ninth century different types of so-called "accession" prayers make their appearance. These first appeared in the form of apologies,[4] then in the form of psalmody—the kind that has continued in use till now. The latter is the case in the Sacramentary of Amiens, which also offers us the first vesting prayers and the first instance of texts for the priest to say quietly during Mass.[5] The preparation has a core of psalmody, namely Psalm 50, with versicles and three orations. This plan of preparatory prayer was not followed very extensively.[6] In its place there appeared about the year 1000, in the Mass *ordo* of the Séez group, a well-planned office of preparation which, with numerous changes, continues to reappear all through the Middle Ages and still stands in our own missal, though in a slightly developed form.

In its original shape this preparation consisted of three psalms: Ps. 83 *(Quam dilecta)* in which the pilgrim expresses his longing for the distant sanctuary; Ps. 84 *(Benedixisti)*, the Advent psalm, which praises God's grace and begs His continued protection; and, to round out the number

---

[2] Eisenhofer, I, 478-480.
Cf. Cuthbert Goeb, O.S.B., "The Asperges", *Orate Fratres*, II (1927-8), 338-342.
Attempts to introduce a more profound, sacramental purification from sin will engage us in connection with the *Confiteor* and especially in connection with the prayers which once were attached to the sermon.
[3] Records since the 10th century in Hanssens, III, 1-7.
[4] Sacramentary of St. Thierry (2nd half of the 9th century; see Leroquais, I, 21): Martène, 1, 4, IX (I, 541-545): 14 penitential prayers, some of them very extended, designated as *orationes ante missam;* to them are added intercessory

prayers. Cf. also the Sacramentary of St. Denis (11th century), *ibid.*, V (I, 518).
Two intercessory prayers intended as preparation, in the Sacramentary of Ratoldus (10th century): PL, LXXVIII, 239.
[5] *Supra*, p. 77.
[6] It recurs again in the Missal of Troyes: Martène, 1, 4, VI (I, 528), and greatly expanded (the seven penitential psalms replacing Ps. 50) in the *Missa Illyrica*: *ibid.*, IV (I, 490-492). In both cases it is followed by the preparatory prayers of the Séez group which we are about to mention. Cf. also the Sacramentary of Lyons (11th century): Leroquais, I, 126.

three, another psalm in the psalter, Ps. 85 *(Inclina)*, which merely invokes God's help in a general way.[7] Of the versicles that immediately follow, two (which emphasize the *motif* once more) are taken from Psalm 84 *(Deus tu conversus; Ostende nobis)*, while others beg the forgiveness of sin (Ps. 142:2: *Ne intres*; Ps. 78:9b: *Propitius esto*) or beg God's mercy (Ps. 43:26: *Exsurge*; Ps. 32:22: *Fiat misericordia*; Ps. 101:2: *Domine exaudi*). The conclusion consists of the oration *Aures tuæ pietatis*, with its petition for the help of the Holy Spirit to render one's service worthy. It is still used as the first oration after the versicles, but the original singular *(precibus meis—merear)* has been altered to the plural.

This office of preparation quickly underwent various augmentations. One addition that gained general acceptance was Psalm 115 *(Credidi)*, which mentions taking up the chalice of sacrifice.[8] Other psalms which were subjoined appear only sporadically,[9] as also did the penitential Psalm 129 *(De profundis)* which, together with Psalm 115, was chosen in Italy about the turn of the twelfth century.[10] It found its way into the Mass *ordo* of the papal chapel by 1290[11] and from there was taken over, in conjunction with Psalm 115, into our Roman Missal. Penitential psalms are not seldom found in the frame of this preparation.[12] In the same document of the papal chapel[13] we find the rest of the details of the prayer-complex belonging to it, just as they are in the missal today: the antiphon again reminding us of penance, *Ne reminiscaris*, then after the *Kyrie* and *Pater noster*[14] the still missing versicles of similar penitential spirit. There is also the increase

---

[7] Sacramentary of Séez: PL, LXXVIII, 245, and related sources (see *supra*, pp. 92 ff.

[8] *Missa Illyrica*: Martène, I, 4, IV (I, 492 D; here with many other accretions); cf. *ibid.*, XVI (I, 594 D). Bernold, *Micrologus*, c. 1; 23 (PL CLI, 979; 992); Sacramentary of Modena (Muratori, I, 86) and most of the later sources.

[9] Among them Ps. 116 *(Laudate)* often appears, either alone (thus, after the 12-13th century, in Styrian Mass books [Köck, 95; 100], and regularly in Hungarian ones [Radó, 23; 40, etc.]) or together with the last octonary of Ps. 118 *(Appropinquet;* thus more than once outside Italy: Köck, 97; Beck, 260; Yelverton, 5). The octonary mentioned is also found in other relationships in Spanish books of the 15-16th century: Ferreres, 54; 67; and already in the Missal of Liége (11th century): Martène, 1, 4. XV (I, 582 E).

[10] Innocent III, *De s. alt. mysterio.*, I, 47 (PL, CCXVII, 791); Sicard of Cremona, *Mitrale*, II, 8 (PL, CCXIII, 86).

In the 13th century the psalms in use today, with appropriate orations, are mentioned in Pseudo-Bonaventure, *De præparatione ad missam*, c. 12 (Bonaventure, opp., ed. Peltier, XII: Paris, 1868), 286; Durandus, IV, 2, 1.

[11] Brinktrine *(Eph. liturg, [1937])*, 199. See also Hoeynck, 367f.; Beck, 260; Yelverton, 5.

[12] The seven penitential psalms are found in the *Missa Illyrica*: Martène, 1, 4, IV (I, 490 E); cf. Sacramentary of Lyons: Leroquais, I, 126. Likewise even at the close of the Middle Ages in: Missal of Seville (1535): Martène, 1, 4, 1, 8 (I, 348 C); Mass-*Ordo* of Regensburg: Beck, 258.

[13] Brinktrine, *op. cit.*, 199f.

Apparently also in a Minorite Missal of the 13th century; Ebner, 313.

[14] The transition to the versicles with *Kyrie* and *Pater noster* is remarked in Bernold, *Micrologus*, c. 1; 23 (PL, CLI, 979:992); in the Missal of St. Vincent at Volturno, about 1100 (Fiala, 197; cf. Codex Chigi: Martène, I, 568 E); in a Seckau Missal of 1170 (Köck, 95), in

of the orations to seven, which all take a very positive turn; the first six, like the original one, begging the grace of the Holy Spirit,[15] and the seventh, the old Advent oration *Conscientias nostras*,[16] in a similar vein asking for a cleansing of the conscience so that it be ready for the coming of the Lord.

This series of prayers shows in outline the general plan followed for a liturgical act according to liturgical laws for common prayer. In fact the later Middle Ages sometimes actually transformed it into a formal canonical hour.[17] From the very beginning these prayers were thought of as suited for common recitation,[18] and even according to present-day rules, at a pontifical Mass the two assisting canons must answer the bishop when he says the "accession" prayer while his sandals are being put on.[19]

the Sacramentary of Modena written before 1174, which also contains an antiphon which, however, reads: *Sanctifica nos, Domine* (Muratori, I, 86).

In certain Hungarian Mass books since the 12th century the *Kyrie* has been built up into a peculiar kind of litany (no names of saints but only groups: *omnes s. patriarchæ*, etc.) : Radó, 23; 40; 76; 96; 18; 123; 155. But for the rest, abstracting from the versicles, these Mass books are most closely akin to the Séez group; e.g. both groups have simply the two prayers—often even combined— as the conclusion: *Fac me, quæso* (see *infra*, p. 286) and *Aures tuas*.

[15] The prevalent attention to the Holy Ghost is shown also in the Seckau Missal where the antiphon *Veni, Sancte Spiritu* follows the psalms; likewise in the late medieval *Ordo* of Gregorienmünster: Martène, 1, 4, XXXII (I, 653 D), where besides the *Veni, Creator* heads the psalms. The isolated antiphon is also found *ibid.*, XXVIII (I, 642 D); Ferreres, LXXXIV.

The *Veni, Creator*, with versicle and the oration *Deus, cui omne cor patet* (without a psalm) as a rule formed the preparation in the usage of Sarum: Legg, *Tracts*, 210; 255; Legg, *The Sarum Missal*, 216; Martène, 1, 4, XXXV (I, 664) ; it was recited while vesting.

Cf. also *infra*, p. 297, note 29.

[16] Sources in Mohlberg-Manz, n. 1359; cf. also Brinktrine, *Die hl. Messe*, 46.

[17] Beginning with *Deus in adiutorium* and the hymn *Veni, Creator*, then the psalms, little chapter (Rom. 5:5), responsory,

preces and several orations; Augsburg Mass-*Ordo* of 1493: Hoeynck, 367 f. Similarly in a Hungarian missal of the 14th century; Radó, 71. Expanded (e.g., with *Appropinquet;* see note 4 above), in the Missal of Seckau about 1330; Köck, 97f. and in the Regensburg Mass-*Ordo*, Beck, 259-261. In curtailed form also in Sweden: Yelverton, 5-7. Hoeynck rightly remarks: "These prayers read like an *Officium de Spiritu Sancto*" (41).

[18] Mass-*Ordo* of Séez: Martène, 1, 4, XIII (I, 574 E) : *cum circumstantibus*. Similarly the parallels: XII, XIV f. (I, 568 D, 580 B, 582 E) ; the *Missa Illyrica* has the clerics praying alone while the bishop vests: *ibid.*, IV (I, 492 C). The Sacramentary of Modena (Muratori, I, 86) also gives a special direction: *cantet per se (episcopus vel presbyter) et per circumstantes psalm. istos cum litaniis et antiphona.* Cf. Ebner, 321.

Further references in Lebrun, *Explication*, I, 32; according to him the litany here included was still sung before High Mass in many places even in 1700.

[19] *Cæremoniale episc.*, II, 8, 7. The same prescription in the Pontifical of Durandus (Andrieu, III, 632f.) : the bishop prays the psalms *cum clericis suis*. Likewise in a Neapolitan missal of the 15th century (Ebner, 115) : the bishop *cum capellanis suis.* The Roman Pontifical of the 13th century still mentions the prayers, beginning with Ps. 83, recited by the bishop while vesting (Andrieu, II, 371, 471, 478 et al.).

Whereas originally this much re-written accession office took the place of the earlier apologies, eventually a very lengthy formula of this latter type was added to the accession, the prayer designated as *oratio s. Ambrosii, Summe sacerdos*, sections of which are now distributed through the seven days of the week. It is an apologia in a wide sense, for the grim tones of dismal self-accusation have faded into a confident voice of humble petition. It did not, in fact, originate during the years when the apologies were rampant, but only in the eleventh century.[20] Like the other prayers and considerations which later Mass books, particularly our present Roman Missal, assigned to the priest,[21] it was not considered obligatory.[22] But the foregoing accession prayers, on the other hand, are always presented in the source books since the eleventh century as part of the liturgy in much the same way as the vesting prayers which are attached to them, and the prayers that follow at the foot of the altar, from which, in point of fact, they are often not very clearly separated. The degree of obligation was more definitely fixed by the law of custom.[23] The Missal of Pius V sets them down as obligatory *pro temporis opportunitate*. On the other hand, it insists on the general admonition, that the priest before going to the altar devote himself to prayer for some time, *orationi aliquantulum vacet.*[24]

[20] F. Cabrol, "Apologies", *DACL, I,* 2599; Wilmart, *Auteurs spirituels,* 101–125, where a critical text is offered and John of Fécamp (d. 1079) is suggested as author. However it must be noted that the prayer is already found by the middle of the 11th century in the Sacramentary of St. Denis, where it stands at the beginning of Mass: Martène, 1, 4, V (I, 522 E); see the dating in Leroquais, I, 142. The prayer was soon widely diffused. It is to be found in the Freising Sacramentary of the 11th century: Ebner, 272; in a mid-Italian sacramentary of the out-going 11th century; *ibid.,* 300; cf. 51; since the 12th century also in Spain: Ferreres, p. LIX, LXXII, CX, 78f.; see also the references in Bona, I, 12, 4 (148f.).

Pseudo-Bonaventure (*op. cit.* note 10 above) advises the priest to append this prayer to the five psalms, etc. It appears to have reached the Roman Missal via the Mass-*Ordo* of Burchard of Strassburg (Legg. *Tracts,* 126ff.), who makes the prayer optional.

[21] The *Ordo missæ* of Regensburg (c. 1500) was a veritable authology of the preparatory prayers and devotions of the later Middle Ages: Beck, 257–261. The *Ordo qualiter sacerdos se præparet* here

contains, after the 15 *gradus beatæ virginis* (that is, three times five psalms, with certain supplements) and the 7 penitential psalms, an introduction to interior recollection, a prayer *de passione Domini,* several other prayers, and besides this the accession office described above in note 17.

The Missal of Vich (1496) starts the preparatory prayers of the priest with an excerpt from the writings of St. Gregory the Great *(Dial.* IV, 58) beginning *Hæc singulariter victima* (Ferreres, p. CIV).

The prayer presented in the Roman Missal with the heading *Oratio s. Thomæ Aquinatis* is found with variants in the preparatory prayers of Linköping (Yelverton. 9 f.); *Omnipotens et misericors Deus, ecce accedo.* The other prayers that follow did not enter the missal until the new revised edition of Clement VIII (1604) and other succeeding editions.

[22] Cf. *supra,* note 20.

[23] The *Tractatus Misnensis de horis canonicis* (c. 1450) ed. Schönfelder (Breslau, 1902), 102, acknowledges an obligation only *ubi hoc est consuetudo vel statutum provinciale vel synodale.*

[24] *Rit. serv.,* I, 1; cf. *Cod. Iur. Can.,* c. 810.

The Tridentine missal is not thinking here of vocal prayer, that seems clear. This is explained by the fact that the movement for meditative prayer, which had developed in the circles of the *devotio moderna*, had been gaining ground year by year since the end of the fifteenth century.[25] In this instance it was a matter of going to the altar with mind alert and with a consciousness of the grandeur of the mystery. It was a matter of drawing near to the sacrifice of the New Covenant, to worship in spirit and in truth. Here, then, the fact had to be acknowledged that a contemplative tarrying in the world of the supernatural was more important by far than any further multiplication of vocal prayer. It was understood, of course, that the day's Matins and Lauds had been said; this rule continued in force.[26] Rightly did morning meditation before Mass become a set part in the order of the day of every priest.[27]

3. Putting on the Liturgical Vestments

Besides the inner preparation there is also an outer one. Before going to the altar the priest must vest himself in the liturgical garments. The natural feeling that we ought to put on better clothing for the celebration of divine worship[1] was something the faithful had learnt long ago. A similar sentiment of reverence had led, even before the end of Christian antiquity, to a special liturgical vesture for the celebrating priest.[2] At first it was merely more costly, more precious than the ordinary holiday clothing of the townspeople.[3] It was not till city fashion ordained a new shorter costume that liturgical dress began to be distinguished from ordinary dress, for our liturgical vesture is nothing else than a stylized form of the holiday attire of the old imperial days of Rome.

In the alb, held together by a cincture, we have a survival of the ancient tunic. To this is joined the amice (*humerale*, shawl or shoulder covering), the neckcloth or scarf of old, which went by various names. As an outer garment there is the chasuble, the Mass garment proper, which by its very name (*casula*, "little house") is reminiscent of an older shape that com-

[25] P. Pourrat, *Christian Spirituality*, III, (trans. W. H. Mitchell; New York, 1927), 4-22.

[26] *Rit. Serv.*, I, 1, Cf. *supra*, p. 248 f.

[27] Regarding some special forms of ascetical preparation which were customary in former centuries for the *hebdomadarius* in certain collegiate churches (complete retirement in the house, fasting, reading of the story of the Passion) see Lebrun, I, 30f. Cf. de Moléon, 173 F.; Binterim, IV, 3, p. 273 f.

[1] Thus Christians acted even in the days of Clément of Alexandria, *Pæd.*, III, 11 (PG, VIII, 657).

[2] For a more detailed study of what follows *vide* J. Braun, *Die liturgische Gewandung* (Freiburg, 1907). Cf. also a series of articles by Dom Raymund James, O.S.B., "The Dress of the Liturgy," *Orate Fratres*, X (1935-6), 28 to 12, and XI (1937-8), 545.

[3] Even in 530 the *Liber pontificalis* (Duchesne, I, 154) ascribes to Pope Stephen a prohibition to wear *vestes sacratæ* outside church; the author is plainly thinking in terms of his own generation.

pletely shielded the body. This shape suggests clearly its origin in the old Roman *pœnula*, which almost entirely replaced the Roman toga in the late imperial period.[4] It was not till the thirteenth century that the ample folds of the ancient bell-shaped *casula* were reduced so that less material—now in various colors—had to be used, and the vestment finally attained its present shape by cutting down the sides. What might first have been induced by the Gothic temper, since the oval outlines suited the style of the period, was eventually pushed to an extreme in the interests of Baroque, which seemed to prefer using heavy, stiff brocades.

The original character of the garment was thus lost, but in the last few years efforts have been made to return to the older shape. As signs of honor and distinction the priest wears two other vestments, both the color of the chasuble, namely, the maniple and the stole. The origin of the stole is not clearly known, but in the maniple we can recognize the fashionable hand-kerchief of Roman times, called *mappa* or *mappula*, which was carried in the hand—hence the later name *manipulus*—or fastened to the arm.

Since Carolingian times the act of vesting in the liturgical garments gradually became a liturgical act fitted out with prayer. It is usually, but not always, preceded by a washing of the hands.[5] This too is accompanied by a short prayer, either by the verse *Lavabo inter innocentes manus meas* (Ps. 25:6),[6] to which in the earlier sources the verse *Asperges me* (Ps. 50:9) is sometimes joined,[7] or by the oration *Largire*, which often recurs after the eleventh century,[8] or, as often happened later, by both verse and prayer.[9] The formula which we at present connect with the handwashing, *Da Domine virtutem manibus meis ad abstergendam omnem maculam* does not appear in this connection until later. Where it does appear earlier, it usually concludes with *Per* and as an addition to the oration *Largire*, it accompanies the drying of the fingers.[10] The preparation of the outer man

---

[4] The same garment, styled here a *planeta*, is already mentioned in the first Roman *Ordo*; see *supra*, p. 68.

[5] In some instances the washing of the hands is placed ahead of the accession psalms; so in the Missa Illyrica: Martène, 1, 4, IV (I, 492); in Styrian missals: Köck, 95; 100; and also in Italy: Ebner, 321.

[6] The Mass-*Ordo* of Amiens, ed. Leroquais (*Eph. liturg.*, 1927), 439.

[7] E.g. Martène, 1, 4, VI ff. (I, 528 E; 534 E; 537 E).

[8] First in the Mass-*Ordo* of the Séez group: *Largire sensibus nostris, omnipotens Pater, ut sicut exterius abluuntur inquinamenta manuum, sic a te mundentur interius pollutiones mentium et crescat in*

nobis sanctarum augmentum virtutum. *Per . . .* (PL, LXXVIII, 245).

[9] Styrian missals, for example; in some of these Ps. 25 is said from its very start; Köck, 95, 96, 98. Also in Hungary: Radó, 23, 41, *et al.*

Seckau missals of the 15th century have interpolated a *Kyrie, Pater noster* and versicle between psalm and oration; Köck, 99, 105; further additions in the Regensburg *Ordo* of circa 1500: Beck, 261.

[10] Missal of St. Vincent (*circa* 1100): Fiala, 196; cf. Martène, 1, 4, XII (I, 568 B). Also the *Ordo* of Gregorienmünster (14-15th century), *ibid.*, XXIII (I, 654 A); Augsburg missal of 1555: Hoeynck, 369; Hungarian missals: Radó, 23, 41 *et al.*

was apparently a very serious concern. In the tenth century and after, there is frequent mention of the comb which the priest uses to arrange his hair,[11] a reference no doubt to the medieval mode of longish hair-cuts.[12]

In medieval sources we find the washing of the hands is preceded, as in present-day pontifical rites, by the ritual putting off of the outer clothing (accompanied by proper prayers)[13] and in the older period also by the putting on of special footwear.[14] At private Mass it was the custom in many medieval churches to prepare the paten and chalice with the offerings right after washing the hands, and to mix the water and wine to the accompaniment of the usual words.[15] After this, followed the vesting.

Vesting did not always occur in the precise order now followed. The amice, for instance, was not put on till after the alb, as would be natural

The formula is used since the 11th century also for putting on the maniple; see *infra.*

[11] Sacramentary of Ratoldus (d. 986; PL, LXXXVIII, 241 a) : *ministretur ei aqua ad manus et pecten ad caput.*

Later on, the comb is always mentioned before the washing : Honorius Augustod., *Gemma an.,* I, 199 (PL, CLXXII, 604) : *deinde pectit crines capitis.* Similarly the rhymed German interpretation of the Mass (12th century), ed. Leitzmann (Kleine Texte, 54), 16, 1. 26 f. Two Seckau missals of the 12th and 14th centuries even contain a special prayer *ad pectinem* : May God remove all that is superfluous and send down the sevenfold gift of the Holy Spirit; Köck, 95, 98. Witnesses of the 15th century, *ibid.,* 103, 104; also in the Hungarian Sacramentary of Boldau (c. 1195) : Radó, 41. See also the illustrations in Ch. Rohault de Fleury, *La messe,* VIII (Paris, 1889), 167-173.

The *Liber ordinarius* of Liége, in agreement with its Dominican model, says about the sacristy : *Solent etiam ibi haberi pectines et forcipes;* Volk, 49, 1. 31.

Cf. Durandus, *Rationale,* IV, 3, 1-3. According to the Pontifical of Durandus (Andrieu, III, 633; cf. 631) the deacon or the court chaplain handles the comb while the bishop is vesting, and a towel is placed around the latter's neck in the process.

[12] According to Simon of Venlo it was also customary to wash one's hands,

mouth and face in the sacristy; see the extracts from his interpretation of the Mass in Smits van Waesberghe (*Ons geestelijk Erf,* 1941), 292.

[13] Examples from the 12th to 15th centuries in Köck, 95-104; Radó, 23, 41; Martène, 1, 4, XXXI f. (I, 649, 654); Augsburg Missal of 1555 : Hoeynck, 369, et al. Just what was taken off is not usually specified further (*vestes*). In all the cases referred to the prayer is almost always the same : *Exue me Domine veterem hominem cum actibus suis, et indue me novum hominem, qui secundum Deum creatus est in iustitia et sanctitate veritatis.* (The prayer is still used at religious investiture ceremonies.)

At an earlier time the phrase from the Psalm was used : *Conscinde Domine saccum meum et circumda me lætitia salutari* (Ps. 29 :12) ; *Missa Illyrica* : Martène, 1, 4, IV (I, 492 C).

[14] Thus in Carolingian sources, e.g. Amalar, *De eccl. off.,* II, 25 (PL, CV, 110), where the *sandalia* of bishop, priest, deacon and subdeacon are all distinct; cf. Braun, *Die liturgische Gewandung,* 390 f.

A prayer *ad calceandum* for priests is seldom mentioned, but it does appear already since the turn of the 11th century : Fiala, 196; Martène, 1, 4, XII (I, 568); here it is the same as that now commanded for the bishop (*Calcea me*). A different formula in Ebner, 332.

[15] Martène, 1, 4, 1 (I, 351, 352) ; *ibid.,* 1, 4, XXVI, XXXVI (I, 635, 671); Ordinary of Coutances: Legg, *Tracts,* 55.

with a scarf or neck-cloth[16]; this usage is still retained in the liturgies of Milan and Lyons.[17] Nor was the manner of putting it on always the same as today's. One practice, which makes its appearance in northern countries about the turn of the ninth century,[18] was to place the amice over the head like a hood and to leave it thus till the other *paramenta* had been donned. For an explanation of the origin of this mode of wearing the amice[19] it might be good to note that the first liturgists who speak of it are the same ones who mention the comb,[20] the work of which would be nullified when putting on the alb and chasuble unless some means were employed to prevent disarranging the hair. This manner of wearing the amice was universally followed in the thirteenth century and so the orders that stem from this time, Franciscans, Dominicans, Trinitarians and Servites, have continued it to the present, while for the rest it disappeared about the same time that the style of hair-cut changed.[21] There were some differences about when the amice thus worn should be pushed back off the head; some removed it right after putting on the chasuble; in the French churches it was customary to keep it on the head till the *secreta* or even till the start of the canon.[22] It is to be noticed, moreover, that the prayer we say at present while putting on the amice, still designates it as a helmet: *Impone, Domine, capiti meo galeam salutis.*

The maniple, too, was not in olden times put on as we do it now, right after girdling the alb. It was not taken up till all the other vestments had been donned. And it had to be thus as long as it was customary to carry it in the hand—that is, up till the eleventh/twelfth century. As soon as the fashion set in of fastening it to the arm, the practice changed and finally

---

[16] The original purpose of the amice is still recalled in the rite of ordination to subdeaconship, in the bishop's phrase about *castigatio vocis,* i.e., discipline in speech. The phrase stems from Amalar, *De eccl. off.,* II, 17 (PL, CV, 1094). It is really unnecessary to follow O. Casel, "Castigatio vocis," JL, VII (1927), 139-141, who seeks the explanation in pre-Christian sacral usage where at the sacrifice every disturbing noise had to be restrained.

[17] Proofs in Braun, 28. Cf. also the succession according to the *Ordo Rom. I,* n. 6; *ibid.* 86.

[18] Braun, 29-32.

[19] Braun, 31 f., lists a series of explanations, but acknowledges himself that they are all unsatisfactory.

[20] Honorius and the rhymed German interpretation (*supra,* note 11). According to the latter the humeral is for the priest "the shelter of the Holy Ghost," and he lays it upon his head that his eyes and ears might not see or hear anything improper (Leitzmann, 16 f.).

[21] It is striking that this mode of putting on the garment first disappears about the 15th century, and in Italy at that; Braun, 30. Italy was the cradle of the Renaissance and consequently of the return to the ancient Roman style of short hair.

This does not exclude the possibility that the primary position of the amice (it was put on first according to the most ancient Frankish sources, in contrast to the older Roman *Ordines*) had its source also in the old Germanic hair style.

[22] In some churches, like Paris, Auxerre, Rochelle, this was done only in the colder season of the year; the practice continued even down to the 18th century; Braun, 31. Thus the amice served not only as a neckcloth and a protection for the hair but also as a winter hood.

shifted to our present use.[23] Only the bishop continues the older manner but with this variation, which became quite general since the thirteenth century, that he takes the maniple only after the *Confiteor.*[24]

There was a great simplification in the ritual of vesting, at least in the eleventh and twelfth centuries, when—as was the practice in various Benedictine monasteries—all the monks on feast days wore albs and maniples during the choir prayer that preceded the Mass.[25] Doubtless the priests in this case regularly wore also a stole since it had been made obligatory by ninth and tenth century legislation to wear the stole at all times, both at home and while traveling.[26]

The prayers which, since Carolingian times, have been said while vesting are extremely diverse. It is hardly an exaggeration to say, as someone actually did, *Quot missalia tot sensus.*[27] There is even a trend to forego any special texts.[28] The diversity of these vesting prayers is in part connected with their half-private nature, but perhaps the most important reason for it is the symbolic interpretation of the vestments, which was based upon various details and continued to produce numerous new formulas in accordance with the changes of thought.

Actually, of course, there is a certain symbolism inherent in the liturgical vestments. The fact that the priest wears garments that are not only better but really quite special, distinct from the garments of ordinary civil life, enhanced where possible by the preciousness of the material and by decoration—all this can have but one meaning: that the priest in a sense leaves this earth and enters another world, the shimmer of which is mirrored in his vesture. But medieval interpreters were not content with such a general explanation; they had to find in each piece of clothing a particular relation to that other world. In one period they directed their attention

---

[23] Braun, 543-548.
[24] Braun, 546 f. The practice will be explained *infra*, p. 289.
[25] Braun, 522 f.

In German cathedrals of the 10th century, the capitulars appeared before Terce *humeralibus et albis, apud quosdam autem casulis induti. Ordo Rom. VI*, n. 1 (PL, LXXVIII, 989).
[26] Braun, 581 f.; 583.

As a matter of fact, in the preparation for both private and conventual Mass the Customs of Cluny make mention only of putting on the chasuble; *Udalrici Consuet. Clun. II*, 30 (PL, CXLVII, 715 D, 724 B); it is different, however, in William of Hirsau (d. 1091), *Const.*, I, 86 (PL, CL, 1015 f.).

Cf. also the monastic Mass-*Ordo* of Rouen (perhaps 13th century): Martène,

1, 4, XXXVII (I, 676): the priest readies himself for Mass simply by putting on maniple, stole (and chasuble) at the altar.
[27] Braun, 706.

In the Missal of St. Lawrence at Liége (1st half of 11th century): Martène, 1, 4, XV (I, 583), there are four formulas *ad zonam.*
[28] Late medieval Mass-books from Normandy and England have the priest saying the entrance prayers (*Veni Creator* and Ps. 42) even while he is vesting; thus in Bayeux and Sarum: Martène, 1, 4, XXIV, XXXV (I, 626, 664). Cf. also the *Alphabetum sacerdotum*: Legg, *Tracts*, 35 f.

At an earlier period, however, Sarum had vesting prayers just as other places did; Legg, *Tracts*, 3.

principally to the moral and ethical order to which the priest must conform; in à second period they kept in view the person of Christ whose place the priest takes; and in the third, Christ's Passion which is commemorated in the celebration.[29]

The concepts in the prayers for vesting are created for the most part out of the explanations of the first period, since they nearly all arose in that period. In our summary view of all these vesting prayers, we will confine our attention mainly to the typical formulas which attained a certain wide distribution or which led eventually to the texts we use today. We cannot consider the many peculiar and idiosyncratic coinages of individual manuscripts.[30] And wherever possible we will try to present the original text and the original ascriptions.[31] For the rest, a summary list of available sources will have to suffice.

In its function as a shoulder cloth which is fastened around the waist with bands,[32] the amice is simply adjusted to the spiritual world and inspires the eleventh century prayer: *Humeros meos Sancti Spiritus gratia tege, Domine, renesque meos vitiis omnibus expulsis præcinge ad sacrificandum tibi viventi et regnanti in sæcula sæculorum.*[33]

Taking the later way of wearing it, the amice suggests a shadow that falls across the head and so it becomes a pertinent image of faith: *Obumbra, Domine, caput meum umbraculo sanctæ fidei et expelle a me nubila ignorantiæ.*[34]

---

[29] *Supra*, 88, 110 ff.

[30] Such are to be found in the Sacramentary of Ratoldus (10th c.; PL, LXXVIII, 240 f.): Over each vestment the bishop says *Jube domine benedicere* and then a blessing composed in hexameters. The vesting formulas of the more ancient Missal of Fécamp (13th-14th century) are quite distinctive, especially in their brevity: Martène, 1, 4, XXVI (I, 635 f.).

[31] For example, formulas that were once allotted to the chasuble were later transferred to the stole or even to the alb.

Conscinde, the formula mentioned above as being recited while taking off the outer garments, was often used since the 11th century as an accompaniment to the donning of the amice; see Martène, 1, 4, VI, XV (I, 529 D, 583 A); likewise in the *Liber ordinarius* of Liége (Volk, 101). Cf. Braun, 712. It was also shifted to the alb: Sacramentary of St. Denis: Martène, 1, 4, V (I, 528).

Cf. also the remarks made about the fate of the formula *Da Domine virtutem*, noted on p. 277.

[32] Kissing certain individual vestments before putting them on is noticed for the first time in an Admont missal of the 15th century, here in reference to amice, alb, stole and chasuble; Köck, 102.

[33] *Missa Illyrica*: Martène, 1. 4, IV (I, 492 D). *Ibid.*, XV (I, 583). Köck, 102; cf. 99, 103, 105.

In Hungarian missals it is combined with the following formula *Obumbra;* in fact the Boldau Sacramentary (*circa* 1195) states: *Dum humerale imponit dicat: Obumbra . . . Dum involvit humerale dicat: Humeros . . .*; Radó, 41; cf. 24, 60 f., *et al.*; Jávor, 112.

In Sweden it is amplified: *Caput meum et humeros meos . . .* Yelverton, 10.

Further sources in Braun, 711, Note 4. The basic ideas recur in the older Mass-*Ordo* of Gregorienmünster, put up in biblical style: *Sub velamento alarum tuarum, Domine, tua me cooperi pietate . . .* (cf. Ps. 16: 8): Martène, 1. 4, XVI (1, 595).

[34] Sacramentary of Séez: Martène, 1. 4, XIII (I, 575); *ibid.*, XII, XXXI (I,

The martial significance is found expressed already in the ninth century, where the amice wrapped around the head is conceived of as a helmet. *Pone, Domine, galeam salutis in capite meo ad expugnandas diabolicas fraudes.*[35] The formula as we have it today seems to have been touched up by some humanists before it was inserted in the present Roman Missal.

Looking at the material of which it was usually made, white linen, which suggests righteousness and nobility, a document of the ninth century combines the amice with the alb and dedicates to both a prayer which later on was appropriated to the alb alone: *Indue me, Domine vestimento salutis et indumento justitiæ circumda me semper.*[36]

The contrast between the white garment and the soiled condition of our sinfulness is emphasized in a prayer that appears quite frequently: *Omnipotens sempiterne Deus, te suppliciter exoro, ut fraude omnium fuscatorum exutus, alba veste indutus te sequi merear ad regna, ubi vera sunt gaudia.*[37] The motif here touched upon, the cleansing blood of the Lamb (Apoc. 7:14) is brought out more clearly in the formula of the Pontifical of Cambrai: *Dealba me, Domine, et a delicto meo munda me, ut cum his, qui stolas suas dealbaverunt in sanguine Agni, gaudiis perfruar cœli. Per.*[38] This formula, rounded out somewhat, is our present-day prayer. But we also encounter the image of the spiritual warrior, accoutred in the armor of faith, in such prayers as: *Circumda me, Domine, fidei armis, ut ab iniquitatum sagittis erutus valeam æquitatem et iustitiam custodire,*[39] or *Indue me vestimento salutis et circumda me lorica fortitudinis.*[40]

568, 649); a different conclusion) in the Mass-*Ordo* of Regensburg: Beck, 262.

The initial words are probably reminiscent of Ps. 139: 8 b.

Cf. Innocent III, *De s. alt. mysterio,* I, 35 (PL, CCXVII, 787): *sacerdos caput suum obnubit.*

[35] Sacramentary of Moissac (11th century): Martène, 1, 4, VIII (I, 538).

Ibid., III, XXVII f. ,XXXIV, XXXVI (I, 480, 639, 642, 661, 671); *ibid.,* 1, 4, 1 (I, 351). The expression *galea salutis* follows I Thess. 5: 8 and Eph. 6:17: hope for salvation is a protecting helmet.

In the Sacramentary of St. Gatien (9-10th century) the formula has the addition: *et omnium inimicorum meorum persequentium me sævitiam superandam;* Martène, I, 4, VII (I, 535). So also in later texts: *ibid.,* II (I, 477); *ibid.,* 1, 4, 1 (I, 350).

Other alterations: *ibid.,* XXVI (I, 635); *ibid.,* 1, 4, 1 (I, 353); Köck, 95, 99. Further sources in Braun, 712, Note 5; cf. 29, note 2.

[36] Mass-*Ordo* of Amiens, ed. Leroquais (*Eph. liturg.,* 1927), 439.

For the alb alone, Martène, 1, 4, II, VI ff., XXVI ff. (I, 477, 529 A, 535, 538, 635, 639, 642); Köck, 95.

Often also with several amplifications (*tunica lætitiæ,* etc.), e.g. the Sacramentary of Modena: Muratori, I, 87.

[37] *Missa Illyrica:* Martène, 1, 4, IV (I, 492).

Ibid., XV (I, 583).

Even in the later Middle Ages: Köck, 99, 102, 103, 105; Radó, 24 et al.; Jávor, 112.

[38] Martène, 1, 4, 1 (I, 353). Further sources: Braun, 713, note 1.

[39] Missal of Liége (1st half of 11th century): Martène, 1, 4, XV (I, 583).

Ibid., IV (I, 492); 1, 4, 1 (I, 350); Volk, 101.

Used for the amice: Martène, 1, 4, V (I, 518).

[40] Sacramentary of Séez and related sources: Martène, 1, 4, XIII, XII, XV f., XXXI (I, 575 A, 568, 595, 649 f.); *ibid.,* 1, 4, 1 (I, 352); Fiala, 196.

For the cincture, the Bible had already furnished a ready symbolism.[41] But this symbolism was brought out more plainly and illustrated from various angles in the prayers that accompany the act of vesting. *Domine, accinge in me custodiam mentis meæ, ne ipsa mens infletur spiritu elationis,*[42] in which the cincture's holding the garment together calls to mind the image of swollen pride. From another viewpoint the alb which enfolds everything represents the virtue of love which is to be held fast by the cincture: *Præcinge me, Domine, zona iustitiæ et constringe in me dilectionem Dei et proximi.*[43] Or there is the thought of the loins girt about by the cincture and the prayer comes to one's lips that temptation might be conquered: *Præcinge, Domine, lumbos mentis meæ et circumcide vitia cordis et corporis mei,*[44] or in another formula which sounds Carolingian and whose original wording is probably retained in the Sacramentary of Moissac (eleventh century): *Præcinge, Domine, cingulo fidei lumbos mei corporis et comprime et extingue in eis humorem libidinis, ut iugiter maneat in eis tenor totius castitatis.*[45] While another setting of this formula—for which there are early sources—has been kept in our missal for the bishop, the one used by the priest has been somewhat simplified.

Remembering that the maniple once served a very practical purpose as a handkerchief or napkin, a formula was composed at latest in the eleventh century which was also spoken while drying the hands, but which we now use while washing them: *Da, Domine, virtutem manibus meis ad abstergendam omnem maculam immundam, ut sine pollutione mentis et corporis*

Used for the amice: Martène, 1, 4, XXXII (I, 654). Likewise, with the variant *galea* instead of *lorica*: Köck, 101, 102; cf. 97.

[41] In some instances just Bible phrases are employed; thus Ps. 17: 33 and (with additions) Ps. 44: 4, in two formulas of the Liége Missal: Martène, 1, 4. XV (I, 583); the first also *ibid.*, 1, 4, 1 (I, 350), and also 1, 4, V (I, 519), but in this latter case used for the maniple; the second psalm phrase is used in a Seckau missal of the 15th century; Köck, 99.

[42] Sacramentary of Séez and related sources: Martène, 1, 4, XIII, XII, XV, XXXI (I, 575, 568, 583, 650); Fiala, 196. Further passages in Braun, 714, note 6.

[43] In a Seckau missal about 1170: Köck, 95; and frequently in more recent Styrian Mass books: *ibid.*, 97, 100 ff. (also with the start *Circumcinge*: *ibid.*, 102 f., 105); Regensburg Mass-*Ordo*: Beck, 262.

With the isolated reading: *constringe in me virtutem caritatis et pudicitiæ* it is already in the older Mass-*Ordo* of Gregorienmünster: Martène, 1, 4, XVI (I, 595).

[44] Sacramentary of Tours (9th-10th century): Martène, 1, 4, 1 (I, 350 B). With tiny variations (among others the beginning *Circumcinge*), *ibid.*, IV f., XV, XXXVI (I, 492, 518, 583, 672); Sacramentary of Modena: Muratori, I, 87.

Hungarian Mass-books since the 12th century: Radó, 24, 41, 71 et al.; Jávor, 112.

Further sources: Braun, 714, note 1.

[45] Martène, 1, 4, VIII (I, 538).

In the remaining texts the words *et virtute castitatis* are regularly inserted after *cingulo fidei;* thus in the Mass-*Ordo* of Amiens, ed. Leroquais (*Eph. liturg.,* 1927), 440.

Martène, 1, 4, 1 (I, 350 f., 352, 353); also II f., VI ff. (I, 477, 480, 529, 535), et al.; see also Braun, 714, note 5.

valeam tibi servire.[46] Its actual significance as an ornamental kerchief which was required for one to be fully dressed up, survived in the consciousness of later ages to this extent, that monastic groups followed the custom already mentioned, of wearing albs and maniples on feast days while the choir sang psalms.[47] To such a use for choir prayer and psalmody[48] corresponded the text which the priest also used while vesting in maniple: *Da mihi, Domine, sensum rectum et vocem puram, ut implere possim laudem tuam.*[49] As a badge of honor with which one was "invested" and which one wore even at work, this is the concept in the prayer: *Investitione[50] istius mappulæ subnixe deprecor, Domine, ut sic operer in temporali conversatione, quatenus exemplo priorum patrum in futuro merear perenniter gaudere.*[51] Finally, the formula we use today (somewhat altered) refers to the modern name of the vestment and makes a cross-reference to Psalm 125:6: *Merear, precor, Domine, manipulum portare mente flebili cum patientia, ut cum exsultatione illud deferendo cum iustis portionem acci-*

---

[46] *Missa Illyrica:* Martène, 1, 4, IV (I, 493).

Without exception in all eight of the Styrian vesting programs of the 12th-15th century in Köck, 96-105. See further in Braun, 715, note 3.

In several places we have a more recent and more precise wording: *Da, Domine, manipulum in manibus meis ad extergendas cordis et corporis mei sordes, ut sine pollutione tibi Domino ministrare merear;* Martène, 1, 4, III, XXVIII (I, 480 f., 639). Further sources in Braun, 715, Note 2.

Variants in Martène, 1, 4, XXVIII (I, 643); Muratori, I, 87.

[47] Rupert of Deutz, *De off. div.,* II, 23 (PL CLXX, 54). Cf. Braun, 522 f.

[48] The connection here is made plainer when we read that at Cluny even in 1700 they had six choir boys who wore albs and maniples at the high Mass on Sundays and feasts; de Moléon, 150. At that time, too, the choir boys at Lyons wore the maniple on their left arm when on Holy Saturday they sang the prophecies; *ibid.,* 63.

[49] Sacramentary of Séez: Martène, 1, 4, XIII (I, 575).

Ibid., XII, XV, XXXII (I, 568, 583, 654); 1, 4, 1 (I, 352); Fiala, 196; Legg, *The Sarum Missal,* 216, note 1; a missal from Fonte Avellana (13-14th century): PL, CLI, 932 B.

Braun, 715, note 6, names some other MSS.; he did not, however, notice the connection with singing.

Somewhat altered: Martène, 1, 4, XVI, XXXVI (I, 595, 672).

Attention should be paid to the musical connotation of the word *sensus;* cf. *infra,* p. 409, note 36.

[50] The word is handed down in corrupt form: *Investione* (Illyr.), *In vestione* (Hittorp), and *Invectione* (the remainder).

[51] *Missa Illyrica*: Martène, 1, 4, IV (I, 493).

Ibid., 1, 4, 1 (I, 353); *Liber ordinarius* of Liége (Volk, 101).

See also Braun, 716, note 1.

The same prayer is spoken by the bishop at the ordination to subdiaconate in *Ordo Rom. antiquus* (circa 950): Hittorp, 91.

In the same sense of duties assumed we have the scriptural phrase *opus manuum* (Ps. 89: 17) in the Missal of Beauvais: Martène, 1, 4, 1 (I, 350).

The maniple is also looked upon as a token of the higher orders which impose the obligation of special virtue; thus in the formula *Manipulum innocentiæ* which puts in a late appearance in Styria (Köck, 103) and in Hungary (Jávor, 112; Radó, 24, 71, 76 *et al.;* at first, in the 13th century, *Stolam innocentiæ:* Radó, 41).

Cf. also Braun, 715 and note 8.

piam.[52] The tearful bundle of earthly care should become the sheaf of a jubilant heritage.

Although the stole had already become, even in the Carolingian period, only a narrow band which was hung around the neck,[53] the name it bore awakened the memory of a garment of the same name which plays so significant a role in the picturesque language of Scripture.[54] The prayer which the bishop says today, and also, slightly changed, the priest, appears as early as the ninth century: *Redde mihi, Domine, obsecro, stolam immortalitatis, quam perdidi in prævaricatione primi parentis, et quia cum hoc ornamento accessi, quamvis indignus, ad tuum sanctum ministerium, præsta ut cum eo lætari merear in perpetuum.*[55] The same garment which alone has value in God's sight is the thought behind another prayer which is of the same age but was not used so frequently: *Stola iustitiæ circumda, Domine, cervicem meam et ab omni corruptione peccati purifica mentem meam.*[56] But there is also another concept that comes to the fore, the stole as a yoke around the neck. In the declining Middle Ages the words of our Lord in Matthew 11:30 are added to the formula mentioned.[57] The yoke of the Lord, and its opposite, is thought of exclusively in a third formula: *Dirumpe, Domine, vincula peccatorum meorum, ut iugo tuæ servitutis innexus valeam tibi cum timore et reverentia famulari.*[58] Here, too, the texts of our Lord from St. Matthew have been added, and that at a very early time.[59]

This scriptural text is today spoken while putting on the chasuble, since this garment with its bell-shape hardly suggested comfort.

[52] Sacramentary of Moissac (11th century): Martène, 1, 4, VIII (I, 538); shortened in the Missal of Narbonne: *ibid.*, 1, 4, 1 (I, 351).
Somewhat altered: *ibid.*, 1, 4, II, VI (I, 477, 529).
Further passages in Braun, 715, Note 5.
In some few late medieval Mass books the scriptural phrase, Ps. 125: 6 (which is at the bottom of the prayer) is used by itself: Martène, 1, 4, 1 (I, 351 D); also 1, 4, XXVI, XXXIV (I, 635, 661).
[53] Braun, 586 f.
[54] Ecclus. 6: 32; 15: 5; Luke 15: 22; Apoc. 6: 11, etc.
[55] Mass-*Ordo* of Amiens, ed. Leroquais (*Eph. liturg.*, 1927), 440. Later sources in Martène, 1, 4, 1 (I, 351, 353); also 1, 4, II, VI, VIII, XXVII f. (I, 477, 529, 538, 639, 643).
[56] Sacramentary of St. Gatien: Martène, 1, 4, VII (I, 535). (In mutilated form also in the Mass-*Ordo* of Amiens, ed. Leroquais, 440).

Numerous sources: among others, Martène, 1, 4, III, IV, VI, XII etc. (I, 481, 492, 529, 568, etc.); Radó, 24, 41, etc.
[57] Styrian Mass books of the 15th century: Köck, 100, 102, 103 f.; Pressburg Missal D (15th century): Jávor, 112; Mass-*Ordo* of Regensburg: Beck, 262; Missal of Upsala (1484): Yelverton, 11.
[58] *Missa Illyrica:* Martène, 1, 4, IV (I, 493).
Ibid., XV (I, 583); Köck, 99; Radó, 41.
Cf. also the formula of a Hungarian missal of 1384: *Stolam innocentiæ pone* . . . Radó, 118.
The formula dependent upon this, *Dirumpe, Domine, omnes laqueos satanæ et confirmato in me hereditatis tu[æ] funicul[um]*, appears in one St. Gall MS. for the maniple (Braun, 715) and in an Admont MS. (14-15th century) for the cincture (Köck, 102, note 1).
[59] Sacramentary of St. Denis (11th century): Martène, 1, 4, V (I, 519).

The formulary to which we are making reference is amongst the oldest: *Domine, qui dixisti: iugum meum . . . præsta ut sic illud deportare in perpetuum valeam, qualiter tuam gratiam consequi merear.*[60] The chasuble, like Christian love, covers everything, and encloses everything fast like a fortress, so it leads to the following words: *Indue me, Domine, ornamento caritatis et pacis, ut undique munitus virtutibus possim resistere vitiis et hostibus mentis et corporis.*[61] A number of other texts begin with the words *Indue me*, but they are not at all alike, differing in their concept of the garment, some presenting an explanation similar to that already considered,[62] others conceiving it as a *lorica (fidei* or *iustitiæ)*[63] or as a *vestis nuptialis*,[64] still others insert *sacerdotalis iustitia*,[65] and the corresponding petition follows.[66]

The *sacerdotalis iustitia* forms the basic motif of another vesting formula we have to mention, *Fac me, quæso.* In later times this was connected with the chasuble but it comes from an earlier era in which the prayers were not said in connection with individual vestments but the whole vesting ceremony was accompanied with a prayer[67] and that of the apologia-

---

[60] Sacramentary of St. Gatien (9-10th century): Martène, 1, 4, VII (I, 535); Mass-*Ordo* of Amiens, ed. Leroquais, 440.

Cf. Martène, 1, 4, II f., VI, VIII (I, 477, 481, 529, 538); also, 1, 4, 1 (I, 351); Braun, 718, note 6.

The phrase from Matt. 11: 30 which we saw used for the stole was in some instances also employed for a formula for the amice, as in the Sacramentary of Tours (9-10th century): Martène, 1, 4, 1 (I, 350).

[61] Sacramentary of Séez, Martène, 1, 4, XIII (I, 575). Often the word *humilitatis* or *humilitatis et castitatis* is set before or after the word *caritatis*, thus stressing, instead of the symbolism of love, the notion of *undique munitus*: *ibid.,* XII, XV, XXXI f. (I, 568, 583, 650, 654); Fiala, 196; Braun, 718, note 2. Also, in a more drastically revised form, Martène, 1, 4, XXVII f. (I, 639, 643).

[62] The phrase *indumenta iustitiæ et lætitæ* finds a place also in a formula (beginning *Creator totius creaturæ*) which appears in the Missal of Liége: Martène, 1, 4, XV (I, 583) and in Seckau: Köck, 99.

[63] Martène, 1, 4, 1 (I, 350, 351); Muratori, I, 87. The expression *lorica fidei* founded on I Thess. 5: 8.

[64] Martène, i, 4, XXVI, XXXIV (I, 636, 662).

[65] *Ibid.,* 1, 4, IV f. (I, 493, 519); also 1, 4, 1 (I, 350).

[66] The formula of the older Mass-*Ordo* of Gregorienmünster: Martène, 1, 4, XVI (I, 595): was rather widespread, taking on, however, a number of variant forms: *Indue me, Domine, ornamento caritatis et concede mihi protectionem contra hostem insidiatorem, ut valeam puro corde laudare nomen tuum gloriosum in sæcula sæculorum.* Cf. the Mass-*Ordo* of Bec: *ibid.,* XXXVI (I, 672 C); Hungarian Mass books: Radó, 24, 41; Jávor, 113. Used for the alb in some German Mass books: Beck, 262; Köck, 97, 100.

A Sacramentary of Fonte Avellana (before 1325) offers: *. . . sacerdotali iustitia, ut induci merear in tabernacula sempiterna*; PL, CLI, 884 D.

Hungarian missals of the 13-14th century also have a formula which ties in with the cross or crucifix on the chasuble: *fac me . . . concupiscentiis crucifigi;* Radó, 118, 123, 155.

[67] Cf. even in the late Middle Ages the rite of Sarum, *supra,* note 28.

type. This formula itself must be reckoned as belonging to this type.[68] The formula, which is part of the supplement of Alcuin,[69] is designated for the Mass *ordo* of the Séez group of the eleventh century[70] together with its derivatives. Here it usually forms the conclusion of the accession psalmody.[71] Even if this whole psalmody did not in some way accompany the vesting, still at least the formula we are talking about was so connected from time past.[72] Sometimes it even carries a corresponding title.[73] In the later Middle Ages it sometimes became the prevalent text when assuming the chasuble.[74]

For putting on the biretta, which was not worn till after the twelfth century, and was not used for going to the altar till much later,[75] no text was specially composed.

As we survey this series of vesting prayers as they are now and as they lie before us in the sources of the Middle Ages, it is plain that there was generally no intention of making these prayers tie in with the opening of the Mass nor, in the main, any effort to conceive a well-ordered plan of thought. The earliest unification of thought was achieved by follow-

---

[68] E.g., in the Pontifical of Halinardus: Martène, 1, 4, XIV (I, 580 B) : *Fac me, quæso, omnipotens Deus, ita iustitia indui, ut in sanctorum tuorum merear exaltatione lætari, quatenus emundatus ab omnibus sordibus peccatorum, consortium adipiscar tibi placentium sacerdotum, meque tua misericordia a vitiis omnibus exuat, quem reatus propriæ conscientiæ gravat. Per.* In the Sacramentary of St. Denis (11th century), Martène, V (I, 519 A) it is found with a variant which might well be the original: *ita iustitiæ indui armis* (the chasuble as armor).

The Mass-*Ordo* of Amiens, ed. Leroquais (*Eph. liturg.*, 1927), 440, contains a formula of this kind which has some of the elements of the *apologiæ: Rogo te,* with the direction: *ad tunicam;* it usually appears among the *apologiæ;* see *infra,* p. 298, note 3.

[69] Muratori, II, 191. Here the formula serves as the collect of a *missa specialis sacerdotis*. This could have been its original function.

[70] *Supra,* p. 94, note 11.

[71] *Supra,* p. 273, note 14.

[72] Thus, e.g., in the Pontifical of Halinardus, where the formula which the bishop recited *cum se ad missam parat* represents the only prayer expressly intended as a vesting prayer.

In later years this vesting, with its accompanying vesting prayers, sometimes precedes the psalmody and the oration *Fac me quæso;* so Martène, 1, 4, XII (I, 568). At other times it is interposed between the psalmody and the oration *Fac me quæso;* so *ibid.,* IV, XV (I, 492 ff., 583); Köck, 95 f., 96 f., 100 f. Sometimes, too, it follows the prayer: thus Martène, 1, 4, XVI (I, 594 f.); Köck, 97 ff.; Hoeynck, 369.

[73] Missal of Troyes (c. 1050): Martène, 1, 4, VI (I, 530): after the psalms the celebrant says this formula, *induens casulam.* The Sacramentary of St. Denis (*supra,* note 20) : *Ad casulam.*

Later the direction reads: *Cum ornatus fuerit;* Ebner, 306; cf. Muratori, I, 87; Franz, 751.

[74] Thus in seven of the eight vesting forms from Styrian missals in Köck, 96-106; the Regensburg Mass-*Ordo*: Beck, 262. As an *alia* for the chasuble also in the Missal of Upsala: Yelverton, 11.

In one case marked *Ad albam:* Martène, 1, 4, XXXII (I, 654).

[75] Braun, 510-514. Cf. Lebrun, *Explication,* I, 84. As we have seen, *supra,* p. 278 f., the amice served as a head covering during the walk to the altar.

ing St. Paul's description,[76] and conceiving the priest putting on the *paramenta* as one donning the armor of God and readying himself for the spiritual combat.[77] In these prayers, therefore—unlike the prayers at the accession or those at the foot of the altar, with which they share both their derivation and their original obligation[78]—there is not to be found any planned progression in the priest's preparation.[79] The individual garments are not explained on the basis of any conscious essential function which is theirs when worn, but it is rather only some ascetical thought, some handy reference to a scriptural text around which the prayer is composed. Thus the external act is raised, easily and without trouble, to the spiritual sphere. For that reason the individual forms are not spread abroad as a rule in a single unit but they are chosen on their own particular merit as taste dictates.[80] Some Mass books since the eleventh century seek to give the prayers a certain rounding off by concluding not only some but all the prayers where possible with *Per Christum Dominum Nostrum.*[81]

Putting on the vestments, even after the prayers were enjoined, was not always connected with the other preparations of the priest. Although in some instances it precedes the accession prayers which are then included in the liturgy proper as parts of equal worth,[82] at other times it is trans-

[76] I Thess. 5: 8; Eph. 6: 14-17.
In the Oriental liturgies, especially the Byzantine, the vesting prayers are restricted almost entirely to scriptural phrases which are used to wonderful advantage; e.g., the Byzantine uses for the idea of girdling, Ps. 17: 33 and Ps. 44: 4 f.; in addition Is. 61: 10; Ex. 15: 6 f.; Ps. 118: 73; Ps. 132: 2. Brightman, 355.
[77] Among the several interpreters, Honorius Augustod., *Gemma an.*, I, 199 (PL, CLXXII, 604 B), mentions this symbolism but did not expand on it; it was carried out more thoroughly by John Beleth, *Explicatio*, c. 32 (PL, CCII, 43). Cf. Braun, 705 f.
[78] Burchard of Strassburg is the first to leave these prayers optional; one could replace them by the *Miserere* or some other psalm; Legg, *Tracts*, 132.
Our Roman Missal, *Ritus serv.*, I, 2, does not make any such reservation. Still most rubricists who discuss the priest's conduct going to the altar and returning, ascribe only a directive character to this direction; thus M. Gatterer, *Annus liturgicus cum introductione in disciplinam liturgicam* (5th ed.; Innsbruck, 1935), 78. But see J. O'Connell, *The Celebration of Mass* (Milwaukee, 1941), I, 22.

[79] The division and gradual mounting which Brinktrine, *Die hl. Messe*, 50 f., attempts to show in our vesting prayers—the first prayer rather negative, the chasuble prayer even stylistically the climax—is something that has been superimposed. But it is true that, by properly choosing from various traditional formulas, such a design has been achieved.
[80] Exceptions see *supra*, p. 281, note 30. Even in the group of the Séez Mass-*Ordo* (*supra*, p. 92) the vesting prayers of the Sacramentary of Séez, which prove to be the original, are found only in the Missal of St. Vincent, in the *Cod. Chigi* and (mixed with others) also in great part in the Missal of Liège.
[81] Martène, 1, 4, 1 (I, 352); also 1, 4, VI, XXXIV (I, 528 f., 661); Köck, 99 99f., 105 f. Likewise the Spanish *Missale mixtum* (PL, LXXXV, 523 f.), where a selection of the formulas we are considering recurs.
The Missal of Evreux-Jumièges (14-15th century) has each formula excepting the last end with *in nomine Patris et Filii et Spiritus Sancti*: Martène, 1, 4, XXVIII (I, 642 f.).
[82] Cod. Chigi (11th century): Martène, 1, 4, XII (I, 568).

ferred to the altar, and sometimes even the donning of the last vestments is joined to the very beginning of Mass.[83] A survival of this practice is possibly to be found in the custom which is to be noticed since the thirteenth century and is still followed today,[84] the custom of handing the bishop his maniple only after the *Confiteor*.[85]

According to the Missal of Westminster[86] the priest had first to vest with the stole, then prepare the chalice and say the prayer for the mingling of the water; only after that did he don the chasuble. In French churches it was customary towards the end of the Middle Ages and thereafter, to recite the psalm *Iudica* and the other prayers that went with it during the vesting, *se revestiendo*.[87] This arrangement is given more in detail in the Missal of the monastery of Bec (probably thirteenth century); after girding himself with the cincture, the priest says Psalm 42 and the conjoined prayer *Aufer*, then he puts on the maniple, stole, and chasuble.[88] In other places the maniple and stole were put on before saying the psalm,[89] which was recited while holding the chasuble lying on the altar.[90] Sometimes, too, the *Confiteor* was said without the chasuble.[91] In this way the preparatory and semi-private character of these prayers was more plainly emphasized. In fact, the psalm *Iudica*, as we shall see, was at that time said as a rule on

[83] This happened especially in private Masses; cf. *supra*, p. 228. In the 11th and 12th centuries this means, for monastic churches, only the stole and the chasuble, which had still to be donned; *Udalrici Consuet. Clun. II*, 30 (PL, CXLIX, 724); cf. *supra*, p. 279. Later this refers to the vestments taken collectively: *Liber ordinarius* of Liège (Volk, 101). Examples from the end of the Middle Ages in Legg, *Tracts*, 34 f., 55 f. Burchard of Strassburg (*ibid.*, 130 f.) also takes the vesting at the altar into account.

[84] *Cæremoniale episc.*, I, 10, 2.

[85] Cf. *supra*, p. 280; Braun, 546-548. The origin and provenience of the custom has not been explained hitherto. Even the attempt at an explanation in Brinktrine, *Die hl. Messe*, 59, is untenable; he would take into account the *prostratio* mentioned in John the Arch-chanter (7th century), where the maniple would certainly prove a hindrance, but the time element must throw this proof aside, since neither the *prostratio*, nor even kneeling at the *Confiteor* was in use after the early Middle Ages.

[86] 14th century; ed. Legg (HBS, 5), 487 ff.

[87] Missal of Tours (1533): Martène, 1, 4, 2, 4 (I, 361 C); *Alphabetum sacerdotum*: Legg, *Tracts*, 35.

[88] Martène, 1, 4, XXXVI (I, 672); similarly in the Mass-*Ordo* of Rouen: *ibid.*, XXXVII (I, 676).

[89] Missal of Châlons (1543): *ibid.*, 1, 4, 1 (I, 352); Missal of Orleans (1504): de Moléon, 200.

[90] *Ordinarium* of Coutances (1557): Legg, *Tracts*, 56. The same rubric (without naming the psalm) is presupposed in the 13th and 14th centuries: Martène, I, 4, XXVI, XXXIV (I, 636 A, 662 A).

Even as late as 1620 St. Vincent de Paul was witness to this manner of starting the Mass; Bremond, *Histoire littéraire du sentiment religieux*, III, 248.

[91] This was presupposed in every case for private Mass in William of Hirsau, *Const.*, I, 86 (PL, CL, 1016): after the *Confiteor* the priest takes the stole in order to pronounce the *Indulgentiam;* only then does he put on the chasuble.

the way to the altar.[92] True, in almost all these arrangements the reference is to private Masses. But amongst the Carthusians in the thirteenth century it was the custom for the priest to put on the chasuble at the altar also in conventual Masses except on the very highest feast days.[93] Even at a later time it was the practice in Orleans to say the psalm *Iudica* in the sacristy, vested in alb and stole, and this before high Mass.[94] So it is not improbable that the same line of thought suggested that at the pontifical Mass the last of the vestments, the maniple—at that time it was really the last of the decorative garments to be donned—should not be handed to the bishop until after the psalm *Iudica*—as the bishop of Minde strikingly testifies with regard to France, the homeland of this special order of vesting[95]—or after the *Confiteor*, as it became customary in Rome later on.[96]

4. The Prayers at the Foot of the Altar as a Unit

When we investigate the beginnings of the prayers at the foot of the altar, we find the seed in the pre-Frankish era not in any definite prayer but rather in the actions which correspond to the two parts of our present-day prayers, the progress towards the altar, all planned in definite forms, and the silent reverence of the celebrant as he bows in front of the altar.[1] In the solemn services of the Roman basilicas the approach to the altar was turned into a procession of the clergy, during which the singers chanted the introit. In the churches of the Frankish Kingdom, according to a law

[92] De Moléon, 167, 427, relates about Sens and Reims that at that time (1718) even the *Confiteor* was said in the sacristy at a high Mass.

[93] *Statuta antiqua:* Martène, 1, 4, XXV (I, 631 B). The psalm *Iudica* was not said by the Carthusians.
See also the case of Evreux-Jumièges: *supra*, p. 269, note 33.

[94] De Moléon, 186; the completion of the statement, *en aube et en étole*, in the Index, p. 535.

[95] Durandus, *Rationale*, IV, 7, 4: *pontifici facturo confessionem* the maniple is put on. In agreement is Durandus's Pontifical (Andrieu, III, 634): *cum confessio coram altari fit*.

[96] Not unequivocal even in the *Ordo Rom. XIV*, n. 53 (PL, LXXVIII, 1159 B).

[1] *Supra*, p. 70. Even though in the stational service of the 7th-8th century—

just as in the present-day pontifical Mass —the fore-Mass centers not on the altar but on the throne where the pope remains during almost its whole length, still in *Ordo Rom. I*, n. 8 the altar is definitely indicated as the terminus of his march; as soon as he enters the sanctuary he *inclinat caput ad altare*, the silent prayer that follows is performed *ante altare*, and finally the salutatory kiss is given: *osculatur evangelia et altare*.
The German expression "Stufengebet" (like the English "prayers at the foot of the altar") is postulated on conditions which obtained only after the year 1000, because before the 11th century there were, as a rule, no steps up to the altar, no platform even; only the sanctuary as a unit was raised above the level of the nave. Braun, *Der christliche Altar*, II, 176-179.

of procedure which was then in force, the clergy themselves, or at least the celebrant, would have to say some prayers even in such circumstances. And from the first, *apologiæ* were considered above all as suited to this spot.[2] Already in the ninth century such prayers had been inserted here,[3] and until the eleventh century the space they thus occupied at the beginning of Mass grew and grew immensely.[4]

But even before the end of the tenth century a new arrangement made its appearance, an arrangement which was retained in the Mass books of the Séez group and which in the time to come was adhered to more or less. The pertinent rubric reads as follows:

> *Postquam ecclesiam intrat episcopus [. . .], osculetur diaconos et presby-*
> *teros duos. Et incipiat per se "Introibo ad altare Dei," cum psalmo "Iudica*
> *me Deus." Cum venerit ad altare dicat has orationes: "Aufer a nobis . . . ,"*
> *"Omnipotens sempiterne Deus, qui me peccatorem . . ." Deinde, cum evan-*
> *gelium osculatus fuerit, dicat: "Pax Christi quam . . ."* [5]

On the way to the altar, therefore, Psalm 42 was spoken in common,[6] and upon arrival at the altar two orations were added in conclusion, one

[2] A prayer upon entering the sanctuary, derived from the Greek liturgy of St. James (Brightman, 33), is also found in 11th century Mass programs: Martène, 1, 4, IVff. (I, 494f., 519 C, 530 B): *Domine Deus omnipotens, qui es magnus.*

In nearly all oriental liturgies *apologiæ* are found at the beginning of the Mass. The priest usually recites them quietly to himself during the external preparations or the introductory incensations.

[3] Mass-*Ordo* of Amiens, ed. Leroquais (*Eph. liturg.*, 1927), 440f.: *Antequam accedat ad altare dicat:* Indignum me . . . *Tunc accedat ad altare dicens:* Ante conspectum . . . Deus qui de indignis.

Similarly in the 10th century the Sacramentary of Ratoldus: PL, LXXVIII, 241f. This corresponds to the rubric of *Ordo Rom. VI*, n. 3 (PL, LXXVIII, 990): *inclinans se Deum pro peccatis suis deprecetur.*

The Sacramentary of St. Thierry (10th century): Martène, I, 4, X (I, 548), has for the first prayer, *dum accedit*, the prayer which now is found at the beginning of the Breviary (with variants): *Aperi, Domine Deus, os meum.*

[4] In some cases even at the end of the Middle Ages there are *apologiæ* (besides the *Confiteor*) at the start of Mass; thus in the Missal of Westminster (c. 1380), ed. Legg (H B S, 5), 489; in some

Mass-arrangements from Normandy: Martène 1, 4, XXVII, XXXVIf (I, 640, 672, 676).

In Spain even printed missals of the 15th and 16th centuries prescribed *apologiæ* to be said *ad introitum altaris* or *ad introitum missæ*; Ferreres, 78f.; cf. 67, 72.

[5] This is the form of the text as handed down in the 10th century Pontifical of Halinardus: Martène, 1, 4, XIV (I, 581f.). From this text, in which the only secondary insertion (four *apologiæ*) is that after *episcopus* (indicated by the brackets), the text of the parallel documents (*vide supra*, p. 92) must have been derived; of these Séez and Verdun-Stablo display only small additions, but the others rather considerable ones. Another point that shows this text to be the original one is the fact that in its rubrics the basic data from *Ordo Rom. I*, n. 8 still peers through plainly while in the other texts it has been almost obliterated: *dat pacem uni episcopo de hebdomadariis et archipresbytero* (two priests are substituted for them) *et diaconibus omnibus . . . Et surgens pontifex* (after quiet prayer) *osculatur evangelia et altare. . . .*

[6] The opinion put forth by Brinktrine, *Die hl. Messe*, 55, and similarly by several others, that this psalm served since the 9th century as a private preparation

of which is our *Aufer a nobis*. In the witnesses to this particular arrangement of the entry there are found in addition various *apologiæ*, forerunners of our *Confiteor*, included in a variety of ways and in an assortment of forms. They are either added at the beginning or inserted somewhere in the middle or subjoined at the end. This arrangement quickly took the lead over other plans of a similar kind.[7]

By the middle of the eleventh century another step was taken in Normandy, at a time when this land was in the forefront of liturgical reform. From these *apologiæ* a formal *Confiteor*, along with the response begging forgiveness, was composed and introduced between the psalm and the oration.[8] This new plan seems to have spread by way of the Cluniac reform into Italy[9] and even into Germany.[10] It prevailed, however, only to this extent that a formal *Confiteor* in some setting or other, along with the corresponding response and the succeeding oration *Aufer a nobis*, became a part of the established design of every Mass *ordo* since the twelfth century.[11] On the other hand the psalm *Iudica* did not gain an entrance into countless Mass arrangements all through the later Middle Ages and after. It will be enough to refer to the monastic liturgies of the Carthusians, the Calced Carmelites and the Dominicans; from all of these the psalm is missing even at present, since, in accordance with the fluctuations of usage, it was not inserted when their Mass arrangements were established during the thirteenth century. Even at the first general chapter of the Society of Jesus, held in 1558, when a unified rite was to be established within the

and thence was taken over into the Mass, first of all into private Mass, I do not find sustained in any of the sources.

[7] The Sacramentary of St. Denis (11th century): Martène 1, 4, V (I, 519f.), assigns the following as preparation: upon entering the church the priest recites an *apologia* and immediately *Aufer a nobis*, then several psalm verses (85:11; 53:8; 49:14) and Ps. 42: 1-4, and again several *apologiæ*.

[8] Mass-*Ordo* of *Cod. Chigi*: Martène, 1, 4, XII (I, 569). Since the section under consideration shows, in many other points a certain dependence upon John of Avranches, who was writing about 1065 (see *supra*, p. 102 f), and since in the present instance there is only a summary report, which is, however, in agreement with the other (a mutual confession right after coming to the altar), it seems certain that the insertion of the *Confiteor* evidenced in the *Cod. Chigi* must be traced to the cycle of the Norman bishop,

despite the Italian origin of the MS. (Bona, I, 12, 4 147f. and App. II, 955).

[9] *Cod. Chigi*, from the *monasterium S. Vincentii O.S.B.* (see the previous note). The same rubrics, but in shortened form, recur in a later MS. from Naples (*Archivio di Stato*, Cod. IV): Ebner, 311f.

The same arrangement of the prayers also in two mid-Italian monastic Mass books at the end of the 11th century (*Bibl. Riccard.*, 299 and 300): Ebner, 297, 300.

[10] Bernold of Constance, *Micrologus*, c. 23 (PL, CLI, 992).

[11] The only exception which I could ascertain is to be found in a missal of Toul dated c. 1400: Martène, 1, 4, XXXI (I, 650), where the *apologia Ante conspectum* precedes the *Aufer a nobis*. Still this Mass-arrangement represents substantially nothing more than a late revision of that of the Séez group, with the interpolation of several more modern elements.

order, it was decided that the psalm be left out.[12] The Missal of Pius V, following the example of most of the Italian Mass books, and particularly the Missal of the Roman curia where it had long had a permanent place, made it a general prescript.

There can be no doubt about the appropriateness of Psalm 42; if any prayer was to be chosen to be said on the way to the altar, this was certainly apt. The fourth verse actually made reference to the very act which was occurring: *Introibo ad altare Dei, ad Deum qui lætificat iuventutem meam*. For one special occasion, the entrance of the newly baptized into the church, this verse must have been incorporated in the Milan liturgy even in the time of St. Ambrose.[13] When it came to inserting the text in the Mass, at first it was only this single verse, just as for the incensing the psalm text is confined to a single verse, *Dirigatur, Domine, oratio mea . . .* , and at the washing of the hands to the words *Lavabo . . .* But to secure a certain richness, the other verses were added whenever their use here made some sense; in this case the whole psalm was included. But the dominant tone is given by this one verse which from the very start was selected as the antiphon: I shall go in to the altar of God, to the God who was the joy of my youth.[14] This approach unto God, which the psalmist longed for, has become fully possible in a proper sense only in the New Covenant; for we gain entrance to God only through Christ "who gives us all confidence, bids us come forward, emboldened by our faith in Him" (Eph. 3:12; cf. Rom. 5:2). The altar of the New Covenant is the place where this meeting with God can be best accomplished this side of heaven. How strikingly pertinent it is, that the Syrians call the Mass simply *Kurobho*, that is, "approach."

But not only is the approach accomplished here, but the situation too in which the psalmist finds himself in his longing for God assumes the nature of a type. When we desire to draw near God, the way is always blocked somehow by the *homo iniquus*. We therefore cry out to Him who is our strength that He may illumine us with His light and sustain us with His faithfulness and guide us in *montem sanctum*, that height upon which the sacrifice of Golgotha will be renewed. The psalmist closes with

---

[12] *Decret. Congr. gen. I*, n. 93 (*Institutum S. J.*, Florence, 1893, II, 176).

[13] Ambrose, *De Myst.*, VIII, 43 (Quasten, *Mon.*, 131); *De Sacr.*, IV, 2, 7 (*ibid.*, 156).

[14] The Hebrew text is translated: I will go up to the altar of God, the God of my triumphant joy. But our problem is rather: What is the meaning of the Vulgate wording, and what is the original conception of the verse in liturgical usage? Ambrose, who cites the verse for

the procession of the neophytes into the Church, understands the *iuventutem* as referring not to biological youth (which is now made joyful) but to the youthful new life of grace which is granted in baptism: *abluta plebs . . . renovata in aquilæ iuventute* (*De myst.*, VIII, 43). *Deposuisti peccatorum senectutem, sumpsisti gratiæ iuventutem* (*De sacr.*, IV, 2, 7). Cf. also J. Pinsk, *Liturg. Leben*, II (1935), 185-187.

shouts of joy and jubilation that anticipate the *eucharistia*, the prayer of thanksgiving.

The rule established in the tenth-century rubric already referred to continued in force throughout the Middle Ages: Psalm 42 was said on the way to the altar in the same way as the canticle *Benedicite* was recited on the way back to the sacristy (as we still do today). In fact, until the Missal of Pius V, this was expressly stated in the rubrics in many cases.[15] Very seldom was there any clear transfer of the psalm to the altar steps.[16] Often this transfer occurred because the chasuble was put on at the altar.[17] as was the custom especially at private Mass. In other cases the rubric was left indefinite. This diversity of practice corresponded to the variety in spatial arrangements. Often the distance from sacristy to altar was very short. In order not to prevent the psalm's being said with proper care and to lend it greater importance, it was not begun until the steps were reached. This must have been the origin of the arrangement now found in the Missal of Pius V.[18]

[15] Thus in Italian Mass books since the 11th century (Ebner, 297, 300, 332) : *Dum ingreditur ad altare*, or (*ibid.*, 345) : *Dum procedunt de secretario*. Similarly in other cases: *ibid.*, 296, 313, 340, 354. Still in the *Missale Romanum* of 1474, ed. Lippe (HBS, 17), 198, but no longer in the editions of 1530 or 1540: Lippe (HBS, 22), 98.

Also in France: Leroquais, I, 131, 163, 211, etc.

The Regensburg Mass-*Ordo* (Beck, 262) : *Transeundo ad altare*. The Augsburg Mass-*Ordo* of 1555 (Hoeynck, 370) : in the sacristy or *dum itur*, with the added remark that the *ministrantes et qui intersunt* should alternate with the priest verse for verse. Similarly a Camaldolese missal from the 13th century (Ebner, 354) notes: *In inceptione processionis dicitur psalmus . . . quem ministri cum eo alternando veniant ante altare*. However in regard to the remark in a mid-Italian Mass-*Ordo* of the 11-12th century (Ebner, 336) : *Quando ingreditur ad altare, sub silentio dicat sacerdos*, it must be observed (*contra* Batiffol, *Leçons*, 13) that this rubric is immediately followed by an apology to which the *sub silentio* directly refers.

[16] Missal of St. Lambrecht (1336; Köck, 107) : *inclinatus ante altare dicat*: *Introibo*. A missal of the Hungarian Her-

mits of St. Paul (15th century; Sawicki, 146) : *ad gradus altaris*.

There is one isolated instance from this era of groping and trying in which the psalm is said only after the altar has been kissed: Missal of Troyes (c. 1050), Martène, 1, 4, VI (I, 530 D).

[17] The older Missal of Fécamp (13-14th c.) : Martène, 1, 4, XXVI (I, 636 A) : *Stans ante altare induat se dicens . . . Postea incipiat antiphonam: Introibo*. The *Ordinarium* of Coutances (Legg, *Tracts*, 50) which is dependent on the older Fécamp Missal. The priest recites Ps. 42 while holding with both hands the chasuble still lying on the alter.

Missal of Evreux-Jumièges: Martène, 1, 4, XXVIII (I, 643).

[18] Italian Mass-arrangements of the 11-13th Century: *accedat ad altare et dicat*: Ebner, 321, 327; cf. 306.

Bernold, *Micrologus*, c. 23 (PL, CLI, 992) : *Paratus autem venit ad altare dicens*.

Even Innocent III, *De s. alt. mysterio*, II, 13 (PL, CXVII, 806), who observes that Ps. 42 precedes the *Confiteor*, does not exclude the possibility that the psalm be said already on the way. The same remark in Durandus, IV, 7, 1.

The *Alphabetum sacerdotum* (after 1495) observes expressly that the priest can say the psalm in front of the altar or even while vesting: Legg, *Tracts*, 35 f.

As early as the eleventh century the characteristic or thematic antiphon was introduced before the start of the psalm. In our present-day manner of handling it, however, the verse is treated not precisely as an antiphon but as a versicle, so that the second half, *Ad Deum qui lætificat* serves as a response. This treatment will be best understood in some situation where a middle way was sought between using the psalm and leaving it out entirely and being satisfied with the one verse which set the tone. With this single verse other versicles could then be joined.[19] This middle way was taken in the Benedictine *Liber ordinarius* of Liége, which in this matter followed the rite of Liége used at that time. The prayers at the foot of the altar began with three verses, *Introibo, Confitemini, Dignare*; in each case the response was supplied by the second half of the verse; the *Confiteor* followed.[20] A similar thing is done in the contemporary Roman Masses in those instances in which Psalm 42 is left out[21]; the confession of faults is preceded by two verses, *Introibo* and *Adiutorium nostrum*. When these verses were joined to the psalm their treatment as versicles was naturally transferred too[22]; however this transfer was not by any

---

[19] Such versicles were in use even independently of the psalm in question. In the *Missa Illyrica*: Martène, 1, 4, IV (I, 494), the bishop, on leaving the sacristy, recites Ps. 85: 11 (*Deduc*); 58: 8 (*Voluntarie sacrificabo*); when entering the church, Ps. 5: 8 f. (*Introibo in domum; Domine deduc*); 118: 37 (*Averte*).
Cf. the French books (11th century); ibid., V f. (I, 519 D, 530 B); further, the Hungarian books of the 12th century: Jávor, 113; Radó, 24, 42, 123.
[20] Volk, 89. Likewise in a 15th century MS. at Tongern; de Corswarem, 110; cf. 112.
The Klosterneuburg Mass-*Ordo* of the 15th century (Schwabes, 61) exhibits the three verses: *Ostende nobis, Et introibo, Confitemini;* a Seckau missal of the 15th century (Köck, 109), *Ostende* and *Introibo;* a Lyons monastic missal of 1531 (Martène, 1, 4, XXXIII [I, 658]): *Et introibo, Pone Domine,* and *Confitemini.* Similarly ibid., XXXIV (I, 662), where the second versicle is missing.
[21] The reason why the Missal of Pius V omits Psalm 42 during Passiontide and at Requiem Masses is to be discovered — with Lebrun, I, 99 — in the feeling that the words *Quare tristis es anima mea* are singularly incongruous on such days of sorrow. Cf. also Kössing, *Liturgische Vorlesungen,* 224-228. Perhaps the fact

that on Passion Sunday the psalm occurs as the Introit of the Mass gave occasion for setting precisely this date as the first for omitting it from the prayers at the foot of the altar.
Even in the 16th century the psalm, with the conclusion *Requiem æternam,* is presupposed by Paris de Grassis (d. 1528), *De cæremoniis,* II, 39 (see Lebrun, I, 99, note a). In the *Directorium of Ciconiolanus* which appeared in 1539 (Legg, *Tracts,* 204) the remark is made that the psalm is to conclude with *Gloria Patri* even at Masses for the Dead.
[22] The versicle form of the verse *Introibo* appears as an introduction to the psalm in the Mass-*Ordo* of the papal chapel about 1290, ed. Brinktrine (*Eph. liturg.,* 1937), 200: the prayers at the foot of the altar start with *Introibo* and *Adiutorium;* Psalm 42 follows; then this rubric: *Et repetatur antiphona Introibo* (an expression similar to that used in the present-day missal); this rubric is the residue of a more ancient arrangement; the next versicle, *Confitemini,* leads into the *Confiteor.* Similarly *Ordo Rom. XIV,* n. 71 (PL, LXXVIII, 1185 A).
Probably the same treatment of the verse as a versicle is intended in the Seckau Missal, about 1170: Köck, 106. In late medieval Mass schemes the appearance of *Introibo* as a versicle before Ps.

means a universal practice.[23]

In our present-day Mass the very first words, even before the *Introibo*, are the words of blessing which accompany the sign of the Cross, words which form a Trinitarian gateway to the whole Mass—*In nomine Patris et Filii et Spiritus Sancti. Amen.* As used here the formula, taken from our Lord's command to preach and baptize, can be traced here and there in the fourteenth century but not any earlier.[24] It had been used as a blessing frequently in the early Middle Ages,[25] and even appears in the Mass itself quite a bit earlier as the characteristic blessing formula.[26] That it should appear at the beginning of Mass as a blessing text—just as it has more recently appeared at the beginning of our other prayers—is probably to be explained by the fact that the sign of "blessing," the *"signum" crucis* is connected with it[27]; we begin the holy action in the power that comes from the triune God through the Cross of Christ.[28] At the same time, in the use of this formula here, we can perceive a bridge between the two great sacraments of Baptism and Eucharist.

42 is quite frequent; see Legg, *Tracts*, 3, 134, 181, 204; Köck, 107 f.; Yelverton, 11.

[23] See e.g., the English Mass books of the declining Middle Ages in Maskell, 8 f; here the verse, undivided, is used as an antiphon.

[24] Cistercian Missal (apparently since the 14th century); Schneider (*Cist.-Chr.,* 1926), 253. The priest says the words immediately after kissing the altar, before he begins the prayers at the foot of the altar.

Admont Missal of the 14-15th century: Köck, 111; here, however, Lk. 1: 28 and the *Salve Regina* with its oration precede.

Late medieval examples in Martène, 1, 4, XXXIII, XXXVII (I, 658, 676).

In other cases the trinitarian formula is found in some other spot; e.g. in the *Ordinarium* of Coutances (1557) at the beginning of the vesting prayers and after Ps. 42 (which is followed in this instance by the donning of the chasuble); Legg, *Tracts*, 55 f. More often it stands at the start of the *Introit*, where today we have simply a sign of the Cross; see infra, p. 332.

[25] Eisenhofer, I. 278.

[26] At the head of a formula for the blessing of incense in the *Missa Illyrica;* Martène, 1, 4, IV I, 494 C), and in related Mass-*Ordines* of the 11th and 12th cen-

turies: Fiala, 197; Muratori, I, 88; cf. Ebner, 333.

Among the earliest witnesses to a linking of the trinitarian phrase with the formulas of Confirmation and absolution is St. Thomas, *Summa theol.,* III, 72, 4; 84, 3 ad 3.

[27] The sign of the Cross at the start of Mass also in *Ordo Rom. I,* n. 8 (PL, LXXVIII, 941 C); also in the Apostolic Constitutions, VIII, 12, 4 (Quasten, *Mon.,* 212 f.), where the bishop at the beginning of the eucharistic prayer signs the τρόπαιον τοῦ σταυροῦ on his brow.

[28] In the same sense the Regensburg Mass-*Ordo* notes an opening sign of the Cross in connection with the words *Sancti Spiritus assit nobis gratia;* Beck, 263. The same in Spanish Mass books of the late Middle Ages together with the trinitarian formula or some other; Ferreres, 66, 67, 71, 76; also in the *Missale mixtum* (PL, LXXXV, 525 B). The phrase quoted seems to be the beginning of an ancient hymn; cf. the text in Yelverton, 5.

Elsewhere there is substituted here the versicle *Adiutorium nostrum* (which also has an introductory function); Pontifical of Durandus (Andrieu, III, 643); cf. Augsburg Mass-*Ordo* of the 15th century: Franz, 751.

Late medieval Mass arrangements often made of this petition for God's blessing a special act of prayer during which the priest knelt at the altar.[29] It was frequently the custom to kneel down first for a few moments' prayer.[30] The psalm *Iudica* was sometimes given a special conclusion, a prayer being said to reaffirm its meaning.[31] In the Norman-English ambit, where such a conclusion was almost universally in use, the *Kyrie* and *Pater noster* were said.[32] A further development of the custom involved going up

[29] *Alphabetum sacerdotum* (Legg, *Tracts*, 35) : *Veni Creator* with versicle and oration (cf. *supra*, p. 278, note 15 and p. 280, note 28, the *Veni Creator* during the vesting in the rite of Sarum). A Styrian missal of the 15th century (Köck, 112) : *Veni S. Spiritus*, *reple* with the versicle and oration, and the added sentence, *Sancti Spiritus assit nobis gratia*. Similarly in Hungary: Jávor, 113 ; Radó, 24, 96, 123; here the elements are already found in the Sacramentary of Boldau c. 1195 (Radó, 42) : at the start *Adsit nobis*, before kissing the altar *Veni S. Spiritus* and oration.

An opening *Veni S. Spiritus* also in the Mass-*Ordo* of the Cistercians; Schneider (*Cist. Chr.* 1926), 253; cf. 222.

According to the Regensburg Mass-*Ordo* (c. 1500) the priest should say Ps. 42 on the way to the altar, then kneeling before the altar he should recite *antiphonam et orationem de B. Virgine vel de S. Spiritu;* Beck, 263. Similarly missals of the Hungarian Hermits of St. Paul; Sawicki, 146 f., with note 27. Cf. the Admont Missal, *supra*, note 24. Augsburg in 1555 had both the *Salve Regina* and the *Veni S. Spiritus,* each with oration; Hoeynck, 370.

The Missal of Evreux-Jumièges (14-15th century) directs that the priest, even before vesting, kneel before the altar and pray first to the Holy Ghost, then to the Blessed Virgin, then to all the saints; Martène, 1, 4, XXVIII (I, 642).

[30] In the ancient Carthusian rite the priest was to say a *Pater noster* kneeling before the altar; Martène, 1, 4, XXV (I, 631 A) ; later an *Ave* was added: Legg, *Tracts*, 99; this is still the present-day custom: *Ordinarium Cart.* (1932), c. 32, 3.

In Holland it was a common practice to pray silently for a few moments or to say the *Pater* three times: Smits van

Waesberghe (*Ons geestelijk Erf*, 1941), 292 f. Or prayers relating to the Eucharist were suggested; Legg, *Tracts*, 130, 204.

In Germany many recited the psalm *Judica* kneeling at the altar; Franz, 574. At the Synod of Brixen (1318), c. 4, *tres genuflexiones ante altare* were appointed for this occasion, to be accompanied by prayer; likewise *missa finita;* J. Baur, "Die Brixner Synode von 1318" (in the *Festschrift zur Feier des zweihundert jährigen Bestandes des Haus-, Hof-, und Staatsarchivs* [Vienna, 1949]).

The Spanish *Missale* (PL, LXXXV, 525 B; cf. 523 A) instructs the priest to say first of all an *Ave Maria;* similarly other Spanish Mass books: Ferreres, 76.

In France the saying of a *Pater* at the start had become such an ingrained practice that St. Vincent de Paul in 1620 still witnessed the practice; Bremond, *Histoire littéraire du sentiment religieux*, III, 248.

[31] Sacramentary of Brescia (11th century; Ebner, 16) : *Omnipotens sempiterne Deus, misericordiam.*

[32] Legg, *Tracts*, 36, 56, 219; Maskell, 10 ff.; Simmons, 90; Martène, 1, 4, XXIV, XXVI ff., XXXV ff. (I, 626, 636, 639, 643, 664, 672, 676). Outside the region mentioned, in which the Sarum Ordinary of the 13th century (Legg, 219) is the earliest witness, I have met the same arrangement only in late sources: in the Regensburg *Ordo* (Beck, 262) and in two printed missals of Chalons and Tours (Martène, 1, 4, 1 [I, 352]; 1, 4, 2, 4 [I, 361]). An exception to this is apparently to be found in two books of the end of the 11th century, the Pontifical of the Biblioteca Casanatense (Ebner, 327) and (but in this case without *Pater noster*) the Missal of St. Vincent-on-Vol-

to the steps of the altar at the conclusion of the *Pater noster (Et ne nos)*, and continuing the prayer with *Confitemini* and *Confiteor*.[88]

5. *Confiteor*

The *Confiteor*, along with its attendant prayers, forms the second portion of the prayers at the foot of the altar. Its beginnings are to be found in the silent worship to which the pope gave himself when, in the course of the stational services of Rome, he came to the altar.[1] But for this quiet prayer words were soon inserted when the Roman Mass reached Frankish territory. The tendency is manifested, for instance in the change of the seventh-century Roman rubric, *prostrato omni corpore in terra*[2]; the Frankish revision of the eighth century makes the addition: *fundens orationem pro se vel pro peccata [!] populi.*[3] Thus the theme of the apologies is sounded.[4]

The prayer in which lowly man humbles himself before the great God is restricted to the expression particularly of man's incapacity and man's unworthiness. Already in the late Carolingian period, prayer of this sort had accompanied the walk to the altar; here at the altar steps it found its proper setting. A formula which highlights the main motifs of the later

turno (Fiala, 198); but the Beneventan script of both documents forces us to conclude that they are of Norman provenance. This arrangement is also contained in a Sacramentary of Fonte Avellana which must be dated before 1325 (PL, CLI, 884 d).

[88] Maskell, 12, 14; Legg, *The Use of Sarum*, I, 64.

In the use of Bec the entrance psalm was given an even greater air of independence; here the *Pater* was followed at once by the oration *Aufer;* similarly other Norman arrangements fitted in a series of versicles and the oration: Martène, 1, 4, XXVII, XXXVI f. (I, 639, 672, 676). Other orations, too, were either substituted or adjoined; see Maskell, 12. In late texts the *Pater noster* was sometimes supplemented with an *Ave*: Martène, 1, 4, XXXV (I, 664 C); Bona, II, 2, 6 (567); Beck, 262.

[1] *Supra*, p. 70.

[2] While *Ordo Rom. I*, n. 8 (PL, LXXVIII, 942) merely says that the pope prays on the *oratorium* which is laid down before him, the *Capitulare eccl. ord.* (Silva-Tarouca, 196) says more definite-

ly: *accedit ad altare et prostrato omni corpore in terra facit orationem.* Since the wording in the *Breviarium eccl. ord.* (*ibid.*) agrees with this, we may rightly trace this method of prayer (which survives even now in the last days of Holy Week) to the Roman Arch-chanter John (Archicantor Johannes).

On the other hand, Frankish tradition of the 9th century recognized in this place only one type of bodily attitude—prayer while standing bowed: Amalar, *De eccl. off.*, III, 5 (PL, CV, 1111 C): *inclinatus stat.* See infra, p. 303.

[3] *Breviarium eccl. ord.* (Silva-Tarouca, 196).

Even intercession for the people often finds a voice in the *apologiæ*, for example in the formula: *Rogo te, altissime Deus Sabbaoth, Pater sancte, ut me tunica castitatis digneris accingere . . . ut pro peccatis meis possim intercedere et adstantibus populis peccatorum veniam promereri ac pacificas singulorum hostias immolare . . .* Mass-*Ordo* of Amiens, ed. Leroquais (*Eph. liturg.*, 1927, 440; and later frequently.

[4] Cf. about this *supra*, p. 78 f.

Confiteor formula, is prescribed in the Sacramentary of Amiens with the rubric:

Tunc accedat ad altare dicens:
Ante conspectum divinæ maiestatis tuæ, Domine, his sanctis tuis confiteor tibi Deo meo et creatori meo, mea culpa, quia peccavi in superbia, in odio et invidia, in cupiditate et avaritia, in fornicatione et inmunditia, in ebrietate et crapula, in mendacio et periurio et in omnibus vitiis, quæ ex his prodeunt. Quid plura? Visu, auditu, olfactu, gustu, et tactu et omnino in cogitatione et locutione et actione perditus sum; quapropter qui iustificas impios, iustifica me et resuscita me de morte ad vitam, Domine Deus meus.[5]

However, this is still a prayer which an individual recites. In the *Confiteor* the prayer becomes a dialogue spoken by several. The celebrant acknowledges his sinfulness not only before God and heaven but also before his brethren around him and begs their mediation, which is offered him at once in the form of a response to his confession. The distinctive transition[6] to this new form was completed within the Mass in the first third of the eleventh century,[7] and soon it was imitated quite generally. It consisted in making one's confession of faults in the same manner as was customary since the ninth century at daily Prime and Compline[8]—a mutual confession of daily faults made two-by-two. This method was now introduced at the beginning of Mass,[9] at first (usually) the priest and deacon alone confessing to each other,[10] later (more generally) the priest and a

[5] Leroquais, *loc. cit.,* 440.

[6] One single instance from the 9th-10th century is represented by the *Confiteor* of the Sacramentary of St. Gatien, Martène, 1, 4, VII (I, 536); in its long list of sins, covering half of a folio column, it still reflects the stylistic form of those *Confiteor* texts which were intended for sacramental confession.

[7] The definite form which eventually prevailed is to be detected for the first time in *Cod. Chigi* (See *supra,* p. 292). But already about 1030 another attempt of a similar sort is presupposed in the *Missa Illyrica,* Martène, 1, 4, IV (I, 495 A), built on the design of the much-altered entry plan of the Séez group (supra, p. 291). While still on the way to the altar, in front of the steps leading to the choir, the bishop recites not *apologiæ* of some sort or another (as in the Pontifical of Halinardus), but a confession or acknowledgment in the narrower sense (*proferens confessionem*). True, there is no mention of a response by the clergy (a thing taken for granted at that time), nor of their corresponding confession, but there follows the absolving reply of the bishop, *Indulgentiam* (see *infra*), and

then, after several intervening orations and Ps. 42, the ingress into the sanctuary.

[8] *Ordo qualiter* (Albers, III, 29). Cf. Jungmann, *Die lateinischen Bussriten,* 282.

[9] For this reason the *Ordinarium O.P.* of 1256 (Guerrini, 250) lays down the rule: Whoever celebrates right after Prime should not say the *Confiteor* during Prime. Amongst the Premonstratensians, according to the *Liber ordinarius* of the 12th century (Lefèvre, 15; Waefelghem, 100), the *Confiteor* of the priest at the early Mass coincided with that of Prime.

[10] This was also given outward expression. At the conventual Mass in Cluny the priest recited his acknowledgment of sin before the altar, at the Gospel side, *inclinis contra diaconum similiter inclinem; Udalrici Consuet. Clun. II,* 30 (PL, CXLIX, 716 A). The two therefore stood to either side of the altar, facing each other. The same rubric amongst the Carthusians (cf. the illustration in Atchley, *A History of the Use of Incense,* 236-7) and in 1380 in the Missal of Westminster, ed. Legg (HBS, V), 489; cf. the commentary (HBS, XII), 1503. In the Westminster case the priest at the same time

number of those in attendance.[11]

The surprising thing is that not only the *Misereatur* (a companion piece to the *Confiteor* which even the layman was permitted to say as the intercessory response to the confession of faults)[12] but also the *Indulgentiam* (or, as often, beginning with the second word *Absolutionem*) was included in this shift from the very start, for the latter was at this time, and continued to be for several centuries, the regular expression of the priests' sacramental absolution.[13] This was, however, nothing else than a feature of the period. It was right around the year 1000 that (as divers witnesses tell us) the custom came into vogue. Shortly before, it had become a general practice to have the absolution follow immediately upon the sacramental confession. The same pattern was therefore followed in the monasteries where it had long been customary to go to confession to one's spiritual father weekly or even oftener[14]; the sacramental absolution was appended to the *Misereatur*.[15]

The *Confiteor* had thus undergone some development before it was ushered into the Mass prayers at the foot of the altar. From the ninth century on, a number of versions are extant which were intended for use in sacramental confession.[16]

The situation we have here outlined helps to explain how it is that the prayer not only makes acknowledgment before God and his priest, but ends with a petition begging the latter to give counsel and judgment and also to act as an intercessor before God.[17] Intercession of the Church, or more particularly of the priest, was, for the first millenary, the form in which the sacramental power of penance was exercised. This petition for intercessory prayer could well be retained in the confession of lay people and

---

makes his confession to his minister and to the people: *stans iuxta sinistrum cornu altaris ministro suo circumstantique populo istam generalem faciat confessionem.* On the contrary, in the rite of Sarum the priest has the deacon at his right, the subdeacon at his left, and both answer him; Martène, 1, 4, XXXV (I, 664 C).
[11] But the case of the Tours Missal (1533) is an extreme; here the *Misereatur*-formula of the priest begins with the words *Fratres et sorores,* Martène 1, 4, 2, 4 (I, 361).
[12] Jungmann, *Die lateinischen Bussriten,* 207 f., 282 f.
[13] *Ibid.,* 200, 217 ff., 251 f.
[14] *Ibid.,* 285.
[15] *Ibid.,* 283 ff.
[16] *Ibid.,* 180, 182, 207 ff.
The most ancient examples contain an often endless catalogue of sins, intended primarily as a confessional guide. Thus

the *Confiteor* in the Pontifical of Poitiers (last third of the 9th century): J. Morinus, *Commentarius historicus de disc. in admin. sacr. poenitentiæ* (Antwerp, 1682), app. 55 f. Similarly in a Tours Sacramentary of much the same age: Martène, 1, 6, III (I, 775-779), and somewhat shorter in the *Ordo Rom. antiquus* of the 10th century (Hittorp, 26 f.). More briefly worded forms of this type have also survived in the vernacular (Slavic and Old High German) since the 9th century. In part they still survive in the "Open Confession" or *culpa;* see *infra,* p. 492.
[17] Sacramentary of Tours (779 B): *ut pro eisdem peccatis meis intercessor existas.*
The confessional order of Regino of Prüm, *De synod. causis,* I, 300 (PL, CXXXII, 252 A): *ut intercedas pro me et pro peccatis meis ad Dominum et creatorem nostrum.*

it was also retained in the confession which the celebrating priest made to his assistants.[18] Another standard element in the early *Confiteor* formula was the mention of the saints, and, in the more ancient texts, an additional mention of the altar was also made.[19] This points to the fact that the formula was used with some eagerness whenever the monastic custom then in vogue was followed, of making the rounds from altar to altar, praying at each one.[20]

The oldest *Confiteor* formulas which were inserted into the Mass were satisfied to follow the fundamental lines just indicated.[21] About 1080 the following version was used at Cluny: *Confiteor Deo et omnibus sanctis eius et vobis, pater, quia peccavi in cogitatione, locutione et opere, mea culpa. Precor vos, orate pro me.*[22] A thing to notice here is something that holds also for later formulas of the *Confiteor*: the acknowledgment in the first part is made first of all to God and the Church in heaven, while the intercession in the second part is asked at once of the Church on earth. It is well to remark that even in the eleventh century lengthier formulas had already put in an appearance.[23]

As time went on a general augmentation may be noted. At the General Chapter of the Cistercians in 1184 it was decreed that the Mother of God should be named before all the other saints: *Confiteor Deo et beatæ Mariæ et omnibus sanctis.*[24] The pious devotion of a St. Bernard is patently at work here.[25] The later Middle Ages continued to add further names to

---

[18] An exception is found in the rite of the Carmelites where, till the 14th century the complementary section, *Ideo precor,* was missing: Zimmermann, "Carmes," DACL, II, 2172. This section is also wanting in Spanish books even in the 16th century; examples in Ferreres, 65-68.

[19] Ps.-Alcuin, *De psalmorum usu* (PL, CI, 498): *Confiteor . . . coram hoc altari sancto.*

[20] Cf. L. Gougaud, *Dévotions et pratiques ascétiques du moyen âge* (Paris, 1925), 57-59.

[21] A large number of examples in Bona, II, 2, 5 f. (565-570).

[22] *Udalrici Consuet. Clun. II,* 30 PL, CXLIX, 716).

Similarly Bernold, *Micrologus,* c. 23 (PL, CLI, 992): *Confiteor Deo omnipotenti, istis sanctis et omnibus sanctis, et tibi, frater, quia peccavi in cogitatione, in locutione, in opere, in pollutione mentis et corporis. Ideo precor te, ora pro me.*

A formula of this short type is used even at present by the Dominicans: *Missale iuxta ritum O.P.* (1889), 17. Simi-

larly the Carthusians: *Ordinarium Cart.* (1932), c. 25, 13.

The formulation, *mea culpa, mea maxima culpa* is evidenced for the first time in Thomas à Becket (d. 1170); A. Wilmart, *Recherches de Théol. Ancienne et mèdièv.* (1935) VII, 351.

[23] In *Cod. Chigi*: Martène, 1, 4, XII (I, 569): *Confiteor Deo omnipotenti et istis et omnibus sanctis eius et vobis fratres, quia ego miser peccavi nimis in lege Dei mei, cogitatione, sermone et opere, pollutione mentis et corporis et in omnibus malis quibus humana fragilitas contaminari potest. Propterea precor vos ut oretis pro me misero peccatore.* The intercessory formula is correspondingly augmented.

[24] Schneider (*Cist.-Chr.,* 1926), 255.

[25] With this compare the way Christian antiquity drew attention to the heavenly powers, e.g. 1 Tim. 5: 21: "I adjure thee in the sight of God and of Jesus Christ, and the angels he has chosen." Further reference in Jungmann, *Die Stellung Christi im liturgischen Gebet,* 239, note 29.

the list[26] usually, however, only in the second part of the *Confiteor* so that they appear as intercessors.[27] This penitential prayer was in danger of becoming a very externalized devotion. The Third Council of Ravenna (1314) decreed that aside from Mary, only Michael, John the Baptist and the Apostles Peter and Paul were to be named.[28] These are names calculated to recall to mind the sin-free glory and holiness of the triumphant Church.

Elsewhere there was often a long listing and detailing of faults[29] that often turned into an acknowledgment of sins *in specie* just as was general and usual at choir Office in many localities. The interpreters of the liturgy voice a disapproval of this, alleging rightly that there is question here

The anti-Arian movement had long since caused Christ to be considered as included (according to his godhead) in the mention of God. Few are the attempts to formulate a *Confiteor* text along the earlier lines. One example is that offered by the Pontifical of Poitiers (note 16 above) : *Confiteor tibi, Domine, Pater coeli et terræ, tibique benignissime Jesu una cum Spiritu Sancto, coram sanctis angelis* . . . Cf. the trinitarian phrasing in a sacramentary of Fonte Avellana (ante 1325: *confiteor Deo omnipotenti Parti et Filio et Spiritui Sancto et omnibus angelis* . . . (PL, CLI, 885 A).

[26] The Augsburg Mass commentary entitled *"Messe singen oder lesen"* (To sing or read Mass; 15th century) instructs the priest to name at least the patrons of the church and of the altar, and then to add those he wants, towards whom he has devotion. Franz, 751, note 4.

[27] Thus the exposition of the Mass mentioned in the last note. Also the Mass-Ordo of Regensburg (Beck, 263), which in the first part names only Mary and "all the saints," but in the second names the Apostles together and then 20 other saints from Stephen to Ursula. Similar, but a little more extensive, is the Styrian Missal of Haus (Köck, 112).

On the contrary, the Missal of the Barberini MS 1861 (14th century; cf. Ebner, 140) makes mention of individual saints mainly in the first part; Bona, II, 2, 5 (567). The theological basis for this confession before the saints is presented in Matt. 19: 28; 1 Cor. 6: 3.

[28] Mansi, XXV, 547.

Michael, who scarcely ever appears in texts from northern countries, is named in a Fonte Avellana missal of the 13-14th century (PL, CLI, 932 C) and in the *Ordo Rom. XIV* (14th century), n. 71 (PL, LXXVIII, 1185) ; in both these instances the symmetrical arrangement of the names in both segments, which became general later on, also emerges.

The Congregation of Sacred Rites had occasion more than once to curb the arbitrary insertion of names; *Decreta auth. SRC*, n. 1332, 5; 2142. However, some religious have the privilege of including the name of their holy Founder, e.g., the Franciscans insert St. Francis.

[29] This may perhaps have been due to the influence of *Confiteor* formulas which were used as a help in sacramental confession; cf. note 16 above. From the late medieval Mass-*Ordo* of the *Breviarium* of Rouen: Martène, 1, 4, XXXVII (I, 677), we get this sample: . . . *quia ego miser peccator peccavi nimis contra legem Dei mei cogitatione, delectatione, pollutione, consensu, tactu, risu, visu, verbo et opere, in transgressione ordinis mei et,omissione servitii mei, participando cum excommunicatis et in cunctis aliis vitiis meis malis, mea culpa.* An analogous form is already found in the Hungarian Sacramentary of Boldau (c. 1195): Radó, 42. Spanish formulas, too, usually list a series of sins, even with the acknowledgment *me graviter peccasse*: Ferreres, 65 ff. Such formulas as these were probably developed from the same sort of thinking that gave rise to the early Scholastic problem, whether it was permissible, for the sake of greater self-humiliation, to confess sins that one had not committed. Cf. H.

not of secret confession but of public.[30] An intensification of the utterance of sorrow is manifested when the subject is described at the beginning: *Ego peccator* or *Ego miser et infelix* or *Ego reus sacerdos confiteor*, and other similar phrases.[31]

As to the external rite, we find from the very outset that the *Confiteor* was recited with body bowed profoundly.[32] But kneeling too must have been rather widespread.[33] Striking the breast at the words *mea culpa* is mentioned quite early.[34] This gesture, copied from the Bible story (Luke 18:13) was so familiar to St. Augustine's audience and so intimately connected with the acknowledgment of sin that the saint had to caution them against beating their breasts every time the word *confiteor* was called out.[35]

According to an old tradition the *Confiteor* of the priest was answered by the deacon or by one of the assistants[36] with the prayer *Misereatur* which corresponded to the final plea of the *Confiteor*.[37] The formulation of the *Misereatur* was just as multiform as that of the *Confiteor*. The ground text which by and large remained in the Mass is to be seen probably in a version which is found in various places in the ninth/tenth century: *Misereatur tui omnipotens Deus et dimittat tibi omnia peccata tua, liberet te ab omni [opere] malo, conservet te in omni [opere] bono et perducat te [per intercessionem omnium sanctorum] ad gloriam sempiternam.*[38] How-

Weisweiler, "Die Busslehre Simons von Tournai" (ZkTh, 1932), 209.

[30] Innocent III, *De s. alt. mysterio*, II, 13 (PL, CCXVII, 806); Sicard of Cremona, *Mitrale*, III, 2 (PL, CCXIII, 95 A); Durandus, IV, 7, 2.

Even John Beleth, *Explicatio*, c. 33 (PL CCII, 43) observed that here it was allowed to confess sins only *generaliter* and not *mensuram excedere*.

[31] Examples in Ferreres, 66 ff.

Ego reus et conscius multorum malorum meorum: Köck, 108; cf. 111; Beck, 263.

Ego reus et indignus: Radó, 42, 61.

Ego reus et indignus sacerdos: Radó, 76; Legg, *Tracts*, 36, 56.

[32] Cf. *supra*, note 2. The express remark is found in the *Ordo. eccl. Lateran.* (Fischer, 80, 1, 16), in the *Liber ordinarius* of Liége (Volk, 89, 1. 22).

[33] The rhymed German Mass-explanation of the 12th century says: He kneels before God's table and confesses his sins; Leitzmann (*Kleine Texte*, 54), 18, 1. 1.

The Mass-*Ordo* of Bec: Martène, 1, 4, XXXVI (I, 672): *ante altare prostratus*. Apparently also in the Styrian Missal

of Haus: Köck, 112 f.; in the Regensburg Mass-*Ordo*: Beck, 263 f.; in the Augsburg Missal of 1555: Hoeynck, 371.

In all the cases mentioned the rubric seems to be intended for a Mass without levites.

[34] Stephen of Baugé (d. 1136), *De sacr. altaris*, 1. 12 (PL, CLXXII, 1283 B); Innocent III, *De s. alt. mysterio*, II, 13 (PL, CCXVII, 806); Durandus, IV, 7, 3.

[35] Augustine, *Serm.*, 67, 1 (PL, XXXVIII, 433). Cf. Roetzer, 245-247.

[36] Cf. *supra*, p. 299. See also the example on p. 301 which imply a confession made now to one *(frater, pater)*, now to several *(fratres)*.

[37] It is worthy of note that the oldest formulas which in the first part name "all the saints," confine the petition for prayer in the second part to the brethren present *(te, vos)*. See *supra*, p. 301.

[38] Sacramentary of Reims: PL, LXXVIII, 442 A. The bracketed expressions are frequently missing in other texts.

Cf. the interpolated rule of Chrodegang: PL, LXXXIX, 1067; Ritual of Durham, ed. Lindelöf (Surtees Society, 140), 170.

ever it is only proper to record that the older Mass books mention this *Misereatur* of the assistants or of the deacon or of the Mass server as infrequently as they do the *Confiteor* that follows. The fact that these two formulas had to follow, was taken as much for granted as the fact that the texts would be almost identical with the priest's.[89] Besides it was hardly necessary to write the formulas down,[40] for not only every cleric but every properly instructed Christian had to know them by heart in some form or other, almost as he did the Lord's Prayer.[41] Still it appears that often the priest used for his *Misereatur* a much more solemn form in which a special phrase was prefixed like *Precibus et meritis sanctæ Dei Genitricis et Virginis Mariæ et omnium Sanctorum suorum*,[42] frequently adding a whole list of names, as in the *Confiteor*[43]; or a phrase like *Per gratiam Sancti Spiritus Paracliti*[44] or *Per auxilium et signum sanctæ crucis*[45] or *Per sanctam misericordiam D. N. J. C.*[46] or *Per amaram passionem D. N. J. C.*[47] or *Per sparsiones sanguinis D. N. J. C.*[48]; or he might use a phrase which changed with the Church year[49]; or several of these phrases together—an

Similar also the later Bernold, *Micrologus*, c. 23 (PL, CLI, 992), in the conclusion with variants that are otherwise quite common: *et perducat nos pariter Jesus Christus Filius Dei vivi in vitam æternam*.

[89] Yet even in the 11th century John of Avranches, *De off. eccl.* (PL, CXLVII, 32 D) says explicitly: *confessione invicem facta*, and William of Hirsau, *Const.*, I, 86 (PL, CL, 1016): *respondente sibi Converso versum Misereatur ac statim adiungente confessionem*. Cf. also *Udalrici Consuet. Clun. II*, 32 (PL, CXLIX, 725): The deacon stands opposite the priest *ut confesso confiteatur*.

The distinction customarily made today (the priest: *vobis fratres, vos fratres;* the server: *tibi pater, te pater*) is remarked in the *Liber ordinarius* of Liége (Volk, 101).

[40] Therefore in some early instances no definite wording is given even for the priest: Martène, 1, 4, IV (I, 495 A); cf. XV (I, 585 B); Köck, 106, 107.

[41] Cf. Jungmann, *Die lateinischen Bussriten*, 283.

St. Vincent Ferrer wanted the people to know the *Pater, Ave, Confiteor* and the Creed by heart; G. Schnürer, *Kirche und Kultur im Mittelalter*, (Paderborn, 1929) III, 232.

In most of the Romance countries this

would probably mean the Latin *Confiteor;* in German countries, the vernacular formula of the "Open Confession" *(culpa)* had to be substituted for the faithful.

[42] *Cod. Chigi:* Martène, 1, 4, XII (I, 569).

[43] *Ordo Rom. XIV*, n. 71 (PL, LXXVIII, 1185).

[44] Missal of St. Pol de Léon: Martène, 1, 4 XXXIV (I, 662 B); Hungarian Mass books of the 15th century: Radó, 24, 123; Jávor, 113.

[45] Missal of St. Pol de Léon: Martène, 1, 4, XXXIV (I, 662 B); *Alphabetum sacerdotum*. Legg, *Tracts*, 36.

[46] *Breviarum* of Rouen: Martène, 1, 4, XXXVII (I, 677); joined with it are several of the formulas already mentioned, including ten Saints' names. Similarly the *Alphabetum sacerdotum*, Legg, *Tracts*, 36.

A Hungarian missal of the 13th century has: *Per virtutem D. N. J. C. et;* Radó, 61.

[47] Regensburg Mass-*Ordo*: Beck, 263.

[48] Missal of Valencia (1417): Ferreres, 71; for the Mass-server a simple *Misereatur* is mentioned.

[49] *Ordinarium* of Coutances (1557): *Per sanctam Incarnationem*, etc.; Legg, *Tracts*, 56 f. Here again the server is given just a simple *Misereatur*.

opportunity for giving the celebrant's devotion ample play.[50] Even though these additions to the intercessory prayer were very meaningful and suggestive of the whole economy of salvation, they were after all—excepting the first of them—embellishments proposed by the Gothic spirit and were in consequence not accepted everywhere,[51] nor were they admitted into the Missal of Pius V. Sufficient that the prayer expressed the wish and hope that God would forgive the faults confessed.

In content the wish expressed in the *Misereatur* differs in nothing except emphasis from the wish expressed in the priest's *Indulgentiam*. The formula, which had gone through no little development long before being taken into the Mass,[52] and had even been shortened in various ways,[53] appears in the Mass in the eleventh century in this simple version: *Indulgentiam et remissionem omnium peccatorum nostrorum tribuat nobis omnipotens et misericors Dominus.*[54] It was only in a few individual instances that it received an augmentation as did its companion piece *Misereatur*.[55]

As already hinted, the *Indulgentiam* had become since the year 1000 a favorite form for absolution in the sacrament of penance—a deprecative or, more properly, optative form. In what sense was it now incorporated into the Mass, in the prayers at the foot of the altar? For the sacrament certain conditions appear to be missing. Contrition might be present, provided the *Confiteor* is said with proper intention, for if we stand before God as sinners and if we see the glance of all heaven directed towards us, we become sufficiently aware of the heinousness of sin and turn away from it. That is perhaps the motive for contrition which is closest to us and therefore also most effectual, even if it is not the highest. But the confession was not at all extensive enough since it was essentially very general. Besides the *Indulgentiam* was spoken only by the priest over the assistants, and not in reverse even when these latter were priests, a surprising thing since it was primarily the celebrant who required the purifying action

[50] Thus expressly in the *Ordinarium* of Coutances, *loc. cit.*
[51] Such additions are missing, for instance, in most of the examples cited from Styrian Mass books, Köck, 107 ff.
[52] The formula is an outgrowth of solemn absolution formulas of the 10th century, which were usually composed of three members and presented in the optative, and which comprised the previous prayers of reconciliation (which had the form of orations), so that they themselves eventually became the conveyors of the sacramental absolution. See Jungmann, *Die lateinischen Bussriten*, 212 ff., 251 ff.
[53] The earliest text within the Mass, in the *Missa Illyrica*, Martène, 1, 4, IV (I, 495), is still quite comprehensive. The text in the *Cod. Chigi:* Martène,

1, 4, XII (I, 569 D), which is a bit later, reads as follows: *Indulgentiam et absolutionem et remissionem omnium peccatorum nostrorum et spatium veræ poenitentiæ per intercessionem omnium sanctorum suorum tribuat nobis omnipotens, pius et misericors Dominus.*

In Spain the following wording often appears: *Absolutionem et remissionem omnium peccatorum nostrorum et spatium et fructus dignos poenitentiæ et emendationem vitæ et cor poenitens per gratiam Spiritus Sancti tribuat nobis omnipotens et misericors Dominus.* Ferreres, 65 ff.
[54] Bernold, *Micrologus*, c. 23 (PL, CLI, 992). Similarly a setting from Limoges: Leroquais, I, 155.
[55] St. Lambrecht Missal (1336): Köck, 107.

of the sacrament.[56] However, we must remember that the development we are considering belongs to a period which had not yet experienced the clarification of its penance theories through Scholasticism. This was the high tide of sacramental general absolutions regarding which, nevertheless, even then the fact was emphasized that the general acknowledgment which was connected with them did not suffice for grave sins.[57] But there was a constant effort to despoil the *Confiteor* formula of its general character by inserting specific references, and doubtless it was not seldom that a personal confession was—by abuse—combined with it. But if the priest does include himself *(tribuat nobis)*, he was surely aware that the formula could have, in his regard, only the value of a petition, which did not however rob it in any way of a more extensive power with regard to others.[58]

It is certain that efforts were made to emphasize the formula by means of ceremonial. According to the use of Cluny the priest at a private Mass, while answering the lay-brother with the *Misereatur*, put on the stole[59] which up to then he had carried in his hand, and then recited the *Indulgentiam*.[60] In other places a special versicle was inserted between *Misereatur* and *Indulgentiam*,[61] or the *Indulgentiam* was introduced by the word *Oremus*.[62] The sign of the Cross which accompanied the formula here as elsewhere, and which *itself* developed out of the laying on of hands by means of which penance and reconciliation were once administered, has survived until the present.

[56] For the priest, especially in monasteries, a sacramental confession before each Mass was customary in the later Middle Ages. Even in the 11th century there is mention of this at Cluny, but with the restrictive clause, *si opus habet; Udalrici Consuet. Clun II*, 12 (PL, CXLIX, 706 f.) ; similarly in a Klosterneuburg source of the 13th century: Schabes, 58; in a missal of Auxerre: Martène, 1, 4, 1 (I, 351 B). In the Dominican order this confession before each Mass was enjoined by various General Chapters down to the 16th century ; Sölch, *Hugo von St. Cher*, 52 f. The *Alphabetum sacerdotum* (after 1495) starts its references to the Mass with a *modus confitendi;* Legg, *Tracts*, 33. Cf. also the missal printed in Venice in 1493: *ibid.*, 114.

[57] Jungmann, *Die lateinischen Bussriten*, 277 ff., 285 ff.

[58] This was a use of the sacramental form outside its own proper sphere analogous to the practice much in vogue in the early Middle Ages of giving absolution to the dead, a practice from which is de-

rived the name still preserved for the corresponding rite, *absolutio ad tumbam, absolutio in exsequiis. Op cit.*, 288 f.

[59] According to the confessional guide of Arezzo of that same 11th century, the remission of sins was granted *per stolam. Op. cit.*, 193. Further passages can be found in the same work cited in the Index *sub verbo* "stola."

[60] *Bernardi Ordo Clun. I*, 72 (Herrgott, 264) ; William of Hirsau, *Const.*, I, 86 (PL, CL, 1016).

[61] But the witnesses to this practice are of a later period: Mass-*Ordo* of Regensburg (Beck, 264) : *Christe audi nos, Salvator mundi adiuva nos.*
Hungarian Mass books of the 15th century, (Jàvor, 113; Radó, 24, 123) : Ps. 120: 7.
Ordinarium of the Carthusians, c. 1500 (Legg, *Tracts*, 99) : *Adiutorium nostrum.*

[62] Styrian missals of the 14th or 15th century: Köck, 111, 112.
Klosterneuburg (15th century) : Schabes, 61.

The original conception of this absolution as a sacramental formula will serve to explain the fact that a penance was not infrequently imposed just as we will find was done at the "Open Confession" which took place after the sermon.[63] The faithful, too, were sometimes drawn into this penitential act. In many churches of Normandy the priest turned towards the people while he spoke the *Indulgentiam*.[64] The nuns at Fontevrauld used to say a *Confiteor* of their own after the priest said his; the introit was not started until after the *Indulgentiam*.[65] According to South-German Mass books of the late Middle Ages, the priest kissed the altar and then turned to the people and pronounced an absolution, using a second formula[66] of the type which was then otherwise employed when administering sacramental forgiveness.[67]

Of these various formations which are in essence—if not in actual time —pre-Scholastic, only the absolution formula *Indulgentiam* has survived. The Church's penitential practice had followed the lead of Scholastic the-

[63] Thus the Pontifical of Durandus in regulating the case when a bishop attends the Mass of a priest: At the prayers at the foot of the altar the bishop stands next to the priest. After the confession of sins and the *absolutio*, the priest recites a few intermediate verses and then says, *Iudicium pro peccatis meis*. Then the rubric continues: *Et pontifex iniungit illi Pater noster vel Ave Maria vel aliud, et sacerdos idipsum vel aliud pontifici.* Andrieu, III, 643.

Quite similar is the arrangement in the monastic Missal of Lyons printed in 1531; here in the same spot the celebrant begins the following dialogue: *Poenitentiam pro peccatis meis. Pater noster. Deo gratias. Et vobis: Ave Maria. R.: Deo gratias.* Only after this penance has been said does the priest kiss the altar. Martène, 1, 4, XXXIII (I, 658 D). The same dialogue, with unessential variations, in the Missal of Vich (1496): Ferreres, 67, and in the later rite of Lyons: Bona, II, 2, 6 (570). Similarly three missals of the 14th century from Gerona, but here the imposition of the penance is provided only for the celebrant: Ferreres, p. XXXII, XXXV, 68.

No doubt the same meaning must be attached to the rubrics of the Carthusian *Ordinarium* of *circa* 1500, according to which the *Confiteor* and *Misereatur* are followed by a *Pater* and *Ave*, to be said bowed, and then there follows the absolution formula (marked with the heading:

absolutio post confessionem privatam). Legg, *Tracts*, 99 f.; cf. *Statuta antiqua*, I, 43: Martène, 1, 4, XXV (I, 631 D). Later on the sacramental confession was anticipated before Mass. The present-day *Ordinarium Cartusiense* (1932), c. 25, 12, still mentions a *signum pro confessionibus* before the procession to the altar. But it also retains the *Pater* and *Ave* referred to above (c. 25, 14).

The same *Pater* and *Ave* are found in the old Cistercian rite, but here only after the *Indulgentiam* and the versicle *Adiutorium nostrum* which is combined with it; Schneider (*Cist.-Chr.*, 1926), 254 (and see the rubric, *ibid.*, 255, according to which the *"confessio"* can be completed later, during the *Gloria*). Cf. Franz, 587; de Corswarem, 111.

[64] Thus in Bayeux: Martène, 1, 4, 2, 5 (I, 363 B). *Ordinarium* of Coutances: Legg, *Tracts*, 57.

Similarly the Bishop of Le Mans as late as 1700: de Moléon, 221.

Cf. the custom of Bec: Martène, 1, 4, XXXVI (I, 672 E).

[65] According to the *Ordinarium* of 1115: de Moléon, 109 f.

[66] Mass-*Ordo* of Gregorienmünster (14th or 15th century): Martène, 1, 4, XXXII (I, 655 B). Augsburg Ritus of the 15th century: Franz, 752. Missal of Chur of 1589: Gerbert, *Vetus liturgia Alemannica*, I, 295.

[67] Cf. Jungmann, *Die lateinischen Bussriten*, 231 ff.

ory and had begun to limit the use of sacramental powers to very definite conditions.[68] As a result, sacramental absolution was neither considered here nor given, and so the pentitential act which began with the *Confiteor*, even in spite of the formula mentioned, continued to have only that meaning which the confession of faults had in the period of monastic lay confession when this formula was not in use. Of course even the confession of faults had long ago assumed a merely formal character; nevertheless it remains an humble acknowledgment of our sinfulness and a worthy expression of our contriteness, and with these the intercession of the Church will continue to be connected as it has been since the beginning.[69]

Besides what we have already described, and even aside from the oration *Aufer a nobis* which from the start had formed the conclusion and before which the *Confiteor*-rite was consciously inserted—besides this, I say, the liturgical mind of the Middle Ages had added a further framework. A versicle or two was introduced before the *Confiteor*, and it made no difference whether the psalm *Iudica* preceded or not. From a time, perhaps, when it was still customary to make a concrete confession of faults, comes the use of the verse (Psalm 140:3); *Pone, Domine, custodiam ori meo . . .*[70] Since the thirteenth century there was an almost general use, chiefly outside Italy, of the verse *Confitemini Domino quoniam bonus* (Ps. 117:1), the original meaning (an invitation to praise God) being twisted into a summons to make a confession of faults to God because He is merciful.[71] In Italy the verse (Ps. 123:8), *Adiutorium nostrum in nomine Domini* had already been used in this same spot in the eleventh century.[72] In the Roman liturgy this last verse was used to introduce not only all blessings[73] but also other liturgical acts, particularly also the *Confiteor* in the Office. The admission which it implies, that in matters of salvation we are helpless without that help from above which—as the accompanying

---

[68] *Ibid.*, 287 ff. Conclusive was the judgment of St. Thomas Aquinas, *De forma absolutionis*, c. 2: *Huiusmodi absolutiones* [at Prime, compline and holy Mass] *non sunt sacramentales, sed sunt quædam orationes quibus dicuntur venialia peccata dimitti.* There is possibly a connection between this decision of St. Thomas and the regulation in the Dominican rite which directs the priest reciting the formula, *Absolutionem et remissionem,* not to make the sign of the Cross: *Signum crucis ne faciat; Missale iuxta ritum O.P.* (1889), 17.

[69] C. Callewaert, *Sacris erudiri,* 191 f., speaks in a similar sense of a sacramental that works *ex opere operantis Ecclesiæ.*

[70] Sacramentary of Modena (before 1174): Muratori, I, 88; Rite of Lyons: Bona,

II, 2, 6 (569); Buenner, 223, note 1. Besides these it appears only in the Mass-Ordo of the Carthusians, which is dependent on Lyons, and there it appears even today.

[71] *Ordinarium O.P.* of 1256 (Guerrini, 235.

Mass-*Ordo* of the papal chapel (*circa* 1290), ed. Brinktrine (*Eph. liturg.,* 1937), 200.

[72] A monastic sacramentary of the outgoing 11th century: Ebner, 297; cf. *ibid.,* 327, 332; Fiala, 198.

Otherwise it is not frequent at this spot. Later in the *Ordo Rom. XIV*, n. 60 (PL, LXXVIII, 1173 C). Outside Italy apparently only since the 15th century; e.g., in Augsburg: Franz, 751.

[73] *Rituale Rom.,* VIII, 1, 7.

sign of the Cross indicates—is disclosed in the Cross of Christ, here fulfills the function of an epiklesis to introduce the act of penance.[74] It is therefore very understandable that in several localities it became customary—and still is today—to pronounce the same little phrase when leaving the sacristy.[75]

A number of versicles was also inserted after the act of penance as a sort of transition to the old oration *Aufer a nobis*. These versicles, which appear quite early, serve a purpose similar to the *preces* before the oration in the Office; the similarity is emphasized by the bowed position the priest assumes while saying them. Even though these are prayers of a semi-private nature, alternate prayer between priest and deacon (or at most the closer assistants)—for the brethren in the choir are busy with singing the introit and the *Kyrie*—still the structural rules for liturgical prayer are carefully observed. The versicles that appear here are seldom newly composed from Holy Writ.[76] Generally they are taken from the verses used

[74] Cf. Callewaert, *Sacris erudiri*, 38 f.

Elsewhere this verse had been put to a different use, at first sight rather surprising, in connection with this same penitential act of the Mass. According to William of Hirsau, *Const.*, I, 86 (PL, CL, 1016) the priest should put on the stole, *"indulgentiam" cum illo versu "adiutorium nostrum, etc."* *adiungens*. As a matter of fact, monastic ordinaries of the years immediately following do actually display this single versicle before the oration *Aufer a nobis*: Seckau Missal of 1170 (Köck, 106); *Ordinarium O.P.* of 1256 (Guerrini, 235); cf. Liége *Liber ordinarius* (Volk, 89).

The verse is here probably a reflex of the absolution, an acknowledgment of the newly-established and confirmed covenant with God, with whose help the work can be begun and the Holy of Holies entered.

Beginning with the 13th century the *Adiutorium nostrum* in this place is usually combined with *Sit nomen Domini benedictum;* thus in the Westminster Missal written between 1362 and 1386, ed. Legg (HBS, V), 490, and in the English and Norman Mass-ordinaries of the following years; it is from this area that the practice must have developed: Maskell, 20; Martène, 1, 4, XXXV ff. (I, 664, 672 E, 677 C). Since the turn of the Middle Ages also outside the area named: *ibid.*, XXXIII (I, 658 D); 1, 4, 2, 4

(I, 360 f.); Legg, *Tracts*, 36 f.; Ferreres, p. XXXII, LXXIX. Also in the Spanish Cistercian Missal of 1762: Schneider (*Cist.-Chr.*, 1926), 254, and in the present-day *Missale Ambrosianum* (1902), 165 f.

In the monastery of Bec: Martène, 1, 4, XXXVI (I, 672 E), the priest would stand turned to the people and add to all this: *In nomine Patris . . .;* it had thus grown into a blessing. Similarly the monastic Mass-*Ordo* of Rouen: *ibid.*, XXXVII (I, 677 CD).

In several late and post-medieval Mass books this set of versicles is placed just before the Introit, again therefore with epicletic meaning: Legg, *Tracts*, 37, 58; Maskell, 27; Martène, 1, 4, XXVII f., XXXIII f. (I, 640 B, 643 E, 658 E, 662 D); also 1, 4, 3 (I, 364 A).

[75] Thus already in the 15th century in the pontifical rite of Trier and of Strassburg; Leroquais, *Les pontificaux manuscrits*, I, 103; II, 165.

In some churches the servers offer the priest the holy water for a blessing as he pronounces these words.

In some places (e.g. in Tyrol) the servers use the formula for asking a blessing: *Benedicite!* and receive the answer: *Deus* [sc. *benedicat*].

[76] As was the case in the Sacramentary of Modena (Muratori, I, 88) where

earlier at the close of the accession prayers. Thus we find here in Italian Mass books of the end of the twelfth century a portion of the versicle which two centuries before had belonged to the oldest accession arrangements and had then disappeared.[77] Amongst these are also the versicles we still use: *Deus tu conversus* and *Ostende*, with which the basic theme of Psalm 84, and therefore of the accession prayers *in toto*, is reviewed in a brief but striking way. It is the same theme which is sounded in Psalm 42: We can gain joy and new life from the well-springs of God; He wants to manifest to us His protection and His saving power. The series of verses in the missal used in the papal chapels about 1290 is confined exclusively to the verses mentioned.[78] But in other places this same group is merely the foundation to which other verses are added.[79] Then after the general petition *Domine exaudi*, which otherwise almost always and even in an earlier period follows the series of versicles,[80] and after the greeting *Dominus vobiscum*, which is not omitted even for this small group of people, the oration *Aufer a nobis* is said. This is the oldest element in the prayers at the foot of the altar, and even after these prayers had been more fully developed, continued to serve as the closing oration.[81] Its glance is turned

verses were chosen all directed towards penance: Ps. 55: 9 (*Deus vitam meam*) and Ps. 31: 5 f. (*Delictum meum*, etc.)

[77] *Supra*, p. 272 f.

In the purest state in *Cod. S.* 1, 19 of the Biblioteca Angelica (Ebner, 322), with Ps. 84: 7, 8 (*Deus tu conversus, Ostende*), Ps. 142: 2 (*Ne intres*), Ps. 78: 9 b (*Propitius*). Cf. Ebner, 354.

In Italian Mass books the versicles appear which today follow the *Confiteor* at Prime and Compline: *Converte nos, Dignare Domine, Miserere nostri, Fiat misericordia.* Ebner, 327, 332, 345.

[78] Brinktrine (*Eph. liturg.*, 1937), 200.

Likewise Ebner, 313.

[79] Thus in the Sarum Ordinary of the 13th century (Legg, *Tracts*, 219; cf. *ibid.*, 3 f.; Legg, *The Sarum Missal*, 217); here Ps. 84: 7 f. is followed by Ps. 131: 9 (*Sacerdotes*); 18: 13 f. (*Ab occultis*); 113 b: 1 (*Non nobis*), the invocation *Sancta Dei Genitrix*, and finally Ps. 79: 20 (*Domine Deus virtutum*). Similarly most of the later English Mass books. The versicles *Ab occultis* and *Sacerdotes* are also frequent elsewhere.

[80] Thus already in the *Ordo Rom. antiquus* (circa 950): Hittorp, 28, 53.

[81] The stamp of conclusiveness is brought out especially in the Mass-*Ordo* of the papal chapel, ed. Brinktrine, 200, where

are added *Dominus vobiscum* and *Exaudiat nos omnipotens et misericors Dominus* just as at the end of the Litany of All Saints.

Just as in the 11th century the Pontifical of Halinardus and other Mass-*Ordines* of the Séez group (*supra*, p. 291 f.) had added to the *Aufer a nobis* a second oration which later disappeared, so also many later Mass books supplemented the *Aufer* with one or more orations. Often these were taken from the accession prayers (*Conscientiæ, Adsit;* both orations, e.g., in Ebner, 341; cf. *supra*, p. 275). Norman books of the late Middle Ages borrowed from the recession prayers (*Ure igne, Actiones;* see Martène, 1, 4, XXVII f.; cf. XXXVII [I, 639 E, 643 D, 676 C]).

But most frequently the penitential oration *Exaudi Domine supplicum preces* (from the *Gregorianum*: Lietzmann, n. 201, 3) was thus used. It is found in the Missal of St. Vincent, added to *Aufer*: Fiala, 198; cf. *Cod. Chigi*: Martène, 1, 4, XII (I, 570 A). But it is especially constant in the German area (e.g. Köck, 108, 109, 110, 113; Hoeynck, 371); also in Hungary: Radó, 42, where later a third oration, *Præsta* is added (this same oration, *Præsta*, also in Tongern; de Corswarem, 111); Radó, 96, 123; Jávor,

backward, back toward the sins we must leave behind, and also forward, toward the sanctuary, the holy of holies[82] that we must enter. The oration derives from ancient Roman tradition. It was used at the beginning of the Easter celebration[83] and later was also said when entering a shrine from which the relics were taken for the consecration of a Church.[84] Now it is used while mounting the steps to the altar, and since the later Middle Ages it is said in a low tone, a practice which spread from England[85] and which seems apparently to have been stimulated by the silence of the canon and the reasons which suggested the latter.[86]

6. Greetings. Kissing the Altar

In the solemn functions of the seventh century, the first thing that occurred when the pope reached the altar was a series of greetings—kisses, according to ancient custom. There was a greeting for the co-liturgists and also for the two objects most intimately connected with the liturgy, objects which represented Christ, the Gospel book and the altar.[1] Of these only the kissing of the altar has been retained in the universal Mass rite. The greeting of the co-liturgists is also to be found at present in solemn papal Masses; three cardinal priests greet the pope with the kiss of peace when he comes to the altar.[2] In France a similar practice is to be noted in many

113; Sawicki, 147; cf. Radó 24. In Augsburg it once even took the place of *Aufer*: Bona, II, 2, 6 (569); likewise in Klosterneuburg: Schabes, 61. In Gregorienmünster the abbot said it kneeling (14-15th century): Martène, 1, 4, XXXII (I, 655 A).

This formula is obviously meant when Henry of Hesse (d. 1397), in his *Secreta sacerdotum* mentions with disapproval the saying of the collect *pro peccatis* after the *Confiteor*: Franz, 521.

[82] The biblical term *sancta sanctorum* was already employed by Jerome, *In Ezech.*, c. 44 (PL XXV, 436 D) for Christian service.

[83] In the *Leonianum* (Muratori, I, 430) on Maundy Thursday; cf. the formulæ that precede and follow. In the older Gelasianum I, 17 (Wilson, 15) at the beginning of Lent. In the *Gregorianum* of Padua (Mohlberg-Baumstark, n. 155) on the Thursday of the first week of Lent.

[84] *Gregorianum* (Lietzmann, n. 194): *oratio quando levantur reliquiæ*. It was used in a like function in the Pontifical of

Donaueschtng: Metzger, n. 101; and in the Sacramentary of Drogo, Bishop of Metz: Duchesne, *Christian Worship*, 487.

[85] Sarum Ordinary (13th and 14th centuries): Legg, *Tracts*, 4, 220; likewise in later Sarum texts. On the continent it was not customary till much later; the custom was probably carried to Rome by Burchard of Strassburg; see *ibid.*, 137; cf. 37, 181.

[86] How far the parallel went can be gauged from a custom found in many French churches and in vogue at Rouen even in the 18th century; here the priest turned to his assistants and said *Orate pro me, fratres* before he ascended to the altar saying *Aufer a nobis*. Lebrun, I, 123; de Moléon, 427.

[1] *Supra*, p. 70.

[2] Brinktrine, *Die feierliche Papstmesse*, 7; 11. For the late Middle Ages cf. *Ordo Rom. XIV*, n. 71 (PL, LXXVIII, 1185 D). Not restricted to the papal Mass in the Mass-*Ordo* of the papal chapel, ed. Brinktrine (*Eph. liturg.*, 1937), 201: *dat pacem diacono*. Cf. Ebner, 313.

churches all through the Middle Ages.[3] Here it was done later on—very significantly—right after the *Confiteor*.[4] In the English use of Sarum this was the spot selected for the kiss of greeting for deacon and subdeacon at every high Mass, even at the Mass of a priest.[5] The priest pronounced the phrase which we will meet again elsewhere at the kiss of peace before Communion: *Habete osculum pacis* . . .

The kissing of the Gospel book was kept in general practice a longer time, and it still takes place in a pontifical service; when the bishop reaches the altar, he kisses the book which the subdeacon presents to him, opened at the beginning of the day's Gospel.[6] Usually the Gospel book was on the altar; so the kissing of the altar followed that of the book, seldom the other way round.[7] Sometimes, in fact, the kissing of the book counted for both.[8] Since the tenth century a more or less regular accompanying prayer was: *Pax Christi quam nobis per evangelium suum tradidit, confirmet et conservet corda nostra et corpora in vitam æternam.*[9]

Since the twelfth century a new object of these greetings was added, the crucifix, now generally standing on the altar.[10] It too is given a reverential kiss.[11] But towards the end of the Middle Ages the kiss is gradually trans-

---

[3] Sacramentary of Ratoldus (10th century) : PL LXXVIII, 242 A; Mass-*Ordo* of the Séez group: *supra*, p. 92 f.

[4] John of Avranches, *De off. eccl.* (PL, CXLVII, 32 D) : the priest salutes deacon and subdeacon.

Similarly the *Ordinarium* of Bayeux: Martène, 1, 4, XXIV (I, 626 D) ; cf. XXI (I, 609 D).

Durandus, IV, 9, 3 f.

[5] All the witnesses of the Sarum rite, e.g., Legg, *Tracts*, 4, 219 f. Normandy is obviously the place of provenience.

[6] *Cæremoniale episc.*, II, 8, 33; I, 10, 2.

Also in *Cod. Chigi* (11th century) : Martène, 1, 4, XII (I, 570 A) : the subdeacon in the same way hands the bishop the book, after having held it towards him all during the *Confiteor*. Cf. Ebner, 311.

[7] Both forms of the practice are witnessed to chiefly in the 11th and 12th centuries: *Udalrici Consuet. Clun. II*, 30 (PL, CXLIX, 716 A) ; Ebner, 328, 345 (cf. also 322) ; Martène, 1, 4, IV f. (I, 496, 520, 530) ; Köck, 110 f.

From a later period there are: *Ordo Rom XIV*, n. 71 (PL LXXVIII, 1185 D) ; Missal of St. Lambrecht (1336) : Köck, 107 (n. 395).

[8] Sacramentary of Ratoldus (10th century) : PL, LXXVIII, 242 C; here the book lies open on the altar, yet a kiss

of the book precedes (241 D).

Missal of Liége: Martène, 1, 4, XV (I, 586 A) : *Deinde osculans evangelium super altare dicat*. The same amalgamation is probably to be supposed in the rest of the books representing the Séez group in which no mention is made of the altar; see *supra*, p. 291. Cf. also Ebner, 332.

[9] Other formulas appear only by way of exception; e.g., *Ave sanctum Evangelium*, *salus et reparatio animarum nostrarum*: Missal of Troyes (15th century) : Leroquais, III, 46. Cf. Sacramentary of St. Denis (11th century) : Martène, 1, 4, V (I, 523 B).

[10] Cf. *supra*, p. 258. Till far into the 16th century the crucifix was but loosely connected with its stand, so that it could be easily lifted out. Thus, by placing it on a proper shaft, it was also used as a processional cross. Braun, *Das christliche Altargerät*, 478-483.

[11] Among the earliest examples we have the Seckau Missal (c. 1170): Köck, 107 (n. 479) and a Sacramentary of the 12th century from Verona (kiss of the Gospel not mentioned) : Ebner, 306.

Along with the kiss of the altar and of the Gospel, also Köck, 109, 109 f; cf. 111 f., 113; Martène, 1, 4, XXXII (I, 655).

ferred from the sculptured crucifix on the altar to the miniature image found in the Missal at the beginning of the canon or elsewhere,[12] so that sometimes the veneration of this image counts also for the veneration of the Gospel book[13] or even of the altar.[14] A typical sample of the Gothic mind is displayed in two fourteenth- and fifteenth-century Mass books of Seckau which stipulate that the same honor (with words of the accompanying prayer) be shown to the images of Mary and John that are connected with the figure of the Cross.[15]

The prayer text selected to accompany the veneration of the Cross evolved many rich forms. Mostly it is derived from the existing treasure of prayers used in the veneration of the Cross,[16] like the text from the Good Friday liturgy, *Tuam crucem adoramus, Domine*[17] or the verse *Adoramus te, Christe.*[18] With this a versicle is usually connected *(Per signum crucis;*

---

[12] Augsburg Mass-*Ordo* in the 15th-16th century: With the words *Pax Christi* the priest first kisses the Gospel of the day, at his left, then, with *Tuam crucem*, the picture of the Crucified in the Mass book. Hoeynck, 372; cf. Franz, 752.

Cf. the Regensburg Mass-*Ordo*: Beck, 264 f.; Missal of Chur (1589): Gerbert, *Vetus liturgia Alemannica*, 296.

[13] Martène, 1, 4, XXVI, XXXIII f. (I, 637 A, 658 E, 662 D).

[14] Missal of Toul (14th or 15th c.): Martène, 1, 4, XXXI (I, 650), where the only rubric pertaining to this matter reads: *Postea osculatur pedes imagini Crucifixi in canone.* Cf. *ibid.*, XXVIII, XXXVI (I, 643 E, 673 A); Legg, *Tracts*, 58.

Sometimes, too, a kiss of the paten (with a cross on it) substitutes in like fashion for all the other reverences; *Alphabetum sacerdotum*: Legg, *Tracts*, 37; Missal of Tours: Martène, 1, 4, 2, 5 (I, 374 A).

Elsewhere, the rite was again split in two, a kiss being appointed both for the *Crucifixus* (the illustration of the Crucified at the start of the Canon—an elaboration of the T of *Te igitur*) and for the *Maiestas Domini* (an illustration of Christ in glory, found at the start of the Preface—an elaboration of the initial letters of *Vere Dignum,* hence usually marked by the sign *VD*). So the Missal of Vich (1547; here along with a kiss of the altar): Ferreres, 66, with a doubled accompanying phrase: *Adoramus te* and

De sede maiestatis benedicat nos dextera Dei Patris. Cf. Mass-*Ordo* of Rouen: Martène, 1, 4, XXXVII (I, 677 C).

Regarding the pertinent representations in the medieval Mass books, see Ebner, 438-441; 444-446 and in the index, "Kreuzigung", "Maiestas." Not seldom are there traces still to be seen of the celebrant's kisses; see Ebner, 166, 449.

[15] Köck, 109, 110, with the acompanying phrases *Ave Maria* and *Sancte Johannes optime, absolve.* . . . The reference is probably to sculptural images of Mary and John which were often since the 13th century associated with the altar cross; Braun, *Das christliche Altargerät*, 485 f.

The development moves a step further in the Missal of Haus (15th century) where the kiss of the crucifix is followed by *Salve Regina*, versicle and oration; Köck, 113.

[16] Newly-composed prayers are but seldom employed; thus one distich (Ebner, 306) begins: *O crux mihi certa salus.*

[17] Köck, 110, 112. Further see note 12 above.

For honoring the *Maiestas Domini* (see note 14 above) the wording is sometimes altered: *Maiestatem tuam adoramus: Breviarium* of Rouen: Martène, 1, 4 XXXCII (I, 677 C).

[18] Very frequent; e.g. Köck, 109, 113; Martène, 1, 4, XXVI, XXVIII, XXXIII f., XXXVI (I 637 A, 643 D, 658 E, 662 D, 673 A).

At Vienne the *Adoramus te* was sung at a high Mass: *ibid.*, XXX (I, 648 C).

Qui passus es; Omnis terra), and an oration, e.g., *Respice quæsumus.* However, these ceremonies of greeting were quite secondary and entailed the danger of disturbing the principal lines of the liturgy and so they disappeared from many of the late medieval Mass arrangements for ordinary Masses[19] and finally vanished altogether from the Missal of Pius V. The only thing remaining is the kissing of the altar, the only thing that was there from the start—a fine example of a return to original forms.

In the first Roman *Ordo* the reverential kiss of the altar on arrival at the beginning of Mass is the only such kiss of the altar during the Mass mentioned expressly.[20] The priest today, after mounting the steps, kisses the altar, just as he does often during the course of the Mass, in accordance with present-day practice; but this first kiss has a very special meaning. It is, as we have already indicated, the salutation of the place where the holy mystery will be consummated.

This ceremony is borrowed from ancient culture.[21] In antiquity it was a natural practice to honor the temple by kissing the threshold. But it was also customary to greet the images of the gods by means of a kiss or to throw them a kiss from a distance, as the pagan Cæcilius, mentioned by Minucius Felix, did when he noticed the statue of Serapis while passing by.[22] In like manner, the ancient altar was greeted with a kiss. And it seems that the family table, as a place enshrined by a religious dedication, was often similarly honored at the start of the meal.[23] It was therefore to be expected that the custom of greeting holy places with a kiss should be continued in Christendom, with only a change of object. And since the practice taken over into Christianity was at bottom a civic custom, though indeed a civic custom in a religious milieu, there was no conflict with the attitude then prevailing against admitting religious practices derived from heathen worship. As early as the end of the fourth century the saluting of the altar with a kiss makes its appearance as a popular practice.[24] The salutation

---

[19] The *Liber ordinarius* of Liége (c. 1285) mentions for high Mass only the "kiss of the text" (Volk, 89, 1. 25), for private Mass only the kiss of the altar (101, 1. 17), and both times without an indication of an accompanying phrase.

[20] However, another kiss is certainly meant when, after collecting the gift-offerings, the pontiff finally approaches the altar and, as the rubric puts it, *salutat altare* (n. 15). This second kiss of the altar is expressly noticed, e.g. in the Pontifical of Laon (13th c.): Leroquais, *Les Pontificaux*, I, 167.

[21] See the study "Der Altarkuss" in F. J. Dölger, *Antike u. Christentum*, 2 (1930), 190-221.

[22] Minucius Felix, *Octavius*, 2, 4 (CSEL, II, 4, 1. 22).

[23] Dölger, 215 f., 217 ff. Cf. *idem., Antike u. Christentum*, 6 (1940), 160.

Kissing the table at the start and finish of a meal is still a practice in the Capuchin order. In Lithuania the bride kisses the table (and the bread and the crucifix) when departing from her parental home (Kl. Razminas, 1948).

[24] Dölger, 201 ff. Medieval witnesses to the same use in L. Gougaud, *Dévotions et pratiques ascétiques du moyen âge* (Paris, 1925), 56 f.

Traces of a corresponding popular custom can be found even at a later time. In Brittany, for instance, the newly-baptized infant was made to touch the

must have been in use in the ecclesiastical liturgy at about the same time. A confirmation of this inference is to be found in the fact that the salutation of the altar at the start of Mass is a custom also in the West Syrian,[25] the Armenian[26] and the Byzantine liturgies.[27]

The kiss is intended first of all simply for the altar, the *mensa Domini.* But subsequently the meaning of the kiss was enlarged by the idea that the altar built of stone represented Christ Himself, the cornerstone, the spiritual rock. Thus the kiss could include Him, too. With the growth of the cult of martyrs, it gradually became a rule from the beginning of the Middle Ages on, that even public churches serving for the assembly of the faithful should have their martyr's grave, and finally that every altar must enclose a "sepulcher" or little reliquary.[28] Thus the kissing of the altar is transformed into the kissing of the martyr and, through him, of the whole Church triumphant. Innocent III therefore explains the bishop's kissing of the altar as representing Christ saluting his spouse.[29]

In the prayer said nowadays while kissing the altar, the memory of the martyrs is combined with a longing for purification from sin reminiscent of the prayers at the foot of the altar: *Oramus te, Domine.* This formula appears for the first time in the eleventh century, and with the rubric, *dum osculatur altare.*[30] The formula is a private and personal prayer of the priest *(peccata mea)* to accompany the kiss; for that reason it is without the conclusion *Per Christum D. N.,* with which the *Aufer a nobis* ends. Other texts also occur, touching on the forgiveness of sin,[31] and in some particular instances a formal oration is found[32] or an apology is connected

altar; something similar was done with the coffin before burial. P. Doncœur, *Retours en chrétienté* (Paris, 1933), 43, 179.

From the region of Strem in the Burgenland (Hungary) comes the following account of a kindred custom: After confession the penitent prays his penance at the altar steps; having finished he mounts to the altar and kisses the center altar card in three places (J. Göndöcz, 1934).

[25] Brightman, 69, 1. 19.
[26] *Ibid.,* 423, 1. 21.
[27] *Ibid.,* 354, 1. 38.
[28] Cf. *supra,* p. 257 f.
The kissing of the grave which was customary in very ancient times (Dölger, 209 ff.) can no longer have had any influence here, because the span of time since the altar was regularly associated with a martyr's tomb was much too long.
[29] Innocent III, *De s. alt. mysterio,* II, 15 (PL, CCXVII, 807).

[30] Ebner, 297. Similarly Martène, 1, 4, V (I, 520 B).
In the *Missa Illyrica* (c. 1030): *ibid.,* IV (I, 508 B), at the kissing of the altar before the Offertory (see note 20 above), still in the singular: *Oro te, Domine.*
A. Reiffenstuel, *Jus canonicum,* III, 40, n. 40 (Venice, 1717; III, 589), mentions some older missals according to which the prayer was omitted when the altar contained no relics.
[31] The formula *Precibus et meritis:* Köck, 107, 113, just as, in older witnesses, at the kissing of the altar at the end of Mass.
The benediction *A vinculis peccatorum* (beside *Oramus*) in the Mass-*Ordo* of the papal chapel, circa 1290, ed. Brinktrine (*Eph. liturg.,* 1937), 201.
[32] Thus in Regensburg: *Descendat, q. D. Spiritus;* Beck, 264; also in the Sacramentary of Boldau (c. 1195): Radó, 42.
A formula much like an oration also at Augsburg: Hoeynck, 372.

with the kiss.[83] The kiss of salutation also survives at the beginning of other functions but without any accompanying text and, in consequence, its original significance is more easily recognizable; thus it is found before the blessing of candles on Candlemas day, before the blessing of palms on Palm Sunday, and before service on Good Friday. Even at the beginning of Mass it is found without any accompanying words in some sources of the declining Middle Ages.[84]

As late as 1240 the altar kiss in the Mass was customary at Rome only on coming in for Mass and on departing, and at one place—not specified —in the canon.[85] A century later, and it had become the prevailing practice to kiss the altar in every instance mentioned in the present-day missal[86]; it was done every time the priest turned around at the altar in salutation, and at the beginning of the canon and at the *Supplices*.[87]

It is not surprising that modern interpreters of the Mass who went into the matter of the kissing of the altar at so many different parts of the Mass were rather uncertain how to explain it, and even found the constant repetition somewhat ample, perhaps excessive.[88] According to one interpretation, the kiss is referred above all to the saints, with whom the priest

---

[83] Ebner, 345. *Ibid.,* 339 the same formula, *Omnipotens s. Deus qui me peccatorem* (see p. 291 above) is used which accompanied the first kissing of the altar in the *Missa Illyrica:* Martène, 1, 4, IV (I, 469 B), in the *Cod. Chigi: ibid.,* XII (I, 570 C) and in the Sacramentary of Boldau (Radó, 42), where a whole collection of relevant accompanying formulas are found (n. 14-19; 22).

[84] So in England: among others Maskell, 22 f.; in Sweden: Yelverton, 12; the Missal of Vich (1547) : Ferreres, 66. Cf. in Italy: Ebner, 328.

The ancient Cistercian rite had the kissing of the altar, without any accompanying phrase, even before the prayers at the foot of the altar, as soon as the altar was reached: Schneider (*Cist. Chr.,* 1926), 253. Similarly also in the Missal of Troyes: Martène, 1, 4, VI (I, 530 D). Cf. *ibid.,* XXVII (I, 640 A).

[85] Innocent III, *De s. alt. mysterio,* III, 11 (PL, CCXVII, 850 C).

The *Liber usuum O. Cist.,* c. 59 (PL, CLXVI, 1434 D) also makes express mention of only three occasions for kissing the altar.

[86] Durandus, IV, 39, 5 f. Pretty much the same in a Minorite missal of the 13th century, where the kissing of the altar each time is so emphasized that it

must have been something very novel; Ebner, 313 ff.

It is at first only the kissing of the altar before the *Orate fratres* and before the kiss of peace that is added in the Missal of St. Vincent (c. 1100) : Fiala, 206, 213; and in the Sacramentary of Modena (*ante* 1174) : Muratori, I, 92 f.; likewise in a sacramentary of the 12th century from Camaldoli: Ebner, 296 f. On the contrary the *Ordo Cluniacensis* of the monk Bernhard (c. 1068) mentions the kissing of the altar before the *Orate fratres,* at the start of the Canon and at the *Supplices te rogamus* (I, 72; Herrgott, 264 f.).

[87] Durandus, IV, 39, 7 mentions also the custom observed by many of tracing a cross on the altar with three fingers, hallowing it through cross and Trinity before kissing it. This complication of the rite was also set aside in the Missal of Pius V, in fact distinctly outlawed by an injunction that is still found in the rubrics (*Ritus serv.,* IV, 1) : *non producitur signum crucis . . . super id quod osculandum est.*

[88] Thus by J. B. Lüft, *Liturgik* (Mainz, 1847), II, 542. Opposed is Gihr, 410, note 1.

In the Dominican rite even today there are only two occasions when the altar is

confirms his communion before he begins the sacrifice and also whenever he salutes the Church on earth.[89] According to another, the priest first receives the kiss of peace from the altar and from Christ in order to pass it on to the rest.[40] Still another interpretation envisions the kiss simply as a symbolic renewal of the bond and union with Christ.[41] All these things may be true as an extension of the meaning. But primarily the kiss, especially at the beginning and the end of Mass, is a proper reverence and honor to the sacredness of the altar, and the same may be said even about the kiss that precedes the greeting of the people.

7. The Incensing of the Altar

At a solemn service the kissing of the altar is followed by the incensing. From the fact that in our present-day rite this action is restricted to the festive form of the Mass,[1] it is plain that incensation is above all a means of heightening the solemnity. Like the flowers and candles, like the beauty of the vestments and the sound of the organ, the clouds of incense rising to the ceiling and filling the whole church with their sweet smell are intended to aid the senses in grasping the greatness of the feast. In ancient times frankincense in its many forms, as the East supplies them, was highly esteemed. In civil life, in better homes, its perfume was in demand. It was used profusely at burials. But above all it played a large part in heathen cult. For Christians, this last circumstance—added to the general objection to any and every materialization of divine service—served rather to exclude incensation from divine worship.[2]

But after the disappearance of paganism it did find its way from profane use into the Christian liturgy. About the year 390 incense was carried

kissed, at the beginning and at the end of Mass: *Missale iuxta ritum O.P.* (1889), 17; 22.
[89] Thus Kössing, *Liturgische Vorlesungen*, 239 ff., 272. Similarly Gihr, 370, 410.
[40] Lebrun, *Explication*, I, 167.
[41] Eisenhofer, I, 260, 262; II, 96. Cf. Parsch, *The Liturgy of the Mass* (trans. Eckhoff; St. Louis, 1936), 74-76.
[1] The restriction just to the *missa sollemnis* was not an absolute rule even in post-medieval times, as is shown by many decrees of the Sacred Congregation of Rites issued even in the 18th century, wherein this restriction is first established; see the compilation of P. Martinucci, *Manuale decretorum SRC*, p. 130 (n. 633-637). From an earlier period see,

e.g., *Ordo Rom. XIV*, n. 61 (PL, XXVIII, 1174 f.).
Even today there is still some leeway, since most dioceses have indults from the Holy See permitting the use of incense on greater feasts even at a simple sung Mass; see Ph. Hartmann-J. Kley, *Repertorium Rituum* (14th ed.; Paderborn, 1940), 459.
Amongst the Capuchins the use of incense at their conventual Mass, which is a low Mass, is an old tradition which the Sacred Congregation of Rites, on Dec. 7, 1888, confirmed for solemn occasions; *Decreta auth. SRC*, n. 3697, 2.
[2] E. G. Atchley, *A History of the use of Incense* (Alcuin Club Collections, 13; London, 1909), 1-96.

in at the Sunday service in Jerusalem, so that the Church of the Resurrection was completely filled with its perfume.[3] And the baptistery of the Lateran possessed a *thymiamaterium* of pure gold, the gift of the Emperor Constantine.[4] In the procession at the papal services described in the first Roman *Ordo* seven torch-bearers and a subdeacon with the *thymiamaterium* preceded the pope,[5] a survival from the Roman court ceremonial.[6]

If incense was thus used quite early in religious assembly it was because its special quality lent itself to religious symbolism. The psalmist used the smoke of incense billowing upwards as an image of prayer rising to God (Ps. 140:2), and in the Apocalypse the golden bowls of incense represented the prayers of the saints.[7] Thus incense could easily express the religious sentiments of the Christian community—the lifting of the heart in prayer, the elevation of the soul to God; and just as easily was it capable of itself becoming a sacred object, a bearer of divine blessing, after the benediction of the Church was pronounced over it. This definitely religious signification and a corresponding intensification of the use of incense, as it had already developed quite some time in the Orient, is met with in the Roman liturgy for the first time in the Frankish area.[8] Amalar mentions the change from Roman practice in the use of incense at the offertory.[9]

By the ninth century, incense was definitely used at the start of Mass. After the celebrant had made his confession of faults and saluted those around him, in many churches a cleric came to the altar and offered incense (*incensum ponens*).[10] The Sacramentary of Amiens presents two prayers for the pertinent *benedictio incensi*,[11] of which the second at least had

---

[3] *Aetheriæ Peregrinatio*, c. 24, 10 (CSEL, XXXIX, 73).

[4] St. Ambrose (d. 397) seems to have been the first to mention the practice of incensing the Christian altar: *Exp. Evang. Lucæ*, i, 28 (PL XV, 1545). In Pseudo-Dionysius (circa 500) it is fully developed.

[4] Duchesne, *Liber pont.*, I, 174.
Hanging thuribles were common in churches all through the early Middle Ages (see Atchley, *Ordo Romanus Primus* [London, 1905], 17-18).

[5] *Ordo Rom. I*, n. 8 (PL, LXXVIII, 941).
Regarding the nature and shape of censers then and later see Braun, *Die christliche Altargerät*, 598-632. A thurible found in the ruins of a basilica at Salona which was destroyed in 624 (*ibid.*, 608; table 127) was held on three chains that came together—the same basic form as today's.

[6] *Supra*, p. 68.

[7] Apoc. 5: 8.

Cf. the explanation of the second gift of the Magi (Matt. 2: 11) which is already in patristic exegesis.

[8] Cf. *supra*, p. 77.

[9] Amalar, *De eccl. off.*, Præf. altera (PL, CV, 992). At the beginning of Mass he expressly mentions the carrying of the *thuribulum*; III, 5 (PL, CV, 1109 f.). Similarly Amalar's *Expositio* of 813-814, ed. Hanssens (*Eph. liturg.*, 1927), 170; 173, according to which three censers could be used, one for incensing the altar, one for the men, and one for the women.

[10] *Ordo Rom. VI* (10th c.), n. 3 (PL, LXXVIII, 990 D).
Yet even down to modern times there were churches where the incense was carried in procession to the altar, but the altar was not incensed. Numerous examples for one usage or the other, along with many variations and degrees, from the 9th to the 19th century in Atchley, *A History of the Use of Incense*, 214-231.

[11] Leroquais (*Eph. liturg.*, 1927), 441.

its origin in the East—an inkling as to the provenience of the custom.[12] A formal incensation of the altar is mentioned as early as the eleventh century.[13] The incensation at the beginning of the fore-Mass is even now less richly developed than the incensation at the beginning of the Mass proper; in the Middle Ages, too, it was only in exceptional cases that it was further expanded. The incense was blessed, of course, just as is done elsewhere,[14] and various formulas for this appear,[15] including the one we use nowadays.[16] But, just as at present, no special prayer was connected with the incensation.[17]

The external action is also mostly very simple. Besides the incensation of the altar there is mention in the later Middle Ages also of the incensation at this place of the celebrant by the deacon.[18] The post-Tridentine Missal carried through the more detailed regulation in this matter by putting in an incensation of the altar cross and the relics as the first items.[19]

[12] *Domine Deus omnipotens, sicut suscepisti munera Abel . . .;* cf. the Greek liturgy of St. James, likewise at the beginning of Mass: Brightman, 32. In the Syrian homeland of this liturgy an incensing at the beginning of Mass is testified to by Pseudo-Dionysius, *De eccl. hierarchia,* III, 2 (Quasten, *Mon.,* 294). Cf. also Hanssens, III, 72, 80.

[13] John of Avranches, *De off. eccl.* (PL, CXLVII, 38 B). In Italy first in that Pontifical of the 11th-12th century which we have already (*supra,* p. 297, note 32) recognized as a carrier of Norman tradition: Ebner, 328.
See also *ibid.,* 312, 313, 347.
Innocent III, *De s. alt mysterio,* II, 14 (PL, CCXVII, 806 f.).

[14] Even in the *Cod. Chigi* the incensation is mentioned without any such blessing: Martène, 1, 4, XII (I, 570 D).

[15] Sacramentary of Amiens (note 11 above). The continuation of the second formula mentioned shows very pointedly the double meaning attached even then to the incense: *suscipere digneris incensum istud in odorem suavitatis—in remissionem peccatorum meorum et populi tui.* The phrasing is turned to good account in the *Missa Illyrica:* Martène, 1, 4, IV (I, 494 C).
Other formulas used here accent only the latreutic value; so a formula which

is allied to the one now in use at the Offertory: *Incensum istud dignetur Dominus benedicere et in odorem suavitatis accipere;* Missal of Toul (14th or 15th cent.); *ibid.,* XXXI (I, 650 D); cf. XV (I, 585 A).
Cf. also the formulas in the Sacramentary of Boldau (c. 1195): Radó, 42.

[16] In Norman-English territories it can be ascertained since the 13th century: *Ab illo sanctificeris in cuius honore crematis, in nomine Patris . . .;* Martène, 1, 4, XXVI; cf. XXXV, XXXVII (I, 637 B, 665 B, 677 D).

[17] So expressly Durandus, IV, 8, 2.
According to John of Avranches, *De off. eccl.* (PL, CXLVII, 38 C) the celebrant performs the incensation while reciting the *Gloria*—a solution akin to that employed nowadays at the *Magnificat* in Vespers.
Yet, by way of exception, Ps. 140:2 (*Dirigatur*) is mentioned; Sacramentary of Amiens: Leroquais (*Eph. liturg.,* 1927), 441; Sicard of Cremona, *Mitrale,* III 2 (PL, CCXIII, 96 B); *Breviarium* of Rouen: Martène 1, 4, XXVII (I, 677 D). Even the Missal of Pius V originally contained Ps. 140: 2-4 here; J. O'Connell, "A Sixteenth Century Missal" (*Eph. liturg.,* 1948) 104.

[18] Missal of Sarum: Martène, 1, 4 XXXV (I, 665 B).

[19] Rit. serv., IV, 4-7.

We will have occasion later[20] to pay greater attention to the transition to the incensing of persons, since it is really from this that the incensing of objects gets its meaning. In the incensing of the altar, the meaning that stood in the foreground was the purification and protection that the incense implied[21]; this became, in turn, a sign of honor. From here the next step was obvious; it could be carried over generally to all sacred objects—and to the most sacred of all, the Blessed Sacrament, where it does today actually find its favorite use.

Thus the incensation at the start of the Mass is manifestly a true opening rite which is repeated at the beginning of the Mass proper; the locale of the sacred action and the *liturgus* himself are removed from this sin-tainted world in a special manner and transported into an atmosphere of sanctity. In the last analysis a biblical example could have had some influence. It was a law in Old Testament worship (Lev. 16:12) that the service of the high priest must not begin without incense. Since Carolingian times it became a favorite interest to discover parallels in the Old Testament and to put them into actual use; this might have had an effect here too.[22]

8. The Introit Chant

After the priest has venerated the altar by means of a kiss and, in given cases, by incensation, he turns to read from the missal the text of the introit which the choir had intoned for the procession of the clergy. This is the practice nowadays. In our modern churches, where the sacristy is built quite close to the sanctuary it is impossible to have a real procession even on feast days unless in some way a circuitous route is deliberately introduced. There could hardly have been any thought of a formal procession in the ruder buildings of primitive Christianity, or even in the modest confines of the average basilica. But when, on the contrary, we view today the colossal ecclesiastical structures which have arisen since the fourth century at prominent points of the Eternal City, and when we notice that the *secretarium* in which the ministers made ready for divine service was at that time situated mostly near the entrance of the basilica, that is, at the end opposite the apse,[1] and when we take into consideration the numerous clergy who, according to the oldest *ordines*, took part in papal

---

[20] *Infra,* p. 451 f.

[21] Durandus, IV, 10, 5.

Also according to the first of the blessings in the Sacramentary of Amiens mentioned on a previous page (319), the incense was to serve as a *munimentum tutelaque defensionis* against the fiend.

[22] The Old Testament concept came to the fore with special clarity in such a setting as that mentioned by Durandus, IV, 8, 1, when in imitation of the activity of the *legalis sacerdos,* the incense was put in and blessed even before the words *Deus tu conversus* were said, therefore before the ascent to the altar.

[1] Beissel, *Bilder,* 255, 302.

worship, it becomes quite clear that the procession of the clergy from entrance to altar was an act of great importance and significance.

Such a procession could hardly have been tolerable if it had been conducted in absolute silence. And since there was no organ and instruments were generally proscribed in the ancient Church, it was left entirely to the singing to give musical color to this entrance procession. We will probably get the best notion of the temper of this chant by thinking of the one genuine introit which is still current in our present-day liturgy, namely the *Ecce sacerdos* to the sound of which the bishop makes his entrance into the gayly decorated church on important occasions.[2] Even in the Roman liturgy of later antiquity this entrance chant, the *introitus* —at a later period also called *officium*[3]—was already arranged as an art-chant performed by a special group of singers,[4] just like the songs for the collecting of the offerings and for Communion, and like these—and like the orations and readings—the introit varied according to the festivity. The texts for these songs were taken essentially from the psalter. By the time that our processional chants were composed, the older hymn creations —from which we derived the *Gloria in excelsis Deo*—had lost the prestige they had once possessed and were reduced to very sparse remnants. The new hymnody, composed on the principles of meter and strophe, which was introduced about the time of St. Ambrose, was not admitted to the Roman Mass for over five hundred years. At Rome a strict rule was observed in the face of the wild and crafty song-propaganda of Manichean and Gnostic groups: We use only the songs dictated by the Spirit of God Himself.[5]

These chants were performed antiphonally, that is, the psalm was sung by two choruses, alternating verse by verse.[6] Already in an early period in ecclesiastical singing, antiphony involved the introduction of a prefatory verse which announced the melody of the following verse, the psalm. This prefatory verse, which we today style an antiphon, appears to have been introduced as the result of a musical exigency; in order to assure a proper intonation it seems to have been the practice in ancient times to play a short prelude on an instrument. But since musical instruments were forbidden in Christian worship as heathenish, the function had to be taken

---

[2] *Pontificale Rom.*, p. III, *ordo ad recipiendum processionaliter prælatum.*
[3] Sölch, *Hugo von St. Cher*, 55 f. The title is already found in the 10th century in Pseudo-Alcuin, *De div. off.* (PL, CI, 1244 C). At the end of the Middle Ages it was generally used in Normandy and in England; see Maskell, 28 f. Regarding the origin of the designation, cf. H. Leclercq, "Introït," DACL, VII, 1213; suggests the influence of the Mozarabic liturgy where the Mass formularies were given the heading: *Ad missam officium.*

[4] See *supra*, pp. 68 ff.
[5] J. Kroll, "Hymnen," in E. Hennecke, *Neutestamentl. Apokryphen*, 596 f.
[6] ἀντιφωνή = counter-melody. Ancient Greek antiphony consisted in singing in octaves, two choirs (men—women or/and children) singing the same melody either alternately or together, thus producing a primitive two-part song. In ecclesiastical antiphony the only essential was interchange, i.e. alternate singing between two choral groups. See A. Gastoué, *Les Origines du chant romain* (Paris, 1907), 50.

over by the human voice. This would lead to a creation such as we have in the antiphon.[7] The first place in which antiphonal song was employed was Antioch where it rode on the swell of a young Catholic movement. When about 350 the leaders of the Catholic monks, Flavian and Diodoros (later bishops), began to gather the people around them and to argue openly against an overmighty Arianism then at its height, they introduced this method of singing at their prayer-meetings in the shrines of the martyrs. From this start antiphonal singing spread everywhere, being carried abroad by the monks, who possessed not only the means of cultivating chant, but also the necessary knowledge of the psalms. The city cathedrals followed, in which special singing groups were formed, the *schola cantorum*.

According to a narrative that has often been repeated, antiphony was introduced into Rome by Pope Celestine I (d. 432), and introduced precisely as a song for the introit. Of him the *Liber pontificalis* recounts: *Constituit ut psalmi David CL ante sacrificium psalli antephanatim ex omnibus, quod ante non fiebat, nisi tantum epistula beati Pauli recitabatur et sanctum evangelium.*[8] Unfortunately the account cannot be relied on as an historical report.[9] However, it does give us this much information, that at the time this section of the book was written, prior to the middle of the sixth century, the introit chant composed of psalm texts[10] had long been in use.[11] In the first description of the papal Mass, a description going back to the seventh century, we come across the introit as a chant of the *schola*. When the pope stands in the *secretarium* ready to make his entry, he beckons to the proper cleric, the *quartus scholæ*, making a sign *ut psallant;* the latter in turn passes the signal on to the director of the *schola*, which stands ready by the passageway to the altar, in two double rows to left and right (corresponding to the two half-choruses), the boys on the inside,

---

[7] H. Leclercq, "Antienne," DACL, I, 2293 f.

[8] Duchesne, *Liber pont.*, I, 230.

[9] Batiffol, *Leçons*, 105, note 1, points out that the data is dependent upon the apocryphal letter of Pope Damasus to Jerome.

[10] A preliminary older form of the Introit chant which, like the *Ingressa* of the Milanese and the corresponding chants of other liturgies, did not as yet include the psalm, has been presumed also for Rome by G. Morin, *Les véritables origines du chant grégorien* (Maredsous, 1890), 54. That the non-psalmodic texts which are still preserved today can be adduced for this older plan—as is done by C. Callewaert, "Introïtus" (*Eph. liturg.*, 1938), 487, and by Righetti, III, 165 f.—

is neither to be excluded nor on the other hand to be considered as absolute proof. For one must remember that it has always —even in more modern times—been hard to express these festal concepts by means of psalm verses. The reference is to such older antiphons as *Gaudeamus omnes in Domino* and *Salve sancta parens* (the beginning of hymn by the 5th century poet Cælius Sedulius).

Regarding the mention of the "150 Psalms" see the various attempts at explanation in H. Leclercq, "Introït", *DACL*, VII, 1214 f.

[11] That all the people originally took part in this is only a later element even in the historical writing of this period; the words *antephanatim ex omnibus* are missing in the older recensions of the text (Duchesne, I, 89).

the men on the outside. At once the leader begins the antiphon. The psalmody is continued until the clergy have passed the rows of singers and reached the altar. After the pope has saluted his assistants with the kiss of peace, he gives a signal to start the *Gloria (Patri)*. At the *Sicut erat* the deacons rise, two by two, to kiss the altar. The pope meanwhile remains kneeling in prayer *usque ad repetitionem versus*, meaning obviously the antiphon.[12] The antiphon was therefore repeated at the end of the psalm. Whether it was also repeated after each single verse of the psalm, cannot be determined so far as the city of Rome itself is concerned.[13] In fact the phrase cited above seems to prove the contrary, for it does not say: *usque ad ultimam repetitionem versus*. But this may well be one of the alterations which were made in the Roman chant when it reached Frankish domains, apparently as the result of Gallican traditions.

The oldest manuscripts of the Roman Mass-chant books, the antiphonaries, surviving from about the year 800, contain only the song-text without the neums; these books do not indicate any explicit shortening of the psalm.[14] This reduction seems to have occurred with varying rapidity in different places. In some places as late as 1000 mention is still made of the

---

[12] *Ordo Rom. I*, n. 8 (PL, LXXVIII, 941 f.).

The same picture in the *Capitulare ecclesiastici ordinis* (Silva-Tarouca): the pope tarries in prayer *usque dum clerici antiphonam ad introitum cum psalmo et Gloria et repetito verso dixerint*.

[13] Still P. Wagner, among others, inclines to this view: *Einführung*, I, 66; cf. also 26 f., 144-147; idem, "Antiphon," LThK, I (1930), 503. Wagner considers the repetition of the antiphon after each verse as the general practice of ancient Christian antiphony. However he has in mind in the main the Frankish sources since the 9th century which also contain the notation of the melody. In the chanting of the Office, indeed, this constant repetition of the antiphon after each psalm verse was occasionally practiced. It is true, moreover, that also for the Mass chant even in the 8th century, there is evidence —in a later passage of the *Capitulare* just referred to above (Silva-Tarouca, 205, 1. 4-9)—of a similar handling of the antiphon as a refrain. Here is the direction: In cases where the antiphon is taken from the psalm, the first verse should be sung after the antiphon, then the antiphon repeated, after that the *Gloria Patri*, then the antiphon again,

then the *Sicut erat*, then the antiphon, then another verse of the psalm (*alio verso de ipso psalmo*) and the antiphon once more. Obviously we have here, within the *Capitulare*, the disclosure of a different source from that which expressly outlined the Roman arrangement of a papal Mass. The procedure of some monastic Mass must have been inserted here (Silva-Tarouca, 204, 1. 41; 205, 1. 41), an arrangement which need not have been of Roman origin at all, for the text of the *Capitulare* as handed down has also included Gallic material (cf. the interpolation p. 206, 1. 21 and the observation p. 219; see also Baumstark, JL, V [1925], 158). For the rest, the text in question, after mentioning the *Gloria in excelsis Deo* for Sundays and feasts, itself continues: on other days *antephona tantum ad introitum psalmo et Gloria, subsequente Kyrie eleison* (205, 1. 14 f.). It is once more the Roman source that is being cited which here, as always, presumes the chanting of a psalm and not of a psalm verse.

[14] Hesbert's edition shows that merely the beginning of the psalm was marked. And there is no limitation to certain verses, as occurs at the Offertory, for instance, on Easter Sunday. Hesbert, n. 80.

nod or gesture to signal for the closing of the psalmody with *Gloria Patri*,[15] or the second (or a second) verse of the psalm is expressly indicated.[16] In other places the psalm was curtailed to the first verse apparently as early as the eighth century.[17] In this abbreviation of the text we have the result, no doubt, partly of a development of the musical forms which had gone on apace, musical forms which we find in the tenth century fully written out, the same melodies that have been once more restored to us in the *Editio Vaticana* of the Roman *Graduale*. Sung thus in solemn fashion, the antiphon itself and its repetition took up no little time in performance.

But a more important factor in producing this reduction of the psalm was the fact that in the more modest circumstances of extra-Roman episcopal and capitular churches there was hardly any room for a lengthy procession like that in the papal liturgy. Moreover a regular formal procession of this sort was not taken into consideration in the planning of new churches[18] and the distance to the altar was shortened to only a fraction of its former length. True, the time at the altar was stretched out by the expansion of the prayers at the foot of the altar and by the introduction of the incensation, so that the shortening of the introit was somewhat counterbalanced. But in any case the introit was no longer the song accompanying a grand procession. Reduced to its essential elements, it became an independent preludial chant, opening up the celebration of Mass. There was even some doubt about the right moment to start it, whether it should be sung in good part before the celebrant and the assistants appeared,[19] or begin only when the clergy have arrived at the foot of the altar, as the later *ordines* usually demanded.[20] The hope that the introit would once more

---

[15] *Ordo Rom. VI*, n. 4 (PL, LXXVIII, 990): *cum Gloria innuente episcopo cantabitur.*

Cf. Remigius of Auxerre, *Expositio* (PL, CI, 1247 D): *ad nutum diaconi.*

[16] Thus in a 10th century Mass book from lower Italy; see Dold, *Die Zürcher und Peterlinger Messbuchfragmente aus der Zeit der Jahrtausendwende* (Beuron, 1934), p. lxiii.

[17] Cf. *supra* the direction interpolated in the *Capitulare eccl. ord.* (note 13 above).

Certainly at Rome by the time of *Ordo Rom. X* (11th century?) the Introit psalm was already reduced to its present state, one verse only (PL, LXXVIII, 1010).

[18] Cf. *supra*, p. 269 f.

[19] Since the 11th century the rubric is often met which directs the priest to go to the altar when the choir begins the *Gloria Patri*. John of Avranches, *De off. eccl.* (PL, CXLVII, 32 B, C); Mass-

Ordo of the *Cod. Chigi*: Martène, 1, 4, XII (I, 569 B). From the 13th-14th century: *ibid.*, XIX (I, 605 A, 615 B). Also in the *Ordinarium O.P.* of 1256 (Guerrini, 235). The *Liber ordinarius* of Liége limits the direction to *missæ maiores* (Volk, 89, 1. 9). The custom was also kept by the Cistercains: see *supra*, p. 270, note 36). At Lyons and Vienne this *Gloria Patri* was sung in a higher register; de Moléon, 29: 52.

Some few Mass schemes direct the priest to start out when the Introit verse is begun; thus a Camaldolese sacramentary of the 13th century; Ebner, 354; cf. the Rituale of Soissons: Martène, 1, 4, XXII (I, 610). Similarly also, in the 8th century, the *Breviarium eccl. ord.* (Silva-Tarouca, 196, 1. 9), where there is question, however, of more than one verse.

[20] Thus partially already in the 11th century.

assume its original character as a processional chant seems to have dictated the rubric in the 1907 *Editio Vaticana* of the songs of the Mass; here the regulation is clear, that the introit is to be intoned *accedente sacerdote ad altare*.

Of the original antiphonal character of the chant—the sort of thing which grew so important in the psalmody of the Office—only a very slight residue is still to be found in the introit. One survival is the sandwiching of the psalm verse between the antiphon and its repetition. Surviving, too, is a recollection of the double chorus[21]: soloists and choir divide the two halves of the psalm verse between them, and the two verses of the doxology.[22] And the liturgical books still employ the sign "Ps." for the beginning of the psalm verse, not the "V." which indicates the part assigned to the soloist in the responsorial chants.

Besides this curtailment of the introit, we have to consider also the very remarkable fact that other trends led to more than one enlargement—to an enlargement and an enlivening. For one thing, the Carolingian reform had sought to have the *Gloria Patri* sung by the people,[23] in line with the original character of this doxology.[24] A hundred years later the prescription was still enjoined.[25] Soon after the Roman liturgy had found its way to the Frankish area we come upon another extension of the introit through the practice, already touched upon, of repeating the antiphon after each verse of the psalm,[26] as was customary also in the psalmody of the Orient under certain conditions.[27] Alongside this there is the puzzling creation of a *versus ad repetendum* which is actually found in some of the oldest manuscript antiphonaries. In these books not only are the antiphon and psalm noted

Already in the *Missa Illyrica*: Martène, 1, 4, IV (I, 496-499) the celebrant is furnished with a series of apologies that he should recite while the choir is singing the *versus ad Introitum*, as well as the *Kyrie* and the *Gloria*, in fact after he has kissed the altar (496 B), therefore after he has reached the altar.

[21] That the introit is sung by two choirs is still mentioned by Honorius Augustod., *Gemma an.*, I, 6 (PL, CLXXII, 545 C) and by Sicard of Cremona, *Mitrale*, III, 2 (PL, CCXIII, 94 A).

[22] *Graduale Vaticanum* (1908), *Ritus serv. in cantu missæ*.

In another way the same rubrics recall the erstwhile intonation of the antiphon by the *prior scholæ* (cf. *supra*, pp. 68, 70), for they direct that the first words (up to the asterisk) be sung by one or several soloists, then taken up by the full choir.

[23] *Admonitio generalis* of Charlemagne (789), n. 70 (MGH, Cap., I, 59).

[24] Cf. Jungmann, *Die Stellung Christi im liturgischen Gebet*, 173.

This tradition has been preserved in the Coptic liturgy: Brightman, 146, 1. 2-126; John, Marquess of Bute, *The Coptic Morning Service* (London, 1908), 52.

[25] Herard of Tours, *Capitula* (858), c. 16 (Hardouin, V, 451). Cf. Nickl, *Der Anteil des Volkes an der Messliturgie*, 15 f.

A modest residue resulting from this arrangement is revealed in the direction of the *Expositio 'Missa pro Multis'*; here we read: *innuente episcopo sive diacono Gloria a cuncto clero decantatur.* Hanssens (*Eph. liturg.*, 1930), XXXII, 1. 4.

[26] *Supra*, p. 323.

Sacramentary of Ratoldus (10th century; PL LXXVIII, 242 A): the psalm should be intoned *cum Introitu reciprocante*. Wagner, I, 66, takes the word in the sense indicated in the text.

[27] Baumstark, *Liturgie comparée*, 116 f.

down for the introit—and likewise for the communion—but there is an additional verse of the psalm under the superscription *ad repet.*[28] Both of these phenomena perhaps belong to the same general plan, as we shall see in more detail in a later chapter.[29] About the twelfth century two other ways of enriching the introit received further attention. They are both mentioned by Beleth (d. 1165).[30] The first method of amplification, followed on feast days, consisted in repeating the antiphon in whole or in part, even before the *Gloria Patri*, so that it was sung three times altogether. This was customary in many places north of the Alps, though not general.[31] The practice was followed from the eleventh century on,[32] and is still in use amongst the Premonstra-

[28] E.g., in the Antiphonary of Compiègne (Hesbert, n. 5), in the Rorate Mass on the Wednesday of the Advent ember week: After the antiphon, *Psalm. Coeli enarrant. Ad repet. In sole posuit.* Of the five oldest antiphonaries printed in Hesbert, that of Rheinau and that of Corbie do not have any verse *ad repetendum,* that of Mont-Blandin has them only on a few greater feasts (n. 73, 80, 87 etc.). The other two seldom agree on the choice of the verse. There cannot therefore be any question of a Roman tradition or traditional material. Further MSS. in Wagner, I, 66, note 4.

Regarding the nature of the *versus ad repetendum* not much is very clear right now. A. Dohmes, "Der Psalmengesang des Volkes in der eucharistischen Opferfeier der christlichen Frühzeit", (*Liturg. Leben*, 1938), 149-151, following E. T. Moneta Caglio, "'Capitulum' e 'Completorium'," *Ambrosius,* IX (1933), 191-209 (with Milan mainly in view), conjectures that this was originally a substitute granted the people when the constant repetition of the antiphon after each verse (here presumed also) was transferred from people to choir (*schola*); after the *schola* had repeated its artistic antiphon, the people would add their simpler verse. This explanation does not, however, take into account the very early (8-9th century) appearance of the *versus ad repetendum* as noticed above, nor the probability that it is this type of verse which is meant by the expression *alio verso de ipso psalmo* in the *Capitulare eccl. ord.* (8th century; note 13 above). As a matter of fact, this *Capitulare* it-

self, in its corresponding and exact presentation of the Communion chant, opens the way to a different explanation. Cf. also the *Breviarium ecc. ord.* (Silva-Tarouca, 196), which expressly mentions a *versus ad repetendum* in the very last place—a thing hardly synonymous with the expression *repetito versu* which parallels it in the *Capitulare.* The same expression in the *Ordo* of St. Amand (Duchesne, *Christian Worship,* 458) will have to be judged differently.
[29] *Infra,* Vol. II, Chap. 3, 14.
[30] John Beleth, *Explicatio,* c. 35 (PL, CCII, 44): [*Introitus*] *diebus profestis bis cani solet, in sollemnitatibus vero ter. Quandoque intermiscentur tropi.*

Cf. also Sicard of Cremona, *Mitrale,* III, 2 (PL, CCXIII, 94); Durandus, IV, 5, 3; 6.
[31] Sölch, *Hugo von St. Cher,* 56-60.

Martène, 1, 4, XX, XXIV, XXIX, XXXV (I, 607 C, 626 C, 646 B, 665 C); de Moléon, 165, 394, 428.

The practice seems to have been quite general in England at the close of the Middle Ages; Maskell, 28 f. Two examples from Spanish Mass books of the 16th century in Ferreres, p. XXVI, CVII.

In German cathedrals the custom obtained down to the 19th century; see R. Stapper, *Katholische Liturgik,* (5th ed.; Münster, 1931), 124.
[32] *Udalrici Consuet. Clun.* I, 8 (PL, CXLIX, 653): *In dominicis diebus ad maiorem missam Introitus post versum dimidius solet recitari, post Gloria Patri totus.* The repetition here mentioned of only half the antiphon also occurs amongst the Premonstratensians, and is referred to

tensians[33] and the Carmelites.[34] The system was called *triumphare psalmis* or *triplicare*. The other method consisted in enlarging the text of the introit by means of tropes.[35] In regard to the introit the favorite device was the introduction of a preliminary phrase.[36]

The Missal of Pius V eliminated all these tropes as parasitic. But in our time the tendency has been manifested more than once to restore the introit to a fuller form, at least on festive occasions, by substituting the original full psalm in place of its vestigial single verse. Thus at the coronation Mass of Pope Pius XI in 1922 the entire *Introitus* psalm was sung.[37]

In an earlier stage of the introit chant the psalm must have been the more important by far. This can be traced quite plainly in the Mass formularies for feast days. A psalm was picked which, taken as a unit (in the sense of the allegorizing psalm-exegesis of the period), could best fit the occasion. The only psalm verse left in our present-day introit—as a rule the first verse, or, if the first verse served as antiphon, the one immediately following—often shows absolutely no connection with the *motif* for the day, whereas the idea is actually conveyed by the continuation of the psalm. Take the Wednesday in the Advent Ember week or the fourth Sunday of Advent; the psalm verse beginning *Cæli enarrant gloriam Dei* conveys no particular impression of Advent. But the psalm from which this verse is derived contains those phrases so often cited in this season with reference to Christ's coming like the orient sun: *Ipse tamquam sponsus procedens de thalamo suo* (Ps. 18:6). In the third Mass of Christmas the introit verse is one that has certainly only a very general meaning: *Cantate Domino canticum novum*; but it is the beginning of Psalm 97 which serves as a Christmas psalm because of the words: *Notum fecit Dominus salutare suum* and *Viderunt omnes fines terræ salutare Dei nostri* (vv. 2f.). In the introit for Epiphany we find the verse: *Deus, iudicium tuum regi da*, from Psalm 71, but a fuller meaning is extracted from what follows, wherein the *reges Tharsis* and the others appear. On the Feast of Holy Bishops we read the introit verse: *Memento, Domine, David* (Ps. 131); it is not till further in the psalm we find the connection with the theme of the day: *Sacerdotes*

by Hugh of St. Cher (d. 1263), who designates it as *imperfecte* chanting; Sölch, *Hugo*, 57; 59.

[33] Waefelghem, 361.

[34] Sölch, 58.

[35] Blume, *Tropen des Missale*, II (Analecta Hymnica, 49), 17-164. Cf. *supra*, p. 123.

[36] E.g., on Christmas: *Laudemus omnes Dominum, Qui virginis per uterum Parvus in mundum venerat, Mundum regens quem fecerat: Puer natus. . . .* Blume, p. 26. The corresponding Easter trope: *Quem quæritis in sepulchro* (Blume, p. 9)

became the starting-point for the development of the medieval drama; see Karl Young, *The Drama of the Medieval Church* (Oxford, 1933).

[37] JL, V (1925), 366. Cf. A. Winninghoff, O.S.B., *Choralmessbuch für die Sonn- und Feiertage* (Düsseldorf, 1938), wherein several extra verses are regularly included at the introit.

In the same spirit the participants at a Community Mass are expected to recite the whole introit psalm; see, e.g., P. Parsch, *Volksliturgie* (Klosterneuburg, 1940), 35 f., 352.

tui induantur iustitiam (v. 9; cf. v. 16). In other cases this characteristic verse is at least given prominence by being selected as the antiphon, but of this more later.

Besides the initial verse of the psalm, the concluding verse has also been retained, namely the *Gloria Patri*. This verse, known as the Little Doxology, has accompanied antiphonal psalm chant as the regular ending of every psalm, joining it in its cradle at Antioch and staying with it in its travels over the world, although not everywhere accepted at once. The opposition to Antiochene Arianism had aided in its introduction. The Arians used as their battle-cry and watch-word the unexceptionable but ambiguous formula, *Gloria Patri per Filium in Spiritu Sancto*, seeing in it the expression of the belief they maintained, of the Son's subordination to the Father. In the Catholic camp the leaders, the very ones who introduced and propagated the new antiphonal chant, set up an opposing formula which had long been traditional amongst the Syrians, *Gloria Patri et Filio et Spiritui Sancto*,[38] a formula derived from the baptismal formula (Matt. 28, 19) which gave unequivocal expression to the essential equality of the three divine Persons. In this way every psalm spoken by the new people of God ended with a shout of praise in honor of the triune God. The succeeding verse is, in its present form, proper to the West, although equivalent phrases are to be found quite early also in the Orient, especially in Egypt.[39] At the Synod of Vaison (529), which is the first to mention it, it is directed against the heretics who denied the eternity of the Son,[40] and therefore likewise against the Arians. The *erat in principio* was the thing that was to be stressed, especially in relation to the Son (and to the Holy Ghost). According to the wording this additional phrase declares that we ascribe to the triune God that glorification which has been God's from the beginning and will ever be.[41]

Why is the *Gloria Patri* omitted during Passiontide? As early as Durandus the reason given was: sorrow and grief.[42] That would be the reason why the phrase is similarly omitted at Requiem Masses. But this is not really the reason. Actually we have here the working of the old "law of retaining the ancient in seasons of high liturgical worth," in other words, we have the residue of an older system. This means, Rome accepted the antiphonal chant without the *Gloria Patri*; later the verse was added at other times

---

[38] Jungmann, *Die Stellung Christi*, 151-177, esp. 160 f., 172 ff.
[39] *Ibid.*, 161, note 41.
[40] Can. 5 (Mansi, VIII, 727).
[41] *Sicut erat* sc. *gloria*. This is especially true if we construe the *Gloria Patri* in the indicative (a construction that is thoroughly possible): Glory *is* to the Father, etc.; cf. Jungmann, *Die Stellung*

Christi, 165 f. But the second clause can still be understood in this way even if the first is taken as subjunctive: Glory be to the Father. . . . as it (glory) was. . . .; cf. Eisenhofer, I, 171. A question however arises whether this should be read: *As it was . . . is now and ever shall be . . .* or *so may it be now and forever.*
[42] Durandus, VI, 60, 4.

of the year, but not during this season.⁴³ The same principle is at work—
only with greater efficacy—at the high point of the Easter service, the Holy
Saturday Mass (which used to be sung in the night before Easter); here
the introit chant, along with the other antiphonal chants, offertory and
communion, is entirely absent. And on Good Friday, the entire opening
rite, including *Kyrie* and oration, was not accepted.

From the viewpoint of music the antiphon is the most important part
of the introit. And even as to contents the opportunity was here presented
to accentuate the tone or temper with which the celebration was to begin.
Thus the antiphon established the tone in a double sense, the musical
note, the psychological mood. This latter was done often by selecting for
the antiphon a psalm verse that seemed to fit the celebration. Thus for the
Christmas midnight Mass Psalm 2 is sung at the introit, and verse 7 is
chosen as the antiphon: *Dominus dixit ad me, Filius meus es tu.* Or in the
introit of a *Confessor non pontifex*, Psalm 91, with the stress on verse 13 as
antiphon: *Iustus ut palma florebit.* An introit of this sort was called in the
Middle Ages *regularis*, while others, where the antiphon was not derived
from the psalm, were styled *irregulares.*⁴⁴ It is understandable that feast
days and festal seasons did much to break through this schema of the
Introitus regularis in order to give free vent to the expression of the mystery of the day. For the most part texts from the Scripture were used.
Thus the introit antiphon for the third Christmas Mass proclaims, with
the Prophet Isaias, the good news of the Nativity: *Puer natus est nobis
et Filius datus est nobis.* And the antiphon for Whitsunday plays upon
the Pentecostal miracle with words from the Book of Wisdom: *Spiritus
Domini replevit orbem terrarum.* A remarkable fact is this, that the text
of the antiphon is frequently derived from the Epistle of the day: *Gaudete
in Domino; Cum sanctificatus fuero; Viri Galilœi; De ventre matris meœ;
Nunc scio vere.*⁴⁵ However, here and there the Bible is sidestepped entirely.
On certain saints' days there is a simple invitation to partake of the joy
of the feast: *Gaudeamus omnes in Domino, diem festum celebrantes . . . ,*
a text which probably comes from St. Gregory the Great, who is said to
have written it for the dedication of St. Agatha's in 592.⁴⁶ One of the Masses

⁴³ A. Baumstark, *Liturgie comparée*, 32;
idem., "Das Gesetz der Erhaltung des
Alten in liturgisch hochwertiger Zeit,"
JL, VII (1927), 1-23.

⁴⁴ Durandus, IV, 5, 5. This irregularity
is increased whenever the "verse" is not
taken from the psalms, as happens on
the Feast of Our Lady of Sorrows.

⁴⁵ In some other instances the pertinent
Epistle subsequently went out of use, so
that the correspondence is no longer per-

ceptible; see the references in C. Callewaert, "Introïtus" (*Eph. liturg.*, 1938),
487.

⁴⁶ G. Verbeke, "S. Grégoire et la messe
de s. Agathe," *Eph. liturg.*, LII (1938),
67-76.
Cf. also Wagner *Einführung*, I, 68,
note 2; P. Pietschmann, JL, XII (1934),
108.
Further comments on the choice of Introit antiphons in Card. Schuster. *The
Sacramentary*, I, 80-81.

of the Blessed Virgin begins with the happy greeting of the poet Sedulius: *Salve, sancta parens.*

Thus, by means as simple as they are masterly, the antiphon of the introit set the tone that should dominate the liturgical assembly. In some examples it is hard to mistake the fact that the text selected had in view both the procession itself and the image of a higher reality from the day's celebration which the procession typified.[47] Thus on Epiphany we read: *Ecce advenit dominator dominus*, and on the Wednesday of Pentecost week: *Deus dum egredereris*. And in Easter week, the crowd of newly baptized who have entered the Church are greeted on Saturday with: *Eduxit populum suum in exultatione, alleluia, et electos suos in lœtitia*, and on Monday: *Introduxit vos Dominus in terram fluentem lac et mel*, and on Wednesday: *Venite benedicti Patris mei*.

But on the other hand there are days—like the Sundays after Pentecost —for which there is no special theme to which the introit antiphon might lead. Then the chant master takes up his psalter and chooses one of the psalms that in some way expresses the relationship of the Christian community to God: trust, praise, petition. It is to be noted that the psalter is gone through straight, starting with Psalm 12 on the first Sunday after Pentecost and moving on, Sunday for Sunday, till Psalm 118 is reached on the seventeenth Sunday.[48] Let us remark here at once that the same rule for the Sundays after Pentecost holds for the other antiphonal chants, offertory and communion, and likewise for the alleluia-verse, but not for the gradual. But it is noteworthy that the choice for the various formularies does not generally fall on the same psalms for any two chants of the day.[49] The following outline shows us all this in greater detail.

The arrangement, as far as the succession of the psalms is concerned, is the same today as it was a thousand years ago.[50] This table makes one thing clear. The succession of the psalms in each row and the divergence between the rows shows that there was no concerted attempt to hold in each case to one specified theme for all four of the chants. Instead, the Book of Psalms was conned from cover to cover, a bit chosen here, a bit chosen there, whatever appeared to suit the fancy of the praying congregation.

---

[47] E. Flicoteaux, "L'introit de la Messe, II": *Cours et Conférences*, VI (Louvain, 1928), 38 ff.
[48] The Introit antiphons that follow show an entirely different plan of arrangement, being taken from other sources and disposed in part with reference to the pre-Advent *cursus;* cf. Jungmann, *Gewordene Liturgie*, 281; Hesbert, *Antiphonale*, p. LXXV.

[49] Only on the 1st, 7th, 8th and 23rd Sundays do two chants coincide on psalms 5, 46, 47 and 129 respectively.
[50] Cf. the survey regarding MSS. of the 8th and 9th centuries in Hesbert, *loc. cit.* Still here the Communion of the 3rd Sunday after Pentecost is taken from Ps. 16 (instead of Luke), thus fitting into the series.

Sunday	Introit from Ps.	Alleluia-verse from Ps.	Offertory from Ps.	Communion from Ps.
1	12	5	5	9
2	17	7	6	12
3	24	7	9	(Luke)
4	26	9	12	17
5	26	20	15	26
6	27	30	16	26
7	46	46	(Dan.)	30
8	47	47	17	33
9	53	58	18	(John)
10	54	64	24	50
11	67	80	29	(Prov.)
12	69	87	(Exod.)	103
13	73	89	30	(Wis.)
14	83	94	33	(Matt.)
15	85	94	39	(John)
16	85	97	39	70
17	118	101	(Dan.)	75
18	(Ecclus.)	101	(Exod.)	95
19	(Salus)	104	137	118
20	(Dan.)	107	136	118
21	(Esth.)	113	(Job)	118
22	129	113	(Esth.)	(16)
23	(Jer.)	129	129	(Mark)

Although in its origin at least, the introit is essentially a part of the solemn high Mass, it soon found its way also into every Mass, even the private low Mass. This last transition can be seen in full detail in a document of the seventh/eighth century. The *Capitulare ecclesiastici ordinis*, already mentioned, an eighth-century Anglo-Frankish document based on the writing of the Roman archcantor John, is in general quite jejune and sober. But in the very midst of its exposition it seems to consider it quite important that the introit should be made a general practice. Twice the author pauses to stress the rule: Every priest at every Mass, in the monastery, in the country, even on weekdays, and even when he celebrates alone, must say the introit with the psalm (-verse) and *Gloria Patri*. That is the arrangement of the *sedes sancti Petri*. Whoever knowingly omits it *non recto ordine offert, sed barbarico*.[51] In the later Middle Ages the rule that the priest had to read the introit at every Mass was transferred also to the solemn Mass in which the choir had already sung it.[52]

---

[51] Silva-Tarouca, 204 f., 206 f. He is a little less emphatic in making the same demand regarding the Communion chant (*ibid.*, 207).

[52] This rule was already proposed (for the priest and his staff) in the Dominican Mass schema of 1256 (Guerrini, 235); likewise in a Minorite missal of the

Holy Saturday, as we noted, has nevertheless remained without an introit, and also without an offertory or communion. The procession of the clergy from the baptistery is accompanied on this occasion by the singing of the litany. Several of the ancient manuscript antiphonaries have a rubric for this day and also for the vigil of Pentecost: *Ad introitum letania.*[52] There are also other instances of the *Kyrie*-litany substituting for the introit. In the Roman *Ordo* of St. Amand, when a church is visited on the way during the procession of the *litania maior*, the church is entered to the accompaniment of the singing of the litany, which had been started while approaching the church, and at the end the pope says an oration.[54]

The introit is the first text amongst the variable parts of the Mass, and the first text in general touching the congregation. The first words of the introit therefore often serve as a designation of the formulary or even of the respective day. We speak of *Lætare* Sunday, or of the *Rorate* Mass and the *Requiem*. The introductory character of the introit is emphasized in our present-day rubrics by the fact that the priest, when he starts to read the introit from the missal, blesses himself with the sign of the Cross,[55] just as he does at the beginning of the prayers at the foot of the altar. But, in contrast to the latter, there is no accompanying formula. This is the present Roman practice although it was often different in the Mass ordinaries of the late Middle Ages. Sometimes *In nomine Patris . . .*[56] was used, sometimes the pair of versicles *Adiutorium nostrum* and *Sit nomen Domini,*[57] sometimes both together,[58] or finally some other words were employed.[59] Another indication of the merely private character of all that precedes the introit is given in some later medieval ordinaries where the preparation of the chalice was inserted before the introit as a final preparation for Mass.[60]

13th century (Ebner, 312). But the *Statuta antiqua* of the Carthusians, which belong to the same period, still say: *dicit vel auscultat introitum;* Martène, 1, 4, XXV (I, 631 D).

[53] Hesbert, n. 79; 105.

[54] Duchesne, *Christian Worship*, 474; on the other hand at the stational church the introit (*antiphona*) is sung after the litany (but no *Kyrie* follows the introit): *ibid.*, 475.

[55] One of the earliest to testify to this practice is the Carthusian *Statuta antiqua* (13th century): Martène, 1, 4, XXV (I, 631 D): *signat se.*

[56] Thus at Salisbury (Sarum; 14th century): Frere, *The use of Sarum*, I, 65, f.—*Missale iuxta ritum O.P.* (1889), 17.

[57] Examples, *supra*, p. 309, note 74 near the end.

[58] Missal of Evreux-Jumièges: Martène, XXVIII (I, 643 E). *Alphabetum sacerdotum*: Legg, *Tracts*, 37.

[59] According to Bernard of Waging (1462) many in Germany prefixed *Domine labia mea* or *Deus in adiutorium* to the introit; Franz, 574 f. The Augsburg Missal of 1555 contains *Adiutorium nostrum* and *Domine labia mea;* Hoeynck, 372. Only the latter formula in the Augsburg Mass-Ordo of the 15th century; Franz, 752. Sometimes there was combined with this the invocation: *Spiritus Sancti assit nobis gratia;* Beck, 265; Köck, 113. The *Deus in adiutorium* alone begins the introit in the ritual of the Hungarian Hermits of St. Paul; Sawicki, 148.

[60] Ancient Cistercian rite: Schneider (*Cist.-Chron.*, 1926), 282 ff.

Hungarian Mass books: Javór, 114, Sawicki, 147 f.

The introit is read by the priest at the Epistle side of the altar. Just as the bishop during the fore-Mass takes his place at his *cathedra*, so one who does not use a *cathedra* should take his place at the right side of the altar, according to an old rule that goes back to the old Roman stational arrangements.[61] Here he should stay till the choir finishes singing the introit, and even for everything which he himself sings or says right up to the Epistle.[62] The exception, which came in only gradually, was the practice of transferring *Kyrie, Gloria* and *Dominus vobiscum* to the center of the altar.[63]

9. Kyrie Eleison

We have already seen in the *Kyrie eleison* a prayer of the people to which the priest's oration is related. Thus considered, there is in this cry for mercy little that is fundamentally puzzling. But looked at more closely the tiny phrase gives grounds for a whole series of questions: Why this repeated cry, and why precisely a ninefold repetition? What is the derivation of this simple cry, so indeterminate in contents? Why in Greek? And who was originally the petitioner?

The Greek form takes us back to the earliest years of the Church. Not that the *Kyrie* is a vestige of that period in the Roman liturgy when the members of the Church in Rome themselves used Greek for the most part, and the language of worship was Greek, as it was till about the middle of the third century. No, the *Kyrie* was not taken into Rome from the Greek liturgy till much later. In the Orient, too, the non-Greek liturgies—the Coptic, the Ethiopian, and the West Syrian—have either borrowed or retained the *Kyrie eleison* untranslated. The *Kyrie* did not get to Rome earlier than the fifth century. And when it was taken over, it was as part of the litany which is traceable in the Orient since the fourth century and

---

[61] *Ordo Rom. I*, n. 22 (PL, LXXVIII, 948 B), regarding the bishop who replaces the pope at the station: *Secundum namque quod non sedet in sede post altare, tertio non dicit orationem post altare, sed in dextro latere altaris.*

[62] The rule that the celebrant should step to the side, *ad dexteram altaris*, after kissing the altar is already found in Amalar, *De eccl. off.*, III, 5 (PL, CV, 1113 A). Cf. Pseudo-Alcuin, *De div. off.* (PL, CI, 1245 B); John of Avranches, *De off. eccl.* (PL, CXLVII, 33 A).

According to Ivo of Chartres, *De conven. vet. et novi sacrif.* (PL, CLXII, 549 f.), the priest stands at the right side while the introit is being sung, and at the *Gloria* and the oration, because the priest represents Christ who, according

to Matt. 15: 24, was to look out only for Israel, typified by the right side.

The Carthusian *Statuta antiqua*: Martène, 1, 4, XXV (I, 631 D): Introit, *Gloria, Dominus vobiscum*—all on the right (the *Kyrie* was not as yet said by the priest); *Ordinarium Cart.* (1932), c. 26, 1.

In the later Middle Ages the rule is formulated as follows: The priest is to perform on the right side of the altar everything up to the Epistle (except the intoning of the *Gloria*), and everything after the Communion; Missal of Sarum: Martène, 1, 4, XXXV (I, 666 E); *Costumarium* of Sarum (end of the 14th century): Frere, *The use of Sarum*, I, 68.

[63] Cf. Sölch, *Hugo*, 60-63.

which has continued in use even today in the liturgies of the Orient as the so-called *ektenes*.

However, the beginnings of the *Kyrie eleison* reach much farther back than that. The petition *eleison* taken by itself, with or without vocative, must surely have been very familiar to the early Christians, even from pre-Christian traditions.[1] As late as the fifth century a preacher in Alexandria felt compelled to denounce the habit many Christians had kept of bowing to the rising sun and crying out ἐλέησον ἡμᾶς.[2] Even the formal κύριε ἐλέησον, directed to the divinity, is traced to heathen times,[3] and the repetition of the cry a given number of times was also not unknown to antiquity.[4] But no need to appeal to pagan custom; Holy Scripture offered examples in plenty of the cry of ἐλέησον directed to God, or, in the Gospels, to Jesus, especially in the book that served as the Church's first prayer book, the Book of Psalms.[5] The Septuagint presented phrases like: ἐλέησόν με κύριε (Ps. 6:3, *et al.*), κύριε ἐλέησόν με (Ps. 40:5, 11). True, none of these have the precise form of our *Kyrie eleison*, but the divergence was not so great it could not have been bridged by someone in prayer.

The proper history of our petition within Christian worship begins for us about the fourth century.[6] The Gallic pilgrim lady Ætheria tells us, about 390, how at Jerusalem at the end of Vespers one of the deacons read a list of petitions and "as he spoke each of the names, a crowd of boys stood there and answered him each time, *Kyrie eleison*, as we say, Lord have mercy (*miserere Domine*); their cry is without end."[7] Corresponding to the mode of pronunciation already then in vogue, Ætheria gives us the transcription *eleison* instead of the *eleeson* we might have expected. At the other hours the bishop himself prays these petitions[8]; this appears to have been the more ancient practice.[9]

From Antioch at about the same time there comes to us the very wording of such petitions which the deacon spoke when, for instance, after the Gospel of the Mass the catechumens were dismissed. And the explicit rubric is appended: "At each of these petitions which the deacon pronounces, the people should say, κύριε ἐλέησον, especially the children."[10]

---

[1] Dölger, *Sol salutis,* 60-103.

[2] *Ibid.,* 61-63.

[3] Epictetus, *Dissertationes,* II, 7; Dölger, 75-77; cf. 80 f.

[4] Dölger, 70 ff., 80 f.

[5] See the general survey in Dölger, 83-86.

Also in Adrian Fortescue, "Kyrie eleison," CE, VIII: 714-716.

[6] Bishop, *Liturgica historica,* 116-136; Eisenhofer, I, 195-201; II, 87-89; Baumstark, *Liturgie comparée,* 77 f., 80-86.

It is therefore hardly possible to justify the specious observation of E. Fiedler,

Christliche Opferfeier (Munich, 1937), 38, that by its use of the fateful title of *Kyrios* which was claimed for the Cæsar-sun cult, the *Kyrie eleison* had been a "Christian song of defiance" before it was incorporated in the liturgy.

[7] *Aetheriæ peregrinatio,* c. 24 (CSEL XXXIX, 72).

[8] *Ibid.,* 71.

[9] Cf. O. Heiming, JL, XIV (1938), 420.

[10] *Const. Ap.,* VIII, 6, 9 (Quasten, *Mon.,* 200). The same arrangement of alternating prayer is presumed for the dismis-

The list of petitions varies from case to case. As a rule there are prayers for the whole Church, for the clergy, for the people and the ruler, for those on a journey and for the sick, for the benefactors of the Church and for the poor, and for peace. This type of prayer, which was called a *litania*, was soon transplanted to the West, perhaps by pilgrims to Jerusalem, and soon came into use everywhere, either in translation or in some free revision. The petition κύριε ἐλέησον is sometimes retained without alteration, sometimes translated,[11] sometimes expanded[12] or otherwise changed to forms like those which still survive in the older part of our Litany of the Saints: *Libera nos, Domine: Te rogamus, audi nos.*[13]

The place where this litany was inserted was sometimes the same one it generally had in the East, namely, at the prayer that followed the lessons. But in the Milanese liturgy—although now restricted to the Sundays of Lent—it is still to be found at the beginning of Mass between the *Ingressa* (introit) and the oration, and therefore exactly where our Roman *Kyrie* is. In the Milanese version the response is made in Latin: *Domine miserere,* but at the end *Kyrie eleison* is repeated three times in succession.[14] Such a litany in a similar part of the Mass must have been proper

sal of the other groups and during the Prayer of the Faithful (VIII, 6-10) and likewise at the close of Vespers (VIII, 35, 2); cf. the reconstruction from Chrysostom in Brightman, 471 f., 477 f.

[11] The translation is also found among the convert Germanic tribes. Thus there is this evidence about the Vandals of North Africa: God is praised also in the language of the barbarians and his mercy sought; even Romans prayed the "Frôja armês": *Domine miserere.* This is found in the *Collatio Pseudo-Augustini cum Pascentio Ariano* (PL, XXXIII, 1162); cf. H. v. Schubert, *Geschichte der christlichen Kirche im Frühmittelalter* (Tübingen, 1921), 24.

Notice that in this as in all other transliterated Greek words (*Paraclitus, Agios, imas*), the spelling supposes the pronunciation of the time when the words were borrowed.

As an answer of the people the *Kyrie eleison* is still used in Spain; Férotin, *Le liber ordinum,* 114 f.

[12] See the examples in Duchesne, *Christian Worship,* 198-201.

[13] Duchesne, 165 f., and following him P. Alfonso, *Oratio fidelium* (Finalpia, 1928), 36-38, express the opinion that a litany formed with words such as these as responses must have been indigenous

to Rome, independently of any oriental pattern. For the possibility of such a thing reference is made to litany-type prayers in pre-Christian Rome, especially to the prayer which Licinius ordered his soldiers to say on the day of his battle with Maximinus; see Lactantius, *De mort pers.,* 46, 6 (CSEL, XXVII, 226): *Summe deus, te rogamus, sancte deus, te rogamus . . ., summe, sancte deus, preces nostras exaudi, brachia nostra ad te tendimus, exaudi, sancte, summe deus!*

Many of the acclamations that are preserved in the *Acta synodorum habitarum Romæ* are also in the same tradition. At a Roman synod of the year 499 the following ejaculations among others were put down in writing (MGH, *Auct. ant.,* XII, 403): *Ut fiat, rogamus,* (*dictum decies*): *ut scandala amputentur, rogamus* (*dictum novies*); *ut ambitus extinguatur, rogamus* (*dictum duodecies*). Cf. also Baumstark, *Liturgie comparée,* 85 f.

On the other hand, the view that at Rome the *Kyrie* was almost never used as a response to the acclamations can hardly be reconciled with what we learn from Gregory the Great, especially with the way he speaks about the Greek practices (see *infra,* note 30).

[14] *Missale Ambrosianum* (1902), 77-81; likewise thus in the older sources of the

also to the Roman liturgy in the fifth century and after. That some form of *Kyrie*-prayer was customary in Rome by the start of the sixth century is unmistakably clear from Canon 3 of the Synod of Vaison (529), which purposed to incorporate this practice in Matins, Mass and Vespers, and appealed to the usage of the Apostolic See where the *Kyrie eleison* was often repeated.[15] But from the remarks of St. Gregory the Great[16] it is clear that even in his time there were two ways of performing the prayer; one a simple repetition of the cry *Kyrie*, the other, combining a further text with the *Kyrie*. This second way must be the litany, in which the *Kyrie* forms the response. However, in the sacramentaries which otherwise permit us to gather a picture of the Mass as it was in the sixth century, no text is presented. The Gregorianum does remark innocently, that the Mass begins with the introit, *deinde Kyrie eleison*.[17] But we need not be amazed, for the celebrant did not intone the litany, and the sacramentary was intended only for his use. There are good reasons for suspecting that the old Roman *Kyrie*-litany survives in the so-called *Deprecatio Gelasii*.[18] For there are various signs to suggest that this prayer had its origin in Rome and that the Pope Gelasius (492-496) named in the title was the redactor. Of this pope the *Liber Pontificalis* recounts that he composed *sacramentorum præfationes et orationes cauto sermone*.[19] It might seem improbable that the Roman liturgy should have had the *Kyrie*-litany at a time when the General Prayer for the Church, which is so akin to the litany in content and form, was still said after the readings. But it is quite likely that the introduction of this *Kyrie*-litany coincided with the correction or revision of the General Prayer for the Church[20] and with the amplification of the intercessory prayers of the canon, which occurred about this time, so that it would have been only one part of a thoroughgoing reform of the Mass-liturgy undertaken by Pope Gelasius.[21] Following is the text of this *Deprecatio Gelasii*:

DEPRECATIO QUAM PAPA GELASIUS PRO UNIVERSALI ECCLESIA CONSTITUIT CANENDAM ESSE.

Dicamus omnes: Domine exaudi et miserere.[22]

Patrem Unigeniti et Dei Filium Genitoris ingeniti et Sanctum Deum Spiritum fidelibus animis invocamus — Kyrie eleison.

Milan liturgy: A. Ratti-M. Magistretti, *Missale Ambrosianum, duplex* (1913), 121 f.; Dölger, 90 f.

[15] Can. 3 (Mansi, VIII, 725).

[16] *Infra*, p. 338 f.

[17] Lietzmann, n. 1.

[18] B. Capelle, "Le Kyrie de la messe et le pape Gélase," *Revue Bénéd.*, XLVI (1934), 126-144.

The results are confirmed and exploited by C. Callewaert, "Les étapes de l'histoire du Kyrie," *Revue d'hist. eccl.*, XXXVIII (1942), 20-45.

[19] Duchesne, *Liber pont.*, I, 255.

[20] Cf. *infra*, p. 483 f.

[21] V. L. Kennedy, *The Saints of the Canon of the Mass* (Rome, 1938), 33-36; cf. C. Mohlberg, *Theol. Revue*, XXXVII (1938), 487-489. The same idea was expressed about this time by B. Capelle, "Le pape Gélase et la messe romaine," *Revue d'hist. eccl.*, XXXV (1939), 22-34.

[22] In place of this word we ought probably

I. *Pro immaculata Dei vivi ecclesia, per totum orbem constituta divinæ bonitatis opulentiam deprecamur — Kyrie eleison.*

II. *Pro sanctis Dei magni sacerdotibus et ministris sacri altaris cunctisque Deum verum colentibus populis Christum Dominum supplicamus — Kyrie eleison.*

III. *Pro universis recte tractantibus verbum veritatis multiformem Verbi Dei sapientiam peculiariter obsecramus — Kyrie eleison.*

IV. *Pro his qui se mente et corpore propter cælorum regna castificant, et spiritalium labore desudant, largitorem spiritalium munerum obsecramus — Kyrie eleison.*

V. *Pro religiosis principibus omnique militia eorum, qui iustitiam et rectum iudicium diligunt, Domini potentiam obsecramus — Kyrie eleison.*

VI. *Pro iocunditate serenitatis et opportunitate pluviæ atque aurarum vitalium blandimentis ac diversorum temporum prospero cursu rectorem mundi Dominum deprecamur — Kyrie eleison.*

VII. *Pro his quos prima christiani nominis initiavit agnitio, quos iam desiderium gratiæ cælestis accendit, omnipotentis Dei misericordiam obsecramus — Kyrie eleison.*

VIII. *Pro his quos humanæ infirmitatis fragilitas, et quos nequitiæ spiritalis invidia, vel varius sæculi error involvit, Redemptoris nostri misericordiam imploramus — Kyrie eleison.*

IX. *Pro his, quos peregrinationis necessitas, aut iniquæ potestatis oppressio vel hostilitatis vexat ærumna, Salvatorem Dominum supplicamus — Kyrie eleison.*

X. *Pro iudaica falsitate . . . aut hæretica pravitate deceptis vel gentilium superstitione perfusis veritatis Dominum deprecamur — Kyrie eleison.*

XI. *Pro operariis pietatis et his, qui necessitatibus laborantum fraterna caritate subveniunt, misericordiarum Dominum deprecamur — Kyrie eleison.*

XII. *Pro omnibus intrantibus in hæc sanctæ domus Domini atria, qui religioso corde et supplici devotione convenerunt, Dominum gloriæ deprecamur — Kyrie eleison.*

XIII. *Pro emundatione animarum corporumque nostrorum, et omnium venia peccatorum clementissimum Dominum supplicamus — Kyrie eleison.*

XIV. *Pro refrigerio fidelium animarum, præcipue sanctorum Domini sacerdotum, qui huic ecclesiæ præfuerunt catholicæ, Dominum spirituum et universæ carnis iudicem deprecamus — Kyrie eleison.*

XV. *Mortificatam vitiis carnem et viventem fide animam — præsta, Domine, præsta.*

XVI. *Castum timorem et veram dilectionem — præsta, Domine, præsta.*

XVII. *Gratum vitæ ordinem et probabilem exitum — præsta, Domine, præsta.*

XVIII. *Angelum pacis et solacia sanctorum — præsta, Domine, præsta. Nosmetipsos et omnia nostra, quæ orta quæ aucta per Dominum ipso auctore suscipimus, ipso custode retinemus, ipsiusque misericordiæ et arbitrio providentiæ commendamus — Domine, miserere.*[23]

This litany or one like it, with the *Kyrie* attached, must have become quite popular in Rome and its environs. Inserting it into the Mass was only one of its uses. In the Rule of St. Benedict the *litania* or the *supplicatio litaniæ id est Kyrie eleison*[24] was part of the ending of every hour,

to follow one of the MSS. by inserting *Kyrie eleison,* that is, the deacon thereby gives the congregation its cue.

[23] Critical text after Capelle, "Le Kyrie . . .," 136-138. There is also a printed text in Migne, PL, CI, 560 f.

[24] *S. Benedicti Regula,* c. 9; cf. c. 12 f., 17.

introducing the *Pater noster* (here used as an oration). In Lauds and Vespers, where there is a more detailed mention of *litania*, the reference is apparently to a fuller text, like that in the *Deprecatio*, while in the other hours only the repeated *Kyrie eleison* seems to have been considered.[25] In the older Gelasianum the litany is mentioned in the rite of the major ordinations; after the candidates have been summoned and the invitation to make objection has been issued, the rubric follows: *Et post modicum intervallum mox incipiant omnes Kyrie eleison cum litania.*[26] From Gregory of Tours (d. 594) we get an account of a penitential procession which Pope Gregory the Great had ordered shortly after his election in the year 590, while pestilence raged in Rome. Seven processions were to assemble at seven Roman basilicas and, with a group of priests in each, were to start for St. Mary Major's in order to beg God's mercy by a *litania septiformis*. The one who told the story to our Frankish historian was himself an eye-witness of the event, and testified how the crowds marched praying through the city: *veniebant utrique chori psallentium ad ecclesiam clamantes per plateas urbis Kyrie eleison.*[27] It is plain that this *Kyrie eleison* was not the entire text, that it was the answer of the throng of people to the invocations spoken by the groups of priests.[28] This manner of saying the litany was retained later and (within limits) even today for the Rogation procession which itself obtained the name of *litania.*[29]

The litany at the beginning of Mass had at any rate undergone a change at the time of Gregory the Great, perhaps partly through his work. In a letter to Bishop John of Syracuse, Gregory took pains to deny that he had been introducing Greek practices into Rome. In this connection he refers also to the *Kyrie.*[30] Gregory stresses the differences from the Greek manner,

[25] In this sense Callewaert, "Les étapes," 29-32.

[26] I, 20 (Wilson, 22).

[27] Gregory of Tours, *Hist. Francorum*, X, 1 (PL, LXXI, 529 B).

[28] *Utrique chori* = the double choir composed of priests and people. Cf. Batiffol, *Leçons*, 106-108.

Septiformis is the term applied to the litany because each of the invocations was repeated seven times; Batiffol, 110 f. A *litania septena* is also mentioned for Holy Saturday in later sources, like the *Gregorianum* of Ménard (PL, LXXVIII, 88 C). According to *Ordo Rom. I,* app., n. 10 (PL, LXXVIII, 964), it was first recited as a *septena,* then as a *quina,* lastly as a *terna*; cf. the *Ordo* of St. Amand (Duchesne, *Christian Worship*, 475) and the Antiphonary of Corbie (Hesbert, n. 79 b); similar data for the *litania maior* in the *Ordo Rom. XI,* n. 57 (PL,

LXXVIII, 1048). Even in the 15-16th century there is witness to the *litania septena* in the Franciscan Missal in Martène, 1, 1, 18, XIX (I, 216 B) and even in the beginning of the 18th in de Moléon, 223 f., 430.

According to present-day rubrics, too, there is a doubling of the invocations on Holy Saturday—each invocation and its response sung first by the chanters, then repeated in full. And for all outdoor processions this is also the accepted method of performing the litany, although it is technically almost impossible to expect the people to repeat the longer texts.

[29] For the history of the litany (*litania*), see R. Hierzegger, "Collecta und Statio," ZkTh, LX (1936), 511-554.

[30] Gregory the Great, *Ep.,* IX, 12 (PL, LXXVII, 956): *Kyrie eleison autem nos neque diximus neque dicimus sicut a Græcis dicitur, quia in Græcis omnes*

which must have been very familiar to him from his stay in Byzantium. The differences are chiefly these: Amongst the Greeks all answer *Kyrie eleison* together, both clergy and people, whereas in Rome the clergy sing and then the people respond. Moreover the Greeks have only the invocation *Kyrie eleison* whereas in Rome the *Christe eleison* is also used, being said as often as the *Kyrie*. Finally Gregory remarks that on ordinary days they leave out whatever is usually said besides the *Kyrie eleison* and *Christe eleison*, in order to linger longer on these two invocations.

What was omitted on ordinary days can only have been the invocations of the litany. On solemn services, therefore, they were still in use, but the manner of rendering included a pre-intonation of the *Kyrie* or *Christe*; the chanters or the *schola* included the *Kyrie* and *Christe* in the invocation, and they were then repeated by the people.[31] In line with this was the practice which lasted far into the Middle Ages—as late as the twelfth century—of omitting the *Kyrie* at Mass on days when the *collecta* with its protracted litany preceded the *statio*.[32] The same thing happened at the major ordinations, since the litany followed.[33] Even at present the litany (with its *Kyrie*) which is said on Holy Saturday counts for the *Kyrie* of the Mass.[34] In all these instances there is a survival of the original form of the *Kyrie* as part of a larger, more complete form of prayer.[35]

A short invocation of this type, using only a word or two to express our beggary, implied, by its very brevity, a tendency to independence and to iteration. This tendency would be all the more pronounced if the *Kyrie eleison* had been known already in pre-Christian antiquity as an independent formula, as a cry repeated many times over, as an acclamation. Actu-

---

simul dicunt, apud nos autem a clericis dicitur et a populo respondetur, et totidem vicibus etiam Christe eleison dicitur, quod apud Græcos nullo modo dicitur. In cotidianis autem missis aliqua, quæ dici solent, tacemus, tantummodo Kyrie eleison et Christe eleison dicimus, ut in his deprecationis vocibus paulo diutius occupemur.
[31] Callewaert, "Les étapes," 36, understands *a clericis* in this wise, that the *schola* took up melodically the invocation which had been delivered by the deacon or lector, e.g. (n. I): *divinæ bonitatis opulentiam deprecamur;* the *Kyrie* cry would be merely spoken by the people as a response; this partition must have been determinative for Gelasius in designing the text; see *ibid., 27.* But with Gregory the *Kyrie* was said by the clerics.
[32] *Ordo* of St. Amand (Duchesne, 475); *Ordo* for Ash Wednesday (9th century) appended to *Ordo Rom. I,* n. 25 (PL, LXXVIII, 950 A); and even as late as

the twelfth century the rule is still outlined in full form in *Ordo Rom. XI* (c. 1140), n. 35 (PL, LXXVIII, 1039): *Quando efficitur Collecta, ad missam non cantatur Kyrie, quia regionarius dixit in litania.* Cf. *ibid.,* n. 34, 63 (1038 C, 1050 A).
[33] *Ordo Rom. VIII,* n. 3 (PL, LXXVIII, 1001).
[34] In the same sense we read in the oldest Antiphonary MSS.: *ad introitum letania;* then follows: *Gloria in excelsis Deo.* Hesbert, n. 79.
[35] From what has been said it follows that the litany under consideration, an older form of our present-day litany of All Saints, could not have represented the litany from which our *Kyrie* derived. But the close intrinsic kinship that existed between it and the *Deprecatio Gelasii* which we have had in view would have been sufficient to establish such a rule.

ally the *Kyrie eleison*, freed from any ties with other prayer-forms and repeated over and over again, is found in the liturgical prayer of the Orient as an ancient traditional usage. And time-honored numbers play a part here: a twelvefold *Kyrie eleison* at the opening of every hour in the Byzantine liturgy, a fortyfold *Kyrie* at the close of every little hour.[36] The fervent *ektene* (ἐκτενὴς ἱκεσία) after the Gospel in a Byzantine Mass has a threefold *Kyrie eleison* after each invocation.[37] The threefold *Kyrie* also appears elsewhere, especially near the end of the *ektene*,[38] and also independent of such a litany. Aurelian of Arles (d. 550) had his monks begin and end the psalmody at every hour of the Office with a *Kyrie* said three times.[39] The Lauds of the Milanese liturgy still contains a threefold *Kyrie* and, near the end, a twelvefold *Kyrie*.[40] Likewise our present-day litanies still have a threefold *Kyrie eleison, Christe eleison, Kyrie eleison* at the beginning and at the end.[41] A parallel to this independence and iteration of a response is to be seen in the history of the alleluia, which served first of all as a refrain which the people sang as they joined in at each verse of the responsorial psalm-chants. It soon turned into a cry of jubilee which could be repeated as long and as loud as you please.[42] The Roman Breviary also has a threefold alleluia on occasion after occasion, and before Pius X it had a ninefold alleluia on the *Dominica in albis*.

We come upon this independent *Kyrie* in the first Roman *Ordo*, even though the service described is a festive one. According to this arrangement, the petition—a song now—is repeated until the pope, after saluting the altar and going to his *cathedra*, turns to the east and gives a signal.[43] But not long afterwards—in fact, still in the eighth century—a specified arrangement for this signal is found, as we learn from other *ordines*, which give us further details about the *Kyrie*-chant. The *schola* sings *Kyrie eleison*, which is repeated three times—that is, most likely, till the number three has been reached. (Custom had thus consecrated the number three.) Then the pope gave a signal for the *Christe eleison*, which was repeated

---

[36] See the list in Dölger, 64, note 2.

[37] Brightman, 373 f.

[38] So in the Greek liturgy of St. James: Brightman, 38; 48.

[39] Aurelian of Arles, *Regula ad monachos* (PL, LXVIII, 393 B).

[40] S. Bäumer, *Geschichte des Breviers* (Freiburg, 1895), 619. The Milanese Mass, too, has a threefold *Kyrie* not only after the *Gloria* but after the Gospel and at the close.

[41] The norm is even plainer in medieval texts of the litany; see the beginning of the litany with a triple *Kyrie eleison* in

Cod. Ottobon. 313: H. A. Wilson, *The Gelasian Sacramentary* (HBS, XLIX), pp. XXXI-XXXIV, and even much later, e.g., the 13th century *Ordinarium* of Lyons, with a triple *Kyrie* and a triple *Christe* at the start: E. Martène, *Tractatus de antiqua ecclesiæ disciplina* (Lyons, 1706), 520, 524.

[42] F. Cabrol, DACL, I, 1229-1246, especially 1234.

[43] *Ordo Rom. I*, n. 9 (PL, LXXVIII, 942): *Schola vero, finita antiphona, inponit Kyrie eleison. Prior vero scholæ custodit ad pontificem, ut ei annuat, si vult mutare numerum litaniæ.*

three times in like manner; then another signal for the triple repetition of the *Kyrie,* and so the end of the chant.⁴⁴

This arrangement based on threes corresponds to a primitive sacral usage, found even in pre-Christian worship, frequent, too, in ancient Rome.⁴⁵ As was to be expected, the number received a new significance once it reached Gallic territory where the struggle against Arianism still rumbled and boomed occasionally. Here it took a trinitarian turn. We meet it in Amalar,⁴⁶ and the same meaning is impressed on us in all our prayer books and Mass interpretations and Mass devotions, right up to the present: God the Father is invoked three times, God the Son three times, and God the Holy Ghost three times.⁴⁷ There is the appearance of truth in the fact that the second group uses the word *Christus.* But in reality the *Kyrie* groups, too, are directed to Christ. That is the Pauline and primitive Christian usage, where χύριος is generally applied to Christ. And it corresponds to the whole tradition in which the *Kyrie eleison* itself arose. True, in some instances in the early period the connection with the Godhead is clear. At other times the meaning of χύριος is undetermined, and it might well be, considering its use as a simple invocation. But in most cases, especially within the Eastern diaconal litanies, where the χύριε ἐλέησον is indigenous, the whole construction of the various invocations of the deacon makes it more or less clear that the χύριε has reference to Christ.⁴⁸ The same is true in the Western litanies; in the oldest versions all the invocations from beginning to *Agnus Dei,* are addressed exclusively to Christ; the invocations of the saints are later insertions.⁴⁹

---

⁴⁴ *Ordo* of St. Amand (Duchesne, *Christian Worship,* 258): *annuit pontifex ut dicatur Kyrie eleison. Et dicit schola et repetunt regionarii. . . . Dum repetierunt tertio, iterum annuit pontifex ut dicatur Christe eleison. . . . Et dum compleverint novem vicibus, annuit ut finiatur.* Somewhat different in the *Capitulare eccl. ord.,* which speaks of two choirs, standing opposite the altar and bowed towards the East, each singing the Kyrie nine times very slowly: *. . . et sic incurvati contra altare ad orientem adorant dicentes Kyrie eleison prolixe unusquisque chorus per novem vicibus.* (Silva-Tarouca, 205; cf. 196 f.).

⁴⁵ Dölger, *Sol Salutis,* 95-103.

There is hardly any need to follow Dix, *The Shape of the Liturgy,* 461 f., in tracing the plan of the ninefold *Kyrie* to Milanese practice, especially since this practice at the time is quite obscured. Rather we might recall the south-Gallic parallels remarked in note·39 above.

⁴⁶ Amalar, *De off. eccl.,* III, 6 (PL, CV, 1113 f.).

It is rather surprising that the *Expositio* of Amalar (of Trier?), which has been traced back to the sea-voyage of 813-814, distinguishes only between *Kyrie eleison* and *Christe eleison,* the former directed to the *forma Dei,* the latter to the *forma servi;* Gerbert, *Monumenta,* II, 150. Cf. the *Expositio 'Missa pro multis',* ed. Hanssens (*Eph. liturg.,* 1930), 33.

⁴⁷ In some few of the *Kyrie*-tropes which developed since the 9th century (see *infra*), the entire piece is still often addressed to Christ; Blume-Bannister, *Tropen des Missale,* I (*Analecta hymnica,* 47), p. 45 f., 101, 102, 103 f., etc.

⁴⁸ Jungmann, *Die Stellung Christi im liturgischen Gebet,* 191 f.

⁴⁹ The invocation of the three divine Persons and of the Holy Trinity after the *Christe audi nos* at the start of the litany does not appear in the oldest texts that have survived. In an English MS. of the

This ninefold invocation of Christos, the Kyrios, serves even at present as a kind of prelude leading very suitably to the priest's oration—an oration which gathers up the prayer of the Church and brings it, through Christ, to the throne of God.[50]

Although we find that in Gregory the Great the arrangement for the *Kyrie* is still: *a clericis dicitur et a populo respondetur*, in the first Roman *Ordo*, the *schola* appears as the only performer. It is the job of the *schola* to sing the *Kyrie*—or perhaps more correctly, to intone it and sing the first part. There is no express statement that no one else participates in the singing, but the directions are all given to the *schola*; it is the *prior scholæ* who has to watch out for the pope's signal to conclude the singing.[51]

8th century the litany begins *Christe audi nos,* then follow invocations of the saints and lastly *Agnus Dei;* A. B. Kuypers, *The Book of Cerne* (Cambridge, 1902), 211 f. In the Sacramentary of Gellone written *circa* 780 the litany on Holy Saturday took the following form: On the way to the baptismal font, *Kyrie eleison;* upon arrival, *Christe audi nos* several times; then the invocations of the saints, plus *Propitius esto,* etc., *Agnus Dei, Christe audi nos*—the same series as today; close with a triple *Kyrie.* Martène, 1. 1, 18, VI (I, 184).

In the *Ordo* of St. Amand the litany that is intoned before the stational church is given as follows: *Kyrie eleison* (3 times), *Christe audi nos,* invocations of the saints, then *Propitius esto,* etc., including the invocation that plainly addresses Christ, *Per crucem tuam,* at the end 3 times *Agnus Dei, Christe audi nos* and again a triple *Kyrie.* Duchesne, *Christian Worship,* 475.

The litany of the Stowe Missal (9th century), which reverts to a Græco-Roman model at the end of the 7th century (Bishop, *Liturgica historica,* 142 ff.), begins: *Christe audi nos* (3 times), *Kyrie eleison,* and the saints' invocations follow; Warner, *The Stowe Missal* (HBS, XXXII), 3.

Further examples of a similar sort from the 9th-10th century: H. A. Wilson, *The Gregorian Sacramentary* (HBS, 49), pp. XXXI-XXXIV; Gerbert, *Monumenta vet. lit. Alam.,* II, 7 f.; H. Ménard in the notes to the *Gregorianum* (PL, LXXVIII, 386 ff., 485, 530 ff.); J. Mabillon, *Analecta* (PL, CXXXVIII, 885);

Beck, *Kirchliche Studien,* 383-387.

It was during the high tide of the Middle Ages that the textual pattern expressing the Trinity, *Kyrie eleison, Christe eleison, Kyrie eleison,* was formed as we now have it at the beginning of the litany as well as at the *Preces* in the office (or as a substitute for these); at this period, too, are inserted the explicit invocations of the three Persons and the Trinity: *Pater de coelis,* etc. It is curious that this insertion is still wanting in today's litany for the dying, *Rituale Rom.,* V, 7, 3.

Suarez, *De oratione,* I, 9, 12 f. (*Opp.,* ed. Berton, 14, 34), faces the objection that this separate invocation of the three divine Persons compromises the unity of the divine nature; he justifies it only in the sense that thus is ackowledged a belief in the difference of the Persons and in their true godhead. Similarly J. Maldonat, *De cæremoniis,* II, 12 (in F. A. Zaccaria, *Bibliotheca rit.,* II, 2 [Rome, 1781], 79), stresses the view that these invocations are not properly addressed to the Son and to the Holy Ghost, *sed ad Deum per enumeratas personas.*

[50] Cf. *supra,* p. 264. f.

The precise meaning of this invocation of Christ who gathers us and heals us, who desires to teach us and even feed us, is handled excellently in an article by J. Gülden, "Kyrie eleison": *Parochia* (ed. by K. Borgmann, Colmar o. J., 1943), 155 f.

[51] *Ordo Rom. I,* 9 (PL, LXXVIII, 942): *Schola vero finita antiphona imponit Kyrie eleison. Prior vero scholæ custodit ad pontificem, ut ei annuat, si*

The Roman *Ordo* of St. Amand confirms this description and adds the detail, that the repetition of the song intoned by the *schola* is the duty of the *regionarii*, that is, of the subdeacons who were organized in Rome according to regions.[52] The people no longer participate, at least in these grander pontifical services. Of course the possibility is not excluded that, in simpler surroundings and under other conditions, the *Kyrie* still remained the people's song. This was surely true in the lands of the North,[53] where *Kyrioleis* was used as a refrain in folk-songs for many centuries, and the "Leise" (Fr. *lais*) represented a special class of spiritual folk-songs.

But at the beginning of Mass, the clergy forming the choir took over the singing of the *Kyrie*, at least in the larger churches where the clergy were numerous—and it is about such churches that most of the accounts are written.[54] We need not necessarily think that the intonation and first-singing was done by a *schola cantorum*; in fact, as a part of the clergy, it was not very carefully distinguished from the rest. Instead the singers, it seems, were divided into two semi-choruses, and thus the tradition that the *Kyrie* was an antiphonal chant was retained. At first the nine invocations of one chorus were, as we have seen, repeated by the other; later the two choirs divided the nine invocations between them.[55] It was but a step to have the first of each of the three sung by one choir and then repeated twice by the other choir, a mode of rendition many propose at the present.[56] But even in the twelfth century it was customary for the choirs simply to alternate, exactly as the priest and the Mass-server alternate while saying the prayer.[57]

---

vult mutare numerum litaniæ. Cf. *Ordo Rom. II*, 5.

[52] Duchesne, *Christian Worship*, 458: *Dicit schola et repetunt regionarii.*
Cf. Nickl, *Der Anteil des Volkes*, 17.
There is mention of two choirs also in the *Capitulare eccl. ord.* (Silva-Tarouca, 205); cf. note 44 above.

[53] Cf. the decree of Bishop Herard of Tours, *Capitula* (558), circa 16 (Hardouin, V, 451): *Gloria Patri ac Sanctus atque credulitas et Kyrie eleison a cunctis reverenter canatur.* The peculiar sequence in the enumeration awakens the doubt whether it is the *Kyrie* at the beginning of Mass that is being mentioned; cf. the data in Nickl, 17-19.
In processions and the like we continue to find the *Kyrie* sung by the people even later, and also at Mass itself, namely after the sermon, in connection with the ancient Prayer of the Faithful; see on this Honorius Augustod. (12th century),

Gemma an., I, 19 (PL, CLXXII, 550 C); Durandus, IV, 25, 14.

[54] Cf. *supra*, p. 124, note 120. See Sicard of Cremona, *Mitrale*, III, 2 (PL, CCXIII, 96 C; 97 B), for the *clerus* and *chorus* as performers of the *Kyrie*-chants.
Innocent III, *De s. alt. mysterio*, II, 19 (PL, CCXVII, 809 C), who speaks of the *chorus;* likewise Durandus, IV, 12, 1.
Even Berthold of Regensburg (d. 1272) still proposes the older usage, though not very enthusiastically (Pfeiffer, I, 496): The laity ought to sing this; it would be all the more correct.

[55] *Ordo eccl. Lateran.* (Fischer, 80, 1. 31): *Deinde Kyrie eleison per distinctiones, sicut mos est, inter se dividunt.*

[56] M. Daras, "Le Kyrie eleison" (*Cours et Conférences*, VI [Louvain, 1928], 67-79), 78.

[57] *Liber usuum O. Cist.*, II, 62 (PL, CLXVI, 1435 f.): only the last *Kyrie* is sung by both choruses together. (The

The plain litany-quality of the old *Kyrie* chants is still recognizable in the Gregorian melody assigned to it in the Requiem Mass where the same simple tune recurs eight times and only in the ninth is there any embellishment.[58] But the process of enhancing the musical form of the *Kyrie* made quick progress, right from the time its performance was given over to the *schola*, as we have seen indicated in the first Roman *Ordo*. When Gregorian chant flourished anew, in the tenth and succeeding centuries, many of the elaborate *Kyrie* melodies of the Roman *Kyriale* were composed.[59] The titles which they bear give us a hint of another remarkable and colorful development in the evolution of the simple *Kyrie* text, the so-called trope. Amalar already suggests a forerunner of this type of troping, for he has the singers chant a fuller text (he is, indeed, merely paraphrasing the contents of their song): *Kyrie eleison, Domine Pater, miserere; Christe eleison, miserere qui nos redemisti sanguine tuo; Kyrie eleison, Domine, Spiritus Sancte, miserere.*[60] But from this time on, from the ninth to the sixteenth century, a full literature of *Kyrie* tropes is developed. Every church possessed a dozen or so, some purely local, others spread far and wide. The collection in the *Analecta hymnica* covers 158 complete numbers.[61] Every one of the nine invocations was amplified into a full verse line in such a way that the notes of the melismas were distributed over the complete text. In rendering this chant one choir would often take up the trope while the other sang the original *Kyrie* with its melismas, till both came together on the word *eleison*. It is from the first lines of these tropes that we derive the labels which many of the melodies of the *Kyriale* bear: *Lux et origo; Kyrie Deus sempiterne; Cunctipotens genitor Deus; Cum iubilo; Alme pater; Orbis factor; Pater cuncta.* As an example let us look at the trope of the first Gregorian Mass; its rhythm follows the melody simply, although several others employ definite verse forms like the hexameter.

1.

a.	b.	c.
Lux et origo	*In cuius nutu*	*Qui solus potes*
lucis, summe Deus,	*constant cuncta, clemens*	*misereri, nobis*
eleison; Kyrie eleison.	*eleison; Kyrie eleison.*	*eleison; Kyrie eleison.*

Roman *Graduale* prescribes something like this, too.)

[58] According to Durandus, IV, 12, 4, the ninth *Kyrie* in some churches had the form: *Kyrie eleison imas* (κύριε ἐλέησον ἡμᾶς).

[59] Cf. Ursprung, *Die Kath. Kirchenmusik,* 57.

[60] Amalar, *De off. eccl.,* III, 6 (PL, CV, 1113 f.).

[61] Blume-Bannister, *Tropen des Missale,* I (*Analecta hymnica,* 47), p. 43-216.

Cf. Blume, "Poesie des Hochamtes im Mittelalter, Die Kyrie-tropen," *Stimmen aus Maria-Laach,* 71 (1906, II), 18-38.

2.

a.
O mundi redemptor
salus et humana
rex pie, Christe,
eleison; Christe eleison.

b.
Per crucem redemptis
a morte perenni,
spes nostra, Christe,
eleison; Christe eleison.

c.
Qui es verbum Patris,
verbum caro factum,
lux vera, Christe,
eleison; Christe eleison.

3.

a.
Adonai, Domine,
Deus, iuste iudex,
eleison; Kyrie eleison.

b.
Qui machinam gubernas
rerum, alme Pater,
eleison; Kyrie eleison.

c.
Quem solum laus et honor
decet, nunc et semper
eleison; Kyrie eleison.[62]

It is clear that such artistic productions could be performed only by a skilled choir. For some of the tropes even many-voiced melodies appear in the thirteenth century.[63] The tropes themselves were not included in the Missal of Pius V, thanks to the stricter tastes of his century. The monumental *Kyrie* was thus freed of overgrowth. But at the same time polyphonic music set to work to give this ninefold plea of mankind to the *Kyrios* a full musical expression.

Originally the celebrating priest took no part in the *Kyrie*. For that reason it is not mentioned in most Mass Ordinaries, not even in those that contain all the texts of the prayers at the foot of the altar, or of the offertory. This held true for all Masses celebrated with singing, right down to the late Middle Ages. It was not till the thirteenth century, when the general principle was formulated that the priest had to read the variable texts from the missal, that a like prescription was made in regard to the *Kyrie*; the celebrant says the *Kyrie* together with his assistant (or assistants).[64] But this novelty did not take everywhere at once. The 1290 Mass *Ordo* of the papal chapels, although it stipulates that the priest should read the introit *cum ministris suis*, says nothing of the sort for the *Kyrie*[65]; but a few centuries later the papal chapels also followed the general custom.[66]

For private Mass, on the other hand, even the eighth-century Archcantor's writings included the *Kyrie eleison*, along with the introit, in the prayers for the priest; he is to say it nine times, bowing low all the while.[67] There is no explicit mention here—nor for some time later[68]—of any par-

[62] Blume, 69 f. In a second text, emphatically stressing the Trinitarian outlook, *ibid.*, 70 f.
[63] Blume-Bannister, p. 92 (on n. 28); 160 (on n. 99).
[64] *Ordinarium O.P.* of 1256 (Guerrini, 235); *Liber ordinarius* of Liége (Volk, 89, 1.30).
The same direction in other Mass-*Ordines* of the late Middle Ages: Martène, 1, 4, XIX, XXIII f., XXXVII (I, 605 B, 616 B, 626 E, 681 B).

[65] Brinktrine (*Eph. Liturg.*, 1937), 201.
[66] *Ordo Rom. XIV*, n. 71 (PL, LXXVIII, 1186 A): cf. *ibid.*, n. 61; 68 (1175 B, 1183 B).
[67] *Capitulare eccl. ord.* (Silva-Tarouca, 205, 1. 11): *Si autem singulus fuerit sacerdos, novem tantum vicibus inclinatus adorando dicit Kyrie eleison, et postea erigit se.* Cf. *ibid.*, 207.
[68] The rhymed commentary of the 12th century remarks only this about the priest: *"Ein Kiriel'er danne singet"*: then

ticipation by the server. Even at solemn service, where the assistants are mentioned as taking part, it seems that the nine invocations were said by all together, since there is no indication of any apportionment.[69] If later on the alternation of the nine between priest and those around him became common, the cause is to be traced to the example of the sung *Kyrie* with its double choir. There is record, however, of another manner of distributing the invocations, the priest taking the first three *Kyries*, the serving cleric the three *Christes*, and the priest the last three *Kyries*.[70]

The priest used often to say the *Kyrie*, as he does the introit, on the Epistle side of the altar.[71] This is still the practice of the Carthusians, the Carmelites and the Dominicans, and we also do the same at a solemn high Mass. It has been suggested that the change to the center was influenced by the wish to stress the prayer-quality of the *Kyrie*; the priest therefore stands facing the image of his crucified Lord, to whom he directs his appeal.[72]

10. *Gloria in excelsis*

The *Gloria*, like the *Kyrie*, was not created originally for the liturgy of the Mass. It is an heirloom from the treasure of ancient Church hymns, a precious remnant of a literature now almost buried but once certainly very rich, a literature of songs for divine service written in the early Church in imitation of the biblical lyrics, especially the psalms. These lyrics were called *psalmi idiotici*, psalms by private persons in contrast to those of Holy Scripture.[1] They are, for the most part, rude creations, and like the biblical psalms and canticles are not constructed on rhythmic and metrical principles. In their literary expression, too, they hold pretty close to

he sings a kyriel. Leitzmann (*Kleine Texte*, 54), 18, 1. 8.

[69] See the passages cited above, note 66.

Cf. also, e.g., the Furtmeyr Missal of 1481 (facsimile of fol. 33 in Ursprung, *Die kath. Kirchenmusik, frontispiece*), where between introit and *Gloria* of a festal Mass the *Kyrie* is inserted nine times without any further remark.

[70] *Ordinarium* of Coutances (1557) : Legg, *Tracts*, 58.

The original relationship of chanters and people, and therefore the basic character of the *Kyrie* as a people's prayer is best achieved in the method of distribution mentioned above, p. 341, where the new text invariably falls to the lot of the choir, that is, of the "intoners."

[71] Lebrun, *Explication*, I, 144.

Cf. *supra*, p. 333.

[72] P. J. B. de Herdt, *sacræ liturgiæ praxis* (2nd ed., Louvain, 1852), II, 84. Cf. also *infra*, p. 370, note 53, regarding the handling of the conclusion of the oration.

[1] J. Kroll, *Die christliche Hymnodik bis zu Klemens von Alexandreia* (*Braunsberger Vorlesungsverzeichnis*, 1921 and 1921-2) ; *idem.*, "Hymn" in E. Hennecke, *Neutestamentl. Apokryphen*, 296-601.

Eisenhofer, I, 207-210.

The expression *psalmi idiotici* is used by the Council of Laodicea (4th century) in contrast to the biblical chants; can. 59 (Mansi, II, 574). See Batiffol, *History of the Roman Breviary* (trans. A. Baylay; London, 1912), 6-8. Cf. also A. Fortescue, "Gloria in Excelsis Deo", CE, VI: 583-585.

their biblical models, and yet in them the religious inspiration of those centuries live on perceptibly. The line begun in the New Testament with the *Magnificat* and Zachary's song of praise and the canticle of aged Simeon, is continued in these works. Few, however, have remained in use to the present, among them the Φῶς ἱλαρόν, already mentioned by Basil, which is still used in the Byzantine liturgy, the *Te decet laus*, which is in use in the monastic liturgy, and the *Te Deum* and the *Gloria* which survive in our Roman liturgy. This last, often called the Greater Doxology,[2] was already so highly esteemed even in the ancient Church that it outlived the fate that overtook so many songs which perished as the result of an adverse attitude towards church hymns created merely *humano studio*.[3]

In the textual tradition of the *Gloria* three principal versions can be distinguished[4]: (1) The Syrian version from the Nestorian liturgy[5]; (2) the Greek version from the *Apostolic Constitutions*[6]; and (3) the Greek version from the Byzantine liturgy, which is found already in the Codex Alexandrinus of the New Testament[7] and which coincides in all essentials with our Western version. Since we can presume that we are acquainted with the last of these, we shall start by comparing the two forms mentioned first.

Syrian Version	Apost. Const. VII, 47
Glory to God in the highest	Δόξα ἐν ὑψίστοις θεῷ
and on earth peace	καὶ ἐπὶ γῆς εἰρήνη,
and a good hope to men.	ἐν ἀνθρώποις εὐδοκία.
We worship thee,	αἰνοῦμέν σε, ὑμνοῦμεν σε, • • • •
we glorify thee,	δοξολογοῦμέν σε
we exalt thee,	προσκυνοῦμέν σε
Being who art from eternity,	
hidden and incomprehensible Nature,	
Father, Son, and Holy Ghost.	
King of kings, and Lord of lords,	
who dwellest in the excellent light,	
Whom no son of man hath seen, nor can see,	

[2] To distinguish it from the little doxology, the *Gloria Patri*.
[3] Cf. IV Council of Toledo (633), can. 13 (Mansi, X, 622 f.).
For the whole study cf. Cl. Blume, "Der Engelhymnus Gloria in excelsis Deo. Sein Ursprung und seine Entwicklung," *Stimmen aus Maria-Laach*, LXXIII (1907), 43-62; J. Brinktrine, "Zur Entstehung und Erklärung des Gloria in excelsis Deo," *Röm. Quartalschrift*, XXXV (1927), 303-315.
[4] A. Baumstark, *Die Textüberlieferung*

des Hymnus angelicus: Hundert Jahre Markus-und-Weber-Verlag (Bonn, 1909), 83-87.
[5] A. J. Maclean, *East Syrian Daily Offices* (London, 1894), 170-171.
[6] *Const. Ap.*, VII, 47 (Funk, I, 454 f.).
[7] Text and variants in Funk, I, 455, note.
In Athanasius, *De virginitate*, c. 20, our hymn is cited as a morning prayer—unfortunately, however, only the beginning is quoted; see Blume, 59, note 2. Cf. *ibid.*, 55 regarding a questionable citation in Chrysostom.

who alone art holy,
(and) alone mighty, (and) alone immortal.

We confess thee through the Mediator
of our blessings,

διὰ τοῦ μεγάλου ἀρχιερέως,
σὲ τὸν ὄντα θεόν,
ἀγέννητον, ἕνα, ἀπρόσιτον, μονον,
διὰ τὴν μεγάλην σου δόξαν,
κύριε βασιλεῦ ἐπουράνιε,
θεὲ πάτερ παντοκράτορ.

Jesus Christ, the Saviour of the world
and the Son of the Highest.
O Lamb of the living God,
who takest away the sins of the world,
have mercy on us.
Thou who sittest at the right hand of
thy Father,

κύριε ὁ θεός, ὁ πατὴρ τοῦ Χριστοῦ
τοῦ ἀμώμου ἀμνοῦ
ὃς αἴρει τὴν ἀμαρτίαν τοῦ κόσμου,

receive our request.
For thou art our God,
and thou art our Lord,
and thou art our King,
and thou art our Saviour,
and thou art the forgiver of our sins.

πρόσδεξαι τὴν δέησιν ἡμῶν,
ὁ καθήμενος ἐπὶ τῶν Χερουβίμ,
ὅτι σὺ μόνος ἅγιος,
σὺ μόνος κύριος,
ὁ θεὸς καὶ πατὴρ 'Ιησοῦ Χριστοῦ[9]
τοῦ θεοῦ πάσης γενητῆς φύσεως
τοῦ βασιλέως ἡμῶν,

The eyes of all men hang on thee,
Jesus Christ.
Glory to God thy Father
and to thee and to the Holy Ghost,
for ever, Amen.

δι' οὗ σοι δόξα, τιμὴ καὶ σέβας.

Aside, perhaps, from the great wealth of attributes predicated of God and Christ, the feature that strikes us in these two versions as different from the form familiar to us, is that the praise is directed to God through Christ, the great high-priest. This is typical of the prayer language of the first centuries. True, the version contained in the *Apostolic Constitutions* can hardly be original in its entirety. Throughout the hymn the prayer is addressed through Christ to the Father, and near the end the line of thought seems somewhat strained. All this is rather the work of the redactor,[9] who appears to have obtruded the notion of mediatorship almost to excess. But the appearance of the formula also in the East Syrian liturgy, where the mediation-formula is no longer found in the orations,[10] proves that even this turn of expression is ancient tradition. The Syrian version probably gives us the basic form of the hymn, not indeed, in its amplifications, but at least in its general structure.

But let us confine our discussion to the western version of our venerable hymn. The oldest witness for the Latin text is the manuscript Antiphonary

[8] Thus according to *Cod. Vat.* 2089; see Funk, 456, apparatus. Cf. C. H. Turner, *Journal of theol. studies,* XVI (1915), 56.

[9] Jungmann, *Die Stellung Christi,* 13 f.
[10] *Ibid.,* 65, 67; cf. 144 ff.

of Bangor, which originated about 690.[11] It forms a connecting link with the Greek tradition, as we can see by comparing it with the nearly duplicate text of the Codex Alexandrinus.

Cod. Alexandrinus	Bangor
῞Υμνος ἑωθινός	Ad Vesperum et ad Matutinam.
1. Δόξα ἐν ὑψίστοις Θεῷ, καὶ ἐπὶ γῆς εἰρηνή, ἐν ἀνθρώποις εὐδοκία.	1. Gloria in excelsis Deo, et in terra pax hominibus bonæ voluntatis.
2. Αἰνοῦμέν σε, εὐλογοῦμέν σε, προσκυνοῦμέν σε, δοξολογοῦμέν σε.	2. Laudamus te; benedicimus te; adoramus te; glorificamus te; magnificamus te.
3. Εὐχαριστοῦμέν σοι διὰ τὴν μεγάλην σου δόξαν, Κύριε, βασιλεῦ ἐπουράνιε, Θεὲ πατήρ, παντοκράτωρ.	3. Gratias agimus tibi propter magnam misericordiam tuam, Domine, rex cælestis, Deus pater, omnipotens.
4. Κύριε, υἱὲ μονογενῆ, 'Ιησοῦ Χριστὲ, καὶ ἅγιον Πνεῦμα.	4. Domine, Fili unigenite, Jesu Christe, Sancte Spiritus Dei. Et omnes dicimus Amen.
5. Κύριε, ὁ Θεὸς, ὁ ἀμνὸς τοῦ Θεοῦ, ὁ υἱὸς τοῦ πατρὸς, ὁ αἴρων τὰς ἀμαρτίας τοῦ κόσμου, ἐλέησον ἡμᾶς.	5. Domine, Fili Dei Patris, agne Dei, qui tollis peccatum mundi, miserere nobis.
6. ῾Ο αἴρων τὰς ἀμαρτίας τοῦ κόσμου, ἐλέησον ἡμᾶς, πρόσδεξαι τὴν δέησιν ἡμῶν, ὁ καθήμενος ἐν δεξιᾷ τοῦ πατρός, ἐλέησον ἡμᾶς.	6. Suscipe. orationem nostram; qui sedes ad dexteram Dei Patris, miserere nobis.
7. ῞Οτι σὺ εἶ μόνος ἅγιος, σὺ εἶ μόνος κύριος, 'Ιησοῦς Χριστὸς, εἰς δόξαν Θεοῦ πατρός. 'Αμήν.	7. Quoniam tu solus sanctus, tu solus Dominus, tu solus gloriosus cum Spiritu Sancto in gloria Dei Patris. Amen.

In the structure of the *Gloria* three sections are plainly discernible; (1) the song of the angels on the night of the Nativity; (2) the praise of God; and (3) the invoking of Christ.

First there is the song of the angels as recorded by St. Luke (2:14). The use of a biblical phrase as the theme at the start of a poem is also found elsewhere in ancient Christian hymns. For instance, the evening hymn which compares with the *Gloria*, a morning hymn, opens with an analogous

[11] F. E. Warren, *The antiphonary of Bangor* (HGS, IV; facsimile and transcription; HBS, X: Text and commentary; London, 1892-1895), fol. 33, p. 31; and commentary, pp. 75-80. The whole version of the present-day text is first found in the Psaltery of Abbot Wolfcoz of St. Gall (9th century); see Blume, 49; references regarding other MSS. and variants, *ibid.*, 47-51. A certain independence is displayed in the ancient Milanese text (DACL, IV, 1534 f.) and in that of the *Antiphonarium mozarabicum* of León; see G. Prado, "Una nueva recension del himne 'Gloria in excelsis'", *Eph. liturg.* XLVI (1932), 481-486.

word of praise utilizing the first verse of Psalm 112: *Laudate pueri Domi-num, laudate nomen Domini.*[12] The same verse is used as the opening of the *Te Deum* in the version found in the Antiphonary of Bangor.[13] And in particular this song of the angels was used as an introduction to prayer.[14]

In all the versions the second section is a praise of God. This consists in a simple accumulation of phrases expressing our activity, and of names for the godhead. In the oldest witnesses of the version we are concerned with, this portion has obtained a certain exclusiveness and independence by making the address to all three divine Persons.[15] The same thing is noticed even earlier in the Syrian version. In the effort to call God by all His grand names it was but a step to rise to the mystery of the Trinity, which had been made known by revelation. There is an exact parallel to be seen in the *Te Deum* where the praise of God also ends in address to the Trinity: *Patrem immensæ maiestatis, venerandum tuum verum et unicum Filium, Sanctum quoque Paraclitum Spiritum.*

And just as in the *Te Deum*, the next section in our present text, clearly distinct from what precedes, is a christological portion; *Domine, Fili uni-genite.* God and Christ—that is not an arbitrary addition nor an unfinished enumeration of the three divine Persons (as some commentators seem to imagine when they make excuses for the fact that the Holy Ghost is mentioned only at the very end, and then only in passing). No, God and Christ are the pillars of the Christian order of the universe: God, the beginning and the end of all things, towards whom all religious seeking is bent and all prayer eventually is turned; but in the Christian order also Christ, the way, the road on which all our God-seeking must be directed. Therefore in St. Paul's letters we find this duality of God and Christ not only in the introductory salutation, but time and time again throughout the writing. And if at times St. Paul rounds out the duality and completes it in the Trinity, this is done not so much to acknowledge the three divine Persons themselves, as rather to mark more distinctly the structure of the Christian order of salvation, in which our ascent to God is vouchsafed through Christ in the Holy Spirit. To this notion the construction of the *Gloria* in its present version corresponds in a very extraordinary way, although the musical compositions of the hymn seldom if ever take note of it. We might add that the two main parts of the hymn are in a way allied to the two members of the introductory biblical motto: To God, glory—we join our voices to the angelic choirs in praising God; to men,

---

[12] *Const. Ap.*, VII, 48 (Funk, I, 456).

[13] Warren, 10.

[14] Cf. Baumstark, *Vom geschichtlichen Werden der Liturgie*, 20, with note 27 (reference to the martyrdom of Cyprian and of Justa).

[15] The same trinitarian termination also in the old Milanese text and in the Mozarabic.

The additional *et Sancte Spiritus* also in a missal of 1519 from Aquileia described by W. Weth, ZkTh, XXXVI (1912), 418.

peace—we turn to Him in whom the peace of heaven was brought to earth, begging Him to fulfill His work in us.

And now let us get down to details.

The oriental liturgies employ the song of the angels as a triple phrase: Δόξα ἐν ὑψίστοις Θεῷ καὶ ἐπὶ γῆς εἰρήνη, ἐν ἀνθρώποις εὐδοκία. This is the form adopted by Luther and the King James Bible: *den Menschen ein Wohlgefallen*—on earth peace, good will towards men. But from the viewpoint of textual criticism the form εὐδοκία in Luke (2:14) is considered untenable; the reading must be εὐδοκίας. This betokens a double phrase in the original text, just as our version has it. But there is another thing to notice. Our ordinary rendering, "Peace on earth to men of good will," does not quite give us the original sense. Εὐδοκία is not the good will of men but the good will of God, God's pleasure, God's favor and grace. The ἄνθρωποι εὐδοκίας are therefore men of God's grace and selection, men to whom the news of God's kingdom has been proclaimed.[16] According to the wording of the text, therefore, there is a limitation in this message of peace: *hominibus bonæ voluntatis*—to those whom God has chosen. But since all men are invited into the kingdom, the only thing clearly enunciated here is that "the children of His kingdom" partake of this peace not because of a turn of fortune's wheel, but because of God's free, merciful decree (cf. Eph. 1:5). The entrance of the Redeemer among the race of men spelt out two things, the glory of God and "peace" for men. Christ's coming to earth really meant the start of Redemption.[17] In this sense it is possible that the angels' song contained not a wish but the expression of a fact, not an optative but a declarative: Glory is given to God and peace to men! It is the same thing that our Lord spoke of at the Last Supper in His great sacerdotal prayer, the only difference being the degree of development: "I have exalted thy glory on earth, by achieving the task which thou gavest me to do."[18] But precisely because the glorification of God and the salvation of mankind was not "achieved" in its fullness till the sacrifice of Christ's Passion, and even then its fruits had still to ripen, and to continue to ripen till the end of time, it is correct to view the angelic song as proclaiming not the work that had already been completed, but the plan and purpose that was yet to be done, step by step: May God be given glory in the highest and may men in His grace find peace! *Gloria sit in excelsis Deo.* And if this was true of the song when the angels sang it, it is truer still when we on earth repeat it. Every day that the Church lives, every time the Church gathers her children in prayer, and particularly when she assembles them for the Eucharist, a new light flashes across

[16] Father Knox's version: "Glory to God in high heaven, and peace on earth to men that are God's friends."

[17] J. Jeremias, Ἄνθρωποι εὐδοκίας: *Zeitschrift f. d. neutest. Wissenschaft,* XXVIII (1929), 13-20.

[18] John 17: 4.

Kindred are the shouts of joy at Christ's entry into Jerusalem, especially Luke 19: 38: "Peace on earth, and glory in heaven above." Cf. Brinktrine, *Zur Entstehung,* 304.

the world and the Church beholds, with mingled joy and longing, the approach of the Kingdom of God, the advent, in spite of every obstacle, of the consummation of the great plan: that glory will come to God, and to men of God's choice, peace and salvation.

In the eastern liturgies which do not use the Greater Doxology at Mass, the opening scriptural words at least are often used, either at the start of the celebration,[19] or at the preparation of the offerings,[20] or at the kiss of peace,[21] or before Communion.[22]

The praises of God, which now follow are plain and clear. We simply list them, inadequate as they are: We praise thee, we bless thee, we glorify thee.[23] The parallels in both of the older versions evidence the fact that the accent is not on the precise and distinctive meaning of each word but on the common basic concept of acclaiming and extolling the greatness of God. If we then construe the next clause, *gratias agimus*, in the same fashion, the pendent phrase, *propter magnam gloriam tuam*, is not so surprising. Still it seems better to take the words at their fullest meaning, for we can really thank God "for His great glory." In the new order of the world, built on grace and love, in which God has given us all things along with His Son (Rom. 8:32), God's kingdom has almost become our kingdom, and the revelation of His glory has become for us an overflowing grace and the beginning of our glory.[24] Still this point of grace must not be overstressed. The magnificent thing about the hymn, and the thing that at the same time makes it so liberal, is the fact that it does not pay God tribute in exact ratio to man's indebtedness, nor does it thank Him only in acknowledgement of benefits received. Love does not recognize any scrupulous distinction; with the pardonable pride of children of God, we direct our glance wholly to God's glory, God's grandeur. We are happy to be allowed to praise His glory.[25] For that reason a song such as this has such wonderful power to free men from any egoistic narrowness and to bring them all together on a higher plane.

The list of God's names which comes next also serves to praise God. These titles follow each other in a distinct gradation[26]; Lord, King of

[19] Nestorian Mass: Brightman, 248, 1. 19; 252, 1. 11; likewise in the Byzantine, *ibid.*, 361, 1. 33.
[20] Liturgy of St. James: Brightman, 45, 1. 3.
[21] Ethiopian liturgy: Brightman, 227, 1. 17.
[22] *Const. Ap.*, VIII, 13, 13 (Brightman, 24, 1. 25).
[23] This expression already in the *Martyrium Polycarpi*, 14, 3: σὲ αἰνῶ, σὲ εὐλογῶ, σὲ δοξάζω. Further parallels in Brinktrine, *Zur Entstehung,* 305-310. Regarding echoes of the acclamations with which the Roman Senate greeted the emperor,

cf. Blume, 56. He is right in saying that words like *laudamus, benedicimus, adoramus,* etc., in this hymn should rather be regarded as reflections of the biblical imperatives (*laudate,* etc.).
[24] Cf. *Did.* 10, 4 (*supra,* p. 12): "Above all, we give thee thanks because thou art mighty." On the other hand, see the wording of the Bangor text, *supra,* p. 349.
[25] For a closer theological study see Gihr, 443-445.
[26] This is especially true if we consider the first *Deus* after *Domine* as purely secondary (see the parallel texts *supra,*

heaven, God, Father, Almighty. The designation, *Deus, Pater omnipotens,* which is also found in the Apostles' Creed, shows again the venerable age of the hymn.

Immediately after this list of God's titles there comes an address to Christ, written in much the same style. It introduces the christological section. The transition is so imperceptible that it goes almost unheeded and we are scarcely aware that something new has started. This can be explained, from the viewpoint of the history of the text, by comparing it with the older versions where an address to the Trinity closed this first section, just as it does in the *Te Deum*; the mention of God the Father was therefore followed by that of the Son and of the Holy Ghost, and at once a new turn of thought set in with an apostrophe to Christ. There is really no doubt about where this section starts. On the other hand, there is no reason for considering this as the beginning of a new theme. Our grateful glance toward God's glory moves naturally on toward Christ, in whom that glory was revealed to us. In this christological section we can distinguish the following framework: (1) the laudatory salutation; (2) the litany-like invocations; (3) the triple predication, *Tu Solus*; and (4) the trinitarian conclusion.

First of all there is a list of names, all of them ancient. They are the same as those found in the oriental creed, in the profession of belief in Christ: Lord, only-begotten Son, Jesus Christ.[27] At the top of the list is the word "Lord," with the connotation of the Pauline κύριος, which is made clear near the end of the hymn in *Tu solus Dominus*. The term "only-begotten Son" also had been highly esteemed in the ancient Church as a special name for Christ.[28] In the *Euchologion* of Serapion the word ὁ μονογενής was often used all by itself as a usual title for Christ.[29] There is a second group of three names, and once again the Kyrios-term *Domine* comes first, in our present-day text amplified to *Domine Deus*, to indicate, no doubt, the essential equality of Father and Son. In the earlier versions this was followed by *Filius Patris*, now transferred to third place obviously because of its special importance. It is a name which appears to say nothing and yet says everything, and it definitely acknowledges our human inability to comprehend the mystery, for Christ is naught else than the radiance of His Father's splendor (Heb. 1:3). Then follows the term *Agnus Dei*, the sacrificial Lamb come from God, a title which refers to Christ's redemptive work. It is no accident that the title "Lamb of God," which recalls our Lord's great mercy, was connected from time immemorial with

p. 349), inserted only to differentiate the word *Domine* (which usually means Christ) in the manner of the Old Testament *Lord God=Yahweh Elohim*.

[27] But with an inversion; cf. in the *Credo* of the Mass: *Et in unum Dominum Jesum Christum, Filium Dei unigentum.*

[28] ὁ μονογενής υἱὸς τοῦ θεοῦ the son of God who, unlike us, "stems from Him in a singular way."

[29] I, 1; II, 1, 3; etc. (Quasten, *Mon.*, 49 ff.).

the cry for mercy in our litanies. Here, too, the term "Lamb of God" is followed by a short litany, likewise composed of three members.[30] But in this case there is a mixture of hymnic predication and pleading. Taking up the words of the Baptist, we remind our Lord of that voluntary abasement to which He, as Lamb of God, subjected Himself; we remind Him of that atoning Passion by which He "took away" the sins of the world; remind Him also of His triumph as He sits, exalted, "at the right hand of the Father,"[31] and there, as Lamb of God, hears the bridal songs of the elect. Thus it is that the same cry breaks forth which was heard in the *Kyrie*: "Have mercy on us, receive our prayer."[32] In order to avoid misunderstanding as much as possible, the Church hesitates to call upon the Savior—through whom she offers her prayer, and of whom it is said that He lives always to make intercession for us—to intercede for us, although there is no theological difficulty to doing so. It seems to suit our reverence and our joy in acknowledging His greatness merely to beg His mercy, for we do not want it to appear even for a moment that He cannot help us through His own power. Still the phrase *suscipe deprecationem nostram* does in some way imply Christ's mediatorship, that office of His which was accented so in older forms of the *Gloria*: Let us lay our pleadings in Thy hands, and carry them up before Thy Father's throne!

By means of a spanning *Quoniam*,[33] the litany once more turns into a word of praise: "For Thou alone art the Holy One, Thou alone art the Lord, thou alone the Most High." In the period when our hymn originated, such expressions very vividly outlined the sharp antithesis between our Catholic worship and heathen worship with its many loosely-given attributes of divinity,[34] its many χύριοι, and its emperor-worship.[35] Above and beyond all these creations of human fancy stands Jesus Christ, radiant and grand, the sole and only Lord. Our own day has great appreciation of this sublime contrast.[36] Taking this as a background there is no need to

[30] See Brinktrine, *Zur Entstehung*, 312 f.

[31] Regarding the text as it appears in the fourth century and the variants, see Blume, 59 f.

[32] The text of an old Milanese Antiphonary which was brought to light by G. Morin here contains an expanded form: . . . *miserere nobis, subveni nobis, dirige nos, conserva nos, munda nos, pacifica nos, libera nos ab inimicis, a tentationibus, ab hæreticis, ab Arianis, a schismaticis, a barbaris; quia tu solus* . . . . H. Leclercq, "Doxologies", DACL, IV, 1534 f.

[33] Cf. the ὅτι at the start of oriental doxologies.

[34] The predicate "holy", ἅγιος, *sanctus*, was originally current among the Semites

as an attribute of the gods; in later paganism the use spread elsewhere; F. Cumont, *Die orientalischen Religionen* (3rd ed.; Leipzig, 1931), 110 f., 266; E. Peterson, Εἷς θεός, (Göttingen, 1926), 135 f.

[35] Cf. A. Deissmann, *Licht vom Osten* 4th ed.; Tübingen, 1923), 287-324; K. Prümm, *Der christliche Glaube und die altheidnische Welt* (Leipzig, 1935), I, 214-225.

[36] Even though today the polytheistic background is lacking, it is not therefore necessary to follow L. A. Winterswyl-F. Messerschmid, *Die Gemeindegesänge der hl. Messe* (Würzburg, 1940), 15, who diminish the ancient Christian emphasis of

reflect that the epithets mentioned can also attach to any of the three divine Persons, for if we refer them to Christ, they must also by that very fact be claimed for the triune God.

Next follows, as the final chord of this great hymn, a mighty act of homage to the Trinity; the name of Christ blossoms out into a naming of the three; "Jesus Christ—with the Holy Ghost—in the glory of God the Father." Again there is no question here of a mere roll-call of the divine Persons. The image of the God-man remains—of Him to whom we have raised our pleading, of Him who is exalted and glorified, who lives on eternally in that glory which He had with the Father before the world began (John 17:5).

The hymn started with the praise of God. It ends with the praise of Christ, in whom God's glory is disclosed to us. This praise of Christ employs terms which we also meet elsewhere in the ancient Christian liturgy. When the priest before Communion showed the blessed Body of Christ he cried out Τὰ ἅγια τοῖς ἁγίοις, and the people answered Εἷς ἅγιος, εἷς κύριος, Ἰησοῦς Χριστός εἰς δόξαν θεοῦ πατρός.[37] Here the same acclamation is enlarged, and modified to a form of address: "Thou alone art the Holy, Thou alone the Lord," and in our Latin rendering another clause is added to the text, a clause from Psalm 82:19, *tu solus altissimus*, which was likewise understood as referring to Christ.[38]

this text; they suggest a translation "alone thou art holy," etc. Cf. also the theological explanation in Gihr, 448, note 32.

This "thou alone art holy" is justified even when we think of the saints of the Church, for their holiness is only a participation in God's.

[37] Brightman, 341.

This formula, still used at present in the Byzantine Mass, is already certified in Didymus the Blind (d. 398), *De Trin.*, II, 7, 8 (PG, XXXIX, 589 B); likewise in the mystagogic Catecheses of Cyril, V, 19 (Quasten, *Mon.*, 107). See further passages in U. Holsmeister, ZkTh, XXXVIII (1914), 128; Peterson, *op. cit.*, 132; 137. Peterson seeks to prove that the εἷς ἅγιος, εἷς κύριος is a shout that greets the appearance of Christ somewhat as the secular acclamations accompanied the appearance of an emperor or an official or the like (140). The present formula he would translate "only holy, only Lord is Jesus Christ" . . . (134), in other words, the εἷς would

be taken as in pre-Christian acclamations wherein any god was designated as εἷς θεος in an "elative sense," not in a "conceptual" sense (cf. 151), so that the god in question was honored for the nonce as "only" or alone, with no thought given to the fact that besides him there were not a few other gods. But as Peterson himself proves, in Christian texts a transit to a profession formula understood in a "conceptual sense," so here the thought must be interpreted in this fashion: Only one is holy, Jesus Christ (and we are all unworthy; 151, 302 f.). Then the acclamation is extended to include the parallel statement of one *Kyrios* in 1 Cor. 8: 6, and tied in with the cry of worship in Phil. 2: 11: ". . . Jesus Christ as the Lord, dwelling in the glory of God the Father."

[38] Cf. U. Holzmeister, ZkTh, XXXVIII (1914), 128.

The Arians wanted to proclaim only the Father as *altissimus;* see *Contra Varimadum*, I, 53 (PL, LXII, 387).

In the Latin Church the *Gloria* was not at first intended for the Mass. Its position must have been somewhat similar to that now occupied by the *Te Deum*.[39] It was a song of thanksgiving, a festival song. And in this role it was sometimes included in the Mass at Rome on occasions especially festive. The account written in the *Liber Pontificalis* in 530 reports Pope Telesphorus (d. 136) as ordering for the nighttime Christmas Mass *ut . . . in ingresso sacrificio missæ hymnus diceretur angelicus*[40]; this shows that by the beginning of the sixth century the *Gloria* had long had a place in the Mass at Rome. Another account from the same source (more trustworthy, because closer in time to the matter reported) relates that Pope Symmachus (d. 514) had permitted the *Gloria* to be used on Sundays and the feasts of martyrs, but only at the Masses of bishops.[41] The rubric in the *Sacramentarium Gregorianum* matches this; after the *Kyrie* it decrees: *Item dicitur Gloria in excelsis Deo, si episcopus fuerit, tantummodo die dominico sive diebus festis, a presbyteris autem minime dicitur, nisi solo in Pascha.*[42] According to the *Ordo* of St. Amand, the priest was allowed to intone it during Easter night, and also on the day of his ordination if he was installed in his titular church and there celebrated his first Mass.[43] Even as late as the eleventh century the carping question was asked, why cannot a priest use the *Gloria* at least on Christmas night, when it certainly is in place.[44] But by the end of the same century the distinction

---

[39] See *supra,* p. 265. Gregory of Tours, *De gloria martyrum*, I, 63 (PL, LXXI, 762). Further references in Martène, 1, 4, 3, 6 (I, 367).

Cf. also the heading in the Antiphonary of Bangor: *Ad Vesperum et ad Matutinam.* As in the *Te Deum*, the christological section of the *Gloria* in this antiphonary is followed by a series of versicles; Blume, 54 f.; Warren (HBS, X), 31; cf. 78 f.

[40] Duchesne, *Liber pont.*, I, 56; cf. I, 129 f. Since the assignment to Telesphorus is pure fiction, it is enough to admit, with older commentators, that Telesphorus meant only the text of Luke 2: 14, since the entire hymn seemingly came to the West only with Hilary.

[41] *Ibid.*, I, 263. In commenting on the prerogative of the bishop to intone the Angelic Hymn, Brinktrine, *Die hl. Messe*, 71, points out that a special relationship was seen between angels and bishops; Apoc. 2, 1 ff.; Leo the Great, *Serm.*, 26, 1 (PL, LIV, 213 A).

[42] Lietzmann, 1; cf. *Ordo Rom. I*, n. 9 (in the version in Stapper, 20 f.) and

the later supplement *Ordo Rom. I*, n. 25 (PL, LXXVIII, 949 f.).

See also the decree of Stephen III (d. 772) for the suburbicarian bishops: Duchesne, *Liber pont.*, I, 478.

[43] Duchesne, *Christian Worship*, 471, 477.

[44] Berno of Reichenau, *De quibusdam rebus ad missæ officum pertinentibus*, c. 2 (PL, CXLII, 1058 ff.).

It might be that in the north the restriction of the *Gloria* was to some extent first induced by the stricter rubrics of the *Gregorianum*. For the 8th century *Capitulare eccl. ord.* (and with it the *Breviarium*) observe that the *Gloria* falls out during Lent (Silva-Tarouca, 206, 1. 39). Amalar, *De eccl. off.*, I, 1; III, 40, 44 (PL, CV, 995 f., 1159 B, 1161 B) makes the same remark about Lent, Advent and Masses for the Dead. The *Gloria* was therefore part of the normal course of a priest's Mass.

A certain popularity for the *Gloria* is apparent in the fact that MSS. of the start of the 9th century contain an Old High German translation; E. v. Steinmeyer, *Die kleineren althochdeutschen Sprachdenkmäler* (Berlin, 1916), 34 f.

between bishop and priest seems to have fallen out,[45] and the present-day rule became universal[46]: The *Gloria* is said in all Masses of a festive character.[47]

Unlike the *Kyrie*, the *Gloria* was from the very outset a song, but it was the song of the congregation, not of a special choir. But it was soon transferred to the clergy gathered in the sanctuary. In contrast to the *Kyrie*, the *Gloria* had the unique distinction of being intoned by the pope himself. He stood at his *cathedra*, facing east; after the *Kyrie* was finished, he turned to the people and intoned the first words,[48] just as is done nowadays.[49] The priest, when he intoned the *Gloria*, stayed originally in the place he took after kissing the altar, namely at the Epistle side,[50] as the Carthusians still do. It was not till the twelfth century that the intonation was transferred to the center of the altar,[51] and then finally the *Gloria* was said through to the end at the same spot.[52] Two things perhaps brought this about, first, symbolism,[53] and second, the desire to underline the importance of the hymn. On feasts of our Lord in the later Middle Ages the

[45] *Udalrici Consuet. Clun. I*, 8 (PL, CXLIX, 653); Bernold of Constance, *Micrologus*, c. 2 (PL, CXLIX, 979).

[46] See the careful regulation contained about 1100 in the Missal of St. Vincent of Volturno (Fiala, 200), somewhat expanded in the Pontifical of Durandus: Martène, 1, 4, XXIII (I, 621 f.); Andrieu, III, 649-651.

[47] To this category belong the entire Pentecost after Easter and also votive Masses of our Blessed Lady on Saturday. The votive Masses of the angels also got the *Gloria*, because it is the song of the angels. Regarding the suppression of the *Gloria* during Advent cf. Jungmann, *Gewordene Liturgie*, 273 f.

[48] *Ordo Rom. I*, n. 9 (PL, LXXVIII, 942): *dirigens se pontifex contra populum incipit Gloria in excelsis Deo. Ordo* of John the Arch-chanter (Silva-Tarouca, 197). *Ordo* of St. Amand (Duchesne, *Christian Worship*, 458).

[49] That the celebrant should himself pray the continuation of the hymn or rather sing it along with those around him was not expressly prescribed, but it was understood and taken for granted.

Around the year 1000, when the apologies were most popular, it was customary for the celebrant to recite one of these during the *Gloria*, since the latter

had already become so elaborate that there was no longer any thought of his taking a part in singing it. Martène, 1, 4, IV; VI, XIII (I, 499, 530, 576).

[50] *Ordinarium* of Laon (13-14th century): Martène, 1, 4, XX (I, 607 D). Cf. Amalar, *De eccl. off.*, III, 8 (PL, CV, 1115).

[51] *Speculum de myst. Eccl.*, c. 7 (PL, CLXXVII, 358).

But then the Gloria was still said to the very end at the Epistle side of the altar. *Ordinarium O.P.* of 1256 (Guerrini, 236); *Liber ordinarius* of Liége (Volk, 90); Missal of Sarum: Martène, 1, 4, XXXV (I, 666 B, E); the older Rite of Lyons (Buenner, 244).

The *Ordinarium O.P.* also prescribes that the priest, while intoning, to lift his hands which had been resting on the altar and to bring them together at the word *Deo*. The *Liber ordinarius* of Liége (Volk, 90) is even more detailed: *elevando et parum extendendo*.

[52] Apparently only since the late Middle Ages. Sölch, 62 f.

[53] Hugh of St. Cher presents as the reason for intoning the *Gloria* in the center (*in medio altaris*) the fact that the angel who appeared at Bethlehem stood *in medio eorum*. Sölch, 60 f.

Gloria was given extra significance also by a special ceremonial in which one of the singers invited the celebrant to intone the hymn.[54] The fact that the bishop when intoning the *Gloria* formerly turned to the people,[55] just as he does at the *Dominus vobiscum* or *Pax vobis*, is an indication that originally the entire congregation was called upon to sing this hymn.[56] The musical setting corresponded to this disposition of the hymn. As Wagner emphasizes, the oldest melodies that are noted down have "the character of a syllabic recitation; it was more like a declamation performed with voice uplifted than a song,"[57] obviously because the hymn was to be sung not by a group of trained singers but by the congregation. Even Radulph de Rivo (d. 1403) still refers to the simplicity of the *Gloria* (and of the *Sanctus*) when he writes: *"in Graduali beati Gregorii Romæ paucæ sunt notæ."*[58] However, the oldest sources are absolutely silent about any real participation of the faithful. This is understandable, considering the limited use of the *Gloria* only at pontifical services where only an ever-changing segment of the people could gather and where there was always a preference for a more festive and a more artistic accompaniment, so that the singing of the people was hardly favored. But when use of the *Gloria* spread beyond the limits of pontifical Mass, we do learn—through Sicard of Cremona—of the actual singing by the people.[59] In smaller surroundings and especially in the Romance countries, this did most likely become the custom. But the accounts that survive, deal for the most part with the cathedral and monastery churches and here the performers of the *Gloria* are almost without exception the chorus, that is, the clerics assembled at the service.[60] They either sang the *Gloria* straight through, or alter-

---

[54] *Liber ordinarius* of Liége (Volk, 43, 1. 13).

Martène, 1, 4, XX-XXII (I, 607, 609, 610). An especially solemn form is found in Blume-Bannister, *Tropen des Missale*, 220: Two chanters approach the bishop with the words: *Sacerdos Dei excelsi, veni ante sanctum et sacrum altare et in laude regis regum vocem tuam emitte, supplices te rogamus; eia, dic domne (tunc dicat pontifex): Gloria in excelsis Deo.* Similarly in other MSS. since the tenth century.

[55] Amalar, *De eccl. off.*, III, 8 (PL, CV, 1115 B) seems to oppose this turning towards the people. At any rate, it is no longer found in later sources.

[56] Leitner, *Der gottesdienstliche Volksgesang*, 192.

[57] Wagner, *Einführung in die gregorianischen Melodien*, I, 87.

The connection can be seen in the fact that the oldest *Gloria* melody (in Mass XV of the Vatican *Kyriale*) is the *Pater noster* melody of the Mozarabic liturgy (*Missale mixtum*: PL, LXXXV, 559). Ursprung, *Die kath. Kirchenmusik*, 28.

[58] Radulph de Rivo, *De can. observ.*, prop. 23 (Mohlberg, II, 135). The elaboration of the melodies he attributes to secular singers (*ibid.*)

[59] Sicard of Cremona (d. 1215), *Mitrale*, III, 2 (PL, CCXIII, 97 B): The priest intones the hymn, *quam populus concinendo recipit lætabundus.* But cf. also Amalar's *Expositio* of 813-814 (Gerbert, *Monumenta*, II, 150), where, commenting on the fact that on the first Christmas first one angel and then the entire heavenly host appeared, he makes this observation regarding the *Gloria: Sicque modo unus episcopus inchoat et omnis ecclesia resonat laudem Deo.*

[60] *Ordo Rom. II*, 6 (PL, LXXVIII, 971): *Deinde vero totus respondet chorus.*

nately in two semi-choruses, as in the *Kyrie*.[61] At Rome in 1140 the *Gloria* is expressly mentioned as the special concern of the *schola cantorum*,[62] but that is an understandable exception in this, the oldest place where Church music was fostered.

But at this time and even quite a bit earlier there are traces of a greater musical development of the *Gloria*. The melodies increase in number.[63] And since the ninth century there appear the farced *Glorias* or *Gloria*-tropes which we have come to recognize as the bases for a melodic amplification of these tropes. Clement Blume edited 51 independent texts, not counting those not written in metrical or rhythmical forms.[64] The reform under Pius V banned the tropes, but gave free rein to the musical composition which the *Gloria* seems to invite.

11. The Collect. The Inclusion of the Congregation Assembled

Keeping in mind the original plan of the Roman Mass, we perceive that the oration is the first place—and, until the so-called *secreta*, the only place —in which the celebrating priest himself steps before the assembly to speak. All the other things are singing and reading which—aside from the intonation of the *Gloria*—are carried on by others, or they are prayers inserted later on which the priest says quietly to himself. Here is a clue to the fact that we have reached the first climax in the course of the Mass. The ceremony of entry reaches a peak in the oration of the priest, in the

See also *Expositio 'Missa pro multis'*, ed. Hanssens (*Eph. liturg.*, 1930), 33.

Similarly the later commentators; cf. Durandus, IV, 13, 1.

[61] This latter arrangement apparently in the *Ordo eccl. Lateran.* (Fischer, 80): *Conventus . . . per distinctiones exultanter decantet.*

[62] *Ordo Rom. XI*, 18 (PL, LXXVIII, 1033 A).

[63] The elaboration affected even the priest's intonation. The Missal of St. Vincent (*circa* 1100) contains 13 Gloria intonations; Fiala, 188.

[64] Blume-Bannister, *Tropen des Missale*, pp. 217-299. In these tropes the *Gloria* is divided into a variety of small sections (as high as 20), with the tropings inserted between the sections. These were written mostly in a given verse form, often hexameters or distichs, in such a way that in each opening a (double-) verse appeared. Frequently there is but

little connection with the basic text. This is especially the case when the trope is fitted to a special festival. A favorite was the trope used on our Lady's feasts, popular all over the West: . . . *Filius Patris, primogenitus Mariæ virginis. . . . Suscipe deprecationem nostram, ad Mariæ gloriam. . . . Quoniam tu solus sanctus, Mariam sanctificans, Tu solus Dominus, Mariam gubernans, Tu solus altissimus, Mariam coronans. . . .* Legg, *Tracts*, 139; Eisenhofer, II, 95. The special popularity of this farcing for our Lady's feasts accounts for the rubric in the Missal of 1570 expressly banning this trope: *Sic dicitur Gloria in excelsis, etiam in missis beatæ Mariæ, quando dicendum est.* (This rubric was still found in the Ordinary of the Mass in the Missal of Leo XIII, but has apparently been dropped since.) At the Council of Trent there was mention of this trope among the *abusus missæ: Concilium Tridentinum*, ed. Görres, VIII, 917.

same way that the presentation of the offerings and the reception of Communion come to a fitting conclusion with an oration. Consequently in the oration the very essence of liturgical prayer is expressed with especial clarity. "Oration" is the name by which the priestly prayer is most often called in the Roman liturgy, even in the oldest Roman *Ordines*. It is a prayer which has, to a certain extent, the character of a public discourse *(Oratio)*; it is as spokesman for the people, that the priest speaks it, and for that reason the people themselves are first summoned to pray. In the same sense the term *collecta* is used at present as a designation for the prayer,[1] particularly (as we shall use it in the following discussion) for the first of the three orations of the Mass which here concerns us, the oration which at Rome was distinguished from the *oratio super oblata* and the *oratio ad complendum* by being called the *oratio prima*.[2] The term *collecta* or *collectio* was native to the Gallican liturgy.[3] When the interpreters of the Romano-Frankish liturgy employ the word in the meaning of oration,[4] this

As a sample of the *Gloria* tropes let the following non-metrical one serve; it is found in many MSS. since the 10th century, and is distinguished not only by its brevity but by the role its last verse has played (Blume, 282 f.).

> *Gloria in excelsis Deo et in terra pax hominibus bonæ voluntatis.*
> 1. Laus tua, Deus, resonet coram te rex;
>   *Laudamus te.*
> 2. Qui venisti propter nos, rex angelorum, Deus,
>   *Benedicimus te.*
> 3. In sede maiestatis tuæ
>   *Adoramus te.*
> 4. Veneranda Trinitas,
>   *Glorificamus te.*
> 5. Gloriosus es, rex Israel, in throno Patris tui,
>   *Gratias agimus tibi . . . Filius Patris.*
> 6. Domine Deus, Redemptor Israel,
>   *Qui tollis . . . deprecationem nostram.*
> 7. Deus fortis et immortalis,
>   *Qui sedes ad dexteram Patris, miserere nobis.*
> 8. Cælestium, terrestrium et infernorum rex,
>   *Quoniam tu solus sanctus . . . altissimus.*
> 9. Regnum tuum solidum permanebit in æternum,
>   *Jesu Christe, cum Sancto Spiritu in gloria Patris.*

The final verse, *Regnum tuum*, is found re-troped in many troparies, the long melismatic neum on the word *per (manebit)* being broken up into a *prosula,* for which, in its turn, a variety of texts are at hand (26 numbers; Blume, 282-299).

[1] In the *Missale Romanum* of Pius V only in the *Ritus serv.*, XI, 1; in our present missal also a number of times in the *Additones et Variationes,* especially c. VI.

[2] *Ordo Rom. III,* n. 9 (PL, LXXVIII, 979); cf. *Ordo Rom. II,* n. 6 (PL, LXXVIII, 971); and also *Ordo Rom. I* (ed. Stapper), n. 9 (p. 21, 1. 2); cf. Batiffol, *Leçons,* 120.

[3] B. Capelle, "Collecta", *Revue Bened.,* XLII (1930), 197-204.

See, e.g., the superscription in the *Missale Gothicum,* Muratori, II, 517 ff. The ancient Roman liturgy recognized the word *collecta* as the designation for an assembly, especially for the assembly that preceded the penitential processions in the stational services; see R. Hierzegger, "Collecta und Statio," ZkTh, LX (1936), 511-554. But the word did not serve as a term for the priestly oration. The *Gregorianum of Hadrian* (Lietzmann, n. 27) does have the heading *Oratio collecta* for the first oration on Candlemas, but a reference to Lietzmann's apparatus shows that the preferred reading would be *oratio ad collectam;* see *ibid.,* n. 35; 172; cf. Hierzegger, 517-521.

[4] Amalar, *De eccl. off.,* IV, 7 (PL, CV, 1183); Remigius of Auxerre, *Expositio*

linguistic usage derives manifestly from Gallican tradition. Despite some
vacillation in the use of the words in the Roman sources at hand, the
knowledge of the only meaning of the word which is here in question was
kept intact, especially in Walafrid Strabo who says: *Collectas dicimus,
quia necessarias earum petitiones compendiosa brevitate colligimus i. e.
concludimus.*⁵

The oration is, as a matter of fact, the prayer in which the priest "collects" the preceding prayers of the people and presents them to God. This
fact explains certain peculiarities in its make-up and in the way it is introduced. Before the priest begins the oration, he summons the congregation
to prayer: *Oremus,* Let us pray. And before he gives this summons, he
turns around to them with a *Dominus vobiscum.* Older commentators
usually cling to a consideration only of the content of this greeting, stressing the fitness of the wish that the Lord might be near and God's favor
accompany their praying, as he, the priest, offers up to God the prayer of
all.⁶ But the form of the salutation, this direct address to the people, is
not explored. For why does the priest just here turn to greet the people?
It will not be easy to answer this if we examine only our present concept
of divine worship. Such a consideration will not explain why the one saying
the prayer should first of all greet the congregation, much less why he
should repeat the greeting several times in the course of the prayer-meeting.
Yet he does just that. The *Dominus vobiscum* recurs every time the congregation receives an invitation or a special announcement: the summons
to join in prayer at the *oratio* and the *gratiarum actio,* or the announcement of the close with the *Ite missa est* or *Benedicamus Domino.*⁷ It is
omitted only when there is question of continuing an activity already
started.⁸ Obviously the formula which introduces the reading of the Gospel,

(PL, CI, 1249); Bernold, *Micrologus,*
c. 3 (PL, CLI, 979).
⁵ Walafrid Strabo, *De exord. et increm.,*
c. 22 (PL, CXIV, 945 D); somewhat less
sure in Bernold, *Micrologus,* c. 3 (PL,
CLI, 979 D).
A discussion of the oration as a résumé
in Jungmann, *Liturgical Worship,* 131-132.
⁶ Gihr, 456, finds another reason for the
greeting in this, that the priest in the
oration performs his office as mediator,
and so, after kissing the altar and thus
binding himself to the Church celestial,
he must turn in greeting to show his
relationship with the Church militant on
earth.
⁷ There is therefore not reason enough
for Brinktrine, *Die hl. Messe,* 277, note 1
(cf. 86, note 1), to take the latter
Dominus vobiscum as the conclusion of
the post-communion, or to give the same

explanation for the greeting after the
oration in the hours of the Office. The
Benedicamus Domino which marks the
close of the hours corresponds exactly,
even in form, to the *Oremus.*
Naturally this *Dominus vobiscum,* even
without any formula of address following,
could be used as a salutation of the people
at the beginning of a solemnity or even
serve as a dismissal. Thus it is witnessed
by Optatus of Mileve, *Contra Parmen.,*
VII, 6 (CSEL, XXVI, 179); Augustine,
De civ. Dei, 22, 8 (CSEL, XL, 2; p. 611,
1. 7); Chrysostom (in Brightman, 476,
note 1). Cf. Dölger, *Antike und Christentum* (1930), II, 204.; 216. In our own
Mass, however, the salutation is never
used in this wise.
⁸ For this latter reason the salutation is
omitted not only before the *Oremus* of a
commemoration that may follow but also

sequentia sancti evangelii, is intended as an announcement and is therefore preceded by the same greeting.[9] Another gesture is to be noticed in this connection. Aside from the beginning of the preface, when the priest already stands at the gates of the Holy of Holies, and aside from the Gospel, the priest always kisses the altar before he turns to the people with his greeting.[10] In the medieval high Mass the deacon always turned around with the priest.[11]

The *Dominus vobiscum* thus has a clear relation to the action that follows; it serves to focus our attention. We might render its monition somewhat prosaically by the use of the vocative: Brethren in Christ, we are going to pray. Devout Christians, listen to today's Gospel.[12] The *Dominus vobiscum* is then, in the first instance, an address to the people and, without overstressing its content (which of course is more than merely an address), it serves to arouse the attention and to denote, each time, an important moment in the course of the liturgy.[13] Besides, the use of a greeting form enables the congregation to return the greeting, and so, through

before the *Oremus* that precedes the *Pater noster*. On the other hand, it was not omitted just because the *Oremus* of the first oration of the Mass was followed by a *Flectamus genua*—the rule that is followed at present (e.g. on Ember Wednesday and Ember Saturday). *Ordo Rom. I*, n. 24 f. (PL, LXXVIII, 949); Hierzegger, *op. cit.*, 544.

[9] In the Greek liturgy of St. James the corresponding formula, which is likewise introduced with a Εἰρήνη πᾶσιν, has also the form of an invitation Ὀρθοὶ ἀκούσωμεν τοῦ ἁγίου εὐαγγελίου (Brightman, 38, 18); in the liturgy of St. Mark the sequence of greeting and invitation is reversed (Brightman, 119, 8).

[10] Regarding this kissing of the altar see *supra*, p. 316 f.; cf. also Dölger, *Antike und Christentum*, (1930, II, 216, who ponders a possible original connection between *Dominus vobiscum* and this altar-kiss, but then rejects it. Because of the late origin of the altar-kiss this connection is actually out of the question.

In the ritual of the late Middle Ages the greeting was sometimes joined with a sign of the Cross over oneself. *Ordinarium* of Coutances (Legg, *Tracts*, 58 f.): *vertens se ad populum et signans seipsum*. Similarly in the later Rite of Sarum: Martène, 1, 4, XXXV (I, 666 C, 671 A, B).

[11] Missal of St. Vincent-on-Volturno (Fiala, 200, 202); *Ordo Eccl. Lateran.* (Fischer, 83, 1. 30).

Martène, 1, 4, XXIV; XXXV (I, 626 f., 666 D).

In the monastic rite the practice is still observed today.

[12] As a matter of fact some such phrase as this latter is often used to introduce the Gospel in the vernacular.

[13] To this extent the explanation given by Amalar, *De eccl. off.*, III, 19 (PL, 105, 1129 C; cf. 1128 C) is pertinent: *Haec salutatio introitum demonstrat ad aliud officium*. The same thought is expanded by Sicard of Cremona, *Mitrale*, III, 5 (PL, CCXIII, 114 A).

The rule for the *Dominus vobiscum* at Mass can be formulated more exactly as follows: It introduces the sacerdotal prayer in each of four main sections: at the opening, at the reading service, at the thanksgiving and in the Communion section. Besides these, it also ushers in both of the proclamations of the deacon, namely the reading of the Gospel and the dismissal. But it is, of course, a matter of only secondary development that it also precedes the oration at the end of the prayers at the foot of the altar, and that it precedes the last Gospel, for both of these are texts audible only to the assistants around the altar.

this religious setting of reciprocal salutation, the feeling of God's nearness is intensified.

Both the greeting and the reply are ancient, their origins hid in pre-Christian times. In the Book of Ruth (2:4) Booz greets his reapers with *Dominus vobiscum*. The salutation was thus a part of everyday life. It is met with several times in Holy Scripture.[14] The reply of the reapers to Booz's greeting was: *Benedicat tibi Dominus*. We employ in its place a phrase which means almost the same thing: *Et cum spiritu tuo*, a formula which betrays its Hebrew origin and has many parallels in St. Paul.[15] We render its full meaning by saying simply, "And with you too."[16]

Since the greeting is Old Testament, the *Dominus* originally meant merely God: God be with you. But there is no difficulty about referring the indeterminate *Dominus* to Christ, and this is more consonant with Christian worship. Take it in the sense of Christ's own promise (the wording is reminiscent anyway) : *"Ecce ego vobiscum sum"* (Matt. 28:20), or that other assurance whose conditions are certainly fulfilled in the liturgical gathering: "Where two or three are gathered in my name, I am there in the midst of them" (Matt. 18:20). Actually this is the sense in which the *Dominus vobiscum* is usually interpreted in modern times.[17] But it

[14] Luke 1: 28; cf. Judg. 6: 12; 2 Chron. 15: 2; 2 Thess. 3: 16.

[15] 2 Tim. 4: 22 (Vulg.): *Dominus (J. Chr.) cum spiritu tuo;* cf. Philem. 25; Gal. 6: 18; also Phil. 4:23.

[16] This is a Semitism: *Spiritus tuus =* your person = you.

Still it is to be remarked that even Chrysostom, *In II. Tim. hom.*, 10, 3 (PG, LXII, 659 f.). had already referred "thy spirit" to the indwelling Holy Spirit. In fact, in his first Whitsun sermon, n. 4 (PG, L, 458 f.) he sees in the word "spirit" in this counter-greeting an allusion to the fact that the bishop performs the sacrifice in the power of the Holy Spirit. That is the reason the *Dominus vobiscum* was even at an early age restricted to those endowed with major orders, bishops, priests and deacons, and not given to subdeacons who were numbered among the higher orders only since the 13th century; cf. Eisenhofer, I, 188 f.

[17] Gavanti explains the altar-kiss that precedes in this sense: *osculatur altare sacerdos salutaturus populum quasi qui accipiat pacem a Christo per altare ut supra significato, ut eandem det populo.* Gavanti-Merati, *Thesaurus*, II, 5, 1 (I,

226). He is followed by many later commentators; see, e.g., Gihr, 456, note 14.

It is quite probable that this was the very reason for the introduction, as early as the 13th century, of the custom of kissing the altar each time the people were greeted. At any rate it was about this time that the analagous kiss of the altar, the one preceding the kiss of peace, was taken in this sense, so much, in fact, that often it was not the altar but the sacred Host that received the kiss, so that the peace was drawn from Christ in all reality.

The reference to Christ is employed in a different way in the recent edition of the *Rituale Rom.* (IX, 5, 5) where the *Dominus vobiscum* is omitted between the *Panem de coelo* and the oration that precede the eucharistic benediction. (This had already been ordered by a decree of the Sacred Congregation of Rites, June 16, 1663; Gardellini, *Decreta*, n. 2223, 7) ; the reason that seems to have prevailed was this, that the desire that God might be with his people finds its expression in the eucharistic blessing itself; so Gatterer, *Praxis celebrandi*, 164. However, this principle was not carried through in all instances; cf. *Rituale Rom.* IV, 4, 24-26.

would be practically the same thing to say, more exactly, that the liturgy leaves the word *Dominus* indefinite; in the greeting the wish is made that "the Lord" may be with the congregation, but we know implicitly that the Lord God does come to us in Christ who is our Emmanuel.

This christological sense is more plainly expressed in the salutation *Pax vobis*, the greeting of the Risen Lord to his Apostles, used by the bishop before the collect. In the Orient, outside Egypt, this formula has taken the place of the *Dominus vobiscum* since the fourth century.[18] There is early testimony regarding its use in North Africa.[19] In Spain in the sixth century it challenged the position of *Dominus vobiscum*, and was forbidden by the second Synod of Braga (563) even as the greeting of a bishop.[20] However, it became firmly established in the West, but under certain conditions; the bishop was to use *Pax vobis* only as his first greeting of the people,[21] and only on days when the Gloria had been sung,[22] a rule which is still binding.[23] After the song of peace sung by the angels, the salute of peace is tendered to the people by those who, as successors of the Apostles, are in a special way entrusted with this greeting.[24]

The greeting is spoken by the bishop in the same way as the priest; at the center of the altar[25] he turns toward the people and stretches out his hands. This gesture, which in its basic form implies great vivacity and a natural pleasure in bodily expression,[26] deepens once more the utterance

For the christological concept in olden times compare *Const. Ap.*, VII, 46, 15 (Funk, I, 454). On the other hand Augustine takes the *Dominus* here usually for God; see Rötzer, 236. Likewise Peter Damian, *Opusc. 'Dominus vobiscum'*, c. 3 (PL, CXLV, 234 B). Cf. also Remigius of Auxerre, *Expositio* (PL, CI, 1248 f.).
[18] Hanssens, III, 194-209. Its form is usually Εἰρήνη πᾶσιν. The first Roman Ordo introduces the collect with the form *Pax vobis* (PL, 78, 942), the second has the form *Pax vobiscum* (*ibid.*, 971). In the use of the greeting in the course of the Mass there were rather large differences between the various rites.
[19] Optatus of Mileve (c. 370), *Contra Parmen.*, III, 10 (CSEL, XXVI, 95); cf. also Augustine, *De civ. Dei*, 22, 8, 22 (PL, XLI, 770).
[20] Can. 3 (Mansi, IX, 777); Eisenhofer, I, 188.
[21] *Ordo Rom. I*, n. 9 (PL, LXXVIII, 942); Amalar, *De eccl. off.* præf. alt.; III, 9 (PL, CV, 992; 1115 f.); cf. Remigius of Auxerre, *Expositio* (PL, CI, 1249). Amalar, *loc. cit.*, observes that the form at Rome was *Pax vobis*, not

Pax vobiscum. The latter form is actually found in the non-Roman *Ordo Rom. II*, n. 6 (PL, LXXVIII, 971).
[22] Leo VII (d. 939), *Ep. ad Gallos et Germanos* (PL, CXXXII, 1086); Durandus, IV, 14, 7.
[23] *Cæremoniale Episc.*, II, 8, 39; II, 13, 8; II, 18, 25.
[24] Matt. 10: 12 f.; Luke 10: 5.
[25] Apart from the pontifical high Mass. Here the bishop remains at his throne, to which he returns after the incensing of the altar.
In the Middle Ages the salutation of the priest was frequently spoken at the Epistle side; see *supra*, p. 333. Even in the present Dominican rite the priest stays at the Epistle side where he has already said the *Gloria* from start to finish.
[26] The starting-point of this gesture was not originally the folded hands, which arise only from the Germanic sacral culture. The motion of both hands naturally expresses an intense gravitation towards the one or ones greeted, but the natural movement has been regulated by the rules of the schools of oratory, which dic-

of a desire to be united with the congregation and to draw them together into the prayer which is about to begin. This can be recognized even in the form we have today.

In the response the congregation for its part also confirms this community of desire, this will to be united. Do we have here only an acclamation in a wider sense?[27] We will surely have to picture these responses in ancient times as acclamations somewhat stormy and unregulated. And it is certain, too, that for centuries the entire people considered this shout, this call as their very own.[28] We can best understand the *Et cum spiritu tuo* as a popular consensus in the work of the priest, not that the congregation here gives the priest authority or power to act in its stead, but that the congregation once more acknowledges him as the speaker under whose leadership the united group will approach almighty God. Thus in the greeting and its response we have the same double note that reappears at the end of the oration; the *Dominus vobiscum* seems to anticipate the *per Christum* of the close of the oration, and the *Et cum spiritu tuo* is a forerunner of the people's agreement expressed in the Amen. How sadly we must admit that, just when we try to recall this simple salutation to its original vitality, we realize how difficult it is for us moderns to make this formality our own in all its former import, even in such surroundings as

tated a certain artistry, and again by the rubrics of worship, which dictated a certain modesty and reserve. Still the rubrical mechanics as found in the Missal of Pius V (*Rit. serv.*, V, 1) were not settled till the later Middle Ages; see the Mass-*Ordo* of Burchard: Legg, *Tracts*, 141; cf. *ibid.*, 100. A preliminary step is formed by the *Ordinarium O.P.* of 1256 (Guerrini, 236).

Regarding the kiss of the altar that precedes, cf. *supra*, 316 f., 361, f.

[27] Acclamations in the strict sense were, in later ancient times, the shouts of a crowd which disclosed the will of the people: veneration when a ruler or his vicar appeared, assent to propositions and resolutions, congratulation, demand and desire. One such is still retained in the consecration of a bishop: *Ad multos annos*. F. Cabrol, "Acclamations," D'ACL, I, 240-265. These shouts often acquired legal significance; cf. E. Peterson, Εἶς θεός, (Göttingen, 1926). 141 ff.

[28] Even in the spacious churches of the 4th century. Cf. Chrysostom, *In s. Pentec. homil.*, 1, 4 (PG, L, 458), who here remarks that his listeners had shouted out,

in common, when their bishop Flavian had ascended his *cathedra* and greeted them, crying "And with thy spirit." Cf. *In Matth. hom.*, 32 (al. 33), 6 (PG, LVII, 384; Brightman, 477, note 6).

For the Gallican liturgy there is the evidence of the *Expositio* (ed. Quasten, 11): the priest gives the salutation, *ut . . . ab omnibus benedicatur dicentibus: Et cum spiritu tuo*. That the salute of the priest should be answered not only by the *clerici et Deo dicati* but by all was also enjoined by several Gallic synods: Orelans (511; Mansi, VIII, 361 f.); Braga (563), c. 3 (Mansi, IX, 777). Even Bernold, *Micrologus*, c. 2 (PL, CLI, 979), still recalls the canon of Orleans when referring to the first greeting, and Durandus, IV, 14, 4 f., also indicates that the answer is given by "choir and people." However in these instances we have probably an indication of the ideal rather than of reality. The most recent remarks of all, those of Sicard of Cremona, *Mitrale*, III, 4, 5 (PL, CCXIII, 107 D, 114 B), might possibly go back to a living practice. Cf. also *supra*, p. 236 f.

the "dialogue" Mass presents, when the outer form is present fully and beyond quibble.[29]

In its chief function as an address, the greeting, as we said, introduces the summons to prayer. This summons in the Roman Mass consists in one single word, *Oremus*. In the oriental liturgies the formula, spoken here mostly by the deacon, is much less concise. Thus in the Byzantine Mass you have: "Let us ask the Lord" (τοῦ κυρίου δεηθῶμεν), "Let us ask the Lord again and again in peace" ("Ετι καὶ ἔτι ἐν εἰρήνῃ τοῦ κυρίου δεηθῶμεν),[30] and then the deacon begins the litany. In Egypt the cry is sometimes quite simple: "Pray" (Προσεύξασθε) or "Stand for prayer" ('Επὶ προσευχὴν στάθητε),[31] but sometimes the object of the prayer is mentioned: "Pray for the emperor," "Pray for the bishop"[32]; in fact sometimes the object is cited in detailed formulas, particularly at the prayer of the faithful after the Gospel, and in the intercessory prayers which are inserted in the canon.[33] In the West this invitation to prayer was especially amplified in the Gallican liturgy. The formula, called a *præfatio*, precedes various prayers and series of prayers, both within the Mass and without; its form is sometimes reminiscent of a little homily.[34] A remarkable thing in regard to the invitation to prayer in the oriental liturgies is this, that the summonses already quoted are usually followed by the prayer of the people put in words. In the Alexandrine liturgy the people respond to the simple summons with a triple κύριε ἐλέησον, or at least with a single one,[35] and even the more detailed summonses of the deacon are thus answered, and meanwhile the priest begins the oration.[36] In the Byzantine Mass a fully developed litany is invariably joined to the deacon's invitation to prayer. The deacon says the invocations and in the meantime, according to present practice, the priest softly speaks the oration (mostly a very extensive one), and only the closing doxology is said out loud. The answer of the people in this instance too is mostly κύριε ἐλέησον. But sometimes another reply

[29] Cf. in this sense the observations of F. Messerschmid, *Liturgie und Gemeinde* (Würzburg, 1939), 22 f., but also the practical reflections of A. Beil, *Einheit in der Liebe* (Colmar, 1941), 12-14; 16 f.

[30] Byzantine liturgy: Brightman, 359 f., 362, 364, etc.
In the Greek liturgy of St. James the formulas are even more varied; Brightman, 38 ff.

[31] Brightman, 113, 115, 117.

[32] Brightman, 114 f.

[33] Brightman, 119 ff., 159 ff., 165 ff.

[34] *Missale Gothicum*: Muratori, II, 520 ff.

[35] Brightman, 113 ff., 117, 119 f.

[36] *Ibid.*, 119 f. Corresponding formulas are still in use in the present-day Coptic liturgy, and in the Greek language, an indication of their great antiquity; *ibid.*, 155, 158 ff., 165 ff. A litany in which the priest takes the lead, *ibid.*, 175. In the Ethiopian liturgy, too, there is a litany at the beginning of the fore-Mass, in which the people respond to each phrase with "Amen, Kyrie eleison, Lord, have mercy on us"; ibid. 206 ff. A sacerdotal prayer of several sections, said after the readings, shows an order the reverse of that in the Roman liturgy: first the call "Stand up to pray," answered by the people with "Lord, have mercy on us"; only then does the priest greet the people and receive their greeting in return; *ibid.* 223 ff., 227. This arrangement is probably due to the insistence that the people receive the salutation standing.

is substituted; thus after the offertory procession the final invocations of the litany are answered with Παράσχου κύριε.[37] There is something very appealing when, in the greater litanies, these petitions resound in the humble but solemn promise: "Mindful of the all-holy ... Mother of God and virgin, Mary ... we will to put ourselves and each other and our whole life in the keeping of Christ our God," and the people cry out in answer Σοὶ κύριε,[38] certainly a worthy chorus for the prayer of the Church of God.

The Roman liturgy has always been more restrained than the liturgies of the Orient in all that concerns the participation of the people. And yet even here we do find in certain instances an extra effort to enlist the cooperation of the people. At the *orationes sollemnes* of Good Friday—amongst the oldest in the liturgy—the Oremus is expanded into a longer phrase, like: *Oremus, dilectissimi nobis, pro Ecclesia sancta Dei*. ... And at the conferring of major orders the *Leonianum* contains invitations to the people to pray which are similarly amplified: *Oremus, dilectissimi, Deum Patrem omnipotentem, ut super hos famulos suos, quos ad presbyterii munus elegit, cœlestia dona multiplicet, quibus quod eius dignatione suscipiunt eius exsequantur auxilio. Per.* ...[39] The later sacramentaries match this.[40]

At the *orationes sollemnes* of Good Friday the invitation is followed by the deacon's imperative, *Flectamus genua*, that is, with the order to kneel down for silent prayer till the deacon himself—later, the subdeacon—gives the further signal, *Levate*, stand up again. The same command is heard on Ember days and on some other occasions, preceded by a simple *Oremus*. Here we are face to face with a custom which possessed a much greater importance in the ancient Church, both West[41] and East, than it does in our own time. It occurs in the Coptic Mass, where the deacon, using the original Greek form, joins his command to the priest's invitation: Κλίνωμεν τὰ γόνατα — ἀνάστωμεν[42]; this is done, for instance, all through Lent after

[37] Brightman, 381.

[38] Brightman, 363 etc.

[39] Muratori, I, 424.

[40] *Gelasianum* I, 20: 22 (Wilson, 22 f., 26), et al.; *Gregorianum* (Lietzmann, n. 3, 1; 4, 1).

[41] In Cæsarius of Arles the custom is found in full swing. Indeed he bemoans the fact that many pay no attention and that he observes them standing *velut columnas* when the deacon has issued his command; Nickl, *Der Anteil des Volkes*, 33-36. Later a *Pater noster*, introduced by *Kyrie eleison*, is inserted for this prayer of the congregation; thus within the General Prayer of the Church (see *infra*): Regino of Prüm, *De synod. causis*, I, 190 (PL, CXXXII, 224 f.);

Burchard of Worms, *Decretum II*, 70 (PL, CXL, 638). In our own rite of adult baptism this *Pater* preceding the oration is still circumscribed with *Ora, electe, flecte genua* and *Leva; Rituale Rom.*, II, 4, 16; 18; etc. Cf. Nickl, 35 f.

On the other hand, the substitute for the genuflection at the beginning of the hours—a *Miserere*—mentioned by Peter of Cluny, *Ep.*, I, 28 (PL, LXXXIX, 153 C) does not belong to this compound. The whole question of the people's silent prayer is discussed in Jungmann, *Liturgical Worship*, 108 ff.

[42] Brightman, 159. The call is repeated three times. The corresponding sacerdotal prayer is no longer extant. We are dealing, therefore, with a fragmentary vestige. Hanssens, III, 233 f.

the Gospel. The practice was not limited in olden times to the Romano-Alexandrian ambit. In the *Apostolic Constitutions* (end of the fourth century), which were compiled within the compass of Antioch, the ordinary Mass—apparently, therefore, without restrictions to special occasions—contains the direction for five different calls to prayer (εὔξασθε) right after the readings, addressed respectively to the catechumens, the energumens, the candidates for Baptism, the penitents and the faithful. The context plainly shows that the command meant, Kneel down for prayer.[43]

The question naturally comes up, why this command, which appears here in the ordinary Mass *ordo*, should in the Roman Mass be restricted to certain extraordinary occasions. The most important source for this restriction is mentioned in Canon 20 of the Council of Nicea (325), which ordered that kneeling be omitted during Eastertide and on Sundays.[44] This arrangement for Easter and Sundays very quickly spread to the feasts (which were already on the increase) and even to saints' days[45]; the only days left were the *dies quotidiani*,[46] and finally only the days which had definite penitential character, and even these were further reduced to the merest remnant, with the loss of the entire Lenten season and all days which did not have two proper orations before the Epistle.[47] And even on the days that remained, kneeling was restricted to the prayer before the real start of the Mass. For even the celebration of the Eucharist, which took place for a long time only on Sundays and feast days, seemed to bear an Easter character.

---

[43] When the deacon, after detailing the contents of the prayer, announces the bishop's prayer, his proclamation in one instance reads as follows: "Stand up, bow down before God through Christ and receive the benediction"; *Const Ap.*, VIII, 9, 6 (Quasten, *Mon.*, 205). For the faithful the first cry reads expressly: Ὅσοι πιστοὶ κλίνωμεν γόνυ, and the second: Ἐγειρώμεθα. *Const. Ap.*, VIII, 10, 2; 22 (Quasten, *Mon.*, 206, 209).

The people kneeling in this same place also in *Testamentum Domini*, I, 35 (Quasten, *Mon.*, 240). Cf. also the data from Chrysostom in Brightman, 471 ff.

[44] Mansi, II, 677.

The canon is repeated in *Decretum Gratiani* III, 3, 10 (Friedberg, I, 1355).

[45] Walafrid Strabo, *De exord. et increm.*, c. 25 (PL, CXIV, 953 A); the prayers are said without kneeling *in dominicis et festis maioribus et Quinquagesima*.

[46] *Ordo* of St. Amand (Duchesne, *Christian Worship*, 475).

[47] Various older *ordines* still insist that the oration of the day, even when it is the only one, should be introduced during Lent with *Flectamus genua: Ordo Rom. I*, n. 24 f. 9th century supplement; (PL, LXXVIII, 949); Bernold, *Micrologus*, c. 50 (PL, CLI, 1014 B): *Ad omnes horas quadragesimales genua flectimus. Item ad missam, etiamsi salutatio præcedat orationem.* Cf. Durandus, VI, 28, 8 ff.; Martène, 4, 17 (III, 162 A B); Martène, *De ant. monach. rit.*, 3, 9, 12 (IV, 316); Missal of Tortosa (1524): Ferreres, 249; cf. *ibid.*, p. LXXXVII. The same procedure still in the Dominican liturgy: *Missale iuxta ritum O.P.* (1889), 50.

The course sketched by Bernold above shows that the *Dominus vobiscum* which appeared to be demanded for the oration of the day was not generally considered compatible with the *Flectamus genua*, and that even then there was a trend to omit the genuflection after the greeting. Radulph de Rivo (d. 1403), *De can. observantia*, prop. 23 (Mohlberg, II, 136

The only problem was to establish just when precisely the Mass really began. A rule of the high Middle Ages fixed this start at the *Gloria*.⁴⁸ Thus the orations which preceded the *Gloria*, that is, those which preceded the proper collect, and only those, remained under the law regarding kneeling.⁴⁹ Or to put it more exactly, only these were subject to the diminished rules of *Flectamus genua;* for in addition kneeling was prescribed for those assisting in choir, and continues to be so prescribed, at all the orations during Advent, Lent, the Embertides, most of the vigils and the Mass for the Dead.⁵⁰

Thus a new thing had appeared, or rather, a substitution: kneeling not *before* the oration but *during* the oration. This change concurred with the gradual contraction of the pause which the *Flectamus genua* implied. The *Ordo Romanus antiquus* (about 950) offers a transitional aspect; in the introduction to the *orationes sollemnes* of Good Friday it includes the ancient prescription after the *Flectamus genua*, namely, *Et orat diutissime* (whereupon the *Levate* would have followed), but in the text of the orations it indicates a different order: *Oremus. Flectamus genua. Omnipotens æterne Deus . . . Levate. Per eumdem . . .* Thus the pause during which the congregation was to pray was filled by the priest's oration.⁵¹

f.), still holds for it but observes that the Franciscans omit these *genuflexiones, quia in capella Papæ non fiunt.* As a matter of fact they were no longer found in the 12th century at the Lateran: *Ordo eccl. Lateran.* (Fischer, 28 f.).

⁴⁸ Cf. *Ordo Rom. XI,* n. 63 (PL, LXXVIII, 1050): On the Ember Saturday after Pentecost: *Finito hymno trium puerorum pontifex incipit missam: Gloria in excelsis Deo.* This corresponds to the arrangement in the Mass on Holy Saturday (and analogously on Maundy Thursday) at the present time: organ and bells once more resound with the beginning of the *Gloria.*

⁴⁹ This method of reckoning was naturally somewhat arbitrary. In the eastern liturgies the rule for kneeling during prayer was regulated by a different system, namely, the start of the sacrifice itself. Moses bar Kepha (d. 903) expressly excludes this kneeling down during the sacrifice (the *kurobho*) because, he explains, kneeling recalls the fall while the *kurobho* appertains to the resurrection; R. H. Connolly-H. W. Codrington, *Two Commentaries on the Jacobite Liturgy* (London, 1913), 43. In the East Syrian Mass, according to the homilies of Narsai (d.

after 503), there was an analogous basis for the rule that genuflection might be permitted up to the epiklesis but not thereafter; Connolly, *The Liturgical Homilies of Narsai,* 23, 127. Thus the East Syrian rule about kneeling is almost directly opposite that which developed in the Roman Mass as the result of eucharistic cult.

⁵⁰ *Missale Rom., Rubr. gen.,* XVII, 5.

⁵¹ Hittorp, *De off. eccl.,* 66; cf. 49 b. This *Levate* just before the *Per eundem* also in the *Liber ordinarius* of the Premonstratensians (12th century; Waefelghem, 220, with note 2, where however the first sentence says too much); the practice has here been retained down to the present (Lentze; cf. p. 100 *supra,* note 44).

Whereas here the rule dictates standing up during the concluding formula, the very opposite is outlined in a directive of Berthold of Regensburg, who tells the people to fall on their knees when they hear the name of Jesus in the *Per Dom. n. J.C.;* Franz, 652.

The bowing of the head at the name of Jesus was ordered by the II Council of Lyons (1274), c. 25 (Mansi, XXIV, 98).

It is self-evident that the Nicene rule for Easter and Sundays was intended to eliminate not the prayer before the priest's oration, but only kneeling during that prayer. This is evident in the oriental liturgies, in which the litanies of the deacon are still customary, unchanged, even on Easter and on Sundays.[62] We must therefore come to the conclusion that the elimination of the *Flectamus genua* after our *Oremus* did not purport to eliminate the pause for prayer which this command ordinarily signalized, but that at least a moment's quiet meditation was still retained.

But just as the pause after the *Flectamus genua* disappeared, leaving only a simple hurried genuflection, so the same fate was bound to overtake the pause after *Oremus* when no *Flectamus* intervened, and even more quickly. After all, the elimination of the pause could be tolerated here more easily, since in the *Kyrie* and the *Gloria* which preceded the *Oremus* the opportunity for prayer was offered, for, although the people did not perform these, yet the clergy assisting in choir did, even in later times. A small vestige of the olden *Oremus* pause is still to be seen in a little notice of Durandus, who records with some emphasis that the priest spoke the *Oremus* before the collect and the post-communion at the middle of the altar and only then went to the right side of the altar to finish the oration.[63] The pause will be seen in full strength and remarkable extent at the *secreta*.

The effort to draw the congregation into the prayer of the priest also found another mode of expression. Carolingian sources of the tenth century contain the prescription that at the *Oremus* of the priest the people were to bow and were to remain in this position *(acclinis)* until the end of the oration.[64] In the Gallican liturgy the practice had already been sev-

---

[62] The same thing is shown in the parallels in our Office: even on Sundays the oration is preceded by the *preces*. Only on feasts of higher rank (considerably on the increase in recent times) are these *preces* left out.

[63] Durandus, IV, 14, 5; IV, 57, 2. The closing formula *Per Dominum nostrum Jesum Christum* was also said at the center; *ibid.*, IV, 57, 2. This latter arrangement is still found in the *Ordo Rom. XIV*, n. 53 (PL, LXXVIII, 1169 B), in Gabriel Biel, *Canonis expositio*, lect. 89, and in the *Ordinarium* of Coutances (1557): Legg, 58. Thus it would seem that the aim was to have the priest's oration recited at the center of the altar as much as possible, the only difficulty being the technical one of reading from the Mass book. Cf. the matching treatment of the *Kyrie*, p. 344 above. On the contrary the rule of the later Middle Ages,

stipulating that everything up to the readings and everything after the Communion takes place at the Epistle side was probably founded on the notion that thus the sacrificial part of the Mass might be differentiated and made prominent. Cf. *supra*, p. 345, note 62.

[64] Remigius of Auxerre, *Expositio* (PL, CV, 1249 C): *Deinde dicit: Oremus, invitans secum populum, ut simul orent. Quapropter acclinis debet esse populus usquequo sacerdos incipiat dicere: Per omnia s. s.*

This posture held also for that part of the year in which kneeling was inadmissible. Regino of Prüm, *De synod. causis*, I, 380 (PL, 132, 265): *Ut presbyteri plebibus annuntient, quod in Quadragesima et in ieiunio quattuor temporum tantummodo ad Missarum sollemnia annuntiante Diacono genua flectere debeant. In dominicis e contra diebus vel ceteris*

eral centuries old.[55] And in the choir rules of many monastic groups the custom was retained for some time,[56] and is, in fact, still retained but with this modification, that the bow is stipulated only for the first oration, not for the commemorations that follow.[57] But elsewhere this rather uncomfortable posture was soon changed either to the usual upright stance—this mostly for festival worship—or to an out-and-out kneeling—this on days of penance.[58] In other words, the old regulation of the *Flectamus genua* before the oration has been replaced more and more—at least since the twelfth century—by kneeling during the oration.[59]

While the priest says the oration, he stands with hands upraised. Until far into the Middle Ages weight was attached to the rule that he stand facing east,[60] and originally the faithful, too, stood facing east and with arms lifted up.[61] Although this orientation lost much of its importance, and the posture of the faithful underwent many changes,[62] the priest still remains standing and his hands are still upraised. For after all, this standing posture has a double purport so far as the priest is concerned, since he is the one who leads the congregation in prayer, since he is the *liturgus*.[63]

---

festis a Vespere usque in Vesperam non flectant genua, sed stantes incurvati orent. The same prescription also in Burchard of Worms, *Decretum XIII*, 3 (PL, CXL, 885).

[55] This bowed bearing during the priestly oration is urged, for example, by Cæsarius of Arles, *Serm.* 76 f. (Morin, 303, 305; PL, XXXIX, 2284 f.); the same demand especially for the Canon: *Serm.* 73 (Morin, 294; PL, XXXIX, 2277). The bow *during* the oration which Cæsarius presumes is still united here with the genuflection *before* the oration in those cases in which the deacons bid it. This arrangement is found also in other Christian sources. In the first instance this bow during prayer was perhaps customary when the orations were really blessings spoken over someone—hence the terms *benedictiones* or *missæ* by which they were often called; cf. Jungmann, *Die lateinischen Bussriten*, 27-31, especially 30, note 101; idem., *Gewordene Liturgie*, 48 f. However the begging character of the orations (*supplices te rogamus*) might also have led to the assumption of this posture.

[56] Cf. *supra*, p. 241, note 42.

[57] Similarly already in the rules of the Canons of St. Victor (12th century): Martène, *App.* (III, 791 f.).

Cistercian rite of the later Middle Ages: Schneider (*Cist.-Chr.*, 1926), 315; cf. *Liber usuum*, II, 53 (PL, CLXVI, 1423 B).

[58] *Supra*, p. 239.

[59] *Ordo eccl. Lateran.*, ed. Fischer, 29, 1. 5 ff. The Pontifical of Durandus prescribes for a bishop attending the Mass of a priest: *Dum collectæ et postcommuniones dicuntur, debet accumbere super faldistorium . . . et iunctis manibus devote accumbens manere.* Andrieu, III, 644; Martène, 1, 4, XXIII (I, 619 A).

[60] *Ordo Rom. I*, n. 8 f. (with the additions of the later recension: PL, LXXVIII, 942). The same posture at the oration is still demanded in the Pontifical of Durandus for a bishop standing at his throne: Andrieu, III, 639, 1. 2; Martène, 1, 4, XXIII (I, 616 E).

[61] *Supra*, p. 239.

[62] *Supra*, p. 240 f.

[63] Kneeling, which since the early Middle Ages made such headway as the preferred posture at prayer, was not thought of for the priest's praying except in certain isolated instances like the prayers at the foot of the altar (cf. *supra*, p. 297) and the intercessory prayers which were inserted (*infra*, vol. II, ch. 3, 3). There is a report from the Japanese mission of the 16th century relating how one of

The raising of the arms heavenward is a fitting accompaniment to the prayer that rises to Him who dwells in heaven.

But even this raising of the hands could undergo some alteration, corresponding to the expression of the prayer; sensitive men of antiquity saw how this pose could imply reverential appeal or even passionate demand. Hence even at an early date we hear the admonition, to lift both hands and glance only moderately and modestly.[64] At the same time the apologists perceive in this posture an image of the Crucified[65] in whose name the Christian appears before God, a thought which recurs again in the commentators of the Middle Ages, who make much of it particularly as regards the posture during the canon of the Mass.[66] In the Roman Mass both during the orations and during the canon this moderate and somewhat stylized raising and stretching out of the hands has become a prescription of law for the priest.[67] However, the priest assumes this posture only in those prayers which have been his since olden times and which he says as speaker for the congregation (the orations, the preface, the canon and the *Pater noster*), but not in those prayers which are only the expression of personal piety and which were given him only later, especially as a contribution from the Frankish Church. For these latter prayers the attitude is one derived from Germanic tradition: praying with hands folded.[68] Thus in the posture of the priest the various strata of prayers, the distinctions between the ancient deposits and the later ones, are made visible to the eye even today.

12. The Collect: Form and Content

The nucleus of that collection of Roman orations which we meet for the first time in the sacramentaries must have been formed in the period from the third to the sixth centuries, that is to say, from the time that the

the fathers sometimes said Mass on his knees; see JL, VII (1927), 380, following L. Fries, *Die Geschichte Japans* (Leipzig, 1926).

Since Leo XIII, kneeling has come into use for the prayers at the end of Mass.

On the other hand, the genuflection at the *Veni Sancte Spiritus* and at *Et incarnatus est* at the high Mass on certain feasts, as is now customary—the prescription is already to be seen in the *Liber ordinarius* of Liége, ed. Volk, 105, 1. 1) —is rather to be regarded as a dramatic element suggested by the festive performance of the hymn and the solemnity of the profession.

[64] Tertullian, *De or.*, c. 17 (CSEL, XX, 190); Cyprian, *De dom. or.*, c. 66 (CSEL, III, 269 f.). Cf. Dekkers, *Tertullianus*, 82-87.

[65] Minucius Felix, *Octavius*, c. 29, 8 (CSEL, II, 43); Tertullian, *De or.*, c. 14; 29 (CSEL, XX, 189; 200). Cf. Eisenhofer, I, 266 f.

[66] See *infra*, Vol. II, Ch. 2, 14.

[67] The rule in force at present is first found in its essentials in the *Ordinarium O.P.* of 1256 (Guerrini, 236): *manuum elevatio sic fieri debet ut altitudinem humerorum sacerdotis non excedat, extensio vero tanta sit ut retro stantibus manus appareant evidenter.* Cf. *Ordo Rom. XIV*, n. 53 (PL, LXXVIII, 1160 C).

[68] *Supra*, p. 78.

Roman Church completed the transfer from Greek to Latin.[1] The formulation of the prayer material was for long left to the *liturgus*, to extemporize freely perhaps, as he did in his admonitions to the people in the homily, or to recite a text previously fixed and written down by himself or by another. St. Augustine bears witness to both methods of composition. In his booklet on *The First Catechetical Instruction (De catechizandis rudibus)* he remarks as an aside that candidates for admission to the catechumenate, if they are well educated or come from schools of rhetoric, ought to be warned not to mock when some bishops or ministers of the Church either fall into barbarisms and solecisms while calling upon almighty God or do not understand or nonsensically separate the words which they are pronouncing; not (he adds) that such faults should not be corrected, so that the people may plainly understand what they are saying "Amen" to, but that at an ecclesiastical *benedictio* the *bona dictio* is not the important thing it is in the forum.[2] But from the territory of the same Augustine we have conciliar resolutions proposing that at divine service only texts which have been approved should be used.[3] Still even in Rome as late as the sixth century some orations show clearly that they were composed for a certain special occasion.[4]

Even for this freely formed prayer, however, a certain style was definitely adopted even from the very beginning of the Latin liturgy. Its external outlines were already conditioned by the laconic spirit of the Roman and his preference for conciseness and clarity. This did not exclude lengthy prayer-formulas. The extended ordination prefaces of the Roman Pontifical (like those for the consecration of bishops and the ordination of priests and deacons) are in substance a part of the most ancient Roman sacramentaries. The Mass-liturgy, too, contains besides the three terse orations which begin with *Oremus* also the rather protracted prayer of thanks introduced with *Gratias agamus*.[5] But when compared with the prayer language of

---

[1] Pope Cornelius (d. 253) was the first to get a Latin inscription on his grave. Baumstark is inclined to date the *orationes sollemnes* of Good Friday back to about his period. A. Baumstark, "Liturgischer Nachhall der Verfolgungszeit" (*Beiträge zur Geschichte des christlichen Altertums und der byzantischen Literatur*, Festgabe A. Ehrhard dargebracht [Bonn, 1922], 53-72), 64-71; idem., *Liturgie comparée*, 84.

[2] Augustine, *De cat. rud.*, c. 9, 13 (PL, XL, 320); cf. J. P. Christopher, *St. Augustine: The First Catechetical Instruction* (Ancient Christian Writers, 2; Westminster, 1946), 33-34.

[3] Synod of Hippo (393), can. 21 (Mansi, III, 922): *quicumque sibi preces aliunde describit non eis utatur, nisi prius eas cum instructioribus fratribus contulerit.* A little later the synod of Mileve, can. 12 (Mansi, IV, 330) speaks of the authorization by a council.

[4] Thus that oration in the *Leonianum* (Muratori, I, 371) in which God is thanked for having granted us, "freed from the furious foes, to receive the paschal sacrament with peaceful mind", takes us back to the year 538 when the long siege of Vitiges was raised just before Easter; Duchesne, *Christian Worship*, 137; F. Cabrol, "Léonien (Sacramentaire)", DACL, VIII (1929), 2552 f.

[5] Cf. the essay to classify the prayer materials of the Roman liturgy in P. Alfonso, *L'Eucologia romana antica. Line-*

oriental or even of Gallic liturgies, the Roman character is still distinctly recognizable even in these longer prayer-formulas. Take just the opening address; in the oriental and Gallic liturgies there is usually an accumulation of divine titles and predicates, arranged in solemn groups of positives and negatives,[6] whereas in the Roman there is seldom more than a single, simple term. But it was in the oration that this Roman mode found its perfect outlet. In its few phrases liturgical prayer was reduced to the most succinct formula, and yet within that small compass there was room for the most dignified development and the greatest variety.

These orations have the character of petitions. This is not something self-evident, fundamentally, for according to Origen the normal course of every properly adjusted prayer—and surely this holds most especially for public prayer—should begin by praising God through Christ in the Holy Ghost; should then pass on to thanksgiving and an acknowledgment of our weakness; and only after that would it be fitting to make petitions, and these, petitions "for great and heavenly things"; and lastly it should close with the doxology repeated over again.[7] But the Roman oration is restricted almost wholly to the petition. The other elements are heard only in the address and in the closing formula. Since the very core of the Mass is entirely circumscribed by the prayer of thanksgiving, it seemed to be enough if the close of the three liturgical complexes which are appended to this core should be confined to petition. This is what actually happened in the orations. They consist of a single main clause or at most of a double clause in which the petition is formulated more plainly in a second phrase connected with the first by et.[8]

Coming now to details, we have to distinguish two types of Roman orations.[9] The *simple type* contains basically nothing except the barest ingredients of the petition, as when a child asks its father: *Pater, da mihi panem*, Father, give me bread. Thus there is nothing more than the address and the designation of what we want God to do for us. The expression can be either imperative or subjunctive, and the word order can be varied (schematized: *Panem da mihi, pater; Da mihi, pater, panem*). This is simple, direct praying, without ornaments or extras. This type is preserved

---

amenti stilistici e storici (Subiaco, 1931).
[6] Thus the beginning of the bishop's oration which concludes the Prayer of the Faithful in the Apostolic Constitutions, VIII, 11, 2 (Quasten, *Mon.*, 209) reads as follows: Κύριε παντοκράτορ, ὕψιστε, ὁ ἐν ὑψηλοῖς κατοικῶν, ἅγιε, ἐν ἁγίοις ἀναπαυόμενε, ἄναρχε, μόναρχε. Cf. the chapter "Sprache und Volksart" in Baumstark, *Vom geschichtlichen Werden der Liturgie* (Freiburg, 1923), 78-88, and the study of the "Genius of the Roman Rite" in Bishop, *Liturgica historica*, 1-19 (cf.

supra, p. 76, note 10).
[7] Origen, *De or.*, c. 33 (PG, XI, 557 f.).
[8] E.g. *Exaudi, Domine, quæsumus, preces nostras et interveniente beato N. . . . placatus intende.*
[9] H. Rheinfelder, "Zum Stil der lateinischen Orationen," JL, XI, (1931), 20-34.
A type-classification founded on the initial words is attempted by P. Salmon, "Les protocoles des oraisons du Missel Romain," *Eph. Liturg.*, XLV (1931), 140-147.

in substance even when there is an additional clause *(ut . . .)* to describe the object petitioned. But there is a second type, the *amplified type*, in which the address to God is enlarged by a phrase praising Him, the so-called *relative predication*[10]: *Deus, qui* . . . This is a definitely literary device, the work of rhetorical art, the sort of oratorical craft one would expect on the occasion of a solemn assembly of the faithful.

The striking thing is that this second type generally does not appear in the secret or post-communion but only in the collect. In the secret and the post-communion, the type commonly used is the simple type, since the object of the petition is already made abundantly clear in the presentation of the offerings and in the reception of Communion. The appearance of this amplified type in the collect is not governed by any strict rule, but we can say that this relative predication is generally found only on days of special solemnity, namely, days of commemoration.[11] It is especially frequent on feast days; in fact, for modern saints' feasts it is a fixed part of the collects, as already indicated in the schema of the *Commune Sanctorum: Deus, qui nos beati N. Confessoris tui solemnitate lætificas, concede* . . . Relative predication is not the only method of incorporating the thought suggested by the feast into the petition, but it is certainly the handiest. This relative clause, which emphasizes the concepts of praise and thanksgiving, thus plays within the priest's oration a part comparable to that which the *Gloria* plays in the preceding prayer of the people. Putting it another way, the *Gloria*, which on festive occasions follows the *Kyrie*, resounds again in this relative clause.

In these and similar ways the festal thoughts have been able to slip into the narrow space of the orations. But by so doing it was almost impossible to avoid burdening, and even overburdening, the traditional schemas. It is, for instance, only right, and indicative of a feeling for the hierarchy of the Christian economy of salvation that the saint of the day be inserted by asking God's help *intercedente beato N.* But it is more than the schema can bear when chunks of the saint's biography are introduced into that pliant form; or lengthy theological reflections are projected into it.[12] Still we must never lose sight of the fact that we are dealing with litur-

---

[10] E. Norden, "Agnostos Theos," *Untersuchungen zur Formgeschichte religiöser Rede* (Leipzig, 1913), 168-176.

Rheinfelder, *op. cit.*, 25 f., with good grounds sees in this use of relative predication in Christian cult an effect of the ancient sacral language so well known to the neo-converts.

[11] Thus, e.g., it appears in Lent only on three Sundays and on the two special week-days, Wednesday and Friday, of the fourth week—a week significant because of the baptismal scrutinies; outside of these only on the first Thursday, which

was not provided with a Mass until much later. But then this relative predication appears in nearly all the orations of Holy Week from Wednesday on, thus, e.g., after ten of the twelve prophecies on Holy Saturday; further on all the days of Easter week from Sunday to Friday, and on all the Sundays from Low Sunday to Pentecost inclusive.

[12] Thus, for the former, the collect of St. Jane Frances de Chantal, and for the latter the oration on the feast of our Lady of Sorrows.

gical, communal prayer which always has a tendency to pass from the simple prayer of inspired feeling to the more rational manner of a profession of faith and the utterance of many thoughts. The classical form of the oration, with its beautiful balance between praying and thinking—this we will always be able to admire in the collects of the Sundays after Pentecost.

Before we turn to the study of the theology and contents of these collects, we must take one further glance at their literary design. The striking feature of the old Roman orations has always been their majestic flow, their rhythm. It is evident that there is here a survival of the rhetorical art of dying antiquity; undoubtedly the earliest writers of these collects had studied in the schools of classical rhetoric. What is the secret of this rhythm? The attempt has been made to show that the ancient orations are still guided primarily by the quantitative meters of the classical era. The orations are composed, as a rule, of several members, all more or less of the same length, and these metrical elements are so repeated (not indeed with the regularity of a verse but with a certain freedom) that the opening phrase and the close are brought close together.[13]

It could well be that these metrical laws of classical poetry did have an influence, unsought perhaps, on the elevated prose of the period of the Empire's decline, but in our case the proof is not easy. But the chief factor in achieving this agreeable harmony in the Roman orations was the *cursus*, the rules for which were followed in Latin artistic prose from the fourth/ fifth century on.[14] By *cursus* is meant the rhythm of the cadences produced by arranging the accents in the last syllables of a literary period or clause according to certain fixed rules. In the sermons of St. Peter Chrysologus and in the sermons and letters of Pope Leo the Great the rules of the *cursus* are observed with meticulous care, with such care in fact, that the absence of the *cursus* has been used as a clue to the spuriousness of some of the pieces ascribed to the latter.[15] We have already discovered on other grounds that the orations of these earliest levels of our liturgy are compositions of the era of Pope Leo the Great and may even be the work of his hands.

There are three chief forms of cadences in the Roman *cursus*:

cursus planus: _/_ __ __ _/_ __   *(esse consortes)*

cursus velox: _/_ __ __ _(/)_ __ _/_ __ *(meritis adiuvemur)*

---

[13] J. Cochez, "La structure rhythmique des oraisons," *Cours et Conférences,* VI (Louvain, 1928), 138-150. Cf. M.L., an English Benedictine, "The Collects of the Roman Office," *American Ecclesiastical Rev.,* XXXVII, 537; XXXVIII, 379; XLI, 397.

[14] H. Leclercq, "Cursus," DACL, III,

3193-3205; Eisenhofer, I, 204.

[15] F. di Capua, *Il ritmo prosaico nelle lettere dei papi,* 2 vols. (Rome, 1937-1939); idem., "De clausulis a S. Leone M. adhibitis" in the C. Silva-Tarouca edition of the Letters of Pope Leo (*Textus et documenta, ser. theol.,* XV; Rome, 1934), pp. xxiii-xxxii.

cursus tardus: $\underline{\prime}$ __ __ $\underline{\prime}$ __ __ (*semper obtineat*)

In the collect of the 13th Sunday after Pentecost these three cadences are found, in a row, in the three members of the text:

Omnipotens sempiterne Deus, da nobis fidei, spei et caritatis augmentum,
et ut mereamur assequi quod promittis,
fac nos amare quod præcipis.

It is remarkable indeed that, for all the care expended on the style of our orations, the Roman liturgy never once overstepped the line dividing prose from verse.[16] We can detect here something of that seriousness that seizes man when he is face-to-face with the majesty of God. There is no object better calculated to inspire poetry and to glorify art than the revelation of God's grandeur and goodness, and the greatest orations of men are replete with just that burden. But when human speech turns directly to God, any possible play of verse dies on the lips of the petitioner who is conscious of what he is doing. This explains, too, why music, which through the centuries has used its treasures to their utmost on the development of every part of the liturgy, especially the prayer of the people, has yet called a halt at the prayer of the priest. The performance of the priest's text has never gone beyond a more or less solemn recitative, the forms of speech-song.[17]

Speech-song or *accentus* is the method of performance most suited to liturgical prayer said aloud. It avoids two extremes; on the one hand that passionate speech whose modulation, directed entirely by emotion and mood, seems alien to a prayer which was not formulated by the speaker, and which at any rate gives the personal and individual element too much play; on the other hand the monotony of the severe *tonus rectus*, unbroken

---

[16] The same is true, moreover, of the sacerdotal prayer of nearly all liturgies. One exception to be found is that in the Gallican liturgy; in the first of the so-called Mone Masses which are traced back to the poet bishop Venantius Fortunatus (d. c. 600), several of the prayers are written in hexameters (PL, CXXXVIII, 876-879). For the Orient see the references to prayers in metrical form in the Syrian liturgies, in Baumstark, *Liturgie comparée*, 76.

[17] Speech-song had already been a practice in the culture of antiquity; see the literary references in O. Casel, *Das Gedächtnis des Herrn in der altchristlichen Liturgie* (*Ecclesia Orans*, 2; Freiburg, 1918), 14, note 1.

Cf. Wagner, *Einführung*, III, 19 ff.

Efforts to do more, to exaggerate the dramatic elements in the prayers, were suppressed by the Church as occasion demanded. An example in point is found in can. 12 of the synod of Cloveshoe in England (747) which ordered: *ut presbyteri sæcularium poetarum modo in ecclesia non garriunt, ne tragico sono sacrorum verborum compositionem ac distinctionem corrumpant vel confundant, sed simplicem sanctamque melodiam secundum morem Ecclesiæ sectentur; qui vero id non est idoneus assequi, pronuntiantis modo simpliciter legendo dicat atque recitet, quidquid instantis temporis ratio poscit* (Mansi, XII, 399). Similar advice also in Walafrid Strabo, *De exord. et increm.*, c. 12 (PL, CXIV, 932 f.).

by any cadence whatever, which does not suit at least the more festive prayer assemblies.[18] But speech-song does not ever rise to the proper art-forms of Gregorian Chant. Hence it happened that even after the chant melodies had long been written down (first in neums and later in full notation), no such means was used for the melodies of the priest's prayers.[19] For these it was sufficient to use the simpler notation of the so-called *positurœ* or *pausationes*, which indicated for public readers the type of cadence and from which our modern system of sentence punctuation derives.[20] The orations and readings in the Roman Missal still contain vestiges of the signs, and they still serve their original function of directing the eyes to the cadence. Thus the drop of a minor third at the end of the first member of the oration (the relative clause) is indicated by a colon *(metrum)*, the drop of a half-tone before the last *ut*-clause by a semicolon *(flexa)*, e.g.:

> *Deus, qui . . . lœtificas:*
> *concede propitius; ut . . .*[21]

Since the collect is a prayer which is supposed to represent within the limits of the introduction to divine service our approach to God, and since, save for an occasional solemnity, no special theme is proposed for it, its content is necessarily very general. It is, in fact, even more general than the nature of a priestly *collectio* demands, even though this *collectio* as such could incorporate only what is general and transsubjective. The Church approaches God in all that indigence and need that must be a part of her in this earthly pilgrimage. Many formulas do not mention any specified object, but merely ask to be heard—for all the desires in the hearts of the assembled petitioners. Or perhaps one or the other constant and ever-recurring desire is mentioned: Help of divine power, overthrow of error and overcoming of danger, inclination to good, forgiveness of sin, attainment of salvation. At the same time, however, these prayers often mirror

---

[18] For like reasons speech-song (declamation) is also suggested for the leader in the German community Mass; see F. Messerschmid, *Liturgie und Gemeinde* (Würzburg, 1939), 90-93; thus (he says) the sacred word is withdrawn from the whim and fancy of the speaker (91). See also Jungmann, *Liturgical Worship*, 131.

[19] Cf. Wagner, *Einführung*, II, 82 ff., 87 f.

[20] The system which was gradually established in the course of the Middle Ages comprised four signs: the *punctus circumflexus*, also called *flexa*, for a simple drop of the voice (a half tone) at a breath-pause; the *punctus elevatus* also called *metrum*, for a longer pause, but where there was a continu-

ation; the *punctus versus* (; or.), for the close of the sentence; and in the lessons the *punctus interrogativus* (?) for the question. Wagner, *Einführung*, II, 87 f., 94.

[21] See the authentic methods in the *Kyriale*, typical edition, Rome, 1905; also in the *Graduale Romanum*, Rome, 1908 (*Toni communes missœ*); cf. D. Johner, *Cantus ecclesiastici iuxta edit. Vaticanum ad usum clericorum* (Regensburg, 1926) or John C. Selner, *Chant at the Altar*. Since the 16th century these symbols were no longer used consistently and accurately in the Mass books, having been adopted in ordinary literature for grammatical and rhetorical purposes even in merely quiet reading; see Wagner, II, 91, who proposes a reform on this point.

the powers that stand opposed to each other in the spiritual combat, especially in the form of pairs of contrasting ideas, a literary device which matched the notorious fondness for antithetical phrasing: Corporal and spiritual, thinking and doing, burden of one's own effort and the heavenly intercession of the saints, abstaining from nourishment and fasting from sin, freedom from oppression and devotion to good works, profession and imitation, faith and reality, earthly life and eternal blessedness. Very often we meet that profound and comprehensive antithesis of external action, temporal service, faithful devotion on the one hand, and internal achievement, eternal welfare, and lasting reality on the other,[22] somewhat as it is expressed for example in the collect of the twenty-second Sunday after Pentecost: *ut quod fideliter petimus—efficaciter consequamur*: what we ask with faith, we may some day obtain in reality.

Above all, however, the collect makes visible to us the grand outlines of that spiritual universe in which our prayer lives and moves and is; it arises in the communion of holy Church and ascends through Christ to God on high. The oration turns to God in an address which, by its very brevity, appears to disclaim all ability to make comprehensible the nature of the unfathomable: *Deus, Domine, Omnipotens Deus*, or at most, *Omnipotens sempiterne Deus*. Even on saints' feasts, and where some special patronage might put us in mind of a particular helper, the oration is still directed to God Himself, begging Him, through the intercession of this saint—presupposing therefore, that he is invoked in the personal prayers of the faithful—to grant us protection and aid. Even the direct address to Christ within the Mass was not permitted in the ancient Church. At the Council of Hippo (393), an explicit decree was written precisely on this point, apparently directed against certain new trends: *Ut nemo in precibus vel Patrem pro Filio, vel Filium pro Patre nominet. Et cum altari assistitur, semper ad Patrem dirigatur oratio.*[23] In the Roman liturgy, which never wavered in its profession of the divinity of Christ, this law, that within the Mass the prayers were to be addressed to God the Father,[24] was kept with-

---

[22] See in this connection O. Casel, "Beiträge zur römischen Oration," JL, XI (1931), 35-45. Especially the term *effectus* is, according to Casel, to be rendered not by effect (result) but by efficacy (realization).

Cf. further W. Kahle, "Vom Stil liturgischen Betens." *Liturg. Zeitschrift*, V (1932/1933). 161-172; P. Schorlemmer, *Die Kollektengebete* (Gütersloh, 1928), especially pp. 29-37; B. Capelle, "Pour mieux comprendre les oraisons du Missel," *Cours et Conférences*, V (Louvain, 1926), 135-145.

[23] Can. 21 (Mansi, III, 922) = can. 23 of the III Council of Carthage (397; *ibid.*,

884). Cf. Jungmann, *Die Stellung Christi*, 150; 198.

[24] In the Roman orations, indeed, no direct address to the Father as such is to be found, but only to God in the sense of a basic relationship of man to his creator; in other words, a trinitarian reflection is wanting. But the *Filium tuum* of the concluding formula opens up the question of the Trinity also for the address, and the only answer must be that "God" refers to the Father. Cf. the theological discussion in Bellarmine, *Disput. de controv.*, III, 3, 6 (*De sacrif. missæ*, II), c. 16 (ed. Rome, 1838: III, 785 f.). Regarding the biblical data see

out exception right down to the year 1000. Till that time not even one collect—nor, for that matter, one secret or one post-communion—can be found to have infringed this rule.[25] It was not till about the end of the millenary, when the native Roman liturgy gave way before the Gallicized form which returned from the north, that any forms of address to Christ Himself appear, as they had previously appeared in the Orient and as they had developed in the Gallic liturgy.[26] In private prayer, in the prayer of the

K. Rahner, " 'Gott' als erste trinitarische Person im Neuen Testament," ZkTh, LXVI (1942), 71-88.

[25] Dom Gaspar Lefebvre, O.S.B., Catholic Liturgy, Its Fundamental Principles (St. Louis, 1937), 30, says: "In the Roman Missal are found only twenty-seven prayers addressed to the Son, and these are almost all later than the thirteenth century."

Pursuing the trinitarian concept even further, especially in view of the prayers addressed to Christ, even medieval interpreters take up the question, why no oration is directed to the Holy Ghost. Hugh of St. Cher, Tract. de missa (Sölch, 15) replies: Quia Spiritus Sanctus est donum et a dono non petitur donum, sed a largitore doni. This is repeated by Durandus, IV, 15, 11. Although speculatively the answer is hardly compelling, it is kerygmatically correct; in other words, the theoretical possibility of prayers addressed to the Holy Ghost should not be exploited for fear that the basic lines of the order of salvation—leading to God through Christ—might vanish in the consciousness of the petitioner. This is particularly true in regard to the sacrifice which Christ offers to the Father; on this Cardinal Bona, Rer. lit., II, 5, 5 (628) lays great stress. But it also holds true generally for all liturgical prayer; cf. supra, p. 80. Besides, the presentation of a distinction in the divine essence should not be encouraged. As a matter of fact orations addressed to the Holy Ghost have gained importance in none of the liturgies save the Armenian; see Jungmann, Die Stellung Christi, 195, note 27.

[26] This change was made in the spirit of the Gallic liturgical tradition with its strong anti-Arian bias, wherein, in consequence of the struggle against the Arians

who disputed the essential unity of the Son with the Father, the ambiguous Per Christum was restricted, and the address to Christ freely exchanged with that to God and thus permitted to appear on a par with it. But even on Frankish soil this change within the Roman liturgy did not go unchallenged; e.g. in the 9th-century collection of Canons ed. by Benedict the Levite, III, 418 (PL, XCVII, 850 f.; cf. also the Capitulare often connected with St. Boniface, in Mansi, XII, App. II, 109), the Canon of Hippo reappears; likewise, about the turn of the 11th century in Bernold, Micrologus, c. 5 (PL, CLI, 980.

Our Missale Romanum, amongst the formularies of Sundays and ferias which otherwise spring from ancient tradition, today exhibits seven collects and two post-communion formulas in which the Per ending certified in the oldest MSS. is replaced by the Qui vivis which presupposes an address to Christ. The fillip inducing the change was probably the mention in these collects of a "coming" of God: in concrete fashion this would be understood of the Christmas coming of Christ. The same is true of two olden orations of the Mass of the Dead; they were provided with the ending because the expressions redemptor, redemptio tua were thought to refer only to Christ.

For new Mass formularies orations were composed which are directed to Christ. But it is significant that they adhere to the tradition of an indifferent address, Deus qui (e.g. on Corpus Christi, or, in modern times, on the feast of St. Gabriel Possenti), instead of Domine Jesu Christe. Cf. Jungmann, Die Stellung Christi, 103 ff.

In the case of the oration pro rege the Congregation of Rites, by the decree of

people, in hymns, and in fact wherever prayer could be more free and not cramped by the need to keep the divine order of the world in full view, prayer to Christ had always been customary; it is attested even in the days of the Apostles.[27] But in the oration, which is the official prayer of the priest, it has always been exceptional.

And still it is evident that Christ also must be mentioned in the official prayer of the Christian community. As a matter of fact His name does appear, and has appeared for ages, in the closing formula. And it appears there in such a way that a much deeper insight is granted into the whole structure of the Christian economy than would be vouchsafed by a prayer addressed simply to Christ even though this latter seems at first glance to be eminently suitable to a Christian assembly.[28] The Roman oration suggests pointedly: We offer up our prayer through our Lord Jesus Christ, Thy Son. This method of prayer or variations of it, already seen in the writings of the New Testament,[29] prevails in the whole Christian service till the fourth century.[30] The expression "through Christ" appears especially as a member of the doxology which usually concludes the prayer: we offer our praise to God through Jesus Christ, or (as sources in the second/third century put it) through our high-priest Jesus Christ.[31] The Roman manner, however, which avoids the doxology except at the end of the canon, builds up the thought of Christ's mediatorship in a different way, which it has retained to the present. Note especially that the *per Christum* does not mean a mere *adiuratio* as some older authors thought, as though we begged a hearing *"by* Christ," for His sake, in virtue of His merits.[32] Nor

March 3, 1761, restored the ancient ending *Per D. n. J. C.*, appealing, as it did so, to the authority of *antiquissima S. Gregorii Magni sacramentaria.* Martinucci, *Manuale decretorum* SRC, n. 423.
[27] A. Klawek, *Das Gebet zu Jesus. Seine Berechtigung und Übung nach den Schriften des N.T.* (Neutest. Abh., VI, 5; Münster, 1921). Regarding his attempt to trace the Christ-payers of the apocryphal Acts of the Apostles back to the worship of the primitive Church (111 f.), cf. Jungmann, 147 ff.
[28] Cf. in the latter sense the criticism by Baumstark, *Vom geschichtlichen Werden,* 90-93.
[29] Rom. 1: 8; 16: 27; 2 Cor. 1: 20; Heb. 12: 15; 1 Pet. 2:5; 4: 11; Jude 25.
[30] Jungmann, *op. cit.,* 118-151.
[31] *Ibid.,* 126 ff.

Another development circumscribes the atmosphere of prayer still more by adding "in the Holy Ghost" or "in the holy Church". *Ibid.,* 130 ff.
[32] Thus, e.g., Suarez, *De oratione,* I, 10, 10-18 (*Opp.,* ed. Berton, 14, 39-41). That the mediatorship of Christ *per modum advocati* should be taken into account in prayer he considers admissible, even in the form of begging for His intercession, but he considers it less suitable for public prayer because we should avoid even the appearance of seeming to pray to Christ *tamquam ad purum hominem.* For this reason he prefers to take *per Christum* to refer to the mediatorship *per modum merentis.* But it is clear that this latter is not the original conception of the formula; numerous texts of the first centuries show this (see the preceding remarks); and besides most of the liturgies left the *per Christum* drop precisely when the Arians obstinately misinterpreted the subordination of the God-man Jesus Christ (which the formula patently attests) as the subordination of the Logos.

does it signify that the gifts we ask *be handed* us through Christ.[33] It must be understood rather as a progressive movement, a mounting upwards. For we declare that we offer up our petitions to God *through the mediation* of Christ, who (as St. Paul says) "lives on still to make intercession on our behalf" (Hebr. 7:25). This kind of prayer is familiar to the Roman Mass, and therefore the concluding formula of the oration must actually be taken in this sense, so that the completed form would read something like: *hoc rogamus per Dominum nostrum Jesum Christum.* Corroboration is seen clearly in the phrase in the canon: *Te igitur . . . per Jesum Christum . . . supplices rogamus ac petimus,* and from allied phrases in other consecratory prayers. We bring our prayer before God "through our eternal high-priest," as the expression is sometimes expanded in medieval Latin texts.[34]

This approach to someone "through" the intervention of someone else was familiar to men in olden times not only in the relationship of attorney or proctor, who represented his client at a legal suit or in a petition for a favor, but perhaps even more in the current version of the greeting in a letter, which at that time could reach its destination only by messenger: "through the bearer I greet you."[35] Just as here a friend is kept in view, so in our case it is God, but in both instances the direct approach is to him who stands in his presence and who speaks to him in our name. It is important to notice that two attributes are attached to the name of Jesus in our formula, two attributes which bring out this connection to both parties: *Dominus noster* and *Filius tuus.* He is our Master; we belong to Him since He has bought us with His blood. And He is God's Son, related by the closest ties and one with Him in the unity of the divine essence.

Such words would, of course, be quite strange and alien to vital prayer unless in our consciousness there was actually the immovable background that made such prayer a matter of course, perhaps not under all circumstances but at least during the solemn prayer of the Church. But such was really the case in the world in which a conclusion to prayer such as this was used for the first time. When this type of conclusion was incorporated into the daily prayer of the Church, this background must have been thoroughly established in the soul of the faithful community—I mean the thought that the earthly Church had its Head in heaven, Jesus Christ, the

---

[33] This point is sharply highlighted by P. Bonhomme, O.P., "Par Jésus-Christ Notre Seigneur," *Cours et Conférences,* VI (Louvain, 1928), 119-137.

[34] Jungmann, *Die Stellung Christi,* 184 f.: *per sacerdotem æternum Filium tuum.* Cf. *ibid.,* 90: *per Jesum Christum Filium tuum Dominum nostrum, verum pontificem et solum sine peccati macula sacerdotem.*

[35] Thus at least in the Greek ambit, where indeed the διὰ Χριστοῦ appears for the first time; cf., e.g., in a letter of introduction from Oxyrhynchos: Receive our brother Heracles well, δι' οὗ σε καὶ τοὺς σὺν σοι πάντος ἀδελφοὺς ἐγὼ καὶ οἱ σὺν ἐμοὶ προσαγορεύομεν. H. Leclercq, "Lettres chrétiennes," DACL, VIII, 2785 (n. 13); cf. *ibid.,* 2781 (n. 3), 2787 (n. 22).

Lord, who in His glorified body returned to the Father as the first-born of many brethren, as King of His holy people, which is bound to Him in the Holy Ghost.[36] It was out of this consciousness that the Roman mediator-formula got its further amplification—a second phrase which is this time an irremovable relative clause referring to Christ: who with Thee liveth and reigneth in the unity of the Holy Ghost,[37] God,[38] world without end.[39]

Here the glory of the Church triumphant shines forth resplendent, to balance the Church terrestrial assembled and made visible in the community at prayer. And this is the third notion with which the spiritual world of liturgical prayer is rounded out in the oration. It is the Church that prays: *Ecclesia tua, populus tuus, familia tua, famuli tui, fideles tui*—these are the terms by which the oration designates the petitioners and the recipients of God's gifts. In every instance the prayer is worded in the plural, "we": *quæsumus, rogamus, deprecamur.* However, the Church is included here not only conceptually, but actually. In liturgical prayer there is—

[36] Inversely this formula, once more given a vital interpretation, can and should make us more aware of this whole series of concepts. Regarding the religious bearing and import of such praying, cf. the chapter "Through Christ our Lord" in K. Adam, *Christ our Brother.* See also Jungmann, *Liturgical Worship,* 137 ff.

[37] *In unitate Spiritus Sancti* = at one with the Holy Ghost, in the unity which the Spirit founds; cf. Eph. 4: 3. The unity is to be considered in the concrete as the Communion of Saints, particularly (in the present instance) the triumphant Church in whose midst the glorified Christ lives and reigns; cf. Jungmann, *Gewordene Liturgie,* 199 ff.

Outside the Roman Mass there is to be found an expression of Christ's reigning *cum (Patre et) Spiritu Sancto,* but this is, of course, an entirely different conception.

[38] The word *Deus* was not originally part of the Roman closing formula; cf. the formula *Conversi* in St. Augustine, *Serm.* 100 (PL, XXXVIII, 605, note 2); 362 (PL, XXXIX, 1634). The spot where it was to be inserted was not plainly fixed till late in the Middle Ages.

The confession of Christ's divinity which the word *Deus* expresses is already contained in the words *Filium tuum.* Regarding its superfluousness, especially in

vernacular translation, see the next note.
[39] The expression *Per omnia sæcula sæculorum,* εἰς τοὺς αἰῶνας τῶν αἰώνων, is a heritage from the service of the primitive Church (cf. Apoc. 1: 6; 5: 13; 7: 12; etc.; Irenæus, *Adv. haer.,* I, 1, 5 [*al.,* I, 3, 1; Harvey, I, 25]) to be found in all the liturgies. It is merely an intensified expression for εἰς τοὺς αἰῶνας (Hebr. 13: 8) and this in turn an intensified expression for εἰς τὸν αἰῶνα (Hebr. 5: 6; 7: 24; etc.): forever, till eternity. This intensified form was already in use in the synagogue service: *min ha'olam we'ad ha'olam,* from era to era. The rabbis gave this explanation: at first the formula was simply: into eternity (*'ad ha'olam*), but in opposition to those who doubted the resurrection and maintained there was but one era, the formula was amplified (Tosephta, Berachoth, 7, 21); see H. Sasse in Kittel, *Theol. Worterbuch,* I (1933), 197 ff., 207.

In the context of this closing formula the *per omnia sæcula sæculorum* is referred to the life and reign of Christ; cf. Apoc. 1: 18: *fui mortuus et ecce sum vivens in sæcula sæculorum.*

The English expression "world without end" must be taken to mean "through all eternity" and must not be referred simply to the preceding word "God" which did not belong to the primitive text.

there must be—in fullest reality a communion in which all those participate who join with the priest as he performs the service, all those who are represented expressly by the greeting and its answer and by the comprehensive *Oremus*. Even in a small group of faithful, with the priest standing at the altar at their head, not only is there present a number of Christians, but the Church itself is there in its hierarchic structure—God's people of the New Covenant in the order and arrangement given them by Christ.

Short and summary though the Roman orations might be, in every one of them the new creation is marked out with monumental lines, and it seems to encompass us most forcefully when the priest, at the head of his congregation, looking up to Christ, approaches God with his pleading prayer.

In the Amen the people are once again called upon to confirm the prayer of their speaker.[40] The word remains untranslated in all the liturgies. Justin renders it by γένοιτο; so be it,[41] and that is obviously the meaning it has here, for it expresses the assent of the people to the priest's praying and pleading. For this purpose it is not the only expression used, but it is by far the most prevalent.[42]

---

[40] Regarding their actually saying *Amen* see *supra*, p. 236.

The *Amen* actually spoken by the people after their prayers is evidenced in Augustine, *De catech. rud.*, c. 9, 13 (*supra*, p. 373); *Ep.*, 217, 26 (CSEL, LVII, 422); *De dono persev.*, 23, 63 (PL, XLV, 1031). That it was particularly expected at this place even in the 8th century is shown in MSS. of the Arch-chanter (Silva-Tarouca, 197, 1. 8, with note 6; 198, 1. 28). Later data, see *supra*, p. 237, note 22 ff.

[41] Justin, *Apol.*, I, 65; likewise already in the Septuagint. To this correspond the customary translations in Italian (*così sia*) and in French (*ainsi soit-il*). In its original use the Hebrew *'amen* means "certainly, truly"; it is the acknowledgment of a statement that is certain and sure; cf. H. Schiller in Kittel, *Theol. Wörterbuch*, I (1939), 339-342; cf. I, 233. Even in the synagogue the *Amen* was used as an acclamation by the people after the doxology; thus the people professed their assent to the praise of God spoken by the leader (Schiller, *loc. cit.*). It was similarly employed in the primitive Church: 1 Cor. 14: 16; Apoc. 5: 14. This primitive use is still to be found in the Egyptian liturgy when the people continually interrupt the account of the institution with an *Amen* after each phrase; Brightman, 132 f., 176 f., 232.

Regarding the liturgical use of the *Amen* there are comprehensive studies like F. Cabrol, "Amen," DACL, I, 1554-1573, especially 1556 ff.; J. Cecchetti, *L'Amen nella Bibbia e nella Liturgia* (Reprint from *Bollettino ceciliano*, v. 37; Vatican City, 1942), 14-37; H. Thurston, "Amen," CE, I, 407-409.

[42] In Egyptian liturgies we find the *Amen* of the people at the close of prayer or even in the course of it, either amplified with a *Kyrie eleison*: thus in the opening litany of the Ethiopian fore-Mass where the response of the people each time is: *Amen, Kyrie eleison, Lord, have mercy on us.* (Brightman, 206; cf. 233, 1. 34: *Amen, grant us!*); or it is replaced by a simple *Kyrie* (B., 223, 1. 34) or by a triple *Kyrie* (B., 117, 1. 33) or by a translation (B. 179, 1. 7). The last form is that found originally in the anamnesis of the West-Syrian Mass (B., 53, 1. 17; 88, 1. 7) and (along with a *Kyrie*) in the intercessory prayer of the same liturgy: Raes, *Introductio*, 90. In the Occident two similar instances are noted by A. Dold, "Die Worte *miserere nobis* als Orationsschluss?" JL, IX (1929), 138; Irish and Glagolitic texts are cited.

The present-day Mass usually has several collects. It was not always thus. The Roman Mass for a thousand years had only one oration. Amalar took the occasion of his visit to Rome in 830 to ask the clerics of St. Peter's about this, and he sets down the results of his inquiry with some emphasis in a special preface to his work.[43] Even in cases (he says) where in the sacramentaries two Mass formularies are stipulated for one and the same day, because a feast coincides with a Sunday or two feasts fall due the same day, they told him that they have only one oration: *unam tantum*. And Amalar tries to assure his readers that this will suffice even where special reasons intervene; if someone wants to pray for the forgiveness of sin, there is opportunity during the offering of gifts; if someone seeks to enlist the cooperation of the angels, the opportunity is found at the end of the preface; if he wishes to plead for peace, the plea is found in the canon *(pacificare digneris)*, etc. But for cases where the same priest wants to fulfill two offices, he suggests the possibility of saying a Mass for each one in particular, that is, several Masses on one day. This possibility was often taken advantage of at the time, until for very good reasons it was finally prohibited.[44] There was another solution which many made use of, namely, to append the fore-Mass of one celebration to the fore-Mass of another, and only then to continue with the Mass proper *(missa bifaciata,* resp. *trifaciata)*, but since this latter would then contain the corresponding number of formulas for the *secreta* and the post-communion the arrangement was rejected as a *monstruosa mixtura.*[45] However one other way remained open: the *missa sicca.*[46] The text of one Mass was tacked on to the other in this fashion: after the (post-) communion the priest removed the chasuble and then, standing at the Epistle side of the altar, he read the second Mass formulary, starting with the introit, but skipping from the offertory-verse to the communion-verse; and thus coming to a conclusion. Everyone was aware that this was but a *nudum missæ officium,* and for that reason it was plainly separated from the real celebration. It was a commemorative rite, a devotion which later on acquired an independent

---

[43] Amalar, *De eccl. off.,* Præf. altera (PL, CV, 987 f.).

The peculiarity that is found in the older *Gelasianum* and partly also in the *Leonianum,* namely, two orations regularly before the secret, will be discussed later *(infra,* p. 484). This is hardly evidence for a practice of having two orations regularly following each other at Mass, certainly not at Rome.

[44] *Supra,* p. 221.

[45] Thus in 1198 by Bishop Odo of Paris;

Pinsk (see note following), 101; Franz, 84 ff.

[46] J. Pinsk, "Die Missa sicca," JL, IV (1923), 90-118. The term *missa sicca* was derived originally from a rite which was customary at the Communion of the sick; even here in the sick-room the Mass formulary was read, skipping however from the fore-Mass (this might even reach to the *Sanctus*) to the *Pater noster,* and then giving Communion in the usual way, but only under the form of bread (hence the *sicca*); Pinsk, 98 f.

existence, being used on various occasions particularly as an extra-eucharistic service till, after the Council of Trent, it was replaced by the Benediction service.[47]

However, besides such a commemoration which comprised all the proper texts, the other type already discovered (and disapproved) by Amalar continued in use. Here for the commemoration of the extra Office or of some other special exigency only the respective orations (collect, secret, and post-communion) were appended.[48] Traces of a tendency to use this expedient are found in the Frankish area quite early. Still the effort was made to work out a scheme whereby both themes would be incorporated in one formula. A hundred years before Amalar, the older *Gelasianum* contains a formulary in which the orations (and the *Hanc igitur* formula) express a double purpose, the remembrance of a holy martyr and a service for the dead.[49] But the *Gregorianum* of Hadrian, in the second Christmas Mass, displays the other expedient, a second oration added for the second theme (St. Anastasia).[50] By the ninth century the second oration appears as an independent formula in many other liturgical texts.[51] Still, as late as the turn of the eleventh century we hear a voice raised to re-establish the old rule that at each Mass, just as there is one introit and one Gospel, there should be but one oration—and at the same time it lauds those who, when adding extra orations, but seldom overstep the number seven.[52] It is quite

---

[47] Pinsk, 101 ff., 117.

The classic example of a "dry Mass" is the one still to be found in the Blessing of Palms on Palm-Sunday. Even the rubric to be found here, not to turn to the people at *Dominus vobiscum*, belongs to this rite.

[48] Inversely in the Byzantine liturgy a commemorative rite has been devised in which it is the readings or at least the Epistle that is added to the reading of the day. Max von Sachsen, *Prælectiones de liturgiis orientalibus*, II (Freiburg, 1913), 226.

[49] III, 95 (Wilson, 303 f.). The first oration reads: *Beati martyris tui (illius), Domine, quæsumus, intercessione nos protege et animam famuli tui (illius) sacerdotis sanctorum tuorum iunge consortiis.*

[50] Lietzmann, n. 7.

Amalar, too, had this case of precedence in view (*loc. cit.*, 989 C).

For extra-eucharistic functions like the conferring of orders or the introduction of Penance and of penitential reconciliation even the older *Gelasianum* had two or more orations following each other (I, 20; 99; I, 15; 38) and this, at least

in part, from genuine Roman tradition; cf. also the formulary for the ordinations in the *Leonianum* (Muratori, I, 422-425) and in the *Gregorianum* (Lietzmann, n. 2-4).

[51] Thus the Mass for penitents in the Pontifical of Poitiers (last third of the 9th century) in J. Morinus, *Commentarius historicus de disciplina in adm. sacr. poenitentiæ* (Antwerp, 1682), App., p. 59 f.

[52] Bernold, *Micrologus*, c. 4 (PL, CLI, 980). At Cluny in the 11th century the rule held that not more than ten orations were to be spoken at the *missa maior; Udalrici Consuet. Clun.* I, 7 (PL, CXLIX, 652); cf. *ibid.*, I, 6; 9 (651, 653). The progressive multiplication of orations can be gauged, e.g., by what happened in the penitential liturgy. Thus in the order of reconciliation on Maundy Thursday the three orations of older sources (8th century) have grown to sixteen in the Romano-German pontifical of the 10th century (Hittorp, 53-55); cf. Jungmann, *Die lateinischen Bussriten, 76, 78f., 96, 187 f.*

possible to see in this trend towards a multiplication of orations the same influence at work that produced the long, wordy prayers of the Gallic liturgies.[53]

As time went on the stress was entirely on this rule, that the number seven should not be exceeded,[54] and that the last should not be an oration *pro defunctis.*[55] Besides there was a new regulation, emphasizing that the number of orations should be uneven—seven or five or three or one.[56] This rule regarding the odd number of orations is still maintained in the present missal for days of lesser rite[57]; manifold are the prescriptions for filling out the orations to the number three. And still the rule is often broken, e.g., by the addition of the *oratio imperata* of the bishop. The numbers five and seven also play a role, but only to this extent that on lesser days these numbers may be taken into account[58]—an example of the rubrical continuance of a rule whose basis has long ago disappeared.

Moreover we will have to point out another development in this growth of orations. The collect (and with it, the secret and the post-communion) has acquired a second function along with the original one. Since the dis-

---

[53] Especially the Irish monks, it seems, were accustomed to such multiplications. At the Council of Mâcon (627) we find a trace of an earnest opposition to the practice aimed especially at this group: A monk Agrestinus had made the charge, *Columbanum . . . sacra missarum sollemnia multiplicatione orationum vel collectarum celebrare.* However the charge was rejected and the opinion of the defender endorsed: *Multiplicationem vero orationum in sacris officiis credo omnibus proficere ecclesiis, quia dum plus Dominus quæritur, plus invenitur.* Mansi, X, 588 f.

[54] John Beleth, *Explicatio,* c. 37; 57 (PL, CCII, 45 f., 51 D).

There is a notable development to be remarked in the series of seven orations in the so-called "gulden mess," a votive Mass which appeared since the 13th century; here an invariable antiphon was added each time to each of the orations. Franz, 282-286.

[55] Beleth, *ibid.*

Beleth adds the enigmatic reason: *quoniam finis ad suum debet retorqueri principium.* This same reason recurs word for word in Innocent III, *De s. alt. mysterio,* II, 27 (PL, CCXVII, 815), in Durandus, IV, 15, 16, and even in Gavanti-Merati, *Thesaurus,* I, 7, 6 (I 89) in their commentary on the rubric which is still in force at present, *Missale Romanum,*

Rubr. gen., VII, 6 (here with the turn that if the first collect is for the living the last must likewise return to the living).

[56] Bernold, *Micrologus,* c. 4 (PL, CLI, 980). These numbers are then given various interpretations in accordance with the medieval number symbolism; see Eisenhofer, II, 97. Seven must be taken as the maximum because it was not exceeded in the petitions of the Lord's Prayer.

As the basis for the unevenness of the number there has been some juggling since Beleth, *Explicatio,* c. 37 (PL, CCII, 46 A), and even before him, of a verse from Virgil's *Eclogs,* VIII, 75: *Numero Deus impari gaudet.* This is but an expression of the high regard which even antiquity had for odd numbers which, as Pliny (28, 23) puts it, are *ad omnia vehementiores;* see E. Riess, "Auberglaube", Pauly-Wissowa, *Real-Encyclopädie d. class. Altertumswiss.,* I (1894), 49 f.

A moral turn is given the concept by Durandus, IV, 15, 15: the uneven number is to be favored because it means indivisibility and unity: *Deus enim divisionem et discordiam detestatur.*

[57] *Missale Rom., Rubr. gen.,* IX.

[58] *Ibid.,* IX, 12; *Additiones et variationes,* VI, 6.

appearance of the Prayer of the Faithful and the curtailment of the *Kyrie*-litany, these orations have become the most obvious place to put into words the special wants of the Church and the needs of the time. To be sure, this was almost entirely the part of the priest and not of the people, so that in very modern times a new substitute was devised, namely the prayers said with the people after Mass. The liturgical practice of older religious orders still gives some indication of the effort to make the oration of the day more prominent and to let the other added orations recede into the shadows; the demeanor in choir manifests the distinction, for it is only during the first oration that the clergy are bowed, showing that this is the priestly prayer they make their own.[59] A similar point is made by a regulation we occasionally meet with, according to which the celebrant says only the first oration out loud, the other being recited *secrete,*[60] *tacite*[61]; this method has been revived by some in the conduct of the "dialogue" Mass. The present rubric that the first oration end with its own concluding formula is apparently derived from the same line of thinking.[62]

Today the Epistle follows right after the orations. At a high Mass this is read by the subdeacon; at a less solemn Mass it is the priest himself who reads it, and he does so at once, without changing his position. As a result, especially in the latter case, we do not get the impression that something new is starting, and that here we have a clear line of separation cutting off the introductory or opening rite from the readings. In the Middle Ages the consciousness of this transition was still alive. This consciousness betrayed itself, for instance, in an abuse which the Roman Council of 743 had to denounce, namely, that many bishops and priests conducted only the procession and said the oration and left the rest of the Mass to another.[63] Many divisions of the Mass in Scholastic times take cognizance of this separation.[64] In greater pontifical functions, too, this spot was singled out for the development of those acclamations which, because of their deriva-tion, are called *laudes gallicanœ.* They are still customary at this very place

---

[59] Cf. *supra,* p. 371.
[60] Pontifical of the Roman Curia circa 1200 (Andrieu, *Le Pontifical Romain,* II, 374); *Ordo Rom. XIV,* n. 15; 30; 45; 53 (PL, LXXVIII, 1129 C, 1136 A, 1142 B, 1160 D).
[61] Pontifical of Durandus: Andrieu, III, 639.
  Bishop Ermengaud of Urgel (d. 1035), in founding a daily Mass for his soul's rest, expressly ordered that in it the oration *Deus qui inter apostolicos* should be spoken, like the other prayers of the Mass, *excelsa voce; Acta SS,* Nov. II, 1, p. 86 B.

[62] This prescription is found already in William of Hirsau (d. 1091), *Const.,* I, 86 (PL, CL, 1016 D). Later in the Missal of Sarum: Martène, 1, 4, XXXV (I, 666 C). But in other medieval Mass ar-rangements we occasionally find that all the orations are concluded under a single closing formula; thus, e.g., Martène, 1, 4, XXXII (I, 655 C).
[63] Can. 14 (Mansi, XII, 365).
[64] *Supra,* p. 114.
  On the contrary, the *Missale Upsalense* of 1513, for example, has the section marked *Lectiones* begin with the collect. Yelverton, *The Mass in Sweden,* 13.

even today, above all at the coronation of the pope.[65] In France until modern times they were a constituent part of the pontifical Mass.[66] After the oration, two (or elsewhere six) knights[67] stood forth, or, in their place, an equal number of clerics; they began: *Christus vincit, Christus regnat, Christus imperat.* The choir repeated. Then the song became a declaration of fealty and homage: *Summo Pontifici et universali Papæ vita!* and then it became a plea to Christ, *Exaudi Christe*, and to a series of saints, *Sancte Petre...*, and after each of the invocations the choir responded: *Tu illum adiuva.* The cry of allegiance to the pope is followed by similar acclamations in honor of the emperor or king, of his wife, of the bishop, of the army, and in each instance the plea *Exaudi Christe* is inserted along with a series of selected saints. If the bishop who was named was present, the whole assembly arose, and the special singers who were chanting the acclamations mounted the steps of his throne, kissed his hand and received his blessing.[68] The *Laudes* closed with a repetition of *Christus vincit*; a doxological ending, calling upon Christ, the victor over all enemies, was often connected with this close, or sometimes a *Kyrie eleison*. In the course of time the acclamations were much altered, place and situation motivating the adaptations.[69]

[65] C. J. Perl, "Die Krönungsmesse des Papstes . . . am 12. III. 1939," *Liturg. Leben*, VI (1939), 13.
Cf. *Ordo Rom. XIV*, n. 16; 31; 45 (PL, LXXVIII, 1129 f., 1136, 1142).
[66] Martène, 1. 4, 3, 13 (I, 369-371). Further texts from Arles and Reims are printed: PL, CXXXVIII, 889 f., 901 f.; U. Chevalier, *Sacramentaire et Martyrologe de l'abbaye de S. Remy* (Bibliothèque liturgique, 7; Paris, 1900), 132 f.
In the 9th century the practice also existed in most German cathedrals: Bona, II, 5, 8 (636). For Rome cf. *Ordo Rom. XI*, n. 47 (PL, LXXVIII, 1044); *Ordo Rom. XII*, n. 2 (1064 f.).
The acclamations are usually subjoined to the collects, but an exception is found in the Pontifical of Durandus, where the *Laudes* follow right after the *Kyrie;* Andrieu, III, 648 f. The same thing is attested by Bonizo of Sutri (d. c. 1095), *De vita christiana,* II, 51 (ed. Perels, Berlin, 1930; 59).
For the history of the acclamations, see H. Leclercq, "Laudes gallicanæ," DACL, VIII, 1898-1910 (here also a series of texts); J. Beckmann, "Laudes Hincmari," LThK, VI (1934), 410; J. Chr. Natter-

mann, "Die Laudes ausserhalb und innerhalb der hl. Messe," *Theologie u. Glaube,* XXXIII (1941), 147-153; Biehl, *Das liturgische Gebet für Kaiser und Reich,* 102-111; 157-160; Eichmann, *Die Kaiserkrönung,* I, 96-101.
A comprehensive study is offered in J. M. Hanssens, "De laudibus carolinis," *Periodica,* XXX (1941), 280-302; XXXI (1942), 31-53. A critical discussion in E. H. Kantorowicz, *Laudes Regiae. A study in liturgical acclamations and medieval ruler worship* (Berkeley, 1946).
[67] Vienne: *milites;* Lyons, *equites;* see Martène, *loc. cit.* (369 C). These are the noble representatives of the people. At the coronation of the *emperor scriniarii, notarii* appear in this capacity; Eichmann, 96 f.
[68] Soissons, Reims; Martène, *loc. cit.* (370 C, 371 B).
[69] Since, in accordance with their origin, the *Laudes* are intended first of all for the ruler, the acclamations for the bishop are not often attested. See, however, besides the examples offered by Martène, in Ebner, 153, note 2; Pontifical of Durandus: Andrieu, III, 649. Also the witness of Bonizo of Sutri, *loc. cit,* belongs here.

It is quite obvious that here in the pontifical liturgy a special finale has been added to the introductory rite, and this with apparent good reason. But this pledge of allegiance to the bishop who has just entered his cathedral could not fittingly take place until after the bishop himself, by means of the oration, had made his own homage and pledge of loyalty to almighty God.[70] This custom is a continuation of a custom stemming from ancient times, of acclaiming the ruler when he ascended his throne or also when he was solemnly received. In the form of prayers now prevalent we have the Christian adaptation of the ancient acclaim.[71]

[70] But we also find the *Laudes* (as suits their character) at the end of Mass, just before the *Ite, missa est;* thus, in a specially ancient form, at Vienne: de Moléon, 18. Probably also the Laudes known as the "Litany of Beauvais" (c. 1005) are to be placed in the same spot, for they conclude: *Multos annos. Amen. Ite missa est. Deo gratias.* St. Baluzius, *Miscellanea* (Paris, 1679), II, 145.

Kindred acclamations ("Long years!") are to be found in the pontifical Mass of the Byzantine liturgy of the Ukrainians, both at the beginning of Mass, namely after the Little Entrance before the start of the readings, and at the departure; M. Hornykevitsch, *Die göttliche Liturgie* (2nd ed.; Klosterneuburg, 1935), 47, note 98. On the other hand the Byzantine liturgy of Constantinople offers the bishop the acclamation Εἰς πολλὰ ἔτη δέσποτα at three different places in the Fore-Mass; Hanssens, *Institutiones,* III, 536 f.; but see Pl. de Meester, DACL, VI, 1636; 1639; 1640.

[71] The transition is discussed by Biehl, 102 f.

II. The Service of Readings

1. Origin and Plan of the Service of Readings

THE SERVICE OF READINGS FORMS THE SECOND SECTION OF THE MASS-liturgy. The reading of Holy Scripture represents the proper content of the fore-Mass in much the same way as the Sacrament forms the heart of the Mass proper; they are both precious treasures which the Church safeguards for mankind.[1] Just as our Lord himself first taught, and only after this foundation was laid did He erect His kingdom, so now too the word of God should first fill our soul before the mystery of the New Covenant is realized amongst us anew. Since the service of readings was at one time an independent entity, it was able to exist even without the continuation in the Mass proper. But since, like every Bible lesson, it demanded some sort of conclusion, we must inquire whether even in the present liturgy its plan stretches out beyond the readings, or at least helps to mould some of the forms now found in the Mass proper. At least the second alternative is plainly verified. And in the oriental liturgies the first is quite apparent; the readings are followed by prayer as is the custom otherwise and the last of the prayers is the Prayer of the Faithful. The same picture is presented in the most important sources of ancient Christian liturgy.

So it is an a priori probability (and the detailed facts will bring this out) that in the Roman Mass too the *Oremus* which follows the readings and the oration which really belongs to it (the so-called secret), if viewed formally, are still part of the reading rite, even if the material shape of the oration and the interval between it and the *Oremus* are concerned with the preparation of the offerings and thus belongs to the opening of the Mass proper. So it is with all the greater right that we speak of a *service* of readings or of lessons.

The beginnings of this service go back, as we have already seen,[2] to the practice in the synagogue, with whose arrangement the Apostles and the Christians of the primitive Church had been acquainted as they grew up. We must, therefore, next turn our attention to the synagogue service.

The very nature of the religion of the Old Testament, as a religion of revelation, implied a heavy leaning on the reading of the sacred Books. This reading took place not in the Temple at Jerusalem but in the many

[1] Cf. *Imitatio Christi*, IV, 11: *Quod corpus Christi et Sàcra Scriptura maxime sint* *animæ fideli necessaria.*
[2] *Supra*, p. 11.

synagogues which were built everywhere after the Exile. Here, on appointed days, above all on the Sabbath, the community was assembled. The reading was disposed in such a way that two passages were read at each meeting, one passage from the "Law" and the other from the "Prophets."[3] The lection from the "Law" (Torah) was first. It was continued from one meeting to the next as a *lectio continua,* so that the whole was finished during a stipulated period and the series started all over again. A fixed cycle, with a certain number of definitely outlined passages *(parashoth)* arranged for each Sabbath, is not traced until the time of the Talmud.[4] The reading of the Law in the Palestinian synagogues was also signalized by the fact that it was not done by one reader but was distributed amongst several, usually at least seven, each of whom read a number of verses. Of the remaining Books, the "Prophets" *(Nebiim),* a passage was usually chosen at will. This formed the conclusion of the service and was therefore called *haphtarah,* "conclusion." Added to the readings was a homily. According to the New Testament accounts[5] this followed the prophetic reading, but the customary arrangement appears to have been to insert the homily after the first reading, which was the more important one.

The assembly was opened with the *shema,* a kind of profession of faith made up of passages from Holy Writ.[6] Every assembly also had a congregational prayer, spoken by one of the members of the group appointed by the ruler of the synagogue; it was introduced with the words "Praise the Lord."[7] However, just how it was done in the time of the Apostles and just where it was inserted, is not clear, since exact and detailed accounts are wanting. Still the groundwork for the *Shemoneh Esreh,*[8] which was developed after the destruction of Jerusalem, can be traced back prior to this.[9] The assembly was concluded with the blessing of a priest, if there was one present, or else with some corresponding prayer.

---

[3] E. Schürer, *Geschichte des judischen Volkes im Zeitalter Jesu Christi* (4th ed.; Leipzig, 1907), II, 497-544; Strack-Billerbeck, IV, 153-1881 Hanssens, II, 422 f.

[4] I. Elbogen, *Der jüdische Gottesdienst in seiner geschichtlichen Entwicklung* (2nd ed.; Frankfurt, 1924), 159-162; Strack-Billerbeck, IV, 154-156. The Palestinians availed themselves of a three-year cycle with 154 sections (or even more, up to 175), the Babylonian tradition on the contrary had a one-year cycle with 54 *parashoth.* There is also question of a three-and-a-half year cycle with 175 *parashoth.*

[5] Luke 4: 16-20; Acts 12: 15 f.

[6] Deut. 6: 4-9; 11: 13-21; Num. 15: 37-41.

[7] Schürer, II, 515; 529; Strack-Billerbeck, IV, 189-249.

[8] *Shemoneh 'esreh =* "Eighteen" (prayer). The text, with emphasis on the portion which is traceable to the first century, in Schürer, II, 539 ff.; cf. Strack-Billerbeck, IV, 211-220.

[9] As the basis of the prayer Schürer, II, 542, note 156, reckons the prayer which in the Hebrew text is appended to Ecclus. 51: 12 (in A. Eberharter, *Das Buch Jesus Sirach* [Bonn, 1925] it is intercalated as verse 51: 12¹ to 12¹⁶). It is a praise of God as protector of Israel; the wording is reminiscent of the great Hallel psalm 135, especially because of the recurring refrain "For His goodness remains forever," which is obviously spoken by the people.

The elements of this arrangement can be found quite unmistakably in the service of the Christian congregations at an early date.[10] According to Justin the readings on Sundays were followed by a homily (spoken by the one presiding) and by the common prayer of the congregation[11]—two elements which continue to be constituent parts of the fore-Mass. The chants or songs which are generally connected with the readings in the Christian liturgies must also go back to some common primitive Christian source. The psalmodic form of the songs carries us back to the synagogue. The *Apostolic Constitutions* of the fourth century[12] makes mention of a singer's psalming the hymns of David after the first of the two readings, and of the people's responding to it. But even two hundred years or so before this, Tertullian makes a cursory reference to the psalmody which follows the readings. Writing as a Montanist, he gives an account of a prophetess who *inter dominica sollemnia* regularly fell into ecstasy, *prout scripturæ leguntur aut psalmi canuntur aut allocutiones proferuntur aut petitiones delegantur*[13]; the allusion to *allocutiones* makes it more or less plain that the narrative deals with an occurrence during a public assembly for reading —obviously the fore-Mass.

The arrangement here to be seen, therefore, is the same as that which, in the oldest sources both East and West, prevailed also in the extra-eucharistic service of the Church,[14] the same that is still in use in the Roman Breviary as the second part of every canonical hour. The series is this: reading, responsorial singing of the assembled congregation, prayer.[15] The only thing added to this plan, as occasion demanded, was the homily.

2. The Choice of Readings

Regarding the number and the selection of the readings a great variety has prevailed and still prevails amongst the Christian liturgies. The only agreement is the rule that there should be at least two lessons, of which the last in all cases is to be taken from the Gospels. And the lessons have all been biblical; aside from the primitive era when the various community letters were read, the lessons were gradually restricted to readings from the Scriptures, although there was some variation here and there.[1] That besides

---

[10] Lines of relationship are pointed out by Baumstark, *Liturgie comparée*, 47-50.

Regarding the reading of Scripture in the primitive Church see the general discussion in Nielen, *The Earliest Christian Liturgy*, 241-250.

[11] Justin, *Apol.*, I, 67.

[12] *Const. Ap.*, II, 57, 6 (Quasten, *Mon.*, 182; Funk, I, 161).

[13] Tertullian, *De an.*, c. 9 (CSEL, XX, 310).

[14] In broad outline also in Hippolytus, *Trad. Ap.*; first the catechumens receive instruction, then prayer follows (Dix, 29). The same arrangement in the assembly of the faithful (60 f.).

[15] Cf. *supra*, p. 268, note 26.

[1] The fluctuation concerned in the main the inclusion of the acts of the martyrs. Reading of the story of the sufferings of the martyrs at the divine service is attested at the earliest in the Acts of

the Old Testament lessons there should be readings from the New Testament—and these even by preference—was to be taken for granted, and was, in fact, explicitly urged in the regulations of St. Paul.[2] For the rest, the various arrangements can be best understood if we contemplate them in their first beginnings, already indicated in the previous chapter, the arrangement of lessons in the synagogue. But we will be amazed to see how strongly Christian principles of choice gradually took over.

The connection with the service of the synagogue is especially recognizable in the order of the lessons in the Syrian liturgies. In the Antiochene Church of the fourth century one lesson was taken from the Law and one from the Prophets, as once they were in the synagogue, and then followed readings from the letters of the Apostles (or, on occasion, from the Acts of the Apostles) and from the Gospels.[3] Even today as a rule two Old Testament readings introduce the reading service of the East Syrian Mass; readings from St. Paul's Epistles and from the Gospels follow.[4] In the West Syrian Jacobite liturgy there are vestiges of the ancient arrangement. The fore-Mass in most cases contains six readings altogether, three from the Old Testament. Of these, the first two are from the Law and the Prophets (in the narrower sense), as usual, and a reading from the Sapiential books is added.[5] Other liturgies have retained at least one Old Testament lection,

---

Apollonius which belong to the second century (n. 47; *Bibliothek der Kirchenväter*, XIV, p. 327 f.). Such a practice was legally sanctioned expressly for the Mass by the III Council of Carthage (397), can. 36 (Mansi, III, 924): *Liceat etiam legi passiones martyrum quorum anniversarii dies eorum celebrantur.* This is matched by St. Augustine's witness to actual practice: Roetzer, 62 f., 107 f.

For the area of the Gallic liturgy there are found accounts of reading the acts of martyrs at Mass even in the centuries that followed. For Gaul see the *Expositio ant. liturgiæ gallicanæ* (ed. Quasten, 13 f.) and the Lectionary of Luxeuil (ed. P. Salmon, *Le lectionnaire de Luxeuii* [Rome, 1944], 27 ff., 181 f.); also Gregory of Tours, *De gloria mart.*, I 86 (PL, LXXI, 781) and *De mirac. s. Martini*, II, 29; 49 (PL, LXXI 954; 963) must be so understood. On the feast-day of the Martyrs of Lyons (June 2) it was the custom at Vienne even circa 1700 to read the pertinent *Passio* from Eusebius (*Hist. eccl.* V, 1) between Gradual and Alleluia: de Moléon, 34. For Milan there is the letter of the Regensburg clerics Paul and Gebhart

of the year 1024 (in J. Mabillon, *Museum Italicum* [Paris, 1724], 2, p. 97): *gestis sanctorum quæ Missarum celebrationibus apud vos interponi solent, non indigemus.* See also Martène, 1, 4, 4, 2 (I, 372 f.).

[2] 1 Thess. 5: 27; Col. 4: 16.

[3] *Const. Ap.*, VIII, 5, 11 (Quasten, *Mon.*, 198). Cf. for this Baumstark, *Nichtevangelische syrische Perikopenordnungen des ersten Jahrtausends* (LF III; Münster, 1921), 17. The sequence: Law — Prophets — Gospel, receives a deeper significance in Maximus Confessor; it reflects the progression: Flesh — Sense — Reason; or again: Shadow — Image — Presence of the reality. H. U. v. Balthasar, *Die 'Gnostischen Centurien' des Maximus Confessor* (Freiburg, 1941), 64.

[4] Baumstark, *Vom geschichtlichen Werden*, 15; idem., *Nichtevangelische syrische Perikopenordnungen*, 16-19. Only during Eastertide and on feastdays is the first reading taken from Isaias, the second from the Acts of the Apostles; cf. Brightman, 256, 1. 2-5.

[5] The three New Testament lessons are taken from the Acts of the Apostles or

besides the two from the New. Thus the Armenian liturgy,[6] which in this continues the older usage of Byzantium.[7] And in the West the ancient Gallican liturgy,[8] along with its sister-forms, the Mozarabic[9] and the older Milanese,[10] which follow this order outside the Easter time. During the Easter time the Acts of the Apostles replace the Old Testament, a rule which we find similarly in the East Syrian liturgy.[11]

It is not surprising that during this festive season of the Church year, when the mystery of our Redemption stands out so plainly, there should be a tendency to restrict the readings from the Old Testament in favor of those from the New. The connection with the eucharistic celebration must have tended in the same direction insofar as there was any consciousness of the Easter character of that celebration.[12] Thus in the Egyptian liturgies we find a fourfold lesson, probably in the beginning an attempt to compromise with readings from both Testaments,[13] but now (in both the Coptic and the Ethiopian liturgies) actually taken from the New Testament only: the Epistle of St. Paul, the Catholic Epistles, the Acts and the Gospels.[14] The Byzantine liturgy, too, since about the seventh century, has only two lessons at Mass, both from the New Testament, the "Apostle" and the Gospel.[15]

The Roman liturgy underwent the same evolution to a degree at least. Here, too, the Mass must once have had three lessons regularly,[16] as it still

the Catholic Epistles, from the letters of St. Paul and from the Gospels. Brightman, 77-70; Baumstark, *Vom geschichtlichen Werden*, 16; idem., *Nichtevangelische syrische Perikopenordnungen*, 78 ff., 175 ff.
[6] Brightman, 425.
[7] Chrysostom attests more than once a prophetic, an apostolic and a Gospel lection; see the passages in Brightman, 531, note 5; cf. Rahlfs (below, note 15), 124 f. The prophetic reading is also mentioned in the life of St. Theodore Sykeota (d. 613), n. 16: *Acta SS*, Apr., III, 37.
[8] Evidence from the sources in Baumstark, *Vom geschichtlichen Werden*, 141, note 13; H. Leclercq, "Gallicane (Liturgie)", DACL, VI, 542 f.
[9] G. Morin, *Liber Comicus* (Maredsous, 1892); *Missale mixtum* (PL, LXXXV, 109 ff.).
[10] It is still attested in the letter (already mentioned) of the Regensburg clerics (note 1 above), in Mabillon, I, 2, 97; cf. Leclercq, *loc. cit.*, 543 note 1. The present-day Milanese liturgy has generally only two lections.

[11] Cf. *supra*, note 4. Cf. also in the Roman Breviary the exclusive choice of New Testament readings (Acts, Apocalypse, Catholic Epistles) during the Paschal season.
[12] Cf. *supra*, p. 239 f. the influence on the posture of the body.
[13] Cf. the numerous homilies of Origen on the Old Testament books.
[14] Brightman, 152-155; 212-219.
[15] H. Rahlfs, *Die alttestamentlichen Lektionen der griechischen Kirche:* Nachrichten der K. Gesellschaft der Wissenschaften zu Göttingen, Phil.-hist. Klasse 1915, 123-125 (= Mitteilungen des Septuaginta-Unternehmens, I [Berlin, 1909-1915], 217-219). The Greek liturgy of St. James and the Greek liturgy of St. Mark, too, in their oldest traditional form, had only these two lessons; Brightman, 36 ff., 118 f.
[16] A fragmentary Mass book from lower Italy recently printed has, besides other pre-Gregorian vestiges, also three lessons as a rule; A. Dold, *Die Zürcher und Peterlinger Messbuchfragmente aus der Zeit des ersten Jahrtausends im Bari-Schrifttyp* (*Texte und Arbeiten*, I, 25;

has on certain of the older liturgical days,[17] and the usual arrangement must have included—in part at least—one reading from the Old Testament and two from the New.[18] But later the Old Testament reading disappeared from the permanent plan of the Mass-liturgy. For on all Sundays the first of the two lessons is always taken from one of the Letters of the Apostles—an "Epistle," therefore, in the strict sense—and all through Paschaltide it is either from the Letters or from the Acts of the Apostles. Outside this season the pre-Gospel reading at the ferial Masses is, as a rule, from the Old Testament, but for feast days, especially for the feasts of saints, no definite rule can be set down.

But it is plain that wherever the Old Testament appears in the readings of the fore-Mass, it is not for its own sake, nor simply to have some spiritual text for reading, but it is chosen for its prophetic worth and its value as an illustration of the New Testament. This is unmistakable in the prophecies of Holy Saturday; here, with gaze fixed on Baptism, the Old Testament illustrations proclaim the new creation, the new people of God, the triumph over death, the new life and the renovating power of God's spirit. It is equally apparent in the Old Testament readings which here and

Beuron, 1934). Of the 20 formularies partially preserved, nine indisputably have the order of lessons: Old Testament, St. Paul, Gospel. Two formularies have only two readings (Old Testament and Gospel); for the rest no verdict is possible (Dold, p. xxx). Regarding the Comes of Murbach, see infra, note 18. Regarding the probability that the Gradual originally had its setting after the first lesson of three see infra.

Batiffol, Leçons, 129, maintained that the ancient Roman liturgy, too, had three lessons only by way of exception. But a different view is held by Kunze, Die gottesdienstliche Schriftlesung, 141, who places the omission of the third lesson in the 6th century.

[17] Ember-Wednesday, Wednesday of the 4th week of Lent, Wednesday and Friday of Holy Week. The longer series of readings on the Saturdays of Ember-week, on the other hand, is the remains of an ancient vigil service. The ancient tradition had on these days 12 lessons, like those still customary on Holy Saturday. The formularies on these days are therefore regularly given the following headings in the liturgical books of the earlier Middle Ages: *Sabbato in duodecim lectionibus,*

[18] This arrangement is retained in the Zurich and Peterling fragments (Dold, loc. cit.). Also in the Comes of Würzburg (ed. Morin: Revue Bénéd., 27 [1910], 46 ff.; cf. the observations of the editor, p. 72) and similarly in the Comes of Murbach (ed. Morin: Revue Bénéd., 30 [1913], 35), in the latter case with the rubric: Si venerit vigilia vel Natale Domini in dominica leg. apostolum, si autem in alia die, legis prophetam tantum.

According to Radulph de Rivo (d. 1403), De canonum observ., prop. 23 (Mohlberg, II, 139), it was still customary in some places at that time to have three readings at the three Christmas Masses and at the Mass of Christmas Eve; in many churches of Italy the Gradual and Alleluia were so apportioned as intermediary chants that the Gradual followed the first lesson, the Alleluia the second. This is also the case in the present-day Dominican liturgy which has three lessons on the days mentioned and in all four instances the first is a reading from Isaias. Cf. also de Moléon, 110; Waefelghem, 152 f., 155.

The African Mass, too,—from what we can learn from Augustine—had three lessons on some days, other times only two. Roetzer, 100.

there appear on feast days, as when on Epiphany the Prophet Isaias views the peoples streaming into the new Kingdom of God, or on feasts of the Blessed Virgin the Son of Sirach praises the divine Wisdom which has built itself a house on earth.[19] Nor is it much different in regard to the Old Testament readings in the ferial formularies for Lent. They illustrate certain relationships in the New Testament economy of salvation or in the ecclesiastical discipline of the Lenten season: forty days of prayer and penance, the call to repentance, Baptism and its effects, the Law of God; or they present little sidelights to the story of the Gospel or to the life of the stational saint; or they suggest some other association with the peculiarities of the stational church.[20]

But we would misunderstand the position of even the New Testament texts and accounts in their liturgical associations if we were to take them solely as primitive accounts of the time of their origin, as mere witnesses of things past, from which we gain no other edification than we might gain from the rest of the testimonials of Christian living. For the words of the Apostles and the accounts of the Evangelists are given a new meaning by being proclaimed anew by the Church to this assembly of Christian men. They must be regarded entirely in the perspective of the present, for they are themselves bearers of the grace-laden message which God gives

[19] The best illustration of the Old Testament lesson in this connection is offered by the grand treasure of homilies delivered by the Fathers on almost all the books of the Old Testament. It is only in virtue of a basic New Testament viewpoint that Origen, for example, could explain in homily not only the prophets but also all five books of the Pentateuch as well as extensive portions of Josue and Judges. He was helped in this, as were most of the other homilists of the ancient Church, by the use of allegorism as a means of explanation and interpretation.

In our liturgical reading of the Old Testament, where the explanation is wanting, formal allegorism plays a part only to the extent that common material from the Fathers is involved, as in the reference of the four beings in Ezechiel (1: 10-14) to the four Evangelists, or the more obvious parallels in the one divine economy.

[20] H. Grisar, Das Missale Romanum im Lichte römischer Stadtgeschichte (Freiburg, 1925).

Hints to the understanding of the choice of pericopes in general, partly retrenching Grisar's opinions, in the chapter "De keuze van Epistel en Evangelie" in Callewaert, Sacris erudiri, 347-378. Callewaert refers, e.g., to the opening and closing words of the pericopes which often contain the main ideas intended (357 ff.).

It seems to have been a peculiarity of the Roman plan which preceded the one which holds at present to have sought as much as possible for some rapport between Epistle and Gospel. In the Masses of Lent this community of theme is still visible in many instances. On Tuesday of the first week of Lent, however, such a connection will be found only if the pericope of the first reading, from Isaias 55: 6-11 (fixed as it is now even in 645) is extended to 56: 7, that is, to include the verse cited in the Gospel. Patently the reading had reached this far at an earlier time and when it was revised and shortened this harmony was no longer so highly prized. B. Capelle, "Note sur le lectionnaire romain de la messe avant s. Grégoire," Revue d'hist. eccl., XXXIV, (1938), 556-559.

to men through His Church. The word of God in Holy Writ sounds with
renewed vigor, waking in the congregation the consciousness of the foundation on which it is built, the spiritual world in which it lives and the home
to which its path is directed. It has a message for this very hour, to arouse
the congregation to find a Christian solution for the problems which face
each of us today.[21]

It is well known that in the service of the ancient Church the various
books of Holy Scripture were read straight through, in the manner of a
lectio continua. The most manifest voucher for this is found in the volumi-
nous commentaries to whole books of both New and Old Testament which
various Fathers have left us—commentaries which are nothing else than
the homilies which they delivered at the end of the reading at worship.
In fact the relationship to this reading is quite often very obvious.[22]

This continuous reading of the Scriptures was broken into, as might
have been expected, first of all by the greater feast days.[23] For such days
a pertinent pericope was selected. For the feasts of martyrs, too, this was
done, as Augustine already testifies.[24] It was but natural that the passages
in question should be used again each year. Still this practice could not
have been very extensive even by the end of the fourth century. For the
Aquitanian pilgrim lady seemed never to weary of pointing out, as a peculiarity of divine service at Jerusalem, that the lessons and the psalms and
antiphons here used on Epiphany or on the days of Holy Week and Easter
week were always *aptœ diei*.[25] But to the Gallic Church of the fifth century
belong the first unmistakable evidences of a system of pericopes.[26] On the
other hand the festal seasons, even at an early period were already given
special consideration by selecting certain more relevant books of the Bible
for the reading. Thus at Antioch in the fourth century the Mosaic books
were read during the weeks before Easter. Elsewhere during Holy Week
first Job and then Jonas were read, in reference to Christ's suffering and
Resurrection.[27] After Easter the reading of the Acts of the Apostles is
affirmed quite early in more than one region.[28] So for the Scripture readings
of the fore-Mass an arrangement was established much like that which
still holds good today in the *scriptura occurrens* of our Roman Breviary.

[21] Regarding the application of Scripture
to the present, both in general and in the
liturgy, cf. A. Stonner, *Bibellesung mit
der katholischen Jugend* (Paderborn,
1933), 191 ff.; A. Miller, "Schriftsinn
und liturgischer Sinn," *Bened. Monatsschrift*, XVI (1934), 407-413. Cf. also
Parsch, *Volksliturgie*, 261, and my remarks in J. Kramp, *Briefe der Kirche*
(Münster, 1940), pp. XX ff.
[22] For Augustine see Roetzer, 109.
[23] St. Beissel, *Entstehung der Perikopen*

des römischen Messbuches (Freiburg,
1907), 41 f.; G. Godu, "Epitre," DACL,
V, 247 f.
     For Augustine, see Roetzer, 103-108,
for Leo the Great, see Baumstark, *Missale Romanum*, 26 f.
[24] Roetzer, 102 f.
[25] *Aetheriæ Peregrinatio*, c. 29; 31; etc.
[26] G. Godu, "Epitre," DACL, V, 249.
[27] Beissel, *Entstehung der Perikopen*, 7.
[28] *Ibid.*, 8. Cf. *supra*, p. 394; Roetzer, 103.

In the Orient the continuous reading of certain books has remained the normal form in the Nestorian and the Jacobite liturgies, and even in modern times it is scarcely ever interrupted.[29] In the Byzantine liturgy for the most part the readings, at least for the Gospels, have continued in so-called serials, just as we have them in the *scriptura occurrens* of our breviary; only selected passages of the respective book are read but the readings are so arranged that the selections follow the course of the text. Thus after Pentecost, Matthew is started and continued for seventeen Sundays (with some few pericopes now displaced from their proper order); then sixteen Sundays follow with readings from St. Luke. This division of the Gospels explains the regular use of expressions like Κυριακὴ πρώτη τοῦ Ματθαίου, κυριακὴ ἑνδεκάτη τοῦ Λουκᾶ, etc.[30] There are also shorter series of readings from Mark and John.

Vestiges of such a progressive reading of the Scriptures are also to be found in our Roman liturgy.[31] The Gospels of the last weeks before Easter, for instance, are taken from St. John and the same is true of the Sundays after Easter. True, the pericopes follow the biblical order only in part, but still the original intent peers through.[32] One other point, noteworthy enough, must be stressed, the fact that at least the title of this continuous type of reading has been retained, for every Gospel is announced with *sequentia sancti evangelii*—the continuation of the reading of the Gospel.

More evident and incontestable are the traces in the Epistles.[33] The Epistles of the Sundays after Pentecost still form a series of pericopes in which the Letters of St. Paul are covered with almost no disturbance of the order of the Scripture canon. Because of the many saints' days which have replaced the weekdays, and which have either special readings or readings taken from the *Commune Sanctorum*, we fail today to recognize such a plan. Actually there are documentary evidences to enable us to trace this plan back to the height of the Middle Ages where it is found to have an even more remarkable extent. The so-called Würzburg *Comes*, the oldest of the documents in question, offers (in addition to the Epistle for specified occasions during the Church year and those for votive Masses) forty-two further readings not stipulated for any precise liturgical function. These forty-two pericopes are taken from the Letters of St. Paul, starting with Romans 5:6-11 and continuing in the order of the accepted canon

[29] Baumstark, *Nichtevangelische syrische Perikopenordnungen*, 173 f.

[30] N. Nilles, *Kalendarium manuale utriusque Ecclesiæ* (2nd ed.; Innsbruck, 1897), II, 442 ff. The pericopes are comprehensively treated in Beissel, 12. Cf. Salaville, *Eastern Liturgies*, 190-192.

[31] Callewaert, *Sacris erudiri*, 375 f.

[32] The reading of the Gospel according to St. John during the Easter-to-Pentecost season is an ancient tradition also in the Orient; cf. Baumstark, *Liturgie comparée*, 133. In the Byzantine liturgy even today the Johannine prologue is read with great solemnity on Easterday, then the lections continue from St. John; Beissel, 11-15.

[33] G. Godu, DACL, V, 245-344; W. H. Frere, *Studies in Early Roman Liturgy*, III. The Roman Epistle-Lectionary (Alcuin Club Collections, 32; Oxford, 1935).

down to Hebrews 13:17-21. The collected Sunday Epistles of that period, insofar as they follow the canonical arrangement, are contained in this group. Of the rest of the pericopes in this Würzburg index, some are found in various reading lists, either as Sunday Epistles, or partly as Epistles appointed for Wednesdays. By a comprehensive investigation[34] of the pertinent lists of lessons, Father Alban Dold, O.S.B., was able to reconstruct the arrangement of the Epistles for the time after Pentecost, as it probably appeared in the start of the fifth century.[35]

SUNDAY EPISTLE	WEDNESDAY EPISTLE
1. Apoc. 4:1-10	
2. I John 4:8-21	
3. I John 3:13-18	
4. I Pet. 5:6-11	
5. I Pet. 3:8-15	
6. Rom. 5:6(8)-11	
7. Rom. 5:18-21	
8. Rom. 6:3-11	
9. Rom. 6:19-23 ———→	Rom. 8:1-6
10. Rom. 8:12-17 ———→	I Cor. 10:6-13
11. I Cor. 12:2-11 ———→	I Cor. 15:39-46
12. II Cor. 3:4-9 ———→	II Cor. 4:5-10
13. II Cor. 5:1-11 ———→	II Cor. 6:14-7:1
14. Gal. 3:16-22	Col. 1:12-18
15. Gal. 5:16-24	Col. 2:8-13
16. Gal. 5:25-6:10	Col. 3:5-11
17. Eph. 3:13-21	Col. 3:12-17
18. Eph. 4:1-6	I Thess. 2:9-13
19. Eph. 4:23-28	II Thess. 2:15-3:5
20. Eph. 5:15-21	II Thess. 3:6-16
21. Eph. 6:10-17	I Tim. 1:5-11
22. Phil. 1:6-11	I Tim. 2:1-7
23. Phil. 3:17-21	I Tim. 6:7-14
24. Col. 1:9-14	II Tim. 1:8-13

That the reading begins with the Catholic Epistles is in accordance with an older arrangement of the canon, in which the Catholic Epistles were placed first immediately after the Acts of the Apostles.[36]

[34] A. Dold, "Das Donaueschinger Comesfragment B II 7, ein neuer Textzeuge für die altüberlieferte liturgische Feier der Stationsfasttage Mittwoch und Freitag. Zugleich ein Beitrag zur Geschichte der Sonn—und Stationsfasttagsperikopen in der Zeit von Pfingsten bis zum Advent," JL, VI (1926), 16-53.
[35] Loc. cit., 37.

[36] Th. Zahn, Geschichte des Neutestamentlichen Kanons, II (Erlangen, 1890), 381 f. "Neither have they [the Catholic Epistles] the same place in the series of the NT books as given in the ancient MSS. versions and catalogues. In most they come between the Acts and the Pauline Epistles. This is the case with the Canon of the Council of Laodicea,

The obvious system of having the weekday readings continue the Sunday ones is followed on only five Wednesdays. The other Wednesdays form an independent series using the material left over from the Sunday series.[37] It is to be noted that the readings from Romans which, in the table above, break off at Romans 8:17, are actually continued in our present-day Roman arrangement on the second to the fourth Sundays after Epiphany.[38] In the course of the Middle Ages other systems for the Epistles were constructed, incorporating Wednesdays and sometimes even Fridays; but these lists never had other than local importance.[39]

We also possess a clear idea of the early medieval Roman arrangement for the Gospel.[40] This, too, agrees fairly well with the arrangement followed today insofar as the same liturgical days come into question. Here, too, weekdays were taken into account, in this case not only Wednesday but Friday, and, as often as not, Saturday also. This involves us in the religious life of the ancient Church, in which the "stational days" as well as the Sundays were taken into account. To the fasting which was an old tradition on these days, was added a prayer-meeting with readings, and gradually—first on Wednesdays, as many evidences indicate—also a eucharistic service.[41] The system of readings which was developed for these services continued to be used throughout the Middle Ages in various places, particularly (it seems) in monastic churches.[42] Some of the references are as late as the sixteenth century.[43] What is not a little surprising is that this

Codices B and A, in the lists of Cyril of Jerusalem, Athanasius, Leontius, the 'Sixty Books,' Cassiodous, John of Damascus, etc." Hasting's *Dictionary of the Bible* (Edinburgh-N.Y., 1904), I, 360.

[37] That exactly 24 Sundays after Pentecost are fitted out with lessons cannot be taken to mean that the time when this plan was outlined there were just 24 Sundays after Pentecost, for there was as yet no Advent.

[38] Rom. 12: 6-16; 12: 16-21; 13: 8-10. It is noteworthy that these pericopes are found also in the Epistle list of the *Codex Fuldensis*, the well-known Vulgate text which stems from the 6th century and from the church of Capua; the first two passages are among the pericopes marked *post epifania* (in Godu, DACL, V, 298, n. 16, 22), the third at the start of Lent (lengthened to include up to 14: 4; Godu, n. 33).

In the *Comes* of Alcuin the same three pericopes are somewhat differently apportioned; in addition, Rom. 12: 1-6 is appointed for the first Sunday after Epiphany; Godu, *loc. cit.*, 302, n. 15.

[39] A. Wilmart, "Le lectionnaire d'Alcuin" (*Eph. liturg.*, 1937), 137, note 5.

[40] Th. Klauser, *Das römische Capitulare Evangeliorum*, I (LQF, XXVIII; Münster, 1935); St. Beissel, *Entstehung der Perikopen* (Freiburg, 1907); G. Godu, "Evangiles," DACL, V, 852-923; W. H. Frere, *Studies in Early Roman Liturgy*, II. The Roman Gospel-Lectionary (Alcuin Club Collections, 30; Oxford, 1934).

[41] Duchesne, *Christian Worship*, 233. The preferential treatment accorded Wednesdays appears to have emerged from Innocent I, *Ep.* 25, 4 (PL, XX, 555 f.); cf. also Hierzegger, "Collecta und Statio", 520, 533 ff.

We can therefore conclude that the assignment of only a Gospel reading to Fridays indicates that on this day there was simply a service of reading.

[42] In the Rule of St. Benedict, c. 41, the observance of the stational days named as fast-days is accentuated.

[43] Dold, "Das Donaueschinger Comesfragment," 21 f, 40; cf. Beissel, 166. With the Premonstratensians this arrangement was not supplanted till the

system of pericopes, although extended to two or three days a week, nowhere gives any signs of any continued series of lessons," not to mention a *lectio continua*. The pericope is chosen very freely, with no regard for previous or succeeding passages. For feast days, those of our Lord and of the saints, the thought of the feast naturally dictated the choice of both Epistle and Gospel. The same thing was true to a rather wide extent also for festive seasons. We have already cited the Sundays after Easter." The choice for Advent was plainly decided by the catch word: the coming of our Lord, the approach of his Kingdom. The Gospels for Sundays after Epiphany" are similarly selected on the basis of a catch-word (especially if we take into account some older Gospel references which no longer obtain): this is the revelation of the wisdom and miraculous might of the God-man who had appeared on earth." In the period from Septuagesima to Easter the theme for both Epistle and Gospel is founded on the prospect of the grand festival and on concern for a proper preparation of the congregation and—to a certain extent—of the candidates for Baptism and the penitents." Above all, however, it is the Roman stational churches with their martyr graves and local reminiscences that offer the key in many cases to an understanding of the choice of a pericope." Least satisfactory is the search for a motive in the choice of the Gospels for the Sundays after Pentecost." In some instances the proximity of the feast of a great saint

Missal of 1622; Th. Szomor, *Das Prämonstratenser Missale im Vergleich zum römischen* (unpublished dissertation, Innsbruck, 1936), 4 f., 22.

" The only thing that does occur is that on a few occasions the reading is concluded, without a break, on a following day; thus the reading of Luke 16: 19-31 on the 2nd Sunday after Pentecost concludes on the next Friday with Luke 17: 1-10, the reading of Luke 16: 1-9 on the 10th Sunday after Pentecost concludes on the following Wednesday with Luke 16: 10-15, the reading of Matt. 13: 24-30 on the Wednesday after the 19th Sunday after Pentecost is continued on the following Friday with Matt. 13: 31-35. Dold, 42-53.

" *Supra*, p. 399.

" The Epistles, as was pointed out, follow a definite course of continued reading; see above, p. 401.

" J. A. Jungmann, "Die Nachfeier von Epiphanie im Missale Romanum," ZkTh, LXVI (1942), 39-46, especially 41 ff. The Gospels of the Sundays after

Epiphany (third to sixth) are arranged according to their order in the Gospel according to St. Matthew, but with lacunæ.

" Baumstark, *Liturgie comparée*, 136 refers to the relationships to the Oriental plan for the Epistles on the Sundays of Lent, particularly to the operation of a reading of Genesis which was once the rule and is so even at present in the Orient and in the Roman Breviary.

" H. Grisar, *Das Missale im Lichte römischer Stadtgeschichte* (Freiburg, 1925), throws much light especially on this portion of the Church year.

" Beissel, 195 f. It has been remarked that all the pericopes are taken from the Synoptics.

In some instances we might suppose that the Epistle, fixed (as we have seen) according to a plan of continuous readings, affected the choice of the Gospel; thus on the 7th Sunday after Pentecost (the mention of good and bad fruit). But the whole series of Epistles is shifted by one Sunday in the oldest MSS. or dif-

honored in the Roman Church appears to have influenced the choice.[51] The other passages, we must conclude, are in substance a group of synoptic passages which were not considered in the lists previously made up, but which seemed to have special value for religious instruction.[52]

When the stational days lost their importance and saints' days (with their own readings) began to appear in ever-increasing numbers, the week-day pericopes in the old Roman lesson-system lost their significance. So by the dawn of modern times they were almost entirely forgotten. But about this very time the Council of Trent heard the plea for an expansion of the system of readings, and the suggestion was made that for each week three unused Pauline and Gospel passages be selected for ferial Masses, to be inserted in the formulary of the preceding Sunday.[53] The plan, however, never came up for consideration and so nothing was done.[54]

3. The Liturgical Setting of the Lessons

The reverence which the Church pays to the written word of God in no way blinds the Church to her task of breaking the bread of God's word to the people. Her consciousness of this duty is revealed in the very fact that some passages are chosen rather than others, and that given passages are used to illustrate certain Church days and feasts. There are even instances in which a passage is put together by omitting some intervening portions of the text,[1] a practice which was widespread in the ancient Gal-

ferently assorted, so that it did not originally fit into the same Gospels as we now have; cf. the table in Godu, DACL, V, 338 ff.

[51] A. Vogel, S.J., "Der Einfluss von Heiligenfesten auf die Perikopenwahl an den Sonntagen nach Pfingsten," ZkTh, LXIX (1947), 100-118. According to this, the pericope of the great catch of fish (Luke 5: 1-11; 4th Sunday) was induced by the feast of the Princes of the Apostles, as Beissel already thought; the pericope of the wise steward (Luke 16: 1-9; 8th Sunday) and the Ephphetha pericope (Mark 7: 31-37; 11th Sunday) by the feast of St. Lawrence, and at least the pericope of the healing of the lame man (Matt. 9: 1-8; 18th Sunday) by the feast of the sainted physicians Cosmas and Damian.

[52] Beissel, 196.

[53] Jedin, "Das Konzil von Trient und die Reform des Römischen Messbuches" (Liturg. Leben, 1939), 55 f.; cf. 34 f. The principle of repeating the Sunday Mass with new lessons was followed even anciently on the Thursday in Pentecost week.

[54] In most recent times R. Guardini, "Die mystagogische Predigt" (Volks-liturgie u. Seelsorge; Colmar o. J. [1942]), 159, calls the extension and development of the pericope-system a "very pressing desideratum." He suggests a two or three-year system that might serve along with the present one.

[1] Thus on the Wednesday of Passion week the Epistle reading is derived from Lev. 19: 1-2, 11-19, 25. This is often the case in regard to Old Testament readings, as can be seen easily in the new edition of the Roman Missal where the exact citation is noted in each instance.

lican liturgy and led to the custom of centonization[2] and to the harmonization of the Gospel accounts.[3]

From the Church the various pericopes have received their setting. First of all, a title telling the origin of the passage: *Lectio libri* . . . , *Lectio epistolæ* . . . ,[4] or announcing whether the passage is the beginning, *Initium*, or a continuation, *Sequentia*,[5] of a certain passage. Then there is an introductory word, either the word of address, *Fratres* (in St. Paul's congregational letters), *Carissime* (in his pastoral letters), *Carissimi* (in the Catholic Epistles), or a phrase suggesting the prophetic character of the reading: *Hæc dicit Dominus*, or a reference to the time of the story, *In diebus illis, In illo tempore, (dixit Jesus . . .).*[6] Sometimes there is a closing

---

[2] *Cento* = "patchwork," a text made up of pieces of various provenience. Centonization was extensively used in the Lectionary of Luxeuil (ed. Salmon [Rome, 1944]; dated circa 700): On the feast of the *Cathedra Petri*, for example, John 21: 15-19 is added to Matt. 16: 13-19 (Salmon, 67 f.); on the *Natale episcoporum* the Epistle from 1 Pet. 1: 3-20 concludes with 5: 1-4 (Salmon, 202 f.). Still greater use is made of it in an old lectionary ed. by A. Dold, *Das älteste Liturgiebuch der Lateinischen Kirche. Ein altgallikanisches Lektionar des 5.-6. Jh.* (Texte und Arbeiten, 26-28; Beuron, 1936). Here for the feast of the dedication of a church an account of the purifying of the Temple is pieced together from 13 passages in the four evangelists, "an original mosaic that is effectively unified". Cf. also in the Bobbio Missal the lesson that is cited as from Colossians: Muratori, II, 914; it is labeled by the editor as a *farrago ex Scripturæ verbis contexta*.

A kindred instance is also to be found in the Roman liturgy: the Epistle *Ecce sacerdos magnus* in the *Commune Confessorum Pontificum* is devised from at least ten texts freely tied together but all taken from the one section of Ecclus. 44:16—45:20. Cf. also the troping of biblical lessons in the Middle Ages; see regarding this Wagner, *Einführung*, I, 286.

[3] A harmonized text from all four evangelists for the lesson on Maundy Thursday and for the Passion on Good Friday is presented in the "oldest" lectionary mentioned above (Dold, pp. LXIII f.,

CV, 45, 47 ff.). As is known, St. Augustine attempted for his church a harmonized lesson of the Passion like that found in the Gallic liturgies, but the project ran aground (*Sermo* 232, 1; PL, XXXVIII, 1108).

[4] In this connection note that the Canticle of Canticles, Proverbs, Ecclesiastes, Ecclesiasticus and the Book of Wisdom are all uniformly introduced as *lectio libri Sapientiæ*.

[5] *Sequentia* = continuation. In the Mozarabic liturgy the Epistle lections are also announced thus: *Sequentia epistolæ Pauli apostoli ad Romanos*. As a matter of fact there are to be found here, e.g., after Epiphany, the remains of a continuous reading of the Pauline letters (PL, LXXXV, 241 ff.).

Some medieval interpreters have proposed a different explanation: *Sequentia sancti evangelii secundum Matthæum* = the following reading of the Gospel is taken from (the Gospel) according to Matthew, etc.; see William of Melitona, *Opusc. super missam*, ed. van Dijk (*Eph. liturg.*, 1939), 325.

Inadmissible is the explanation offered by Brinktrine, *Die hl. Messe*, 104, note 2, who seeks to link *Sequentia* with ἀκολουθία

[6] The ancient Gallican lectionary cited in note 2 above also makes use of other freer phrases, e.g., *Quae postquam gesta sunt* (Dold, 6). The word *Dominus* is joined to the name of Jesus: *In tempore illo ait Dominus Jesus* (Dold, 55 *et al.*). In the present-day Roman liturgy, too, there is often found a supplementing of the subject, the addition of a clarifying word; thus in Luke 2: 33 on the Sunday

formula corresponding to this introduction, but in the Mass this has not become the rule as it did, for example, in our Matins.[7] Only at the closing of the reading of the prophecies is there always a regular concluding formula, *dicit Dominus omnipotens*. In some of the readings from St. Paul there is also a tacked-on phrase, the words reminiscent of the very theme of all Pauline concepts: *in Christo Jesu Domino nostro.*[8]

The setting of the holy texts in the oriental liturgies is much the same[9]; it has been especiallly developed in the Coptic.[10]

Besides this immediate setting, the readings also generally have an introduction designed to arouse the attention of the audience. The people are addressed, just as they are before the priestly oration, with the salutation *Dominus vobiscum*, to which the people respond. In the Roman Mass this salutation is in use only before the Gospel, whose higher worth is also emphasized by the extra richness of the liturgical framework. In the Milanese liturgy the same greeting precedes the Epistle also,[11] and in the

within the Christmas octave; or in Jer. 18: 18 on Passion Saturday where instead of *contra Jeremiam* is substituted *contra iustum*. Cf. further Callewaert, *Sacris erudiri*, 355.

[7] *Tu autem Domine miserere nobis;* cf. Eisenhofer, II, 513.

[8] Thus in the first two Christmas Masses (Tit. 2: 15; 3: 7). Other times the words which actually end the piece, *in Christo Jesu,* are extended by the addition of *Domino nostro,* as on the 3rd Sunday of Advent.

[9] Hanssens, III, 178-180; Droosten, "Proems of liturgical lections and gospel," *Journal of Theological Studies,* VI (1906), 99 ff.

Already Chrysostom is witness to various introductory (and concluding) formulæ of this type in the liturgical readings; Brightman, 531, note 5. According to Chrysostom, *In Hebr. hom.,* 8, 4 (PG, LXIII, 75), the lector should not only announce what book is being read from but even state the motive behind what is being related (Τὴν αἰτίαν τῶν γεγραμμένων).

[10] The first lesson, from the Pauline Epistles, is ushered in with the Apostle's own solemn self-introduction in Rom. 1: 1, and has various closing formulæ, e.g., "May grace be with you and peace, Amen, so may it be," whereupon a prayer follows for a right understanding of the Apostle's teaching. The second lesson,

from the Catholic Epistles, begins: "Katholikon. Our father (James): Beloved," and closes with the warning of the Apostle John regarding the world and its transitoriness (1 John 2: 15, 17). The third lesson, from the Acts of the Apostles, opens with "The deeds of our fathers, the Apostles; may their holy blessing be with us," and closes with the benediction composed from Acts 12: 24. "But the word of the Lord should grow and spread wide and become mighty and be firmly established in the Church of God. Amen." Finally the Gospel, preceded by various invocations addressed to the people, is concluded by the reader with the words, "Glory to our God for eternity. Amen". Brightman, 152-156.

Cf. the formulas in the Ethiopian liturgy which are in part identical with these and therefore indicative of their great antiquity, *ibid.,* 212-222. Here the Pauline lection concludes with an expanded version of St. Paul's own words, "Whoever does not love our Lord Jesus Christ, let him be anathema" (1 Cor. 16:22). At the Gospel a special closing statement is formulated, taken from the evangelist in question; thus for Mark there is "Whoever has ears to hear, let him hear!" (Mark 4: 9, 23; 7: 16).

[11] *Missale Ambrosianum* (1902), 167. After the greeting there is the softspoken *Iube Domine benedicere* and the blessing formula: *Apostolica lectio* (with

Mozarabic Mass it is found before each of the three readings[12] and the people answer Amen at the close of each.[13] Similarly in the Orient the corresponding salutation, Εἰρήνη πᾶσιν, whenever it is used before the readings, precedes (in part) the pre-Gospel lesson.[14] In some instances the admonition of the deacon, warning the congregation to pay attention, is also placed here before the first reading, although it is far more generally placed just ahead of the Gospel, and then in a more extended phrase.[15] Moreover, in the Byzantine orbit a song (conceived, it seems, as a preamble) is premised to each of the readings, in accordance with a general rule that had penetrated through the whole Byzantine liturgy where even in the Office the προκείμενον precedes the readings[16] in the same way that, in other liturgies (according to ancient tradition), a responsory follows them.[17] In the non-Greek liturgies in Syrian and Egyptian areas a preparatory prayer (begging for a fruitful attendance to the word of God) serves a similar purpose before each of the lessons.[18] These prayers are later crea-

the Old Testament reading Prophetica lectio) sit nobis salutis eruditio.
[12] Missale mixtum (PL, LXXXV, 109 ff.). After the greeting preceding the second lesson another song is inserted (psallendo), whereupon the deacon calls for quiet: Silentium facite.
[13] Ibid.
[14] Thus in the Greek liturgy of St. James (Brightman, 35), with repetition before the Gospel (38); likewise in the Greek liturgy of St. Mark (Br., 118 f.).
[15] Greek liturgy of St. Mark (Brightman, 118): Πρόσχωμεν. Notice the parallel to the Oremus which in the Roman Mass is likewise preceded by the greeting. In the Byzantine liturgy the Πρόσχωμεν precedes the Pauline lection without the greeting (Brightman, 370 f.).
In the interpretation of the Syrian liturgy written by Pseudo-George of Arbela (9th century), Explicatio off. eccl., IV, 4 ff., the deacon, before the first lesson, cries out: "Sit down and be quiet!", before each of the other lessons, "Be quiet!" Hanssens, III, 173, 181, 221. A similar command before the Epistle in the rite of the (Catholic) Chaldeans; Hanssens, III, 179.
There is also evidence here and there in the West of an admonition to be quiet; G. Godu, "Epitres," DACL, V, 255. The warning command was also customary at Rome before each of the four Gospels when these were solemnly introduced to

the catechumens at the scrutinies: State cum silentio audientes intente! Gelasianum I, 34 (Wilson, 51).
At the Duomo in Milan the custom is still preserved of having a deacon and two custodi call out to the people at the start of the Gospel at high Mass: Parcite fabulis, silentium habete, habete silentium! G. Luzzatti, "La s. Messa Ambrosiana," Ambrosius, VIII (1932), 294; cf. JL, XII (1932), 247 f. See also Archdale A. King, Notes on the Catholic Liturgies (London, 1930), 233.
This is in agreement with the custom witnessed to by the Ordo of Beroldus (12th century; ed. Magistretti, Milan, 1894, 51).
[16] In the Byzantine Mass the προκείμενον before the Pauline reading (Brightman, 371); in the Armenian Mass a chant before each of the two pre-Gospel readings (Brightman, 425 f.). Hanssens, III, 169 ff., 174 ff.
[17] The προκείμενον before the reading of the Apostle is first mentioned at Byzantium in the interpretation of the liturgy by the Patriarch Germanus (PG, XCVIII, 412 A). Cf. however the ancient Armenian lectionary in F. C. Conybeare, Rituale Armenorum (Oxford, 1905), 517 f. For the whole question see O. Heiming, JL, XI (1931), 298 f.
[18] East Syrian liturgy (Brightman, 225 ff.), West Syrian (78 f.), Ethiopian (212

tions,[19] comparable to the *Munda cor meum* of the Roman liturgy, but this latter prefaces only the Gospel and deals only with the worthiness of the one who is reading.[20] The blessing of the reader, which in the Roman Mass appears only before the Gospel, in some cases stands at the very start of all the lections.[21] Note, too, that sometimes, after the reader has completed his task, he is greeted with the complimentary words, *Pax tibi*.[22]

In the summons to the people to be attentive, there is revealed a wish that the faithful might really understand the readings. But the big obstacle to this is the fact that the liturgical language retained from ancient times has become incomprehensible to the people. Sometimes, however, we find that in such cases an actual shift was made to the current vernacular; thus amongst the Maronites and other groups of Syrians a switch was made from the Syrian, which the people no longer understood, to Arabic.[23] Even in the Roman liturgy (which at a papal Mass has at least a symbolic bilingualism in the readings),[24] a similar change was made, but only in the territory where the Croatian language is spoken. In these places use is made of the *"Schiavetto,"* a collection of Sunday and feast-day Epistles and Gospels translated into "Slavic," that is, modern Croatian. From this book the lessons are produced, whether the Mass is sung in Old Slavic or in Latin.[25] Amongst the Copts every lesson is read first in Coptic and then in Arabic. This has its parallel in our own Roman Mass, when, after the

ff.); only in part and with displacement in the Coptic (152 ff.).

[19] Cf. Hanssens, III, 177 f., 184 f., 191 f.

[20] The Byzantine Mass also contains a corresponding prayer before the Gospel (Brightman, 371 f.), and it reappears in the Greek liturgy of St. James.

[21] In the East Syrian Mass the priest pronounces a blessing over the reader of the first two lessons and over the deacon who is to read the Apostle (Brightman, 255, 1. 30; 257, 1. 4); the Gospel he reads himself. On the contrary a similar blessing is not given except before the Gospel in the Greek liturgy of St. Mark (*ibid.*, 118 f.); cf. the West Syrian liturgy of St. James (*ibid.*, 79). Other liturgies do not have any formal blessing of the reader.

[22] With these words the pope saluted the deacon after the Gospel, according to *Ordo Rom. I*, n. 11 (PL, LXXVIII, 943 A); cf. *Ordo* of Johannes Archicantor (Silva-Tarouca, 197). According to. Augustine, *Ep.*, 43, 8, 21 (CSEL, XXXIV, 2, p. 102 f.) it was customary among the Donatists for the reader to be

greeted after the Epistle with *Pax tecum*. Roetzer, 99.

In the Byzantine liturgy too the priest greets the reader after the Epistle: Εἰρήνη σοι τῷ ἀναγινώσκοντι, and after the Gospel: Εἰρήνη σοι τῷ εὐαγγελιζομένῳ. Brightman, 371 ff.

[23] Cf. D. Attwater, The Christian Churches of the East (Milwaukee, 1948), 160, 174, 206.

Regarding MSS. of oriental pericopes in two languages, in which (consequently) this transition to the vernacular can be traced, see Kunze, *Die gottesdienstliche Schriftlesung*, 79-83.

[24] Cf. *infra*, p. 444, note 12.

[25] C. Segvic, "Le origini del rito slavo-latino in Dalmazia e Croazia," *Eph. liturg.*, LIV (1940), 38-65, especially 41. Thus in the Schiavetto the principle which has been followed in the South-Slavic area since the introduction of Christianity, the principle (which Segvic tries to establish) of the vernacular within the (Roman) liturgy, has once more become operative for the readings.

reading of the Latin Gospel, there follows a reading (of Epistle and Gospel) in the vernacular, but with this difference, that the reading in the vernacular is viewed by the general law of the Church only as an introduction to (or a substitution for) the sermon and is left devoid of any liturgical framing.[26]

Examples of a bilingual reading of the Scriptures are known also from more ancient times. But in these instances the basis is usually to be found in the bilingual character of the congregation. Thus we learn from our Aquitanian pilgrim lady that the readings in Jerusalem at the end of the fourth century were in Greek, but that they were also presented in Syrian.[27] Similar arrangements are likewise mentioned in other historical sources.[28] It would, indeed, seem that these methods go back to traditions from Apostolic times, to surroundings in which, for the texts in question, no authentic translations into the vernaculars were as yet available for use.[29] We have already made reference to the solution of the problem of a congregation of mixed language, where the service of readings was conducted in groups separated according to language.[30]

It is here in the matter of the lessons that we can see most plainly the great rift that exists—a rift growing wider with the centuries—between the holy text in its traditional sacred language and the natural objective of being understood by the audience. From time to time some sort of decision was inevitable. Sometimes the solution is made in favor of understanding the text; this is done especially where the reading at divine services (by means of a planned catechesis or a sermon) is the only form of relig-

---

[26] Custom, however, and perhaps diocesan regulation do dictate certain procedures regarding the introduction and the conclusion (e.g. the sign of the Cross at the start of the Gospel and the closing words "Thus far the words of today's holy Gospel"). Some of these practices are very old. Gerbert, *Vetus Liturgia Alemannica*, I, 125 f., offers a number of instances and mentions a collection of Epistles and Gospels in German made in 1210, patently for public use. Formulas like those used at present were used in the 13th century; cf. A. Linsenmayer, *Geschichte der Predigt in Deutschland* (Munich, 1886), 138.

[27] *Aetheriæ Peregrinatio*, c. 47 (CSEL, XXXIX, 99).

[28] Here belongs the account from Eusebius, *De mart. Palæst.*, I, 1 (a longer recension ed. by B. Violet, TU, XIV, 4, p. 4; 110; cf. A. Bigelmair, *Bibliothek der Kirchenväter*, 9, p. 275 and in the intro-

duction); the martyr Procopius (d. 303) had done the Church a service in several ways: as lector (reader) and by his translation from the Greek into Aramaic.

The office of translator of lessons and homilies is mentioned in Epiphanius, *Expositio fid.*, c. 21 (PG, XLI, 825). Also in the *Euchologium* of Serapion of Thmuis there is a prayer ὑπὲρ τῶν... ἀναγνώστων καὶ ἑρμηνέων (XI, 4; Quasten, *Mon.*, 57 f.)

[29] Cf. P. Gächter, "Die Dolmetscher der Apostel," ZkTh, LX (1936), 161-187. According to Gächter it seems probable that the remark of Papias about the aramaic Gospel of St. Matthew (in Eusebius, *Hist. eccl.*, III, 39, 15), that at first each one rendered it as best he could, is to be understood of just such a translation at the public assembly for worship (186). Thus the ancient practice of the synagogue regarding the Hebrew Bible was continued in the Christian community (171 ff.).

[30] *Supra*, p. 262.

ious instruction, as in many oriental countries.[81] In other places, where there were other opportunities for religious teaching, reverence for tradition was too strong to permit such a change. The liturgical lesson then became merely a symbolic presentation of God's word. But even then, whenever a new tide of liturgical thought set in, the reading felt the brunt of the forces that sought a more intelligible form of divine service and desired the use in the lesson of a language which the congregation could understand.

Still the liturgical reading cannot long remain on the level of a prosaic presentation that looks only to the congregation's practical understanding of the text. The performance must be stylized, much in the same way as we have found in the case of the priestly oration.[82] The reader must never inject his own sentiments into the sacred text, but must always present it with strict objectivity, with holy reverence, as on a platter of gold. He must recite the text. This can be done by avoiding every change of pitch —the *tonus rectus*. As a matter of fact the Roman *tonus ferialis* has no modulation whatsoever, outside the questions. But in addition there have been, since time immemorial, many forms of elevated performance with certain cadences, little melodic figures which are indicated by punctuation marks.[83] They serve especially to signalize the Gospel above the other readings. Augustine makes mention of a *sollemniter legere* for the reading of the Passion on Good Friday.[84] The Epistles, too, were fitted out more richly than the prophetic lessons.[85] In the ninth century we hear of a festive tone for the lessons which was used at Rome for the reading of St. Paul's Epistles on Sundays.[86] However, the readings in the fore-Mass were consciously kept free of melodic overgrowth. Compared with the Office lessons on feast days, the readings at Mass even now display a great severity, which is, however, well suited to the dignity of the sacrifice.

Early in the Church's history a special reader was appointed for the performance of the readings—always someone other than the leader of the divine service, as we see already in Justin.[87] There is a certain amount of drama in this; the word which comes from God is spoken by a different

[81] Note in this connection that in the most extended compass, that of the Byzantine rite, the whole liturgy is, in the main, understood by the people at least to some extent.

[82] *Supra*, p. 377.

[83] Cf. *supra*, p. 378.

[84] Augustine, *Serm.* 218, 1 (PL, XXXVIII, 1084).

[85] According to Hugh of St. Cher, *Tract. super missam* (ed. Sölch, 17) the Old Testament lessons resound *in gravem accentum*, those of the New Testament on the contrary *in accentum acutum*.

Cf. Statutes of the Carthusians of the year 1368 (ed. Le Messen, p. 271; cited JL, 1924, 96).

[86] *Ordo Rom. IX*, n. 8; 9 (PL, LXXVIII, 1008 AB): *in sensu lectionis sicut epistolae Pauli diebus Dominicorum*. Cf. Jungmann, "Der Begriff 'sensus' in frühmittelalterlichen Rubriken," *Eph. liturg.*, XLV (1931), 124-127. For *sensus* with the same meaning see also Duchesne, *Liber pont.*, I, 415, 1, 3 (cf. ZkTh, 1942, 8, note 90) and a sacramentary of the 12th century in Ebner, 194.

[87] *Supra*, p. 23.

person than the word which rises from the Church to God. Even if Justin does not actually present the office of lector, that office does certainly appear in the second century as a special position; the lector is the oldest of the lesser degrees of ordination.[38] It is clear that the lector has to have, or to receive, a certain amount of education. But this was not the only thing kept in view in choosing him. It is a remarkable fact that since the fourth century in the West—especially in Rome—boys appear preponderantly as lectors. In many places these youthful lectors live under ecclesiastical tutelage in special communities, which thus become the foremost seed-beds for promotion to the higher degrees of spiritual office.[39] Childish innocence was considered best suited to lift the word of God from the sacred Book and to offer it, unadulterated, to the congregation.[40] But at the same time an effort was made to lay greater stress on the Gospel reading by turning it over to someone in higher orders.[41] While in the Orient the position of the lector was not disturbed by this shift,[42] in the West the reading of the Epistle in the Roman stational services of the seventh/eighth century had become the work of the subdeacon,[43] and so it has remained at high Mass even now. On the other hand, the service of a lector or of some other cleric to read the Epistle continued to be put to use for hundreds of years at the celebration of the pastor in his parish.[44] Even in private Mass the reading of the Epistle by a Mass-server is mentioned a number of times as late as the thirteenth century.[45] And even now in the Roman Mass the desirable thing at a *missa cantata* is to have the Epistle sung not by the celebrant but by *aliquis lector superpellicio indutus.*[46]

[38] F. Wieland, *Die genetische Entwicklung der sog. Ordines minores* (Rome, 1897), 67-114; Eisenhofer, II, 369 f.; J. Quasten, "Lektor," LThK, VI, 479 f.

[39] For Rome see J. M. Lungkofler, "Die Vorstufen zu den höheren Weihen nach dem Liber Pontificalis," ZkTh, LXVI (1942), 1-19, especially 12.

[40] E. Peterson, "Das jugendliche Alter der Lectoren," *Eph. liturg.*, XLVIII (1934), 437-442.

[41] See *infra*, p. 443.

[42] Besides the ἀναγνώστης the ὑποδιάκονος is the only degree in the Greek Church corresponding to the minor orders. Reading has continued to be his duty. If no ἀναγνώστης is present in a congregation, the reading of the Epistle becomes the honorary office of a layman.

[43] *Ordo Rom. I*, n. 10. Further evidences in Godu, "Epitres," 251 f. Still Amalar, *De eccl. off.*, II, 11 (PL, CV, 1086) is puzzled over this matter, since in the ordination the subdeacon was given no particular charge. Handing the book to the subdeacon at his ordination was not a general custom till the 13th century; cf. de Puniet, *Das römische Pontifikale*, I, 174.

[44] Cf. *supra*, p. 208. In Spain as late as 1068, in can. 6 of the Synod of Gerona (Mansi, XIX, 1071) there is question of lectors who belong to the clergy but yet are permitted to wed.

[45] *Supra*, p. 227, note 106.

[46] *Missale Rom., Rit. serv.*, VI, 8.

According to a decree of the Congregation of Rites dated April 23, 1875, the priest himself should simply read the Epistle, not sing it, in the absence of a lector; *Decreta auth. SRC*, n. 3350.

But in Germany custom appears to sanction the practice of chanting it; so Brinktrine, *Die hl. Messe*, 91.

A lector is also mentioned for the first reading on Good Friday and for the prophecies on the vigils of Easter and Whitsunday. In the *Liber ordinarius* of

When the reader performed his duty, this was made visible in the older Roman liturgy by the way he wore his official garb. He is now definitely "in service" and should not seem to be hindered by his garments. This vesture was—as with all clerics—the bell-shaped *planeta* or *casula*. But the deacon and subdeacon wore this tucked up in front, so that their hands were free, and the subdeacon's formed a sort of envelope or pocket so that he could pick things up and carry them around not with bare hands but holding them through the garment.[47] So when the deacon got ready to read the Gospel he arranged the *planeta* in such a way that it lay tightly folded over his left shoulder and fell across his breast at an angle. Thus he kept it all through his service till after the Communion. But the subdeacon or other cleric, when getting prepared for the reading, took the *planeta* off.[48] Thus the gradation of office was kept somewhat in a recognizable form. This practice, which appears about the ninth century, is still retained in broad outline at high Masses which take place during Lent or on other days of similar dignity; the deacon and subdeacon make use of the *planeta* (since replaced by dalmatic and tunicle), but the deacon, before the reading, substitutes the *stola latior*, and the subdeacon takes off his outer vestment before he reads the Epistle.[49]

For the presentation of the sacred text the reader also chooses a special place. To be better understood he will turn to the listeners, perhaps—if possible—take an elevated place, as Esdras did,[50] and as the Roman Pontifical actually prescribes for the lector.[51] As early as the third and fourth centuries there is mention of an elevated place where the reading-desk stood or where the lector stood even without a desk.[52] Later this was turned into

---

Liége (Volk, 82, 1. 25) the lessons on Ember Saturday were also assigned to a lector.

Further, it is permitted at present for a cleric in minor orders to substitute for the subdeacon at a high Mass when the latter is not available; he may be vested—*paratus absque manipulo;* decree dated July 5, 1698; *Decreta auth. SRC,* n. 2002. The question of such a substitution was likewise raised in the Middle Ages, but answered in the negative because reading the Epistle was the exercise of a power which a cleric in minor orders did not possess. The priest himself, in this case, should read the Epistle. Bernold, *Micrologus,* c. 8 (PL, CLI, 982); Beleth, *Explicatio,* c. 38 (PL, CCII, 46 A):

[47] Braun, *Die liturgische Gewandung,* 166-169; Callewaert, *Sacris erudiri,* 233-239.

[48] Braun. 166.
  Cf. *Ordo Rom. V,* n. 3 (PL, LXXVIII, 985); Amalar, *De eccl. off.,* III, 15 (PL, CV, 1122 f.); *Ordo Rom. I,* n. 51 (PL, LXXVIII, 960).
[49] *Missale Rom., Rubr. gen.,* XIX, 6; cf. Braun, 149 f.
  The "broad stole" (*stola latior*) is really a stylized folded chasuble—a limp chasuble that was folded over the shoulder and pinned there; eventually the folds were sewed in and the cloth cut down to its present nondescript shape.
[50] Nehem. 8: 4.
[51] *Pontificale Rom., De ord. lectoris: Dum legitis, in alto loco ecclesiæ stetis, ut ab omnibus audiamini et videamini.*
[52] Cyprian, *Epist.* 38, 2 (CSEL, III, 580 f.); 39, 4 (583 f.): *pulpitum;* Council of Laodicea, can. 15 (Mansi, II, 567); *Const. Ap.,* II, 57, 5 (Quasten, *Mon.,* 182).

an ambo[53] or pulpit, a podium fitted out with a balustrade and lectern, set up at some convenient spot between sanctuary and nave, and either standing free or else built into the choir railing or into the side-railings of the enclosure, which, in many basilicas, surrounded the space for the *schola cantorum*. The ambo also served—as we will see later in greater detail— for the singer in the responsorial chant. Frequently the preaching was done from here. In the Orient the deacon ascended—and still ascends—the ambo to lead the prayer of the people in the *ektene*, but it was especially intended for the reader who presented the Sacred Scriptures. This is indicated, *inter alia*, by the names it has: *lectrinum, lectionarium,*[54] *analogium*. Frequently it was very richly adorned with mosaics, sculpture and the like.[55]

But now the Roman Mass contains hardly a trace of an arrangement which seemed so well suited to making the reading as understandable as possible. As far as the people are concerned, the readings have, during the past thousand years, become a mere symbol. The subdeacon who reads the Epistle stands at his accustomed place, facing the altar[56] and therefore with his back to the people. The deacon who sings the Gospel, should indeed turn *contra altare versus populum,*[57] but the latter direction, *versus populum*, seems to be countermanded by the first, *contra altare*.[58] So, for a practical suggestion as to the position to be taken by deacon, the rubric from the pontifical Mass is usually given, since it is plainer: the deacon turns in that direction which corresponds to the north side of an oriented church.[59]

---

[53] The word is derived from the verb ἀναβαίνειν, to mount or climb up. It first appears at the Council of Laodicea, can. 15 (Mansi, II, 567).
A. M. Schneider, "Ambo," RAC, I, 363-365.
[54] The word "lectern."
[55] H. Leclercq, "Ambon," DACL, I, 1330-1347. Cf. Caryl Coleman, "Ambo," CE, I : 381-2.
[56] *Missale Rom., Ritus serv.*, VI, 4: *contra altare*. According to the Mass-*Ordo* 'Indutus planeta' (Legg, *Tracts*, 184) which appeared in Mass books after 1507, the subdeacon reads the Epistle in front of the steps *contra medium altaris*. This latter expression is already in the *Liber usuum O. Cist.* (12th century), c. 53 (PL, CLXVI, 1423 B), and after that in the *Liber ordinarius* of Liége (Volk, 90). But the Missal of St. Vincent-on-Volturno (circa 1100) directs: *versus contra altare* (Fiala, 200). Cf. also Durandus, IV, 16, 5.
[57] *Missale Rom., Ritus serv.*, VI, 5.

[58] Gavanti is right when he declares: *verba rubricæ . . . videntur pugnare invicem*. He therefore settles for a direction halfway between altar and people; Gavanti-Merati, II, 6, 5 (I, 242). As a matter of fact the same expression, *contra altare*, is used shortly before in the rubrics of the Mass book, as we noticed already (VI, 4), and here it is used to describe the stance of the subdeacon at the Epistle, with face directed towards the altar. The expression is used unequivocally in this sense by Paris de Grassis (d. 1528) when he gives the rule: In a non-oriented church the deacon should stand ·at the Gospel *non collateraliter* to the altar, but *facie ad faciem altaris, id est contra ipsum altare* (PL, LXXVIII, 934).
[59] *Cæremoniale episc.*, II, 8, 44: The subdeacon should hold the book *vertens renes non quidem altari, sed versus ipsam partem* (i.e., towards the "Gospel side"; this phraseology was not used till near the end of the Middle Ages) *quæ pro aquilone figuratur*.

Or recourse is had simply to local custom, which is actually diversified.[60]

On the contrary there are no differences of opinion regarding the further rule, that the Epistle is read on the south side of the sanctuary, the Gospel on the north—a rule which the priest himself must observe at the altar even at the simplest private Mass. In addition, a more detailed regulation regarding the Gospel is this, that he does not face straight ahead but towards the corner of the altar,[61] that is, in an oriented church he turns just a bit to the north. This is almost the same rule as that for the deacon at solemn Mass. From the standpoint of the ordinary participant, this means that the Epistle is said at the right side, the Gospel at the left. Further it means that at every Mass the book has to be carried over from one side to the other. The difference in the locale of the readings and the accompanying conduct of the Mass-server are some of the peculiarities of the external Mass rite which make the strongest impression. "Epistle side" and "Gospel side" are phrases that even poorly instructed Catholics are acquainted with. It is therefore very much in place to go into greater detail regarding this regulation.

The north side as the place for the Gospel is specifically mentioned for the first time in the commentary of Remigius of Auxerre (d. c. 908)[62]; the north, he says, is the region of the devil whom the word of God must contend with. And Ivo of Chartres (d. c. 1117) continues the line of thought,[63] remarking that the Gospel is proclaimed against paganism, which is represented by the northern part of the world, and in which the coldness of unbelief had so long prevailed. And Ivo does not mean merely the direction of the body which the reader assumes in the ambo, but the actual position on the north side of the sanctuary, for he speaks of the passage of the levite or of the priest "to the left side of the church" in order to read the Gospel.[64] And that too has a meaning, for it represents the transfer of preaching from the Jews to the Gentiles.[65] The suspicion is forced upon one that these are but later attempts to explain by allegory a practice which was long in

[60] W. Lurz, *Ritus und Rubriken der hl. Messe* (2nd ed.; Würzburg, 1941), 454, note 58: The exact stance—whether diagonally towards the altar or towards the people, or parallel to the altar steps—is determined by the custom of the particular church. According to M. Gatterer, *Praxis celebrandi*, 248, note o, the deacon should stand *sicut sacerdos in missa privata*, therefore diagonal to the altar; on the other hand Ph. Hartmann-J. Kley, *Repertorium rituum* (14th ed.; Paderborn, 1940), 502, direct the deacon to stand turned somewhat towards the people. And J. O'Connell, *The Celebration of Mass* (Milwaukee, 1940), III, 100-101, takes the third position, insisting that the deacon takes his place facing directly "north," that is, towards the left-hand side of the church.

[61] *Missale Rom., Ritus serv.*, VI, 1.
Substantially the same direction in the Mass-*Ordo* of Burchard: Legg, *Tracts*, 146; cf. *ibid.*, 145, note 6.

[62] Remigius, *Expositio* (PL, CI, 1250 f.).
Cf. John of Avranches, *De off. eccl.* (PL, CXLVII, 35 A).

[63] Ivo of Chartres, *De conven. vet. et novi sacrif.* (PL, CLXII, 550).

[64] *Ibid.*

[65] Cf. *supra*, p. 110.

use and no longer understood, a practice which did not concern north and south at all, but had an entirely different viewpoint.

An inkling of this is to be found in the author of the *Micrologus*,[66] a work almost contemporaneous with Ivo. The author writes that it is almost a general custom that the deacon reading the Gospel turn toward the north. But he takes exception to this, not only because the north side is the side for the women, and it is therefore unbecoming that the deacon turn that way, but also because it is plainly *contra Romanum ordinem*, according to which the deacon stands on the ambo turned to the south, that is, the side of the men. He explains the variant practice, which had already become fixed and rooted, as a conscious imitation of the movement and position of the priest who, when saying Mass without a deacon, does really have to say the Gospel at the north side of the altar in order to leave the other side free for the sacrificial activity, and who thus could give the appearance of actually turning towards the north. But this explanation, suggesting the private Mass as the origin of the practice, although it has been repeated in our own day,[67] is presented only for lack of something better.

Just what is to be said about this "Roman order" which Bernold had in view? He is thinking, one might say, of Mabillon's second Roman *Ordo*, but this order he could not have known since it was not compiled till the tenth century and in Franco-German territory.[68] The real Roman arrangement was not as precise as Bernold supposes. We can reconstruct it as it actually was, better perhaps from archeological evidences than from literary sources.[69]

The spot from which the deacon at a solemn function could read the Gospel most conveniently and fittingly had to be chosen in such a way that on the one hand the reader had the people before him, and on the other he did not turn his back on the bishop and the clergy surrounding him. In the basilicas of the dying ancient period, where the *cathedra* of the bishop

---

[66] Bernold, *Micrologus*, c. 9 (PL, CLI, 982 f.) : *De evangelio in qua parte sit legendum.*
Similarly somewhat later Honorius Augustod., *Gemma an.*, I, 22 (PL, CLXXII, 551).
[67] M. Daras, "La position du diacre durant l'évangile," *Les questions liturgiques et paroissiales* (1930), XV, 57 ff. Similarly Brinktrine, *Die hl. Messe*, 106 f.
[68] *Ordo Rom. II*, n. 8 (PL, LXXVIII, 972) : *Ipse vero diaconus stat versus ad meridiem, ad quam partem viri solent confluere.*
The position looking towards the south is already appointed for the deacon in

Amalar's *Expositio* of 813-14, ed. Hanssens (*Eph. liturg.*, 1927), 164 f. (= Gerbert, *Monumenta*, I, 154 f.) ; this direction means *Ecclesiam ferventem animo in amore Dei*. Likewise in the *Expositio 'Missa pro multis'*, ed. Hanssens (*Eph. liturg.*, 1930), 36, and in the *Ecloga* (PL, CV, 1322 f.). It is also admitted in the Missal of St. Vincent (c. 1100; Fiala, 201) : *versus ad septemtrionem sive meridiem*. The same direction is still mentioned in Durandus, IV, 24, 21.
[69] Cf. the anonymous study "Pourquoi ces différents endroits pour la lecture de l'épître et de l'évangile?" *Les Questions liturgiques*, IV (1914), 314-320.

stood in the apse, he would therefore have to stand to the side, in the forward part of the choir, to the right of the presiding bishop (for all the ranks of honor were reckoned with the *cathedra* of the bishop as the point of departure).[70] He would thus face either north or south depending on the position of the apse and the *cathedra*, whether to the west, as they were in the older Roman structures, or to the east, as later became customary. As a matter of fact we find the ambo is arranged in many places in accordance with these notions.[71] In the latter case, where the apse is towards the east, the deacon who wanted to talk to the people, turned toward the south. This position is evinced both by the placement of ambos[72] and by literary documents[73]; this is the position which Bernold wanted observed (Fig. 1). In the Roman churches of the older type, which had the apse toward the west, the deacon would, under the same circumstances, assume a position facing north, and many Roman basilicas actually indicate this layout (Fig. 2).[74]

---

[70] Cf. *Ordo Rom. I,* n. 4 (PL, LXXVIII, 639) : the clergy should take their place in the semicircle of the *presbyterium* in such wise *ut quando pontifex sederit ad eos respiciens episcopos ad dexteram sui, presbyteros vero ad sinistram contueatur.* In those early churches in the Occident which faced west the men and women were also seated in the nave to right and left of the *cathedra* : the women were assigned the north side. This continued to be their side also in the oriented churches; Beissel, *Bilder,* 56 f. For meanwhile the point of view that had become established was the orientation at prayer : as before the men were to be at the right, the women at the left; H. Selhorst, *Die Platzordnung im Gläubigenraum der altchristlichen Kirche,* Diss. (Münster, 1931), 33.

Only later, when the rear wall was built out and the *cathedra* was moved from the vertex of the apse to the side, did the arrangement in the sanctuary (opposite that in the nave) become unintelligible. From the viewpoint of the entrance (or, what is the same, from the viewpoint of prayer-orientation), the Gospel is said at the "left" side—a terminology that continued to be used throughout the Middle Ages (e.g. in the Missal of Westiminster, circa 1380; see *Supra,* p. 299, note 10), and allegorical interpretations were employed to explain this fact (*supra,* p. 110; Durandus, IV, 23). Still Durandus himself notes in his pontifical that there are great feast-days *quibus pontifex sedet post altare* (Andrieu, III, 648; cf. 641). Paris de Grassis (d. 1528) offers an additional explanation of the matter when he points out that the Gospel side is to the right if viewed from the altar itself, not from the viewpoint of the celebrant, *Nam et crucis et crucifixi super ipso altari stantis dextra ad praedictum cornu evangelii vergit* (PL, LXXVIII, 934 B). The *Cæremoniale Episcoporum* again calls the Epistle side the left (II, 8, 40); cf. *supra,* note 59. The Missale Romanum mentions only a *cornu epistolæ* and a *cornu evangelii.*

[71] In the Roman *Ordines* both the one design and the other are considered. For instance there is an ancient recension of *Ordo Rom. I* which presupposes a basilica facing west (ed. Stapper) and a later recension in which the oriented structure is basic (ed. Mabillon); see the instruction at the *Gloria* (*Ordo Rom. I,* n. 9).

[72] The cathedral of Torcello; F. X. Kraus, *Geschichte der christlichen Kunst* (Freiburg, 1896), I, 334; cathedral of Grado: DACL, I, 2657.

[73] *Supra,* p. 414, note 68.

[74] Examples of churches facing west in which the ambo was set according to this sense: St. Peter: Duchesne, *Liber pont.,* I, 192-193; S. Maria Maggiore: H. Grisar, *Geschichte Roms und der Päpste*

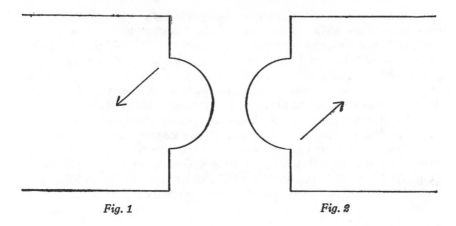

Fig. 1   Fig. 2

It is this latter position, set free of its natural foundation, that continued to be the fixed norm in the conception of the medieval liturgists and
still survives in the rubrics of the *Cæremoniale episcoporum*. But in the
transfer to the oriented churches two possibilities remained open. The deacon could place himself to the left of the *cathedra* (still standing at the
center of the apse) and thus speak from the south side of the church, facing
the nave and the north (Fig. 3) ; again there are actual examples.[75] But it
was hardly possible to tolerate for long the reading of the Gospel at the
left of the *cathedra* and with face towards the women's side of the church.
So the second possibility came to mind; the deacon could stand to the
right and still face northwards, too—as we are accustomed to seeing it
done (Fig. 4).

This last solution is basically in complete correspondence with the intellectual and cultural condition of the Middle Ages. It seemed more important to hold on to the symbolism of the northward direction (since this had
a message for the symbol-hungry eyes of the people of that era) than to
turn to the people (since the contents of the Latin lesson were not grasped
by them anyway). This arrangement then became a norm for the priest
in reading the Gospel at the altar. Thus, besides this symbolical northward

(Freiburg, 1901, I, 344; S. Clemente
(Gospel ambo with Easter candle) : Th.
Gsell Fels, *Rom* (6th ed.; Leipzig, 1906),
364; cf. *Les Questions liturg.*, (1914),
IV, 319, Fig. 9.
[75] S. Maria in Cosmedin: R. Stapper,
Katholische Liturgik (5th ed.; Münster,
1931), p. 48-49; cf. *Les Questions liturg.*,
(1914), IV, 319, fig. 10; S. Lorenzo
fuori le mura: Gsell Fels, *Rom*, 783 f.

See also Ch. Rohault de Fleury, *La
messe* (Paris, 1883), III, p. 39, where,
in consequence of the position of the
Easter candle, this position of the Gospel
ambo *"sur la face opposée"* is indicated
also in the cathedrals of Salerno and
Beneventum, Lebrun, *Explication*, I, 201,
refers to the minster of Aachen (ambo
of the year 1011).

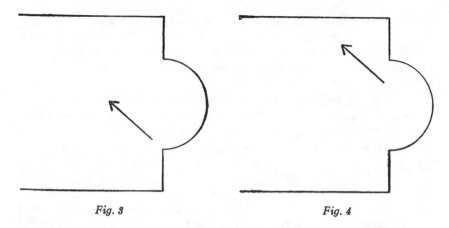

Fig. 3   *Fig. 4*

direction both at solemn and simple Masses another rule remained in force, that the Gospel should be read at the right side (reckoning from the viewpoint of the bishop's *cathedra*). The opposite side was then the Epistle side, but this only at a comparatively late date. Even in the late eleventh century, at the private monastic Masses at Hirsau, if the priest read the Epistle himself, he did so at the "Gospel side" of the altar,[76] while, on the other hand, according to a Monte Cassino *ordinarium* of about 1100, the Gospel is still read on the "Epistle side."[77] Beleth in 1160 objects that the priest generally reads the Gospel at the altar instead of at a special lectern.[78] It appears that up to that time the norm mostly followed was a very practical one, to keep the right side of the altar—our Epistle side— free for the gift-offerings at least from the offertory on.[79]

Interest in a gradation amongst the readings was early at work in the choice of readers, as we have seen. But in localizing the reading the process was slower. Even in the early Middle Ages there was, as a rule, but one ambo, which served for all the lessons. Amalar is the first to mention an *excellentior locus* at which the Gospel was read.[80] The *Ordo Romanus II*, which originated in the north in the tenth century, directs the subdeacon

[76] William of Hirsau, *Const.* I, 86 (PL, CL, 1016 D): *lecturus epistolam librum ponit ad sinistram ibique reliqua dicit usque ad communionem.* "Gospel side" therefore means here only the position of the book (probably a complete missal) at the left of the priest, just as now during the sacrificial portion of the Mass. Similarly also *Bernardi Ordo Clun.* (circa 1068), I, 72 (Herrgott, 264), where

nevertheless we read: *lecturus epistolam ad sinistram transit.*
[77] Lebrun, I, 205 f.
[78] John Beleth, *Explicatio,* c. 37 (PL, CCII, 45 C).
[79] Thus even circa 1100 the Missal of St. Vincent orders at the Offertory: *diaconus . . . ornet altare in dextro latere;* Fiala, 203.
[80] Amalar, *De eccl. off.,* III, 18 (PL, CV, 1126 C).

who reads the Epistle to mount the ambo, *non tamen in superiorem gradum, quem solum solet ascendere qui evangelium lecturus est*,[81] a rule which is often repeated later on.[82] At the same time we hear of a specially built desk for the reading of the Gospel; it had the form of an eagle with wings outspread.[83]

In the church architecture of the later Middle Ages the ambo is no longer considered, or, to be more precise, it is moved away from the *cancelli* farther into the nave of the church where it becomes a pulpit. Obviously the smaller churches did not possess an ambo even in earlier times. Ivo of Chartres apparently has this case in mind.[84] The Gospel thus retained the place it got either by tradition or by symbolic interpretation—a place on the level of the choir (sanctuary), on the north side. The subdeacon became the bearer of the Gospel book, replacing the lectern or desk—a new honor for the Gospel. But the Epistle later obtained its place on the opposite side, with the subdeacon reading toward the altar,[85] and himself holding the book.[86] Thus the "Epistle side" of the altar was evolved. Ivo of Chartres seems to stipulate some such thing,[87] although in many other places, even at a much later date, there is still no fixed rule.[88] In an intervening period, when the division of readings to right and left was recognized and still at the same time the need was felt for an ambo, two ambos were sometimes constructed,[89] one more ornamental on the Gospel side, the other more modest on the Epistle side.[90] In our modern buildings we sometimes

[81] *Ordo Rom. II*, n. 7 (PL, LXXVIII, 971); cf. *Eclogæ* (PL, CV, 1321 C).

On the contrary *Ordo Rom. XI* (a plan for the city of Rome, but originating only circa 1140), n. 40 (PL, LXXVIII, 1040), says without further distinction: *subdiaconus legit epistolam in ambone*.

Martène, 1, 4, 4, 3 (I, 373 f.) presents examples from his own time of French churches that followed the one plan as well as some that followed the other.

[82] Durandus, IV, 16, 2.

[83] Durandus, IV, 24, 20. He makes reference to Ps. 17: 11: *et volavit super pennas ventorum*.

Regarding medieval pulpits in the form of an eagle see Eisenhofer, I, 383 f.

[84] *Supra*, p. 413.

[85] It is possible that love for symbolism helped to tip the scales, once the reason for turning to the people had lost its force. According to Durandus, IV, 15, 5. the subdeacon looks towards the altar, which signifies Christ, *quia Johannis praedicatio se et alios dirigebat in Christum*.

It is precisely in this portion of the Mass, the Epistle, that the allegorical significance (preaching of the prophets, of John) is of ancient tradition and quite unanimous; cf. *supra*, p. 89; p. 110, note 41.

[86] For this reason the priest, while reading the Epistle, is even at present directed to place his hands on the book or to hold the book, whereas he reads the Gospel with hands folded, like the deacon whose hands are free. *Missale Rom., Rit. serv.*, VI, 1, 2; 5.

[87] *Supra*, p. 413.

[88] Cf. the expression *contra medium altaris* for the reading of the Epistle, note 58 above.

[89] The study of H. Leclercq, "Ambon," DACL, I, 1330-1347, which covers the period up to the 9th century, maintains that in this time there is nowhere any evidence of two ambos (1339).

[90] Thus in S. Clemente which was rebuilt in 1100 but kept the form that it had had at the time. In S. Lorenzo the Gospel

see this plan followed, since the regulations in force at the present time[91] leave room for such an arrangement.

4. The Epistle

The first of the two readings of the Roman Mass is called simply "the Epistle" although it is not always taken from the Letters of the Apostles. This usage, which the *Missale Romanum* retains,[1] existed even in the twelfth century.[2] The reading was also called *"lectio,"* corresponding to the designation by which the title of the book being read is introduced: *lectio Isaiæ prophetæ, lectio epistolæ.* . . . Since enough was already said previously about the selection of the Epistle, the choice of a reader and his position in the sanctuary, it is only necessary to state that in our Roman liturgy it seems that the principle of the highest simplicity has been followed in the framing of the Epistle itself at high Mass. Consequently there is no address to the people and no reply on their part, no blessing of the reader (as is customary otherwise even in the Office before the longer readings at Matins[3]) and no prayer by the reader for purification, no solemn escort to the ambo (in recent times only the accompaniment of an acolyte has been allowed[4]). Even the melody to which it is sung is kept much simpler than at the Gospel.[5]

ambo dates from the 8th century; Gsell Fels, *op. cit.,* 784.
[91] *Cæremoniale episc.,* I, 12, 18.
[1] *Missale Rom., Rit. serv.,* VI.
[2] John Beleth, *Explicatio,* c. 38 (PL, CCII, 46 B). The Epistle can be taken from all books of the Scriptures except the Psalms and the Gospels.
[3] All the more surprising then is the practice of having the subdeacon at high Mass, after the reading of the Epistle, bring the book to the celebrant, and kiss his hand and receive his blessing. Thus already in Durandus, IV, 17. According to the Missal of St. Vincent (circa 1100) he gives the book to the thurifer and simply receives the priest's blessing with head bowed (Fiala, 200). It seems, therefore, that the older element is not the return of the book but the reverence and the blessing. Cf. for this also Martène, 1, 4, 4, 5 (I, 374). Still the original significance may perhaps be seen in the *Ordo* of the Lateran church (middle of the 12th century) ; according to this the subdeacon offers the bishop the Epistle *legendam;* only after the latter has read

it does the subdeacon kiss his hand (Fischer, 81). Later the bishop read the Epistle at the same time that the subdeacon did.

That the ceremony was continued ties in very well with the rather commonly accepted allegorical interpretation of the Epistle as the preaching of the prophets or the Baptist: by means of a symbolic ceremony it was possible to suggest the fulfillment of the Old Covenant through Christ who is represented by the priest; cf. Durandus, *loc. cit.*

In some isolated instances this blessing of the subdeacon is found fitted out with a petition and a formula of benediction: *Ordinarium* of Bayeux (13th c.) : Martène, I, 4, XXIV (I, 627 B).
[4] Cf. Innocent III, *De s. alt mysterio,* II, 29 (PL, CCXVII, 816 C). In the *Ordinarium O.P.* of 1256 (Guerrini, 236) this is done only on Sundays and feasts.
[5] It is therefore all the more striking that since the 11th century tropes were composed for some of the Epistles, but not for the Gospels. These tropes expanded the text either by means of Latin phrases

This sobriety was evidently intentional, in order to let the Gospel stand out more strongly. Putting it more exactly, it was retained when the richer fitting-out of the Gospel was begun. In general an older manner in the fitting-out of the lection still survives in the Epistle. Here, too, the role of the lector is still acknowledged at least in part—which agrees with what we have said. To sit during the Epistle was also one of those olden reading practices.[6] On the other hand, this sobriety is not quite so pronounced as at the readings which bear the stamp of greatest antiquity—those of Good Friday and Holy Saturday. About these the rubric still remarks that they are read *sine titulo* and the answer *Deo gratias* is omitted at the end—two elaborations which have nevertheless been accorded the Epistle.

The *Deo gratias* at the end is not necessarily proper to the Epistle only. It is repeated at the end of the last Gospel, just as it follows at the lessons of the Office, and also at the *Ite missa est*. In truth only in the last case does the response bear the marks of primitiveness, since it is made by the choir and not by the servers.[7]

It is without doubt sensible and very becoming for one to thank God after being permitted to receive His word. But it is questionable whether the *Deo gratias* is here intended as a spoken thanks. Primarily its function seems to be quite different. In this *Deo gratias* we have a formal shout which was much used outside of divine service especially in the North African Church, e.g. as an acclamation in the sense of approval, and as a greeting of Christians on meeting each other.[8] The *Deo gratias* seems to have come from North Africa into the Arabian liturgy, where it is used along with *Amen* as a response after the reading.[9] We find also that it was

---

or, later, by means of French farcings. Blume, *Tropen des Missale,* II (Analecta hymnica, 49), p. 165-207, especially 167 f.; idem., "Epitre farcie," LThK, III, 734.
[6] At one time it was customary at high Mass for the celebrant to sit during the Epistle, even if only a simple priest, along with the deacon, as is still the practice in the Carthusian and Dominican rites and as I myself saw it done at Lyons in 1929. This custom is attested also in the *Udalrici Consuetudines Clun.* (circa 1080), II, 30 (PL, CXLIX, 716); in the Missal of St. Vincent: Fiala, 200; in the old Cistercian rite: Schneider, (*Cist.-Chron.,* 1926), 315 f.; in the *Liber ordinarius* of Liége: Volk, 90; and in Durandus, IV, 18. Sitting also became customary for the faithful (*supra,* p. 241), and in many lands, especially those following English and French practices, it has con-

tinued customary; Kramp, "Messgebräuche der Gläubigen in den ausserdeutschen Ländern" (StZ, 1927, II), 355.

For the papal and episcopal Mass see *Ordo Rom. I,* n. 9 (PL, LXXVIII, 942); cf. *Ordo Rom. II,* n. 6 (PL, LXXVIII, 971). At a pontifical Mass the bishop sits even today and reads the Epistle the while: *Cæremoniale episc.,* II, 8, 39; 41.
[7] On the contrary in the Office the whole choir answers the readings with *Deo gratias.* Thus the *Deo gratias* at the Epistle, which is apparently not mentioned in medieval *Ordines* or Mass books, becomes a secondary development, derived from the Office.
[8] F. Cabrol, "Deo gratias," DACL, IV, 649-652; cf. the examples from inscriptions which are there cited by H. Leclercq, *ibid.,* 652-659.
[9] *Ibid.,* 650.

a part of the Roman liturgy at an early period. At the stational service in the eighth century when the deacon made the announcement of the next station, right after the Communion of the Pope, the people answered, *Deo gratias.*[10] The sense in which the formula is here used is plain. The only purpose is to express the fact that the hearers have understood the announcement. It is the same situation as that predicated in the rule of St. Benedict where the gate-keeper is told to answer *Deo gratias* whenever anyone knocks at the monastery doors.[11] Surely he is not shouting his gratitude for any benefit received; he is merely indicating that he has heard the summons. But he does use a formula which goes down deep into Christian concepts, a formula which has become so much a part of everyday life that it can serve as a simple signal. It is in this sense that we must understand the *Deo gratias* which is said after the *Ite missa est* and on other occasions in the Roman liturgy,[12] especially after the Epistle and the lessons. We can trace here the prevailing tone that dominates the Roman liturgy, the strong, religiously accented consciousness of the community, the realization that after the proclamation made to all, after the presentation of God's word, no doubt should be left about its reception. The proclamation has been heard, the reading has been received, and the reply that resounds from the people is one which the Christian should use in every challenging situation in life: *Deo gratias*, Thanks be to God.

5. The Intervenient Chants

It is in the very nature of things that the grace-laden message which God proclaims to men would awaken an echo of song. In the chant which is linked with the readings we have the most ancient song of the Christian liturgy, and in particular of the Roman liturgy. In contrast to the more modern strata of the Mass chants: introit, offertory and communion, which were antiphonal in design and so demanded a special singing group for performance, the gradual and alleluia still show plainly the traits of the older responsorial method which dominated the field till at least the fourth century. For this type of music only one trained singer was required, with the people all answering together. Only this solo singer had any continuous text to reproduce; the people answered by repeating after each passage the unchanging verse, the refrain or *responsum.*[1] This is a very simple procedure, but for a vital participation of the people a procedure suitable in the highest measure, since neither any special preparation nor a written

---

[10] *Ordo* of St. Amand: Duchesne, *Christian Worship,* 462; cf. *Breviarium eccl. ord.*: Silva-Tarouca, 200.

[11] Rule of St. Benedict, c. 66.

[12] Cf. the enumeration in Eisenhofer, I, 192 f.

[1] The Greeks had various designations for

this: ἀκροτελεύτιον, ἀκροστίχιον, ὑπακοή, ἀφύμνιον; the singing itself they called ὑποψάλλειν, ὑπακούειν, *succinere, respondere.* Leitner, 207 f.

In Spain it was called *subpsalmare;* Férotin, *Le Liber mozarabicus sacramentorum,* p. XLI f.

text were necessary for the people. This responding of the people was customary both in the singing of the races of the ancient Orient and in the divine service of the Old Covenant.[2] But in the pre-Christian and primitive Christian eras there was in the texts scarcely any distinction between song and prayer, nor was there any definite singing tune for use only in the performance of the psalms, since certain recitatives and even formal melodies were customary also for the other books of the Bible.[3] But responsory itself was to some extent inherent in the very text of the psalms. It was a legacy which the synagogue inherited from the services in the Temple.[4] And thence it passed to the primitive Church where it is found in full practice.

According to the arrangement of the agape outlined by Hippolytus of Rome, the faithful were to say "alleluia" when the psalms were read at the beginning of the agape.[5] The reference is to the alleluia psalms in which the biblical text already contains the entry, "alleluia," either at the beginning or at the end, as an indication that the word was to be inserted as a response after every verse.[6] St. Athanasius on one occasion mentioned the deacon's reciting a psalm before the entire people, while the people responded repeatedly: *Quoniam in æternum misericordia eius*,[7] just as we find it sketched in Psalm 135.

Since the third century, contemporaneous with the vanishing of the vogue of privately composed hymns,[8] the use of the Scriptural psalms became more pronounced. And the opposition to these hymns probably led to a greater stressing of the musical character of the psalms.[9] In the fourth century there is explicit evidence of the use of psalm chant in the reading

[2] Leitner, *Der gottesdienstliche Volksgesang im jüdischen und christlichen Altertum*, 26-93; Elbogen, *Der jüdische Gottesdienst*, 494 ff. Cf. also Nielen, *The Earliest Christian Liturgy*, 281-289.

[3] Elbogen, 503 ff. The accent marks of the Masoretic texts contained (as we know) indications also of the method of production. Much information regarding cantillation signs (*ta'amin*) may be obtained from Solomon Rosowsky, "The Music of the Pentateuch," *Proceedings of the Music Association*, XLVIII (1934), 38.

[4] Elbogen, 494 f. The fundamental elements of Hebrew cantillation are thoroughly discussed in Abraham Z. Idelsohn, *Jewish Music* (New York, 1929).

[5] Hippolytus of Rome, *Trad. Ap.* (Dix, 51 f.; Hennecke, 581); cf. *supra*, p. 13, note 29.

Cf. Tertullian, *De or.*, c. 27; see for this Dekkers, 35.

[6] In this way the Hallel was prayed at the synagogue service; see Elbogen, 496: The leader began with "halleluja," the congregation repeated it, and after each half-verse chimed in again with "halleluja," in all (as the ancient sources report) 123 times.

In much the same way the alleluia is used as a refrain after a rather lengthy series of verses in the Stowe Missal.

A discussion of the relation of the alleluia to the liturgy of the synagogue in P. Wagner, *Einführung*, I, 31.

[7] Athanasius, *De fuga*, c. 24 (PG, XXV, 676 A).

[8] Cf. *supra*, p. 346.

[9] During the first two hundred years of the Christian era the Psalter appears to have served the Church only as a prayerbook, not as a songbook, just like the other books of the Bible. B. Fischer, *Die Psalmenfrömmigkeit der Märtyrenkirche* (Freiburg, 1949), 3, 10, referring to R. Knopf.

service of the fore-Mass, and its performance followed the method of responsorial song already in vogue.[10] In this process the alleluia gained considerable importance. It is, at any rate, a phenomenon worth remarking, that nearly all the liturgies both East and West still display the alleluia in the Mass in some form or other.[11] And usually the alleluia follows the second-last reading, either immediately[12] or (as in the Roman liturgy too) mediately, so that it looks like a prelude to the Gospel[13]; but sometimes it does not appear till after the last lesson.[14]

In the sermons of St. Augustine we are introduced to the fully developed form of the responsorial psalming as it was done between the lessons. He speaks of a psalm "which we heard sung and to which we responded." [15] Augustine himself was wont to select the psalm. Even lengthier psalms were sung right through without curtailment.[16] The refrain seems always to have consisted of an entire verse of the respective psalm. It could be taken either from the beginning of the psalm or from the context. The first alternative we see exemplified in Psalm 29, where the response is: *Exaltabo te Domine quoniam suscepisti me nec iucundasti inimicos meos super me.*[17] Due to their constant recurrence these refrains were quite familiar to the people. Like Augustine, another preacher, St. Chrysostom, takes occasion time and time again to refer to these refrains as a starting point for a deeper study of the contents of the psalms.[18] St. Leo the Great, too, makes reference to this community singing of the psalms with the people.[19]

[10] *Const. Ap.*, II, 57, 6 (Quasten, *Mon.*, 182): When the reader has finished two readings, another shall psalm the Psalms of David, καὶ ὁ λαὸς τὰ ἀκροστίχια ὑποψαλλέτω.

[11] The only exceptions are the Ethiopic and the Gallican liturgies. Still even in the Ethiopian there is a trace; see Hanssens, III, 187. In the Gallican the *canticum trium puerorum*, which is itself arranged in responsorial fashion, seems to have taken over the role of the alleluia chant.

[12] West Syrian liturgy (Brightman, 36; 79), Greek liturgy of St. Mark (*ibid.*, 118), Byzantine (371) and Armenian liturgies (426); the Milanese liturgy (present-day missal; Daniel, *Codex liturg.*, I, 60).

[13] Coptic liturgy (Brightman, 156), East Syrian liturgy (*ibid.*, 258 f.).

[14] Mozarabic liturgy (PL, LXXXV, 536). As A. Lesley notes (*ibid.*, note), it was decreed by the IV Council of Toledo (633), can. 12 that the alleluia be sung not before the Gospel but after it; cf. Isidore, *De eccl. off.*, I, 13, 4 (PL, LXXXIII, 751), who took part in the proposal and who presents the following reason: Thus it could be suggested that our life after the revelation of the Gospel must be one praise of God. Obviously, then, even here a different plan had previously been followed.

[15] Augustine, *Enarr. in ps. 119*, 1 (PL, XXXVII, 1596). Further texts in Wagner, *Einführung*, I, 81 f. and likewise in Roetzer, 101 f.

[16] Augustine, *Enarr. in ps. 138*, 1 (PL, XXVII, 1784).

[17] Wagner, I, 82. The text named, along with the following verse (as the remainder of the psalm) today forms the gradual for the Wednesday in Passion week.

[18] Chrysostom, *In ps. 117 expos.*, 1 (PG, LV, 328); *in ps. 144*, 1 (464); Leitner, 208 f.

[19] Leo the Great, *Serm.*, 3, 1 (PL, LIV, 145): *Davidicum psalmum . . . consona voce cantavimus.*

It is really remarkable that now only a few remnants remain of this responsorial singing which was once so flourishing. Quite early it invaded the domain of art.[20] In the Oriental Church the refrain was first expanded into a ṣtrophe, the *heirmos*, then further verses were intercalated for the repetition of the refrain, and these groups of strophes, called a "canon," entwine around the psalm or canticle of the singer like an ivy-vine. These canons were performed by a choir, or by two choirs.[21] The next step in the evolution was to drop most of the psalm at a solemn Office, retaining a few verses which were hymnically interwoven in the manner indicated. Finally in the canticles the basic text disappeared entirely and all that was left was an elaborate store of hymn poetry, redolent of the biblical songs upon which they had been founded.[22]

Between the readings of the fore-Mass, however, the development did not reach these lengths even in the Eastern liturgies. The basic form did not disappear entirely. True, only a fragment of the psalm remains, a few verses that vary with the church year. But this remnant is linked with the alleluia which appears in some sort of repetition, so that the responsorial character is still plainly recognizable. Amongst the East Syrians a triple alleluia follows after every three verses[23]; amongst the Copts, a triple alleluia after two verses, and a single alleluia after another verse[24]; amongst the West Syrians, a double alleluia precedes, and a single alleluia follows the one verse of the psalm.[25] Similarly in the Byzantine liturgy the variant verse is enclosed between an alleluia at the beginning and one at the end.[26] On Holy Saturday a whole psalm is sung, with alleluia inserted as a response after each verse.[27] But less extended chants which are found within the compass of the lessons display few of the responsorial features[28]; they are, in fact, mere preludes to the later readings rather than echoes of those that went before. Even the alleluia, paralleling this, seems to have been

[20] In folk song responsorial singing was retained and the alleluia, like the *Kyrie eleison,* continued to be used as a refrain in both spiritual and secular songs; see the references in Leitner, 205, Note 6.

[21] This line of progress is described in greater detail by O. Heiming, *Syrische 'Eniânê und griechische Kanones* (LQF, 26; Münster, 1932). Among the psalms which were thus intercalated with new compositions, a special role was played by Ps. 113 ff. and Ps. 148 ff., allelulia-psalms which were from the start suited to the responsorial performance (Heiming, 42).

Andrew of Crete (d. 740) is accounted the first great composer of these canon-poems.

[22] Cf. the study in Baumstark, *Liturgie comparée,* 26 ff.

[23] Brightman, 258 f.

[24] Brightman, 156.

[25] Brightman, 79.

Cf. the Armenian liturgy (*ibid.,* 426; Hanssens, III, 188 f.).

[26] Brightman, 371.

[27] Baumstark, *Die Messe im Morgenland,* 92. Cf. Max von Sachsen, *Praelectiones de liturgiis orientalibus* (Freiburg, 1913), II, 239 f.

The allelulia as a response to each verse of a complete psalm is also preserved in the Byzantine burial service, P. Matzerath, *Die Totenfeiern der byzantinischen Kirche* (Paderborn, 1939), 10; 101 f.; 105 f.

[28] Baumstark, *Die Messe im Morgenland,* 92 f.

conceived predominantly as a preparation for the Gospel,[29] if it is possible to judge in the midst of such a variety and irregularity in the forms of the chants as well as the prayers.

In the Roman liturgy, too, this curtailment of responsorial song has been allowed a free hand, and not one single chant has retained the original type unimpaired. Aside from the ferial formularies, in which only one responsorial chant follows the Epistle,[30] as is also the case after the several lessons of the vigil Masses on Ember Saturdays—aside from these instances the full form of the Sunday and feast-day formularies includes two songs, the gradual and the alleluia (resp. Tract), and in addition the more recently composed sequences also belong in this grouping. There are various indications that tend to show that the gradual originally followed the first of the three readings (which disappeared very early).[31] That is manifested even at present on the few days that have three readings; one of the chants follows the first reading, one the second.[32] Similarly in the Milan liturgy the psalmellus follows the first of the three readings, and the alleluia chant follows the second.[33] In fact, even in the Roman liturgy a fragment of a Mass book has recently come to light which regularly has the gradual follow the first of its three lections, and the alleluia the second.[34]

When the first reading disappeared, it was hard to sacrifice either the gradual or the alleluia, probably because both had become by that time— the sixth century—jewels of the Roman Mass; perhaps, too, because by that time the alleluia was more and more considered an Easter piece[35]

[29] Hanssens, III, 187-191.

[30] This rule is followed, among others, in the Commune formulary In vigiliis apostolorum; likewise in the ferial Masses of Advent (see the rubric after the first Sunday of Advent). In Lent there is an exception insofar as the tract Domine non secundum comes into question (see below, p. 431, note 66). It is therefore inconsequent if votive Masses, even those which are matched by a violet color, are decked out with gradual and allelulia or tract. Still such inconsequences are found quite early; see, e.g., the Antiphonary of Senlis (9th century): Hesbert, n. 154, compared with n. 121 (vigils of Apostles).

The appearance of a single chant in ferial Masses bears a relationship to the fact that here (aside from Ember week and such) three lessons were not usual. Cf. the outline of lessons as apportioned to various week-days, above, p. 400.

[31] Cf. supra, p. 395.

[32] There is only an apparent exception in the Wednesdays of the 1st and 4th weeks of Lent, insofar as a tract, in addition to the second gradual, follows the second reading; cf. below, p. 431, note 66. On Good Friday the first lesson is followed nowadays by a tract only, but it was different in the most sacred antiphonaries; Hesbert, n. 78.

[33] The psalmellus is a double verse that changes with the Church year, much like our gradual; Missale Ambrosianum (1902), p. 167 etc. The Gospel, too, is followed by a chant, the antiphona post evangelium, but (as the name implies) it has no responsorial character.

[34] A. Dold, Die Zürcher und Peterlinger Messbuchfragmente (see above, p. 395, note 16), p. XXX. According to Durandus, IV, 19, 2 the gradual was at that time sung before the Epistle in many churches.

[35] This was the arrangement, at any rate, in the closely related liturgy of North Africa. Here the alleluia was in use only in the Easter-to-Pentecost season and on Sundays; Isidore, De eccl. off., I, 13, 2

admirably suited to the eucharistic celebration especially on Sundays and feast days. And then it was no longer regarded simply as an echo of the Epistle but a presentiment of the joyous Gospel message, as the later interpreters regularly explain it.[36]

All the more, then, must the texts of the two chants be shortened, and all the more thoroughly in proportion to the melodic elaboration which by this time they had gained. If in the Orient it was poetics that proved to be the enemy of the ancient responsorial technique, in the Western world it was musical art. Already in St. Augustine's time the singers displayed the tendency more and more to enhance the chant with richer melodies.[37] The external beauty of God's house had been enhanced, the service increased in splendor; it was but natural that the music should follow suit. The formation of the elaborate melismas must have been accomplished in the solo singing of the psalmist long before a similar development could be inaugurated in the *schola cantorum*.[38] This hypothesis is confirmed by the fact that even later melodies of the responsorial songs, compared with those of the antiphonal songs of the *schola*, show an unevenly greater embellishment. This can be seen to best advantage only since the *Graduale Romanum* has been republished with the fuller ancient melodies. The richness of the solo chant must have had a reaction also in the *responsum* of the people. Gradually this response slipped away from the congregation and into the ranks of the singers, that is, the *schola*. With this new development another fact was closely related, namely that even the most ancient books containing the texts for the Roman chants between the readings—with a few exceptions that were fast disappearing—indicate for both grad-

(PL, LXXXIII, 750). In the church of St. Augustine it was heard, in the main, only during the Easter season; Roetzer, 234 f. Vigilantius wanted the same thing in Gaul; Jerome, *Contra Vigilantium*, c. 1 (PL, XXIII, 339).

This latter restriction to Eastertide had its sponsors also within the territory of the Roman liturgy at the time of Gregory the Great, who was reproached *quia Alleluja dici ad missa extra pentecostes tempora fecistis*. For his own praxis the pope invokes the old tradition stemming from the church of Jerusalem. Gregory the Great, *Ep. IX*, 12 (PL, LXXVII, 956). Perhaps it was Gregory who had ordered the omission of the Alleluia after Septuagesima, a reform that did not seem radical enough to his correspondent; cf. below, note 67. A different explanation of the spare accounts which have been preserved is sought by J. Froger, "L'Alle-luja dans l'usage romain," *Eph. liturg.*, LXII (19-48), 6-48.

A certain connection between the Alleluia and Easter is even a pre-Christian tradition, for the allelulia belonged especially to the paschal Hallel.

[36] See the results of this interpretation in Durandus, IV, 20.

[37] Augustine, *Confessiones*, IX, 6 f.; X, 33 (CSEL, XXXIII, 208; 263 f.); Cassian, *De coenob. inst.*, II, 2 (CSEL, XVII, 18).

[38] Wagner, *Einführung*, I, 33-40. Wagner believes he is able to date the introduction of the rich melismatic style into the responsorial Mass chants about the period between 450 and 550 (83 f.). But since the explanation of the Gallican liturgy ascribed to St. Germanus belongs at earliest to the 7th century, it seems better to stretch out this period to the time of Gregory the Great.

ual and alleluia only a single verse instead of the full psalm.[39] This is what we are accustomed to at present, and so the responsorial design of these songs is scarcely ever noticed.

Still this abbreviation of the texts did not make such progress in other parts of our liturgy. In these places it came to a halt. Thus in the invitatory in Matins we have an example of the original form of responsorial singing. In order to render the design of the songs we are considering more plainly visible we might do well to outline and compare the forms of responsorial song still preserved in our liturgy.

1. Invitatory	2. Responsory at the Little Hours	3. Responsory at Matins
Response intoned	Response intoned	
Response of the choir	Response of the choir	Response of the choir
Verse 1 of the Psalm	Verse	Verse
Response of the choir	Response of the choir	Response of the choir
Verse 2 of the Psalm		
Response of the choir		
....		
Gloria Patri	*Gloria Patri*	(*Gloria Patri*
Response of the choir	Response of the choir	Response of the choir)

4. Alleluia Chant	5. Gradual
Response intoned	Response of the choir
Response of the choir	(Response of the choir)
Verse	Verse
Response of the choir	

In the gradual almost nothing of the original responsory character is retained, though the older sources did keep the names *responsorium* or *responsorium graduale*.[40] Still the second half of the text is designated as *versus* (℣.). This verse takes the place of the once complete psalm sung by the precentor. Even now all of it except the final cadence is performed (according to rule) by one or two soloists. But the preceding portion of the text which corresponds to the older response of the people is now begun by the soloist(s) and continued by the choir. This method of performance, of which there are evidences even at an earlier period,[41] is a substitute for the more ancient plan according to which the *responsum* was first pre-intoned by the precentor and then repeated by all.[42] The further repetition

[39] It can now be easily studied in the editions of the six oldest MSS. (8th and 8-9 centuries), which appear in parallel columns in R. J. Hesbert, *Antiphonale Missarum sextuplex* (Brussels, 1935). Cf. *supra*, p. 64.

[40] *Expositio 'Primum in ordine'* (PL, CXXXVIII, 1174) : *Et dictum respon-*

sorium, quod uno cessante hoc ipsum alter respondeat.

[41] *Ordo* of the Lateran church (middle of the 12th century) : Fischer, 81, 1. 19.

[42] Wagner, *Einführung*, I, 87 f. This repetition is clearly attested in Amalar's exposition of 813-14, ed. Hanssens (*Eph. liturg.*, 1927), 162 = Gerbert, *Monumenta*, II, 151 (see *supra*, p. 89, note 73) ; in

of the *responsum* after the verse was still customary in the thirteenth century, and in many places even later.[43] As a rule" it was at first omitted only in those instances in which another chant, the alleluia or a tract, followed,[45] but in most churches it soon disappeared entirely. In order to avoid an unsatisfactory ending[46] it then became the practice to have the entire choir join in during the closing cadence of the verse,[47] as usually happens today. But in the new edition of the *Graduale Romanum* (1908), the original plan was also permitted, that namely of repeating the *responsum* after the verse.

In Holy Week two graduals are retained which even today show several verses instead of the usual one.[48] The repetition of the response after the individual verses which was still customary in the Carolingian period[49] and even later[50] has disappeared, it is true, so that the chants are no longer to be distinguished from the *tractus*; indeed they have actually taken this title from the latter form. In Easter Week also a lengthy section of the Easter psalm *Confitemini*, with a constant repetition of the refrain, *Hæc*

the *Expositio 'Missa pro multis,'* ed. Hanssens (*Eph. liturg.*, 1930), 34; in the *Eclogæ* (PL, CV, 1321); in the *Ordo Rom. II* (10th century), n. 7 (PL, LXXVIII, 971 B); and also in the late medieval *Ordinarium* of Chalon: Martène, 1, 4, XXIX (I, 646 CD).

[43] Wagner, 87 f.

Honorius Augustod., *Gemma an.*, I, 96 (PL, CLXXII, 575 C); Sicard of Cremona, *Mitrale*, III, 3 (PL, CCXIII, 106 A); Ordinal of Exeter (1337), ed. Dalton (HBS, 37), 295. Also, according to the *Alphabetum sacerdotum* (in printed missals between 1495 and 1530), the response *Beata gens*, in the Pentecost Mass which is presented as a paradigm, is repeated after the verse; Legg, *Tracts*, 38.

The repetition after the verse was done on a higher tone: Amalar, *De eccl. off.*, III, 11 (PL, CV, 1120); Sicard, *Mitrale*, III, 3 (PL, CCXIII, 105 f.).

On the other hand in *Ordo Rom. V* (10th century), n. 7 (PL, LXXVIII, 987 C), the repetition is left to the discretion of the bishop, who gives the choirmaster a sign if he wants the repetition. Durandus, IV, 19, 9, then makes the general statement that at Mass, differently from the Office, the repetition is not customary. This ties in naturally with the fact that the gradual had become music-

ally much richer than the responsories of the Office.

[44] Every repetition is suppressed in the *Ordinarium O.P.* of 1256 (Guerrini, 145).

[45] Thus, e.g., in the 1312 Ordinal of the Carmelites (Zimmerman, 71). Cf. Ursprung, *Die Kirchenmusik*, 57.

[46] In the Mass for the feast of John the Baptist the omission of the repetition brought with it an unnatural and infelicitous break in the text. For the verse reads as follows: *Misit Dominus manum suam et tetigit os meum et dixit mihi;* this naturally demands the repetition of the response: *Priusquam.* (If need be we could take the Alleluia-verse as a continuation of the phrase: *Tu puer* . . .)

[47] Wagner, 88 f. Thus in the 13th century at Bayeux, but here in the same way the response after the verse was begun by the chanters and continued by the choir to the finish. U. Chevalier, *Ordinaire et Coutumier de l'église cathédrale de Bayeux* (Bibliothèque liturgique, 8; Paris, 1902), 27.

[48] On Wednesday: *Domine exaudi orationem meam*, with five verses; on Good Friday: *Domine audivi*, with four verses.

[49] Wagner, 89 f.

[50] Robert Paululus (d. circa 1184), *De cæremoniis*, III, 17 (PL, CLXXVII, 449 A).

dies quam fecit Dominus, exsultemus et lœtemur in ea, long survived.[51] But as time went on the verses of the psalm were distributed throughout the week. Just as here in the Easter octave a store of antique responsorial song is to be found, so (to cite another example) in the second Christmas Mass, too. The head-piece of the gradual, *Benedictus qui venit in nomine Domini, Deus Dominus et illuxit nobis,* was the song which the Christian people in the fourth century repeated tirelessly during the Christmas procession from Bethlehem to Jerusalem.[52]

If in the gradual only a rudiment of the ancient responsorial singing has been retained, in the alleluia, as it is presented now, the original design still peeps through. The singer chants alleluia,[53] just a he usually intones the refrain. The congregation repeats it. The singer begins the psalm, that is, he sings the verse which replaces the psalm. The choir again repeats the alleluia.[54] In Eastertide, from Low Sunday to Whitsunday, where a double alleluia is inserted in place of the gradual and alleluia, a second verse follows and then the alleluia once more.[55]

The present-day manner of executing the alleluia really corresponds in substance to this description: the first alleluia is sung by one or two soloists and then, with the *jubilus* added, is repeated by the choir; the verse again is the soloist's; and in the repetition after the verse the choir joins in once more at least with the *jubilus.*[56]

---

[51] Antiphonal of Mont Blandin (8-9th century): Hesbert, n. 80, with verse 1, 2, 3, 4, 16, 22, 26. Cf. *Ordo Rom. XI,* n. 47 (PL, LXXVIII, 1044 B): *Duo cantores in pulpito cantant Graduale: Hœc dies quam fecit Dominus. Primicerius cum schola respondet.*
There is evidence also for the feast of the Cathedra of St. Peter of a *responsum* with three verses: PL, LXXVIII, 655 A.
[52] *Aetheriœ Peregrinatio,* 25, 6; cf. 31, 2 (CSEL, XXX, 75; 83 f.); Baumstark, *Liturgie comparée,* 166 f.
[53] *Hallelu-yah* = Praise Yahweh.
[54] For this conception cf. A. Eizenhöfer, "Der Allelujagesang vor dem Evangelium," *Eph. liturg.,* XLV (1931), 374-382. According to the explanation which predominated till then, only the word "alleluia" with its *jubilus* was at first used at Mass, and only later on was a verse added as a support; Eisenhofer, II, 108 f. This opinion runs counter to the fact, already established, of the common acceptance, even at Rome (see above, p. 422) of the alleluia in responsorial psalmody; for the essentially responsorial character of the allelulia see H. Eng-

berding, "Alleluja," RAC, I, 293-299, especially 295.
It is true that in the MSS. the alleluia-verse is not presented uniformly, that therefore in its present state it is of later date. But that is not the same as saying that even previously the allelulia at Mass was not connected with a verse.
[55] That this is not the case also in Easter week is explained by the fact that the psalm *Confitemini* had an even stronger and more original Easter character than the alleluia. The reflections in Gihr, 501, therefore, miss the main point.
It must be remarked that the double alleluia of Eastertide is, musically and textually, really two separate alleluias juxtaposed.
[56] Thus according to the rubric in the *Graduale Romanum* (ed. Vaticana, 1908), *De rit. serv. in cantu Missœ,* IV: *Si Alleluia, alleluja cum versu sunt dicenda, primum Alleluja cantatur ab uno vel a duobus usque ad signum* *. *Chorus autem reptetit Alleluja et subiungit neuma, seu iubilum, protrahens syllabam a. Cantores versum concinunt, qui ut supra occurente asterisco a toto choro terminatur. Finito*

The tendency to drop the repetitions, particularly the repetition after the verse, was also manifested in the alleluia,[57] but, excepting the days of lesser solemnity,[58] the tendency was overcome. The nearness of the joyous message of the Gospel probably helped to produce this result.[59]

In the *jubilus* of the alleluia Gregorian chant achieved its highest expression, and, no doubt, in the ages before people were spoiled by the charms of harmony, the untiring reiteration of the melismatic melodies with their endless rise and fall must have been a wonderful experience for the devout congregation.[60]

In penitential periods the *tractus* takes the place of the alleluia. Its one big peculiarity today is the fact that it consists of a lengthy series of psalm verse, each marked with the designation *V(ersus)*. The tract for Palm Sunday, for instance, embraces the greater part of Psalm 21, that of the first Sunday of Lent the complete Psalm 90. The Carolingian liturgist thought the chief distinction between tract and gradual was the lack of a response (refrain) after the verses in the former, where it was still customary in the latter.[61] Musically the distinctive mark is the scantier store of melody.[62] This in fact may possibly be the derivation of the name: *tractus* = εἱρμός, a typical melody, which recurs according to fixed rules in the course of the piece.[63] Medieval interpreters sought the derivation in the "drawn-out" method of singing, a style appointed for penitence and

---

versu cantor vel cantores repetunt Alleluja et chorus addit solum neuma. This distribution to choir and soloists (*pueri*) is already to be found in the *Ordinarium* of Bayeux of the 13th century; Chevalier (note 47 above), 27.

[57] *Ordo Rom. V,* n. 7 (PL, LXXVIII, 987 C).

[58] Both repetitions are omitted in paschal Masses of a ferial character (Rogations, vigil of Pentecost and partly Pentecost Ember days). In this case there is the same design as is now found in the gradual.

Only the repetition after the verse has disappeared on Holy Saturday. It is only this last phenomenon that is explained in Wagner, I, 95. This is really only a sort of toning-down of the festal jubilee in accordance with the type of celebration; cf. *Ordo Rom. I,* n. 26 (PL, LXXVIII, 950 A): *in quotidianis diebus* it is alright to be satisfied with the first Alleluia.

Spanish missals of the later Middle Ages had only one alleluia outside the paschal season, and only the verse followed; Ferreres, 106.

[59] Cf. Durandus, IV, 20, 7: *Per hoc vero quod Alleluja cum pneuma repetitur, laus et gaudium ineffabile patriæ significatur.*

[60] Even in the ancient Church the alleluia was sung with rich melismas. Pertinent remarks of St. Augustine (who speaks of wordless jubilation) in Roetzer, 233-235. Further particulars in Wagner, I, 36 ff. Regarding the singing of the Alleluia among oriental Christians, see Wagner, 92. From his own experience Wagner confirms the report of older authors that the Copts often sing just alleluia for a quarter of an hour.

[61] Amalar, *De eccl. off.,* III, 12 (PL, CV, 1121): *Hoc differt inter Responsorium, cui chorus respondet, et Tractum, cui nemo. . . .*

[62] Many of the tracts belong to the second or to the eighth (ecclesiastical) mode, and the preference is for the same melodies. The same musical melodies are repeated from verse to verse and from tract to tract. Wagner, I, 99 f.

[63] Wagner, I, 99.

grief[64]; but this was hardly the original notion of these chants, for amongst them are found several that begin with *Jubilate, Laudate Dominum*. Wagner has good grounds for his opinion that in the tract we have simply graduals—perhaps we ought to say responsorial chants—of the fourth/fifth century, chants which, in their melodic design and partly in the range of their text, stem from the more ancient period of Roman solo-psalmody and so reflect the condition of the chants before the art of the singer had succeeded in embellishing it and thus led to the shortening of the psalm.[65] This traditionally simpler manner was later used more and more exclusively for fast-day Masses,[66] in which we generally find the older forms retained, especially in the last days of Lent.[67] Later the tract was given a certain animation by being divided amongst the whole choir in alternate fashion, as is the rule now.[68]

It was really an important moment in the liturgy when, at the Roman stational service of the seventh century, right after the Epistle the singers

[64] Durandus, IV, 21, 1.

Later the name was usually derived from the fact that the tract was sung straight through, "in one strain" (*tractim*), without interruption by a refrain; cf., e.g., Gihr, 493.

[65] Wagner, *loc. cit.* Cf. idem, *Geschichte der Messe* (Leipzig, 1913), I, 4, with the hint that in the medieval tract melodies are probably concealed the remains of synagogue song.

[66] Wagner, *Einführung*, I, 100 f.

More in detail we refer to the Sundays from Septuagesima on, a few incidental feasts, as well as Ember and Holy Weeks. It is only here that the oldest chant books indicate the tract; see the survey in Hesbert, p. 244.

The tract *Domine non secundum peccata*, which we use every Monday, Wednesday and Friday in Lent, is a more recent composition. It was introduced in Frankish territory, and not before the 8th century. Its origin is due to the then prevailing penitential discipline which exacted from public penitents special penitential works on the three *feriæ legitimæ* all through *Quadragesima*. Jungmann, *Die lateinischen Bussriten*, 70 f.

[67] Since these are regularly the chants which stand in the second place, especially on the Sundays in the pre-Easter fasting season, there is an explanation for the loss of the *responsum*. This latter would have had to stay in the alleluia, but this too was excluded during this season.

About 400 the alleluia was still compatible with sorrowful solemnities, like the burial of Fabiola, even at Rome; Jerome, *Ep.*, 77, 12 (CSEL, LV, 48, 1. 12). But a few decades later Sozomen, *Hist. eccl.*, VII, 19 (PG, LXVII, 1476), was under the impression that the alleluia was originally sung at Rome only on Easterday. What is behind his report, which is at any rate quite questionable (cf. Cabrol, DACL, I, 1236), might possibly be the fact that the alleluia was removed from Quadragesima. This was already a fixed rule in Spain and in Africa at the time of St. Isidore, *De eccl. off.*, I, 13, 3 (PL, LXXXIII, 750 f.), and perhaps also in Rome. Gregory the Great seems to have banned the alleluia further, from Septuagesima; Callewaert, *Sacris erudiri* 650, 652 f. On the part of the Greeks the omission of the alleluia during the Lenten season was for the first time made a matter of complaint and accusation by Leo of Achrida in 1053; A. Michel, *Humbert und Kerullarios II* (Paderborn, 1930), 94, note; 124.

[68] *Graduale Romanum* (ed. Vaticana, 1908), *De rit. serv. in cantu Missæ*, IV: *cuius versiculi alternatim cantantur a duabus sibi invicem respondentibus chori partibus, aut a cantoribus et universo choro*.

Reporting from Rouen, de Moléon, 361, tells of an older manner of performance.

ascended the ambo, first the one who intoned the *responsorium* and after him the one who did the alleluia. For these songs were not like those of the *schola*, intended merely to fill out a pause, nor were they, like the latter broken off at the signal of the celebrant. They were independent, self-sufficient members inserted between the readings like a moment of pious meditation, like a lyrical rejoicing after the word of God had reached the ears of men.[69] The name of the singer like that of the reader of the Epistle had to be made known to the pope at the beginning of the service.[70] Previous to Gregory the Great these chants were done by deacons,[71] but St. Gregory forbade this[72] since he wanted to avert the possibility of a beautiful voice counting in the promotion to diaconate. So the duty fell to the subdeacon's lot.[73] When the singer mounted the ambo, he was not allowed to stand at the top—at least this was true later, in the territory of the Romano-Frankish liturgy. This platform was reserved to the Gospel. Instead, like the reader of the Epistle, he had to be satisfied with one of the steps *(gradus)* of the stairway.[74] Hence the chant took the name *"graduale."*[75] And his vesture, too, was that of the reader of the Epistle—that

---

[69] The time occupied by these chants seems to have meant nothing even in the 11th century; this is gathered from the lengthy prayers that the celebrant was expected to recite during these intervening chants. Those in the *Missa Illyrica* and in the Mass-*Ordo* of *Cod. Chigi* would take at least a quarter of an hour even for a hurried recital; Martène, 1, 4, IV; XII (I, 499-504; 570-574).

[70] *Ordo Rom. I*, n. 7 (PL, LXXVIII, 940). Apparently two different singers are here meant; see Stapper in his edition of the *Ordo Rom. I* (Stapper, 17). The duality is patent in the *Ordo* of St. Amand (Duchesne, *Christian Worship*, 456) and in the *Ordo Rom. III* (11th century), n. 9 (PL, LXXVIII, 979).

[71] This Office is emphasized more than once in the grave inscriptions, e.g., in that of the archdeacon Deusdedit (5th century):

Hic levitarum primus in ordine vivens
Davitici cantor carminis iste fuit.

(Duchesne, *Christian Worship*, 170).

[72] At the Roman Synod of 595 (PL, LXXVII, 1335).

[73] This seems to be at least suggested in *Ordo Rom. I*, n. 7 (PL, LXXVIII, 940). Later on every grade of orders was waived; see below, note 81.

[74] *Expositio 'Primum in ordine'* (circa 800; PL, CXXXVIII, 1174 C); *Ordo*

Rom. II, n. 7 (PL, LXXVIII, 971 B); *Expositio 'Missa pro multis'*, ed. Hanssens (*Eph. liturg.*, 1930), 34 f.

Amalar's interpretation of 813-14, ed. Hanssens (*Eph. liturg.*, 1927), 184, does indeed refer to this rule, but also allows a second step.

[75] The name and the corresponding practice were certainly to be found in the Frankish kingdom towards the end of the 8th century. Antiphonary MSS. of this period, as found in Hesbert, regularly use the superscription *Grad.* or *Resp. Grad.*

But even at Rome, where the older *ordines* simply use the term *Responsorium* for this song, in the *Gregorianum* of Hadrian the designation handed down is uniformly this one, in some form or other: *(sequitur) gradale, gradalis, gradalem;* Lietzmann, n. 1.

A suspicion that the term might be traced back to Frankish transcribers is strengthened by an explicit remark of Amalar's, *De ord. antiph., prol.* (PL, CV, 1245 B), that he had ascertained at Rome *quod dicimus gradale, illi vocant cantatorium.* However this is said about the book.

Gastoué suggests another derivation for the word *graduale (gradale)*, recalling that the adjective *gradalis* meant "well-ordered, composed with care," and that this adjective was applied to the

is, he first took off the *planeta*.[76]

For the text of the chant the singers of the responsorial songs looked to a special book which is called, in the Roman *Ordines*, simply *cantatorium*. This he carried along to the desk. Amongst the six oldest manuscripts which give us the Mass chants, only one is devoted entirely to the solo-songs.[77] All the others combine these in one book with the antiphonal chants of the *schola;* this shows that by the ninth century the singer had become simply a member of the ensemble,[78] and the latter, in turn, had long since taken over the response and therefore needed to have the text in view. Nor was the singer separated from the choir in space, particularly when the ambo gradually disappeared from the plan of the church. About the same time the soloist was replaced by two or three singers[79]; soon even four were mentioned.[80] In other places the boy singers appeared as performers of the solo chants, apparently as a continuation of the arrangement followed in the Gallic liturgies[81]—an arrangement which must have been car-

---

responsorium; A. Gastoué, *L'art gregorien,* 174.

In English the gradual is sometimes referred to as "grail."

[76] Amalar, *De eccl. off.,* III, 15 (PL, CV, 1122 f); cf. also the references given *Supra,* p. 411, note 48.

[77] The Gradual of Monza (8th century); see the ed. in Hesbert.

Whereas in Rome and Italy at this time the *cantatorium* is still a separate book, in the Frankish kingdom it is united with the Mass antiphonary. Amalar, *De ord. antiph.,* prol. (PL, CV, 1245 B).

The *cantatorium* is also referred to under the term *tabulæ,* as Wagner, *Einführung,* I, 85, note 5, opined and J. Smits van Waesberghe proves, for the *tabulæ* which Amalar, *De eccl. off.,* III, 16 (PL, CV, 1123), says the singers held in their hands, were probably the *cantatorium,* bound (as usual) in ivory; see JL, XII (1934), 423; 457; JL, XIII (1935), 453; cf. also de Moléon, 54; 284.

[78] In the Roman stational services this situation seems to have been brought about already in the 8th century, as seems clear from the papal notification referred to in *Ordo Rom. I,* n. 7 (PL, LXXVIII, 940 C): *talis de schola cantabit.* (In Stapper's ed. the *de schola* is missing; 18).

[79] Rabanus Maurus, *De inst. cleric.,* II, 51 (PL, CVII, 363). According to

Ordo Rom. XI, n. 20 (PL, LXXVIII, 1033), on festive occasions two *cantores* mount the ambo and together sing gradual and Alleluia. According to the *Ordinarium* of Laon (c. 1300), the gradual was sung by two subdeacons, the Alleluia by two deacons; Martène, 1, 4, XX (I, 607 D).

[80] John of Avranches, *De off. eccl.* (PL, CXLVII, 38 B).

For great feasts: *Ordinarium O.P.* (Guerrini, 145); *Liber ordinarius* of Liége (Volk, 47, 1. 17).

[81] In the *Expositio ant. liturgiæ gallicanæ* (ed. Quasten, 12; 14), mention is made of *parvuli* who sing the *Kyrie* and also the responsory after the lessons.

About the same time singing boys also appear in the Orient in the role of precentors; see *Testamentum Domini,* I, 26; II, 11 (Rahmani, 55; 135). Cf. J. Quasten, *Musik und Gesang in den Kulten der heidnischen Antike und christlichen Frühzeit* (LQF, XXV; Münster, 1930), 137 f.

Singing boys are found in Rome at a very early time, but only for antiphonal chant within the *schola cantorum;* Wagner, I, 23; 29; 216 ff. In the Roman liturgy boys as performers of the gradual are expressly mentioned for the first time by Sicard of Cremona, *Mitrale,* III, 3 (PL, CCXIII, 106 A). However they are already presupposed in *Ordo Rom. V* (10th century), n. 7 (PL, LXXVIII, 987 B); here there is a prescription that

ried over into the Roman liturgy only after encountering great opposition.[81] The text of these chants is derived, as a rule, from the psalms and canticles; after all, this matches their origin as psalmodic chants. But where two songs follow each other, they are totally independent and the choice of one in no way inruences the choice of the others.[83] The tracts follow the rule strictly and are taken, without exception, from the psalms. For the gradual and the alleluia chant, texts not taken from the psalter are very infrequent in the pre-Carolingian Roman liturgy. They do appear now and then on feast days, when the remarkable art which was able to adapt the psalm verses to the occasion did not seem able to achieve its aim.[84] On Sundays no effort was made to draw a particular connection between the chants and the readings; the effort would probably have been fruitless anyhow.[85] But on feasts there is a certain agreement between them. Thus on the feast of St. Stephen, after the account of the hearing before the High Council, the gradual continues with Psalm 118:23: *sederunt principes et adversum me loquebantur*. And on Epiphany the closing sentence of the lesson is simply taken up and amplified: *Omnes de Saba venient*.

the singers, if they are clerics, should, after the alleluia, kiss the knee of the bishop seated at his throne; *si vero extra gradum fuerint, pedibus eius pervolvantur.*
[82] Here we might cite the order of the canons of Theodore of Canterbury (II, 1, 10): *Laicus non debet in Ecclesia recitare lectionem nec Alleluja dicere, sed psalmos tantum et responsoria sine Alleluja* (H. J. Schmitz, *Die Bussbücher und die Bussdisciplin der Kirche* [Mainz, 1883], 539; Finsterwalder, 313, cf. 243; 268; 283), that is, a layman may not be a precentor, at least for the sacred alleluia. The explanation given by Leitner, 193, is unsatisfactory.

A similar prohibition had already issued from the Council of Laodicea (4th century), without any such restriction; only the κανονικοὶ ψάλται are allowed to sing psalms (can. 15); cf. Leitner, 184. But there was a way out; the boys could be joined to the ranks of the clergy as lectors; cf. *supra*, p. 410. For the performance of the responsorial psalms was, in early times, scarcely distinguished from a reading. For both a lector was required. Thus Augustine, referring to boys whom God had inspired to sing a psalm (which he, Augustine, had not foreseen): *Serm.* 352, 1 (PL, XXXIX, 1550 A): speaks of them in the same way as

cordi etiam puerili imperavit, as he speaks of *pueri* who, *in gradu lectorum*, read the Holy Writ: *De cons. evang.*, 9, 15 (PL, XXXIV, 1049). See also Quasten, *Musik und Gesang*, 138 ff.

[83] On the other hand in the gradual itself the response and the verse or verses are taken from the same psalm.

[84] Here we must mention among the texts still used today: gradual and alleluia-verse on the feast of St. John the Evangelist (John 21: 23, 19; 21: 24) and on the Epiphany (Is. 60: 6, 1; Matt. 2: 2); the gradual on the feast of John the Baptist (Jer. 1: 5, 9) and on the Commemoration of St. Paul (Gal. 2: 8 f.); the alleluia-verse on Easter Sunday (1 Cor. 5: 7); Hesbert, n. 14, 18, 80, 119, 123.

[85] While the Mass songbook counted the Sundays right through from Pentecost to Advent, the pericope lists (which differed among themselves) usually started a new Sunday series after the feast of the Apostles Peter and Paul, a list independent of the Easter group. So the chants after the 29th of June combined with different lessons from year to year— much as in the present breviary from August on the lessons of the 2nd and 3rd nocturns fall in with different lessons of the *Scriptura occurens*.

Indeed there is even an instance where the chant is an actual continuation of the reading, namely on Ember Saturday when the lesson from Daniel concludes with the canticle.[86]

For the alleluia verse in the Sunday formularies there was from the very start no fast connection with certain psalms. But Amalar does advise choosing those verses which would most appropriately lead to the repetition of the alleluia, those (in other words) which gave expression to the joy of the Church or the praise of God.[87] The antiphonaries often contained a list of suitable alleluia verses to be chosen at will.[88] It is therefore evident that later on, after the various churches had settled on a certain alleluia verse for each formula there should be very little uniformity on this matter amongst the Mass books.[89] And this also explains why the present *Missale Romanum* should contain amongst these verses such a great number of non-psalmodic and even non-Biblical texts, for the connection with the original psalm-chanting had meanwhile been loosened even more.

In medieval liturgical practice the alleluia obviously received greater attention than the gradual. The gradual was allegorically interpreted only as a re-echoing of the penitential preaching of John the Baptist and at best as a transition from the Old Testament to the New, and therefore, despite its content and its musical form, it was often accounted penitential in character.[90] But the alleluia was the first of the Mass chants to be treated with troping.[91] The alleluia verses which were performed by a soloist were the very first texts of the Mass to be set to multi-voiced compositions.[92] But in general, the stress was put not on the verse but on the alleluia

---

[86] Add the parallel case with regard to the prophecies on Holy Saturday.

As Hesbert, p. XLII remarks, in such cases the reader also performed the chant which followed at once in his Bible text and was here often accompanied by notes or corresponding signs as well as by a rubric (*Hic mutes sonum* or the like); cf. *Paléographie musicale*, XIV (1931-4), 272; see also the Antiphonary of Senlis in Hesbert, n. 46 a.

[87] Amalar, *De eccl. off.*, III, 13 (PL, CV, 1122).

[88] Hesbert, n. 199; cf. the editor's introduction, p. CXIX f. The list of Compiègne contains 78 numbers.

[89] See the samples in Hesbert, *Antiphonale missarum sextuplex*, n. 199 and p. CXIX f.

[90] Cf. Innocent III, *De s. alt. mysterio*, II, 31 (PL, CCXVII, 817) : the gradual signifies *poenitentiæ lamentum;* therefore it is more correct to sing it not *festivis*

aut modulationis vocibus but *quasi cantum gravem et asperum.*

Durandus, *Rationale*, IV, 19, 1: *per Graduale conversio de Judæis, per versum conversio de Gentilibus, per Alleluia utriusque in fide lætitia, per sequentiam canticum victoræ figuratur.* Cf. *ibid.*, IV, 19, 4; IV, 20.

[91] Blume, *Tropen des Missale*, II (Analecta hymnica, 49), p. 211: the alleluiatic verse on the contrary, with its closing Alleluia, is the proper medium for the growth of the tropes. The oldest tropes to the Alleluia-verse reach back to the 9th century (214). *Ibid.*, p. 215-287, the edition of the text of the *"Tropi ad Responsorium graduale et ad versum Allelujaticum".*

[92] In the Winchester Troper (11th century), ed. Frere (HBS, VIII), of the 100 or so multi-voiced compositions, 54 are for alleluia-verses, besides about a dozen for sequences; cf. Ursprung, *Die kath. Kirchenmusik*, 119-121.

itself. On its final vowel tune was piled upon tune, florid melodies called *jubili* or, to follow medieval precedent, *sequentiæ*.[93]

Singers found it no easy task to memorize these long intricate tonal figures. But since about the middle of the ninth century certain texts begin to make an appearance in Normandy and then in St. Gall—texts intended to support the melodies[94] and at the same time (and perhaps even primarily) to render the melodies more agreeable to the musical sensibilities of the northern peoples to whom up to now the melismatic chant was strange. Soon this new art was also extended to newer and more protracted melodies.[95] It is the same routine that was later repeated in the tropes, but with this difference that in the latter case brief texts already in existence were expanded.[96] Notker Balbulus, a monk of St. Gall (d. 912), set to work to supply texts on the principle of one note to a syllable. This text was then itself called *sequentia*. They were written in a free rhythmic style, a kind of elevated prose, and were therefore also called "proses," a term which is still used in French for church hymns. But since each of the musical phrases or strophes of the complete melody was repeated with a different text, the result was a series of paired strophes which were then usually performed by alternate choirs. However, the first and last strophes—the introduction and the conclusion—were not usually paired.[97]

After the year 1000 a new type of sequence began to develop, a type founded on rhythmical principles and, in general, composed of even verses

[93] Amalar, *De eccl. off.*, III, 16 (PL, CV, 1125). Even earlier in the Antiphonary of Mont-Blandin (c. 800), in the list of alleluia-verses the note is added to several: *cum sequentia.* Hesbert, n. 199 a; cf. *ibid.*, p. CXIX f.

Cf. also in the *Ordo Rom II*, n. 7 (PL, LXXVIII, 971, note d): *sequitur jubilatio quam sequentiam vocant.*

[94] A. Manser, "Sequenz," LThK, IX (1937), 482-485; here a good bibliography. Wagner, I, 248-276.

On the other hand even in the 12th century the *Speculum de myst. Eccl.* (PL, CLXXVII, 359 C) maintains: *quædam ecclesiæ mystice pneumatizant sequentiam sine verbis.* Cf. Blume-Bannister, *Tropen*, I, p. 12 f.

[95] According to Wagner, I, 253 ff. these richer melodies must have been brought over by oriental monks from the Byzantine music treasury. But Cl. Blume and H. Bannister, *Liturgische Prosen erster Epoche* (Analecta hymnica, 53; Leipzig, 1911), pp. XXI-XXVIII, differ with him, referring to the fact that the traditional sequence melodies—the oldest traceable to the 9th century—fit in perfectly with the Gregorian melodies of the final syllable of the alleluia and in fact build up upon it (XXVI f.). In this continuation they prefer to see rather the independent "improvisations" of the sequence-poets (*ibid.*). A preliminary step to the sequence proper they find in the *versus ad sequentias* of French MSS, which are based only on part of the Alleluia *jubilus.* In a similar vein also Ursprung, *Die kath. Kirchenmusik*, 67 ff. Cf. also Anselm Hughes, *Anglo-French Sequelæ* (1934), *passim*, and Jacques Handschen, "The Two Winchester Tropers," *Journal of Theological Studies*, 37 (1936), 35.

A new and comprehensive study of the whole question in W. v. d. Steinen, "Die Anfänge der Sequenzedichtung," *Zeitschr. f. schweiz. Kirchengeschichte*, XL (1946), 190-212, with continuations to XLI (1947). 122-162.

[96] *Supra*, p. 344 f.

[97] Cf. the examples in Wagner, I, 256 ff.

and strophes; they also make use of rhyme. This is the flourishing period in the composition of sequences, the most famous writer of which was Adam of St. Victor (d. about 1192). Some 5000 sequences have been collected from the manuscripts[98]; they form an important branch of literature in the Middle Ages.

In northern countries the Mass books of the later Middle Ages contain a sequence for almost every feast day, or even (you might say) for every Mass formula that uses the alleluia. A Cologne missal of 1487 has 73 of them, the Augsburg missal of 1555 has 98.[99] But elsewhere, above all in Rome, their reception was very cool,[100] or at least (in line with their origin) they were not used at low Mass.[101] In the reform of the Mass books under Pius V, out of all the luxuriant crop only four were retained—the same, approximately, as those which are encountered earlier here and there in Italian Mass books.[102] The Italian tradition and the humanist attitude were probably both at work in bringing this result about.[103]

Of the sequences kept,[104] the Easter sequence, *Victimæ paschali*, belongs to a traditional form halfway between the older and the newer type. Its author is the Burgundian Wipo (d. after 1048), court-chaplain of Emperor Conrad II. This sequence, which, for all its freshness and the happy, genuinely paschal play of its thoughts, still gives us the impression of a somewhat clumsy poem, is in its original form actually very strictly fashioned; there are an introduction, and four verse-pairs matched line for line and syllable for syllable.[105]

---

[98] In the *Analecta Hymnica Medii Aevi* ed. by Cl. Blume and G. M. Dreves, the portion given over to *"Sequentiæ ineditæ"* comprises vols. 8, 9, 10, 34, 37, 39, 40, 42, 44. Other sequences are contained in vols. 7, 53, 54, 55; cf. also v. 47, 49.

A selection is presented in G. M. Dreves-Cl. Blume, *Ein Jahrtausend lateinischer Hymnendichtung* (Leipzig, 1909).

[99] The figures according to Eisenhofer, II, 113. English Mass books often contain a rubric to the effect that the sequences that follow are to be sung above all in Advent and at greater saints' feasts outside the period from Septuagesima to Easter. J. W. Legg, *The Sarum Missal* (London, 1916), 461-496; cf. Ferreres, 109.

[100] Cf. Innocent III, *De s. alt. mysterio*, II, 33 (PL, CCXVII, 820 A); Wagner, I, 275 f.

[101] Thus among the Dominicans and the Carmelites; Manser, 484.

It is in this same sense that the Missal of Benedict XV (1925) permits the priest to omit the sequence at private Masses within the octave of Corpus Christi, and likewise at private daily Masses for the Dead.

[102] See in the index in Ebner.

Cf. also Wagner, I, 276.

Some few other sequences are preserved in the propers of various orders and of some French dioceses; thus, e.g., the sequence *Lætabundus exultet* on Christmas and Epiphany in the present-day Dominican rite.

[103] Cf. *supra*, p. 136.

[104] Data regarding the literary history in Eisenhofer, I, 112-114.

An edifying exposition in Gihr, *Die Sequenzen des römischen Messbuches dogmatisch und aszetisch erklärt* (2nd ed.; Freiburg, 1900).

[105] Wagner, I, 268.

In the reform under Pius V the 5th strophe was left out; in strophe 4a the *suos* was replaced by *vos*, but the Vatican edition of the *Graduale Romanum* has once more restored the *suos*.

1. *Victimæ paschali laudes*
Immolent Christiani.

2. *Agnus redemit oves, Christus innocens Patri reconciliavit peccatores.*	2a. *Mors et vita duello conflixere mirando, dux vitæ mortuus regnat vivus.*
3. *Dic nobis, Maria, quid vidisti in via?*	3a. *Angelicos testes, sudarium et vestes.*
4. *Sepulchrum Christi viventis et gloriam vidi resurgentis.*	4a. *Surrexit Christus, spes mea, præcedit suos in Galilæam.*
5. *Credendum est magis soli Mariæ veraci quam Judæorum turbæ fallaci.*	5a. *Scimus Christum surrexisse a mortuis vere, tu nobis, victor rex, miserere.*

It might be well to note the structure of the latter part of the sequence: a question by the congregation, the answer of the biblical person, a common paen of praise from both. This is really a formal type, often employed especially in oriental church poetry.[106] From the fact that in the first half of the sequence, unlike the second, there is no rhyme but only assonance, it has been argued with some probability that the first part of the hymn must have been in existence already before Wipo.[107]

The Pentecost sequence, *Veni, Sancte Spiritus*, which was formerly ascribed to a number of different authors, is the work of Stephen Langton, Archbishop of Canterbury (d. 1228).[108] Here the sequence, although built on the alleluia-*jubilus*, has become an independent hymn. Still the text is tied up with the second alleluia verse, *Veni, Sancte Spiritus*[109] and so becomes an earnest prayer, a cry for that vivifying power from above which overcomes all the weakness of nature. Thus it came to be an expression of medieval devotion to the Holy Ghost, which had revealed itself in the dedication of so many hospitals and hospital churches to the Holy Ghost.

In the *Lauda Sion*, the sublime didactic poem on the Holy Eucharist which St. Thomas Aquinas composed in 1263, the spirit of Scholasticism created within the liturgy a memorial which bears witness at once to the penetrating search for knowledge and the deep devotion of those generations.

The *Stabat Mater* was long assigned to Jacopone da Todi (d. 1306),

---

[106] Baumstark, *Liturgie comparée*, 113 f.
[107] A. Arens, "Wipos Oster-Sequenz," *Theologie u. Glaube*, XVIII (1926), 149-154.
[108] G. Morin, *Revue Bénéd.*, XXX (1913), 121; Wilmart, *Auteurs spirituels*, 37-45. See also Card. Pitra, *Spicilegium solesmense* (Paris, 1855), III, 130.

Stephen Langton is well-known as a theologian and as the originator of the present system of dividing the Scriptures into chapters.
[109] This itself is of later origin. In its stead in older antiphonaries the verse *Spiritus Domini* or *Hæc dies* was to be found; Hesbert, n. 106.

but appears to be the work of an even more ancient Franciscan; of late St. Bonaventure has been designated as author.[110] At first it was accepted in Mass books only exceptionally,[111] and for long it was used only in Books of Hours and prayer books. Not till 1727, when Pope Benedict XIII extended the feast of Our Lady of Sorrows to the whole Church, was it admitted into the Roman Missal. And it actually exhibits a character that is not properly liturgical, an accent that is emotionally lyrical rather than hymnic, and in its immersion in the sufferings of Christ—reminiscent of St. Francis's mysticism—it shows traces of individual piety, of Franciscan devotion to the Passion and our Lady hardly consonant with the objective spirit of common prayer.

Almost the same is true, at least in part, of the *Dies iræ* which put in an appearance at the end of the twelfth century.[112] But the *Dies iræ* has its basis in the liturgy, since it grew out of a rhymed trope added to the responsory *Libera me, Domine.*[113] Besides, various portions of the hymn have been borrowed from older liturgical songs.[114]

The possibility of giving the alleluia a musical elaboration was the tiny crevice in the structure of the Mass liturgy which the medieval mind was able to widen to such an extent that there was space for its own liturgical language and its own liturgical creations. The sequence, along with the alleluia, became the first crown and climax in the Mass. Here it was that polyphony found its first outlet.[115] At the sequence the organ seems to have been used as an accompaniment from the start.[116] Later we hear of a solemn pealing of bells to accompany the sequence.[117] Dramatic art, too, found

---

[110] A. Manser, "Stabat mater," LThK, IX (1937), 759 f.; cf. M. Grabmann, *Zeitschr. f. Assese u. Mystik*, 19 - ZkTh, LXVIII (1944), 27.

[111] However see Ebner, 168: a later entry in a Minorite missal of the 13th century.

[112] M. Inguanez, "Il Dies iræ in un codice del secolo XII," *Rivista liturgica*, XVIII (1931), 277-288, called attention to a text — partially variant — of this time; Brinktrine, *Die hl. Messe*, 102. As a consequence the ascription to Thomas of Celano (d. circa 1255) can no longer be maintained.

[113] The 9th responsory in the Office for the dead, also used for the *Absolutio ad tumbam.*

Cf. the occurrence in a Burial rite of a Franciscan missal of the 13th century: Ebner, 120.

[114] Eisenhofer, II, 114, after Cl. Blume, "Dies iræ," *Cäcilienvereinsorgan*, XLIX, (1914), 55 ff.

[115] See *supra*, p. 125.

[116] Wagner I, 264 f.

[117] *Liber ordinarius* of the Liége St. James monastery (Volk, 53, 1. 13).

In many parts of Germany it is customary to ring a bell at the Gospel. It is as good as proven that here we have a case of transfer; the sequence being omitted, the bell was rung at the Gospel instead. A transitional stage is seen in de Moléon, 245, 365, 426; according to these accounts, it was the custom in French churches about 1700 to ring a bell "during the gradual," "shortly before the Gospel and during it," "during the *prosa*"; the reporter thought that this was done to usher in the Mass of the Faithful. It is remarkable that an English source about 1529 mentions the ringing of a large bell at the Gospel; see Maskell, 63. Also a Trier Synod of 1549, can. 9, speaks of a signal of the bell at the Gospel; Mansi, XXXII, 1447.

an opening here for its first efforts. As is well known, the older type of sequence, with its double-strophe that seemed to invite the use of dialogue (as we still have it in the *Victimæ paschali*), was the most important starting-point for the religious play. The dramatic development properly so-called did not, it is true, intrude here, just before the Gospel, where the link with the liturgical action was too pronounced, but it is found usually at the beginning of Mass where on Easter the dialogue-trope, *Quem quæritis in sepulchro, o Christicolæ*, introduced the introit *Resurrexi*.[118]

But the verse-pairs with the repetition of the melody did give rise to the possibility of a popular amendment and elaboration at this very spot. There is proof that in the *Victimæ paschali* the step so important for the development of a German vernacular hymnody was actually taken; vernacular verses were written in imitation of the Latin, and were then sung by the whole congregation right after each strophe of the Latin.[119] This is the origin of the ancient *Christ ist erstanden*, a German Easter hymn traced back to the twelfth century, whose melody gives a clear indication of the connection between German hymn and Latin sequence.[120]

The ancient Pentecost songs, *Nun bitten wir den Heiligen Geist* and *Komm, Heiliger Geist, Herre Gott* stand in the same relation to the Whitsun sequence, *Veni, Sancte Spiritus;* likewise the *vulgaris prosa* known as *Christ fuer gen Himmel* is linked with the sequence for Ascension, *Summi triumphum*.[121] The syllabic character which distinguished the sequences from the more ancient melismatic chants, along with the accentual versification (as distinguished from the quantitative), was from the start a popular element that made such a transformation easier. But when these songs became distinct and independent of the sequences they could no longer keep their place within the liturgy of the Mass. Performance by alternate voices—either precentor *versus* choir, or two choirs—has continued, even till now, as the rule for the sequences.[122]

[118] K. Young, *The Drama of the Medieval Church* (Oxford, 1933), I, 201-222. Ursprung, 77; cf. 79.

[119] W. Bäumker, *Das katholische deutsche Kirchenlied* (Freiburg, 1883), II, 12, quotes a school plan of Crailsheim, 1480: *Item circa alia festa Resurrectionis, Ascensionis et Corporis Christi habentur plures canciones convenientes cum sequentiis; videlicet in sequentias 'Victime paschali laudes':* 'Crist ist erstanden,' *circa quoslibet duos versus, etc., regulariter fit. Vel aliud: 'Surrexit Christus hodie, alleluja, alleluja, humano pro solamine, alleluja', vulgus:* Erstanden ist der heilig Christ, Alleluja, Der aller Welt ein Tröster ist, Alleluja, usw.

For Ingolstadt about 1530 Dr. Eck attests this usage: *Sub Alleluja solet ali-*

quando cani: 'Christ ist erstanden'. Greving, *Johann Ecks Pfarrbuch*, 152, note c.

Bäumker, *op. cit.*, (1886) I, 199, also cites the Mainz Cantual of 1605 and 1627, where German verses within the sequence of great feasts are presupposed.

[120] See the comparison presented by Ursprung, 72, cf. 101. Also printed in P. Gennrich, *Der Gemeindegesang in der alten und mittelalterlichen Kirche* (Welt des Gesangbuches, 2; Leipzig o. J.), 27. Other older forms of the song in Bäumker, I, 502-510.

[121] Bäumker, II, 12.

Cf. also W. Bäumker, *Zur Geschichte der Tonkunst* (Freiburg, 1881), 132 f.

[122] *Graduale Romanum* (ed. Vat., 1908), *De rit. serv. in cantu Missæ*, IV.

In the period of Baroque it was especially the sequence *Lauda Sion* that received a ceremonial embellishment. At the high Mass celebrated before the Blessed Sacrament exposed, the celebrant near the end of the sequence, before the words *Ecce panis angelorum*, took the monstrance from the throne and turned with it to face the people; or he himself intoned the words just mentioned.[123]

The fact that here the swift course of the Mass seemed to reach a point of rest, a breathing spot before the triumphal entry of the divine word in the Gospel, was early manifested in the possibility of making various insertions here. In contrast to a more ancient arrangement, which placed the ordinations (without any fore-Mass) immediately before the start of the Mass proper,[124] it was customary at Rome as early as 600 to insert the conferring of the major Orders before the Gospel, or more precisely, between gradual and alleluia, *resp.* tract.[125] This has remained the rule even today, at least for ordination to priesthood and episcopacy. Like the consecration of abbots and virgins and the crowning of kings, these are introduced before the alleluia or, as the case may be, before the last verse of the sequence or the tract.[126]

In the later Middle Ages it became customary at a high Mass to start the preparation of the offerings during these interposed chants before the Gospel.[127] This custom was then taken over here and there into the less

---

[123] The latter was the case at the Corpus Christi high Mass as celebrated at Klosterneuburg in the 18th century; Schabes, 171.

For the Premonstratensians of Brabant a provincial chapter of 1620 decreed: Each time, when the conventual Mass *de Venerabili* was celebrated, *Ecce panis* should be sung after the Alleluia, *et sub istis omnibus* (viz., also at the *Tantum ergo* and *Genitori* before and after the service) *venerabile sacramentum a celebrante exhibeatur, acolythi tædas accensas teneant, cymbala pulsent et thuribularius thurificet.* J. E. Steynen, *Capitula provincialia Circariæ Brabantiæ* (Supplemet to the *Analecta Præm.*, 17-18 [1941-42], 4).

Countless other examples since the 14th century in Browe, *Die Verehrung der Eucharistie im Mittelalter*, 150-153.
[124] Hippolytus, *Trad. Ap.* (Dix, 6).
[125] *Ordo Rom. VIII*, n. 3, 4, 8 (PL, LXXVIII, 1001-1004); cf. de Puniet, *Das römische Pontifikale*, I, 131 f. Since the 10th century the other orders which were previously conferred outside Mass or ·after Communion were often inserted

here, until later the Gallican fashion of conferring the orders at various places in the fore-Mass finally won the day; *ibid.*, 132.
[126] *Pontificale Rom., De ordinibus conferendis.*
[127] Thus already in the *Ordo eccl. Lateran.* (Fischer, 81): The subdeacon washes his hands and then puts wine into the chalice and the requisite hosts on the paten. Cf. *Ordinarium O.P.* (Guerrini, 237); *Ordo Rom. XIV*, n. 53 (PL, LXXVIII, 1161 B).

We learn that in French episcopal churches of the late Middle Ages this preparation took place on a side altar and that the deacon spoke the accompanying words (*Deus qui humanæ substantiæ* or *De latere*) at the commingling of the water. Frequently the chalice and paten were then carried to the altar during the *Credo*; Martène, 1, 4, 4, 10 (I, 375 f.). Further examples, *ibid.*, 1, 4, XXIV, XXIX, XXXVII (I, 627 D, 646 D, 677 D).

Cf. also the Mass-plan *Indutus planeta* (in Mass books since 1507), in Legg, *Tracts*, 184.

solemn Mass.[128] At the same time we hear occasionally that during these chants and preparations the celebrant was to say certain *apologiæ* quietly to himself, or at least that he could do so; in fact some Mass books of the eleventh and twelfth centuries offer a large store of them in this place.[129] It is hard to say whether this is the expression of an exaggerated sin-consciousness or of a remarkable *horror vacui* which could not tolerate a pause not filled with vocal prayer. Both practices disappeared in the course of time.

6. The Gospel

It is a strict rule which holds true in all liturgies, that the last of the readings should consist of a passage from the Gospels,[1] but this is not something self-explanatory. If the order of the biblical canon or the time sequence of the events were the norm, the Acts of the Apostles would, at least on occasion, come last. But obviously there had to be some order of precedence, and there was never any doubt that the Gospels hold the highest rank; they contain the "good tidings," the fulfillment of all the past, and the point from which all future ages radiate. And just as in a procession of the clergy the highest in rank comes last, so too in the series of readings.[2]

How highly the Gospels were regarded is seen in the care and the wealth that was expended on the manuscripts containing them. The Gospels were long written in stately uncials even after these had otherwise gone out of use. Not a few manuscripts were prepared in gold or silver script upon a purple ground, or they were richly decorated with miniatures. What Christian antiquity had begun in this regard, was even surpassed in the Carolingian era. Not seldom was the binding of the evangeliary covered with ivory and pure gold or silver.[3] The Gospel book alone was permitted

---

[128] See the rite in the Regensburg Missal of 1500 (Beck, 265).

Elsewhere the priest should here merely see whether chalice and paten are ready for the sacrificial offerings; thus in two Mass-plans in Legg, *Tracts*, 39, 58.

[129] Ebner, 297, 337.

Cf. *supra*, note 69.

See also the account from the life of St. Thomas of Canterbury (d. 1170), who used to say St. Anselm's penitential prayers during the chants of the fore-Mass; Martène, 1, 4, 4, 9 (I, 375).

[1] Only in the enumeration of the lessons in Justin, *Apol.*, I, 67, are the "memoirs of the apostles" (= Gospels) named first, and then the prophets; but no argument can be built on the order here outlined.

The oldest attestations for the Gospel as the last lesson will be found in Th. Zahn, *Geschichte des Neutestamentl. Kanons,* II (Erlangen, 1890), 380, note 2.

[2] Remigius of Auxerre, *Expositio* (PL, CI, 1250 A): the Epistle precedes, just as the Lord sent his apostles before him (Luke 10: 1). Later expositors unanimously see in this precedence of the Epistle a representation of the activity of the Forerunner; thus Amalar, *De eccl. off.*, III, 11 (PL, CV, 1118); Durandus, IV, 16, 2 ff.; Eisenhofer, II, 103.

[3] St. Beissel, *Geschichte der Evangelienbücher in der ersten Hälfte des Mittelalters* (Freiburg, 1906); H. Leclercq, "Évangeliaire," DACL, V, 775-845; F. Cabrol, *Books of the Latin Liturgy* (London, 1933), 144-147.

on the altar which otherwise bore only the Blessed Sacrament, a conception which survives in the Greek Church down to the very present.[4]

In the liturgy itself the effort was made from earliest times to enhance and stress the *evangelium* as much as possible. It was to be read not by a lector but by a deacon or a priest.[5] On feast days perhaps the bishop himself read the Gospel[6]; in Jerusalem this was the case every Sunday.[7] In the West the delivery of the Gospel was the deacon's duty from earliest times,[8] for he was the first cleric amongst all those assisting. On Christmas night it became the privilege of the Roman emperor to stand forth in full regalia to deliver the Gospel: *Exiit edictum a Cæsare Augusto.*[9]

In the latter part of the ancient Christian period the question was agitated, whether the Gospel was not too sacred to be heard by the profane ears of the catechumens. The Roman baptismal rite as revised in the sixth century[10] at all events puts the sharing of the Gospel on a par with the sharing of the confession of faith and the Our Father which were always regarded as restricted by the *disciplina arcani.* And as a matter of fact the catechumens—as a rule children who were subjected to the forms of adult baptism—were dismissed before the Gospel at the Scrutiny-Masses. Similar endeavors must have made themselves felt in Gaul even earlier, for the Council of Orange in 441 had occasion to insist that the catechumens were

[4] Leclercq, 778.

[5] Thus according to the *Ap. Const.,* II, 57, 7 (Quasten, *Mon.,* 182). The deacon is mentioned by Jerome, *Ep.,* 147, 6 (PL, XXII, 1200).

According to Sozomen, *Hist. eccl.,* VII, 19 (PG, LXVII, 1477 A), the Gospel was reserved in his time in many places to the priest, in Alexandria to the archdeacon, elsewhere to the deacon.

[6] Sozomen, *loc. cit.* In the Byzantine-Slavic rite even at present the celebrant (and therefore, on occasion, the bishop) on Easter Sunday himself reads the Gospel (John 1: 1-17), and does so in this manner: each sentence is repeated by each of the priests and deacons present, and at the finish the bells are rung. A. v. Maltzew, *Fasten- und Blumen-Triodion* (Berlin, 1899), 723-725.

[7] *Aetheriæ Peregrinatio,* c. 24, 10 (CSEL, XXXIX, 73 f.). In the Syrian liturgies and in the Ethiopian it is still the practice at present for the celebrant always to read the Gospel; Baumstark, *Die Messe im Morgenland,* 93.

[8] *Ordo Rom. I,* n. 11 (PL, LXXVIII, 942 f.). Jerome, too, speaks of the deacon as reader of the Gospel, *Ep.,* 147, 6

(CSEL, LVI, 322). The deacon also reads the Gospel in the Byzantine and the Armenian liturgies; in the Coptic liturgy the deacon has several readings; Baumstark, 93 f.

[9] In the Roman *ordines* this right is assigned to the emperor only for the pertinent lesson at Matins; *Ordo Rom. XIV,* n. 67 (PL, LXXVIII, 1182); *Ordo Rom. XV,* n. 9 (1278). But the right was also exercised at Mass, e.g., by Charles IV and by Sigismund; see Biehl, *Das liturgische Gebet für Kaiser und Reich,* 100 f. Frederick III did the same at Rome in 1468; see the account in Browe, JL, XII (1934), 166. The rite included the ceremonial in which the emperor drew his sword and brandished it three times as a sign that he upheld the Gospel. In virtue of his consecration as ruler the emperor was granted the spiritual honors of a canon. By many, in fact, he was considered a deacon or at least a cleric. Biehl, 100 f., 121 ff.; Eichmann, *Die Kaiserkrönung,* I, 282 f.

[10] *Ordo Rom. VII,* n. 5 (PL, LXXVIII, 997); *Sacramentarium Gelasianum* I, 34 (Wilson, 50-53); P. de Puniet, "Catéchuménat," DACL, II, 2605 ff.

also to hear the Gospel.[11] This latter attitude paralleled the counsel of our Lord: Preach the Gospel to the whole of creation (Mark 16:15), and was always the standard in the Church as long as the catechumenate continued to be a vital institution for the instruction of candidates for Baptism. The word of the Gospel should resound throughout the world—this idea sometimes found (and finds) a special symbolical expression in the practice of reciting the Gospel-pericope on festive occasions in several languages.[12]

The deportment of the deacon, too, as he walked to the place where the Gospel was to be read, was built up gradually into a formal procession. The beginnings of such a ceremonial are already to be seen in the first Roman *Ordo*[13]; the deacon kisses the feet of the pope, who pronounces over him the words: *Dominus sit in corde tuo et in labiis tuis.*[14] Then he goes to the altar where the Gospel book has been lying since the beginning of the service (having been placed there ceremoniously by a deacon, accompanied by an acolyte).[15] He kisses it and picks it up.[16] As he betakes himself to the ambo, he is accompanied by two acolytes with torches, and by two subdeacons, one of whom carries a *thymiamaterium*.

[11] Can. 18 (Mansi, VI, 439). The same prescription is repeated by later councils. Amalar, *De eccl. off.*, III, 36 (PL, CV, 1156 B), calls the dismissal before the Gospel *consuetudo nostra*, but finds it unreasonable. Cf. P. Borella, "La 'missa' o 'dimissio catechumenorum'," *Eph. liturg.*, LIII (1939), 60-110, especially 63 ff.

[12] In the Byzantine-Slavic rite of the Catholic Ukrainians it is still the custom to sing the Gospel on Easter Sunday in several languages, including the modern one of the locality in which the church is built. Usually the various languages follow verse for verse or section for section; see note 6 above.

In the solemn papal Mass not only the Gospel but the Epistle also is read in both Latin and Greek; Brinktrine, *Die feierliche Papstmesse*, 14-16. There is evidence for the practice since the early Middle Ages: *Liber pont.*, Vita of Benedict III (d. 858; Duchesne, II, 147); *Ordo Rom. XI*, n. 20; 47 (PL, LXXVII, 1033, 1044), etc. The custom held also for Easter and Pentecost and for the Ember Saturdays; see Kunze, *Die gottesdienstliche Schriftlesung*, 105 f.

Similar customs were still in existence at St. Denis about 1700; Martène, 1, 3, 2, 10 (I, 281 D). Further accounts, *ibid.*

1, 3, 2, 7 (280 f.). At the coronation of Alexander V at the Council of Pisa (1409) both readings were done in Latin, Greek and Hebrew; Martène, *loc. cit.*

[13] *Ordo Rom. I*, n. 5; 11 (PL, LXXVIII, 942 f.).

[14] In this short form also in Sicard of Cremona, *Mitrale*, III, 4 (PL, CCXIII, 106).

[15] This was obviously done to show that the sacred message comes from Christ. Amalar, *De eccl. off.*, III, 18 (PL, CV, 1125) and later interpreters; with special exactness Hugh of St. Cher (ed. Sölch, 18).

[16] In the Middle Ages it was the rule (to a great extent) to place the Gospel book on the altar at the beginning of Mass. However, according to the Cistercian and Carmelite rites, it was laid on the reading desk at once; Sölch, 66.

When, in the present-day high Mass, the deacon lays the Gospel book on the altar after the Epistle, it is doubtless a reminiscence of the ancient symbolic ritual. The older, fuller ceremony was probably omitted from the Missal of Pius V (*Rit. serv.*, VI, 5) because the Gospel is contained in the missal, and the latter is on the altar from the start. Sölch, 67.

In the Gallican liturgy of this period we come upon somewhat the same picture as that at Rome, but heightened a little. The well-known commentary on this ancient liturgy—a work of the seventh century—sees in the solemn entry of the *evangelium* (which is accompanied by the chanting of the *Trisagion* and at which seven torches are carried) a representation of Christ's triumphal coming.[17] We can also include as parallel the Little Entry of the oriental liturgies, although this is placed at the very beginning of the reading service.[18] Its center, too, is the Gospel book—if not exclusively, at least predominantly.[19] A procession which apparently centers on the Gospel book is also found in the Coptic liturgy. The procession is formed immediately before the reading of the Gospel; lights are carried in front of the book, and the altar is circled.[20]

As seems plain from what has been said, the carrying of tapers before the Gospel tallies with an ancient Christian practice that must have been common to all the liturgies. In fact St. Jerome testifies that it was customary in all the churches of the Orient to light lights when the Gospel was to be read, and this on the brightest day; in this way an air of joy could be lent to the gathering.[21] More precisely, however, the practice was palpably an honor paid to the holy book. The Roman *Notitia dignitatum*[22] of the fifth century, amongst the official insignia of the various dignitaries of the Roman State which are there illustrated, shows for the *præfectus prætorio* a picture in which a book stands opened on a covered table between two burning candles—a book whose cover bears a likeness of the

---

[17] *Expositio ant. lit. gallicanæ* (ed. Quasten, 14 f.) : *Egreditur processio sancti evangelii velut potentia Christi triumphantis de morte, cum prædictis harmoniis et cum septem candelabris luminis, quæ sunt septem dona Spiritus Sancti . . . ascendens in tribunal analogii velut Christus sedem regni paterni, ut inde intonet dona vitæ clamantibus clericis: Gloria tibi Domine, in specie angelorum qui nascente Domino: Gloria in excelsis Deo, pastoribus apparentibus cecinerunt.* The seven torches (after Apoc. 1: 12, 20) still found in *Ordo Rom VI* (Germany, 10th century), n. 7 (PL, LXXVIII, 991). On the contrary only at the entry for the start of services in *Ordo Rom. I*, n. 8 (PL, LXXVIII, 941).
[18] Cf. *supra*, p. 263.
[19] See above all the rite in the Byzantine liturgy (Brightman, 367). Here, too—apparently about the same time as in Gaul—the reference to the entrance of the Son of God into the world; Hanssens, III, 105.

For the other rites of the Orient, cf. the indications in Baumstark, *Die Messe im Morgenland*, 82. B. sees the prototype of the μιχρὰ εἴσοδος in the procession from the church of the Resurrection to that of the Holy Cross after the fore-Mass of Sunday morning's service, as described in the *peregrinatio Aetheriæ*, c. 24 (CSEL, XXXIX, 74). The explanation does not seem to be wholly warranted, for the procession here mentioned took place after the Gospel and had an entirely different function (cf. *supra*, 261 f.).

[20] Renaudot, *Liturgiarum orient. collectio*, I (1747), 189* f. Cf. for the Ethiopian liturgy, Brightman, 220, 1.5.
[21] Jerome, *Contra Vigilantium*, c. 7 (PL, XXIII, 346).
[22] Regarding this remarkable document cf. H. Leclercq, "Notitia dignitatum," DACL, XII, 1711-1715; cf. Batiffol, *Leçons*, 81, note 3.

emperor on a ground of gold; it is the *liber mandatorum* which contains the powers granted to this official by the emperor.[23] We can also recall the custom of carrying lights and incense before the bishop at a solemn entry —one of the honors which, since the time of Constantine, was transferred from the higher civil officials to church dignitaries.[24] It is but a step to explain the carrying of lights and incense before the Gospel book on the basis of the personal honor paid to the bishop; in the Gospel book, which contains Christ's word, Christ Himself is honored and His entry solemnized.[25] This custom is on a level with the practice of erecting a throne at synods and placing the Gospel book thereon to show that Christ is presiding,[26] or with that other practice, followed as late as the tenth and twelfth century, of carrying the Gospel book in the Palm Sunday procession to take the place of Christ.[27]

In the later Middle Ages the processional character of this act was emphasized in many places by having a cross-bearer precede the group.[28] The cushion for the book was probably also carried in the procession.[29] This stately escort of the Gospel book at a high Mass is sometimes reflected in the action of private Mass, when the priest himself transfers the Mass book for the Gospel.[30] At Le Mans it was even the custom for the priest to

[23] *Notitia dignitatum,* ed. O. Seeck (Berlin, 1876), p. 8; 107; cf. E. Böcking, *Über die Notitia dignitatum* (Bonn, 1834), 96 f., 101.

[24] *Supra,* p. 68 f.

[25] Cf. Remigus of Auxerre, *Expositio* (PL, CI, 1248 A), who says of the Gospel-book in the procession at the beginning of Mass: the Gospel of Christ is surrounded by a grand retinue *tamquam persona præpotentis.*

[26] Thus, e.g., at the Council of Ephesus (431); Cyril of Alexandria, *Apol. ad Imperatorem,* (PG, LXXVI, 472 B).

[27] Eisenhofer, I, 506.
It is not necessary, therefore, to follow Atchley, 184 f., in considering the use of lights and incense at the Gospel procession as originally intended to honor the bishop.

[28] Durandus, IV, 24, 16; Frere, *The use of Sarum,* I, 73.
The custom existed among the Premonstratensians and even today is preserved by the Dominicans and in many French churches; Sölch, *Hugh,* 69 f.

[29] Innocent III, *De s. alt. mysterio,* II, 41 (PL, CCXVII, 823 B); Durandus, IV, 24, 1. Also at a later period; de Moléon, 55; 229.

In this procession the Middle Ages found ample opportunities for allegorical interpretation: The deacon must proclaim the Crucified. The cushion reminds him of the reward. The two candles recall the fact that he must have a knowledge of both Testaments, or they refer to Enoch and Elias who will precede Christ's second coming, etc. Durandus, IV, 24, 12-16; cf. A. van Dijk(*Eph. liturg.,* 1939), 324, with the references to older expositors. That the deacon carried the book supported on his left arm was also a matter of moment, because the preaching of Christ in the Gospel passed from the Jews to the Gentiles (indicated by the left); Sölch, 67 f.

[30] *Alphabetum sacerdotum* (15-16th century): Legg, *Tracts,* 39; *Ordinarium* of Coutances (1557), *ibid,* 58.
Even in the present *Missale Rom., Ritus serv.,* VI, 1, the priest at a private Mass is given to understand that he himself carries the book to the other side: *ipsemet seu minister.* C. M. Merati (d. 1744) was the first to think it more fitting that the server transfer the book, and he has him carry it over closed, *pollice sinistro inter folia interiecto;* Gavanti-

carry the Gospel book to the altar at a high Mass, and only then to turn it over to the deacon.[31] That Christ Himself is honored in the Gospel book[32] is also revealed in the acclamations that are uttered. Here we have another of those dramatic elements which the Roman Mass gradually acquired in the countries of the North. The deacon greets the people and receives their greeting in return.[33] Then he announces the pericope and the cry is heard: *Gloria tibi, Domine.*[34] After the lection the Mass-server answers: *Laus tibi, Christe.*[35] And in one Italian church of the twelfth century use is made of the shout of homage with which the crowds greeted our Lord: *Benedictus qui venit in nomine Domini.*[36] In some isolated instances the deacon himself, at the end of the reading, is saluted by the celebrant with a *Pax tibi.*[37]

Merati, *Thesaurus,* II, 5, 5 (I, 233). Practical considerations have here won out over the esteem for symbolism. Cf. however the stressing of the ancient rubric by J. ·M. Hanssens, "Cuius est in Missa privata transferre Missale?" *Eph. liturg.,* XLVIII (1934), 328-330.

[31] As a practice still circa in de Moléon, 221.

[32] Cf. Augustine, *In Joh. tract.,* 30, 1 (PL, XXXV, 1632): *Nos itaque sic audiamus evangelium quasi præsentem Dominum.* Similarly already Ignatius of Antioch, *Ad Phil.,* 5, 1: The Gospel is his refuge, "like the flesh of Jesus."

[33] Thus first in the Carolingian *Ordo Rom. II,* n. 8 (PL, LXXVIII, 972).

[34] From the Gallican Mass of the 7th century; see above, note 17. With the wording *Gloria Deo omnipotenti* already in Gregory of Tours, *Hist. Franc.,* VIII, 4(PL, LXXI, 451 D).

Amalar, *De eccl. off.,* III, 18 (PL, CV, 1125 f.) is the first to attest its presence in the Roman Mass and he wishes that everyone should join in saying it, even if he cannot understand the words of the Gospel.

Cf. in the later part of *Ordo Rom I,* n. 27 (PL, LXXVIII, 950 C); also Innocent III, *De s. alt. mysterio,* II, 46 (PL, CCXVII, 826), who apportions it to the people.

According to the *Ordinarium* of Coutances (1557) the priest adds to the response given by the clerics (*Gloria tibi Domine*) the words: *Qui natus es de Virgine* or *Qui apparuisti hodie,* etc.; Legg, *Tracts,* 59.

The phrase may ultimately spring from the Orient. In the Greek liturgy of St. James (Brightman, 38), the people cry out before the Gospel: Δόξα σοι κύριε. In the Coptic liturgy (Br. 156) the choir does this. The Greek form in the Coptic Mass may possibly reach back to the 7th century. Similarly in the Armenian liturgy (Br., 426) where the words "God speaks" are added.

[35] That it is the Mass-server and not the choir that answers ties in with its recent (late Middle Age) origin. Still the Armenian liturgy repeats the acclamation which the clerics spoke before the Gospel: "Glory be to thee, O Lord, our God!" (Brightman, 426).

[36] Sicard, *Mitrale,* III, 4 (PL, CCXIII, 112 A); the same circa 1300 in Tours: Martène, 1, 4, 5, 6 (I, 379 C). The same exclamation is used by the Jacobites after the announcement of the Gospel; Brightman, 79.

According to John Beleth, *Explicatio,* c. 39 (PL, CCII, 48 Dʲ), all should cry after the Gospel: *Amen,* or *Deo Gratias.* A rule for nuns of about 1115 has the choir answer *Amen;* de Moléon, 110. Other later authors attest the practice: cf. van Dijk, 326. It probably stems from the Rule of St. Benedict (c. 11) according to which all should answer *Amen* when the abbot has finished the reading of the Gospel. Cf. the Mozarabic liturgy (*supra,* p. 406).

This *Amen* was said with hands uplifted, according to Durandus, IV, 24, 30; 34.

[37] *Supra,* p. 407. The practice still ap-

If, in these cries, the clergy answer the message of joy rather than the people, still the faithful also take a part in showing honor to the Gospel, at least by their bodily posture. From ancient times it has been customary to listen to the Gospel *standing*.[38] The practice prevails generally in the Orient, too,[39] and is provable there as far back as the fourth century.[40] In the West also there is early and manifold evidence of standing at the Gospel.[41] The medieval interpreters place a great deal of weight on the usage and describe it in minute detail. When the deacon's greeting sounds, all stand up and turn to him. Thereupon all the people face east, till the words of our Lord begin.[42] Meanwhile the canes that are used to support oneself[43] are put aside and the people either stand erect (like servants before their Lord)[44] or else slightly bowed.[45] The men are to remove every head covering, even the princely crown.[46] Mention is made, too, of setting

pears in Mass books of the 11-12th century: Ebner, 300, 337. But it is no longer understood even in *Ordo Rom. III* (11th century; Germany), n. 10 (PL, LXXVIII, 980). In the *Missa Illyrica* all the clerics cry out to the deacon: *Pax tibi;* Martène, 1, 4, IV (I, 505 B).

[38] Today it is prescribed as the one exception to the kneeling position at private Mass; *Missale Rom., Rubr. gen.,* XVII, 2.

[39] Hanssens, III, 214.

[40] *Const. Ap.,* II, 57, 8 (Quasten, *Mon.,* 182); Sozomen, *Hist eccl.,* VII, 19 (PG, LXVII, 1477 A). Cf. the reading of the law by Esdras: 2 Esdr. 8: 5.

[41] *Liber pont.* (Duchesne, I, 218): *Hic* [Anastasius I] *constituit, ut quotiescumque evangelia sancta recitantur, sacerdotes non sederent, sed curvi starent.* This order, which belongs to the oldest portion of the book (dated *circa* 530 according to the generally accepted norm), is found again in an expanded form (*sacerdotes et ceteri omnes*) in the pseudo-Isidorean Decretals (PL, CXXX, 691), whence it crept into various later canonical collections; for this last see Browe, *Eph. liturg.,* L (1936), 402.

[42] Amalar, *De eccl. off.,* III, 18 (PL, CV, 1125 C); *Ordo Rom. II,* n. 8 (PL, LXXVIII, 972).

[43] These sticks, later in the form of crutches, usually took the place of pews; Sölch, Hugh of St. Cher, 74. Canes of this sort are still used for the same purpose by Abyssinian monks.

[44] Amalar, *loc. cit.*

Further illustrations below, note 45 f., and in van Dijk (*Eph. liturg.,* 1939), 325; Durandus, IV, 24, 23-25.

[45] Thus according to the ancient canon; see note 41 above. John Beleth, *Explicatio,* c. 39 (PL. CCII, 49 B): *erecti . . . aut capite inclinato.* This regulation is still found in the 13th century; see van Dijk, 323: *erecto corpore . . . et capite aliquantulum inclinato.* The folding of the hands (the practice in Spain) was probably inspired by the same reasons which fostered the bowing of the head; see the evidence from a lectionary of the year 1073 in Férotin, *Le Liber mozarabicus sacramentorum,* p. 904; cf. Ferreres, 112.

[46] *Ordo Rom. II* (10th century), n. 8 (PL, LXXVIII, 972): *Sed et baculi omnium deponuntur de manibus, et in ipsa hora neque corona neque aliud operimentum super capita eorum habetur.* Cf. *Eclogæ* (PL, CV, 1322).

Similarly most of the later interpreters, e.g. Hildebert of Le Mans (d. 1133) in his poetic exposition of the Mass: *Plebs baculos ponit, stat retegitque caput* (PL, CXI, 1178). Women, however, were to keep their heads covered, *propter pomum vetitum.* In case of necessity the mother should lay a handkerchief on the head of a girl: John Beleth, *Explicatio,* c. 39 (PL, CII, 49).

aside one's weapons and outer mantle or cloak,[47] as well as gloves.[48] Elsewhere the knights laid their hand on the hilt of their sword, or they drew the sword and held it extended all during the reading[49]—expressions, both, of a willingness to fight for the word of God.

When the Gospel ended it was customary in the Roman stational services for a subdeacon to take the book (not with bare hands, however, but holding it *super planetam*),[50] and to bring it around to the attending clergy to be kissed[51] before it was returned again to its casket, sealed and brought back to its place of safekeeping.[52]

In countries of the North the people were, for a time, permitted to share in this veneration of the Gospel book.[53] Later the right was limited to *personis inunctis*.[54] And from there on it was usually handed only to clerics

[47] Durandus, *loc. cit.*; mentions *arma* and *chlamys*.

[48] Albert the Great, *De sacrificio missæ*, II, c. 7, 7 (*Opp.*, ed. Borgnet, 38, 56).

[49] Thus above all among the religious orders of knights; Bona, II, 7, 3 (669). This is attested as still the practice of these military orders by J. M. Cavalieri (d. 1757), *Commentaria in authentica SRC decreta*, V (Augsburg, 1764), 31. See also note 9 above.

Some student fraternities have taken over the usage of drawing their weapons at the Gospel. A custom having a similar aim is that of waving banners, as is done by certain Catholic organizations.

[50] *Ordo Rom. I*, n. 11 (PL, LXXVIII, 943). The subdeacon, like other clerics of the 8th century, wore a bell-shaped chasuble which he therefore rolled up. In like manner the acolyte covered his hands when he picked up the book before the entrance procession and carried it to the altar. *Ordo Rom. I*, n. 5 (PL, LXXVIII, 940); Beissel, *Bilder*, 304 f., 313.

[51] In *Ordo Rom. I*, n. 11 (PL, LXXVIII, 943) it seems at first only a small group were concerned, at least if Batiffol's explanation of the phrase *per ordinem graduum* pertains here; *Leçons*, 82.

This kiss of the Gospel book by the bishop and the assembled clergy is attested as an ancient tradition by Jonas of Orleans (d. 843), *De cultu imag.*, II, *præf.* (PL, CVI, 342 f.).

The book is honored by a kiss from the pontiff upon entering the church, and by a kiss from the deacon before he ascends the ambo (*supra*, p. 445). *Ordo Rom. II*, n. 5; 8 (PL, LXXVIII, 950 C, 971 C), which mentions the same reverences, also names the bishop as the first to kiss the book after the Gospel; n. 8 (972 B).

In the Byzantine liturgy the celebrant kisses the Gospel-book at the finish of the Little Entrance; Brightman, 368, 1. 19 f.

[52] *Ordo Rom. I*, n. 11 (PL, LXXVIII, 943).

[53] *Expositio 'Missa pro multis'*, ed. Hanssens (*Eph. liturg.*, 1930), 36; *Ordo Rom. II*, n. 8 (PL, LXXVIII, 972 B). According to William of Hirsau (d. 1091), *Const.*, I, 86 (PL, CL, 1017), the priest at a private Mass kissed the book after the reading, then handed it to the Massserver *et aliis communicare volentibus* to be kissed. Also according to the Lay Folks Mass Book of the 13th century (Simmons, p. 18), the faithful still kiss the book. Later there is no mention of it any more.

In the Coptic liturgy it is also customary for those present to kiss the book after the reading of the Gospel, the priest kissing the open book, the faithful kissing the silken covering; Renaudot, *Liturgiarum orient. collectio*, I, 190. Notice the similarity to the practice at Bayeux, note 56 below.

[54] Thus according to a decision of Honorius III, March 8, 1221 (A. Potthast, *Regesta pont. Rom.*, I [Berlin, 1874], p. 573); cf. J. M. Cavalieri, *Commentaria*, V, 31.

450   THE MASS CEREMONIES IN DETAIL

to be kissed,[55] and the celebrant used to do so with the book opened, just as it is customary nowadays, while the rest of the choir did so with the book closed.[56] Gradually, however, since the thirteenth century, the custom of having the clergy kiss the book disappeared,[57] although it was still to be found in some places as late as the eighteenth century.[58] According to present-day practice even the deacon no longer kisses the book,[59] but only the celebrating priest[60] or (but only in his stead) an attending higher prelate,[61] even at a private Mass. And while doing so the priest says: *Per evangelica dicta deleantur nostra delicta*. Similar formulas have attended the kissing of the Gospel since around the year 1000.[62] And traces of the original mean-

Even according to present usage a Gospel book (not the same as that kissed by the celebrating bishop) can be handed to a *maximus princeps* for a kiss, likewise to a high prelate. *Cæremoniale episc.*, I, 29, 9. For the rest, however, the prohibition to hand the book to lay people has been repeatedly stressed in decrees; Gavanti-Merati, II, 6, 2 (I, 237 f.).
[55] Thus in John of Avranches, *De off. eccl.* (PL, CXLVII, 35 B).
[56] Hugh of St. Cher, *Tract.* (Sölch, 21).
At Bayeux the book was handed to all the priests open, to other clerics closed; Martène, 1, 4, XXIV (I, 628 C). Similar customs also existed elsewhere; see Lebrun, *Explication*, I, 204, note b.
In this case the open book was understood in the light of Luke 8: 10: "To you it is granted to understand the secret of God's kingdom; the rest must learn of it by parables." Durandus, IV, 24, 32.
[57] Durandus, IV, 24, 32, cites it only in the following form: *Postea in quibusdam ecclesiis liber clausus illis qui sunt in choro ostenditur*. However it did endure for a long time in many places in France: Martène, 1, 4, XX, XXIV; cf. XXIX (I, 608 A, 628 B, 646 E).
In England we see the practice, but in a later part of the Mass, at the Offertory when the clergy are incensed and then each is given the book to kiss; Missal of Sarum: Martène, 1, 4, XXXV (I, 667).
[58] According to Martène, 1, 4, 5, 6 (I, 379 D), it was at that time customary at Vienne and Tours to hand each one the open book with the words: *Hæc est lex divina*. Likewise Lebrun reports the custom at Paris: After the thurifer has

incensed each individual, the subdeacon presents the Gospel book to be kissed with the words: *Hæc sunt verba sancta*, whereupon the other answers: *Credo et confiteor;* Lebrun, *Explication*, I, 203 f. Similarly amongst the Premonstratensians in the *Ordinarius* of 1739; Waefelghem, 56, note 2.
[59] The subdeacon often kissed the book as soon as the reading was finished: Sicard of Cremona, *Mitrale*, III, 4 (PL, CCXII, 112 B); Durandus, IV, 24, 30.
In the rite of the Dominicans and of the Carthusians he kisses it after the priest; Sölch, *Hugh*, 75.
In some places the deacon also kissed the book before starting to read: thus in the *Missa Illyrica*: Martène ,1, 4, IV (I, 505 B), in the Missal of St. Vincent (Fiala, 201), likewise in Sicard, *loc. cit.* (110 B). According to a mid-Italian sacramentary of the 11th century he kissed not only the book but the altar, saying *Munda cor* and *Domine labia mea;* Ebner, 340. The same formulas, without the kissing of the altar, also at St. Vincent: Fiala, 201.
[60] The possible exceptions, note 54 above.
[61] *Missale Rom., Rit. serv.*, VI, 2; 5. The same direction in the *Ordo Missæ* of John Burchard; Legg, *Tracts*, 147.
[62] Specially frequent is the formula which appears about 1030 in the *Missa Illyrica*, mostly with slight variations: *Per istos sanctos sermones evangelii Domini nostri Jesu Christi indulgeat nobis Dominus universa peccata nostra*: Martène, 1, 4, IV (I, 505 B). Likewise in a mid-Italian book about the same time: Ebner, 300 (*quando salutant omnes evangelium, dicat unusquisque . . .*); likewise later:

THE GOSPEL

ing of reverent and grateful greeting are to be seen in a formula from that early period: *Ave verba sancti evangelii quæ totum mundum replestis*[63]; or in the words found in a more recent arrangement of the private Mass: *Deo gratias, credo et confiteor.*[64]

In contrast to this sharp retrenchment of the kissing of the book, the use of incense—again in the northern countries—has been on the increase. Originally the censer was merely carried in the procession of the book to the ambo; no special incensing took place. Then later it was to be carried up the ambo with the deacon,[65] if there was room. In fact a second *thuribulum* was probably employed.[66] Now the fragrant smoke emanating from the censer and swirling around the Gospel book gains a special value; everyone wants to be touched by it, to be blessed by the blessing of this consecrated incense, and therefore after the reading the censer is carried through the crowd. This usage is, significantly, mentioned first by the same witness who testifies to the ceremony of handing the book to the people to be kissed.[67] The practice was curtailed and only the celebrant was incensed, but even then this incensation retained its special meaning (already men-

ibid., 322, 355; Fiala, 202. Cf. Martène 1, 4, XIII, XVI (I, 576 D, 596 f.).

In a somewhat exuberant fashion the *Alphabetum sacerdotum* (after 1495; Legg, *Tracts*, 40) directs the priest to make a sign of the Cross over the book while saying: *Deo gratias. Per evangelica dicta deleantur delicta. Amen. Hæc sunt verba sancta. Credo et confiteor.* The formula in use at present I find only one other place, in the Pontifical of Noyon (end of the 15th century); V. Leroquais, *Les pontificaux* (Paris, 1937), I, 170.

[63] Missal of St. Denis (11th century; cf. Leroquais, I, 142): Martène, 1, 4, V (I, 523 B); here at the same time the formula already referred to (note 62), *Per istos*. Some mid-Italian Mass books of the 11th century use here the formula that is also used at the start of Mass: *Pax Christi quam* (see pp. 291, 312, *supra*); Ebner, 298, 300.

[64] Missal of St. Pol de Léon 15th century; cf. Leroquais, III, 230 f.): Martène, 1, 4, XXXIV (I, 662 E). Here, however, there is a further formula, our *Per evangelica dicta*, which is otherwise hard to find in medieval Mass books.

The first-named formula should be compared with that used in the Jacobite Mass, in which the deacon, after intro-

ducing the Gospel, cries out: "We believe and confess." (Brightman, 80, 1. 6).

[65] Amalar, *De eccl. off.*, c. 18 (PL, CV, 1126 B); *Expositio 'Missa pro multis'*, ed. Hanssens (*Eph. liturg.*, 1930), 35.

[66] *Ordo Rom. II*, n. 8 (PL, LXXVIII, 971).

[67] *Ordo Rom. II*, n. 9 (PL, LXXVIII, 972): *thuribula per altaria portantur et postea ad nares hominum feruntur et per manum fumus ad os trahitur.* Cf. *supra*, p. 449. In part more precise in the *Ordo Rom. V* which likewise belongs to the 10th century, n. 7 (PL, LXXVIII, 987): *Acolythorum autem gestantium incensoria unus pergat ad altare incensionem exhibere circa illud, necnon et episcopo ac presbyteris atque diaconibus cunctoque clero, alius vero pergat ad populum.*

The connection between incensing and kissing the book is plain in the *Missa Illyrica*, which also has a prayer for each: *Tunc allato incenso simulque evangelio ad salutandum dicant singuli: Per istos sanctos sermones* . . . [see note 62 above] *Quando incensum offertur dicant singuli: Dirigatur oratio mea sicut incensum in conspectu tuo, Domine;* Martène, 1, 4, IV (I, 505 B). The same connection still existed in the time of Lebrun in some of the churches of France; see note 58 above.

tioned),[68] different from others,[69] until it, too, was gradually lost.[70] The incensing of the book before the start of the reading is mentioned since the eleventh century.[71] This has been retained and was, in fact, at one time even duplicated after the reading—another instance of the new (and yet basically ancient) concept of honoring the Gospel.[72] It is only in the Máss for the Dead that the kissing of book and hand is omitted, and so also this incensing.[73]

The desire to grasp the sacred word of God and to secure its blessing (a desire that proved transiently effective in the case of the incensing), also found a lasting expression in another symbol—the sign of the Cross. In the ninth century for the first time do we come across this practice of the faithful signing a cross on their foreheads after the deacon greets them.[74] Then we hear of another custom, the deacon and all those present imprinting the cross on forehead and breast after the words *Sequentia sancti evangelii.*[75] About the eleventh century mention is made of forehead,

[68] *Ordo Rom. VI* (10th century), n. 7 (PL, LXXVIII, 992 A): *episcopus . . . accepto odore incensi.*

William of Melitona, *Opusc. super missam* (ed. van Dijk, 326): *Lecto evangelio liber et thuribulum ad episcopum defertur . . . et ipse thus adolet.* A middle stage is seen in the *Ordo eccl. Lateran.* (Fischer, 81): After the reading, the deacon is presented with *incensum odorandum,* likewise then the bishop and the assisting priest. (Similarly the Missal of St. Vincent: Fiala, 201.) In fact here the deacon is offered this *incensum* also at the very beginning of the reading. Also in the *Liber ordinarius* of the Liége monastery of St. James (Volk, 91) we read much the same thing at the beginning of the Gospel: *thuriferarius debet diaconum interim incensare et ad finem evangelii similiter faciat,* whereas the celebrant is not incensed.

[69] This special meaning is expressed, to some extent, in the prayer which the celebrant says while putting in the incense: *Odore coelestis inspirationis suæ accendat Dominus et impleat corda nostra ad audienda et implenda evangelii sui præcepta. Qui vivit.* This is to be found in Mass books since the 11th century, e.g., in the Missal of Troyes (circa 1050): Martène, 1, 4, VI (I, 531 A); in a mid-Italian missal of the 11th century: Ebner, 297 (later examples, *ibid.,* 332,

337, 345); also, with the addition of a second formula of blessing, in the *Missa Illyrica*: Martène, 1, 4, IV (I, 504 f.).
[70] Durandus, IV, 24, 34, is aware only of the incensing of the bishop after the Gospel, and sees in it an invitation to prayer.
[71] John of Avranches, *De off. eccl.* (PL, 147, 35 A); Sicard of Cremona, *Mitrale,* III, 4 (PL, CCXIII, 110 B). Other interpreters know nothing of it, not even Durandus.

According to the Sarum Ordinary (c. 1320) it is not the book but the altar that is incensed; Legg, *Tracts,* 4.
[72] Cf. *supra,* p. 445 f.
[73] According to the present-day *Missale Romanum.* At the time of Durandus (IV, 24, 33) the basic principle regarding Masses for the Dead was formulated: *omnis solemnitas subtrahitur,* but it was applied only in part to the kiss, not as yet to the incensing.
[74] Amalar, *De eccl. off.,* III, 18 (PL, CV, 1125 D); *Eclogæ* (PL, CV, 1322 A). Also, according to Remigius of Auxerre (d. circa 908), *Expositio* (PL, CI, 1251 A), the people make the sign of the Cross on their foreheads, the deacon on both forehead and breast.
[75] *Ordo Rom. II,* n. 8 (PL, LXXVIII, 972).

There is mention only of the deacon in the Missal of St. Vincent (Fiala, 201)

mouth and breast,[75] and since that time also of the signing of the book.[77] At the end of the Gospel it was the custom for all those present to sign themselves with the cross once more.[78] The original idea of this signing of oneself is probably indicated in the scriptural text frequently cited in this connection, the quotation about the wicked enemy who is anxious to take the seed of the word of God away from the hearts of the hearers.[79] This, in any case, makes the sign of the Cross at the close intelligible,[80] since it is practically as ancient as the other at the beginning. This opening act, which alone has continued to exist, indeed has grown somewhat, was at first explained in a similar sense.[81] And it is a "blessing" of oneself,[82] that is true. But another explanation takes over by degrees; an ever-increasing stress

and in Bernold, *Micrologus,* c. 9 (PL, LI, 983); likewise in Hugh of St. Cher, *Tract. super Missam* (ed. Sölch, 20), where besides the crossing of the book comes first. The same ritual in the *Liber ordinarius* of Liége (Volk, 91). According to the Regensburg Missal of 1500 (Beck, 265 f.), the priest at a non-solemn Mass stands at the center of the altar and crosses his breast and lips with the words: *Jube Domine benedicere. Dominus sit in corde † meo in labiis † meis, ut . . .,* and thereupon he signs the altar, adding the words: † *Pax mecum. Et cum spiritu meo.* Then he starts the reading of the Gospel with *Dominus vobiscum,* and once more signs the book, his forehead and breast; likewise at the end he signs the book.

[76] William of Hirsau, *Const.,* I, 86 (PL, CL, 1017); cf. as a preliminary step *Bernardi Ordo Clun.,* I, 72 (Herrgott, 264).

Honorius Augustod., *Gemma an.,* I, 23 (PL, CLXXII, 551); John Beleth, *Explicatio,* c. 39 (PL, CCII, 4803); Innocent III, *De s. alt. mysterio,* II, 43 (PL, CCXVII, 824); *Ordinarium O.P.* (Guerrini, 238); Durandus, IV, 24, 28. The threefold sign of the Cross is attested for the first time, in general, by these authors of the 11th and 12th centuries.

[77] John Beleth, *loc. cit.*

Alexander of Hales, *Summa de sacrif. missæ,* and following him William of Melitona (in van Dijk, *Eph. liturg.,* 1939, 325). That the faithful, too, should sign

themselves with the Cross these interpreters declare is only the opinion of *quidam* (van Dijk, 325). As a matter of fact among the Saxon Franciscans of the 15th century it was still thought sufficient that the deacon should make a single sign of the Cross, and this upon himself; *ibid.,* note 149.

[78] Remigius of Auxerre, *Expositio* (PL, CI, 1251 C); *Ordo Rom. II,* n. 8 (PL, LXXVIII, 972 B); John Beleth, *Explicatio,* c. 39 (PL, CCII, 48 D). Further witnesses from the 12-13th century in van Dijk, 326.

This last sign of the Cross was customary among the Dominicans from the outset and is still prescribed; Sölch, *Hugh,* 74; at present it is the large Latin Cross that is prescribed both here at the end and also after the triple Cross at the beginning; *Missale iuxta ritum O.P.* (1889), 26.

[79] Luke 8: 12.

[80] The quotation is connected with this closing sign in Remigius, *loc. cit.,* Beleth, *loc. cit.*

Further illustrations in van Dijk, 326.

[81] Amalar, *De eccl. off.,* III, 18 (PL, CV, 1125 f.).

[82] The Sacramentary of St. Denis (11th century) presents a special prayer for this sign of the Cross with the rubric: *Quando se signant;* the prayer is as follows: *Crucis vivificæ signo muni, Domine, omnes sensus meos ad audienda verba sancti evangelii corde credenda et opere complenda;* Martène, 1, 4, V (I, 523 A).

is placed on the readiness to acknowledge God's word with courage[83] in the sense of St. Paul's assertion: I am not ashamed of this Gospel.[84] Probably it was in this sense that the signing of the forehead grew into a triple signing of forehead, lips and breast, and in addition, the signing of the book. The meaning is this: For the word which Christ brought and which is set down in this book we are willing to stand up with a mind that is open; we are ready to confess it with our mouth; and above all we are determined to safeguard it faithfully in our hearts.[85]

Pursuing this conception of a blessing with which we ought to prepare for the Gospel, Amalar remarks that the deacon who is about to scatter the seed of the Gospel stands in need of a *major benedictio*.[86] The simple word of blessing which, according to the first Roman *Ordo*, the pope pronounces over the deacon,[87] is soon broadened out into formulas that reproduce[88] or resemble the one we use today, for example, *Dominus sit in corde tuo et in labiis tuis ut nunties competenter evangelium pacis*,[89] or it is replaced or supplemented by other blessing formulas, for instance: *Benedictio Dei Patris et Filii et Spiritus Sancti descendat super te et aperiat Christus os tuum ad pronuntiandum digne idoneeque sanctum evangelium suum*,[90] or: *Corroboret Dominus sensum et labia tua, ut recte pronunties nobis eloquia divina*,[91] or by a biblical phrase *Deus misereatur vestri et benedicat*,[92] or: *Spiritus Domini super te, evangelizare pauperibus*.[93] Then too, the deacon formally begs for the blessing with *Iube, domne, benedicere*.[94] Since the eleventh century there appears, either before or after the

[83] Amalar, *loc. cit.* (1126 A); Beleth, *loc. cit.* (PL, CCII, 48 A); Durandus, IV, 24, 27.

[84] Rom. 1: 16.

[85] This interpretation in its essentials already in Beleth, *loc. cit.* Regarding the history of the sign of the Cross in general, and the various ways of making it, see Eisenhofer, I, 273-281.

The West Syrians have a custom that gives apt expression to the desire to cling to the Gospel; the faithful are wont to murmur the closing word of each phrase along with the reader; thus according to several accounts from Jerusalem, e.g. Chr. Panfoeder, *Das Persönliche in der Liturgie* (Mainz, 1925), 129.

[86] Amalar, *De eccl. off.*, III, 18 (PL, CV, 1125 D).

[87] *Supra*, p. 444.

[88] Mid-Italian missal of the 11th century: Ebner, 300.

[89] *Missa Illyrica*: Martène, 1, 4, IV (I, 505 A). From then on frequent everywhere, e.g. Sarum Ordinary (14th c.):

Legg, *Tracts*, 4; Hungarian Mass books since the 12th century: Radó, 42; Jávor, 114. Also still in the *Ordinarium Cart.* (1932), c. 26, 14.

[90] Missal of Troyes (c. 1050): Martène, 1, 4, VI (I, 531 A); cf. *ibid.*, IV, V, XV f. (I, 505 A, 523 A, 589 E, 596 E). Almost duplicated in mid-Italian Mass books of the 11th century: Ebner, 297, 300, 337.

[91] Mass-*Ordo* of Amiens (9th century), ed. Leroquais (*Eph. liturg.*, 1927), 441; Martène, 1, 4, VIII, XXV (I, 539 A, 631 D); Ebner, 325.

[92] *Udalrici Consuet. Clun. II*, 30 (PL, CXLIX, 716).

[93] Missal from Bobbio (10-11th century): Ebner, 81.

[94] Mid-Italian Mass books of the 11th century: Ebner, 300, cf. 355; *Ordo Rom. XIV*, n. 53 (PL, LXXVIII, 1161). Already in the 7th century the reader begged a blessing at the table-prayers of Roman monasteries by using this formula:

celebrant pronounces the blessing, another prayer by which the deacon prepares himself, our *Munda cor meum*.[95] But it was far from common even as late as the sixteenth century, and in the Dominican use is lacking even today. Elsewhere the deacon recites the psalm verse: *Domine, labia mea aperies et os meum annuntiabit laudem tuam.*[96]

In a non-solemn Mass the priest, before starting to read the Gospel, was satisfied with a little petition, *Dominus sit in ore meo*[97] or with Psalm 50:17[98] or with one of the formulas already mentioned (revised with reflexives): *Corroboret Dominus sensum meum et labia mea ut recte pronunciem verba sancti evangelii. Per Christum,*[99] or with the sentence used in the present-day Dominican rite: *Dominus sit in corde meo et in labiis meis ad pronuntiandum sanctum evangelium pacis.*[100] In the *Ordo Missæ* of John Burchard (1502) the *Munda cor meum*, with the petition for the blessing and the blessing, both unchanged, were taken over into the private Mass just as we have them today.[101]

Thus the same thought of a proper preparation is disclosed: Pure must be the heart and chaste the lips of him who is to set forth the word of God, as the Lord Himself had declared in His message to Isaias when the seraph had touched the seer's lips with the glowing coal[102]; lips that were to pronounce the word of God; and the heart, too, because this pronouncement was not to be a mere mechanical movement but an intellectual and intelligent speech, because the messenger of the glad tidings (and this holds also for one who only reads the message to the assembly) must first take the lesson to heart before he conveys it to the congregation.

Ordo of Johannes Archicantor, *De convivio* (Silva-Tarouca, 213 f.).

Jube = *dignare* = "deign"; it is a courteous formula which implies that great lords do not themselves act but charge servants with the task. The *domnus* here used is also customary in other cases to distinguish earthly masters from the heavenly *Dominus*.

[95] Ebner, 300, 314, 340, 342; *Ordo Rom. XIV*, n. 53 (PL, LXXVIII, 1161).

[96] Ps. 50: 17; *Ordo Rom. VI* (10th century), n. 6 (PL, LXXVIII, 991).

Also Esth. 14: 12 f. (in Old Latin phrasing: *Conforta me rex . . .*) is often found in monastic texts: Fiala, 201; Ebner, 355; De Corswarem, 121; cf. Missal of Hereford (1502): *Da mihi, Domine, sermonem rectum . . .* Maskell, 66.

[97] *Liber ordinarius* of Liége (Volk, 101).

[98] Lyons Mass book of the 13th century: Ebner, 326.

[99] Lyons Missal of 1531: Martène, 1, 4, XXXIII (I, 659 A).

[100] *Missale iuxta ritum O.P.* (1889), 18. Similarly already a Hungarian missal of the 13th century: Radó, 61.

[101] Legg, *Tracts*, 146. In the Mass-plan 'Indutus planeta' (since 1507) it is left to the option of the priest to pray either *Sit Dominus in cor meum* or *Munda cor meum*: Legg, *Tracts*, 184.

Older Mass-*ordos* direct the priest to kiss the altar while saying the pertinent prayer at private Masses: *Liber ordinarius* of Liége (Volk, 101, 1. 27). Cf. Sarum Ordinary of the 14th century: Legg, *Tracts*, 4.

[102] Is. 6: 6 f.

A similar prayer for purity, based on this passage from Isaias, is found at the beginning of the liturgy of St. James (Brightman, 32, 1. 4). But here the glowing coals are referred to the two natures in Christ, to his humanity aglow with the divinity; this interpretation is quite frequent in the exegesis of the Fathers since Origen.

7. The Homily

The sermon, which (together with its embellishments) is delivered in the vernacular after the Gospel,[1] is currently regarded as an interpolation in the course of the liturgy rather than as a step forward in its progress. As a matter of fact, however, it belongs to the earliest constituent parts, indeed to the pre-Christian elements of the liturgy. The Sabbath Bible reading in the synagogue, which according to rigid custom had to be followed by a clarifying explanation, was for our Lord the main opportunity for preaching the word of God to receptive hearers and to proclaim His kingdom.[2] At Antioch in Pisidia Paul and Barnabas, in similar circumstances, were ordered by the rulers of the synagogue to direct "a word of encouragement" to the assembly.[3]

It stands to reason, therefore, that in Christian worship the homily was similarly joined at the very start to the reading of the Scriptures.[4] Indeed, the homily appears almost as an indispensable part of public worship,[5] which took place, of course, only on Sundays. The Bishop who presided over the community-worship would himself address the congregation after the reading. This was a particular duty of his. Still the priests also were allowed to preach; thus we have the numerous homilies of an Origen,[6] or those of Hippolytus of Rome or later those of Jerome, and—

---

[1] According to Durandus, IV, 26, 1, the sermon took place only after the *symbolum,* which served as a subject for exposition. This is still the custom in some places, like the diocese of Trier.

According to the *Ordo* of the Lateran church (Fischer, 78), the sermon (on the worthy reception of Communion) took place here on Easter Sunday *post acceptam oblationem;* cf. Sicard of Cremona, *Mitrale,* III, 5 (PL, CCXIII, 116 B). The Low German "Rule for Lay People" (15th century; R. Langenberg, *Quellen und Forschungen zur Geschichte der deutschen Mystik* [Bonn, 1902], 87) also assumes that the preaching is done at this spot; similarly the Pontifical of Noyon (15th century; V. Leroquais, *Les pontificaux* [Paris, 1937], I, 170). In France and England the sermon in the later Middle Ages was usually inserted after the *Orate fratres;* in France this practice continued till the 18th century; Simmons, *The Lay Folks Mass Book,* 317 ff., especially 318, note 2. The explicit prescription in the *Missale Romanum, Ritus serv.,* VI, 6, according to which the

sermon follows the Gospel, was first inserted in 1604 by Clement VIII.

[2] Luke 4: 16 ff.; Mark 1: 21, and parallels.

[3] Acts 13: 15.

[4] Justin, *Apol.,* I, 67; cf. Irenæus as in Eusebius, *Hist. eccl.,* V, 20, 6.

[5] Towards the end of the Middle Ages, therefore at a time when the sermon was becoming more and more separated from the Mass, emphasis was frequently laid on the obligation of the faithful to attend Mass *and* the sermon on Sundays. J. Ernst, *Die Verlesung der Messperikopen in der Volkssprache* (Separate print from *Theol.-prakt. Monatsschrift,* 1899; Passau, 1899), 14-16.

[6] Origen had incurred the displeasure of his bishop by preaching outside his diocese, even though with the permission of the bishop of the place. About 230 he had himself ordained priest but again, because of his self-mutilation, this was contrary to the canons. O. Bardenhewer, *Geschichte der altkirchlichen Literatur* (2nd ed.; Freiburg, 1914), II, 108 f.

from Antioch—those of Chrysostom. In the fourth century it was the general custom in the East, when several priests were present at the divine service, that each one would preach after the reading; and finally, as a rule the bishop himself.[7]

In other places, the presbyters were not allowed to preach at public gatherings, whereas for the work of catechizing no grade of Orders was required at all. Thus, after the fall of Arius, preaching was forbidden to priests in Alexandria[8]; likewise in North Africa, where the prohibition was not cancelled till the time of St. Augustine who himself was permitted to preach when only a priest. A similar practice obtained for a long time in Rome and in Italy. In fact under Pope Celestine[9] a letter of disapproval was sent out from Rome to the bishops of Provence where a contrary custom was in vogue. Sozomen made it known that in his day, as he thought, no preaching whatsoever was done in Rome.[10] As a matter of fact there is no provision for preaching in the ancient Roman *Ordines*, which (of course) record primarily only the divine service for the major stations.[11] Still the homiletic works of a Leo the Great and of a Gregory the Great prove that this was not altogether a period of absolute silence.[12] From the beginning of the Middle Ages, at any rate, there was in general a strong return to the preaching of the word of God.[13]

---

[7] *Const. Ap.*, II, 57, 9 (Quasten, *Mon.*, 182 f.); *ibid.*, VIII, 5, 12 mentions only the preaching of the bishop.

Likewise the pilgrim lady Aetheria reports regarding Jerusalem that as many of the priests as wanted to preached, but after them came the bishop; *Aetheriæ Peregrinatio*, c. 25, 1 (CSEL, XXXIX, 74); cf. *ibid.*, c. 43, 2 (93). St. John Chrysostom, too, while a priest at Antioch, frequently refers to the fact that after his sermon other addresses would follow, occasionally that of the bishop. Similarly Jerome, in the homilies which he delivered at Bethlehem. See the passages in A. Bludau, *Die Pilgerreise der Ätheria* (Paderborn, 1927), 63 f. Baumstark, *Die Messe im Morgenland*, 98, recognizes in this succession of several speakers an echo of the charismatic preaching of the primitive period.

[8] Socrates, *Hist. eccl.*, V, 22 (PG, LXVII, 640); Sozomen, *Hist. eccl.*, VII, 19 (PG, LXVII, 1476 f.).
[9] Celestine I, *Ep.*, 21, n. 2 (PL, L, 528-530).

[10] *Op. cit.* (PG, LXVII, 1476).
[11] The first Roman descriptions of the Mass which also mention the sermon are: *Ordo eccl. Lateran.* (Fischer, 50, 1. 32; 78; 1. 22; 82, 1. 9); *Ordo Rom XI* (n. 20; PL, LXXVIII, 1033 C) of the 12th century and *Ordo Rom. XIV* (c. 53; PL, LXXVIII, 1162 A, C) of the 14th.

A number of sermons by Innocent III have been handed down. In numerous passages in *Ordo Rom. XV* (circa 1400) the sermon after the Gospel of the papal service is alluded to (PL, LXXVIII, 1274 ff.).

In Germany in the 10th century, in *Ordo Rom. VI*, n. 7 (PL, LXXVIII, 992 A), which had its origin there, the sermon is presumed in the plan of the episcopal service. The Lombard, Bonizo of Sutri (d. c. 1095), *De vita christiana*, II, 51 (ed. Perels, 59), also testifies to the same arrangement.
[12] Cf. also Batiffol, *Leçons*, 137.
[13] In some oriental communities the sermon has long since gone out of use. In the texts of the Coptic Mass, however, the place of the sermon after the Gos-

But if in Christian antiquity the preaching to the assembled congregation was chiefly restricted to the bishop, there resulted from this the clear and indubitable expression of his teaching authority. Furthermore such a restriction was quite necessary because of the none too high ability of the priests. But the restriction was carried through without considerable harm in the well-established provinces of North Africa and middle Italy, where every little town had its own bishopric. In Gaul the case was quite different. There the Council of Vaison (529), at the urgent request of St. Cæsarius,[14] expressly gave the priests in the city and in the country the right to preach[15]; and in case the priest was hindered by sickness, the deacons were to read from the homilies of the Fathers. In fact the ancient commentary on the Gallican Mass has the homily follow the Gospel in the ordinary course of the service; there, apparently, the mere reading of the homiliæ sanctorum was practically on a par with the real sermon.[16] In regard to this latter it was the duty of the preacher (stressed by the author of the Expositio) above all to find, by his own efforts, the proper medium between the language of the people and the pretensions of the more highly educated. And even when the homilies of the Fathers were read, they had to be rendered more or less freely in the language of the people. The Carolingian Reform-Synods of 813 expressly demanded the translation of the homilies in rusticam Romanam linguam aut Theotiscam quo facilius cuncti possint intelligere quæ dicuntur.[17] The requirements of the clergy were supplied by various collections of homilies, such as were prepared for reading at monastic choir prayer (as, for example, those of Paul Warnefried), or others that offered an explanation of the Epistle and Gospels intended directly for the laymen's service.[18] In this modest form the homily must have been used quite regularly in the following centuries even in the country—at least in Germany—in such a way, at any rate, that it shared the Sunday pulpit along with the repetition of the elementary Christian truths taken from the Symbol and the Our Father.[19] The crest of the Middle Ages, and the appearance of the mendicant Orders,

pel is still marked; Brightman, 158, 1. 5.

Regarding the sermon among the West Syrians, see Baumstark, Die Messe im Morgenland, 98.

Among the Greeks the sermon was still zealously practiced during Byzantine times; see A. Ehrhard in K. Krumbacher, Geschichte der byzantinischen Literatur (2nd ed.; Munich, 1897), 160 f.

[14] Cf. Vita Cæsarii, I, 54 (MGH, Scriptores rer. Merov., III, 478 f.).

[15] C. 2 (Mansi, VIII, 727): placuit ut non solum in civitatibus sed etiam in omnibus parochiis verbum faciendi daremus presbyteris potestatem.

[16] Expositio ant. lit. gallicanæ (ed. Quasten, 15 f.) ; cf. Duchesne, 197.

[17] Tours, can. 17 (Mansi, XIV, 85) ; similarly Reims, can. 15 (Mansi, XIV, 78). Cf. H. v. Schubert, Geschichte der christlichen Kirche im Frühmittelalter (Tübingen, 1921), 654. Here also the reference to remnants preserved in the Old French and Old Slovenian languages.

[18] A. Manser, "Homiliar," LThK, V, 128 f.; E. Hosp, "Il sermonario di Alano di Farfa" (Eph. liturg., 1936), 375 f.; Kunze, Die gottesdienstliche Schriftlesung, 147-159.

[19] H. v. Schubert, 652-654.

brought a new blossoming, if not of the homily, then surely of the sermon in general.

Although it would be an exaggeration to say that all church preaching should be limited to the framework of the Mass or perhaps even the homily,[20] still there was from olden times a definite and restrictive pattern for the spiritual talk that followed on the reading, a pattern exacted by the circumstances in which it appeared. The talk was to be about the word of God that had been read from the Sacred Scriptures, it was not to stifle it but to apply it to the present day. Therefore the talk is basically a *homily* —the application of the Scripture just read.[21] To this day, in the ordination of the Lector, his office is still designated as: *legere ei qui prædicat.*[22] This neither is nor was the spot to unfold the entire preaching of the Church. The homily was the living word of the Church taken up into the liturgy as proof of the higher world in which it lives and into which it enters after being renewed by the sacred mysteries.[23]

Hence also the trend to make visible the hierarchical structure of the Church in the person of the homilist. Hence, too, the guarding as much as possible of the liturgical structure even in its outward appearance. As a rule the Bishop talks from his *cathedra*,[24] and, as an expression of his authority, he is seated,[25] or else standing on the steps that lead to the *cathedra.*[26]

---

[20] Cf. the extensive and detailed explanation of the "liturgical sermonette" in Parsch, *Volksliturgie*, 423-441; according to Parsch not only Christian instruction (catechetics) but also evening sermons lie outside the compass of the Mass.

[21] Not necessarily only the Gospel. What Augustine, for instance, as a rule explains in his homilies is "a text of Scripture, usually taken from one of the three lessons"; Roetzer, 109.

[22] The *Pontificale Romanum* selects this wording in preference to the other: *legere ea quæ prædicat*. This last reading, which appears to presume preaching on the part of the lector himself, is indeed to be found in the Roman Pontifical of the 12th century and in that of the 13th (Andrieu, I, 125; II, 330), but the earliest evidence of the formula in Cod. 14 of Vendôme (first half of the 11th century; see Andrieu, *Les ordines Romani*, I, 351 f.) gives us the reading: *legere ei qui prædicat*; see de Puniet, *Das Römische Pontifikale*, I, 283. Only this latter reading is taken into account. True, de Puniet, I, 139, does raise a doubt, referring to Isidore, *De off. eccl.*, II, 11,

where there is mention of *lectores qui verbum Dei prædicant*, but it is to be noted that *prædicare* at that time meant not only "preaching" but also "solemn reading"; see IV Synod of Toledo (633), can. 17 (Mansi, X, 624). Similarly even *Ordo Rom. III*, n. 8 (PL, LXXVIII, 972 A): *prædicante eo* [sc. *diacono*] *evangelium*.

[23] That the sermon in the liturgy is not an *instruction* but an *initiation*, an introduction into the *mysterium*, is stressed by J. Hartog, *The Sacrifice of the Church* (Barrn, 1939), 23 f., 26 ff.

[24] Eisenhofer, I, 382 f.; Dölger, *Antike und Christentum*, I (1929), 61.

[25] Thus, e.g., Augustine (Roetzer, 111 f.). This corresponds to the archeological findings; H. Leclercq, "Chaire épiscopale," DACL, III, 19-75. Following the custom in the synagogue, our Lord himself spoke while seated (Luke 4: 20). Regarding the symbolism of this sitting, see Th. Klauser, *Die Cathedra im Totenkult* (LF, IX; Münster, 1927), 11; 179 ff.

[26] Augustine, *De civ. Dei*, 22, 8 (CSEL, XL, 2, p. 611, 1. 18; Roetzer, 112).

A preacher like Chrysostom of course mounts the ambo for the convenience of his audience.[27] According to a rule of the Egyptian Church, the bishop—but not the priest—holds the Gospel book in his hand.[28]

The revival of the sermon during the height of the Middle Ages involved a separation from the liturgy, and also a departure from its homiletic character. It leaves the confines of the Mass in the form of a mission sermon of the new Orders.[29] Even the stand of the preacher is moved into the body of the church, though it takes with it the old name: in French, for example, it takes the name of the *cathedra* (*chaire*; cf. the German *Predigtstuhl*), and in German the name is derived from the ambo as an extension of the chancel (*Kanzel*), but the English word "pulpit" is a mere descriptive term (from Lt. *pulpitum*, a platform or scaffold).[30] Its site on the Gospel side still shows its connection with the reading of the Gospel.[31] On the other hand, the very high pulpit towering over the heads of the listeners is apparently the result of the impassioned oratorical form of the sermon, a condition that also contributed to the fact that now the preacher generally speaks standing.[32]

Although the teacher was seated, the audience (according to the prevailing custom of the ancient Church) was obliged to hear the lecture while standing. Augustine felt that such a rule was quite a strain during long delivery[33] and therefore he praised the custom followed in other places, *in quibusdam ecclesiis transmarinis*, where the people were seated.[34] Cæsarius of Arles permitted the more feeble people to sit during the sermon or the readings, though they probably used the floor for this.[35] Only the clerics were provided quite generally with seats in those early days.[36] The faithful helped themselves with canes on which to lean.[37] Only in modern times in

---

[27] Eisenhofer, I, 383.

[28] *Canones Basilii*, c. 97 (Riedel, 273).

[29] Honorius of Augustodunum and Sicard of Cremona (d. 1215), however, mention the sermon in the course of the Mass. Eisenhofer, II, 120.

[30] G. Gietmann, "Pulpit," CE, XII: 563-5.

[31] However there is no prescription to this effect.

[32] It might be remarked in this connection that nowadays the "meditations" which are preached at a retreat—suited to the tone of a simple ὁμιλία ("conversation")—are often given while seated. The *Cæremoniale episcoporum*, II, 8, 48, even today presumes that the bishop preaches while seated, whether from the throne (if it is turned to the people) or from the faldstool which is set on the *suppedaneum* of the altar. Likewise the

priest, too, might preach, sitting at the Gospel-side of the altar; see Gavanti-Merati, *Thesaurus*, II, 6, 6 (I, 247 f.). But we must remark that pacing up and down while preaching is often determined and affected by the antics customary in profane speaking.

[33] Augustine, *De catech. rud.*, I, 13, 19 (PL, XL, 325).

[34] In the earliest times seats in church are often mentioned; see H. Achelis, *Das Christentum in den ersten drei Jahrhunderten* (Leipzig, 1912), II, 61, note 4.

[35] Cæsarius of Arles, *Serm.*, 78, 1 (Morin, 309; PL, XXXIX, 2319). Cf. *supra*, p. 240.

[36] *Ordo Rom. I*, n. 4 (PL, LXXVIII, 939). Cf. *supra*, p. 70.

[37] *Supra*, p. 448.

our countries did the laity obtain pews, perhaps copying the Protestant churches.[38]

As a simple homily, the address of the celebrant could follow upon the reading of the Gospel without any further intermediary or any special prayer-introduction. The preacher addressed the people at the beginning and end of his sermon with the usual greeting[39] and began his delivery. Toward the end of the Middle Ages, however, it was the practice for the preacher to begin with an *Ave Maria* while everybody knelt.[40] The custom is possibly traceable to the mendicant preachers. It is prescribed in the *Cæremoniale episcoporum*[41] and seems to have been in use for a long time within the Mass.[42] Alongside of the *Ave*, however, the *Veni, Sancte Spiritus* or the Lord's Prayer was also permitted.[43]

Together with the prayer-introduction in this or that form, there was often also a special song to introduce the sermon, taken over from the independent sermon and adapted here to the sermon that followed the readings at Mass. The patterns that thus arise remind us of the preparatory prayers or songs which precede the readings in the oriental liturgies.[44] And contrariwise, the independent Sunday parochial sermon at times had a very rich prayer ending, the basis of which was borrowed for its connection with the Mass or more precisely (as we shall see), taken from the old "Prayer of the Faithful."

8. The Credo

On Sundays and on certain feast days the last lesson (or the homily, as the case may be) is followed by the *Credo* as a sort of re-enforced echo. Although it is but a supplement on these days, still it gets such a performance at solemn service that both in duration and in musical splendor it

---

[38] Eisenhofer, I, 379 f.; cf. H. Bergner, "Ausstattung, kirchliche," *Religion in Geschichte und Gegenwart* (1909), I, 811-813.

[39] Illustrations from Chrysostom, see Brightman, 470, 476 f. Notice there, 470, 1. 37, the doxological ending which was a fixed rule in the ancient Christian sermon as in prayer.

Compare the custom in German-speaking lands, of starting and ending the sermon with *"Gelobt sei Jesus Christus"* (Praised by Jesus Christ). Or the practice of making the sign of the Cross with the Trinitarian formula before and after the talk.

[40] *Ordo Rom. XV* (c. 1400), n. 43 (PL, LXXVIII, 1295 A).

[41] I, 22, 3.

[42] In France the *Ave* was inserted after the exordium of the sermon; J. Mabillon in the note to *Ordo Rom. XV*, n. 43 (PL, LXXVIII, 1295). J. M. Cavalieri, *Commentaria*, V (1764), 32, still stresses the obligation of this prayer.

[43] Thus Jerome Dungersheym in a writing of his which appeared ab. 1514, *De arte prædicandi;* see R. Cruel, *Geschichte der deutschen Predigt im Mittelalter* (Detmold, 1879), 232.

[44] *Supra*, p. 406 f.

In the later Middle Ages a song (*Ruf* or *Leis*) was sung at the end of the sermon. Regarding German hymns before and after the sermon, see W. Bäumker, *Zur Geschichte der Tonkunst* (Freiburg, 1881), 133.

often surpasses all the other portions of the Mass. It is precisely in this role of the *Credo* at the high Mass that a contrast is marked out—despite its import, the *Credo* offers the great masters of music only a simple and rather unpoetic verbal text. In addition, this text is stylized as the profession of an individual *(Credo, Confiteor)*, exactly like other professions of faith. All the more reason to ask, why this formula of profession of faith secured the singular honor of being used at the celebration of Mass.

Our symbol was not composed just for the Mass. It first appears in the acts of the Council of Chalcedon (451) as the profession of "the 150 holy fathers who were assembled in Constantinople."[1] As time passed the symbol was taken as a compilation summing up the belief proclaimed at the preceding councils of Nicea (325) and Constantinople (381) ; this is borne out by the current name of Nicene or Niceno-Constantinopolitan Creed. Not that its wording was immediately formulated by these councils. The symbol drawn up at Nicea,[2] which concludes with the words *Et in Spiritum Sanctum*—only an anathema follows—does not coincide exactly with our *Credo* even in the foregoing parts. In the acts of the Council of Constantinople no symbol whatever was handed down and in the interval till Chalcedon there is never a reference to any such profession of faith drawn up there.[3] The only matter ascribed to the synod at Constantinople is the expansion of the statement regarding the Holy Ghost.[4]

In the Niceno-Constantinopolitan symbol we have the draft of a profession which, of all the various forms in use in the episcopal cities of the East, gained the widest acceptance, particularly after the approval accorded it at the Council of Chalcedon.[5] We can track this draft even a little distance back into the fourth century. We discover it, almost complete, about 374 in Epiphanius,[6] and, in a slightly simpler form, about 350 in Cyril of

---

[1] Mansi, VI, 957 and again VII, 112 (only two linguistic variants). A different text is offered in the critical edition of E. Schwartz, *Acta conciliorum oecum.,* II, 1, 2 (Berlin, 1933), 128, where, among others, the phrases φῶς ἐκ φωτός, καὶ παθόντα, κατὰ τὰς γραφάς and the ἁγίαν before the word Church—all these are missing. According to Schwartz it was the insertion of these phrases and words that produced the new formulation of the symbol undertaken by Chalcedon; the older text he thinks can be traced to the Council of Constantinople; see E. Schwartz, "Das Nicænum und das Constantinopolitanum auf der Synode von Chalkedon," *Zeitschrift f. d. neutest. Wissenschaft,* XXV (1926), 38-88. Opposed to both these hypotheses is J. Lebon, "Les anciens symboles dans la définition de Chalcédoine," *Revue d'hist.*

eccl., XXXII (1936), 809-876. Cf. also B. Capelle, "Le Credo," *Cours et Conferences,* VI (Louvain, 1928), 171-184.
[2] Denzinger-Umberg, n. 54.
[3] Lebon, 847 ff. The only name ever used for the creed was "the confession of Nicea," but in various church provinces this creed was enlarged by various additions (Lebon, 837 ff.). One such expanded version was proposed to the Council of 451 by the representatives of the imperial court as the confession "of the 150 holy Fathers" (855 ff.).
[4] Lebon, 860, 870.
[5] A. Hahn, *Bibliothek der Symbole* (3rd. ed., Breslau, 1897); H. Lietzmann, *Symbole der alten Kirche* (4th ed.; *Kleine Texte,* 17-18; Berlin, 1935).
[6] Epiphanius, *Ancoratus,* c. 118 (Lietzmann, *Symbole,* 19 f.).

Jerusalem, who explained it to his candidates for Baptism.[7] We may therefore see in this basic text of the Niceno-Constantinopolitanum the ancient baptismal symbol of Jerusalem.[8] Our Mass *Credo* thus had originally the same purpose which our Roman "Apostles' Creed" had, the same purpose which it still serves at present, namely, as a profession of faith before Baptism. That is the reason why even in its original form the Mass Creed, like the Apostles', is set in the singular: *Credo*.

In the two texts mentioned we clearly have the typical instances of the basic form of the profession of faith in West and East. And these in turn give us an inkling of the common design underlying both. In both cases the content of our belief falls into three sections, comprising our belief in God the Creator, in Christ our Lord, and in the goods of salvation. And what is more to the point in a baptismal profession, these three sections are linked with the naming of the three divine Persons. Further, in both of these main forms the second section is enlarged through the inclusion of a more detailed profession of Christ. A peculiarity of the oriental type is that its structure was influenced not only by the command to baptize (Matt. 28:19) but also by a second scripture text, Eph. 4:4, which emphasizes the praise of unity: "one body and one spirit . . . one Lord, one faith, one baptism, one God and Father of all." This is the apparent clue to the stressing of oneness in this symbol: *Credo in unum Deum . . . in unum Dominum . . . in unam sanctam catholicam et apostolicam Ecclesiam . . . Confiteor unum baptisma.*[9] With a certain pride the contrast is drawn between the division caused by error and the oneness of God and the oneness of his revelation in Christ, Church and Sacrament.

The design of the *Credo* will probably be rendered clearer in the following abstract, in which the texts of the older drafts are also indicated:

CREDO IN UNUM DEUM, PATREM OMNIPOTENTEM, FACTOREM CŒLI ET TERRÆ,
  VISIBILIUM OMNIUM ET INVISIBILIUM.
  ET IN UNUM DOMINUM JESUM CHRISTUM, FILIUM DEI UNIGENITUM
    et EX PATRE NATUM ANTE OMNIA SÆCULA,
      Deum de Deo, *lumen de lumine, Deum verum de Deo vero,*
      genitum non factum,
      consubstantialem Patri,
      PER QUEM OMNIA FACTA SUNT.
    Qui propter nos homines et propter nostram salutem descendit de cœlis et
    incarnatus est de Spiritu Sancto ex *Maria virgine et* HOMO FACTUS EST.
    CRUCIFIXUS *etiam pro nobis sub Pontio Pilato, passus et sepultus est.*

[7] Cyril of Jerusalem, *Cateheses,* VII-XVIII (Lietzmann, *Symbole,* 19).

[8] F. Kattenbusch, *Das Apolostische Symbol* (Leipzig, 1894), I, 233-244.

[9] The Pauline expression "one Spirit" is wanting in the wording of our symbol, but it is found in its antecedent, the symbol of Jerusalem: εἰς ἓν ἅγιον πνεῦμα (Lietzmann, *Symbole,* 19) as well as in the recension which is used in the Syrian liturgy (Hanssens, III, 298).

Et RESURREXIT TERTIA DIE *secundum* Scripturas, ET ASCENDIT IN CŒLum,
SEDET AD DEXTERAM PATRIS
ET ITERUM VENTURUS EST CUM GLORIA IUDICARE VIVOS ET MORTUOS, CUIUS
REGNI
NON ERIT FINIS.
ET IN SPIRITUM SANCTUM, *dominum et vivificantem,*
qui ex Patre Filioque *procedit, qui cum Patre et Filio simul adoratur*
et conglorificatur,
QUI LOCUTUS EST PER PROPHETAS.
ET UNAM SANCTAM CATHOLICAM *et apostolicam* ECCLESIAM.
Confiteor UNUM BAPTISMA IN REMISSIONEM PECCATORUM.
Et *expecto* RESURRECTIONEM *mortuorum* ET VITAM *venturi sæculi. Amen.*[20]

The character of this symbol is distinguished by one trait—its theological clarity. While in our Apostles' Creed the faith is asserted simply and forthrightly, in this by contrast we have a theological and polemical profession aimed at giving orthodoxy a clear exposition.[21] Still, after comparing this with other oriental forms of the symbol, we come to recognize the fact that but a few of the phrases are the result of the struggles of the fourth century. In the christological section these are the words *Deum verum de Deo vero, genitum non factum, consubstantialem Patri,* words with which the Council of Nicea had countered the heresy of Arius.[22] All the other statements circumscribing the divinity of Christ are found in the baptismal confessions, and even where they are wanting in that of Jerusalem, they are contained in the more ancient one of Eusebius of Cæsarea (d. 340), who for his part was never suspected of having gone too far in any opposition to the Arians.[23] But in contrast to this, all the older baptismal professions contained only one assertion regarding the Holy Ghost: *Qui locutus est per prophetas.* Everything else was occasioned by the struggle against the Macedonians who drew the conclusions inherent in the Arian doctrine of the Logos and denied also the divinity of the Holy Ghost. Still the more complete profession regarding the Holy Ghost in its present-day wording appeared (as we can see above), in the symbol of St. Epiphanius even before the solemn condemnation of this heresy which took place at the Council of Constantinople (381).[24]

Even aside from these additions which were first incorporated in opposition to heresy,[25] there still remains in this Mass *Credo,* compared with

[20] The text as found in Epiphanius is printed in small capitals; the parts already attested by Cyril of Jerusalem are in italics.
No account is taken of those additions in Epiphanius or Cyril which have not survived in the received version.
[21] Capelle, *Le Credo,* 173.
[22] Denzinger-Umberg, n. 54.
[23] Lietzmann, *Symbole,* 18; in Eusebius also the phrase: *Deum de Deo.*

[24] Macedonius was already condemned in 360 at a synod in Constantinople.
[25] The form which is basic to all oriental symbols is reconstructed by H. Lietzmann as follows: "I believe in one God, the Father, the Almighty, the Creator of everything visible and invisible. And in one Lord Jesus Christ, the only-begotten Son of God, who was born from the Father before all eons, through whom all was made, who for our salvation's sake

the extreme terseness of our Apostles' Creed, a notable wealth of statement which serves not so much to oppose heresy as rather to unfold the contents of our faith. In the very first assertion about "God the Creator of heaven and earth," the creation is described by a second double phrase "of all things visible and invisible."

But in this basic text one point is given special prominence, the divinity of Christ. In its kerygma of Christ, our Apostles' Creed also goes into detail regarding the mystery of the person of our Lord whom it introduces as the only-begotten Son of God; He was born of the Virgin Mary, conceived by the Holy Ghost. But these assertions refer immediately to His human nature, even if its wonderful origin suggests His godhead. The oriental *Credo*, however, adverts at once expressly to the eternal divinity of the Logos: "Born of the Father before all ages, God of God, light of light, through whom all things were made." Only the last phrase is taken word for word from St. John (1:3), but in the rest we can detect the tone of his language.[16] The additions which the Nicene Creed here embodies, expressing with inexorable lucidity the uncreated divinity of Christ and His essential unity with the Father, dovetail easily with the rest even stylistically, despite the unavoidable abstractness of the ideas. They round out the profession of faith into a tiny hymn.

The additional assertions which describe the entrance of the Logos into the world and His assumption of a human nature from the Virgin wind up the picture of the mysterious person of the Redeemer. One significant feature is the prominence given here to the work of salvation: "for us men and for our salvation came down down from heaven." Rightly does this article become the center and turning point of the whole creed. In His mercy God wanted it that way, and so the inconceivable became a reality. We therefore fall upon our knees at the words *Et incarnatus est*, in awe of the mystery.[17] Some of the grandest creations of ecclesiastical music have

became man, suffered and rose again on the third day and ascended into the heavens and will come again in majesty to judge the living and the dead. And in the Holy Ghost." H. Lietzmann, "Apostolikum," *Die Religion in Geschichte und Gegenwart* (2nd ed.,) (1927), I, 445.

[16] For the expression φῶς ἐκ φωτός cf. Justin, *Dial.*, c. 61 (PG, VI, 616 A).

[17] This genuflection is mentioned as being done by many, in Radulph de Rivo (d. 1403), *De canonum observ., prop.* 23 (Mohlberg, II, 141 f.), but it is opposed by him as a novelty. However it is already mentioned in Durandus, IV, 25, 10. Reference to it also occurs in the Statutes of the Carthusians: Martène, 1, 4, XXV

(I, 632 C); with them, however, even today, the celebrant himself here only kisses the altar: *Ordinarium Cart.* (1932), c. 26, 18.

A decision of Peter of Cluny (d. 1156) calls the genuflection at the singing of the words *et homo factus est* a custom which *longo iam usu* is observed almost everywhere (PL, CLXXXIX, 1027). As a matter of fact it is assumed in the *Liber usuum Θ. Cist.,* c. 56 (PL, CLXVI, 1431). The Premonstratensians, too, followed the practice already towards the end of the 12th century (Lefèvre, 21). In this case the genuflection was later lengthened out up to the words *et sepultus est*, as is still done at present (Waefelghem, 121, note O). This use of a genu-

here made the devout offering of their greatest endeavor, in the effort to help us conceive the meaning of that tremendous descent of the Son of God from heaven to bring peace to earth.

After the mystery of the person of the God-man is thus sketched out, the *Credo* turns to His work, which is again clearly designated in two steps: first the lowly path of pain and the cross and the grave (with a stressing of *pro nobis*), then the victorious surge of His Resurrection "according to the Scriptures," which even in the Old Testament had announced the concluding triumph of the Messias,[18] His return to the glory of His Father, His judgment, and His kingdom without end, as these were already foretold in the message of the angel.[19]

The third section of the symbol surveys the fruit which has become ours as a result of the work of redemption. In various texts of the ancient Church the first thing mentioned in this connection is the Holy Ghost, who is poured out over the believing congregation.[20] This concept is likewise to be supposed in the basic form of our symbol. That He had already spoken through the prophéts[21] was the start of His activity. Its completion is the bestowal of the new life, as is added in the later supplement to the older text of the symbol.[22] This supplement also takes into account His divinity; He is the Lord.[23] He proceeds from the Father and from the Son.[24] Right-

---

flection therefore obviously originated as early as the 11th century.

[18] The expression *secundum Scripturas*, as well as the words that follow, *qui locutus est per prophetas*, corresponds to the era of the Apologists of the 2-3rd century who were very much concerned to show the agreement between the acts of our Saviour and the prophecies of the Old Testament. Cf. J. Creyghton, *Credo* (Hertogenbosch, 1941), 25-27.

[19] Luke 1: 33.

[20] Jungmann, *Gewordene Liturgie*, 178 f.

[21] This characterization of the Holy Ghost recurs frequently even in the 2nd century, especially in Irenæus, e.g. *Epid.*, c. 42; J. Brinktrine, "Beiträge zur Entstehung und Geschichte des Credo," *Eph. liturg.*, XLII (1928), 48-58.

[22] The expression ζωοποιός goes back to John 6: 63; 1 Cor. 15: 45; 2 Cor. 3: 6. It is found early in Egypt (Brinktrine, "Beiträge," 52 f.) and also in Syria. Here is the wording at the bottom of the newly-discovered Catecheses of Theodore of Mopsuestia (d. 428): Καὶ εἰς ἓν πνεῦμα ἅγιον, τὸ ἐκ τοῦ πατρὸς ἐκπορευόμενον, πνεῦμα ζωοποιόν (the Church follows);

A. Rücker, *Ritus baptismi et missæ quem descripsit Theodorus ep. Mopsuestenus* (Münster, 1933), 43 f.

[23] The Greek word κύριον which corresponds to the Latin *Dominum* seems to be meant as an *adjective*, like the preceding ζωοποιόν. It would then· mean something like "divine". Brinktrine, "Beiträge," 51, explains the insertion of the words as resting on the formula Εἷς ἅγιος, εἷς κύριος. But cf. the phrase in the *Athanasianum*: *Dominus Pater, dominus Filius, dominus Spiritus Sanctus*.

[24] The *Filioque*, which corresponds to a theological confession already discussed in Augustine, was incorporated into the symbol in Spanish territories in the 5th or 6th century. Still there were Latin versions which did not contain this addition, and they were widely circulated. Even Leo III (d. 816) disapproved (for disciplinary reasons) its insertion. The Greeks opposed it since Photius (869), claiming it to be heretical. Since the 11th century, however, it had a firm place in the Latin text of the *Credo*. E. Krebs, "Filioque," LThK, III, 1039 f.

fully is He given in the doxology the same adoration and the same honor as the other two.²⁵ The series of predications seems to have been dictated mainly by certain formal considerations, as the Greek text indicates more clearly.²⁶

After the mention of the Holy Ghost there follows in nearly all the creeds—and here, too—the mention of the Church which is inspired and vitalized by His activity. It is one, as God is one, and as Christ is one. This one Church, to which we pledge ourselves, is holy, because it is filled by the Holy Ghost²⁷; it is catholic, because it stands open to all peoples²⁸; it is apostolic, because it rests on the foundation of the Apostles.²⁹ The Church transfers its own life to its children by means of the sacraments. Baptism, mentioned in the creed, stands for all the others which are based on it. In fact Confirmation and the Eucharist are linked with it. Its wonderful efficacy in taking away sin was mentioned by our Lord Himself amongst the basic elements of the glad tidings.³⁰ A prospect of our final transformation to the likeness of the Risen One in the resurrection from the dead and in the life of eons to come—with this the creed concludes. The outpouring of the Spirit, holy Church, sacrament, glorious resurrection—that is the way by which the new creation and the new creature reach their perfection.

This symbol was in use at Constantinople as a baptismal creed formula. Here on Good Friday it was also pronounced at public worship while the bishop catechized the candidates for Baptism.³¹. The same historian who

According to W. M. Peitz, *Das vorephesinische Symbol der Papstkanzlei* (Rome, 1939), 46-50, a formula of the confession of the Roman Church which is preserved in the *Liber diurnus* (PL, CV, 57 f.) must have contained the *Filioque* even before 400 (57 A).

It might be noted that Greek Catholics need not insert the phrase in their traditional liturgical symbol.

²⁵ The συνδοξαζόμενον obviously goes back above all to a form of the doxology which gained ground since the middle of the 4th century: (Christus) μεθ' οὗ σοι ἡ δόξα σὺν ἁγίῳ πνεύματι, by which the older δι' οὗ... ἐν ἁγίῳ πνεύματι was supplanted. It was directed against the heresy of the Arians and the Macedonians. Jungmann, *Die Stellung Christi*, 158 f., 162 ff.

²⁶ First three adjectives, τὸ ἅγιον, τὸ κύριον, τὸ ζωοποιόν, then the fuller statements. Brinktrine, *Die hl. Messe*, 113.

²⁷ This connection is visibly intimated in the older form of the Roman symbol: Καὶ εἰς πνεῦμα ἅγιον, ἁγίαν ἐκκλησίαν. Lietzmann, *Symbole*, 10. "Holy" is here the only qualifying word for Church, a word for which there is also other very early evidence.

²⁸ F. Kattenbusch, *Das Apolostische Symbol* (Leipzig, 1900), II, 922 ff.

²⁹ This attribute of the Church is first found in Egypt at the start of the 4th century, apparently confined in the beginning to congregations founded by the Apostles. Brinktrine, "Beiträge," 56.

³⁰ Luke 24: 47; cf. Acts 2: 38; 10: 43; 13: 38; 26: 18.

³¹ Thus still today in the Byzantine liturgy. At Rome too, from the time of the Byzantine ascendancy on, the Niceno-Constantinopolitanum was for a long time used at the Easter baptismal rites, and provision was made for its being recited in both Latin and Greek. Duchesne, *Christian Worship*, 301.

mentions this[32] also records that Timotheus, the Patriarch of this city (511-517), a man whose thinking was tainted with Monophysitism, was the first to order the symbol recited at every Mass. He did this in order to put his Catholic predecessors to shame and to emphasize his own zeal for the truth.[33] This example was soon aped everywhere in the Orient. Thus the symbol attained a place in every Mass in all the oriental liturgies.[34] Usually it was the Niceno-Constantinopolitan that was thus taken up,[35] but not without a number of rather significant variants.[36] However, it is not placed right after the Gospel,[37] but only after the Prayer of the Faithful and the Great Entry, either before or after the kiss of peace—a location that makes it less a conclusion to the fore-Mass than rather a foundation and start for the sacrifice.[38] Since the symbol was restricted by the *disciplina arcani*, it is not by chance that the dismissal of the catechumens (the formula for which has retained its ancient place in most rites of the East) had to precede.[39]

The symbol is, as a rule, spoken by the people—thus in the Egyptian liturgies and mostly also in the Byzantine.[40] Or it is spoken by a representative of the people.[41] But it is never said by the priest,[42] and it is never sung.[43] In most of the oriental liturgies—but not in all[44]—the communion

---

[32] Theodorus Lector, *Hist. eccl. Fragm.*, II, 32 (PG, LXXXVI, 201).

[33] The account that, a generation earlier, Petrus Fullo (476-488), Monophysite Patriarch of Antioch, had given such an order, is also found in the same historian's book (II, 48; PG, LXXXVI, 209), but appears to be a later interpolation and without historical value; Capelle, *Le Credo*, 174 f. Still it must be observed that Pseudo-Dionysius, *De eccl. hierarchia*, III, 3, 7 (Quasten, *Mon.*, 305 f.), talks about the use of the symbol at Mass; it must therefore have been current in Syria at latest about 515.

[34] Hanssens, III, 293-308.

[35] One exception is the East Syrian liturgy which uses an ancient Syrian baptismal symbol, the same as that attested by Theodore of Mopsuestia (cf. note 22 above). Also in the Ethiopian Mass a special symbol is used in part. Hanssens, III, 295 f.

[36] Hanssens, III, 297-299.

[37] Outside the later Armenian liturgy, which is influenced by the Roman; Hanssens, III, 303.

[38] The same place was occupied, it seems by the so-called *Mystagogia*, a symbol-

like outline of the teachings of faith with special emphasis on the Easter mystery. It is handed down in a somewhat different version in Egyptian and Syrian sources, among them the *Testamentum Domini* (I, 28), and was to be said on the highest feast-days after the departure of the catechumens *ante oblationem, ante sanctam liturgiam*. Text with parallels in Quasten, *Monument.*, 242-249.

[39] In the Byzantine Mass the symbol was preceded in addition by a special warning: Τὰς θύρας, τὰς θύρας! Brightman, 383.

[40] Brightman, 162, 226, 383.

[41] Some of the editions of the Byzantine liturgy assign the symbol to the lector. Thus also it is said by a lector in the Byzantine-Slavic liturgy of the uniat Ukrainians. At the court of the Byzantine Patriarchs the Great Logothet was the chief of the laity permitted to recite the symbol during the liturgy. K. Lübeck, *Die Christlichen Kirchen des Orients* (Kempten, 1911), 65.

[42] Outside the Syrian liturgies. Hanssens, III, 294.

[43] Baumstark, *Die Messe im Morgenland*, 174.

[44] Except, that is, in the Byzantine and the Jacobite liturgies. Hanssens, III, 297 f.

of all the faithful is given expression by means of the plural form: we believe, we profess. It is also usually heralded by a call from the deacon.

In the same century in which the Niceno-Constantinopolitanum was for the first time admitted into the Mass in the Orient, it appears also in a similar employ in Spain, a portion of whose coastline was under Byzantine domination. When in 589 King Reccared and his Visigoths renounced Arianism, they made their profession of faith in this creed and it was then ordered said by all the people at every Mass right before the *Pater noster* so that, before the Body and Blood of the Lord were received, the hearts of all might be purified by faith.[45] Thus the symbol here shares in the function of the *Pater noster* as a prayer of preparation for Communion; this was the position it also held, in passing, in the Byzantine Mass,[46] and still holds today in the rite of Communion for the sick.

Two centuries later the creed also makes an appearance in France, just about the time that a reaction was setting in against the last offshoot of christological error, the Adoptionism of the Spanish bishops Elipandus and Felix who had been condemned at various synods since 792. It must have been about this time that Charlemagne introduced the symbol in his palace chapel at Aachen.[47] Various indications point to the theory that the custom came to the Irish from the Spaniards, and was by them carried to the Anglo-Saxons and so, through Alcuin, the custom reached Aachen.[48] In Aachen the symbol was sung after the Gospel. Charlemagne obtained the consent of Pope Leo III to his innovation, perhaps with the subsequent restriction to leave out the *Filioque*. But the custom took long to spread. Of the Carolingian sources of the ninth century a few mention it, others appear to know nothing about it.[49] Not till the next century did it become general in the North. When the emperor Henry II came to Rome in 1014 he was surprised that at Rome the *Credo* was lacking in the Mass. The Roman clerics explained to him that the Roman Church had never been

[45] C. 2 (Mansi, IX, 993).

This place also in the present Mozarabic Mass of the *Missale mixtum* (PL, LXXXV, 556 f.). The priest here sings: *Fidem quam corde credimus, ore autem dicamus,* and lifts the Body of the Lord aloft so that it can be seen by all the people. Then the choir begins: *Credimus in unum Deum.* The text shows several variants from ours.

[46] The pertinent decree of Emperor Justin II (d. 578) is transmitted to us by John of Biclaro, *Chron.* (PL, LXXII, 863 B); cf. Jungmann, *Gewordene Liturgie,* 153, note 64.

[47] Capelle, *Le Credo,* 178 f. But a new translation was used, one which probably

stems from Paulinus of Aquileia. It is more careful than that in the *Missale mixtum;* B. Capelle, "L'origine anti-adoptianiste de notre texte du symbole de la messe," *Recherches de théol. ancienne et médiévale* (1929), I, 7-20. Regarding textual variants see Fiala, 221.

[48] B. Capelle, "Alcuin et l'histoire du symbole de la messe," *Recherches de théol. ancienne et médiévale* (1934), VI, 249-260. Remaining doubts indicated by Th. Klauser, JL, XIV (1938), 453 f.

[49] The illustrations in Capelle, *Le Credo,* 180 f. What Walafrid Strabo, *De exord. et increm.,* c. 22 (PL, CXIV, 947), says about the spread of the *Credo* is, to say the least, inexact; Capelle, 178.

disturbed by error and therefore had no reason to profess the *Credo* so often. However the pope, Benedict VIII, gave in to the emperor's importunings.[50] Still an instruction must have issued from Rome, restricting the *Credo* to Sundays and to those feasts of which mention is made in the symbol.[51] As such the feasts of our Lord from Christmas to Pentecost are named, those of the Blessed Virgin, of the Apostles,[52] of All Saints and the Dedication of a Church.[53] The principle of selection, namely, *quorum in symbolo fit mentio*,[54] recurs regularly in the liturgical commentators of the twelfth and thirteenth centuries.[55] Gradually, however, other regulations were adopted till, with Burchard of Strassburg, the present-day rule came into being, according to which only the feasts of martyrs, virgins and confessors are without a *Credo*.[56] Of the confessors, the Doctors of the Church —whose number, before Pius V, was restricted to the "Four great Doctors" (Ambrose, Jerome, Augustine and Gregory the Great)—took a place next to the Apostles as outstanding heralds of the faith to whom a *Credo* was due. And even the feast days of the other saints had the creed when they were celebrated with special solemnity. The *Credo* was thus conceived simply as a means of enhancing the festivity.[57]

Our *Credo* was therefore originally a profession of faith at Baptism; one vestige of this, in the draft of the creed as we know it, is the singular in the formula: *credo*. Just as before Baptism, so here, too, it is the individual

---

[50] As an immediate witness we have Abbot Berno of Reichenau, *De quibusdam rebus ad missæ officium spectantibus*, c. 2 (PL, CXLII, 1060 f.): The pope ordered *ut ad publicam missam illud decantarent*. Many have thought that the *Credo* must have belonged to the Mass much earlier; among them Mabillon; more recently F. Probst, *Die abendländische Messe* (Münster, 1896), 129; Wagner, *Einführung*, I, 103; cf. also Fortescue, *The Mass*, 288. But this is a misunderstanding; Capelle, *Le Credo*, 180 and note 25. *Ordo Rom. II*, n. 9 (PL, LXXVIII, 972), cannot be considered as evidence since this *Ordo* is not Roman.

However, the *Credo* does seem to have been in use at Beneventum in the 8th century. From here it went to Aachen; this is the opinion of R. J. Hesbert, "L'Antiphonale missarum de l'ancien rit bénéventain," *Eph. liturg.*, LII (1938), 36-40.

[51] Bernold, *Micrologus*, c. 46 (PL, CLI, 1011 f.), and contemporaneously in the Missal of St. Thierry (11th century); Capelle, 181 f.

[52] Because of the *apostolica Ecclesia;* Durandus, IV, 25, 13.

[53] All Saints' was accounted a feast of dedication and therefore of the church; Durandus, *loc. cit.*

A very extensive list is presented in the Missal of St. Vincent (Fiala, 202).

[54] John Beleth, *Explicatio*, c. 40 (PL, CCII, 49).

[55] In some details the interpretations were at variance, thus in regard to the Evangelists. Some wanted to allow John the Baptist a *Credo* because he was "more than a prophet" (cf.: *qui locutus est per prophetas*). For the angels the words *creatorem coeli* were made to do, for Mary Magdalen the fact that she was *apostola apostolorum;* Durandus, IV, 25, 13. Cf. also Radulph de Rivo, *De can. observ.*, prop. 23 (Mohlberg, II, 141).

[56] Capelle, *Le Credo*, 183.

[57] Thus today three titles are taken into account as reason for the *Credo*, namely *mysterium, doctrina, solemnitas*. Gihr, 529-533. For details see Gavanti-Merati, *Thesaurus*, I, 11 (I, 111-118).

who professes his faith. But it is also a profession influenced by the war against the christological heresies. Because of these its statements were augmented, and it was set up as a barrier against them even in the celebration of Mass, first of all in those lands which had become the battleground. By the subsequent restriction to certain days—days which show a certain internal relation to the contents of the symbol—a middle way was found between the early almost belligerent affirmation of the right belief and the calm inwardness of prayer to almighty God—a solution which in a certain sense bespeaks the peace which the Roman Church has continued to maintain, ever vigilant for the purity of faith, yet never permitting the movement of prayer and worship to be disturbed by loud protests against heresy. Thus the creed, the profession of faith, is simply the conclusion of the reading service, the joyous "yes" of the faithful to the message they have received. Even when viewed in its systematic setting, the creed is an organic extension of the line begun in the readings. Just as the sermon is joined to the lessons on certain occasions to further the teaching of God's word through His Church, so on appointed days the catechetic and theological formulation of that teaching is likewise annexed. And so the profession of faith forms a solemn entrance-gate to the Mass of the Faithful.

The *Credo* was introduced into the Mass as the avowal of the whole believing congregation. Necessarily, then, it ought to be spoken by the whole congregation. In the East this was as a general rule always maintained, and at the start also in Spain. In France, too, the same idea was kept in mind—the priest intoned the creed[58] while standing at the center of the altar[59]; and the people carried it through to the end. Bishop Herard of Tours, in 858, lists the *credulitas* along with *Sanctus* and *Kyrie* as texts to be sung devoutly by all.[60] More unequivocal is a decree of Bishop Walter of Orleans, of the year 871.[61] The Mass commentators of the period also ascribe the *Credo* to the people,[62] and even at a much later time it con-

---

[58] This intonation takes the place of the invitation which is elsewhere customary; see note 45 above. The accompanying gesture, spreading, lifting and folding the hands, is exacted (as for the *Gloria*) in the *Ordinarium O.P.* of 1256 (Guerrini, 238). Cf. Durandus, IV, 25, 4, who also mentions the sign of the Cross at the close.

[59] While, according to the Roman rite, the *Credo* is recited by the priest in its entirety at the center of the altar, in the Dominican rite the priest returns to the Gospel side after intoning the creed and continues it there. But the *Et incarnatus est*, like the start, is said at the

center; *Missale iuxta ritum O.P.* (1889), 18. This movement seems to be a late medieval custom, since the Dominican Missal of the 13th century in Legg, *Tracts*, 77, and the *Ordinarium O.P.* of 1256 (Guerrini, 238) do not contain it.

[60] See *supra*, p. 343, note 53.

[61] *Ut Gloria Patri et Filio et Spiritui Sancto et Credo in unum Deum apud omnes in missa decantetur.* Martène, 1, 4, 5, 10 (I, 383 A).

[62] Amalar, *Expositio* of 813-14, ed. Hanssens (*Eph. liturg.*, 1927), 163 (= Gerbert, *Monumenta*, II, 152): *Postquam Christus locutus est populo suo fas est ut dulcius et intentius profiteatur credulitatem*

tinued in many places to be entrusted to them.[63]

When one considers how much trouble must have been taken during the era of the Carolingian reform to teach the people to recite the simple Apostles' Creed in the vernacular, it is easy to imagine what results were achieved with the much longer—and still Latin!—*Credo* in the Mass. A practicable way out—a solution which agrees with that followed sometimes in the Orient—was to have the faithful recite the symbol they knew. This seems to have been tried in northern France during the twelfth century,[64] but whether or not the vernacular was used is not certain.[65] At any rate the attempt was not very widespread at that time, though nowadays the practice is again being introduced in many places in the dialogue Mass.

The difficulty of having the people perform the *Credo* was all the greater when—contrary to the practice usual in the Orient—the words were to be sung.[66] True, *Credo*-songs played a conspicuous role in vernacular singing,[67] but right now we are concerned with the Latin text of the symbol.

---

suam. . . . Sicque convenit populum post evangelium, quia Christi verba audivit, intentionem credulitatis suæ præclaro ore proferre. The same in *Ecloga* (PL, CV, 1323); cf. also *Expositio 'Missa pro multis'*, ed. Hanssens (*Eph. liturg.*, 1930), 36.

[63] *Ordo eccl. Lateran.* (Fischer, 82, 1. 14): *Ab universis sc. clero et populo communiter decantetur.*

In France it is still occasionally sung by all the people, a special melody being used in this case.

[64] Ivo of Chartres, *De conven. vet. et novi sacrif.* (PL, CLXII, 550 B): *Post evangelium profitetur Ecclesia fidem suam cantando symbolum Apostolicum.* Still the term *Apostolicum* is not unambiguous. In the *Missa Illyrica* it stands for our Mass creed; Martène, 1, 4, IV (I, 505 D); cf. Ebner, 80, note. But it is striking that the Apostle's Creed is actually marked with neum signs in certain MSS. (St. Gall, Rheinau, Winchester); it is therefore intended for singing, but the words are in Greek, with Latin letters; Wagner, I, 102, note 5. It therefore belongs obviously in the series of Greek Mass chants which were mentioned *supra*, p. 91, note 79.

[65] As is often done in the Orient; see Raes, *Introductio*, 215, 218.

[66] This cannot be concluded from the oc-

casional use of the word *cantare*, but it does seem inherent in Amalar's *dulcius* (cf. note 62 above), and more especially in the phrase of Walafrid Strabo (*De exord.*, c. 22; see note 49 above) who is patently trying to explain an existing practice by the hypothesis that the Greeks had brought our symbol *in cantilenæ dulcedinem.*

[67] For Germany Berthold of Regensburg (d. 1272) mentions with praise the practice he found in several places where the people joined the *Credo in unum* by singing a German song which he cites as follows: *Ich gloube an den Vater, ich gloube an den Sun miner frouwen sant Marien, und an den Heiligen Geist. Kyrieleys.* Berthold von Regensburg, *Predigten*, ed. Pfeiffer, I, 498.

The pre-Reformation hymn, "Wir glauben all' an einem Gott", must have had the same purpose. W. Bäumker, *Das kath. deutsche Kirchenlied*, I (Freiburg, 1886), 683-688. Here we must also mention the report that the people sang *Kyrie eleison* while the clergy said the *Credo*; Honorius Augustod., *Gemma an.*, I, 19 (PL, CLXXII, 550); Sicard of Cremona, *Mitrale*, III, 4 (PL, CCXIII, 113); Durandus, IV, 25, 14. This probably refers to Credo-songs which used *Kyrie eleison* as a refrain—in other words, simply *leis*, as they were called.

It is not surprising to find that even in the tenth century the performance of the *Credo* was turned over to the clergy who formed the choir at high Mass. This transfer was especially easy since the *Credo* was at that time apparently considered a substitute for the sermon.[68] But the choir was then retained even independently of this.[69]

Even so the chant at first remained in the simplest forms of a syllabic recitation. In addition, in many churches objection was raised to performing the *Credo* in two choruses, since everyone had to profess the entire creed.[70] In contrast to the other chants of the Ordinary the manuscripts and even the early printed copies seldom contain more than a single tune, the ancient recitative.[71] The Gregorian melodies remained generally plain; the melodies included in the present *Graduale Vaticanum* show this clearly. How different, once the *Credo* was set to polyphony. Often it became the show-piece amongst the chants of the Ordinary. In fact, because of its broad presentation and because of the musical unfolding of its inexhaustible contents, it has attained such an importance in the full course of the Mass that it leaves the eucharistic prayer (which, in its design, is much akin to it) quite in shadow. For the sacerdotal eucharistic prayer has much the same aim: to survey, in the form of a thanksgiving, the achievements of the divine plan of salvation which we grasp by faith. So true is this that words like *prædicatio, contestatio* and even ἐξομολόγησις appear as names for this prayer,[72] names which could only be applied to a profession of faith; just as, contrariwise, the profession of faith itself is sometimes designated an εὐχαριστία.[73] And so true is this, that the older formulations of the eucharistic prayer are distinguished in little from a profession of faith.[74] Because the text of the prayer of thanksgiving is kept plain and simple in the Roman Mass, the *Credo* has taken on an even

[68] *Ordo Rom. VI*, n. 7 (PL, LXXVIII, 992): *Sin autem episcopus praedicare noluerit, alta voce incipiat canere: 'Credo in unum Deum,' et ita omnis chorus incipiens 'Patrem omnipotentem' ad finem usque perducat.*

[69] Honorius Augustod., *Gemma an.*, I, 19 (PL, CLXXII, 550 C): *clerus.*

For Rome: *Ordo Rom. XI* (City of Rome, circa 1140), n. 20 (PL, LXXVIII, 1033): *basilicarii* = clergy of the particular basilica; Innocent III, *De s. alt. mysterio*, II, 52 (PL, CCXVII, 830: at the papal high Mass the *subdiacones*, who are distinguished from the *cantores* (= *schola*).

[70] De Moléon, 167. At Sens, for similar reasons, the organ was excluded (*ibid.*). This is expressly ordered in 1583 by the

Synod of Bordeaux (Hardouin, X, 1340 D).
The same is reported of other churches in Lebrun, *Explication*, I, 217 f.

[71] Wagner, I, 105.

[72] Cf. *infra.*

[73] Pseudo-Dionysius, *De eccl. hierarchia*, III, 3, 7 (Quasten, *Mon.*, 305 f.).

[74] On the intrinsic relationship between the creed and the eucharistic prayer, F. Probst, *Liturgie der drei ersten christlichen Jahrhunderte* (Tübingen, 1870), 47 f., 208 f., was the first to remark (giving examples from Novatian, *De Trinitate*, c. 8); see also Kattenbusch, *Das Apostolische Symbol*, II, 347-353. Further references in Dekkers, *Tertullianus*, 194, note 5. Most impressively is this relationship seen in the *Eucharistia* of Hippolytus of Rome; see *supra*, p. 28 f.

greater importance. In the reawakening of all those concepts of our faith which center on Christ's life-work, in that reawakening with which every celebration of the Eucharist must begin, that reawakening which is the prime purpose of the whole reading service, that reawakening to which the anamnesis after the consecration recurs in a short and hurried word—in that reawakening the *Credo* has become a main element.

On the other hand, in tracing this tremendous growth of the *Credo* we encounter—very early, at that—the phenomena that manifest fatigue, the attempts to counterbalance the musical expansion by cutting down the text.[75] It is an abuse that is to be found frequently enough even today where small choirs try to emulate bigger and more capable groups; in fact, it is an abuse that is almost unavoidable when small choruses pretend to do a many-voiced *Credo* that is beyond their power. But it is a practice that the Congregation of Sacred Rites has repeatedly condemned.[76] In any case the plain recitation of the creed by the whole congregation, as is done in the dialogue Mass, is far more in harmony with the original design of the *Credo* and with its place in the plan of the Mass-liturgy, far more in harmony than such and similar residua of a musical culture that is past.

9. The Dismissals

With the *Credo*, which we have for the moment surveyed, we have strictly speaking gone out of the sphere of the Mass of the Catechumens; for the symbol is a hallowed formula, matter only for the faithful. However, it got its place at a time when there was no longer a question of the *disciplina arcani*, and one merely felt its close, intimate connection with the Gospel. But now, as we return to that early period during which there still existed a sharp boundary between the Mass of the Catechumens and the Mass of the Faithful, we must direct our attention to those forms which were attached to that boundary-line, and of which several remnants still exist.

It was always self-evident and (thanks be to God) still is for the most part even today, that a Christian instruction, a catechesis and a common reading from the Bible are concluded with a prayer. Therefore prayer had also to follow the readings and the instructions of the fore-Mass. And all the less could people forego a special prayer when the fore-Mass was felt to be an independent entity. Actually the prayer of the entire congregation at this spot we find already attested in the oldest accounts. The prayer that was supposed to be said here, however, coincided with the dismissal

---

[75] Wagner, *Einführung*, I, 105, tells of one late medieval MS. of St. Gall (Cod. 546) in which several *Credo* melodies close with *et homo factus est. Amen*, while another skips from *et homo factus est* to *Confiteor unum baptisma*.
[76] The decrees in Eisenhofer, II, 126. Especially SRC 3827 ad II.

of those whose presence at the further course of the holy sacrifice did not
seem permissible. For the instructional service did not form a part of the
introduction into the Christian world of faith for the catechumens alone;
heretics as well as pagans were admitted as guests in the hope that many
would in this way find the path to the faith.[1] After the instructional service, however, they had to leave the congregation. The celebration of the Eucharist was the exclusive privilege of the children of the
house. This conception was not a result of the *disciplina arcani*, which first
came into existence in the third century and was in full force for only a
comparatively short time[2]; rather it was the simple expression of a sound
Christian feeling, that at least the most sacred possession of the Church
ought not be presented to the eyes and ears of all. This conception did not
lose ground till the beginning of modern times, as a result of the conditions
of a divided Christendom.[3]

Then the question arose, whether these participants of the fore-Mass
who were not of the same class as the rest, should be given a part in the
community prayer, or whether they were to be dismissed beforehand. When
the catechumens had their usual instruction this had to be concluded with
a prayer, according to a third-century law. But a prayer said together with
the faithful—that was to be avoided.[4] Their common prayer would be
looked upon as a strange, coarse and debasing admixture in the prayer of
the Church—an idea which somehow continued effectual even later on.[5]
Nevertheless several solutions were possible. These participants could be
let go after the readings without prayer or any further ado, or they could
be permitted to say a certain prayer right at the beginning of the series of
community prayers that followed, or they could be allowed to stay at least
till that part of the prayer of the Church[6] where, according to an estab-

---

[1] This reason explicit in the Council of
Valence (524), can. 1 (Mansi, VIII,
620); cf. also p. 443 *supra*. The most
famous example is Augustine, who listened to St. Ambrose while he was still
only an inquirer.

[2] J. P. Kirsch, "Arkandisziplin," LThK,
I, 652 f.; O. Perler, "Arkandisziplin,"
RAC, I (1943), 667-676.

[3] Cf. *supra*, p. 234.

The same reasons are behind the antag-
onistic reactions of rectors of churches
towards photographers at solemn church
functions.

[4] Hippolytus of Rome, *Trad. Ap.* (Dix,
29).

[5] See the arrangement in the liturgy which
Chrysostom explains: even when prayer
is said for the catechumens, only the
faithful are invited, for the catechumens
themselves are still ἀλλότριοι; only at the

last petitions of the deacon are they also
invited to rise and, presumably, to
answer with Κύριε ἐλέησον; Chrysostom,
In II Cor. hom., 2, 5 (PG, LXI, 399-404).
When, on the contrary, prayer was said
for the ἐνεργούμενοι, this latter invitation
was omitted; for it was not fitting
(οὐ θέμις), that they should pray with the
assembly of the brethren. *De incompr.
Dei nat. hom.*, 3, 7 (PG, XLVIII, 727).

In a similar vein Hippolytus of Rome
stresses the fact that the kiss which follows the prayer should not be exchanged
with catechumens, "for their kiss is not
yet pure." (Dix, 29)

[6] Some few liturgical monuments show
that the presence of the catechumens was
permitted during all of the General
Prayer of the church; see the ecclesiastical *Canones* of Sahidic transmission,
c. 64 f. (Brightman, 462, 1. 6; cf. 461,

lished procedure, the faithful would pray for them and their own act of prayer could then be inserted here.

The first solution, a rather cold one, seems to have been employed in early times.[7]

In the prime of the catechumenate at Antioch,[8] the second solution was taken as a basis. It was so arranged that when the readings and sermon were over, the people were summoned to pray for those who had to leave, that is, to add their κύριε ἐλέησον to the series of supplications which the deacon pronounced for them and during which these persons lay stretched on the floor. Then they were summoned to rise and bow for the blessing which the bishop in solemn prayer bestowed on them. Only then were they asked to leave. During St. Chrysostom's time an independent prayer-act of this sort was devoted to the catechumens, the energumens[9] and the public penitents.[10] The Apostolic Constitutions (belonging to the same area) inserted before the public penitents, as a particular class, the candidates for Baptism who were undergoing their last preparation (φωτιζόμενοι).[11] Each one of these groups, when it had received the blessing of the celebrant, in the manner previously stated, was summoned by a call from the deacon

1. 22), the *Canones Basilii*, c. 97 (Riedel, 273 f.) and also the present East Syrian liturgy (Brightman, 267). The old Gallican Mass might also belong to this class; see note 24 below. The simple presence of a repeated warning before the start of the Eucharistic prayer (cf. *Const. Ap.*, VIII, 12, 2) would naturally be no proof that catechumens were actually allowed to remain till this moment.

[7] This is the explanation given by Baumstark, *Die Messe im Morgenland*, 104, for Justin's silence.

[8] For Egypt compare the *Euchologion* of Serapion, n. 3 f. (Quasten, *Mon.*, 51 f.), where the prayer for the catechumens is preceded only by a prayer closing the homily.

[9] Cf. *Const. Ap.*, VIII, 7, 2 (Funk, I, 480 f.; Quasten, *Mon.*, 202): ἐνεργούμενοι ὑπὸ πνευμάτων ἀκαθάρτων, possessed in the widest sense, obviously including specified sicknesses which were thought to be due to Satan's special influence; cf. the paraphrase in Chrysostom, *De incompr. Dei nat hom.*, 4, 4 (PG, XLVIII, 733); he called them δαιμονῶντας καὶ μανία τῇ πονηρᾷ κατεχομένους. Regarding the judgment of epilepsy in Christian antiquity and the exclusion of epileptics and possessed from oblation and Communion,

see the studies of F. J. Dölger, *Antike und Christentum*, IV (1934), 95-137.

[10] Brightman, 471 f., 477 f.

[11] *Const. Ap.*, VIII, 6-9 (Funk, I, 478-488; Quasten, *Mon.*, 199-206). Here the first thing is the call to each group for (silent) prayer: Εὔξασθε οἱ κατηχούμενοι, but the κύριε ἐλέησον is here said by the faithful for them. After the oration of benediction by the bishop, the invitation is given each time: Προέλθετε οἱ κατηχούμενοι etc. Besides the four classes named, and preceding them, the same document also mentions the ἀκροώμενοι. The first call of the deacon reads as follows: Μή τις τῶν ἀκροωμένων, μή τις τῶν ἀπίστων (VIII, 6, 2; cf. 12, 2). The ἀκροώμενοι receive no special act of prayer. They are the non-obligatory audience whose presence was merely tolerated. But that the term had a particular meaning—this despite the remark of Funk, I, 478 f.—can be gathered from the fact that in the organization of the classes of penitents in the Orient the second stage of the full ecclesiastical penitence (i.e. that after the πρόσκλαυσις) in the promotion passed to the degree of the ἀκροώμενοι. E. Schwartz, *Bussstufen und Katechumenatsklassen* (Strassburg, 1911), 37 ff.

to leave: (Προέλθετε οἱ κατηχούμενοι, ᾿Απολύεσθε οἱ ἐν μετανοίᾳ. After all these had been dismissed the doors were closed[12] and the formal Prayer of the Faithful in the narrower sense followed.

However, in the majority of the liturgies with which we are familiar, the third solution was chosen, namely the insertion of a procedure like the above in the place where prayers were usually said for these respective groups.[13] Moreover, outside the Syrian ambit,[14] only catechumens and penitents were taken into consideration already at an earlier period,[15] and in many provinces of the church, even of the East,[16] and almost commonly in the West, only the catechumens came under consideration, since as a rule public penitents (who after all were baptized) were permitted to remain during the sacrifice.[17] True, they were only allowed to remain there as mute spectators, and not till at the end of Mass was a blessing (at least for a time) devoted to them.

The rite of this dismissal was of a form similar to the one at Antioch, although it did not always possess such solemn pageantry as there. It was essential that a blessing with prayer be imparted to the group concerned; this was often done by the celebrant's laying his hands on each one individually.[18] With this was conjoined the deacon's cry for dismissal: Go,

---

[12] Brightman, 316, 1. 7; 478; 1. 6; 531, 1.3.

[13] Cf. Baumstark, *Die Messe im Morgenland*, 106 f.

[14] For Syria there is evidence in Chrysostom (p. 476 *supra*), as well as in Pseudo-Dionysius, *De eccl. hierarchia*, III, 3, § 6 f. (Quasten, *Mon.*, 301 ff.) and later in Jacob of Edessa (see note 18 below), of a dismissal of catechumens, energumens and penitents.

[15] Thus in Asia Minor, according to a decree of the Council of Laodicea (4th century); Brightman, 518.

[16] Only a dismissal of catechumens is attested by the *Euchologion* of Serapion, n. 3 f. (Quasten, *Mon.*, 51 f.) and in the Pilgrimage of Aetheria, c. 24 ff. (CSEL, XXXIX, 71 ff.).

[17] H. Koch, "Die Büsserentlassung in der alten abendländischen Kirche," *Theol. Quartalschr.*, LXXXII (1900), 481-534; Jungmann, *Die lateinischen Bussriten*, 7 f.

There is one exception to take into account, namely can. 29 of Epaon (517; Mansi, VIII, 562), according to which penitents were to leave with the catechumens.

It is possible, too, that the prayer for penitents which the Spanish *Missale mixtum* (PL, LXXXV, 307 A) indicates

before the Offertory at the ferial Masses of Lent might be the remnant of such a dismissal of penitents; cf. Borella (see note 22 below), 85, 89. Regarding the formula transmitted by St. Gregory the Great: *Si quis non communicat, det locum,* which most (e.g. Batiffol, Borella) interpret as prime evidence for the exclusion of penitents at the start of the sacrifice even at Rome, cf. below, Vol. II, Chap. 3, 8.

[18] Cf. Council of Laodicea, can. 19 (Brightman, 518, 1. 34): After prayer has been offered for them, the catechumens go to the celebrant ὑπὸ χεῖρα.

Jacob of Edessa depicts the same rite, but notes that about that time, 703, it was already a thing of the past (in Brightman, 490): "[After the prayer over the catechumens] the deacon calls loudly: 'Go, catechumens,' that is, they should present themselves under the hands of the bishop or presbyter, receive the laying-on of hands and depart." The same procedure here for the energumens and penitents. Because of this regular laying-on of hands, which under no circumstance could take place within the Mass, it is said in the Orient of a certain

catechumens! In this consisted the *missa catechumenorum*.[19]

With the disappearance of the catechumenate the corresponding dismissals had naturally to be omitted or at least contracted. In the Byzantine Mass alone not only is the cry of dismissal retained—and this is a fourfold phrase![20]—but even the prayer for the catechumens (as a second prayer after the Gospel) is still continued today. In the West and particularly in the sphere of the Roman liturgy, as we shall see more in detail, even the prayer of the congregation in this place has been sharply curtailed. In Rome it had completely disappeared, even in an early period, perhaps at a time when there were still catechumens. So the prayer for them, too, was dropped in the ordinary service.[21]

Elsewhere corresponding forms survived somewhat longer.[22] As a matter of fact a formal dismissal of the catechumens right after the reading service, in which the celebrating bishop had a share, is reported in Milan, Gaul, Spain and North Africa.[23] The *Expositio* of the Gallican liturgy (a work of the seventh century) still makes particular mention of a prayer for the people, and of one for the catechumens after the readings and the sermon. Both prayers were performed by "Levites" and priests; that is, in form of a litany-like alternating prayer and a collect following. The deacon's voice directed the catechumens and finally called upon them to go.[24] The

---

group of penitents that they are *sub manus impositione;* cf. Jungmann, *Die lateinische Bussriten,* 308 and in the index s.v. "Handauflegung."

[19] For the expression see Jungmann, *Gewordene Liturgie,* 38; cf. *supra,* p. 261, note 1.

[20] "Ὅσοι κατηχούμενοι προέλθετε· οἱ κατηχούμενοι προέλθετε· ὅσοι κατηχούμενοι προέλθετε· μήτις τῶν κατηχουμένων! Brightman, 375.

Before the *Credo* the call of the deacon resounds once more: τὰς θύρας, τὰς θύρας! Brightman, 383, 1. ϑ. Other liturgies also have a call of dismissal. In the Armenian liturgy the penitents are also named. See the survey in Hanssens, III, 265 f.

[21] That at the beginning of the prayer which follows the readings a prayer was spoken for the catechumens, is clear from the testimony of Felix II (483-492), *Ep.,* 7, al. 13 (PL, LVIII, 925 C; Thiel, 263) who decrees as a penance for certain clerics who had done wrong by rebaptizing: *nec orationi non modo fidelium sed ne catechumenorum (quidem) omnimodis interesse.* This *oratio catechumenorum* therefore must at that time have

been arranged within the framework of the Mass somewhat differently than in today's Good Friday prayers.

[22] P. Borella, "La 'missa' o 'dimissio catechumenorum' nelle liturgie occidentali," *Eph. liturg.,* LIII (1939), 60-110.

[23] Borella, 63-67.

[24] *Expositio ant. lit. gallicanæ* (ed. Quasten, 16 f.): *Caticuminum ergo diaconus ideo calmat iuxta antiquum Ecclesiæ ritum ut tam Judæi quam hæretici vel pagani instructi . . . audirent consilium Veteris et Novi Testamenti, postea deprecarent pro illis levitæ, diceret sacerdos collectam post precem, exirent postea foris.* An *ostiarius* then had the duty of seeing *ne quis retardaretur in templo.* The author makes it clear that in his day the rite was little more than a memory.

The doubt that hinders some from recognizing here a second prayer besides the preceding *pro populo* (Borella, 88 f.) is not right at all. In the Orient, too, as seen above, pp. 475, 477, there was a previous prayer of the Church which was definitely not the "Prayer of the Faithful" in the narrowest sense.

Upper-Italian churches had a similar rite for dismissing the catechumens with prayer. It was employed with certain individual acts of preparation for Baptism. That it was also used at the end of Mass we know to be true only about Milan, where the twelfth-century documents still prescribe the rite for the Sundays in Lent.[25]

Even in the various acts of preparation for Baptism, Rome did not have any such solemn dismissal. The scrutinies which the candidates for Baptism had to undergo during the course of Lent did indeed contain exorcisms, layings-on of hands, and priestly blessings. But even (for instance) after the solemn sharing of Gospel, symbol and Our Father, in the great scrutinium of the *aurium apertio*, the conclusion did not contain any further blessing, but simply the cry of the deacon: *Catechumeni recedant. Si quis catechumenus est recedat. Omnes catechumeni exeant foras.*[26] This manner of dismissal was used in cathedrals along with the complete rite of the scrutinies until the very end of the Middle Ages[27]; within the Mass on the days during Lent it occurred at first before the Gospel[28] then, from the great scrutinium on, after it, but only on the few occasions which were kept for this.[29] For it seems that according to Roman regulations the catechumens, as a closed group, did not appear regularly at the usual divine service even in more ancient times. Formulas similar to the previously mentioned Roman ones were also used in other churches in requesting withdrawal.[30]

A somewhat enlarged cry for dismissal was customary on solemn occasions in various parts of Italy. It was used not only on Holy Saturday before the consecration of the baptismal water, but also (at least in Milan, it would seem) within the Mass, namely, when the bishop confided the *Credo* to the candidates for Baptism, after the Gospel on the evening before Palm Sunday.[31] In this case it is meant for the sacred text of the symbol which came under the *disciplina arcani*. The six-fold cry of the deacon, which was solemnly sung like our *Ite missa est*[32] and the individual phrases of which were repeated by a second deacon or a subdeacon, was as follows:

[25] Borella, 90 ff.; cf. 71. The candidates for Baptism receive the following call for silent prayer: *Orate competentes, cervicem flectite!* Then they were to stand upright and again bow for the blessing. Finally the deacon cries out: *Procedant competentes!* and acolytes repeat the call. M. Magistretti, *Manuale Ambrosianum* (Milan, 1904), II, 123 f.

[26] *Ordo Rom. VII*, n. 6; (PL, LXXXVIII, 998 f.) and the parallels.

[27] Eisenhofer, II, 255; see the examples in Martène, 1, 1, 12 (I, 89 ff.).

[28] Cf. p. 443, *supra.*

[29] The Roman basic text of the older *Sacramentarium Gelasianum* (6th century) presupposes only three scrutinies, on the 3rd, 4th and 5th Sundays of Lent; the Frankish recension reckons seven. The great scrutiny was still held at Bamberg as late as 1631. Eisenhofer, II, 250-255.

[30] Borella, 96 f.

Isidore, *Etymol.*, VI, 19 (PL, LXXXII, 252) reports the formula: *Si quis catechumenus remansit, exeat foras.* It was used before the beginning of the sacrifice.

[31] Borella, 104.

[32] Editions of the traditional melodies are noted in Borella, 107, note 166.

Si quis catechumenus est, procedat!
Si quis hæreticus est, procedat!
Si quis Judæus est, procedat!
Si quis paganus est, procedat!
Si quis Arianus est, procedat!
Cuius cura non est, procedat![33]

Considering the wide circulation of this last formula, from Milan and Aquileia to Beneventum and Bari, it is not difficult to conclude that Rome was, if not the point of origin, at least a point of intersection. Still the formula must have gone out of use here quite early, because Roman documents make no mention of it.

10. The General Prayer of the Church

Just as the readings of the fore-Mass were everywhere the most excellent form of the reading service, so the prayer which followed upon it—apart from the *eucharistia*—was from ancient times regarded as the most excellent prayer, *the* prayer, simply, of the Church. Its importance became clear already in the earliest accounts. After the sermon by the bishop (here is the description of Sunday service as given by Justin) "we all stand up and recite prayers."[1] These prayers of the assembled brethren are the first in which the neophyte takes part. In them prayer is said "for ourselves, for the neophyte, and for all others everywhere."[2] Prayer "after the delivery of the homily" is a common term in the third and fourth century in Egypt.[3] Later on we meet the prayer after the readings in all the liturgies of the East. In the West it is plainly indicated by Hippolytus[4]; besides, Cyprian clearly refers to it when he speaks of the *Communis oratio.*[5] In Augustine's time a large number of sermons ended with the

---

[33] Borella, 98 ff. First published by J. M. Tommasi; see Tommasi-Vezzosi, *Opp.,* VII, 9 ff.

When at Milan and elsewhere on the occasion mentioned this formula was used to dismiss those catechumens who were not yet *competentes,* these latter had to have a special dismissal within the Mass itself, after the *traditio symboli.* This was done after a prayer of benediction, the formula being a repeated and somewhat varied *Competentes secedant.* Borella, 103 f.

Ibid., 103; 105 f. are found vastly enlarged variants of the formula of dismissal given above, among them one from Aquileia of nine members which were spoken by priest and deacon together; each time there followed a response from the choir which affirmed: *Nec quis Arianus est,* etc.

[1] Justin, *Apol.* I, 67.
[2] *Ibid.,* 65.
[3] *Euchologion* of Serapion, n. 2. Further citations in Quasten, *Mon.,* 50, note 2.
[4] *Supra,* p. 393, note 14.
[5] Cyprian, *De dom. or.,* c. 8 (CSEL, III, 271). Cf. Kennedy, *The Saints of the Canon,* 13. Further information from Cyprian in Fortescue, *The Mass,* 45.

The expression *communis oratio* for the prayer under consideration is certain in Augustine, *Ep.,* 55, 18, 34 (CSEL, XXXIV, 209; cf. Roetzer, 115).

formula: *Conversi ad Dominum,*[6] that is to say, common prayer followed upon the sermon, and during it, as was always customary, the congregation turned towards the East.[7] In the beginning this prayer was antiphonally recited by celebrant and congregation, a practice that remained in the Roman liturgy and partly in the Egyptian. The bishop led, by first inviting to prayer; then recited his own portion and the congregation answered.[8] Then as time went on, the deacon, who at first only announced short directions, began to take a more prominent place in most liturgies.[9] By the end of the fourth century he took over the invitation to prayer, the announcing of the special intentions which combined into a litany (*ektene*[10] or *synapte,)*[11] and to which the congregation answered with the *Kyrie eleison* or some other similar invocation; only then did the celebrant start to pray.[12]

In the Roman liturgy, in which the older and simpler form was preserved, this general prayer is still in use once a year, on Good Friday. Even in the eighth century this practice was still customary also at least on the Wednesday of Holy Week.[13] It is a well-grounded hypothesis that in these Good Friday prayers, whose echo goes back to the first century,[14] we have

[6] See the passages in Dölger, *Sol salutis,* 331, note 4 f.
Further illustrations from Augustine for the prayer at this part of the Mass in Roetzer, 113-115.

[7] Dölger, 331-333. Standing turned towards the sun is also accentuated in the Apostolic Constitutions, II, 57, 14 (Quasten, *Mon.,* 184 along with the notes). In so doing the hands were raised and stretched out in the attitude of prayer; Baumstark, *Die Messe im Morgenland,* 100.

[8] Baumstark, 100 f. Here you will find many details regarding the development which we can only briefly hint at in the following sketch.

[9] In Rome and Egypt: *Flectamus genua. Levate,* insofar as these calls come under consideration; cf. *supra,* p. 367 f. This gradually increasing prominence given to the deacon is evidenced, so Baumstark thinks, *loc. cit.,* in the *Aetheriæ Peregrinatio,* c. 24, where the deacon appears as leader in prayer only at Vespers, but not yet at Mass.

[10] From ἐκτενής = "extended, stretched out," with the undertone: intent, earnest.

[11] συνάπτη = joined, united.

[12] Cf. *supra,* p. 366 f.

[13] *Ordo Rom. I,* n. 28 (PL, LXXVIII, 950). The *orationes sollemnes,* as they

are here called, are at any rate on this day also separated from the Mass which follows some hours later, just as on Good Friday they are disjoined from the following rite by a pause; the fore-Mass is therefore treated as an independent unit.

[14] Clement I, *Ad Corinth.,* c. 59-61: "We beseech thee, O Lord, be our helper and provide for us; save those of us who are in tribulation; take pity on the oppressed, raise up those that have fallen, reveal thyself to those who beg, heal the sick, lead those of thy people who have gone astray once more into the right path. Feed the hungry, deliver those in prison, bring health to the sick, and comfort to the faint-hearted. Let all peoples recognize that thou art the only God and that Jesus Christ is thy servant and that we are thy people and the sheep of thy pasture. . . . Yea, Lord, make thy face to shine upon us for our well-being and our peace, so that we may be protected by thy strong hand and guarded against every sin by thy mighty arm, and save us from those who hate us groundlessly. Give unity and peace to us and to all who dwell on earth, as thou didst give them to our fathers when they called upon thee devoutly with faith and sincerity. Let us be obedient to thy all-

the general prayer of the Roman Church in the exact wording in which it was performed after the readings and the homily in the Roman congregation at their regular services since the third century.[15] The petitions that are here offered in nine parts: for the church, for the pope, for the assembled clergy, for the ruler, for the catechumens, for all who are in straits and in danger, for the heretics and schismatics, for the Jews and for the heathens, show up, except for the last two mentioned, and for occasional different groupings, in the general church prayer of other liturgies.

Still in the eastern liturgies, and especially in the litanies introduced by the deacon, which correspond to the invitations to prayer in the Roman Good Friday prayers, numerous other petitions are mentioned, and here they are answered by a supplication of the people. Peace on earth, prosperity in the field, the country or the city or the monastery, the sick, the poor, widows and orphans, travelers, benefactors of the poor and of the Church, eternal rest for the dead, forgiveness for sinners, an untroubled life, a Christian death—these are the intentions recommended to prayer. In the Egyptian liturgies the proper rising of the Nile and beneficial rains are not forgotten. The respective prayers of the celebrant are mostly kept

dominant and powerful name and to our rulers and princes on earth. . . . Grant them, O Lord, health, concord, peace and stability, that they may exercise unhindered the authority with which thou hast entrusted them . . . so that they may piously exercise in peace and meekness the authority which thou hast granted them, and may participate in thy grace. . . . Who alone hast power to give these and more good things, thee we praise through the high priest and protector of our souls, Jesus Christ, through whom be glory and majesty to thee now and from generation to generation, forever and ever. Amen."

It might be noted that the identification of the Good Friday prayers with the ancient general prayer, proposed by Msgr. Duchesne, *Christian Worship* 172-173, was disputed by E. Bishop, "Kyrie eleison," *Downside Review*, XVIII (1899), 294-303, but Bishop's view is hardly sustained.

[15] For the great antiquity of the Good Friday orations preserved today and already extant in the oldest sacramentaries, Baumstark, *Missale Romanum*, 20 f., refers to the naming of *confessores* after the series of clerics: the prayer belongs to the period of persecution, when those

who suffered for the faith were given the honors and rights of clerics; cf. Hippolytus, *Trad. Ap.* (Dix, 18 f.).

From the 5th century we have the evidence of the *Indiculus*, which is transmitted to us as an appendix to a letter of Celestine I on the Pelagian heresy, and which is traced back to Prosper of Aquitaine (M. Cappuyns, *Revue Bénéd.*, 1929, 156-170). Here, in c. 11 (PL, L, 535; Denziger-Umberg, *Enchiridion*, n. 139) which contains the famous sentence: *ut legem credendi lex statuat supplicandi*, to bolster an argument for the necessity of grace, reference is made to the prayer of the Church (*obsecrationes sacerdotales*), which was handed down from the Apostles and is in use throughout the world: the bishops pray therein *tota secum Ecclesia congemiscente* for unbelievers, idolaters, Jews, heretics, schismatics, penitents, catechumens. Echoes of the traditional text are not recognizable in this reference, as in the mention of the prayer for the Jews: *ablato cordis velamine.* Felix II (483-492) likewise testifies to the existence of such a prayer (*supra*, p. 478, note 21); here, however, the *oratio catechumenorum* must have stood right at the beginning.

Cf. Kennedy, 29-32.

on more general terms. They follow the pattern of invocations spoken by deacon and people, but bunch several of them together and thus give the course of the prayer its divisions. Usually three such parts are noticed. In Egypt the ending of the general prayer said after the dismissal of the catechumens, "the Prayer of the Faithful"—the only portion that has survived—still retains the name of "the three," αἱ τρεῖς; in it prayer is offered for the peace of the Church, for the bishop and clergy, for the entire Church and for the worshippers present.[16] Opposed to this, the Byzantine liturgy distinguishes only a first and a second prayer of the faithful, the contents of which very early underwent quite a process of change.[17]

In the other eastern liturgies, the retrogressive evolution ended up with only one such prayer form, made up of the diaconal litany and the celebrant's prayer,[18] similar in structure to the type handed down from older times, though with richer developments.[19] Finally, the East also has the one instance to prove that almost the last trace of the former general prayer of the Church has disappeared.[20]

This is also the case in our Roman Mass as we know it since the sixth century. After the Gospel or the *Credo*, it is true, the priest addresses himself to the congregation with the usual greeting, and adds the invitation to pray: *Oremus*. But he himself then reads out of the missal the text of the offertory which the choir immediately begins. Nor is any form of prayer anywhere indicated for the congregation.[21] In the oldest sacramentaries and *ordos*, which hand down this isolated invocation, no other prayer follows except the *oratio super oblata*, our *secreta*. There is nothing to keep us from recognizing in the secret the corresponding prayer of the priest. For the *oratio super oblata* was at that time spoken, as we shall see, in a loud voice just like the other orations. Likewise it is patterned as a prayer

[16] Brightman, 121 f., 160 f., 223 ff.

"Three prayers" of the faithful were appointed by the Synod of Laodicea, can. 19, of which the first was spoken διὰ σιωπῆς, the second and third διὰ προσφωνήσεως, that is, in the second and third, but not in the first, the deacon was to "call out" to the people the individual prayers in the manner of the *ektenes*. Brightman, 519 f.

The North-African liturgy of Augustine also appoints the prayer in three members: for the unbelievers, for the catechumens, for the faithful; Roetzer, 113-115.

[17] Brightman, 316 f., 375 f. The prayers of the celebrant in the 9th century have both times as object the worthy service at the altar; the related short synapte of the deacon, on the other hand, prays in

a general way for "protection, help, mercy and shelter." One is forced to conclude that in the homogeneous εὐχὴ τῆς προσκομιδῆς, which follows (Brightman, 319 f., 380 f.), in reality εὐχὴ πιστῶν γ′ is to be found, all the more since the litany expressly enters as a continuation of what precedes: πληρώσωμεν τὴν δέησιν ἡμῶν.
[18] Greek liturgy of St. James (Brightman, 38-40) and Armenian liturgy (*ibid.*, 428-430).
[19] Liturgy of the West Syrian Jacobites (Brightman, 80 f.); cf. Baumstark, *Die Messe im Morgenland*, 107.
[20] *Const. Ap.* VIII, 10 f.
[21] The silent prayers of the Offertory do not come into consideration as an explanation of the isolated *Oremus*, since they are all much more recent.

said in the name of the congregation, just as the other orations are, and therefore it requires, no less than these, an introductory invitation to pray and a greeting. Both these elements are present at the offertory, only separated from the oration by a pause. But even the pause involves nothing surprising. It is a time for the prayer by the people, though not announced by a *Flectamus genua*, since in the stricter compass of the sacrifice a bending of the knee, according to ancient modes, is not to be thought of.[22] That is the explanation for the lone *Oremus*.

The only thing standing in the way of our recognizing in this formula the ancient concluding oration of the faithful is that in content the prayer is simply and indubitably an *oratio super oblata*. But this need not surprise us. For even in the Byzantine liturgy we noted the same process of change, indeed in two instances at least, namely, in the "first" and the "second" prayer of the faithful. But while here prior to the dismissal of the catechumens a first section of the general prayer of the Church remained unshortened, viz., the fervent *ektene* with the corresponding prayer of the priest, nothing corresponding to it was kept in the Roman liturgy. This almost complete disregard of the Roman Mass for the general prayer of the Church ties in with the fact in its place some substitution was or would be made: in the intercessory prayers that meanwhile found entrance within the canon, and also in the *Kyrie*-litany which begins to emerge at the start of the Mass simultaneously with the disappearance of the prayer of the Church.[23] Probably the general prayer of the Church no longer had (if it ever had) the same extent in connection with the sacrifice which it showed when it was the conclusion of an independent prayer service. And therefore very probably the offertory procession was inserted a long time ago in the pause after the last *Oremus*,[24] and correspondingly also the content of the oration was newly devised. What preceded was at last naturally dropped.[25]

Nevertheless there are traces still to be found of the foregoing prayer of the Church. With a certain regularity the Gelasian Sacramentary—and partly also the Leonine—has an addition to the present-day pattern of one oration (our collect) preceding the *oratio super oblata* (our secret); instead we find not one but two, both having the same form and both of a similar general character. Several conjectures have been made about this twofold prayer.[26] We will be nearest to the truth if we assume that the sec-

---

[22] See *supra*, p. 368.
[23] See *supra*, p. 336 ff.
[24] The consciousness of this still survives in Sicard of Cremona, *Mitrale*, III, 5 (PL, CCXIII, 114 B): While among the Greeks prayer follows at this spot, amongst us the *oblatio* of the people precedes (*præcedit*).

The intervention of a different rite in a prayer-pause is repeated elsewhere,

e.g., in the ordination liturgy in regard to the laying-on of hands.
[25] In some instances the *Oremus* was omitted; it is missing in the Wolfenbüttel MS. of *Ordo Rom. I* (Stapper, 22) and in *Ordo Rom. III*, n. 10 (PL, LXXVIII, 980).
[26] According to Baumstark, *Das Gesetz der Erhaltung des Alten* (JL, 1927), 6 f., and *Missale Romanum*, 29, these two

ond oration was to be said after the Gospel, and if we see in it a parallel with the *oratio super sindonem*, which follows the Gospel in the Milanese Mass.[27] Even in the earlier Roman liturgy we occasionally find examples of an *oratio post evangelium*,[28] innovations such as could arise at a time which no longer coupled the secret with the *Oremus*, but which had a living realization that a real closing prayer should follow the readings. Still such an intermediary oration did not survive. The secret in the Roman Missal remained the only formula in which, in place of the former general prayer of the Church between readings and sacrifice, the priest takes up the prayer according to the style and language of the orations. And when in it the *preces populi* are often explicitly mentioned alongside of the *oblationes* which are presented to God, we can see here the traces of the prayer of the faithful which formed a lower level over which was laid the thought of the offertory.

Besides all this we still have to dwell on a special evolution of the old prayer of the faithful, a development in the territory of the early Gallican liturgy, within the frame of the Roman Mass, though not in the Roman Missal. Gallican traditions here proved very tenacious.

In the year 517 a council of Lyons mentions the *oratio plebis*.[29] What this was we learn more precisely when the exposition of the Gallican Mass in the seventh century speaks of *preces* after the homily which the Lévites

orations correspond to the two pre-Gospel readings. Similarly P. Alfonso, *L'Euchologia romana antica* (Subiaco, 1931), 131, 135. But notice that the instances which come to mind of two orations preceding the two pre-Gospel readings in the present-day *Missale Romanum*, among them those on the Ember Wednesdays, do not represent the original arrangement and plan; Hierzegger, "Collecta und Statio" (ZkTh, 1936), 520 f.

[27] Thus, among others, Wilson, *The Gelasian Sacramentary* (1894), p. LXXIV, note 1; A. Wilmart in his new edition of E. Bishop, *Le génie de Rit Romain* (Paris, 1920).

In the Milanese liturgy each Mass has, besides the orations corresponding to our collect, secret and post-communion, a proper oration *super sindonem;* it is preceded, as is the *oratio super oblata* (= secret) by the *Dominus vobiscum.* The designation *super sindonem* is derived from the moment in which it is said; cf. the "prayer of the chalice-cover" in the West-Syrian anaphoras, which Jacob of Edessa considers as developing from the

third member of the prayer of the faithful; Hanssens, III, 332 f. Regarding the function of the *oratio super sindonem* there is little clarity; see Borella (*Eph. liturg.,* 1939), 94, who rejects the opinion that it is in reality the closing prayer of the dismissal of the catechumens, and rightly believes it is a development from the *oratio fidelium.*

A different view is taken by V. L. Kennedy: "The two collects of the Gelasian," *Miscellanea Mohlberg* (1948), I, 183-188.
[28] In the Mass book fragments from lower Italy edited by A. Dold (see *supra,* p. 395, note 16) the Mass formularies regularly have, between Gospel and Offertory, an *oratio post evangelium;* see Dold, p. XXX f. It is obviously of secondary development; cf. the remarks on this in ZkTh, LIX (1935), 320.

Within the *Ordo Missæ* in a mid-Italian sacramentary of the 11th century there is an *oratio post evangelium,* but its contents have taken over the thoughts regarding the oblation and remind one of the *apologiæ;* Ebner, 298.
[29] Can. 6 (Mansi, VIII, 370).

solemnly recited for the people and in which the priests made intercession for the sins of the people.[30] There is reference here apparently to a single litany spoken by the deacon or deacons with a collect following *post precem*. Under this name, the contemporary Gothic Missal also actually contained a corresponding formula for the priest for Christmas and Easter services.[31] Likewise examples of the litany of the people are preserved in certain texts in which the Gallican material has been fitted to the Roman: in the Irish Stowe Missal,[32] where each of the petitions is followed, after the Gallican manner, by the people's response, *Oremus te, Domine, exaudi et miserere* or *præsta, Domine, præsta*,[33] and in the Freiburg Pontifical of the ninth century,[34] where the schema of the litany of All Saints forms the groundwork.

When in the eighth century the Frankish Church turned to using the Roman liturgy and found in the newly received forms no palpable traces of the erstwhile general prayer of the Church, there must have been some repercussions also here in Frankish territory in regard to this prayer. For what now appear are either remnants of an old tradition or even products obviously created in an untimely attempt to achieve new forms.

It was a matter of preserving old relics in those various cases in which, after the readings and the sermon, we find the people repeating the *Kyrie eleison*. But the meaning of this isolated *Kyrie eleison*, still found today in the Milanese liturgy,[35] was unclear already in the height of the Middle Ages. The people repeated the cry of *Kyrie*, not only after the clergy had recited the symbol but even during its recitation, and it was explained as signifying among other things a praise of God for the faith received.[36] Then here and there the *Kyrie* turned into a *Leis*, the German hymn which is

---

[30] *Expositio* (ed. Quasten, 16): *Preces vero psallere levitas pro populo ab origine libri Mosiaci duxit exordium ut . . . levitæ pro populo deprecentur et sacerdotes prostrati ante Dominum pro peccatis populi intercedant.* There follows the prayer act for the catechumens; see *supra*, p. 478 f.

[31] Muratori, II, 520.

The intercessions are emphasized to some extent only in the Christmas formula. Notice that in the Gallican Mass the reading of the names still follows, along with a pertinent *collectio post nomina*, in which most often prayers are said expressly for the living and for the dead. For the Gallican formulas from the Leofric Missal, see note 39 below.

[32] Warner (HBS, 32), 6 f. That the litany here stands before the Gospel is naturally something secondary. A parallel case is to be seen in the Abyssinian Mass where the

initial portion of the general prayer of the Church today likewise precedes the Gospel; Brightman, 216, 1. 31; cf. 210 f. and resp. 150 f.

[33] Nickl, *Der Anteil des Volkes*, 12 f.

[34] Metzger, *Zwei karolingishe Pontifikalien vom Oberrhein*, p. 68*-70*. The introductory rubric says: *tempore ieiunii aut in aliis statutis diebus recitantur quando missa celebratur.* Within the Mass at this time the only spot that could be considered is after the readings.

[35] *Missale Ambrosianum* (1902), p. 167: After the reading of the Gospel there follows *Dominus vobiscum* and three times *Kyrie eleison*. Thus already in the oldest sources of the Milan liturgy.

[36] Durandus, IV, 25, 14.

Honorius Augustod., *Gemma an.*, I, 19 (PL, CLXXII, 550 C), interprets as a promise to observe the teaching of the Gospel the *Kyrie eleison* which the people

to be found in many places since the twelfth century at the close of the sermon.[37] But alongside of all this, new forms sprang up, the basic pattern of which is seen in Regino of Prüm (d. 915). On Sundays and feast days after the sermon the priest is to recommend to the faithful a general prayer for various needs: for the rulers, for the heads of the churches, for peace, against plagues, for the sick, and for the departed. The people were to recite quietly an Our Father each time, while the priest recited the corresponding Latin oration.[38] The votive Masses of the Gelasian Sacramentary offered the priest a sufficient supply of such orations. Other orations survived from the Gallican liturgy, as the Leofric Missal indicates.[39]

In many French-speaking dioceses the tradition of Regino has been preserved to this day with remarkable purity in the so-called *prières du prône*. Their wording, while keeping to the basic structure, varies in different places. A form very widespread today has the following outline[40]: After

sing at the same time that the clergy say the *Credo;* cf. supra, p. 472, note 67. The fact that this *Kyrie* accompanies the creed (*symbolo cantato ante et dum cantatur*) is also attested by Sicard of Cremona, *Mitrale,* III, 4 (PL, CCXIII, 113 D).

[37] Cf. A. Linsenmayer, *Geschichte der Predigt in Deutschland* (Munich, 1886), 142 f.

[38] Regino of Prüm, *De syno. causis,* c. 190 (PL, CXXXII, 224 f.): . . . *in quibus singillatim precibus plebs orationem Dominicam sub silentio dicat, sacer dos vero orationes ad hoc pertinentes per singulas admonitiones sollemniter expleat. Post hæc sacra celebretur oblatio.* Regino's careful wording hardly confirms the theory maintained by H. v. Schubert, *Kirchengeschichte des Frühmittelalters* (Tübingen, 1921), 654, that the entire intercessory prayer was said in German. Regino obviously has in mind a plan similar to the Roman arrangement for Good Friday. Certainly the silent *Vaterunser* corresponds to the pause (then still customary) after the *Flectamus genua* (see *supra,* p. 369 f.). The oration that followed would be in Latin. But one can not maintain this for the preceding *admonitio;* see the conditions in the French and English tradition, note 43 f. below.

[39] F. E. Warren, *The Leofric Missal* (Oxford, 1883), 207 f. In this Mass book

(9-10th century), from either Lotharingia or the Rhine, there is, outside a Mass formulary and without any special designation (being thrown in among various formularies), a remarkable group of four orations of which the third, by its closing formula, betrays the Gallican origin which would otherwise be recognized from the vocabulary and its temper. The titles of the individual formulas indicate the contents only imperfectly: *Oratio pro familiariis* (a prayer for benefactors, relatives, for those recommended to our prayers, *vel qui nobis eleemosinarum suarum reditus erogaverunt*), *Oratio pro omni populo catholico* (for the king and his family, for believers and unbelievers), *Oratio generalis pro omni populo* (for all princes and leaders, for the clergy and the monasteries, for married people and children, for sinners, for the poor and oppressed, for all our departed *quorum nomina tu scis*), *Oratio in agenda mortuorum* (for the deceased *quorum et quarum nomina commendata sunt nobis,* with several further specifications).

[40] According to the text in G. Lefebvre, O.S.B., *Missel-Vespéral romain* (Lophemlez-Bruges, 1923), 77-79. Here, to correspond to actual use, there is reference to the text of the "prône" between Gospel and *Credo* in the *Ordo Missæ* (p. 100).

The word "prône" is translated in many modern Latin texts as *pronaos,* antechamber, but this is incorrect. The word

an introductory reference to the Sunday and feast-day offering, there is mention first of a list of prayer intentions: for Church and clergy, for secular rulers, for benefactors, for the soldiers of the parish, for the sick and for sinners. Here follows a *Pater* and *Ave* recited in common, or—what must have been the original—Psalm 122, a silent *Pater noster* and, after the corresponding versicles, the Latin oration.⁴¹ Then follows a second invitation to prayer, this time for the departed. Psalm 129 is recited, the *Requiem æternam*, and again the corresponding oration.⁴² Then follow the announcements for the coming week.

A formula prescribed for a church in Paris shortly before 1300 shows exactly the same design.⁴³ A similar order was probably in use in northern France as early as the eleventh century, because it is already found, though somewhat more developed, in England after the Norman conquest,⁴⁴ where-

derives from *præconium;* cf. A. Gastoué, *Les Questions liturgiques et paroissiales,* 12 (1927), 243. The "Announcements" continue to play a great role in the *prône;* cf. the chapter "Du prosne" in G. Grimaud, *La liturgie sacrée* (Paris, 1678), II, 52-58; de Moléon, 418 f.

⁴¹ The oration for the 22nd Sunday after Pentecost (*Deus noster refugium*) is used.

⁴² *Deus veniæ largitor.* In both cases only the invitation to prayer is in the vernacular, as this already seems to be assumed in Regino of Prüm.

The same arrangement is found as a *formula pronai singulis Dominicis legenda* in the *Rituale Parisiense* (Paris, 1839), 433-441, but with a greater extension of the invitation and of the intentions of the first part.

At the present time, when the liturgical movement in France has grown apace, attention has been drawn to this venerable piece of liturgical tradition; cf., e.g., *Etudes de Pastorale liturgique* (Paris, 1944), 279 (G. Chevrot); Pastoral-liturgical Congress of St. Flour: *La Maison-Dieu,* IV (1945), 39 f. (A. M. Roguet and H. Ch. Chery).

⁴³ The prayer for the living is introduced by a formula of 18 members, each beginning: *Nous prierons Dieu pour;* thereupon follows Ps. 122, with *Kyrie, Pater,* versicles and threefold oration. After a later invitation in the vernacular there follows a prayer for the dead, *Pater*

noster, and Ps. 129 (obviously a secondary re-arrangement) with versicle and two orations. A. Gastoué, "Les prières du prône à Paris au 14ᵉ siècle," *Les Questions liturgiques et paroissiales* (1927), XII, 240-249.

⁴⁴ Manuscript evidence apparently starts only in 1405; see the four texts (bidding prayer, n. II-V) which are reprinted in Simmons, *The Lay Folks Mass Book,* 64-80. They start with the Latin formula: *Deprecemur Deum Patrem omnipotentem pro pace* (or *pro statu*) *et stabilitate sanctæ matris Ecclesiæ* (*et pro pace terræ*). Then in three of the four pieces (the fourth, p. 74, shows a condensed, secondary form) there follows a threefold prayer-act: the English exhortation to pray closes each time with the invitation, a *Pater* and an *Ave* (in the second member in two instances: five *Aves.*). At the end of the first member, for spiritual and secular authorities, for benefactors of the Church, etc. (remarkable is the naming of those who build roads and bridges, as well as pregnant women), Ps. 66, and after the *Kyrie, Pater noster* and several versicles, three orations. At the end of the second member, begging for the intercession of the Mother of God (and in part other intentions), a Marian hymn and after several versicles a Marian oration. At the end of the third member, again for the dead, Ps. 129, and after *Kyrie, Pater noster* and versicle the oration *Fidelium.*

as a British text of the "bidding prayer" just prior to the conquest shows a different form.[45]

On German soil, on the contrary, no such well-adorned form was able to unfold. Of course one can still see a trace of the forms of the older traditions in a German formula of the twelfth century in which a long drawn-out invitation to prayer is divided into two parts: for the living and for the dead, and closes both times with the command to raise a "cry."[46] But for the rest the practice we find from this time on,[47] is that the priest mentions a fairly long list of prayer intention after the sermon, which usually begin with the temporal and spiritual rulers, but outside of that follows no strict order. Selection, grouping and wording are much interchanged. Even in the same diocese differing practices occur.[48] The participation of the laity was limited to a high degree and tended gradually to disappear entirely. Maybe in the beginning there was a *Kyrie eleison* by the parish after each part. Nevertheless we meet such a chant usually at the end of the entire list.[49] But this too faded out.[50] Towards the end of the Middle Ages we note the practice of inviting the faithful to recite an *Ave*,[51] or a *Pater* and *Ave* after each part.[52] Later a single *Pater* and *Ave* was recited

[45] *Ibid.* 62 f. The Old English text has four sections, each section closes simply with the exhortation to say the "Our Father." Worthy of note is the emphasis put on the mention of godfather and godmother. In the fourth section, for the dead, the naming of names is presupposed.

The Bede-rolls in English churches contained the list of petitions and the names of those for whom prayer was asked. Details on giving out the bidding-prayers in English cathedrals and parish churches in D. Rock, *The Church of Our Fathers*, i, chap. 7 (in the edition cited, vol. 2, p. 292); also A. Gasquet, *Parish Life in Medieval England*, 222 ff.

[46] Linsenmayer, *Geschichte der Predigt*, 143, 145, 146. The term *Ruf* probably refers to songs in the vernacular which developed out of the *Kyrie-eleison;* see *supra*, p. 342 f. and also 472, note 67.

[47] Honorius Augustod. *Speculum Ecclesiæ* (PL, CLXXII, 827-830), produces 13 members, of which each closes with an *Amen* that was probably spoken by the leader. The "Homiliary of the Bishop of Prague" ed. by F. Hecht (Prague, 1863), p. 17, presents a much shorter series which is not so clearly divided. The text in both instances is Latin.

[48] Cf. the examples from Regensburg mentioned in note 52 below. A more careful study would note distinction in type and typical form-elements. One recurrent introduction is, e.g., this one from the Regensburg *Obsequiale* of 1570 (Beck, 354): ". . . help me diligently to invoke and pray God the almighty."

[49] Honorius Augustod., *Speculum Eccl.* (PL, CLXXII, 830): After the preacher has announced the intentions for prayer, he exhorts the faithful: *Nunc, carissimi, corda vestra et manus ad Deum levate, ut pro his omnibus dignetur vos clementer exaudire. . . . Eia nunc preces vestras alta voce ferte ad coelum et cantate in laude Dei: Kyrie eleison.*

[50] In the homiliary mentioned in note 47 above, the list of intentions is introduced with a formula much like the close of that of Honorius: *Modo, fratres, cum timore Dei levate corda et manus et invocate. . . .* But no mention is made of any formula by which the people could answer. Hecht, 17

[51] According to one MS. from St. Florian about 1480, the petitions were announced in 21 sections, each followed by an *Ave*. K. Eder, *Das Land ob der Enns vor der Glaubensspaltung* (Linz, 1933), 249 f.

[52] In the "Announcement" from Brandenburg, of 1380, ed. by A. Schönfelder

at the end,[63] or once more all noticeable prayer activity of the faithful drops out.[64].

In these circumstances it was indeed a step forward when St. Peter Canisius in 1556-57 wrapped the long list of the current prayer intentions into one single all-embracing and theologically excellent prayer, and began to spread this around. He found sympathy almost everywhere for this idea.[65] His composition prevails to this day as the "general prayer" of the German dioceses; more than this, it has in many places taken the spot in the divine service which belonged to the ancient general prayer: after the sermon, where Sunday after Sunday it is said by the entire congregation in chorus,[56] and in places, in fact, it has for a long time been said within the Mass itself.[67]

11. Further Adjuncts to the Sermon

Alongside the General Prayer of the Church, other texts in the course of time were also adjoined to the end of the sermon, but no particular order of succession was ever made standard for them. Some of these have come and gone like the wind, others have at least left a permanent mark. The chief of these additions are the announcements, the formulas for popular catechesis, and the *culpa* or *Offene Schuld* ("open confession").[1]

(*Liturg. Zeitschrift*, 1929), 58-62, the *Pater* and *Ave* are expected in six places in the 14-sectional prayers.

Likewise in the "Announcement for Sundays in Parish Churches," written about 1500 at Regensburg (Beck, 274 ff.) a *Pater* and *Ave* are appointed in six of the sections: for spiritual and secular authority, for all believers, especially the sick and oppressed, for each one's wants, for all deceased priests, for all deceased faithful, for deceased members.

The Regensburg *Obsequiale* of 1570 (Beck, 354) has a shorter formula of petition, chiefly prayer for the peace of Christendom and for spiritual and secular authority, and only twice are *Pater* and *Ave* recited.

Practices of this sort have not gone out of use entirely. The announcements in many churches begin or end with a recommendation of the souls of the sick and dead of the parish to the prayers of the congregation.

[63] Thus, after a long list of intentions, according to the Basle parish priest John Ulrich Surgant, *Manuale curatorum*

predicandi prebens modum (Strassburg, 1508), fol. 78-79.

[64] Thus in the plan which R. Cruel, *Geschichte der deutschen Predigt im Mittelalter* (Detmold, 1879), 224 f., presents as the usual phraseology.

[65] P. F. Saft, "Das 'Allgemeine Gebet' des h. Petrus Kanisius im Wandel der Zeiten," *Zeitschrift f. Aszese u. Mystik*, XIII (1938), 215-223, with a presentation of five different recensions. The original form, published by Canisius in 1560, was still in use in the diocese of Brixen in 1900.

[56] Thus, e.g., in my own parish of Taufer in Pustertal. From such public use it spread also to private use at night prayer.

[67] An important attempt to reconstruct the general prayer of the Church along the lines of the Litany, taking into account variations for various feasts and seasons and various needs, is found in the plans projected by J. Gülden, "Fürbittgebete": *Parochia*, ed. by K. Borgmann, 387-408.

[1] R. Cruel, *Geschichte der deutschen Predigt im Mittelalter*, 221 ff. The development was in the direction of order and

First of all, the end of the sermon was always considered a good spot—though not the only one—to make the announcements to the people, telling them of the future plans for worship or of other matters of interest to the congregation. Pope Leo the Great (to cite one example) at the end of his Embertide sermon always reminded his hearers of the fast days during the coming Ember week and invited them to attend the vigil on the eve of the next Sunday.[2] The practice during the late Middle Ages was much the same, detailed explanation being given of the sanctoral calendar for the week following.[3] Indeed the custom is still maintained to a great extent at the present.[4]

Secondly, this spot right after the homily, or perhaps even in its place, was usually selected for a modest form of popular catechesis, in accordance with the decrees of Charlemagne. The heart of this catechetical instruction consisted of the Our Father and the Apostles' Creed.[5] These formulas had to be explained or at least recited with the people.[6] Often in the course of the Middle Ages the prescription was inculcated anew.[7] Later, from the

design, so that the many different formulæ and prayer activities were gradually reduced to this list (and this order): Announcements, creed, *culpa* (with granting of indulgence), recommendations for prayer, Our Father and Hail Mary. Cruel, 222-225; Linsenmayer, 140 f. Already by the 12th century the creed and *culpa* had been reduced to a single formula. For a different order see note 9 below.

[2] Leo the Great, *Serm.*, 12, 13 (PL, LIV, 172 f.), *et al.*

Augustine, at the end of his sermon (*Sermo* 3) announces the anniversary of the consecration of the old bishop which would occur the following day and invites all to the basilica of Faustus (Roetzer, 112 f.; further examples here).

Cf. in the later *Gelasianum* (Mohlberg, n. 1460 f.) the formula of the *denuntiatio natalicii unius martyris*.

In an earlier period these announcements took place at Rome just before the Communion of the faithful, therefore before the non-communicants had departed; see below, Vol. II, Ch. 3, 8.

[3] See two formulas from Regensburg in Beck, 274, 353. One from Brandenburg (1380) in A. Schönfelder, "Die 'Verkündigung' im mittelalterilchen Gottesdienst," *Liturg. Zeitschrift*, 1 (1929), 58-62.

Cf. Cruel, 227-230, regarding a custom very extended in the 15th century: the village priest would free himself from the duty of preaching a real sermon by making a little announcement about the feast of the saint, filling it out with examples from the legends.

[4] Cf. F. Schubert, "Die 'Verkündigung'," *Theologie u. Glaube*, XXIV (1932), 736-750, who bemoans the present-day style of announcements, curt as a telegram, and suggests a return to an earlier sacral type especially for the announcements regarding feasts and festal seasons.

[5] The directions appeared in various capitularies and in episcopal synodal writings; see also Synod of Frankfurt (794), c. 33 (MGH, Cp. I, 77).

P. Göbl. *Geschichte der Katechese im Abendlande vom Verfalle des Katechumenats bis zum Ende des Mittelalters* (Kempten, 1880), 78 f., 82-84.

[6] Such an explanation is connected with the Our Father, but not with the symbol in Honorius Augustod., *Speculum Eccl.* (PL, CLXXII, 819-824); likewise in the contemporaneous homiliary of the Bishop of Prague (Hecht, 60 f.).

[7] Göbl, 82-97.

K. Schrems, *Die religiöse Volks- und Jugendunterweisung in der Diozese Regensburg vom Ausgang des 15. Jh. bis gegen Ende des 18. Jh.* (Munich, 1929),

thirteenth century on, the Ave Maria and the Ten Commandments were added to the materials for catechism,[8] besides the seven sacraments, and at least several times a year other lists or enumerations, as built up in the systematic instruction of the later Middle Ages,[9] and finally "Acts of Faith, Hope and Charity"[10] with other allied formulas.

Insofar as prayer-texts were concerned, the saying of these formulas was on the borderline between an impressive repetition and real praying. General prayer and popular catechesis were therefore often intermixed and combined. Here, too, French tradition has maintained a fixed arrangement with clear limits right down to the present.[11]

Sometime after the year 1000 another act of purification put in an appearance, connected loosely either with the Prayer of the Church or with the catechetical texts. This act, which was to precede all further prayer and the start of the sacrifice itself, was called the "Open Confession" (*Offene Schuld*). It is an expanded *Confiteor* said in the vernacular. The German texts for this are amongst the most ancient monuments of the German language.[12] At first (since the ninth century) they served patently

24 ff., *et al.* (see the Index). Examples from Silesia (13-15th century) in J. Klapper, "Religiöse Volkskunde im gesamtschlesischen Raum," *Volk und Volkstum*, I (Munich, 1936), 75, note 2.

[8] Thus, e.g., in the formulary of Pastor Surgant, *Manuale*, fol. 79-83. Surgant had in view the prescriptions of the Synod of Basle, 1503; Göbl, 95 f.

[9] The Regensburg "Announcement" follows up the prayer intentions already mentioned (p. 489, note 62) with Our Father, Hail Mary and creed; then, within the framework of the *culpa*, as possible objects of sin, there follows the enumeration of the Ten Commandments, the nine ways of sharing the sins of others, the eight beautitudes, the seven gifts of the Holy Ghost, the seven sacraments, the seven deadly sins, the six works of mercy, the five senses, the four sins "crying to heaven for vengeance," the six sins against the Holy Ghost. The same schema in the Brandenburg "Announcement" of 1380, ed. by Schönfelder (*Liturg. Zeitschrift*, 1929), 61 f. Other examples in J. Geffcken, *Der Bildercatechismus des 15. Jh. und die catechetischen Hauptstücke in dieser Zeit bis auf Luther* (Leipzig, 1855), 21 f.

[10] For private prayer there are formulas of the theological virtues already in the *Manale catholicorum* of St. Peter Canisius (1587); see A. Schrott, "Das Gebetbuch" (ZkTh, 1937), 215.

By the 17th and 18th centuries they already play a great part in catechisms; J. Hofinger, *Geschichte des Katechismus in Österreich von Canisius bis zur Gegenwart* (Innsbruck, 1937), 195 f, with note; 232 f.

Benedict XIII and Benedict XIV granted indulgences for their use; F. Beringer, *Die Ablässe*, (14th ed., Paderborn, 1915), I, 167 f. In the bull "Etsi tamen" (Feb. 7, 1742) Benedict XIV prescribed them—the acts of the three theological virtues, plus an act of contrition—*intra missarum sollemnia*.

[11] Twice a year the *prières du prône* are replaced by the reading of a prescribed section of Christian doctrine.

According to the *Rituale Parisiense* of 1839 (*supra*, p. 488, note 42), the reading of this epitome of doctrine should follow the *prône*.

[12] The more ancient texts, traceable to the 10th century, marked "Beichten" (Confessions) in E. v. Steinmeyer, *Die kleineren althochdeutschen Sprachdenkmäler* (Berlin, 1916), 309-364.

for the sacramental confession of individuals.[13] But just as the profession of faith in its original singular form was transferred from the baptismal rite into public worship, so now the formula of acknowledging our sin was transferred from the sacrament of Penance. In this instance, however, the complete sacramental rite was originally united with the formula, at least in a limited way, even at Holy Mass. For after the tenth century it became customary to include all the faithful congregated in church in the rite of the reconciliation of penitents on Holy Thursday. And soon this grew into the practice of granting a similar benefit to the faithful also on other days. Already by the middle of the eleventh century it was the custom in Rhenish churches for the preacher after every sermon[14] to make the faithful raise their hands and confess their faults. Then they pronounced over them the then customary formula of sacramental absolution, a variant of our *Indulgentiam*[15]—to which the *Misereatur* was soon prefixed.[16]

Of course it was well-known even then that this type of general absolution, without a special individual confession, was not in itself enough for mortal sins; in fact this was inculcated very emphatically.[17] But the practice was so highly treasured that it continued for long even after the sacramental character was denied it (in the period of Scholasticism),[18] and it was no longer performed with sacramental intent.[19] It is even practiced today to some extent,[20] but usually only at the end of the Sunday sermon preached outside Mass.

But it is also retained in the solemn pontifical Mass, in the course of which our rite was already taken for granted as a fixed constituent as early

---

[13] Jungmann, *Die lateinischen Bussriten*, 180.

[14] A German collection of sermons from the 12th century is satisfied with Communion days: *si sit festivitas quod ad corpus Domini aliqui accedere velint.* Linsenmayer, 144.

[15] Jungmann, *Die lateinischen Bussriten*, 275-295 (General absolutions), especially 279 ff.

[16] In the examples of Steinmeyer, 345-349, it is possible to visualize the following reconstruction: act of faith (creed), followed by a confession of guilt, both in the vernacular. Then *Misereatur* and *Indulgentiam*. Then, again in the vernacular, a series of intentions for prayer. Cf. Steinmeyer, 357-361; Also the *Confiteor* and the *allocutio* which follows (a freely worded form of absolution) in the homiliary of the Bishop of Prague (Hecht, 60).

[17] Honorius Augustod., *Speculum Eccl.* (RL, CLXXII; 826 f.; cf. 829 B).

[18] In the Regensburg "Announcement" (*supra*, 489, note 52), at the end of the *culpa* the preacher grants the absolution (*Misereatur* and *Indulgentiam*), then he imposes a penance, to be said during Mass, five *Paters* and seven *Aves.* Beck, 277-281. Similarly at Ingolstadt; see Greving, *Johann Ecks Pfarrbuch*, 214 f. Pastor Surgant (LXXXV) indicates the same order, but remarks that other preachers (whose practice he opposes) give out the penance before the *Misereatur*.

[19] *Misereatur* and *Indulgentiam* are designated as mere blessings in Ph. Hartmann, *Repertorium rituum* (11th ed., Paderborn, 1908), 402.

[20] In the Diocese of Brixen even today the *Offene Schuld* after the Sunday sermon as well as in the introduction to service for the dead, is always concluded with *Misereatur* and *Indulgentiam.* The

as the twelfth century,[21] and is still, in a way, taken for granted even today. At present it is merely a substitute for the sacramental absolution after the announcement of the indulgences,[22] and the formula of blessing is superadded to that of absolution.[23]

What we have here in substance is an attempt—only halfway successful —to find for the faithful here at the start of the sacrifice a counterpart to that preparation and purification which was provided for the celebrant and his assistants at the beginning of the fore-Mass in the *Confiteor* and the prayers accompanying it. Thus an idea which had once been realized in the primitive Church[24] once more strove to take tangible shape.

opinion of some Protestant historians that this form of absolution—which they surmise is a substitute for private confession —reaches back to the time of Charlemagne, cannot be sustained; Jungmann, *Die Lateinischen Bussriten,* 291, note 198.

[21] Even in Rome itself; see the *Ordo eccl. Lateran.* (Fischer, 82): After the homily *confessio a diacono fit populo. Et episcopus dicit: Misereatur vestri.* Cf. *Ordo Rom. XI,* n. 20 (PL, LXXVIII, 1033 C): *benedicit.*

[22] In the late Middle Ages there was undoubtedly at this spot an announcement of the granting of an indulgence to all those present at the sermon; this was a widespread custom even for the ordinary service; see Linsenmayer, 148 f.

[23] *Cæremoniale episc.,* II, 30: after the homily the deacon sings the *Confiteor;* the preacher (see II, 8, 50 and II, 8, 80, the *presbyter assistens*) announces the indulgence of 40 days; the bishop pronounces the absolution, turning to the people: *Precibus et meritis B. M. semper virginis . . . misereatur vestri . . .* then the *Indulgentiam;* finally, with mitre on his head, the blessing: *Et benedictio Dei omnipotentis. . . .*

The same rite already in the Pontifical of Durandus (Andrieu, 639); but the addition of the blessing was here still left to the discretion of the bishop (*si velit*). Similarly, with even more exact rubrics, in the Pontifical of Castellani (1520): Martène, 1, 4, 5, 8 (I, 381); cf. also *Ordo Rom. XIV,* n. 53; 72 (PL, LXXVIII, 1294 D).

In the *Cærem. episc.,* I, 25, 2, when the rite is first described, the *Indulgentiam* is omitted, thus emphasizing the character of blessing. According to *Cærem. episc.,* II, 8, 80, it is also permissible to unite this rite, now simply described as the granting of an indulgence, with the blessing at the end of Mass, the solution most frequently employed nowadays.

The change of the original character of a general absolution has a parallel in the case of the dying, the general absolution being replaced by the granting of a papal blessing to which is attached a plenary indulgence; cf. Jungmann, *Die lateinischen Bussriten,* 294 f.

[24] *Supra,* p. 51.

END OF VOLUME ONE